# Navigating
## the *Mindfield*

# NAVIGATING THE MINDFIELD

A Guide to Separating Science
from Pseudoscience in Mental Health

Edited by
*Scott O. Lilienfeld,*
*John Ruscio,*
*and Steven Jay Lynn*

Prometheus Books

59 John Glenn Drive
Amherst, New York 14228-2119

Published 2008 by Prometheus Books

Inquiries should be addressed to
Prometheus Books
59 John Glenn Drive
Amherst, New York 14228–2119
VOICE: 716–691–0133, ext. 210
FAX: 716–691–0137
WWW.PROMETHEUSBOOKS.COM

12  11  10  09  08      5  4  3  2  1

Library of Congress Cataloging-in-Publication Data

Navigating the mindfield : a guide to separating science from pseudoscience in mental health / edited by Scott O Lilienfeld, John Ruscio, and Steven Jay Lynn.
        p. cm.
    ISBN 978–1–59102–467–5
    1. Psychiatry—Popular works. 2. Psychiatric errors. 3. Mental health. 4. Pseudoscience. 5. Alternative medicine—Evaluation. I. Lilienfeld, Scott O., 1960– II. Ruscio, John. III. Lynn, Steven J.

RC460.N38 2008
616.89—dc22

2008016553

Printed in the United States on acid-free paper

*To Barry Lane Beyerstein (1947–2007),*
*wonderful friend, courageous inquirer, and tireless proponent of*
*rationality in mental health practice*

# CONTENTS

# ACKNOWLEDGMENTS

The authors are grateful to Steven L. Mitchell for his support and encouragement of this book project and to the staff at Prometheus Books for helping us to shape it into a form that both mental health consumers and mental health professionals can benefit from and enjoy. We also thank Therese Hammond for her invaluable assistance with locating and scanning the articles in this collection. The project would have been virtually impossible to complete without her hours of patient, tireless, and conscientious work. In addition, the authors thank Lorenza Houser and Jack Murray for technical assistance and Christine Kramer and Heather Ammermuller for their help with production and copy editing. Last but not least, we thank the authors of the articles in this collection for their willingness to impart their psychological knowledge to the general public. Their writings will help thousands of readers to better navigate the confusing mindfield of mental health practices.

# INTRODUCTION

## A TALE OF TWO WORLD*VIEW S*

*Tales of 2 Types of Treatment*

he vast realm of modern mental healthcare is a tale of two worlds. The first is scientific psychology. There, researchers nestled comfortably in the safe confines of the ivory tower of academia investigate the causes, treatment, and prevention of serious mental disorders, including schizophrenia, depression, panic disorder, obsessive-compulsive disorder, and alcoholism. They have made significant discoveries in the treatment of these and other disorders, helping millions of people lead happier and more fulfilling lives. This world is also inhabited by a substantial number of psychotherapists who ground their practices in solid scientific evidence. Although not necessarily researchers themselves, these therapists function as scientists in the clinical setting. They rely on the best available research knowledge to guide their selection of assessment techniques, diagnostic procedures, and interventions.

The second world of mental healthcare is vastly different. There, in the often strange terrain of popular psychology, intuition and clinical experience frequently reign supreme. This is a land populated by media self-help "gurus," television talk shows, Hollywood movies, Internet sites, entrepreneurs enthusiastically marketing a motley assortment of products for self-improvement, and authors of popular self-help books and manuals. Perhaps most worrisome, this second world also consists of the swelling ranks of psychotherapists who base their practices on unsubstantiated subjective judgments rather than on scientific research.

## POPULAR PSYCHOLOGY

For most laypersons, *psychology* is pretty much synonymous with *popular psychology*. That's not surprising, because far more Americans get their psychological knowledge from the self-help industry and popular media than from academic researchers. Over two thousand self-help books appear every year, and this number shows no sign of abating. Although a handful have been tested and found to be helpful, scientific researchers have never examined the vast majority of them. In many bookstores, the size of the "self-help" and "recovery" sections dwarfs that of the psychology section; indeed, some bookstores no longer even contain a psychology section at all. The television talk show of Dr. Phil McGraw (*Dr. Phil*) attracts approximately 6.7 million viewers, and Dr. Laura Schlessinger's radio talk show attracts approximately 18 million listeners. (Incidentally, "Dr." Laura's doctoral degree was in physiology, not psychology or psychiatry, although she received a certification degree in marriage, family, and child counseling.)

Why is any of this problematic? It's because much of popular psychology is a loose collection of practices derived from folk knowledge, clinical lore, and untested assumptions. In contrast to scientific psychology, a good deal of popular psychology relies on what clinical psychologist Paul Meehl of the University of Minnesota called *fireside inductions*, informal conclusions derived from common sense, word of mouth, and hearsay. Some of these beliefs are quite reasonable. Regrettably, many others—like the idea that memory works like a video camera or that we need to psychologically "relive" past events to solve current life problems—are scant more than urban legends.

The realm of popular psychology thus contains a mixture of trustworthy and untrustworthy information. On the positive side, the popular media accurately report a good deal of cutting-edge scientific knowledge to the general public. As a consequence, the average American of the early twenty-first century knows considerably more about effective treatments for depression and anxiety, for instance, than did the average American of fifty or even ten years ago. Moreover, many self-help books contain useful advice for solving everyday life problems, and some even offer scientifically supported tips for overcoming psychological ailments (see chapters 25–26). Most encouragingly, even many psychotherapists who use one unscientific technique base many other clinical practices on well-supported scientific findings. When passing judgment on popular psychology, it's crucial not to throw the scientific baby out with the unscientific bathwater.

On the negative side, however, much of popular psychology has drifted progressively from its moorings in scientific psychology. More than ever, large sectors of popular psychology have become dominated by the ethos of "almost anything goes." Indeed, in the world of popular psychology, scientific findings are sometimes neglected or even treated with outright disdain as irrelevant to the rough-and-tumble world of daily clinical practice. Some proponents of popular psychology, imbued with the widespread but misguided belief that "science is only one way of knowing," are convinced that they can safely ignore scientific findings when they conflict with clinical experience or personal judgment. Yet if the history of science teaches us anything, it's that we should be profoundly skeptical of the "I know it works" claim when it clashes with the results of systematic investigations (see chapters 2–3).

Because the world of popular psychology is a bewildering mix of claims—some poorly supported and others well supported—the general public sorely needs guidance for distinguishing the wheat from the chaff in mental healthcare. Moreover, there are at least five hundred brands of psychotherapy, many or most untested. This makes it remarkably difficult for mental health consumers to figure out which treatments to choose—and which to avoid. As psychologists John Riolo and his colleagues noted in a 2004 article in the *Scientific Review of Mental Health Practice*:

> Finding one's way through the plethora of available mental health treatments and therapies can be confusing and even dangerous to both consumers and therapists. Numerous theories, approaches, techniques, and schools of thought—some with empirical grounding and

some without—create such a puzzling maze that even guides need a roadmap. It is a formidable task for practitioners, patients, and their families to decide what is beneficial and what is not.

Nevertheless, precious few books are available to assist mental health consumers or interested laypersons with that critically important goal. This edited book of user-friendly readings will do precisely that.

## NAVIGATING THE *MIND*FIELD

As we have already seen, what we term the mental health "*mind*field" is a bewildering maze of claims that can be remarkably challenging to navigate. If you are a mental health consumer wondering how best to traverse this often perilous landscape, you are in good company. A 2006 *Newsweek* poll found that about 20 percent of Americans have received psychological treatment at some point in their lives, and about 4 percent are presently in psychotherapy. Moreover, published surveys show that about a quarter of Americans suffered from at least one major mental disorder in the past year. Yet many or most wander aimlessly through the *mind*field, with scant guidance for where to turn.

The confusing mental health maze leaves consumers with a plethora of questions:

- How should I select a therapist?
- How can I tell the difference between well-supported and poorly supported psychotherapy?
- What psychotherapies should I be sure to avoid?
- What self-help books are trustworthy?
- Are the psychological tests I'm taking based on adequate scientific evidence?
- What does the diagnosis I've received really mean, and can I trust it?
- When should I consult a mental health professional for a second opinion?

- Will the drug that I was prescribed help me?
- How do I know whether I'm really getting better?
- In what situations should I consider switching to a different therapist?

In this book, we offer helpful suggestions for answering these and many other questions. More broadly, we intend to provide readers with guidance for finding their way through the mental health maze without stepping on major land mines.

## LOOKING BACK: THE POPULAR PSYCHOLOGY OF YORE

In reality, the problems we describe are not all that new. The myriad fields of mental healthcare have long been associated with more than their share of dubious claims and even blatant hucksterism. Let's look at three historical examples.

In the early and mid-nineteenth century, thousands of "phrenologists" claimed to discern individuals' personality traits by examining the size and pattern of bumps on their skulls. The familiar expression "having one's head examined" derives from phrenology. The best-known phrenologist, a Viennese physician named Franz Joseph Gall, claimed to have pinpointed twenty-seven areas of the skull linked to specific psychological "faculties," such as aggressiveness, vanity, friendliness, and even a love of colors; subsequent phrenologists expanded the number to forty-three. For decades, phrenology was all the rage in the United States and Europe. Phrenology "parlors" sprouted up in dozens of locations. Thomas Edison and Ralph Waldo Emerson, among others, were passionate devotees of phrenology who reveled in having their skull bumps measured using a "psychograph," a metallic, spring-loaded device that clamped down on an individual's head and provided a detailed readout of personality traits. Interest in phrenology finally subsided in the late nineteenth century when it became obvious that patients with damage to specific brain areas didn't suffer the kinds of psychological changes that phrenologists had predicted.

During the 1940s and 1950s, the German psychiatrist Wilhelm Reich and his followers marketed a large number of "orgone accumulators"—or "orgone boxes"—which resembled small telephone booths in which patients sat. These boxes purportedly cured mental illnesses by releasing the stored energy of the human orgasm, which Reich regarded as the universal life force that explained the origin of the solar system and the color of the sky. According to Reich, a deficiency in orgone produces almost every mental disorder under the sun, not to mention political revolutions and cancer. (Incidentally, the orgone box was the inspiration behind the "orgasmotron" in Woody Allen's film *Sleeper.*) Reich was finally put out of business by the US Food and Drug Administration, which confiscated his orgone boxes on the grounds that he had made fraudulent claims to the American public. Even today, you can purchase an orgone box on the Internet, and a few hundred people still adhere to Reich's weird brand of therapy.

As recently as 1971, the American Academy of Psychotherapy bestowed its prestigious "Man of the Year" award to John Rosen, a psychologist who claimed to treat schizophrenics by yelling at them, sucking on their nipples, and threatening to cut them into pieces. In some cases, he even enlisted psychiatric aides to dress up as FBI agents to interrogate patients about their fantasies. Rosen called his bizarre technique "direct analysis" because it supposedly allowed him to communicate directly with patients' unconscious minds. By terrifying his patients, Rosen believed, he could break through their conscious defenses and get to the root of their deep-seated conflicts. Rosen never bothered to conduct any research to find out whether direct analysis worked, and neither did anyone else.

# FADS, FALLACIES, AND FABLES OF THE TWENTY-FIRST CENTURY

Given the remarkable advances in scientific psychology over the past few decades, one might assume that the bizarre fads of popular psychology would be a thing of the past. Yet in growing enclaves of twenty-first-century popular psychology, clinical practices are influenced by doubtful claims and New Age concepts of questionable validity. Even today, novel and untested approaches are frequently marketed as "breakthroughs" or "miracle cures" despite a wholesale absence of research evidence. Promises of quick fixes for long-standing or intractable psychological problems abound, as do an almost unimaginable variety of therapeutic and diagnostic fads.

Here's a sampling of a few of the unusual—and in some cases deeply troubling—practices we'll encounter in this book.

- In anticipation of the upcoming revision of the American Psychiatric Association's classification manual, scores of mental health professionals are lobbying vigorously for the inclusion of novel psychiatric diagnoses. Among them are "road rage disorder," "sexual addiction," "codependency," "celebrity worship syndrome," "Internet addiction," and "post-traumatic slavery disorder," a condition supposedly afflicting individuals traumatized indirectly by the slavery of previous generations. In a recently published article, one psychiatrist has even proposed formal diagnostic criteria for "oppressive supernatural states disorder," a form of multiple personality disorder (now known as "dissociative identity disorder") ostensibly produced by demonic possession. The research evidence for the clinical utility of these diagnostic labels ranges from slim to none (see chapter 12).
- In the mid-1980s, a young woman named Nadean Cool entered psychotherapy suffering from fairly typical problems: mild depression, family conflict, and residual symptoms of bulimia. After five years of treatment with a psychiatrist, she emerged with over 130

"alter" personalities, including demons, angels, children, and a duck. In 1997, after becoming convinced that her therapist had inadvertently implanted these alters, she won a $2.7 million malpractice suit against him. Other therapists have supposedly uncovered as many as forty-five hundred alter personalities in a single client. In recent years, clients with multiple personality disorder have reported alters of Madonna, Mr. Spock, the Teenage Mutant Ninja Turtles, aliens from other galaxies, lobsters, chickens, gorillas, God, and the bride of Satan. Although the diagnosis of dissociative identity disorder remains popular among many clinicians, accumulating evidence indicates that this condition is largely a product of inadvertent therapist prompting and cueing, rather than naturally occurring splits into alter personalities (see chapters 12 and 14).

- Many clinicians use hypnotic age-regression techniques in an effort to "return" clients psychologically to childhood. Some purport to reinstate clients' exact memories of the womb or even of their past lives. Nevertheless, a large body of psychological research demonstrates that regression techniques do not return individuals to the psychological state of childhood. Instead, age-regressing adults are merely role-playing behaviors they believe to be characteristic of younger ages. Moreover, age-regressed individuals exhibit the brain waves of adults, not of children, and they respond to advanced language that only adults can comprehend (see chapters 13–14).

- Hundreds of psychotherapists have recently been trained in a technique known as Thought Field Therapy (TFT), which ostensibly treats anxiety by manipulating clients' "energy fields." Clients undergoing TFT perform a sequence of specific actions, such as humming a happy tune, counting, and rolling their eyes, while the therapist taps repeatedly on the back of their hands and other bodily areas. Roger Callahan, the developer of this increasingly popular method, says that it has proven effective in the treatment of young children, not to mention horses, dogs, and cats. He has reported cure rates of 90 to 95 percent and even claims to be able to cure anxiety disorders over the telephone. As of this writing, not a single published study supports any of these assertions (see chapter 20).

• Numerous companies produce subliminal self-help tapes, which purport to help listeners increase their self-esteem or improve their memory by presenting them with deeply embedded messages (e.g., "You are a good person"). In carefully controlled studies, however, researchers have found these tapes to be useless. Remarkably, sophisticated auditory analyses of commercially available subliminal tapes reveal that many contain no signal whatever (see chapter 28). That is, the tapes are essentially blank!

These are by no means isolated developments. As we'll discover throughout the book, these practices are merely the tip of a growing iceberg of myth, misconception, and misinformation. As a consequence, a great deal of popularly available knowledge about psychology is woefully inaccurate.

## SOME TELLTALE SYMPTOMS OF PSEUDOSCIENCE

Many of these practices appear to be symptoms of a deeper underlying disease afflicting a good deal of popular psychology, the disease called *pseudoscience*. You can think of these as "warning signs" to keep in mind when evaluating information about mental health practices (see chapter 2). The more of these symptoms you see, the more suspicious you should become.

Among the recurring telltale symptoms of psychological pseudoscience are:

• Promises of simple, rapid, and dramatic cures for complex emotional problems. The history of psychology suggests that such promises are usually false.

- Extravagant claims of effectiveness that greatly outstrip a meager base of research evidence. Such claims typically constitute little more than wishful thinking.
- Promotion and marketing of novel techniques before well-controlled scientific studies to evaluate them have been carried out. Putting promotion ahead of testing raises troubling ethical questions.
- The dubious assumption that all untested techniques are bound to be helpful or, at worst, harmless. Researchers have found that some treatments are in fact harmful, and even "harmless" approaches can be wasteful when effective ones exist.
- Failure to consider alternative explanations for apparently supportive research results. There are often many plausible interpretations of data, and it is unsound to assume the best and adopt the most favorable view.
- Cavalier dismissal of negative scientific results on flimsy or illogical grounds. Practitioners genuinely interested in helping their clients give due consideration to all evidence rather than ignore inconvenient or unflattering findings.
- Failure to attend to decades of well-established scientific findings. Knowing the history of the discipline often sheds light on new and questionable practices.
- Placing the burden of proof on skeptics, rather than proponents, of extraordinary claims. Just as our legal system requires evidence of guilt to counter the presumption of innocence, scientific mental health practice requires evidence of benefit from those promoting new types of assessment, diagnosis, or treatment.
- Many of these symptoms contribute to what we term the "Rasputin effect," after the Russian monk who miraculously survived multiple attempts to slay him: Questionable techniques tend to live on despite overwhelmingly negative evidence.

# GRAND CANYON:
# THE SCIENTIST-PRACTITIONER GAP

Over the past few decades, the worlds of scientific and popular psychology have become increasingly isolated from one another. This disconnection has resulted in a worrisome fact: many well-substantiated research findings have exerted surprisingly little influence over many therapists' clinical practices. Former American Psychological Association president Ronald Fox even coined a term for this worrisome disconnection: the *scientist-practitioner gap* (see chapters 1–3). Yet this very term is itself emblematic of a more fundamental problem because it inadvertently implies that scientists and practitioners compose two mutually exclusive camps. They need not be. Indeed, our central thesis is that these two disparate worlds must be united. Just as popular mechanics is based on physical science, popular psychology can and must be based on psychological science.

As Princeton University psychologist George Miller argued in his presidential address to the American Psychological Association in 1969, one of the great and noble ambitions of scientific psychology should be to "give psychology away," that is, to furnish the general public with the fruits of hard-won scientific knowledge regarding human thought and behavior. Four decades later, George Miller has ample reason to be proud of scientific psychology. Psychologists have put scientific findings to good use in improving productivity in the workplace, reducing airplane accidents, assisting cancer patients to cope with the pain and anguish of terminal illness, improving the accuracy of eyewitness identifications of criminal suspects, and treating depression.

Yet in other respects, scientific psychology has fallen conspicuously short in its mission to enhance human welfare. For example, although researchers have shown that several forms of psychotherapy are effective, the majority of individuals with major mental disorders are still not receiving treatments based on good scientific evidence. A large-scale US survey published in 2003 by Harvard University epidemiologist Ronald Kessler and his colleagues revealed that only about 20 percent of individuals with clinical depression receive adequate treatment. The majority of depressed individuals receive no treatment at all, grossly suboptimal treatment, or psychological treatments that have not been shown to be effective in scientific studies. A 1999 survey by Harvard psychiatrist Robert Goisman and his co-workers indicated that the number of clients with anxiety disorders who receive demonstrably effective treatments—namely, behavioral and cognitive-behavioral therapies—has declined in recent years. They also found that the treatments most commonly administered to anxiety-disordered individuals were psychodynamic therapies—those premised on gaining insight into the unconscious causes and childhood roots of one's problems. Yet researchers have not found these to be effective in the treatment of anxiety disorders.

The vacuum left by scientific psychology has been occupied by a growing cadre of mental health professionals who administer scientifically questionable or pseudoscientific techniques. For example, a large 2001 national survey by Kessler and his colleagues revealed that substantial numbers of clinically depressed and anxious individuals receive such interventions as energy therapies (like TFT), massage therapy, aromatherapy, acupuncture, and even laughter therapy (a technique premised on the scientifically unsupported notion that laughing will make you feel better in the long run). Again, none of these techniques has been shown to be effective in the treatment of clinically significant mood or anxiety disorders.

Researchers and scientifically minded therapists often know precious little of the world of popular psychology, and they often care to know even less. Most simply choose to ignore this alien world, perhaps believing that it poses little threat to either them or the general public. Others are blissfully unaware of this world, believing that pseudoscientific practices are merely an occasional blemish marring the otherwise pristine landscape of psychology. A recent past president of the American Psychological Association, Robert Sternberg of Tufts University, recently expressed this view in print, maintaining that irresponsible psychological practices are limited to only a small number of practitioners. Survey data demonstrate that Sternberg's view is overly sanguine.

For example, about 25 percent of American and Canadian psychotherapists regularly use highly suggestive techniques, like hypnosis, dream interpretation, guided imagery, and even "trance writing" (a technique in which clients write out past memories while in an apparent trance) to recover purportedly long-forgotten memories of early child abuse. Yet we'll later learn that that these techniques can generate false memories of abuse in many clients (see chapters 13 and 14). Survey data also show that about 30 to 40 percent of American psychologists frequently use the Rorschach Inkblot Test and human figure drawings to draw inferences regarding their clients' mental state, even though we'll later discover that these instruments have been found to be of little value for the substantial majority of clinical purposes to which they are put (see chapters 6–7). Moreover, surveys reveal that more than a third of therapists who work with children suspected of having been sexually abused use anatomically detailed dolls to detect such abuse. Nevertheless, these dolls are of doubtful validity and have been found in numerous studies to misidentify many nonabused children, especially African American children, as abused (see chapter 6).

Psychologists and laypersons must beware of the all-too-common mistake of assuming that pseudoscientific practices are rare, as it can easily lull us into a false sense of complacency. On the bright side, many psychotherapists avidly consult the research literature and, whenever possible, base their practices on trustworthy scientific evidence. On the dark side, disconcertingly large numbers do not.

Why does the scientist-practitioner gap exist, and why does it appear to be widening? First, because of the burgeoning popular psychology industry, inaccurate information about psychological treatments is more readily available than ever before. Radio and television talk shows, self-help books and magazines, and now the Internet permit psychological misinformation to spread like wildfire. These media also permit unscientific therapists to market their claims to the public and to other practitioners with unprecedented efficiency. The popular psychology industry has grown into a myth-making machine—a powerful mechanism for disseminating psychological misconception and misunderstanding (see chapters 24–28).

Of course, on the positive side, the increasing availability of these media sources allows the public unprecedented access to accurate psychological information as well. Yet because few laypersons possess the extensive background knowledge needed to distinguish scientifically supported from unsupported psychological information, they are understandably confused about what to believe. In appendixes I and II, we'll provide you with suggestions for useful book and Internet resources for distinguishing science from pseudoscience in mental health.

Second, as we'll discover later in the book, the academic standards of many clinical psychology–training programs have declined markedly in recent decades (chapter 29). More and more, these programs are encouraged to adopt their own training models rather than to provide students with a core curriculum of basic scientific knowledge. Although a number of excellent clinical psychology programs exist, some are little more than diploma mills that mass-produce large numbers of practitioners with questionable scientific training.

Third, many areas of popular psychology have been riding the wave of the enormously successful "alternative medicine" movement. Capitalizing on people's understandable frustration with treatments that can be lengthy, expensive, invasive, or painful, growing numbers of medical practitioners over the past decade have been offering untested "quick-fix" treatments. Psychologists have increasingly followed suit. A growing number of well-controlled studies suggest that, with only a few possible exceptions, such as St. John's wort for mild depression, most alternative medical treatments have fallen well short of expectations.

## THE HIGH PRICE TAG OF PSEUDOSCIENCE

Pseudoscience can be hazardous to mental health consumers and their loved ones. Later in the book, we'll encounter the tragic story of Candace

Newmaker, a ten-year-old-girl smothered to death by therapists administering a variant of rebirthing therapy, a technique premised on the scientifically dubious assumption that reenacting the trauma of birth can alleviate the symptoms of certain psychological conditions (see chapters 21 and 30). Candace Newmaker was not alone. Several other children have been killed by therapists administering variants of so-called attachment therapy. We'll also learn that about nine thousand well-intentioned therapists descended on New York City in the aftermath of the terrorist attacks of September 11, 2001. Many therapists administered crisis debriefing to witnesses or victims. There is only one problem: several carefully conducted studies suggest that crisis debriefing may actually increase the risk of post-traumatic stress reactions (see chapters 4 and 11). Some mental health practices can be bad for your mental health.

One of the most frequent questions we hear is "If something is by itself harmless, who cares?" Some psychological techniques we will discuss in this book, like subliminal audiotapes for enhancing self-esteem, are ineffective but probably innocuous. Yet even techniques that are by themselves harmless can lead mental health consumers to pass up effective interventions. Economists term this unappreciated adverse effect *opportunity cost.* Such techniques also deprive mental health consumers of valuable time, money, and effort, sometimes leaving them with precious little of all three. Finally, nonscientific practices can tarnish the reputation and credibility of all mental health professionals, rendering members of the general public more reluctant to turn to them for sorely needed psychological help that is based on sound evidence.

## HOW WE CAN BE FOOLED

It's tempting to blame the general public for the popularity of pseudoscientific treatments. That would be a grave mistake. There are many reasons why thoughtful and rational people can be drawn to techniques that don't work.

For one thing, excepting experts and science writers, few of us possess the time or specialized knowledge to keep up with the enormous body of scientific literature on mental disorders and their treatment. With well over two thousand journals in psychology, psychiatry, and related areas (e.g., counseling, social work, psychiatric nursing, school psychology) alone, reading even a tiny percentage of research articles concerning mental health is an overwhelming task. Thus, we are forced to place our trust in the hands of practitioners, some of whom may not be familiar with recent research findings. Others may simply reject research evidence that conflicts with their clinical intuition.

In addition, because of how our memory works, we are easily influenced by vivid and subjectively compelling anecdotes. Often, our judgments are affected by testimonials involving dramatic improvement in single cases far more than by dry statistical reports based on hundreds of individuals. This is an example of what psychologists call *the availability heuristic,* which refers to the fact that the events most easily recalled (or easily imagined) tend to exert a greater impact on our thinking than less vivid or emotionally compelling information. Compounding this tendency, the media typically prefer to report treatment successes rather than treatment failures, leaving us with a skewed portrait of a treatment's actual effectiveness.

Even entirely worthless techniques can appear to work (see chapter 5), for several reasons. For example, some mental conditions, like depression, often go away on their own accord. Such cases of spontaneous remission can fool us into attributing improvement to the treatment. *Placebo effects,* the tendency of some conditions to get better because of the mere expectation of improvement, can be a further source of error. Recent analyses suggest that perhaps 75 to 80 percent of the apparent effectiveness of antidepressant medication, for example, is attributable to such effects. Finally, "effort justification" and "demand characteristics" can lead patients to report improvement where none has occurred. The former refers to patients who have devoted time and effort to a treatment to convince themselves that their investment was worth it; the latter refers to patients who report what they think their therapists want to hear.

Only the scientific method, which consists of an expanding, evolving set of tools designed to prevent us from fooling ourselves, permits us to evaluate whether therapies really work. Without it, even the most intelligent individuals can mistake a useless treatment for an effective one. As the Nobel Prize–winning physicist Richard Feynman reminded us, good scientists bend over backwards to prove themselves wrong.

Science isn't a perfect safeguard against human error. But in the long run, it's the best collection of methods we have for sorting fact from fiction in mental health practice. We'll rely on it throughout this book.

In the book's opening section, we examine the scientist-practitioner gap and its implications for mental health consumers and clinicians. Opening readings by Barry Beyerstein and Scott Lilienfeld and his colleagues make a compelling case that all is not well in the vast land of mental health practice. These authors lay out the scope and dimensions of the scientist-practitioner gap and provide tangible evidence that this gap poses grave threats to the general public. In addition, these authors, especially Lilienfeld and his colleagues, delineate useful warning signs for identifying pseudoscientific claims. For example, mental health consumers should be especially wary of claims that are difficult to disprove, lack connection with established scientific disciplines, are dressed up in fancy jargon, or rely on anecdotes and testimonials rather than systematic scientific evidence.

Finally, Stuart Vyse addresses the fascinating question of how mental health fads originate, with particular reference to those in the treatment of infantile autism and other developmental disabilities. As he observes, fad treatments are especially likely to spread when effective treatments are unavailable, when existing treatments are unpleasant, and when the fad treatments are supported by a powerful and plausible ideology. By placing therapeutic fads in a historical context, Vyse sets us on the path toward resisting their seductive influence.

# SECTION I. THE SCIENTIST-PRACTITIONER GAP AND ITS ORIGINS

# 1.

# FRINGE PSYCHOTHERAPIES: THE PUBLIC AT RISK

### Barry L. Beyerstein
Brain Behavior Laboratory

*Knowledge consists in understanding the evidence that establishes the fact, not in the belief that it is a fact.*

—Charles T. Spraling

From Hippocrates to the present, the first duty of the helping professions has been "Do no harm." Unfortunately, a widening gap between science and the further reaches of psychotherapy has allowed certain practices to flourish that have the potential to do much harm. Although the vast majority of counselors who engage in "talking therapies" continue to act responsibly, the profession has not always been as quick as it should in curtailing fringe practitioners whose antics put the unsuspecting public at risk. At the outset, it must be said that although fringe practices such as "rebirthing" and Neurolinguistic Programming are based on what Richard Rosen has aptly dubbed "psychobabble," most of them probably do little damage in the long run—providing we overlook the costs of pandering to the narcissistic irrationalism of society's more affluent worriers.[1] Despite their absurd premises, these therapeutic outliers at least provide clients of a certain metaphysical bent with comforting mythologies that explain why their lives are not as fulfilling as they had expected. Indirectly, these

Reprinted with permission from *Scientific Review of Alternative Medicine* 5 (2002): 5–13.

quaint rituals can supply existential support, emotional consolation, and even some useful spurs to change troublesome habits. Thus, on balance, psychotherapies founded on ill-conceived assumptions may still prove beneficial if they furnish needed reassurance in an atmosphere where clients can mull over solutions to their dissatisfactions in life.

That said, the dangers posed by fringe therapists arise principally in three ways. One is the potential for manipulation and fraud. Cultlike pseudotherapies can prey on the dependency needs of vulnerable people while extracting unconscionable sums of money. The nonsensical prattle of Scientology is but one example.[2] Other fringe operators have been known to victimize clients sexually as well as monetarily. All told, these victims could have been helped much more ethically, effectively, and cheaply by scientifically trained counselors who would target specific, tractable problems in their lives. Another concern is that inadequately trained therapists may fail to recognize early signs of serious psychopathologies that, left untreated, could prove disastrous. And finally, much hardship has been created, albeit often with the best of intentions, by ill-informed counselors who encourage their clients' delusions while claiming to "recover" repressed memories of childhood sexual abuse, ritual satanic abuse, or abduction by extraterrestrials.[3]

## HOW DID THIS STATE OF AFFAIRS COME ABOUT?

As scientific psychology emerged from wholesale reliance on intuition and folk wisdom, its pioneers argued that the best way to train psychotherapists was the so-called scientist-practitioner model (also called the "Boulder model" after the Colorado campus whose psychology department was an early proponent). It was assumed that if therapists had a strong background in behavioral research, they would base their professional activities on a valid understanding of human memory, cognition, emotion, motivation, personality, and brain function. Sad to say, this linkage has become increasingly strained as an assortment of new players has been drawn into the lucrative therapeutic-industrial complex. The practice of psychotherapy is drifting further from its scientific underpinnings as a growing percentage of the therapeutic workforce is graduated from stand-alone schools of professional psychology and a variety of programs in schools of social work and nursing.

To make matters worse, a number of for-profit, nonaccredited diploma mills have sprung up, offering degrees of questionable quality to aspiring psychotherapists on the run. And with the growth of the "New Age" movement, the market has also been flooded by a growing cadre of therapists with little formal training but an immense investment in pop-psychology and "post-modernist" psychobabble. In most jurisdictions, these entrepreneurs cannot call themselves psychologists or psychiatrists because licencing statutes restrict these titles to professionals with specified credentials and training. They can, however, offer their services (where local laws permit) by appropriating unreserved titles such as counselor, psychotherapist, psychoanalyst, sex therapist, pastoral counselor, Dianetics auditor (one of several pseudonyms for Scientology), New Age guide, relationship advisor, mental therapist, etc.

To the extent that many of these people are kind, empathetic individuals possessed of some common sense, they undoubtedly help more than a few troubled clients. This, of course, is all to the good and, as Dawes[4] points out, research shows that, for most everyday psychological difficulties, there is not much evidence that therapists with extensive professional training have greater rates of success than these sympathetic listeners armed with the conventional wisdom of the ages. The dangers arise, however, when their lack of training makes untutored advisors more likely to venture into the risky pursuits discussed below. There is also the possibility that bad advice could exacerbate rather than alleviate clients' complaints. The public is generally unaware of the fact that regulations in most jurisdictions governing who can perform psychotherapy are fairly weak. This invites increasing numbers of self-styled entrepreneurs whose training is of the "watch one, do one, teach one" variety. Unless he or she checks in advance, the average client arriving at the clinic door will have little way of knowing which brand of therapist the luck of the draw will provide.

The thinning of the bond between psychotherapy and empirical research is reflected in the fact that even the more respectable stand-alone professional schools generally offer a "PsyD" (Doctor of Psychology) degree rather than the traditional PhD. The PhD is a research degree, requiring competence in experimental design and statistics and the ability to understand and criticize, if not actually contribute, to the scientific literature. In the scientist-practitioner model, critical thinking skills are honed as trainees acquire a grounding in the science of psychology at the post-graduate level before specializing in psychodiagnostics and psychotherapeutics. In this way, the need for impartial follow-ups to gauge the effectiveness of therapeutic techniques is impressed upon would-be providers. Most stand-alone professional psychology schools, catering to the demands of those eager to achieve professional status with less of this tedious exposure to the science of psychology, have reduced that portion of their curriculum in favor of an apprentice-ship approach where particular therapeutic techniques are assimilated by rote. Even in many university-based clinical psychology programs that still require the methodology courses and research participation, there has been a growing tendency for clinical training to become isolated from other parts of their departments where the bulk of the theoretical and experimental work is done. One result of this estrangement has been that many clinical trainees leave these programs insufficiently committed to the idea that therapeutic interventions should be tied to research that supports their safety and effectiveness.

This failure to instill a self-critical attitude in many therapists-in-training was deplored by Paul Meehl,[5] a former president of the American Psychological Association, over a decade ago:

> When I was a student, there was at least one common factor present in all of the psychology faculty . . . namely, the general scientific commitment not to be fooled and not to fool anyone else. Some things have happened in the world of clinical practice that worry me in this respect. That skepsis, that passion not to be fooled and not to fool anyone else, does not seem to be as fundamental a part of all psychol-

ogists' mental equipment as it was a half century ago. One mark of a good psychologist is to be critical of evidence . . . I have heard of some psychological testimony in court rooms locally in which this critical mentality appears to be largely absent.

At the highest levels of the profession, the erosion of the linkage between science and clinical practice was further aggravated in recent years when many research psychologists left the American Psychological Association (APA) to form the rival American Psychological Society. The defectors felt that the APA was undervaluing the scientific side of its mandate as it devoted more effort to lobbying and other professional issues primarily of concern to clinicians. Many also felt that the APA had been too timid in disciplining those of its members who engage in scientifically dubious practices. On several occasions, I have witnessed this reluctance to chastise peddlers of outlandish wares myself. My disappointments sprang from fruitless attempts to get various psychological associations to rein in their members who charge clients for scientifically discredited services such as subliminal audiotapes, graphology (handwriting analysis), dubious psychological tests, bogus therapy techniques, and various so-called rejuvenation techniques for recovering supposedly repressed memories. I continue to be appalled to see journals of various psychological associations with advertisements for courses carrying official continuing education credits for therapists that promote this kind of pseudoscience. The political will to sanction well-connected, dues-paying mavericks is obviously weak.

In the case of psychiatry, one would have hoped that, as a specialty of medicine, the basic science taught in the pre-medical curriculum, and medical training itself, would make practitioners less susceptible to pseudoscience. Unfortunately, many departures from science-based theories have been perpetrated by psychiatrists.[6] For example, there are well-known psychiatrists among those who advocate treating current maladjustments by encouraging patients to "re-live" mental trauma that supposedly occurred in utero, during birth, or even in previous incarnations."[7] There are others who still support the discredited views of "hidden memories" criticized below, and the most prominent advocate of the "alien abduction" hypothesis was the late John Mack, a professor of psychiatry at the Harvard Medical School.[8] Modern biologically oriented psychiatrists overwhelmingly reject such views, but many in the older generation of psychodynamically trained (i.e., Freudian) analysts cling to other diagnoses and therapies based on scientifically dubious rationales.[9]

Summarizing the foregoing trends, Lilienfeld,[10] a model for the hard-nosed scientist-practitioner, concluded that many cherished assumptions "taken for granted by most [clinicians] are little more than pseudoscientific beliefs built upon an edifice of myth and misconception." Let us now examine some of those myths.


## PSYCHOTHERAPEUTIC FICTIONS

*Mainstream psychotherapies are highly successful.* Scientific understanding of how best to alleviate emotional distress and other problems of living has been steadily accumulating, but those who specialize in talk therapy still have much to be modest about. With respect to the effectiveness of psychotherapy in general, Dawes[11] summarized several meta-analyses of the therapy outcome literature. Meta-analysis is a mathematical technique for combining and differentially weighting the results of many individual studies in a way that can provide a more reliable estimate of the effects of the manipulation in question than simply tallying up the number of studies "for and against." As Hagen[12] points out, however, meta-analyses can be misleading, especially in the realm of psychotherapeutic outcome research. The conclusions drawn from a meta-analysis are only as sound as the studies that were included in it and the judgment of the reviewer who chooses and weights them. It is the contention of Epstein that even the modest claims of therapeutic efficacy conceded by Dawes, Lilienfeld, the Consumer Reports survey, and others are overstated because the methodologies employed in most studies of therapeutic outcome suffer from substantial defects.[13]

Be that as it may, Dawes[14] argues that when psychotherapists base their interventions on the reliable research at their disposal, there is reason to believe that recipients will be helped—though not to the extent that many assume and all would wish. While research shows that there is a tendency for psychological complaints to get better, even if they are not treated, and that there is a placebo effect with psychological interventions, just as with medical treatments, there is some evidence that psychotherapy has more than just a placebo effect. The upshot is that the *process* of interacting with a sympathetic mentor in all but the most nonsensical psychotherapeutic settings can promote real, albeit often modest, improvements in emotional adjustment. While these data provide some comfort to treatment providers, the same studies consistently indicate that the effectiveness of treatment is unrelated to the specific type of training the therapist has had or the length of time he or she has been practicing. Looking at the same data, Lilienfeld[15] concluded, "there is no compelling evidence that clients need to pay high-priced professionals to enact psychological change; relatively straightforward behavioral interventions implemented by para-professionals will often suffice."

Even if minimally trained therapists can do some good, there remains the danger that they will divert clients from treatments that would help them more. More worrisome is the possibility that their limited knowledge will lead them to apply risky procedures that can exacerbate existing conditions or even create serious problems of their own. When such malpractice occurs, these uncertified therapists have no professional associations and disciplinary boards to whom dissatisfied customers can turn. It is when therapeutic fads emerge from a research vacuum and treatments lack proper outcome evaluations to back them up that these safety concerns arise.

*Clinical Judgment.* One of the most prevalent misconceptions in the field of psychotherapy is that "clinical judgment" is a reliable basis for deriving predictions about clients' behavior (e.g., regarding recidivism, violence-proneness, etc., or even job suitability). In fact, the kind of reasoning involved in these judgments tends to be quite fallible.[16] As Dawes[17] concluded in his devastating review, predictions based on simple statistical formulas almost always outperform those based on the ad hoc reasoning touted as "clinical intuition." Research also indicates that increased experience or specialized training in the field is unlikely to improve a clinician's hit rate for such judgments. Dawes goes so far as to assert that the clinician's role in making these predictions should be restricted to gathering the raw data that researchers will use for deriving reliable statistical decision-making rules. Once these rules have been formulated, their strict application will produce far better predictions than therapists' subjective impressions.

*Psychoanalysis.* Psychoanalysis, the system invented by Freud and developed by followers such as Jung, Adler, Fromm, Reich, and Sullivan, is almost synonymous with psychotherapy in the public mind. Its concepts are so ingrained in literature, cinema, and everyday discourse that most laypersons are surprised when they hear that psychoanalysis has been widely attacked as a nonfalsifiable pseudoscience.[18] Its detractors also point to its culture-bound and misogynistic views of personality, the excessive duration and cost of its treatments (weekly, over many years), and its poor track record in helping any but the mildest of psychological complaints. The psychoanalytic movement has also been largely responsible for perpetuating several popular misconceptions, discussed below. Among these dubious conjectures are: (a) that most psychological problems in adults stem from trauma or abuse in childhood; (b) that people are inevitably damaged, psychologically, by tragedies that befall them; (c) that the mind routinely "represses" memories of events that would be too disconcerting if allowed to enter awareness; and (d) that the mind, when traumatized, readily "splits" to form multiple, experientially isolated personalities.

*The Trauma/Psychopathology Connection.* With respect to the causes of emotional dysfunction, much personal and societal harm has resulted from the uncritical acceptance (among some therapists, as well as the public) of the assumption that most psychological problems stem from trauma or maltreatment early in life. In an excellent critique of this supposition, Pope[19] points out that, alongside those who *were* mistreated and *do* bear emotional scars in later life, many others were abused as children but grew into surprisingly well-adjusted, high-achieving adults. On the other hand, many people enjoyed a loving, supportive upbringing but nonetheless suffer great emotional torment as adults. The conjecture that psychopathology necessarily results from past trauma is easy to accept because it fits our intuition that horrible problems should have horrible causes and because clinical practice typically lacks the appropriate control groups for sorting out such causal attributions.[20] Once again, familiarity with scientific psychology would alert people to the fact that, as far as general happiness or unhappiness with one's lot in life is concerned, inherited constitutional factors account for more variance than one's objective situation.[21] Because abuse sometimes does lead to psychopathology, there is also a tendency to jump to the conclusion that mistreatment necessarily underlies most cases of maladjustment. Many unsuspecting persons, seeking help for vaguely focused problems of living, have stumbled upon recovery-obsessed therapists who assume (and sometimes aggressively suggest) that the cause of the client's unhappiness must lie in forgotten abuse at the hands of family, friends, satanic cults, or visitors from outer space. In their zeal to uncover this mistreatment, these counselors have been known to create false beliefs in their clients that they were victimized.[22]

In a related vein, concern has been raised about the growing number of doubtful diagnoses of posttraumatic stress disorder (PTSD).[23] With the aid of well-meaning therapists, many people are now seeking compensation for emotional difficulties supposedly caused by incidents that are little more than what used to be considered the vicissitudes of life. In fact, most people are far more resilient than is generally believed, and this mounting number of questionable demands for compensation is beginning to threaten the solvency of some insurance plans. As with the aforementioned survivors of abusive childhoods, Bowman[24] has shown that there are substantial individual differences in how people react to major adversity in their lives. Once again, the problem arises from the lack of appropriate comparison groups for forming clinical judgments. Just as someone who spends too much time in the vicinity of the divorce courts might be hard pressed to believe that anyone has a successful marriage, reliance on clinical experience alone can produce an inflated estimate of the likelihood that PTSD will follow a personal misfortune. According to Bowman,[25] many clinicians develop a faulty baseline for making such diagnoses because they typically see only a subset of those who survive catastrophic events, that is, the ones who subsequently seek help for protracted emotional disturbances. The rest, who overcome their horrific experiences in one way or another, get on with their lives and do not show up in therapists' offices, and hence in clinicians' subjective tallies. Consequently, therapists who do not read beyond their narrow professional specialties are in danger of developing unrealistically high expectations that emotional debility will follow a cataclysmic event. This, in turn, can foster an undue willingness to support those who claim to suffer PTSD after relatively mild incidents.

This inclination can be magnified if the therapist is insufficiently mindful of the base rate of similar symptoms in the population at large. In fact, the sorts of difficulties typically attributed to PTSD (mood swings, fatigue, headaches, rotating bodily pains, and difficulties with concentration, memory, sleep, digestion, etc.) are fairly prevalent in those who suffered no comparable trauma.[26] To assume automatically that the symptoms one sees are necessarily the result of past trauma is to commit the logical fallacy known as *post hoc, ergo propter hoc* ("after this, therefore because of this"). The trauma and symptoms may be causally connected, but not necessarily.

*Multiple Personality.* If proof were needed that conventionally trained psychotherapists can succumb to pseudoscientific thinking, a case in point would be the current diagnostic fad Multiple Personality Disorder (MPD), also known as Dissociative Identity Disorder.[27] The mere fact that a psychological syndrome could rocket from obscurity to near epidemic proportions in a remarkably short interval should, in itself, raise suspicions of an iatrogenic component. The MPD fad could only have taken hold where proponents lacked a firm grasp of the relevant empirical literature and insurance carriers were willing to pay for the prolonged treatment that proponents say is required. The modern advocates who revived the formerly discarded diagnosis of MPD seriously underestimated the power of social conditioning in conjunction with the high suggestibility of some individuals to *create* rather than *reveal* apparent multiple personalities. These misconceptions spread rapidly by way of plots in novels and movies, uncritical media reports, and an endless parade of "pop psychology" books aimed at the general public.[28]

The history of the MPD craze has been analyzed in a penetrating volume by the late Nicholas Spanos.[29] It shows how patients with a weakly developed sense of self can interpret the complex, ambiguous communications of therapists in ways that engage imaginal and other cognitive skills to create the subjective experience of as many "alternate" personalities as the therapist will unwittingly reward. In earlier times, these patients would probably have been diagnosed as suffering from hysteria. Like the excellent hypnotic subjects that they are, these "multiples" become totally absorbed in the personas they concoct, focusing on them one by one, as the setting demands.[30]

Unfortunately, Spanos did not live to see a revealing interview with Borch-Jacobsen[31] given by the Columbia psychiatrist Herbert Spiegel. In it, Spiegel revealed for the first time how, in the 1960s, a fellow psychiatrist, Cornelia Wilbur, essentially created the diagnostic category of MPD out of whole cloth. A highly suggestible patient of Wilbur's, whom Spiegel felt was suffering from hysteria, was depicted instead by Wilbur as a "multiple personality." With the help of Flora Schreiber, a popular writer, Wilbur sensationalized the case in a resulting book, *Sybil*.[32] Predictably, it became a runaway best-seller and highly popular movie. Although Spiegel declined Wilbur's offer of coauthorship, because he disbelieved her account, *Sybil* engendered a thriving cottage industry among therapists and self-diagnosed sufferers who believed its far-fetched speculations.

Passing familiarity with the work of T. X. Barber and his colleagues on "fantasy-prone personalities" and other hypnosis-like phenomena would have prompted a greater awareness that social conditioning and compliance with the implied suggestions of an authority figure can create not only "alternate personalities" but also vivid pseudomemories of abduction and sexual molestation by Satanic covens or space aliens.[33] Although client sincerity is not at issue in these cases, there is no reason to believe these experiences are anything but constructions of their own minds.[34]

*Ignorance of research into the nature of memory and social influence: "Recovered" Memories of Childhood Abuse, Satanic Ritual Abuse, or Alien Abduction.* Nonsensical beliefs cease to be merely amusing when pseudo-scientific theories destroy the lives of innocent people. Ignorance of modern research in the areas of memory and interpersonal influence misguides the efforts of counselors who are persuaded by books such as Bass and Davis's *Courage to Heal.*[35] Neither author of this best-selling tome of the recovery movement has any psychological credentials, a fact they proudly proclaim along with their questionable practices for uncovering supposedly repressed memories of sexual abuse.

Sexual abuse of children is a social problem of greater magnitude than most professionals used to think. Nonetheless, in the belated rush to curtail this evil, the pendulum may have swung too far in the opposite direction, fomenting witch-hunts wherein unfounded accusations, based on allegedly "recovered" memories, are automatically believed. As a result, jobs have been unfairly lost, reputations destroyed, and family ties shattered. More than a few innocent people have been sent to jail, and a few were even driven to suicide.[36] It is a concern that, as more of these false accusations become widely known, a backlash might develop that would threaten many of the salutary reforms achieved by those who have led the crusade against real, as opposed to imagined, sexual abuse. An organization has been founded for purposes of helping people who claim to be falsely accused in this way and promoting more scientific views of memory and psychopathology: The False Memory Syndrome Foundation, 3401 Market St., Ste. 130, Philadelphia, PA 19104-3315.

It is doubtful that the "hidden memory" craze could have gained the momentum it did if proponents in the "recovery movement" had been familiar with the relevant research on human memory. Many of their practices are predicated on outmoded views, such as the misconception that memory records every aspect of every experience, much like a videotape that is simply "replayed" verbatim when an event is recalled. In fact, memory is much more abbreviated, inferential, and reconstructive than it feels like when we experience it.[37] As a result, it is also much more prone to confabulation and error than many people believe.

Moreover, as with the credulous espousal of MPD, many in the recovery movement were also unaware of research on suggestibility and interpersonal influence that shows how easy it is to implant false memories, quite unintentionally, during therapy. This, in conjunction with the questionable views about the etiology of psychological distress discussed earlier, led many recovery-oriented counselors to use scientifically unsupportable techniques in ill-advised attempts to ferret out the memory traces they were sure must be hidden in their clients' minds.

Clients' denials of initial suggestions that they had been abused were often ignored because most therapists of this persuasion also subscribe to dubious notions of repression, that is, that traumatic memories are forcibly kept from awareness until they are "recovered" in therapy. It is supposed that a subconscious censor actively keeps troublesome memories out of consciousness until the barrier can be circumvented by special therapeutic techniques. This idea of "strong repression" is also derived from Freudian speculation that has never enjoyed much empirical support.[38] Unfortunately, much research shows that the methods advocated for breaking through the repressive wall are the very ones likely to create false memories. These risky "rejuvenation" techniques include hypnosis, guided imagination, role playing, dwelling on childhood photos and mementoes, and participation in exhortative "recovery group" sessions. Misuse of the much overrated technique of hypnosis in this regard has been widely documented.[39] The ability of subtle suggestions and probing techniques to create highly convincing pseudomemories has been demonstrated repeatedly. The initial comeback of many in the recovery movement was that only a few "bad apples" in the profession lead their clients in this fashion. However, a large-scale survey of relevant beliefs among doctorate-level psychotherapists disputes this.[40] The level of belief in the foregoing misconceptions was found to be very high. Similar pseudomemories can be created when therapists encourage clients' fantasies that they have been abducted and mistreated by extraterrestrials or by underground satanic cults.[41]

A more pernicious side of this mutual delusion of patient and therapist is that many self-professed victims are led to believe that, in order for them to recover, some suspected (often innocent) abuser must pay. In the "satanic ritual abuse" version of this scenario, the abuse supposedly occurs during orgiastic rites of devil worship, sexual perversion, torture, and human sacrifice. Concerted efforts by law enforcement agencies around the world have failed to find any evidence that these allegedly pervasive satanic conspiracies exist.[42] This has not prevented charges being laid and convictions being obtained, however.[43] The fact that supporters of alleged victims of satanic abuse and extraterrestrial abduction firmly believe their "memories," despite the implausibility of such events, should give pause to therapists and prosecutors who accept virtually every patient "recollection" of abuse at face value.

From a purely practical standpoint, encouraging patients to dwell on early traumas, even if they are undeniably real, is questionable in that there is little research to show that it helps victims get better. Instead of pressing patients to ruminate incessantly about tragedies from long ago (which may well exacerbate rather than alleviate their emotional distress), they would probably be better served by sympathetic, practically oriented counselors who will help them pick up the pieces in the here-and-now and aid them in finding workable strategies for achieving a more satisfying future.[44]

*Ignorance of modern brain research.* There are a variety of devices, exercises, and potions vigorously marketed by entrepreneurs who claim they can improve well-being and performance by "reprogramming" or improving the chemical efficiency of the brain. Most proponents have little or no understanding of modern neuroscience and offer even less evidence for their wares.

Descriptions and critical reviews of these New Age sellers' claims can be found in the following references.[45] An example of how even well-trained professionals can fall prey to "neurobabble" and thus promote highly questionable therapies based on outdated notions about brain function is contained in a critical review by Hines.

In a similar vein, questionable notions about brain biochemistry have spawned a large industry selling herbs and supplements that are alleged to have therapeutic effects for various neurological conditions and/or to improve brain function in normal people.[46] Brue and colleagues report on a test of one such combination of products claimed to alleviate the symptoms of attention deficit hyperactivity disorder in children. While the authors find some reason to pursue further research with some components of the supplement cocktail they tested, the results offer little support for the supplement industry's claims in general.

## OTHER QUESTIONABLE PRODUCTS IN THE THERAPEUTIC MARKETPLACE

Space does not permit detailed critiques of the large number of scientifically suspect practices vying for customers in the therapeutic marketplace. Here, I can only list a selection of currently fashionable pseudoscientific psychological products and provide references where the case against them is made in detail.

*Aromatherapy.* Believers claim that the odors of certain "essential oils" have unique and lasting effects on various psychological problems.[47] There are many theoretical and practical difficulties with this notion.[48] In an issue of *SRAM*, Sgoutas-Emch and colleagues present a well-controlled study that fails to support aroma therapists' claims to alleviate stress. These results are in line with those of the present author, who also found (in a blinded study done with the encouragement of professional aroma therapists) no support for the contention of aroma therapists that there are uniquely arousing and sedating essential oils.

*Eye-Movement Desensitization and Reprocessing (EMDR) Therapy.*
Shapiro[49] has promoted the doubtful claim that back-and-forth eye-tracking of a therapist's finger while imagining traumatizing events from the past can cure patients of debilitating anxiety. Several reviews have raised strong doubts about Shapiro's claims.[50] Critics argue that Shapiro merely borrowed elements from existing cognitive-behavior therapies and added the superfluous ingredient of finger waving, with no scientific rationale or data to back up this highly improbable practice. When EMDR works with traumatized people, it is likely because of its overlap with validated treatments such as "cognitive restructuring,"[51] where clients are repeatedly forced to experience traumatic memories, along with desirable thoughts, in order to extinguish their disturbing emotional reactions to recollections of distressing events.

*Handwriting Analysis.* The pseudoscience of graphology claims psychological traits and diagnoses can be derived from the analysis of handwriting. While no scientific case can be made for these claims, even more far-fetched assertions are made by "graphotherapists." The latter contend that undesirable psychological attributes can be eliminated by learning to remove the signs that indicate those traits from one's handwriting. Graphology firms routinely offer marital and psychological advice and consultations on hiring and promotion, the credit worthiness of borrowers, and the guilt or innocence of criminal defendants. Although the evidence against graphology is overwhelming,[52] advertisements continue to appear in journals directed at psychotherapists for graphology seminars that carry continuing education credit for licenced psychologists and psychiatrists. In some advertisements, the promoters promise to teach techniques for identifying secret drug abusers, philanderers, and both perpetrators and victims of sexual abuse from signs supposedly encoded in their handwriting.

*Meditation as Psychotherapy.* Marketing schemes such as Transcendental Meditation (TM) have profited handsomely from those seeking release from the psychological and physical ills attributed to the stresses of today's fast-paced lifestyles. Research papers from TM devotees, largely from the TM-owned Maharishi International University, have claimed special efficacy for the mental exercises prescribed by the TM organization. In addition to their claims of improved physical and psychological health, TM-ers assert that meditators can learn to levitate and that if one percent of the local population takes up TM, the crime rate in that locale will drop. As far as TM's psychological pretensions are concerned, outside evaluators with no personal stake in the outcome find that TM, or any other form of meditation, is no more efficacious than simple rest.[53]

*Therapies That Encourage Clients to Recall Their Thoughts While In Utero, During Birth, or in Early Childhood.* Rebirthing, Primal Scream Therapy, and Dianetics (Scientology) all assert that people can and should recall times in their lives when their brains and cognitive processes were too immature to lay down memories of the sort posited by these theorists.[54] As I have noted elsewhere,[55] our understanding of neural development makes such claims extremely unlikely. As discussed above, the idea that early trauma frequently leads to adult psychopathology is equally questionable. As we have also seen, clients in situations like this are capable of responding to suggestions that they are recalling such events, fooling themselves with pseudomemories of such early times before, during, or after birth.

*Self-Help Psychotherapy Books.* A spate of do-it-yourself therapy and self-improvement books also continues to sell well to an anxious public. The advice they offer runs the gamut from reasonable and useful to bizarre and unsupported.[56]

## CONCLUSION

As long as people refuse to think critically and to put psychotherapy methods to hard-nosed empirical tests, bogus treatments will continue to flood the market. It continues to amaze me that many people who demand extensive, impartial evaluations of automobiles or televisions before making a purchase will put themselves in the hands of psychotherapists with little or no prior investigation of their credentials, theoretical orientations, professional affiliations, or records of successfully helping their clients in the past. For reasons I have summarized earlier,[57] testimonials from satisfied customers are essentially useless in deciding the efficacy of both psychological and medical treatments.

For those who agree that advance screening of psychotherapists by potential consumers is at least as good an idea as checking the qualifications and achievements of would-be home renovation contractors, several sources come to mind. A good overview and critique of various fringe psychotherapies is contained in a special edition of the *International Journal of Mental Health*, edited by Loren Pankratz.[58] Another good source of such information is a volume by Gambrill.[59] A thought-provoking, if occasionally overly strident, critique from within the psychotherapy industry (by one who voluntarily left the profession because of concerns not unlike those voiced in this article) has been penned by Tana Dineen.[60] A thoroughly disillusioned Dineen attacks her former colleagues for making mental illnesses out of what used to be considered the normal hardships of life and for promulgating questionable treatments lacking in scientific rationales and proof of efficacy.

Potential consumers should also know that most state and provincial psychological and psychiatric associations maintain consumer advocacy and quality assurance boards to assist the public in this regard—even though, as we have seen, these organizations have not always been as ready to police their own as one would wish. Good discussions of the latest therapeutic fads by skeptical clinicians are obtainable at sscpnet@ listserv. acns.nwu.edu. The abbreviation "sscp" stands for "Society for a Science of Clinical Psychology," a group of academics and clinicians dedicated to restoring a strong scientific basis for psychotherapy. And finally, it is a pleasure to announce that a new journal has recently been founded that will be dedicated to exposing junk science in psychotherapy. Under the editorship of Scott Lilienfeld, this companion to SRAM's efforts in the biomedical field will be called the *Scientific Review of Mental Health Practice.* In light of the transgressions discussed above, it should be apparent that this is a necessary corrective whose time is long overdue.

*The author would like to express his thanks to Drs. James Alcock, Scott Lilienfeld, and Gerald Rosen for their helpful comments on an earlier version of this paper. The conclusions expressed herein are, of course, those of the author.*

Editor's Note: The *Scientific Review of Mental Health Practice* has since been founded. Interested readers can consult www.srmhp.org for information and access to some past articles.

## NOTES

1. R. D. Rosen, *Psychobabble: Fast Talking in the Era of Feeling* (New York: Atheneum, 1978).

2. C. Evans, *Cults of Unreason* (New York: Farrar, Straus, and Giroux, 1973); R. Miller, *Bare-Faced Messiah: The True Story of L. Ron Hubbard* (Toronto, ON: Key-Porter Books, 1987); R. Behar, "The Thriving Cult of Greed and Power," *Time*, May 6, 1991, pp. 50–57.

3. R. Baker, *Child Sexual Abuse and False Memory Syndrome* (Amherst, NY: Prometheus Books, 1998).

4. R. M. Dawes, *House of Cards: Psychology and Psychotherapy Built on Myth* (New York: Free Press, 1994).

5. P. Meehl, "Psychology: Does Our Heterogenous Subject Matter Have Any Unity?" *Minnesota Psychologist* (Summer 1986): 4.

6. P. McHugh, "Psychiatric Misadventures," *American Scholar* (Autumn 1992): 498–510.

7. Rosen, *Psychobabble*; B. L. Beyerstein, "The Brain and Consciousness: Implications for Psi Phenomena," *Skeptical Inquirer* 12, no. 2 (1988): 163–73.

8. J. E. Mack, *Abduction: Human Encounters with Aliens* (New York: Scribner's, 1994).

9. F. Crews, "The Unknown Freud," *New York Review of Books*, November 18, 1993.

10. S. O. Lilienfeld, "Arguing from a Vacuum," *Skeptical Inquirer* 19, no. 1 (1995): 50–51.

11. Dawes, *House of Cards.*

12. M. A. Hagen, "Damaged Goods?" *Skeptical Inquirer* 25, no. 1 (2001): 54–59.

13. Dawes, *House of Cards*; Lilienfeld, "Arguing from a Vacuum"; "Does Therapy Help?" *Consumer Reports* (November 1995): 734–39.

14. Dawes, *House of Cards.*

15. Crews, "Unknown Freud."

16. T. Gilovich, *How We Know What Isn't So: The Fallibility of Human Reason in Everyday Life* (New York: Free Press/Macmillan, 1991); D. A. Levy, *Tools of Critical Thinking: Metathoughts for Psychology* (Boston: Allyn and Bacon, 1997); L. Chapman and J. Chapman, "Illusory Correlation as an Obstacle to the Use of Valid Psychodiagnostic Signs," *Journal of Abnormal Psychology* 74, no. 3 (1969): 271–80; M. Bowman, *Individual Differences in Posttraumatic Distress: Problems in the Adversity-Distress Connection* (Hillsdale, NJ: Lawrence Erlbaum, 1997).

17. Levy, *Tools of Critical Thinking.*

18. Crews, "Unknown Freud"; A. Grunbaum, *The Foundations of Psychoanalysis: A Philosophical Critique* (Berkeley: University of California Press, 1984); E. F. Torrey, *The Freudian Fraud* (New York: HarperCollins, 1992); P. Gray, "The Assault on Freud," *Time*, November 29, 1993, pp. 47–50; P. Horgan, "Why Freud Isn't Dead," *Scientific American* (December 1996): 106–11.

19. H. G. Pope Jr., *Psychology Astray: Fallacies in Studies of "Repressed Memory" and Childhood Trauma* (Boca Raton, FL: Upton Books, 1997).

20. Gilovich, *How We Know What Isn't So*; Levy, *Tools of Critical Thinking*; Chapman and Chapman, "Illusory Correlation as an Obstacle"; Bowman, *Individual Differences in Posttraumatic Distress.*

21. D. Lykken and A. Tellegen, "Happiness Is a Stochastic Phenomenon," *Psychological Science* 7, no. 3: 186–89.

22. Baker, *Child Sexual Abuse and False Memory Syndrome*; Pope Jr., *Psychology Astray*; E. Loftus and K. Ketcham, *The Myth of Repressed Memory* (New York: St. Martin's Press, 1994); R A. Baker, *Hidden Memories* (Amherst, NY: Prometheus Books, 1992).

23. G. M. Rosen, "Posttraumatic Stress Disorder, Pulp Fiction, and the Press," *Bulletin of the American Academy of Psychiatry and the Law* 24 (1996): 267–69.

24. Bowman, *Individual Differences in Posttraumatic Distress.*

25. Ibid.

26. Ibid.; E. Shorter, *From Paralysis to Fatigue: A History of Psychosomatic Medicine in the Modern Era* (New York: Free Press, 1992).

27. McHugh, "Psychiatric Misadventures."

28. M. Borch-Jacobsen, "Sybil—The Making of a Disease: An Interview with Dr. Herbert Spiegel," *New York Review of Books,* April 24, 1997, pp. 60–64.

29. N. P. Spanos, *Multiple Identities and False Memories* (Washington, DC: American Psychological Association Press, 1996).

30. A. Piper, "Multiple Personality Disorder: Witchcraft Survives in the Twentieth Century," *Skeptical Inquirer* 22, no. 3: 44–50.

31. Borch-Jacobsen, "Sybil—The Making of a Disease," pp. 60–64.

32. F. R. Schreiber, *Sybil* (New York: Regency, 1973).

33. T. X. Barber and S. Wilson, "The Fantasy Prone Personality: Implications for Understanding Imagery, Hypnosis, and Parapsychological Phenomena," in *Imagery: Current Theory, Research and Application,* ed. A. Sheikh (New York: J. Wiley and Sons, 1983), pp. 340–87; R. A. Baker, *They Call It Hypnosis* (Amherst, NY: Prometheus Books, 1990).

34. S. Clark and E. Loftus, "The Construction of Space Alien Memories," *Psychological Inquiry* 7, no. 2 (1997): 140–43.

35. E. Bass and L. Davis, *The Courage to Heal: A Guide for Women Survivors of Child Sexual Abuse* (New York: Harper and Row, 1988).

36. Baker, *Child Sexual Abuse and False Memory Syndrome;* Pope Jr., *Psychology Astray;* F. Crews, "The Revenge of the Repressed (Part 1)," *New York Review of Books,* November 17, 1994, pp. 54–60; F. Crews, "The Revenge of the Repressed (Part 2)," *New York Review of Books,* December 1, 1994, pp. 49–58.

37. Baker, *Child Sexual Abuse and False Memory Syndrome;* Loftus and Ketcham, *Myth of Repressed Memory;* D. S. Lindsay and J. D. Read, "Psychotherapy and Memories of Childhood Sexual Abuse: A Cognitive Perspective," *Applied Cognitive Psychology* 8 (1994): 281–338.

38. Pope Jr., *Psychology Astray;* Loftus and Ketcham, *Myth of Repressed Memory;* Lindsay and Read, "Psychotherapy and Memories of Childhood Sexual Abuse"; D. Holmes, "The Evidence for Repression: An Examination of Sixty Years of Research," in *Repression and Dissociation: Implications for Personality Theory, Psychopathology and Health,* ed. J. Singer (Chicago: University of Chicago Press, 1990).

39. Spanos, *Multiple Identities and False Memories;* Piper, "Multiple Person-

ality Disorder"; M. Yapko, "Suggestibility and Repressed Memories of Abuse: A Survey of Psychotherapists' Beliefs," *American Journal of Clinical Hypnosis* 36, no. 3 (1994): 163–71.

40. D. A. Poole, D. S. Lindsay, A. Memon, and R. Bull, "Psychotherapy and the Recovery of Memories of Childhood Sexual Abuse: U.S. and British Practitioners' Opinions, Practices, and Experiences," *Journal of Consulting and Clinical Psychology* 63, no. 3 (1995): 426–37; Z. Katz, "Canadian Psychologists' Education, Trauma History, and the Recovery of Memories of Childhood Sexual Abuse," doctoral dissertation, Department of Psychology, Simon Fraser University, Burnaby, BC, Canada, 2000.

41. P. A. Klass, *UFO Abductions: A Dangerous Game* (Amherst, NY: Prometheus Books, 1988); R. D. Hicks, "Police Pursuit of Satanic Crime," *Skeptical Inquirer* 14, no. 3 (1990): 276–86.

42. Hicks, "Police Pursuit of Satanic Crime."

43. R. Wright, *Remembering Satan* (New York: Vintage Books, 1995).

44. Bowman, *Individual Differences in Posttraumatic Distress*.

45. B. L. Beyerstein, "Brainscams: Neuromythologies of the New Age," *International Journal of Mental Health* 19 (1990): 27–36; B. L. Beyerstein, "Pseudoscience and the Brain: Tuners and Tonics for Aspiring Superhumans," in *Mind-Myths: Exploring Everyday Mysteries of the Mind and Brain*, ed. S. Della Sala (Chichester, UK: John Wiley and Sons, 1999), pp. 59–82.

46. Beyerstein, "Pseudoscience and the Brain," pp. 59–82.

47. M. Scholes, *Aromatherapy* (n.p.: Aroma Press International, 1993), p. 50; L. McCutcheon, "What's That I Smell? The Claims of Aromatherapy," *Skeptical Inquirer* 20, no. 3 (1996): 35–37.

48. H. Lawless, "Effects of Odors on Mood and Behavior: Aromatherapy and Related Effects," in *The Human Sense of Smell*, ed. Laing et al. (Berlin: Springer-Verlag, 1991), pp. 361–87.

49. F. Shapiro, "Eye Movement Desensitization: A New Treatment for Posttraumatic Stress Disorder," *Journal of Behavior Therapy and Experimental Psychiatry* 20 (1989): 211–17.

50. S. O. Lilienfeld, "EMDR Treatment: Less than Meets the Eye?" *Skeptical Inquirer* 20, no. 1 (1996): 25–31; G. M. Rosen, "A Note to EMDR Critics: What You Didn't See Is Only Part of What You Didn't Get," *Behavior Therapist* 16 (1993): 216; G. M. Rosen, "Treatment Fidelity and Research on Eye Movement Desensitization and Reprocessing (EMDR)," *Journal of Anxiety Disorders* 13,

nos. 1–2 (1999): 173–84; J. M. Lohr, R. A. Kleinknecht, D. F. Tolin, and H. Richard, "The Empirical Status and the Clinical Application of Eye Movement Desensitization and Reprocessing," *Journal of Behavior Therapy and Experimental Psychiatry* 26, no. 4 (1995): 285–302.

51. D. Meichenbaum, "Examination of Model Characteristics and Reducing Avoidance Behavior," *Journal of Personality and Social Psychology* 17 (1971): 298–307.

52. B. Beyerstein and D. Beyerstein, eds., *The Write Stuff—Evaluations of Graphology* (Amherst, NY: Prometheus Books, 1992).

53. M. A. West, ed., *The Psychology of Meditation* (Oxford, UK: Clarendon Press, 1987); S. Blackmore, "Is Meditation Good for You?" *New Scientist* (July 6, 1991): 30–33.

54. Rosen, *Psychobabble: Fast Talking in the Era of Feeling*.

55. Beyerstein, "The Brain and Consciousness."

56. G. M. Rosen, "Self-Help Treatment Books and the Commercialization of Psychotherapy," *American Psychologist* 42, no. 1 (1987): 46–51; E. Gambrill, *Critical Thinking in Clinical Practice* (San Francisco: Jossey-Bass, 1990).

57. B. L. Beyerstein, "Social and Judgmental Biases That Make Inert Treatments Seem to Work," *Scientific Review of Alternative Medicine* 3, no. 2 (1999): 20–33.

58. L. Pankratz, ed., "Unvalidated, Fringe, and Fraudulent Treatment of Mental Disorders," *International Journal of Mental Health* 19, no. 3 (1990).

59. Gambrill, *Critical Thinking in Clinical Practice*.

60. T. Dineen, *Manufacturing Victims: What the Psychology Industry Is Doing to People* (Montreal: Robert Davies, 1996).

# 2.

# SCIENCE AND PSEUDOSCIENCE IN CLINICAL PSYCHOLOGY: INITIAL THOUGHTS, REFLECTIONS, AND CONSIDERATIONS

*Scott O. Lilienfeld, Steven Jay Lynn, and Jeffrey M. Lohr*

— ORI the Problem -

As Bob Dylan wrote, "The times they are a-changin'." Over the past several decades, clinical psychology and allied disciplines (e.g., psychiatry, social work, counseling) have borne witness to a virtual sea-change in the relation between science and practice. A growing minority of clinicians appear to be basing their therapeutic and assessment practices primarily on clinical experience and intuition rather than on research evidence. As a consequence, the term "scientist-practitioner gap" is being invoked with heightened frequency (Fox 1996), and concerns that the scientific foundations of clinical psychology are steadily eroding are being voiced increasingly in many quarters (Dawes 1994; Kalal 1990; McFall 1991).

Some might contend that the problem of unsubstantiated treatment techniques is not new and has in fact dogged the field of clinical psychology virtually since its inception. To a certain extent, they would be correct. Nevertheless, the growing availability of information resources (some of which have also become misinformation resources), including popular psychology books and the Internet, the dramatic upsurge in the number of mental health training programs that do not emphasize sci-

> ORIGIN, nature, validity, values.

entific training (Beyerstein 2001), and the burgeoning industry of fringe psychotherapies, has magnified the gulf between scientist and practitioner to a problem of critical proportions.

# THE SCIENTIST-PRACTITIONER GAP AND ITS SOURCES

What are the primary sources of the growing scientist–practitioner gap? As many authors have noted (see Lilienfeld 1998; 2001, for a discussion), some practitioners in clinical psychology and related mental health disciplines appear to making increased use of unsubstantiated, untested, and otherwise questionable treatment and assessment methods. Moreover, psychotherapeutic methods of unknown or doubtful validity are proliferating on an almost weekly basis. For example, a recent and highly selective sampling of fringe psychotherapeutic practices (Eisner 2000; see also Singer & Lalich 1996) included neurolinguistic programming, eye movement desensitization and reprocessing, Thought Field Therapy, Emotional Freedom Technique, rage reduction therapy, primal scream therapy, feeling therapy, Buddha psychotherapy, past lives therapy, future lives therapy, alien abduction therapy, angel therapy, rebirthing, Sedona method, Silva method, entity depossession therapy, vegetotherapy, palm therapy, and a plethora of other methods.

Moreover, a great deal of academic and media coverage of such fringe treatments is accompanied by scant critical evaluation. For example, and edited volume (Shannon 2002) features twenty-three chapters on largely unsubstantiated psychological techniques, including music therapy, homeopathy, breath work, therapeutic touch, aromatherapy, medical intuition, acupuncture, and body-centered psychotherapies. Nevertheless, in most chapters, these techniques receive minimal scientific scrutiny (see Corsini 2001 for a similar example).

Additional threats to the scientific foundations of clinical psychology and allied fields stem from the thriving self-help industry. This industry produces hundreds of new books, manuals, and audiotapes each year, many of which promise rapid or straightforward solutions to complex life problems. Although some of these self-help materials may be efficacious, the overwhelming majority of them have never been subjected to empirical scrutiny. In addition, an ever-increasing contingent of self-help "gurus" on television and radio talk shows routinely offer advice of questionable scientific validity to a receptive, but often vulnerable, audience of troubled individuals.

Similarly questionable practices can be found in the domains of psychological assessment and diagnosis. Despite well-replicated evidence that statistical (actuarial) formulas are superior to clinical judgment for a broad range of judgmental and predictive tasks (Grove et al. 2000), most clinicians continue to rely on clinical judgment even in cases in which it has been shown to be ill advised. There is also evidence that many practitioners tend to be overconfident in their judgments and predictions, and to fall prey to basic errors in reasoning (e.g., confirmatory bias, illusory correlation) in the process of case formulation. Moreover, many practitioners base their interpretations on assessment instruments (e.g., human figure drawing tests, Rorschach Inkblot Test, Myers-Briggs Type Indicator, anatomically detailed dolls) that are either highly controversial or questionable from a scientific standpoint.

Still other clinicians render confident diagnoses of psychiatric conditions, such as dissociative identity disorder (known formerly as multiple personality disorder), whose validity remains in dispute (see Gleaves, May & Cardena 2001, for a different perspective). The problem of questionable diagnostic labels is especially acute in courtroom settings, where psychiatric labels of unknown or doubtful validity (e.g., road rage syndrome, sexual addiction, premenstrual dysphoric disorder) are sometimes invoked as exculpatory defenses.

## STRIKING A BALANCE BETWEEN EXCESSIVE OPEN-MINDEDNESS AND EXCESSIVE SKEPTICISM

It is critical to emphasize that at least some of the largely or entirely untested psychotherapeutic, assessment, and diagnostic methods reviewed in this volume may ultimately prove to be efficacious or valid. It would be a serious error to dismiss any untested techniques out of hand or antecedent to prior critical scrutiny. Such closed-mindedness has sometimes characterized debates concerning the efficacy of novel psychotherapies (Beutler & Harwood 2001). Nevertheless, a basic tenet of science is that the burden of proof always falls squarely on the claimant, not the critic (see Shermer 1997). Consequently, it is up to the proponents of these techniques to demonstrate that they work, not up to the critics of these techniques to demonstrate the converse.

As Carl Sagan (1995b) eloquently pointed out, scientific inquiry demands a unique mix of open-mindedness and penetrating skepticism (see also Shermer 2001). We must remain open to novel and untested claims, regardless of how superficially implausible they might appear at first blush. At the same time, we must subject these claims to incisive scrutiny to ensure that they withstand the crucible of rigorous scientific testing. As space scientist James Oberg observed, keeping an open mind is a virtue, but this mind cannot be so open that one's brains fall out (Sagan 1995a). Although the requirement to hold all claims to high levels of critical scrutiny applies to all domains of science, such scrutiny is especially crucial in applied areas, such as clinical psychology, in which erroneous claims or ineffective practices have the potential to produce harm.

## WHY POTENTIALLY PSEUDOSCIENTIFIC TECHNIQUES CAN BE HARMFUL

Some might respond to our arguments by contending that although many of the techniques reviewed in this book are either untested or ineffective, most are likely to prove either efficacious or innocuous. From this perspective, our emphasis on the dangers posed by such techniques is misplaced, because unresearched mental health practices are at worst inert.

Nevertheless, this counterargument overlooks several important considerations. Specifically, there are at least three major ways in which unsubstantiated mental health techniques can be problematic (Lilienfeld 2002; see also Beyerstein 2001). First, some may be harmful per se. The tragic case of Candace Newmaker, the ten-year-old Colorado girl who was smothered to death in 2000 by therapists practicing a variant of rebirthing therapy, attests to the dangers of implementing untested therapeutic techniques (see Mercer 2002). There is also increasing reason to suspect that certain suggestive techniques (e.g., hypnosis, guided imagery) for unearthing purportedly repressed memories of childhood trauma may exacerbate or even produce psychopathology by inadvertently implanting false memories of past events. Even the use of facilitated communication for infantile autism has resulted in erroneous accusations of child abuse against family members. Moreover, there is accumulating evidence that certain widely used treatment techniques, such as critical incident stress debriefing, peer group interventions for adolescents with conduct disorders (Dishion, McCord & Poulin 1999), and certain self-help programs (Rosen 1987) may sometimes be harmful. Consequently, the oft-held assumption that "doing something is always better than doing nothing" in the domain of psychotherapy is likely to be mistaken. As psychologist Richard Gist reminds us, doing something is not license to do anything.

Second, even psychotherapies that are by themselves innocuous can indirectly produce harm by depriving individuals of scare time, financial resources, or both. Economists refer to this side effect as "opportunity cost." As a consequence of opportunity cost, individuals who would otherwise use their time and money to seek out demonstrably efficacious treatments may be left with precious little of either. Such individuals may therefore be less likely to obtain interventions that could prove beneficial.

Third, the use of unsubstantiated techniques eats away at the scientific foundations of the profession of clinical psychology (Lilienfeld 1998; McFall 1991). As one of us (Lilienfeld 2002) observed:

> Once we abdicate our responsibility to uphold high scientific standards in administering treatments, our scientific credibility and influence are badly damaged. Moreover, by continuing to ignore the imminent dangers posed by questionable mental health techniques, we send an implicit message to our students that we are not deeply committed to anchoring our discipline in scientific evidence or to combating potentially unscientific practices. Our students will most likely follow in our footsteps and continue to turn a blind eye to the widening gap between scientist and practitioner, and between research evidence and clinical work. (p. 9)

In addition, the promulgation of treatment and assessment techniques of questionable validity can undermine the general public's faith in the profession of clinical psychology, and lead citizens to place less trust in the assertions of clinical researchers and practitioners.

## THE DIFFERENCES BETWEEN SCIENCE AND PSEUDOSCIENCE: A PRIMER

To distinguish scientific from pseudoscientific claims in clinical psychology, we must first delineate the principal differences between scientific and pseudoscientific research programs. As one of us has noted elsewhere (Lilienfeld 1998), science probably differs from pseudoscience in degree rather than in kind. Science and pseudoscience can be thought of as Roschian (Rosch 1973) or open (Meehl & Golden 1982; Pap 1953) concepts, which possess intrinsically fuzzy boundaries and an indefinitely extendable list of indicators. Nevertheless, the fuzziness of such categories does not mean that distinctions between science and pseudoscience are fictional or entirely arbitrary. As psychophysicist S. S.

Stevens observed, the fact that the precise boundary between day and night is indistinct does not imply that day and night cannot be meaningfully differentiated (see Leahey & Leahey 1983). From this perspective, pseudosciences can be conceptualized as possessing a fallible, but nevertheless useful, list of indicators or "warning signs." The more such warning signs a discipline exhibits, the more it begins to cross the murky dividing line separating science from pseudoscience (see also Herbert et al. 2000). A number of philosophers of science (e.g., Bunge 1984) and psychologists (e.g., Ruscio 2001) have outlined some of the most frequent features of pseudoscience. Among these features are the following (for further discussions, see Herbert et al. 2000; Hines 1988; Lilienfeld 1998):

1. *An overuse of ad hoc hypotheses designed to immunize claims from falsification.* From a Popperian or neo-Popperian standpoint (see Popper 1959) assertions that could never in principle be falsified are unscientific (but see McNally 2003 for a critique of Popperian notions). The repeated invocation of ad hoc hypotheses to explain away negative findings is a common tactic among proponents of pseudoscientific claims. Moreover, in most pseudosciences, ad hoc hypotheses are simply "pasted on" to plug holes in the theory in question. When taken to an extreme, ad hoc hypotheses can provide an impenetrable barrier against potential refutation. For example, some proponents of eye movement desensitization and reprocessing (EMDR) have argued that negative findings concerning EMDR are almost certainly attributable to low levels of fidelity to the treatment procedure. But they have typically been inconsistent in their application of the treatment fidelity concept (Rosen 1999).

   It is crucial to emphasize that the invocation of ad hoc hypotheses in the face of negative evidence is sometimes a legitimate strategy in science. In scientific research programs, however, such maneuvers tend to enhance the theory's content, predictive power, or both (see Lakatos 1978).

2. *Absence of self-correction.* Scientific research programs are not necessarily distinguished from pseudoscientific research programs in the verisimilitude of their claims, because proponents of both programs frequently advance incorrect assertions. Nevertheless, in the long run, most scientific research programs tend to eliminate these errors, whereas most pseudoscientific research programs do not. Consequently, intellectual stagnation is a hallmark of most pseudoscientific research programs (Ruscio 2001). For example, astrology has changed remarkably little in the past 2,500 years (Hines 1988).

3. *Evasion of peer review.* On a related note, many proponents of pseudoscience avoid subjecting their work to the often ego-bruising process of peer review (Ruscio 2001; see also Gardner 1957, for illustrations). In some cases, they may do so on the grounds that the peer-review process is inherently biased against findings or claims that contradict well-established paradigms (e.g., see Callahan 2001a for an illustration involving Thought Field Therapy). In other cases, they may avoid the peer-review process on the grounds that their assertions cannot be evaluated adequately using standard scientific methods. Although the peer-review process is far from flawless (see Peters & Ceci 1982 for a striking example), it remains the best mechanism for self-correction in science and assists investigators in identifying errors in their reasoning, methodology, and analyses. By remaining largely insulated from peer review, some proponents of pseudoscience forfeit an invaluable opportunity to obtain corrective feedback from informed colleagues.

4. *Emphasis on confirmation rather refutation.* The brilliant physicist Richard Feynman (1985) maintained that the essence of science is a bending over backwards to prove oneself wrong. Bartley (1962) similarly maintained that science at its best involves the maximization of constructive criticism. Ideally, scientists subject their cherished claims to grave risk of refutation (Meehl 1978; see also Ruscio 2001). In contrast, pseudo-

scientists tend to seek only confirming evidence for their claims. Because a determined advocate can find at least some supportive evidence for virtually any claim (Popper 1959), this confirmatory hypothesis-testing strategy is not an efficient means of rooting out error in one's web of beliefs.

Moreover, as Bunge (1967) observed, most pseudosciences manage to reinterpret negative or anomalous findings as corroborations of their claims (see Herbert et al. 2000). For example, proponents of extrasensory perception (ESP) have sometimes interpreted isolated cases of worse-than-chance performance on parapsychological tasks (known as "psi missing") as evidence of ESP (Gilovich 1991; Hines 1988).

5. *Reversed burden of proof.* As noted earlier, the burden of proof in science rests invariably on the individual making a claim, not on the critic. Proponents of pseudoscience frequently neglect this principle and instead demand that skeptics demonstrate beyond a reasonable doubt that a claim (e.g., an assertion regarding the efficacy of a novel therapeutic technique) is false. This error is similar to the logician's ad ignorantium fallacy (i.e., the argument from ignorance), the mistake of assuming that a claim is likely to be correct merely because there is no compelling evidence against it (Shermer 1997). For example, some proponents of unidentified flying objects (UFOs) have insisted that skeptics account for every unexplained report of an anomalous event in the sky (Hines 1988; Sagan 1995a). But because it is essentially impossible to prove a universal negative, this tactic incorrectly places the burden of proof on the skeptic rather than the claimant.

6. *Absence of connectivity.* In contrast to most scientific research programs, pseudoscientific research programs tend to lack "connectivity" with other scientific disciplines (Bunge 1983; Stanovich 2001). In other words, pseudosciences often purport to create entirely new paradigms out of whole cloth rather than to build on extant paradigms. In so doing, they often neglect well-established scientific principles or hard-won scientific

knowledge. For example, many proponents of ESP argue that it is a genuine (although heretofore undetected) physical process of perception, even though reported cases of ESP violate almost every major law of physical signals (e.g., ESP purportedly operates just as strongly from thousands of miles away as it does from a few feet away). Although scientists should always remain open to the possibility that an entirely novel paradigm has successfully overturned all preexisting paradigms, they must insist on very high standards of evidence before drawing such a conclusion.

7. *Overreliance on testimonial and anecdotal evidence.* Testimonial and anecdotal evidence can be quite useful in the early stages of scientific investigation. Nevertheless, such evidence is typically much more helpful in the context of discovery (i.e., hypothesis generation) than in the context of justification (i.e., hypothesis testing; see Reichenbach 1938). Proponents of pseudoscientific claims frequently invoke reports from selected cases (e.g., "This treatment clearly worked for Person X, because Person X improved markedly following the treatment") as a means of furnishing dispositive evidence for these claims. For example, proponents of certain treatments (e.g., secretin) for autistic disorder have often pointed to uncontrolled case reports of improvement as supportive evidence.

As Gilovich (1991) observed, however, case reports almost never provide sufficient evidence for a claim, although they often provide necessary evidence for this claim. For example, if a new form of psychotherapy is efficacious, one should certainly expect at least some positive case reports of improvement. But such case reports do not provide adequate evidence that the improvement was attributable to the psychotherapy, because this improvement could have been produced by a host of other influences (e.g., placebo effects, regression to the mean, spontaneous remission, maturation; see Cook & Campbell 1979).

8. *Use of obscurantist language.* Many proponents of pseudoscience use impressive-sounding or highly technical jargon in an effort to

provide their disciplines with the superficial trappings of science (see van Rillaer 1991 for a discussion of "strategies of dissimulation" in pseudoscience). Such language may be convincing to individuals unfamiliar with the scientific underpinnings of the claims in question and may therefore lend these claims an unwarranted imprimatur of scientific legitimacy.

For example, the developer of EMDR explained the efficacy of this treatment as follows:

[The] valences of the neural receptors (synaptic potential) of the respective neuro networks, which separately store various information plateaus and levels of adaptive information, are represented by the letters Z through A. It is hypothesized that the high-valence target network (Z) cannot link up with the more adaptive information, which is stored in networks with a lower valence. That is, the synaptic potential is different for each level of affect held in the various neuro networks. . . . The theory is that when the processing system is catalyzed in EMDR, the valence of the receptors is shifted downward so that they are capable of linking with the receptors of the neuro networks with progressively lower valences. . . . (Shapiro 1995, 317–18)

9. *Absence of boundary conditions.* Most well-supported scientific theories possess boundary conditions, that is, well-articulated limits under which predicted phenomena do and do not apply. In contrast, many or most pseudoscientific phenomena are purported to operate across an exceedingly wide range of conditions. As Hines (1988; 2001) noted, one frequent characteristic of fringe psychotherapies is that they are ostensibly efficacious for almost all disorders regardless of their etiology. For example, some proponents of Thought Field Therapy have proposed that this treatment is beneficial for virtually all mental disorders. Moreover, the developer of this treatment has posited that it is efficacious not only for adults but for "horses, dogs, cats, infants, and very young children" (Callahan 2001b, 1255).

10. *The mantra of holism.* Proponents of pseudoscientific claims, especially in organic medicine and mental health, often resort to the "mantra of holism" (Ruscio 2001) to explain away negative findings. When invoking this mantra, they typically maintain that scientific claims can be evaluated only within the context of broader claims and therefore cannot be judged in isolation. For example, some proponents of the Rorschach Inkblot Test have responded to criticisms of this technique by asserting that clinicians virtually never interpret results from a Rorschach in isolation. Instead, in actual practice clinicians consider numerous pieces of information, only one of which may be a Rorschach protocol. There are two major difficulties with this line of reasoning. First, it implies that clinicians can effectively integrate in their heads a great deal of complex psychometric information from diverse sources, a claim that is doubtful given the research literature on clinical judgment. Second, by invoking the mantra of holism, proponents of the Rorschach and other techniques can readily avoid subjecting their claims to the risk of falsification. In other words, if research findings corroborate the validity of a specific Rorschach index, Rorschach proponents can point to these findings as supportive evidence, but if these findings are negative, Rorschach proponents can explain them away by maintaining that "clinicians never interpret this index in isolation anyway" (see Merlo & Barnett 2001 for an example). This "heads I win, tails you lose" reasoning places the claims of these proponents largely outside of the boundaries of science.

We encourage readers to bear in mind the aforementioned list of pseudoscience indicators (see Ruscio 2001 for other useful indicators) when evaluating the claims in this volume. At the same time, we remind readers that these indicators are only probabilistically linked to pseudoscientific research programs. Scientists, even those who are well trained, are not immune from such practices. In scientific research programs, however, such practices tend to be weeded out eventually through the slow but steady process of self-correction. In contrast to sciences, in which erroneous claims tend to be gradually ferreted out by a process akin to natural selection (e.g., see Campbell's [1974] discussion of evolutionary epistemology), pseudosciences tend to remain stagnant in the face of contradictory evidence.

# 5. CONSTRUCTIVE EFFORTS TO ADDRESS THE PROBLEM

Until fairly recently, the field of clinical psychology has shown relatively little interest in addressing the threats posed by pseudoscientific or otherwise questionable practices. Paul Meehl (1993), perhaps the foremost clinical psychologist of the latter half of the twentieth century, observes,

> It is absurd, as well as arrogant, to pretend that acquiring a Ph.D. somehow immunizes me from the errors of sampling, perception, recording, retention, retrieval, and inference to which the human mind is suspect. In earlier times, all introductory psychology courses devoted a lecture or two to the classic studies in the psychology of testimony, and one mark of a psychologist was hard-nosed skepticism about folk beliefs. It seems that quite a few clinical psychologists never got exposed to this basic feature of critical thinking. My teachers at [the University of] Minnesota . . . shared what Bertrand Russell called the dominant passion of the true scientist—the passion not to be fooled and not to fool anybody else . . . all of them asked the two searching questions of positivism: "What do you mean?" "How do you know?" If we clinicians lose that passion and forget those questions, we are little more than be-doctored, well-paid soothsayers. I see disturbing signs that this is happening and I predict that, if we do not clean up our clinical act and provide our students with role models of scientific thinking, outsiders will do it for us. (pp. 728–29)

Nevertheless, the past decade has witnessed a number of constructive efforts to address the problems posed by questionable and potentially pseudoscientific methods in clinical psychology. Two of these efforts have originated within the American Psychological Association (APA), an organization that has been chastised for turning a blind eye to the festering problem of pseudoscience within clinical psychology (Lilienfeld 1998). First, Division 12 of the APA has advanced a set of criteria for empirically supported treatments (ESTs) for adult and childhood disorders, along with provisional lists of therapeutic techniques that satisfy these criteria (see Chambless & Ollendick 2001 for a thoughtful review). Vigorous and healthy debate surrounds the criteria established for identifying ESTs as well as the current list of ESTs (Herbert 2000). Despite this controversy, it seems clear that the increasing push toward ESTs reflects a heightened emphasis on distinguishing interventions that are scientifically supported from those whose support is negligible or nonexistent. Second, there is suggestive evidence that certain APA committees have begun to move in the direction of addressing the threats posed by unsubstantiated psychotherapies. For example, several years ago, the APA Continuing Education (CE) Committee turned down workshops on Thought Field Therapy for CE credit on the grounds that the scientific evidence for this treatment was not sufficiently compelling (or even suggestive) to warrant its dissemination to practitioners (Lilienfeld & Lohr 2000).

In addition, the Committee for the Scientific Investigation of Claims of the Paranormal established a new subcommittee dedicated to evaluating the validity of questionable or untested mental health claims. Finally, Prometheus Books launched an interdisciplinary journal, the *Scientific Review of Mental Health Practice*, which is devoted to distinguishing scientifically supported from scientifically unsupported claims in clinical psychology, psychiatry, social work, and allied disciplines. These and other recent developments (see Lilienfeld 2002) suggest that careful attention is at long last being accorded to questionable and potentially pseudoscientific practices in clinical psychology and to distinguishing them from practices with stronger evidentiary support.

# REFERENCES

Bartley, W. W. 1962. *The Retreat to Commitment.* New York: Knopf.

Beutler, L. E., and T. M. Harwood. 2001. Antiscientific attitudes: What happens when scientists are unscientific? *Journal of Clinical Psychology* 57: 43–51.

Beyerstein, B. L. 2001. Fringe psychotherapies: The public at risk. *Scientific Review of Alternative Medicine* 5: 70–79.

Bunge, M. 1967. *Scientific Research.* New York: Springer.

———. 1983. Speculation: Wild and sound. *New Ideas in Psychology* 1: 3–6.

———. 1984. What is pseudoscience? *Skeptical Inquirer* 9 (Fall): 36–46.

Callahan, R. J. 2001a. The impact of Thought Field Therapy on heart rate variability. *Journal of Clinical Psychology* 57: 1154–70.

———. 2001b. Thought Field Therapy: Response to our critics and a scrutiny of some old ideas of science. *Journal of Clinical Psychology* 57: 1251–60.

Campbell, D. T. 1974. Evolutionary epistemology. In *The Philosophy of Karl R. Popper,* edited by P. A. Schilpp. LaSalle, IL: Open Court, pp. 412–63.

Chambless, D. L., and T. H. Ollendick. 2001. Empirically supported psychological interventions: Controversies and evidence. *Annual Review of Psychology* 52: 685–716.

Cook, T. D., and D. T. Campbell. 1979. *Quasi-Experimentation: Design and Analysis Issues for Field Settings.* Boston: Houghton Mifflin.

Corsini, R. J., ed. 2001. *Handbook of Innovative Therapy.* 2nd ed. New York: Wiley.

Dawes, R. M. 1994. *House of Cards: Psychology and Psychotherapy Built on Myth.* New York: Free Press.

Dishion, T., J. McCord, and F. Poulin. 1999. When interventions harm: Peer groups and problem behavior. *American Psychologist* 54: 755–64.

Eisner, D. A. 2000. *The Death of Psychotherapy: From Freud to Alien Abductions.* Westport, CT: Praeger.

Feynman, R. P., with R. Leighton. 1985. *Surely You're Joking, Mr. Feynman: Adventures of a Curious Character.* New York: Norton.

Fox, R. E. 1996. Charlatanism, scientism, and psychology's social contract. *American Psychologist* 51: 777–84.

Gardner, M. 1957. *Fads and Fallacies in the Name of Science.* New York: Dover.

Gilovich, T. 1991. *How We Know What Isn't So: The Fallibility of Human Reason in Everyday Life.* New York: Free Press.

Gleaves, D. H., M. C. May, and E. Cardena. 2001. An examination of the diagnostic validity of dissociative identity disorder. *Clinical Psychology Review* 21: 577–608.

Grove, W. M., D. H. Zald, B. S. Lebow, B. E. Snitz, and C. Nelson. 2000. Clinical versus mechanical prediction: A meta-analysis. *Psychological Assessment* 12: 19–30.

Herbert, J. D. 2000. Defining empirically supported treatments: Pitfalls and possible solutions. *Behavior Therapist* 23: 113–34.

Herbert, J. D., S. O. Lilienfeld, J. M. Lohr, R. W. Montgomery, W. T. O'Donohue, G. M. Rosen, and D. F. Tolin. 2000. Science and pseudoscience in the development of eye movement desensitization and reprocessing. *Clinical Psychology Review* 20: 945–71.

Hines, T. 1988. *Pseudoscience and the Paranormal: A Critical Examination of the Evidence.* Amherst, NY: Prometheus Books.

———. 2001. The Doman-Delacato patterning treatment for brain damage. *Scientific Review of Alternative Medicine* 5: 80–89.

Kalal, D. M. 1990. Critical thinking in clinical practice: Pseudoscience, fad psychology, and the behavior therapist. *Behavior Therapist* (April): 81–84.

Lakatos, I. 1978. *Philosophical Papers*, vol. 1: *The Methodology of Scientific Research Programmes*, edited by J. Worrall and G. Currie. New York: Cambridge University Press.

Leahey, T. H., and G. E. Leahey. 1983. *Psychology's Occult Doubles: Psychology and the Problem of Pseudoscience.* Chicago: Nelson-Hall.

Lilienfeld, S. O. 1998. Pseudoscience in contemporary clinical psychology: What it is and what we can do about it. *Clinical Psychologist* 51: 3–9.

———. 2001. Fringe psychotherapies: Scientific and ethical implications for clinical psychology. Paper presented at the Annual Meeting of the American Psychological Association, San Francisco.

———. 2002. The Scientific Review of Mental Health Practice: Our raison d'etre. *Scientific Review of Mental Health Practice* 1: 5–10.

Lilienfeld, S. O., and J. M. Lohr. 2000. News and comment: Thought Field Therapy educators and practitioners sanctioned. *Skeptical Inquirer* 24: 5.

McFall, R. M. 1991. Manifesto for a science of clinical psychology. *Clinical Psychologist* 44: 75–88.

McNally, R. J. 1978. Theoretical risks or tabular asterisks: Sir Karl, Sir Ronald, and the slow progress of soft psychology. *Journal of Consulting and Clinical Psychology* 46: 816–34.

————. 1993. Philosophy of science: Help or hindrance? *Psychological Reports* 72: 707–33.

————. 2003. The demise of pseudoscience. *Scientific Review of Mental Health Practice* 2, no. 2 (Fall/Winter): 97–101.

Meehl, P. E., and R. R. Golden. 1982. Taxometric methods. In *Handbook of Research Methods in Clinical Psychology*, edited by P. C. Kendall and J. N. Butcher. New York: Wiley, pp. 127–81.

Mercer, J. 2002. Attachment therapy: A treatment without empirical support. *Scientific Review of Mental Health Practice* 1, no. 2: 105–12.

Merlo, L., and D. Barnett. 2001. All about inkblots. *Scientific American* 285 (September): 13.

Pap, A. 1953. Reduction sentences and open concepts. *Methodos* 5: 3–30.

Peters, D. P., and S. J. Ceci. 1982. Peer-review practices of psychological journals: The fate of published articles, submitted again. *Behavioral and Brain Sciences* 5: 187–255.

Popper, K. R. 1959. *The Logic of Scientific Discovery*. New York: Basic Books.

Reichenbach, H. 1938. *Experience and Prediction*. Chicago: University of Illinois Press.

Rosch, E. 1973. Natural categories. *Cognitive Psychology* 4: 328–50.

Rosen, G. M. 1987. Self-help treatment books and the commercialization of psychotherapy. *American Psychologist* 42: 46–51.

————. 1999. Treatment fidelity and research on eye movement desensitization and reprocessing. *Journal of Anxiety Disorders* 13: 173–84.

Ruscio, J. 2001. *Clear Thinking with Psychology: Separating Sense from Nonsense*. Pacific Grove, CA: Wadsworth.

Sagan, C. 1995a. *The Demon-Haunted World: Science as a Candle in the Dark*. New York: Random House.

————. 1995b. Wonder and skepticism. *Skeptical Inquirer* (January/February): 19, 24–30.

Shannon, S., ed. 2002. *Handbook of Complementary and Alternative Therapies in Mental Health*. San Diego, CA: Academic Press.

Shapiro, E. 1995. *Eye Movement Desensitization and Reprocessing: Basic Protocols, Principles, and Procedures*. New York: Guilford Press.

Shermer, M. 1997. *Why People Believe Weird Things: Pseudoscience, Superstition, and Other Confusions of Our Time*. New York: Freeman.

————. 2001. *The Borderlands of Science: Where Sense Meets Nonsense*. New York: Oxford University Press.

Singer, M. T., and J. Lalich. 1996. *Crazy Therapies: What Are They? Do They Work?* San Francisco: Jossey-Bass.

Stanovich, K. 2001. *How to Think Straight about Psychology.* 6th ed. New York: HarperCollins.

van Rillaer, J. 1991. Strategies of dissimulation in the pseudosciences. *New Ideas in Psychology* 9: 235–44.

# 3.
# WHERE DO FADS COME FROM?

## Stuart Vyse
### Connecticut College

*But, above all, let it be considered that what is more wholesome
than any particular belief is integrity of belief, and that to avoid
looking into the support of any belief from fear that it may turn
out rotten is quite as immoral as it is disadvantageous.*
— Charles Sanders Peirce (1992, p. 123)

## WHAT'S IN A FAD?

**B**efore anything can be said about how fad therapies emerge and
why they are often adopted over more valuable approaches, we
must understand what we are talking about. What is a fad therapy in the
field of developmental disabilities and how does it stand in relation to
other, non-fad therapies? When language is used to define social or functional categories, it is often because doing so benefits someone by codi-
fying an inherent value system. The motivations behind the establishment of these categories may be honorable or dishonorable. For
example, the application of the label "mental retardation," based on definitions involving intellectual and adaptive functioning, makes it possible for a segment of the population to receive educational and social
services that enhance their lives. At the same time, applying this label—

Reprinted with permission from John W. Jacobson, Richard M. Foxx, and James A. Mulick, eds., *Controversial Therapies for Developmental Disabilities: Fad, Fashion, and Science in Professional Practice*
(Mahwah, NJ: L. Erlbaum Associates, 2005), pp. 13–15. Copyright 2005.

as well as providing the services—may make these individuals more susceptible to stigmatization, prejudice, and discrimination (Danforth 2002; Goode 2002). Indeed, the current preference for the phrase "person with mental retardation" is aimed at diminishing the stigmatizing effect of the label. Furthermore, the concept of a "developmental disability" is even more effective in this regard because it more clearly refers to a specific aspect of the person—one ability among many—and is less likely to be taken as a global assessment of the individual.

Throughout this volume, the treatments that are its subject will be described using adjectives such as "fad," "alternative," "controversial," "pseudoscientific," and "unsubstantiated," among others. It must be acknowledged that these are—in some sense—terms of derision, and they reveal the value system of the authors who use them. I will return to the definition of a fad later, but what of the other terms? For example, if a therapy is "alternative," it can only be so in relation to some other standard or orthodox therapy (Wolpe 1999). That which distinguishes orthodox from alternative or unorthodox therapies may or may not be the level of scientific support. A therapy is "controversial" in relation to some issue of controversy brought, presumably by those who are critical of its use. Thus, just as being honored has more to do with the honorers than the honored, being controversial has more to do with the behavior of a therapy's critics than with the therapy. Absent arguments against it, a therapy might be free of controversy, but being so says nothing of its value. The label "pseudoscientific" is a pejorative adjective that suggests the treatment in question appears to be—but is not—scientific. The therapy may employ a technical jargon that sounds authoritative, and it may include a theoretical support structure that makes reference to genuinely scientific content (e.g., neurotransmitters, the sensory system, the brain), all of which give it the look and feel of a scientifically based treatment. But if these trappings of science are not backed up by reliable evidence, the treatment is a sham that steals some of its appeal from the positive reputation genuine science has acquired over its history. Despite the abundant evidence to the contrary (e.g., Shermer 1997), we live in an age of science. Although many people reject scientific thinking in important aspects of their lives, appeals to the scientific basis of a belief, product, or treatment often lend credibility to it. So powerful is the allure of science as a method of argument that some have even attempted to use it to support beliefs that are clearly beyond its limits, such as the existence of an afterlife and the possibility that the dead can communicate with the living (Schwartz et al. 2001).

But the label "unsubstantiated" or similar terms, such as "non-evidenced-based treatments" or "treatments unsupported by evidence," are a more direct indication of the philosophy of this chapter. If it has a bias, it is that treatments should be backed up by evidence and that scientific evidence is to be valued over other forms. The only way to obtain this kind of evidence is through research conducted according to accepted standards of methodology in the behavioral, social, and medical sciences. This is an admittedly positivist stance, and there have been many recent postmodern arguments about whether objective truth can ever be obtained in the social sciences (Gergen 2001). But these arguments do not hold much sway in this arena. People with developmental disabilities and those who work with and care about them do not always leap to scientific evidence—or *sound* scientific evidence—as the best way of evaluating treatments for developmental disabilities, but most agree in principle that this is the kind of evidence that should matter. Most believe that a treatment should be chosen on the basis not of whether it is enjoyable to administer, is consistent with the user's personal philosophy, or seems logical, but whether it works. Unfortunately, there is less agreement about what constitutes proof of success. Although most of those concerned about people with developmental disabilities are seeking evidence for the treatments they are using, some have not embraced scientific evidence as the most valued kind, and others cannot separate the good and bad information they encounter. The purpose of this book is to outline the standards for evaluating treatments and help differentiate treatments that have strong scientific support from those that have little or no support.

By using these labels to distinguish various treatments and therapies for developmental disabilities, we are establishing categories on the basis of the presence or absence of scientific support. This value system is also evident in the definition of a "fad." A fad, for the purposes of this chapter, is defined as "a procedure, method, or therapy that is adopted rapidly in the presence of little validating research, gains wide use or recognition, and then fades from use—usually in the face of disconfirming research, but often due to the adoption of a new fad" (J. W. Jacobson, personal communication, November 11, 2001). So a fad is a therapy that is not supported by scientific evidence and that has a fairly rapid rise and fall. The basic concern, however, is the question of evidence. There are other techniques—equally lacking in support—that nonetheless manage to maintain their popularity over relatively long periods of time. Though they are not fads, these more resilient therapies are also the appropriate concern of many of the chapters to follow. Understanding that these are relative terms, the short lifespan of a fad may sometimes be evidence of its lack of value, but conversely, the longer life of another therapy is not necessarily evidence of value. If popularity and longevity were correlated with usefulness, a book like this one might not be necessary. But for a variety of reasons, this is not so. In Darwinian terms, scientific support is not the only measure of a treatment's evolutionary fitness. Other factors may allow it to fill an ecological niche and survive repeated rounds of natural selection.

As we set up these categories of scientifically supported and unsupported—essentially, good and bad—treatments, it is useful to examine our motives. Science has a long history of theoretical and technological triumphs, but over the years, scientific arguments have often been used to further political or professional social agendas. The eugenics movement of the late nineteenth and early twentieth centuries attempted to ground class and race discrimination in science (Gould 1981). The system of classification known as the *Diagnostic and Statistical Manual of Mental Disorders (DSM;* American Psychiatric Association 1994) was intended as a scientific aid to research, diagnosis, and treatment, but its publication by a professional organization, the American Psychiatric Association, serves to keep this profession at the top of the heap as the final arbiter of what represents a bonafide mental illness (Kutchins &

Kirk 1997). The link between this manual and health insurance reimbursement policies raises additional questions. One need only ask who benefits if the manual contains many mental disorders (the current total is 374) rather than just a few?

Yes, we believe in science. This is an ideological stand of sorts. But we believe in a science that promotes no particular product or profession. The most effective treatments described in these chapters have been and are being used by a variety of professionals and nonprofessionals. The use of scientific therapies is not restricted to certain individuals by professional standards, ethical guidelines, or licensing laws. In addition, there are few products being sold in connection with a scientific approach to developmental disabilities treatment, and the professional books, periodicals, and manuals that have been spawned provide little profit motive for their authors and publishers. Certainly individual careers have benefited from the adoption or promotion of scientific therapies, but nothing remotely similar to the relationship between the American Psychiatric Association and the health insurance and pharmaceutical industries exists in the field of developmental disabilities. The primary social motive is improving the lives of people with developmental disabilities, and truly effective treatments have the best chance of providing the skills needed for them to participate as fully and independently as possible in the community.

## WHERE DO FADS COME FROM AND WHY ARE THERE SO MANY?

In a world where scientifically validated, effective treatments exist for people with developmental disabilities, where do all the ineffective fad treatments come from? Why are they not naturally eliminated from the landscape and replaced by treatments that work? In the remainder of this chapter, I will outline the circumstances—especially the market demands—that appear to encourage the development and promotion of fad therapies, and I will outline some of the reasons why consumers—

parents and professionals—choose them over other options. The story is one of the gradual adoption of science as the final arbiter of value, and it mirrors, in many respects, the history of modern medicine. Thus, as an introduction to the circumstances facing the field of developmental disabilities treatment, I will first outline the history of medicine in America. Although the following section is about US history, the arc of the plot—from nonscientific therapies to scientifically validated ones—takes a similar path in Europe and other areas that have endorsed Western medical procedures. The specific events are different, but the endpoints are the same.

# A BRIEF HISTORY OF AMERICAN MEDICINE

In the United States and other Westernized nations, effective research-validated procedures are now the dominant approach to medical problems, but this is a relatively new development. Rigorous medical research of the kind we value today became a widespread phenomenon only at the beginning of the twentieth century. Before then, medical practice both here and in Europe was characterized by a diverse array of practitioners and techniques. Today, in the field of developmental disabilities, scientifically validated techniques exist, but unlike contemporary medicine, these methods have yet to emerge as the single dominant approach to treatment. An examination of the history of Western medicine provides a number of clues to the popularity of alternative, unsubstantiated treatments in developmental disabilities treatment.

### American Medicine before the Revolution

In the colonial period, medical services were provided by a variety of practitioners, the great majority of whom had no formal academic training. Barbers in England and the colonies were authorized to perform surgery, and training was passed on by the apprenticeship method. It was not until 1745 that surgeons separated from barbers to form their own guild (Duffy 1993). Surgeons were not officially authorized to practice medicine, but in fact, they often served as general practitioners for the lower classes. Apothecaries also served the poor, providing drugs for the treatment of illness, and they were joined by a variety of other trades offering medical services, including folk healers, bloodletters, bonesetters, midwives, and herb doctors, among others.

In the American colonies, particularly in New England, a class of minister physicians emerged. While studying theology, many ministers who dissented from the prevailing church in England had also studied medicine as an alternative means of employment in the event they were dismissed from the church. As a result, a number of the ministers who arrived in the colonies also provided medical services. Cotton Mather was such a minister-physician, and he wrote a very eloquent medical essay on a measles epidemic of 1713, which claimed five members of his household (Duffy 1976).

In the seventeenth century, those colonialists who had received formal training—such as the minister-physicians—were at the top of the medical hierarchy and were the practitioners most likely to treat the ailments of the wealthy. Often these physicians had studied at the great hospitals and universities in England and on the continent. The American Revolution interrupted contact with British institutions and slowed the adoption of new medical techniques, but by the time of the Revolution, one hospital and two medical schools were in operation in America. A number of medical societies had been formed, and several colonies had established medical licensure laws (Duffy 1976). Nonetheless, the limited access to academic training meant that the majority of physicians acquired their skills by apprenticeship.

### From the Revolution to 1900

Many of the forces that led to modern medicine of the twentieth century were present in the period following the Revolution. Throughout the eighteenth century, physicians had attained the highest status of all those providing medical services, but medicine rarely brought them wealth.

Furthermore, their methods were not free of criticism. The most important American doctor of the late eighteenth and early nineteenth centuries was Benjamin Rush. Rush attended college in New Jersey and
apprenticed with a physician in Philadelphia, but to improve his chances
of success as a doctor, Rush traveled to Britain to study medicine. He
attended the University of Edinburgh and studied with noted physicians
in London and Paris. On his return to America, Rush was appointed
professor of chemistry at the College of Philadelphia. During the 1770s,
Rush was swept up in the political furor of the times, and he was eventually elected to the Second Continental Congress and became a signer
of the Declaration of Independence (Duffy 1993). Following the war,
Rush returned to his medical practice and, until his death in 1813, he
was one of the most influential forces in American medicine.

During the eighteenth century and into the nineteenth century,
physicians who used the traditional methods taught in the medical
schools of Europe sought to distinguish themselves from the other
forms of medical practice. They called themselves the "regulars" and
referred to various purveyors of folk medicine and nonstandard treatments as the "irregulars." Despite being of higher status and having the
attention of the wealthy sick of the colonies, the regulars did not achieve
dominance until the beginning of the twentieth century, and their eventual success was achieved only after adopting very different methods.

The problem with American medicine before the end of the nineteenth century is that it was not based on what we would now think of
as scientific evidence. Techniques that were extremely harmful to the
patient were not recognized as such, and as a result, for several centuries,
the regulars of the medical profession—both in Europe and America—
did more harm than good. This situation led Oliver Wendell Holmes to
deliver this now famous assessment in a lecture given at Harvard Medical School: "I firmly believe that if the whole *materia medica* could be
sunk to the bottom of the sea, it would be all the better for mankind and
all the worse for the fishes" (cited in Wolpe 1999, 222). Holmes's indict-
ment was justified. The standard medical philosophy of the day was
based on a theory first articulated by the ancient Greek physicians, Hip-

pocrates and Galen. It asserted that illnesses were caused by an imbalance of four basic bodily humors: yellow bile, black bile, phlegm, and blood. Imbalances could be caused by an excess of one of the humors or by the putrefaction or fermentation of one of them. The standard treatment was something that became known as heroic medicine. Physicians sought to alter the balance of humors by bleeding, cupping, or purging the patient. Cupping was accomplished by heating a glass cup or jar and placing it on the patient's skin. As the air in the cup cooled, it created a vacuum that was thought to draw materials out of the body. Wet cupping involved cutting the skin under the cup so that blood was drawn out of the wound. Purging involved the administration of strong herbal formulas that created violent vomiting and diarrhea.

Bloodletting was perhaps the most popular of all heroic treatments, involving the draining of large amounts of blood from the patient's body. Benjamin Rush erroneously believed that the body contained twenty-five pounds of blood (in fact, it contains less than half that amount), and he recommended bleeding until four-fifths of the fluid had been removed from the body. He used this technique throughout his career, and a paradoxical result of the Philadelphia yellow fever epidemic of 1793 was that Rush's popularity increased. The fever simply ran its course throughout the city, and Rush's methods of bleeding and purging patients undoubtedly increased the number of deaths. Nonetheless, perhaps due to his warm and enthusiastic personality, he drew many adherents to his techniques (Duffy 1976).

Throughout the colonial period and well into the nineteenth century, heroic medicine was the standard approach of the most highly trained physicians. But the brutality of these methods fueled the development of other medical theories and techniques. In addition, the higher cost of treatment by physicians meant that people of the middle and lower classes continued to bring their ailments to a variety of irregular physicians.

During the nineteenth century, several strong, rival therapies rose up to challenge the regulars. One of these was Thomsonianism. Samuel Thomson was born into a poor New Hampshire family in 1769, and as an adult he developed an interest in botanicals. He had witnessed the death of his mother, which he blamed on the harsh medicines of her orthodox physician, and when his wife became ill and was subjected to bloodletting and purging, he rejected the physician in favor of a root-and-herb doctor. Based on these experiences, Thomson began to experiment with the use of botanicals to treat disease, and in 1822, he published a book describing his methods. During the next twenty years, Thomsoniansim grew in popularity, both because it was a more humane alternative to the prevailing wisdom and because of its connection with a number of social movements of the time. Samuel Thomson was a religious fundamentalist, and his approach to medicine was aimed in large measure at returning the practice of medicine to the common person—a message that was consistent with the democratic ideals of Andrew Jackson's presidency. During the Jacksonian period, restrictions on eligibility to vote were greatly reduced, and more states moved toward popular elections for president. The period from the mid-nineteenth century through the early twentieth century was one of great social reform movements, and Thomsonians fought the establishment of medical licensure laws and supported efforts against the use of alcohol, tobacco, coffee, and tea (Duffy 1976).

Another popular but irregular treatment in the nineteenth century—which retains considerable popularity today—was homeopathy. Homeopathic medicine was developed by the German physician Samuel Christian Hahnemann, who had obtained a medical degree from the University of Erlangen. Homeopathy was based on two principles. First, *similibus curantur*, or "like cures like." This principle suggested that to cure a disease, one must find an herb or a substance that produces the same symptoms as the disease in a healthy person. Hahnemann developed this principle after taking doses of cinchona bark, which produced fever in him and, when given to a patient with malaria, cured the patient's fever. The second principle of homeopathy effectively nullified any possible therapeutic effect of its treatments. Hahnemann believed that his medicines were most effective when they were highly diluted—a process that turned all homeopathic medicines into functional placebos. Nonetheless, because they did no harm to the patient, homeo-pathic physicians undoubtedly enjoyed better results than regular physicians using heroic methods because the body's own restorative functions were given a chance to operate (Duffy 1993).

Homeopathy arrived in the United States in 1825, brought by physicians who had studied in Europe. It quickly made inroads in the eastern part of the country, and by 1935 the first homeopathic college in America was established in Allentown, Pennsylvania. The growing popularity of Thomsonianism and homeopathic medicine, as well as other competitors to the regulars, led to a number of defensive moves on the part of orthodox physicians—chief among these was the "consultation clause." The American Medical Association (AMA) was formed in 1847, but it is a testament to the strength of homeopathy that the first national medical organization in the United States was the American Institute of Homeopathy, which had been created three years earlier. By this time, the country had suffered epidemics of yellow fever and Asian cholera, and the benign interventions of the homeopathic physicians were far more effective than the standard methods of bleeding and purging. In southern states, which were more affected by these epidemics, homeopathy gained many converts. So when the AMA was formed in 1847, it adopted its first Code of Ethics. This document included a number of useful principles regarding the physician-patient relationship, but it also included a clause regarding consultation:

But no one can be considered as a regular practitioner, or fit associate in consultation, whose practice is based on an exclusive dogma, to the rejection of accumulated experience of the profession, and of the aids actually furnished by anatomy, physiology, pathology, and organic chemistry. (Bell & Hays 1847/1999, chapter II, article IV. 1)

The effect of the consultation clause was to forbid any regular physician from taking on a patient who was also being seen by a homeopath, and no physician could consult with a homeopath, even if the patient requested it (Duffy 1993). The consultation clause effectively defined who was a physician, and it also helped to solidify the regulars' control over municipal and state hospitals. During the Civil War, homeopaths were not allowed in the Army Medical Corps; however, it is noteworthy that homeopathy was sufficiently strong in New York that in 1882 the Medical Society of the State of New York deleted the consultation clause from its version of the ethics code (Warner 1999), an action that led to the establishment of two competing state medical societies. In addition, the exclusion of homeopathic physicians from regular hospitals forced them to establish their own, many of which achieved reputations superior to those of the regulars. Finally, homeopaths fought back rhetorically by labeling orthodox medicine "allopathy," a term that angered the regulars (ibid.).

A particular irony of this history is that science was lost in the battle for professional dominance. If anything, those physicians who were the most scientifically based, such as the advocates for experimental physiology, tended to be among the opposition to the AMA code of ethics, and those who most harshly criticized experimental therapeutics were among the code's defenders (ibid.). But by the late nineteenth century, the war of competing dogmas was beginning to fade, and many of the influential physicians of the era stressed the importance of scientific evidence in support of medical therapies. In a move that helped to break down divisions within the profession, the University of Michigan, which had previously maintained separate departments of regular and homeopathic medicine, admitted a professor of homeopathy to the regular medicine department. Finally, by the beginning of the twentieth century, scientific medicine began to emerge as the new orthodoxy. In the 1903 revision of its Code of Ethics, the AMA eliminated the consultation clause, and by 1910, Abraham Flexner, the president of the AMA, described allopathy and homeopathy alike as "medical sects" and urged that both must be abandoned in favor of "scientific medicine" (ibid., p. 65). Furthermore, during the early twentieth century, gifts made by the Carnegie and Rockefeller foundations and other wealthy philanthropists helped build important new research institutes (Duffy 1976). Although it represented a great step forward, the adoption of scientific methods by the field of medicine did not lead automatically to a morally sound and value-free profession. The late nineteenth and early twentieth centuries was the era of social Darwinism, in which scientific arguments were used to further social agendas (Gould 1981). Nonetheless, the rise of scientific medicine in the twentieth century led to rapid technical advancement and rejection of medical dogma as the guide for medical practice.

## THE ORIGINS OF FAD THERAPIES

The history of medicine in America suggests a number of factors that can lead to the success of nonscientific therapies. Since 1900, science has become the dominant judge of value in many domains, but it does not mean that science-based therapies or beliefs are universally endorsed. Here are some of the conditions that appear to lead to the popularity of alternative, nonscientific therapies.

*Incomplete Effectiveness of Available Therapies.* When a person is ill or when a child is diagnosed with a developmental disorder, the current circumstance stands in stark contrast to normal expectation. As a result, the sick person is highly motivated to return to health, and the parents of the developmentally disabled child have a similar strong desire to bridge the gap between the child they hoped would be theirs and the one they have. In the case of a medical condition, if the available therapy is effective enough to eliminate the disease entirely (e.g., smallpox, tuberculosis) or to make it no longer a significant threat (e.g., infections treated with modern antibiotics), then alternative therapies are not needed. However, there are many conditions for which science has to produce a uniformly successful treatment. This was true earlier in the HIV epidemic in the United States, before the introduction of protease inhibitors and the more effective polypharmacy therapies now available ("People with AIDS" 1991), and it is the current state of affairs in the field of developmental disabilities. For example, a study of applied behavior analysis (ABA), the most effective therapy for autism, produced the highest levels of success in only 47 percent of participants (Lovaas 1987), and there is considerable debate about whether the effectiveness of ABA has been exaggerated (e.g., Herbert & Brandsma 2002). Under these circumstances, an alternative therapy—for example, facilitated communication (FC)—can gain rapid acceptance. In the absence of a completely effective treatment, FC is attractive because it instantly erases the intellectual gap for all children. The physical deficit that is purported to hide the child's true abilities remains, but FC's promise—the exchange of a pervasive developmental disability for a mere physical one—is very appealing to many.

*Best Available Treatment Is Onerous or Distasteful for Parent or Client.* Heroic medicine was an easy foil for more mild forms of treatment such as Thomsonianism and homeopathy. Contemporary alternative cancer therapies undoubtedly gain popularity from the substantial discomfort produced by chemotherapy and radiation therapy (Okie 2000). In the field of developmental disabilities, the best therapies are expensive and demanding to administer and take years to complete—or are never fully completed. Thus, a gluten- and casein-free diet (Whitely et al. 1999) or holding therapy (Welch 1988) may be appealing to some parents because it appears easier to administer or because the more effective treatment is thought to be "cold and manipulative" (Maurice 1993, 63).

*Alternative Treatment Supported by Ideology.* Many treatments in both medicine and developmental disabilities have survived because the proponents and consumers have adopted a theory about the disease or disorder in question. All the regular and irregular treatments of American medicine before 1900 were based on a theory of disease: the heroic/humorial system of the regulars, Thomson's botanical treatments, and Hahnemann's homeopathy. Often belief, based on the ideological appeal of a therapy, is sufficient to sustain the use of a treatment in the absence of any evidence that it is effective.

The attractiveness of ideology is greatest if it extends beyond the specific condition and makes contact with a more general personal philosophy or, alternatively, draws credibility from its apparent relationship to another, validated theory. The success of Thomsonianism was spurred by its association with Jacksonian democracy and a variety of nineteenth-century social reform movements. Similarly, a variety of modern alternative medical therapies derive much of their appeal from broad cultural trends that reject traditional organized medicine in favor of approaches emphasizing diet, exercise, vitamins, and holistic health (Cassileth 1989; Vyse 1997a). In the field of developmental disabilities, treatments based on holding (Welch 1988) and dietary restrictions (Whitely et al. 1999) may benefit from their coherence with contemporary theories of parenting and nutrition, respectively. In addition, despite limited evidence of the effectiveness of gluten- and casein-free diets in the treatment of autism (Herbert, Sharp & Gaudiano 2002), these treatments gain a veneer of plausibility from their apparent similarity to dietary programs for validated metabolic disorders, such as phenylketonuria and diabetes. However, without sound evidence in support of these diets, they represent another case of pseudoscience.

*Treatment Promoted by a Proprietary Professional Group.* Quite often, a therapy originates with a professional group and goes on to be promoted by members of that group. Ineffective treatments can survive if they are based on an appealing ideology and are backed up by the authority of the profession. Furthermore, the promotion of a proprietary therapy strengthens the professional group. The regulars, who were most likely to be academically trained and who represented the orthodox medical approach from colonial times into the nineteenth century, had a proprietary interest in the methods of heroic medicine, and they sought to protect their professional turf with state licensing laws and the consultation clause of the AMA (Wolpe 1999).

Even today there are examples of unsubstantiated alternative therapies that have emerged from specific professional groups. In medicine, therapeutic touch (TT; Mackey 1995) is a practice developed by a Dolores Krieger, a professor of nursing, based on the premise that the body is surrounded by energy fields. Proponents argue that a variety of diseases and conditions can be treated by passing the hands a few inches above the body to smooth these energy fields. A recent review found that "the 'facts' of TT are that it has an unknown mechanism of action and its efficacy is questionable" (O'Mathuna et al. 2002, 171). TT is not exclusively practiced by nurses, but it remains closely associated with the nursing profession. In the field of developmental disabilities, sensory integration therapy (Ayres 1994/1979) has its origins in occupational therapy and is most often promoted by members of that profession—despite the absence of support for this therapy in the research published to date (see Herbert et al. 2002 for a review).

It should be acknowledged that not all therapies primarily promoted by a single professional group are worthless. The use of drugs to treat physical, psychiatric, and developmental disorders has, until recently, been the exclusive privilege of physicians, and that privilege has been protected by state licensing laws and educational and accreditation standards. Without question, drug therapies are very effective in treating a wide variety of ailments; thus, promotion by a professional group alone is not proof of ineffectiveness. Nonetheless, any therapy, whether effective or ineffective, gains strength from the authority granted to the professionals who promote it. In some cases, when combined with the ideological appeal of the therapy, the force of professional authority is surprisingly influential in maintaining the popularity of unsubstantiated treatments.

These are some of the broad historical and cultural factors—the market trends—that contribute to the development of questionable therapies, but what about the individual consumer? When there are better options available, why do parents and professionals often choose unsubstantiated treatments over those with better support? Much of the answer is beyond the scope of this chapter, but in the most general sense, the question is one of belief. How do parents and professionals acquire the beliefs they use to guide their decisions? In 1877, the American pragmatist philosopher Charles Sanders Peirce published an article titled "The Fixation of Belief" that has become a classic of the philosophy of science. In it, Peirce describes four ways people acquire beliefs and assesses the relative value of each method. Peirce's categories apply to beliefs of all kinds, and they provide a useful framework for understanding the adoption of fad therapies.

*Authority.* Beliefs are acquired by the method of authority if we accept the word of another. Often we grant others the power to change our beliefs if they have higher social status or are assumed to have special knowledge. Religious beliefs are acquired by the method of authority, as are, in fact, most of our everyday beliefs. As a practical matter, it is impossible for any individual to test more than a few ideas empirically; thus, we must acquire much of our knowledge by the method of authority. For example, I believe the light on my desk glows because of the movement of electrons through its copper wires and tungsten element, but I have never observed this phenomenon directly—only its effects. Some authority instilled my belief in the action of electrons years ago. Although it is often necessary to take the word of others, authorities are frequently wrong. Unless we know the basis of a person's statements, we have little reason to trust in their authority.

The regulars of early American medicine were the authorities of their day, and it is a testament to the power of their position that their methods were dominant for centuries. In addition, early American homeopathic physicians undoubtedly gained some influence from the authority they commanded. Today, physicians and other health professionals are the primary medical authorities, and although most of them recommend procedures based on scientific evidence, much of the influence they enjoy is based on the authority granted them by contemporary society. In the field of developmental disabilities, where cures are hard to come by, parents are confronted with authorities from many helping professions advocating different—often contradictory—therapeutic approaches. To the extent they find these professionals persuasive solely because of their standing, parents fall into the trap of choosing therapies by the method of authority.

*Tenacity.* Sometimes we hold onto a belief out of loyalty—merely because it is our own. According to Peirce, the tenacious man "goes through life, systematically keeping out of view all that might cause him to change his opinions" (1992, 116). At times we are all guilty of defending our beliefs in the face of strong contradictory evidence, but to do so will often lead us astray. It is a basic tenet of scientific thinking that theories must be jettisoned or modified in the face of clear conflicting data.

The regulars of early American medicine represent a striking example of tenacity. Somehow most were able to maintain belief in their methods in the face of what were often devastating effects. Of course, their judgment was undoubtedly affected by professional and financial incentives, as well. Recognizing the superior effectiveness of homeopathic and Thomsonian therapies would have led many physicians to sacrifice the status afforded by association with orthodox medicine. Nonetheless, as previously noted, some doctors, particularly in the southern states during the yellow fever and Asian cholera epidemics, were not blind to the devastating effects of heroic medicine and adopted the more benign methods of homeopathic medicine.

In the field of developmental disabilities, tenacity allows professionals and parents to remain committed to a therapy despite evidence that it is ineffective. If the ideology behind the therapy has a strong appeal, adherents will be reluctant to give it up. Today, despite ample evidence that facilitated communication is an ineffective, pseudoscientific technique (Herbert et al. 2002; Jacobson, Mulick & Schwartz 1995), several Web sites are devoted to promoting FC, and the technique remains popular with many parents. Of course, the promise (or dream) of FC—that one's child is merely physically disabled, not developmentally disabled—would be difficult to relinquish.

*A Priori.* Beliefs are fixed by the a priori method if they make sense or feel right. This is a subjective measure of value, which is necessarily dependent on the accidents of one's prior experiences. Although the a priori method is widely used, it cannot be a path to objective truth. Honest people using this method of reasoning will come to very different conclusions, and unless one embraces fully the postmodernist view of science, this is an unacceptable situation. Nonetheless, many people make judgments and choose actions on the basis of this kind of subjective assessment. In the fields of medicine and developmental disabilities treatment, a priori reasoning is particularly evident when an appeal is made directly to the consumer, as in the case of Thomsonianism. Thomson's approach was to remove the intervening authority of the physician and return medicine to the people. By aligning his approach with dominant political and social themes of the day, he increased the likelihood that his theory would conform to the sensibilities of his audience.

Any approach that makes use of a plausible ideology—particularly one that draws on other broad, cultural themes—will make subjective sense to large numbers of people in search of a solution. For example, biological autism therapies, such as secretin (Horvath et al. 1998) and gluten- and casein-free diets (Whitely et al. 1999), gain an air of plausibility from the assumption that the etiology of autism is genetic or, in some sense, "biological." The underlying logic is that biological therapies are best for biological conditions. Dietary treatments may also benefit from popular contemporary beliefs about nutrition and food allergies. But it is dangerous to rely on our intuitive response to a treatment because the subjective appeal of an idea is no more reliable than the word of an authority.

*The Scientific Method.* Peirce's answer to the problem of fixation of belief was the scientific method, but, of course, there is no one scientific method. There are several ways of conducting science, and researchers have long debated how behavioral science, in particular, should be done (Cohen 1994; Johnston & Pennypacker 1993; Sidman 1960). Nonetheless, according to Peirce, when empirical methods are used with adequate controls they should lead to beliefs that have "external permanency" (1992, 120). Taking a strongly positivist stance, he asserted that there are "real things, whose characters are entirely independent of our ideas about them" (ibid.), and if the appropriate tests are devised, we can find out what those real things are. In support of this view, he pointed to the many scientific advances that were evident to his readers in 1877.

The authors of this volume share Peirce's enthusiasm for the scientific method. Empirical evidence rigorously obtained is the best way to settle disputes about the value of a treatment. Of course, science is an iterative process that can lead in unexpected directions, particularly early in the process of discovery. For example, in researching the use of prism glasses as a treatment for children with autism, Kay and Vyse found only two published studies in the available databases, both of which reported positive effects. Thus, their case study may be the only published report of a negative outcome with this rather improbable therapy. Nonetheless, given adequate time, science typically produces an unequivocal estimate of the value of any therapy.

## IN SEARCH OF BARTHOLOW'S FUTURE

Peirce's list makes good sense. Most, if not all, the beliefs we hold have been acquired by one or more of his four methods. But, if as individuals, we are to live by his suggestions, we will have a difficult time. If we are to use the scientific method to form our beliefs, a lifetime of testing will provide us with only a fraction of what is needed to live our lives. Because the goal of testing every important idea is impossible to achieve, we must rely on authorities to help us make our daily decisions, and parents of developmentally disabled children making decisions about their children's therapy have the same problem. They cannot all be scientists—indeed, there is no reason for them to be. There are plenty of behavioral scientists at work on these problems today. The person who wants to acquire sound beliefs about disabilities treatment need not conduct research him- or herself. Instead, the consumer must value scientific evidence, seek it out, and recognize it when he or she sees it.

And this is where the problem lies. We live in an age of science. The effects of science, in the form of technological innovations, are obvious throughout the Westernized world. In professional medicine, the scientific method is the dominant approach to settling issues of opinion. It does not always lead to uncontroversial truth (e.g., Taubes 2002), but the profession has fully adopted the view that arguments must be based on scientific evidence. Fewer professionals in the field of developmental disabilities have made a similar commitment to science. But the fundamental problem that faces us is one of cultural values. We may have adopted the fruits of science in the form of advances in technology and medicine, but not enough of us have adopted scientific thinking as the primary way of "fixing knowledge" (Vyse 1997a; 1997b). To be certain, science does not have the answer to every question. Science will not tell you whom to marry, what is the most meaningful part of your life, or whether there is a god. But for matters of testable fact, there is no better tool, and claims about treatments for people with developmental disabilities are easily testable. If we are to help people with developmental disabilities reach their fullest potential, we must teach the larger community the benefits of scientific evidence and thought (Vyse 1997a).

In 1872, Roberts Bartholow, an early advocate for the scientific approach to medicine, wrote in a textbook of the day:

> Homeopathy and allopathy are dreams of a by-gone time. Modern science is indifferent to Hippocrates and Hahnemann. The therapeutics of today rejects dogmas, and the therapeutics of the future will accept nothing that cannot be demonstrated by the tests of science. (Bartholow 1872, 636)

Bartholow's future may be here for medicine, but it has not yet arrived for the field of developmental disabilities treatment. But if the history of American medicine is an example, the effort will not be in vain. Bartholow's future is within our grasp.

## ACKNOWLEDGMENT

The author would like to thank John H. Warner for his comments on an earlier draft of this chapter.

# REFERENCES

American Psychiatric Association. 1994. *Diagnostic and Statistical Manual of Mental Disorders.* 4th ed. Washington, DC: American Psychiatric Association.

Ayres, A. J. 1994/1979. *Sensory Integration and the Child.* Los Angeles, CA: Western Psychological Services.

Bartholow, R. 1872. Experimental therapeutics: Introductory address. *Cincinnati Lancet and Observer* (Medical College of Ohio) 15: 635–36.

Bell, J., and I. Hays. 1999. *Code of Ethics.* In *The American Medical Ethics Revolution: How the AMA's Code of Ethics Has Transformed Physicians' Relationships to Patients, Professionals, and Society,* ed. R. B. Baker, A. L. Caplan, L. L. Emanuel, and S. R. Latham. Baltimore: Johns Hopkins University Press, pp. 324–34. Original work published 1847.

Cassileth, B. R. 1989. The social implications of questionable cancer therapies. *Cancer* 63, no. 1: 1247–50.

Cohen, J. 1994. The earth is round (p < .05). *American Psychologist* 49: 997–1003.

Danforth, S. 2002. New words for new purposes: A challenge for the AAMR. *Mental Retardation* 40, no. 1: 51–55.

Duffy, J. 1976. *The Healers: A History of American Medicine.* Urbana: University of Illinois Press.

———. 1993. *From Humors to Medical Science.* Urbana: University of Illinois Press.

Gergen, K. J. 2001. Psychological science in a postmodern context. *American Psychology* 56, no. 10: 803–13.

Goode, D. 2002. Mental retardation is dead: Long live mental retardation. *Mental Retardation* 40, no. 1: 57–59.

Gould, S. J. 1981. *The Mismeasure of Man.* New York: Norton.

Herbert, J. D., and L. L. Brandsma. 2002. Applied behavior analysis for childhood autism: Does the emperor have clothes? *Behavior Analyst Today* 3, no. 1: 45–50. Available from http://www.behavior-analyst-online.org /BAT/.

Herbert, J. D., I. R. Sharp, and B. A. Gaudiano. 2002. Separating fact from fiction in the etiology and treatment of autism: A scientific review of the evidence. *Scientific Review of Mental Health Practice* 1: 25–45.

Horvath, K., G. Stefanatos, K. N. Sokoloski, R. Wachtel, L. Nabors, and J. T. Tildon. 1998. Improved social and language skills after secretin administration in patients with autistic spectrum disorders. *Journal of the Association for Academic Minority Physicians* 9: 9–15.

Jacobson, J. W., J. A. Mulick, and A. A. Schwartz. 1995. A history of facilitated communication: Science, pseudoscience, and antiscience. *American Psychologist* 50: 750–65.

Johnston, J. M., and H. S. Pennypacker. 1993. *Strategies and Tactics of Behavioral Research.* 2nd ed. Hillsdale, NJ: Lawrence Erlbaum Associates.

Kutchins, H., and S. A. Kirk. 1997. *Making Us Crazy: DSM: The Psychiatric Bible and the Creation of Mental Disorders.* New York: Free Press.

Lovaas, O. I. 1987. Behavioral treatment and normal educational and intellectual functioning in young autistic children. *Journal of Consulting and Clinical Psychology* 55: 3–9.

Mackey, R. B. 1995. Discover the healing power of therapeutic touch. *American Journal of Nursing* 95, no. 4: 26–34.

Maurice, C. 1993. *Let Me Hear Your Voice: A Family's Triumph over Autism.* New York: Knopf.

Okie, S. 2000. Maverick treatments find U.S. funding: Cancer therapy to be tested despite mainstream medical doubts. *Washington Post,* January 18, p. A1.

O'Mathuna, D. P., S. Pryjmachuk, W. Spencer, M. Stanwick, and S. Matthiesen. 2002. A critical evaluation of the theory and practice of therapeutic touch. *Nursing Philosophy* 3: 163–76.

Peirce, C. S. 1992. The fixation of belief. In *The Essential Peirce,* ed. N. Houser and C. Kloesel, vol. 1, pp. 109–23. Bloomington: Indiana University Press. (Original work published in 1877.)

People with AIDS are targets of phony cure schemes. December 29, 1991. *St. Louis Post-Dispatch,* p. 10C.

Schwartz, G. E. R., L. G. S. Russek, L. A. Nelson, and C. Barentsen. 2001. Accuracy and replicability of anomalous after-death communication across highly skilled mediums. *Journal of the Society for Psychical Research* 65, no. 1: 1–25.

Shermer, M. 1997. *Why People Believe Weird Things: Pseudoscience, Superstition, and Other Confusions of our Time.* New York: Freeman.

Sidman, M. 1960. *Tactics of Scientific Research: Evaluating Experimental Data in Psychology.* Boston: Authors Cooperative.

Taubes, G. July 7, 2002. What if it's all been a big fat lie? *New York Times Magazine,* 22–27, 34, 45, 47.

Vyse, S. A. 1997a. *Believing in Magic: The Psychology of Superstition*. New York: Oxford University Press.

———. 1997b. Superstition in the age of science. *World Review* 2, no. 4: 13–15.

Warner, J. H. 1999. The 1880s rebellion against the AMA code of ethics: "Scientific democracy" and the dissolution of orthodoxy. In *The American Medical Ethics Revolution: How the AMA's Code of Ethics Has Transformed Physicians' Relationships to Patients, Professionals, and Society*, ed. R. B. Baker, A. L. Caplan, L. L. Emanuel, and S. R. Latham, pp. 52–69. Baltimore, MD: Johns Hopkins University Press.

Welch, M. G. 1998. *Holding Time: How to Eliminate Conflict, Temper Tantrums, and Sibling Rivalry and Raise Loving, Successful Children*. New York: Simon & Schuster.

Whitely, P., J. Rodgers, D. Savery, and P. Shattock. 1999. A gluten-free diet as an intervention for autism and associated spectrum disorders: Preliminary findings. *Autism* 3: 45–65.

Wolpe, P. R. 1999. Alternative medicine and the AMA. In *The American Medical Ethics Revolution: How the AMA's Code of Ethics Has Transformed Physicians' Relationships to Patients, Professionals, and Society*, ed. R. B. Baker, A. L. Caplan. L. L. Emanuel, and S. R. Latham, pp. 218–239. Baltimore, MD: Johns Hopkins University Press.

# Section II. How to Distinguish the Wheat from the Chaff in Mental Healthcare

# INTRODUCTION

Without a map, navigators can become hopelessly lost. Similarly, to navigate the mental health mindfield, we need a set of directions for how to avoid hidden land mines. Without them, as psychologist John Riolo wisely reminds us, we can easily fall prey to ineffective or even harmful therapeutic fads. In this section, we will provide you with a road map for finding your way through the mental health *mind*field.

If psychologists have learned anything over the past few decades, it is that we humans are fallible creatures. Although we often trust the raw data of our perceptions, these data can—and frequently do—mislead us in a host of ways. As a consequence, we must all work hard to combat what psychologist Lee Ross calls "naïve realism": the erroneous belief that the world is exactly as we see it. In the domain of mental healthcare, we can easily be fooled into believing that a psychological test works even though it doesn't or that a new brand of psychotherapy is effective even though it isn't.

That's because none of us is immune to what Italian psychologist Massimo Piatelli-Palmarini terms "cognitive illusions"—mistaken beliefs that we find subjectively compelling. Like visual illusions, most cognitive illusions stem from what is generally an adaptive psychological tendency: our propensity to make sense out of nonsense and to seek order in disorder. This tendency typically works well for us, as it helps us to simplify the remarkably confusing world in which we live. Yet in some cases, it can lead us to perceive associations that aren't there.

To take just one example, we can easily become convinced that vaccines trigger the symptoms of infantile autism, even though numerous carefully controlled studies have disconfirmed this connection. In this case, our tendency to find meaningful patterns in essentially random data leads us to perceive an association that is in fact nothing more than a mental mirage. We may also "see" improvement following a few sessions of psychotherapy and conclude that the treatment must have been responsible for the change. But as we will learn in this section of the book, this inference isn't necessarily justified.

To avoid cognitive illusions, we must develop skills for distinguishing science from pseudoscience and wheat from chaff. In an invaluable selection that should be required reading for all mental health consumers and professionals, Barry Beyerstein describes a variety of factors, such as spontaneous remission, initial misdiagnosis, and placebo effects, that can lead the unwary to conclude that entirely ineffective treatments actually work. These factors can easy trick all of us if we're not vigilant, because we're often unaware of their existence in the day-to-day process of psychotherapy. Beyerstein's points remind us that randomized placebo-controlled trials, in which research subjects are randomly assigned to two groups—one that receives the active treatment and one that receives a placebo (such as a dummy pill)—are the best way to determine whether a therapy is effective.

Hal Arkowitz and Scott Lilienfeld discuss the implications of the scientist-practitioner gap for evaluating psychotherapies and examine the raging controversies over recent efforts to establish standards of evidence-based care for psychological conditions. They attempt to steer a middle ground between an overly rigid adherence to unrealistic practice standards on the one hand and a loose, "almost anything goes" approach on the other. In doing so, they describe psychological techniques that have been found to be effective as well as those that have been found to be ineffective or even harmful.

# 4.

# PSYCHOTHERAPY ON TRIAL

## *H. Arkowitz and Scott O. Lilienfeld*

In the past half a century, psychotherapy research has blossomed, with thousands of studies confirming its positive effects for a wide array of clinical problems, including depression, anxiety, eating disorders and sexual dysfunction. Yet in recent years, intense controversy over whether and how to put these findings into practice has erupted, further widening the "scientist-practitioner gap," the deep gulf that has separated many researchers and psychotherapists for decades.

The current debate centers on the growing use of empirically supported therapies, or ESTs, which are specific therapies for specific problems—for example, depression and bulimia—that meet certain criteria (such as a given number of well-designed studies showing positive effects) for treatment efficacy. Proponents have welcomed ESTs for their clear guidelines on what works for patients and their explicit manuals prescribing administration of treatment. Critics have sharply questioned ESTs on a number of grounds, namely, whether their research base is adequate, whether their one-size-fits-all approach can address the needs of individual patients, and whether their focus should be primarily alleviation of symptomatic distress or changes in underlying dispositions and vulnerabilities.

The debate's resolution bears important implications for treatments that psychotherapy patients seek and receive. A survey of nearly ten thousand adults published in 2005 showed that one out of four Americans meets the criteria for a diagnosis of a psychological disorder in any given year and that slightly less than half of all people in the United States will suffer from a psychological disorder over the course of their lifetimes.

Before we wrote this article, one of us (Arkowitz) had been highly critical of ESTs (though not of placing psychotherapy on a more scientific basis). The other one of us (Lilienfeld) had been a strong advocate of ESTs. Ultimately we found considerable common ground on many points regarding the proper role of research in informing clinical practice. In this chapter, we hope to offer a modest step toward reconciling opposing views on ESTs.

## LAYING THE GROUNDWORK

Fifty years ago, the foundations of modern psychotherapy research were just being laid. One participant at a 1950 conference was being only partially facetious when he commented: "Psychotherapy is an undefined technique applied to unspecified problems with unpredictable outcomes. For this technique we recommend rigorous training."

Just two years later, an eminent British psychologist named Hans Eysenck questioned the scientific basis of talk therapy in a landmark paper—asserting that it was no more effective than the absence of treatment. Researchers soon rose to Eysenck's challenge, and thousands of studies over the ensuing decades demonstrated conclusively that psychotherapy does help many patients. But which are the most effective therapies and for which problems? Further studies sought answers.

In 1995 a task force of a division of the American Psychological Association (APA), chaired by Boston University psychologist David H. Barlow, issued the first of several reports that set forth initial criteria for ESTs, along with lists of therapies that met those criteria. The current task force list is widely used today, especially in university settings in which future clinical psychologists are educated.

We should note that the list tells only whether a treatment has been found to work in controlled studies but not necessarily in clinical practice outside the laboratory. Most experiments have examined cognitive-behavioral therapy; psychoanalytic, humanistic and integrative methods have received less research attention. If a treatment is absent from the list, it means one of two things: either studies have shown that the treatment does not work, or it has not been tested and, therefore, we do not know whether or not it works. Most of the more than five hundred "brands" of psychotherapy are not on the EST list, because they fall in the second category.

## THE CASE FOR ESTs

Advocates have advanced three major arguments in favor of a list of efficacious therapies for specific disorders: it protects patients against fringe psychotherapies, it empowers mental health consumers to make appropriate choices for their care, and it aids in training future therapists.

First, in recent years, consumers have been beset by a seemingly endless parade of fad therapies of various stripes. Despite scant scientific support—or sometimes outright debunking—some fringe treatments continue to be used widely. For example, surveys of doctoral-level therapists in the 1990s indicated that about one quarter regularly employed two or more recovered-memory techniques. Facilitated communication, discredited by scientific research in the 1990s, is still popular in some communities. Counselors who administer crisis debriefing number in the thousands; in the aftermath of the September 11 terrorist attacks, one crisis-debriefing outfit in Atlanta alone dispatched therapists to two hundred companies. All these treatments have been found to be ineffective or even harmful. Some studies have discovered that crisis debriefing, for example, increased the risk of post-traumatic stress disorder in trauma-exposed individuals. The EST list makes it harder for practitioners who administer these and other questionable techniques to claim that they are operating scientifically.

Second, the EST list benefits patients because by providing them with information regarding which treatments have been proven to work, it puts them in a better position to make good choices for their care. Like the Food and Drug Administration's list of approved medications, the EST list performs a quality-control function. It serves a similar purpose for managed care organizations and healthcare agencies, which want to make scientifically informed decisions about which treatments should—and should not—be reimbursed. By placing the burden of proof on a treatment's proponents to show that it is efficacious, the EST list helps to ensure that therapies promoted to the general public have met basic standards.

Third, the EST list can improve the education and training of graduate students in clinical psychology, social work and other mental health fields. The sprawling psychotherapy research literature is often confusing and contradictory; without such a list, novice clinicians have no clear research guidance concerning which treatments to administer and which to avoid.

## THE CASE AGAINST ESTs

Critics have responded with four concerns: EST research findings may not apply to psychotherapy as practiced in the "real world"; the list may be biased toward cognitive-behavioral therapies; the EST view of psychotherapy is narrow; and techniques emphasized by such lists may not be the key ingredients of therapeutic change.

First, critics have attacked ESTs for both the science underlying their "empirical support" and their applicability to clinical practice. "The move to worship at the altar of these scientific treatments has been destructive to clients in practice, because the methods tell you very little about how to read the real and complex people who actually come in for therapy," said psychiatrist Glen O. Gabbard of the Baylor College of Medicine in a 2004 *New York Times* article.

To satisfy requirements for good research, which seeks to eliminate any variables that could confound the results, investigators must sacrifice a great deal of what practicing psychotherapists believe is important. EST manuals often sharply constrain therapists' flexibility to tailor the treatments to clients' needs, resulting in a one-size-fits-all approach. Researchers reject up to 90 percent of subjects who are initially recruited, in the name of ensuring a "pure" group with the diagnosis of interest. As a result, participants in these studies typically represent only a small percentage of those who might be seen in actual practice.

The all-or-none nature of the EST list also has been criticized. By categorizing treatments as either empirically supported or not, the list omits potentially useful information, such as the degree of efficacy of different EST therapies. Further, many of the ESTs have modest or even relatively weak effects. That is, they leave many clients slightly improved or not helped at all, with a high likelihood of relapse. Is it reasonable to call such therapies "empirically supported"?

In 2001 psychotherapy researchers Drew Westen, now at Emory University, and Catherine M. Novotny, now at the Department of Veterans Affairs Medical Center in San Francisco, published an analysis of a large number of efficacy studies for depression and some anxiety disorders. Most of the therapies they examined were variants of cognitive-behavioral therapy. Their findings revealed a glass that is both half full and half empty. On the positive side, they learned that 51 percent of depressed clients and 63 percent of those with panic disorder were significantly better or no longer had symptoms. But the glass seems emptier if we recognize that many patients who had improved still exhibited symptoms at the end of treatment and that others were not helped at all. If we include people who dropped out of therapy, the success percentages plunge considerably. In addition, follow-up studies reveal high rates of relapse. For example, only 37 percent of those depressed clients who completed treatment remained improved one to two years later.

Second, some critics have argued that EST therapies are biased in favor of cognitive-behavioral techniques. Reviews of research on psychoanalytic and humanistic therapies suggest positive effects broadly comparable to those of cognitive-behavioral therapies. Although less research has been conducted on these therapies than on cognitive-behavioral therapy, their underrepresentation on EST lists raises questions of bias.

Third, ESTs focus almost exclusively on symptoms and distress to the exclusion of other important factors that lead people to seek therapy. These considerations include predispositions, vulnerabilities and personality characteristics that often persist after the symptoms are gone. Many psychotherapists believe that it is important to focus on these types of problems in therapy, in order to enhance the quality of the client's life and help reduce the chances of a relapse. The emphasis of ESTs on standardized techniques similarly ignores not only the uniqueness of individuals but also the salutary power of the therapist-client relationship.

Fourth, the techniques emphasized by the EST list may not be what produces change in many cases. Most studies comparing the efficacy of two or more therapies find that they all do about equally well. This surprising result is termed the "Dodo Bird verdict," after the Dodo Bird in *Alice's Adventures in Wonderland,* who declares (following a race) that "everybody has won and all must have prizes." Psychotherapy researchers intensely debate the meaning of the Dodo Bird verdict. Some argue that actual important differences exist among therapies but that problems with study design have masked them. Such problems include small samples and the limited range of therapies that have been compared. It is also possible that although average outcomes of various therapies may not differ, some clients may do better with one therapy, whereas other clients may do better with another.

Still other researchers have accepted the Dodo Bird verdict and attempted to account for it. One explanation suggests that therapeutic change is caused more by "common factors" that therapies share rather than by specific techniques. Such factors include instilling hope and providing a believable theoretical rationale with associated therapeutic "rituals," which can make clients feel that they are taking positive action to solve their problems. This perspective also emphasizes the healing power of the therapist-patient relationship.

## FUTURE DIRECTIONS

The EST movement has succeeded in placing the importance of evidence-based practice squarely on the agenda of clinical psychology. Because EST lists have many inherent problems, however, they may prove more useful as a catalyst for helping the field move toward scientifically informed practice than they will be as the final word.

Several promising proposals recently have attempted to refine or replace ESTs in ways that retain their emphasis on science-based practice. One comes from the work of University of New Mexico psychologist William R. Miller. Miller constructed a list of all researched therapies for alcoholism, ranking them by the quality of the research and magnitude of the effects. His method provides access to all relevant information about all therapies studied, not just those that meet the all-or-none criteria for inclusion on the EST list.

Others have suggested that we seek empirically based "principles of change" rather than empirically supported therapies. For example, repeated exposure to feared objects and events is a central principle underlying most effective treatments for anxiety disorders. Therapists can derive many ways of flexibly implementing a principle of change to fit clients without being constrained by a specific technique or manual. In a similar vein, others have recently suggested that we focus on "empirically supported relationship factors," such as therapist empathy and warmth. But there is not yet sufficient agreement concerning which change or relationship principles should qualify as empirically supported.

Another alternative to ESTs was proposed by a committee appointed by past APA president Ronald F. Levant. The concept, which is called evidence-based practice, has been widely embraced in many areas of medicine. In its 2005 policy statement, the APA committee defined evidence-based practice as "the integration of the best available research with clinical expertise in the context of patient characteristics, culture, and preferences."

The term "best available research" is much broader than evidence based on psychotherapy studies alone. It encompasses research across the entire field of psychology, including personality, psychopathology and social psychology. "Clinical expertise" relates to therapist competencies that are not tied directly to research but that are believed to promote positive therapeutic outcomes. These capabilities inform the ability to form therapeutic relationships with clients and to devise and implement treatment plans. Finally, inclusion of client characteristics, culture and preferences points to the importance of tailoring treatments to individuals.

Although this APA report is a noble effort to grapple with some of the controversies, its long-term impact remains unclear. Many EST proponents have been dissatisfied with the recommendation to employ "the best available research" as being so vague, at least compared with the specificity of ESTs, as to be of little value. Many EST advocates have also objected to the inclusion of clinical expertise in a definition of evidence-based practice.

Given the shortcomings of ESTs and the existing alternatives to them, it is clear that the field is just beginning to incorporate science-based practice. Nevertheless, we can begin to see the broad outlines of promising positions that are less dogmatic than earlier ones. Such trends may help assuage the legitimate concerns of both researchers and practitioners. Ultimately we believe that the field must move beyond a narrow definition of ESTs toward views that bridge the gap between researchers and practitioners. After all, whatever their differences may be, aren't all clinical psychologists seeking better ways to help troubled people feel happier and live enriching lives?

# 5

# WHY BOGUS THERAPIES SEEM TO WORK

*Barry L. Beyerstein*

*Nothing is more dangerous than active ignorance.*

—Goethe

hose who sell therapies of any kind have an obligation to prove, first, that their treatments are safe and, second, that they are effective. The latter is often the more difficult task because there are many subtle ways that honest and intelligent people (both patients and therapists) can be led to think that a treatment has cured someone when it has not. This is true whether we are assessing new treatments in scientific medicine, old nostrums in folk medicine, fringe treatments in "alternative medicine," or the frankly magical panaceas of faith healers.

To distinguish causal from fortuitous improvements that might follow any intervention, a set of objective procedures has evolved for testing putative remedies. Unless a technique, ritual, drug, or surgical procedure can meet these requirements, it is ethically questionable to offer it to the public, especially if money is to change hands. Since most "alternative" therapies (i.e., ones not accepted by scientific biomedicine) fall into this category, one must ask why so many customers who would not purchase a toaster without consulting *Consumer Reports* shell out, with trusting naïveté, large sums for unproven, possibly dangerous, health remedies.

Reprinted with permission from *Skeptical Inquirer* (September/October 1997): 29–34.

For many years, critics have been raising telling doubts about fringe medical practices, but the popularity of such nostrums seems undiminished. We must wonder why entrepreneurs' claims in this area should remain so refractory to contrary data. If an "alternative" or a "complementary" therapy:

a. is implausible on *a priori* grounds (because its implied mechanisms or putative effects contradict well-established laws, principles, or empirical findings in physics, chemistry, or biology),
b. lacks a scientifically acceptable rationale of its own,
c. has insufficient supporting evidence derived from adequately controlled outcome research (i.e., double-blind, randomized, placebo-controlled clinical trials),
d. has failed in well-controlled clinical studies done by impartial evaluators and has been unable to rule out competing explanations for why it might *seem* to work in uncontrolled settings, and,
e. should seem improbable, even to the lay person, on "common-sense" grounds, why would so many well-educated people continue to sell and purchase such a treatment?

The answer, I believe, lies in a combination of vigorous marketing of unsubstantiated claims by "alternative" healers (Beyerstein and Sampson 1996), the poor level of scientific knowledge in the public at large (Kiernan 1995), and the "will to believe" so prevalent among seekers attracted to the New Age movement (Basil 1988; Gross & Levitt 1994).

The appeal of nonscientific medicine is largely a holdover from popular "counterculture" sentiments of the 1960s and 1970s. Remnants of the rebellious, "back-to-nature" leanings of that era survive as nostalgic yearnings for a return to nineteenth-century-style democratized healthcare (now wrapped in the banner of patients' rights) and a dislike of bureaucratic, technologic, and specialized treatment of disease (Cassileth & Brown 1988). Likewise, the allure of the "holistic" dogmas of alternative medicine is a descendant of the fascination with Eastern mysticism that emerged in the sixties and seventies. Although the philosophy and the science that underlie these holistic teachings have been severely criticized (Brandon 1985), they retain a strong appeal for those committed to belief in "mind-over-matter" cures, a systemic rather than localized view of pathology, and the all-powerful ability of nutrition to restore health (conceived of as whole-body "balance").

Many dubious health products remain on the market primarily because satisfied customers offer testimonials to their worth. Essentially, they are saying, "I tried it and I got better, so it must be effective." But even when symptoms do improve following a treatment, this, by itself, cannot prove that the therapy was responsible.

## THE ILLNESS-DISEASE DISTINCTION

Although the terms *disease* and *illness* are often used interchangeably, for present purposes it is worth distinguishing between the two. I shall use *disease* to refer to *a pathological state* of the organism due to infection, tissue degeneration, trauma, toxic exposure, carcinogenesis, etc. By *illness* I mean the *feelings* of malaise, pain, disorientation, dysfunctionality, or other complaints that might accompany a disease. Our subjective reaction to the raw sensations we call symptoms is molded by cultural and psychological factors such as beliefs, suggestions, expectations, demand characteristics, self-serving biases, and self-deception. The experience of illness is also affected (often unconsciously) by a host of social and psychological payoffs that accrue to those admitted to the "sick role" by society's gatekeepers (i.e., health professionals). For certain individuals, the privileged status and benefits of the sick role are sufficient to perpetuate the experience of illness after a disease has healed, or even to create feelings of illness in the absence of disease (Alcock 1986).

Unless we can tease apart the many factors that contribute to the perception of being ill, personal testimonials offer no basis on which to judge whether a putative therapy has, in fact, cured a disease. That is why controlled clinical trials with objective physical measures are essential in evaluating therapies of any kind.

## CORRELATION DOES NOT IMPLY CAUSATION

Mistaking correlation for causation is the basis of most superstitious beliefs, including many in the area of alternative medicine. We have a tendency to assume that when things occur together, they must be causally connected, although obviously they need not be. For example, there is a high correlation between the consumption of diet soft drinks and obesity. Does this mean that artificial sweeteners cause people to become overweight? When we count on personal experience to test the worth of medical treatments, many factors are varying simultaneously, making it extremely difficult to determine what is cause and effect. Personal endorsements supply the bulk of the support for unorthodox health products, but they are a weak currency because of what Gilovich (1997) has called the "compared to what?" problem. Without comparison to a similar group of sufferers, treated identically except that the allegedly curative *element* is withheld, individual recipients can never know whether they would have recovered just as well without it.

## TEN ERRORS AND BIASES

The question is, then: *Why might therapists and their clients who rely on anecdotal evidence and uncontrolled observations erroneously conclude that inert therapies work?* There are at least ten good reasons.

### 1. The disease may have run its natural course.

Many diseases are self-limiting—providing the condition is not chronic or fatal, the body's own recuperative processes usually restore the sufferer to health. Thus, before a therapy can be acknowledged as curative, its proponents must show that the number of patients listed as improved exceeds the proportion expected to recover without any treatment at all (or that they recover reliably faster than if left untreated). Unless an unconventional therapist releases detailed records of successes *and* failures over a sufficiently large number of patients with the same complaint, he or she cannot claim to have exceeded the published norms for unaided recovery.

## 2. Many diseases are cyclical.

Arthritis, multiple sclerosis, allergies, and gastrointestinal complaints are examples of diseases that normally "have their ups and downs." Naturally, sufferers tend to seek therapy during the downturn of any given cycle. In this way, a bogus treatment will have repeated opportunities to coincide with upturns that would have happened anyway. Again, in the absence of appropriate control groups, consumers and vendors alike are prone to misinterpret improvement due to normal cyclical variation as a valid therapeutic effect.

## 3. Spontaneous remission.

Anecdotally reported cures can be due to rare but possible "spontaneous remissions." Even with cancers that are nearly always lethal, tumors occasionally disappear without further treatment. One experienced oncologist reports that he has seen twelve such events in about six thousand cases he has treated (Silverman 1987). Alternative therapies can receive unearned acclaim for remissions of this sort because many desperate patients turn to them when they feel that they have nothing left to lose. When the "alternatives" assert that they have snatched many hopeless individuals from death's door, they rarely reveal what percentage of their apparently terminal clientele such happy exceptions represent. What is needed is statistical evidence that their "cure rates" exceed the known spontaneous remission rate and the placebo response rate (see the next page) for the conditions they treat.

The exact mechanisms responsible for spontaneous remissions are not well understood, but much research is being devoted to revealing and possibly harnessing processes in the immune system or elsewhere that are responsible for these unexpected turnarounds. The relatively new field of psychoneuroimmunology studies how psychological variables affect the nervous, glandular, and immune systems in ways that might affect susceptibility to and recovery from disease (Ader & Cohen 1993; Mestel 1994). If thoughts, emotions, desires, beliefs, and so on, are physical states of the brain, there is nothing inherently mystical in the notion that these neural processes could affect glandular, immune, and other cellular processes throughout the body. Via the limbic system of the brain, the hypothalamic pituitary axis, and the autonomic nervous system, psychological variables can have widespread physiological effects that can have positive or negative impacts upon health. While research has confirmed that such effects exist, it must be remembered that they are fairly small, accounting for perhaps a few percent of the variance in disease statistics.

### 4. The placebo effect.

A major reason why bogus remedies are credited with subjective, and occasionally objective, improvements is the ubiquitous placebo effect (Roberts, Kewman, & Hovell 1993; Ulett 1996). The history of medicine is strewn with examples of what, with hindsight, seem like crackpot procedures that were once enthusiastically endorsed by physicians and patients alike (Barrett & Jarvis 1993; Skrabanek & McCormick 1990). Misattributions of this sort arise from the false assumption that a change in symptoms following a treatment must have been a specific consequence of that procedure. Through a combination of suggestion, belief, expectancy, cognitive reinterpretation, and diversion of attention, patients given biologically useless treatments can often experience measurable relief. Some placebo responses produce actual changes in the physical condition; others are subjective changes that make patients feel better although there has been no objective change in the underlying pathology.

Through repeated contact with valid therapeutic procedures, we all develop, much like Pavlov's dogs, conditioned responses in various physiological systems. Later, these responses can be triggered by the setting, rituals, paraphernalia, and verbal cues that signal the act of "being treated." Among other things, placebos can cause release of the body's own morphinelike pain killers, the endorphins (Ulett 1996, ch. 3). Because these learned responses can be palliative, even when a treatment itself is physiologically unrelated to the source of the complaint, putative therapies must be tested against a placebo control group—similar patients who receive a sham treatment that resembles the "real" one except that the suspected active ingredient is withheld.

It is essential that the patients in such tests be randomly assigned to their respective groups and that they be "blind" with respect to their active versus placebo status. Because the power of what psychologists call expectancy and compliance effects (see below) is so strong, the therapists must also be blind as to individual patients' group membership. Hence the term *double blind*—the gold standard of outcome research. Such precautions are required because barely perceptible cues, unintentionally conveyed by treatment providers who are not blinded, can bias test results. Likewise, those who assess the treatment's effects must also be blind, for there is a large literature on "experimenter bias" showing that honest and well-trained professionals can unconsciously "read in" the outcomes they expect when they attempt to assess complex phenomena (Chapman & Chapman 1967; Rosenthal 1966).

When the clinical trial is completed, the blinds can be broken to allow statistical comparison of active, placebo, and no-treatment groups. Only if the improvements observed in the active treatment group exceed those in the two control groups by a statistically significant amount can the therapy claim legitimacy.

### 5. Some allegedly cured symptoms are psychosomatic to begin with.

A constant difficulty in trying to measure therapeutic effectiveness is that many physical complaints can both arise from psychosocial distress and be alleviated by support and reassurance. At first glance, these symptoms (at various times called "psychosomatic," "hysterical," or "neurasthenic") resemble those of recognized medical syndromes (Merskey 1995; Shorter 1992). Although there are many "secondary gains" (psychological, social, and economic) that accrue to those who slip into "the sick role" in this way, we need not accuse them of conscious malingering to point out that their symptoms are nonetheless maintained by subtle psychosocial processes.

"Alternative" healers cater to these members of the "worried well" who are mistakenly convinced that they are ill. Their complaints are instances of somatization, the tendency to express psychological concerns in a language of symptoms like those of organic diseases (Alcock 1986; Shorter 1992). The "alternatives" offer comfort to these individuals who for psychological reasons need others to believe there are organic etiologies for their symptoms. Often with the aid of pseudoscientific diagnostic devices, fringe practitioners reinforce the somatizer's conviction that the cold-hearted, narrow-minded medical establishment, which can find nothing physically amiss, is both incompetent and unfair in refusing to acknowledge a very real organic condition. A large portion of those diagnosed with "chronic fatigue," "environmental sensitivity syndrome," and various stress disorders (not to mention many suing because of the allegedly harmful effects of silicone breast implants) look very much like classic somatizers (Huber 1991; Rosenbaum 1997; Stewart 1990).

When, through the role-governed rituals of "delivering treatment," fringe therapists supply the reassurance, sense of belonging, and existential support their clients seek, this is obviously worthwhile, but all this need not be foreign to scientific practitioners who have much more to offer besides. The downside is that catering to the desire for medical diagnoses for psychological complaints promotes pseudoscientific and magical thinking while unduly inflating the success rates of medical quacks. Saddest of all, it perpetuates the anachronistic feeling that there is something shameful or illegitimate about psychological problems.

### 6. Symptomatic relief versus cure.

Short of an outright cure, alleviating pain and discomfort is what sick people value most. Many allegedly curative treatments offered by alternative practitioners, while unable to affect the disease process itself, do make the illness more bearable, but for psychological reasons. Pain is one example. Much research shows that pain is partly a sensation like seeing or hearing and partly an emotion (Melzack 1973). It has been found repeatedly that successfully reducing the emotional component of pain leaves the sensory portion surprisingly tolerable. Thus, suffering can often be reduced by psychological means, even if the underlying pathology is untouched. Anything that can allay anxiety, redirect attention, reduce arousal, foster a sense of control, or lead to cognitive reinterpretation of symptoms can alleviate the agony component of pain. Modern pain clinics put these strategies to good use every day (Smith, Merskey, and Gross 1980). Whenever patients suffer less, this is all to the good, but we must be careful that purely symptomatic relief does not divert people from proven remedies until it is too late for them to be effective.

### 7. Many consumers of alternative therapies hedge their bets.

In an attempt to appeal to a wider clientele, many unorthodox healers have begun to refer to themselves as "complementary" rather than "alternative." Instead of ministering primarily to the ideologically committed or those who have been told there is nothing more that conventional medicine can do for them, the "alternatives" have begun to advertise that they can enhance conventional biomedical treatments. They accept that orthodox practitioners can alleviate specific symptoms but contend that alternative medicine treats the *real* causes of disease—dubious dietary imbalances or environmental sensitivities, disrupted energy fields, or even unresolved conflicts from previous incarnations. If improvement follows the combined delivery of "complementary" and scientifically based treatments, the fringe practice often gets a disproportionate share of the credit.

### 8. Misdiagnosis (by self or by a physician).

In this era of media obsession with health, many people can be induced to think they have diseases they do not have. When these healthy folk receive the oddly unwelcome news from orthodox physicians that they have no organic signs of disease, they often gravitate to alternative practitioners who can almost always find some kind of "imbalance" to treat. If "recovery" follows, another convert is born.

Of course, scientifically trained physicians are not infallible, and a mistaken diagnosis, followed by a trip to a shrine or an alternative healer, can lead to a glowing testimonial for curing a grave condition that never existed. Other times, the diagnosis may be correct but the time course, which is inherently hard to predict, might prove inaccurate. If a patient with a terminal condition undergoes alternative treatments and succumbs later than the conventional doctor predicted, the alternative procedure may receive credit for prolonging life when, in fact, there was merely an unduly pessimistic prognosis—survival was longer than the expected norm, but within the range of normal statistical variation for the disease.

### 9. Derivative benefits.

Alternative healers often have forceful, charismatic personalities (O'Connor 1987). To the extent that patients are swept up by the messianic aspects of alternative medicine, psychological uplift may ensue. If an enthusiastic, upbeat healer manages to elevate the patient's mood and expectations, this optimism can lead to greater compliance with, and hence effectiveness of, any orthodox treatments he or she may also be receiving. This expectant attitude can also motivate people to eat and sleep better and to exercise and socialize more. These, by themselves, could help speed natural recovery.

Psychological spinoffs of this sort can also reduce stress, which has been shown to have deleterious effects on the immune system (Mestel 1994). Removing this added burden may speed healing, even if it is not a specific effect of the therapy. As with purely symptomatic relief, this is far from a bad thing, unless it diverts the patient from more effective treatments, or the charges are exorbitant.

## 10. Psychological distortion of reality.

Distortion of reality in the service of strong belief is a common occurrence (Alcock 1995). Even when they derive no objective improvements, devotees who have a strong psychological investment in alternative medicine can convince themselves they have been helped. According to *cognitive dissonance* theory (Festinger 1957), when experiences contradict existing attitudes, feelings, or knowledge, mental distress is produced. We tend to alleviate this discord by reinterpreting (distorting) the offending information. To have received no relief after committing time, money, and "face" to an alternate course of treatment (and perhaps to the worldview of which it is a part) would create such a state of internal disharmony. Because it would be too psychologically disconcerting to admit to oneself or to others that it has all been a waste, there would be strong psychological pressure to find some redeeming value in the treatment.

Many other *self-serving biases* help maintain self-esteem and smooth social functioning (Beyerstein & Hadaway 1991). Because core beliefs tend to be vigorously defended by warping perception and memory, fringe practitioners and their clients are prone to misinterpret cues and remember things as they wish they had happened. Similarly, they may be selective in what they recall, overestimating their apparent successes while ignoring, downplaying, or explaining away their failures. The scientific method evolved in large part to reduce the impact of this human penchant for jumping to congenial conclusions.

An illusory feeling that one's symptoms have improved could also be due to a number of so-called *demand characteristics* found in any therapeutic setting. In all societies, there exists the "norm of reciprocity," an implicit rule that obliges people to respond in kind when someone does them a good turn. Therapists, for the most part, sincerely believe they are helping their patients and it is only natural that patients would want to please them in return. Without patients necessarily realizing it, such obligations are sufficient to inflate their perception of how much benefit they have received. Thus, controls for compliance effects must also be built into proper clinical trials (Adair 1973).

Finally, the job of distinguishing real from spurious causal relationships requires not only controlled observations, but also systematized abstractions from large bodies of data. Psychologists interested in *judgmental biases* have identified many sources of error that plague people who rely on informal reasoning processes to analyze complex events (Gilovich 1991, 1997; Schick & Vaughn 1995). Dean and colleagues (1992) showed, using examples from another popular pseudoscience, handwriting analysis, that without sophisticated statistical aids, human cognitive abilities are simply not up to the task of sifting valid relationships out of masses of interacting data. Similar difficulties would have confronted the pioneers of prescientific medicine and their followers, and for that reason, we cannot accept their anecdotal reports as support for their assertions.

## SUMMARY

For the reasons I have presented, individual testimonials count for very little in evaluating therapies. Because so many false leads can convince intelligent, honest people that cures have been achieved when they have not, it is essential that any putative treatment be tested under conditions that control for placebo responses, compliance effects, and judgmental errors.

Before anyone agrees to undergo any kind of treatment, he or she should be confident that it has been validated in properly controlled clinical trials. To reduce the probability that supporting evidence has been contaminated by the foregoing biases and errors, consumers should insist that supporting evidence be published in peer-reviewed scientific journals. Any practitioner who cannot supply this kind of backing for his or her procedures is immediately suspect. Potential clients should be wary if, instead, the "evidence" consists merely of testimonials, self-published pamphlets or books, or items from the popular media. Even if supporting articles appear to have come from legitimate scientific periodicals, consumers should check to see that the journals in question are published by reputable scientific organizations. Papers extolling pseudoscience often appear in official-looking periodicals that turn out to be owned by groups with inadequate scientific credentials but with a financial stake in the questionable products. Similarly, one should discount articles from the "vanity press" journals that accept virtually all submissions and charge the authors for publication. And finally, because any single positive outcome—even from a carefully done experiment published in a reputable journal—could always be a fluke, replication by independent research groups is the ultimate standard of proof.

If the practitioner claims persecution, is ignorant of or openly hostile to mainstream science, cannot supply a reasonable scientific rationale for his or her methods, and promises results that go well beyond those claimed by orthodox biomedicine, there is strong reason to suspect that one is dealing with a quack. Appeals to other ways of knowing or mysterious sounding "planes," "energies," "forces," or "vibrations" are other telltale signs, as is any claim to treat the whole person rather than localized pathology.

To people who are unwell, any promise of a cure is especially beguiling. As a result, false hope easily supplants common sense. In this vulnerable state, the need for hard-nosed appraisal is all the more necessary, but so often we see instead an eagerness to abandon any remaining vestiges of skepticism. Erstwhile savvy consumers, felled by disease, often insist upon less evidence to support the claims of alternative healers than they would previously have demanded from someone hawking a used car. Caveat emptor!

# REFERENCES

Adair, J. 1973. *The Human Subject*. Boston: Little, Brown and Co.

Ader, R., and N. Cohen. 1993. Psychoneuroimmunology: Conditioning and stress. *Annual Review of Psychology* 44: 53–85.

Alcock, J. 1986. Chronic pain and the injured worker. *Canadian Psychology* 27, no. 2: 196–203.

————. 1995. The belief engine. *Skeptical Inquirer* 19, no. 3: 14–18.

Barrett, S., and W. Jarvis. 1993. *The Health Robbers: A Close Look at Quackery in America.* Amherst, NY: Prometheus Books.

Basil, R., ed. 1988. *Not Necessarily the New Age.* Amherst, NY: Prometheus Books.

Beyerstein, B., and P. Hadaway. 1991. On avoiding folly. *Journal of Drug Issues* 20, no. 4: 689–700.

Beyerstein, B., and W. Sampson. 1996. Traditional medicine and pseudoscience in China. *Skeptical Inquirer* 20, no. 4: 18–26.

Brandon, R. 1985. Holism in philosophy of biology. In *Examining Holistic Medicine,* edited by D. Stalker and C. Glymour. Amherst, NY: Prometheus Books, pp. 127–36.

Cassileth, B., and H. Brown. 1988. Unorthodox cancer medicine. *CA—A Cancer Journal for Clinicians* 38, no. 3: 176–86.

Chapman, L., and J. Chapman. 1967. Genesis of popular but erroneous diagnostic observations. *Journal of Abnormal Psychology* 72: 193–204.

Dean, G., I. Kelly, D. Saklofske, and A. Furnham. 1992. Graphology and human judgement. In *The Write Stuff,* edited by B. and D. Beyerstein. Amherst, NY: Prometheus Books, pp. 342–96.

Festinger, L. 1957. *A Theory of Cognitive Dissonance.* Stanford: Stanford University Press.

Gilovich, T. 1991. *How We Know What Isn't So: The Fallibility of Human Reason in Everyday Life.* New York: Free Press/Macmillan.

————. 1997. Some systematic biases of everyday judgment. *Skeptical Inquirer* 21, no. 2: 31–35.

Gross, P., and N. Levitt. 1994. *Higher Superstition.* Baltimore: Johns Hopkins University Press.

Huber, P. 1991. *Galileo's Revenge: Junk Science in the Courtroom.* New York: Basic Books.

Kiernan, V. 1995. Survey plumbs the depths of international ignorance. *New Scientist* (April 29): 7.

Melzack, R. 1973. *The Puzzle of Pain.* New York: Basic Books.

Merskey, H. 1995. *The Analysis of Hysteria: Understanding Conversion and Dissociation.* 2nd ed. London: Royal College of Psychiatrists.

Mestel, R. 1994. Let mind talk unto body. *New Scientist* (July 23): 26–31.

O'Connor, G. 1987. Confidence trick. *Medical Journal of Australia* 147: 456–59.

Roberts, A., D. Kewman, and L. Hovell. 1993. The power of nonspecific effects in healing: Implications for psychosocial and biological treatments. *Clinical Psychology Review* 13: 375–91.

Rosenbaum, J. T. 1997. Lessons from litigation over silicone breast implants: A call for activism by scientists. *Science* 276 (June 6): 1524–25.

Rosenthal, R. 1966. *Experimenter Effects in Behavioral Research*. New York: Appleton-Century-Crofts.

Schick, T., and L. Vaughn. 1995. *How to Think about Weird Things: Critical Thinking for a New Age*. Mountain View, CA: Mayfield Publishing.

Shorter, E. 1992. *From Paralysis to Fatigue: A History of Psychosomatic Illness in the Modern Era*. New York: Free Press.

Silverman, S. 1987. Medical "miracles": Still mysterious despite claims of believers. *Psientific American* (July): 5–7. Newsletter of the Sacramento Skeptics Society, Sacramento, Calif.

Skrabanek, P., and J. McCormick. 1990. *Follies and Fallacies in Medicine*. Amherst, NY: Prometheus Books.

Smith, W. H. Merskey, and S. Gross, eds. 1980. *Pain: Meaning and Management*. New York: SP Medical and Scientific Books.

Stalker, D., and C. Glymour, eds. 1985. *Examining Holistic Medicine*. Amherst, NY: Prometheus Books.

Stewart, D. 1990. Emotional disorders misdiagnosed as physical illness: Environmental hypersensitivity, candidiasis hypersensitivity, and chronic fatigue syndrome. *International Journal of Mental Health* 19, no. 3: 56–68.

Ulett, G. A. 1996. *Alternative Medicine or Magical Healing*. St. Louis: Warren H. Green.

# SECTION III. HOW TO EVALUATE ASSESSMENT METHODS

# INTRODUCTION

To find out what psychological problems a person is experiencing, we first need to be able to detect them accurately. Similarly, to find out whether a treatment works, we first must be able to measure its effects.

That's where the science of what psychologists call "assessment" enters the picture. The field of assessment comprises the myriad practices that psychologists use to measure psychological characteristics, like mental illness, personality traits, intelligence, and interests. As is so often the case in psychology, there's some good news and some bad news when it comes to the world of assessment.

First, the good news. Psychologists have developed a large number of assessment instruments that work reasonably well. How do we know? There are two major criteria. First is "reliability," which refers to the consistency of a measuring instrument. A psychological test is reliable if its scores are stable over time (so-called test-retest reliability) and if the items composing the test are positively related to each other (so-called internal consistency). A third form of reliability, "inter-rater reliability," applies primarily to interviews; it tells us whether two different interviewers or observers agree on the presence of individuals' psychological conditions. In short, a test is reliable if it yields systematic rather than random measurements.

The second major criterion is "validity," which refers to the extent to which a test measures what it purports to measure. Validity refers to truth in labeling: a valid test is true to its name. If a supposed measure of depression in fact assesses schizophrenia, it is not valid for its intended purpose. In contrast, if a supposed measure of depression predicts things that we expect to be related to depression—like neurochemical or hormonal abnormalities (e.g., elevated cortisol) or a tendency to perceive oneself and others negatively—it possesses at least some validity.

Many psychological tests boast fairly high levels of both reliability and validity. This is particularly true of "structured" personality tests, which consist primarily of fairly clear-cut statements (like "I enjoy going to parties" or "I frequently stole things when I was a youngster") and a limited number of response options (like "true" and "false"). Among the best known of such tests are the old workhorse, the Minnesota Multiphasic Personality Inventory (MMPI), revised in the late 1980s as the MMPI-2; the California Psychological Inventory; and the Personality Assessment Inventory.

The bad news? The reliability and validity of some widely used psychological tests are, to be charitable, less than impressive. As we will discover in this section, many "projective" techniques have come under particular attack in the scientific community. These techniques consist mostly of ambiguous stimuli (like inkblots or pictures of people interacting with each other) and allow clients an essentially infinite number of response options. Among the best known of these tests are the Rorschach Inkblot Test, which is simultaneously the most revered and reviled of all psychological measures; the Thematic Apperception Test; and the Draw-a-Person Test. All of these tests, although widely administered, are of questionable clinical utility for most purposes. Nevertheless, structured tests aren't immune from shortcomings either. For example, the wildly popular Myers-Briggs Type Indicator, a familiar fixture in many counseling and vocational settings, doesn't fare especially well in either reliability or validity.

❦

In the first chapter in this section, Scott Lilienfeld and colleagues describe a plethora of reasons for the popularity of dubious assessment devices. Echoing Barry Beyerstein's chapter in the previous section, they point out that mental health consumers and practitioners can easily be fooled into concluding that an invalid psychological instrument is actually valid. Among these reasons are the "P. T. Barnum effect," the tendency to accept highly vague and generalized statements as self-descriptive, and "illusory correlation," the tendency to perceive connections that aren't present.

In the next three chapters, James Wood and his colleagues examine the scientific status of projective techniques, with particular emphasis on the exceedingly controversial Rorschach Inkblot Test. They observe that despite its widespread use, most of the scores derived from this test have at best doubtful validity for their intended clinical purposes. Nevertheless, Wood and collaborators also note that a handful of Rorschach scores, especially those designed to detect the thought disorder characteristic of schizophrenia and bipolar disorder (manic-depression), perform reasonably well.

David Myers next discusses the promises and perils of clinical intuition. As Myers points out, studies show that clinical judgments frequently predict important psychological outcomes at better-than-chance levels. Nevertheless, clinical intuition has its limits. For example, an enormous body of psychological research demonstrates that statistical formulas derived from real-world data do at least as well as, and often better than, clinical judgments when it comes to combining data to generate predictions (such as whether a client will attempt suicide or benefit from a specific type of psychotherapy). Moreover, if left unchecked by the safeguards of scientific evidence, unbridled clinical intuition can lead us to embrace ineffective treatments, such as subliminal self-help tapes.

One domain in which psychological assessment plays a key role is child custody law. Nevertheless, as Robert Emery and his colleagues observe in the concluding chapter in this section, there appears to be considerably less than meets the eye when it comes to the science of child custody disputes. They argue that precious few psychological tests have been validated for assisting triers of fact with custody decisions, and psychologist expert witnesses should play a far more limited role in such decisions than they do at present.

# 6.

# WHAT'S WRONG WITH THIS PICTURE?

## By Scott O. Lilienfeld, James M. Wood, and Howard N. Garb

What if you were asked to describe images you saw in an inkblot or to invent a story for an ambiguous illustration—say, of a middle-aged man looking away from a woman who was grabbing his arm? To comply, you would draw on your own emotions, experiences, memories and imagination. You would, in short, project yourself into the images. Once you did that, many practicing psychologists would assert, trained evaluators could mine your musings to reach conclusions about your personality traits, unconscious needs and overall mental health.

But how correct would they be? The answer is important because psychologists frequently apply such "projective" instruments (presenting people with ambiguous images, words or objects) as components of mental assessments and because the outcomes can profoundly affect the lives of the respondents. The tools often serve, for instance, as aids in diagnosing mental illness, in predicting whether convicts are likely to become violent after being paroled, in evaluating the mental stability of parents engaged in custody battles, and in discerning whether children have been sexually molested.

We recently reviewed a large body of research into how well projective methods work, concentrating on three of the most extensively used and best-studied instruments. Overall our findings are unsettling.

## BUTTERFLIES OR BISON?

The famous Rorschach inkblot test—which asks people to describe what they see in a series of ten inkblots—is by far the most popular of the projective methods, given to hundreds of thousands, or perhaps millions, of people every year. The research discussed below refers to the modern, rehabilitated version, not to the original construction, introduced in the 1920s by Swiss psychiatrist Hermann Rorschach.

The initial tool came under severe attack in the 1950s and 1960s, in part because it lacked standardized procedures and a set of norms (averaged results from the general population). Standardization is important because seemingly trivial differences in the way an instrument is administered can affect a person's responses to it. Norms provide a reference point for determining when someone's responses fall outside an acceptable range.

In the 1970s John E. Exner Jr., then at Long Island University, ostensibly corrected those problems in the early Rorschach test by introducing what he called the Comprehensive System. This set of instructions established detailed rules for delivering the inkblot exam and for interpreting the responses, and it provided norms for children and adults.

In spite of the Comprehensive System's current popularity, it generally falls short on two crucial criteria that were also problematic for the original Rorschach: scoring reliability and validity. A tool possessing scoring reliability yields similar results regardless of who grades and tabulates the responses. A valid technique measures what it aims to measure: its results are consistent with those produced by other trustworthy instruments, or are able to predict behavior, or both.

To understand the Rorschach's scoring reliability defects, it helps to know something about how reactions to the inkblots are interpreted. First, a psychologist rates the collected reactions on more than a hundred characteristics, or variables. The evaluator, for instance, records whether the person looked at whole blots or just parts, notes whether the detected images were unusual or typical of most test takers, and indicates which aspects of the inky swirls (such as form or color) most determined what the respondent reported seeing.

Then he or she compiles the findings into a psychological profile of the individual. As part of that interpretive process, psychologists might conclude that focusing on minor details (such as stray splotches) in the blots, instead of on whole images, signals obsessiveness in a patient and that seeing things in the white spaces within the larger blots, instead of in the inked areas, reveals a negative, contrary streak.

For the scoring of any variable to be considered highly reliable, two different assessors should be very likely to produce similar ratings when examining any given person's responses. Recent investigations demonstrate, however, that strong agreement is achieved for only about half the characteristics examined by those who score Rorschach responses; evaluators might well come up with quite different ratings for the remaining variables.

Equally troubling, analyses of the Rorschach's validity indicate that it is poorly equipped to identify most psychiatric conditions—with the notable exceptions of schizophrenia and other disturbances marked by disordered thoughts, such as bipolar disorder (manic-depression). Despite claims by some Rorschach proponents, the method does not consistently detect depression, anxiety disorders or psychopathic personality (a condition characterized by dishonesty, callousness and lack of guilt).

Moreover, although psychologists frequently administer the Rorschach to assess propensities toward violence, impulsiveness and criminal behavior, most research suggests it is not valid for these purposes either. Similarly, no compelling evidence supports its use for detecting sexual abuse in children.

Other problems have surfaced as well. Some evidence suggests that the Rorschach norms meant to distinguish mental health from mental illness are unrepresentative of the US population and mistakenly make many adults and children seem maladjusted. For instance, in a 1999 study of 123 adult volunteers at a California blood bank, one in six had scores supposedly indicative of schizophrenia.

The inkblot results may be even more misleading for minorities. Several investigations have shown that scores for African Americans,

Native Americans, Native Alaskans, Hispanics, and Central and South Americans differ markedly from the norms. Together the collected research raises serious doubts about the use of the Rorschach inkblots in the psychotherapy office and in the courtroom.

## DOUBTS ABOUT TAT

Another projective tool—the Thematic Apperception Test (TAT)—may be as problematic as the Rorschach. This method asks respondents to formulate a story based on ambiguous scenes in drawings on cards. Among the thirty-one cards available to psychologists are ones depicting a boy contemplating a violin, a distraught woman clutching an open door, and the man and woman who were mentioned at the start of this chapter. One card, the epitome of ambiguity, is totally blank.

The TAT has been called "a clinician's delight and a statistician's nightmare," in part because its administration is usually not standardized: different clinicians present different numbers and selections of cards to respondents. Also, most clinicians interpret people's stories intuitively instead of following a well-tested scoring procedure. Indeed, a recent survey of nearly a hundred North American psychologists practicing in juvenile and family courts discovered that only 3 percent relied on a standardized TAT scoring system. Unfortunately, some evidence suggests that clinicians who interpret the TAT in an intuitive way are likely to overdiagnose psychological disturbance.

### RORSCHACH TEST: WASTED INK?

"It looks like two dinosaurs with huge heads and tiny bodies. They're moving away from each other but looking back. The black blob in the middle reminds me of a spaceship."

Once deemed an "x-ray of the mind," the Rorschach inkblot test remains the most famous—and infamous—projective psychological technique. An examiner hands ten symmetrical inkblots one at a time in a set order to a viewer, who says what each blot resembles. Five blots contain color; five are black and gray. Respondents can rotate the images.

Responses to the inkblots purportedly reveal aspects of a person's personality and mental health. Advocates believe, for instance, that references to moving animals—such as the dinosaurs mentioned above—often indicate impulsiveness, whereas allusions to a blot's "blackness"—as in the spaceship—often indicate depression.

Swiss psychiatrist Hermann Rorschach probably got the idea of showing inkblots from a European parlor game. The test debuted in 1921 and reached high status by 1945. But a critical backlash began taking shape in the 1950s, as researchers found that psychologists often interpreted the same responses differently and that particular responses did not correlate well with specific mental illnesses or personality traits.

Today the Comprehensive System, meant to remedy those weaknesses, is widely used to score and interpret Rorschach responses. But it has been criticized on similar grounds. Moreover, several recent findings indicate that the Comprehensive System incorrectly labels many normal respondents as pathological.

Many standardized scoring systems are available for the TAT, but some of the more popular ones display weak "test-retest" reliability: they tend to yield inconsistent scores from one picture-viewing session to the next. Their validity is frequently questionable as well; studies that find positive results are often contradicted by other investigations. For example, several scoring systems have proved unable to differentiate normal individuals from those who are psychotic or depressed.

A few standardized scoring systems for the TAT do appear to do a good job of discerning certain aspects of personality—notably the need to achieve and a person's perceptions of others (a property called "object relations"). But many times individuals who display a high need to achieve do not score well on measures of actual achievement, so the ability of that variable to predict a person's behavior may be limited. These scoring systems currently lack norms and so are not yet ready for application outside of research settings, but they merit further investigation.

## THEMATIC APPERCEPTION TEST: PICTURE IMPERFECT

The Thematic Apperception Test (TAT), created by Harvard University psychiatrist Henry A. Murray and his student Christiana Morgan in the 1930s, is among the most commonly used projective measures. Examiners present individuals with a subset (typically five to twelve) of thirty-one cards displaying pictures of ambiguous situations, mostly featuring people. Respondents then construct a story about each picture, describing the events that are occurring, what led up to them, what the characters are thinking and feeling, and what will happen later. Many variations of the TAT are in use, such as the Children's Apperception Test, featuring animals interacting in ambiguous situations, and the Blacky Test, featuring the adventures of a black dog and its family.

Psychologists have several ways of interpreting responses to the TAT. One promising approach—developed by Emory University psychologist Drew Westen—relies on a specific scoring system to assess people's perceptions of others ("object relations"). According to that approach, if someone wove a story about an older woman plotting against a younger person in response to the image [of an older woman looking over a younger woman's shoulder] the story would imply that the respondent tends to see malevolence in others—but only if similar themes turned up in stories told about other cards.

Surveys show, however, that most practitioners do not use systematic scoring systems to interpret TAT stories, relying instead on their intuitions. Unfortunately, research indicates that such "impressionistic" interpretations of the TAT are of doubtful validity and may make the TAT a projective exercise for both examiner and examinee.

# FAULTS IN THE FIGURES

In contrast to the Rorschach and the TAT, which elicit reactions to existing images, a third projective approach asks the people being evaluated to draw the pictures. A number of these instruments, such as the frequently applied Draw-a-Person Test, have examinees depict a human being; others have them draw houses or trees as well. Clinicians commonly interpret the sketches by relating specific "signs"—such as features of the body or clothing—to facets of personality or to particular psychological disorders. They might associate large eyes with paranoia, long ties with sexual aggression, missing facial features with depression, and so on.

As is true of the other methods, the research on drawing instruments gives reason for serious concern. In some studies, raters agree well on scoring, yet in others the agreement is poor. What is worse, no strong evidence supports the validity of the sign approach to interpretation; in other words, clinicians apparently have no grounds for linking specific signs to particular personality traits or psychiatric diagnoses. Nor is there consistent evidence that signs purportedly linked to child sexual abuse (such as tongues or genitalia) actually reveal a history of molestation. The only positive result found repeatedly is that, as a group, people who draw human figures poorly have somewhat elevated rates of psychological disorders. On the other hand, studies show that clinicians are likely to attribute mental illness to many normal individuals who lack artistic ability.

## HUMAN FIGURE DRAWINGS: MISLEADING SIGNS

Psychologists have many projective drawing instruments at their disposal, but the Draw-a-Person Test is among the most popular—especially for assessing children and adolescents. A clinician asks the child to draw someone of the same sex and then someone of the opposite sex in any way that he or she wishes. (A variation involves asking the child to draw a person, house, and tree.) Those who employ the test believe that the drawings reveal meaningful information about the child's personality or mental health.

In a sketch of a man, for example, small feet would supposedly indicate insecurity or instability—a small head, inadequacy. Large hands or teeth would be considered signs of aggression; short arms, a sign of shyness. And feminine features—such as long eyelashes or darkly colored lips—would allegedly suggest sex-role confusion.

Yet research consistently shows that such "signs" bear virtually no relation to personality or mental illness. Scientists have denounced these sign interpretations as "phrenology for the twentieth century," recalling the nineteenth-century pseudoscience of inferring people's personalities from the pattern of bumps on their skulls.

Still, the sign approach remains widely used. Some psychologists even claim they can identify sexual abuse from certain key signs. For instance, in a child's drawing, alleged signs of abuse could include a person older than the child, a partially unclothed body, a hand near the genitals, a hand hidden in a pocket, a large nose, and a mustache. In reality, the connection between these signs and sexual abuse remains dubious, at best.

Certain proponents argue that sign approaches can be valid in the hands of seasoned experts. Yet one group of researchers reported that experts who administered the Draw-a-Person Test were less accurate than graduate students at distinguishing psychological normality from abnormality.

A few global scoring systems, which are not based on signs, might be useful. Instead of assuming a one-to-one correspondence between a feature of a drawing and a personality trait, psychologists who apply such methods combine many aspects of the pictures to come up with a general impression of a person's adjustment. In a study of fifty-two children, a global scoring approach helped to distinguish normal individuals from those with mood or anxiety disorders. In another report, global interpretation correctly differentiated fifty-four normal children and adolescents from those who were aggressive or extremely disobedient. The global approach may work better than the sign approach because the act of aggregating information can cancel out "noise" from variables that provide misleading or incomplete information.

Our literature review, then, indicates that, as usually administered, the Rorschach, TAT and human figure drawings are useful only in very limited circumstances. The same is true for many other projective techniques, some of which are described in the sidebar below.

We have also found that even when the methods assess what they claim to measure, they tend to lack what psychologists call "incremental validity": they rarely add much to information that can be obtained in other, more practical ways, such as by conducting interviews or administering objective personality tests. (Objective tests seek answers to relatively clear-cut questions, such as, "I frequently have thoughts of hurting myself—true or false?") This shortcoming of projective tools makes the costs in money and time hard to justify.

## Other Projective Tools: What's the Score?

Psychologists have dozens of projective methods to choose from beyond the Rorschach Test, the TAT, and figure drawings. As the sampling below indicates, some stand up well to the scrutiny of research, but many do not.

### Hand Test

Subjects say what hands pictured in various positions might be doing. This method is used to assess aggression, anxiety, and other personality traits, but it has not been well studied.

### Handwriting Analysis (Graphology)

Interpreters rely on specific "signs" in a person's handwriting to assess personality characteristics. Though useless, the method is still used to screen prospective employees.

### Lüscher Color Test

People rank colored cards in order of preference to reveal personality traits. Most studies find the technique to lack merit.

### Play with Anatomically Correct Dolls

Research finds that sexually abused children often play with the dolls' genitalia; however, that behavior is not diagnostic, because many nonabused children do the same thing.

### Rosenzweig Picture Frustration Study

After one cartoon character makes a provocative remark to another, a viewer decides how the second character should respond. This instrument, featured in the movie *A Clockwork Orange*, successfully predicts aggression in children.

### Sentence Completion Test

Test takers finish a sentence, such as, "If only I could . . ." Most versions are poorly studied, but one developed by the late Jane Loevinger of Washington University is valid for measuring aspects of ego development, such as morality and empathy.

### Szondi Test

From photographs of patients with various psychiatric disorders, viewers select the ones they like most and least. This technique assumes that the selections reveal something about the choosers' needs, but research has discredited it.

## WHAT TO DO?

Some mental health professionals disagree with our conclusions. They argue that projective tools have a long history of constructive use and, when administered and interpreted properly, can cut through the veneer of respondents' self-reports to provide a picture of the deepest recesses of the mind. Critics have also asserted that we have emphasized negative findings to the exclusion of positive ones.

Yet we remain confident in our conclusions. In fact, as negative as our overall findings are, they may paint an overly rosy picture of projective techniques because of the so-called file drawer effect. As is well known, scientific journals are more likely to publish reports demonstrating that some procedure works than reports finding failure. Consequently, researchers often quietly file away their negative data, which may never again see the light of day.

We find it troubling that psychologists commonly administer projective instruments in situations for which their value has not been well established by multiple studies; too many people can suffer if erroneous diagnostic judgments influence therapy plans, custody rulings or criminal court decisions. Based on our findings, we strongly urge psychologists to curtail their use of most projective techniques and, when they do select such instruments, to limit themselves to scoring and interpreting the small number of variables that have been proved trustworthy.

Our results also offer a broader lesson for practicing clinicians, psychology students and the public at large: even seasoned professionals can be fooled by their intuitions and their faith in tools that lack strong evidence of effectiveness. When a substantial body of research demonstrates that old intuitions are wrong, it is time to adopt new ways of thinking.

## HOW OFTEN THE TOOLS ARE USED:
## POPULARITY POLL

In 1995 a survey asked 412 randomly selected clinical psychologists in the American Psychological Association how often they used various projective and nonprojective assessment tools, including those listed below. Projective instruments present people with ambiguous pictures, words, or things; the other measures are less open-ended. The number of clinicians who use projective methods might have declined slightly since 1995, but these techniques remain widely used.

| PROJECTIVE TECHNIQUES | USE ALWAYS OR FREQUENTLY | USE AT LEAST OCCASIONALLY |
| --- | --- | --- |
| Rorschach | 43% | 82% |
| Human Figure Drawings | 39% | 80% |
| Thematic Apperception Test (TAT) | 34% | 82% |
| Sentence Completion Tests | 34% | 84% |
| CAT (Children's version of the TAT) | 6% | 42% |

| NONPROJECTIVE TECHNIQUES | USE ALWAYS OR FREQUENTLY | USE AT LEAST OCCASIONALLY |
| --- | --- | --- |
| Wechsler Adult Intelligence Scale (WAIS) | 59% | 93% |
| Minnesota Multiphasic Personality Inventory-2 (MMPI-2) | 58% | 85% |
| Wechsler Intelligence Scale for Children (WISC) | 42% | 69% |
| Beck Depression Inventory | 21% | 71% |

* Those listed are the most commonly used nonprojective tests for assessing adult IQ (WAIS), personality (MMPI-2), childhood IQ (WISC), and depression (Beck Depression Inventory).

SOURCE: C. E. Watkins et al., "Contemporary Practice of Psychological Assessment by Clinical Psychologists," *Professional Psychology: Research and Practice* 26, no. 1 (1995): 54–60.

# 7.

# THE RORSCHACH INKBLOT TEST, FORTUNE TELLERS, AND COLD READING

## James M. Wood, M. Teresa Nezworski, Scott O. Lilienfeld, and Howard N. Garb

*Famous clinical psychologists used the Rorschach Inkblot Test to arrive at incredible insights. But were the astounding performances of these Rorschach Wizards merely a variation on astrology and palm reading?*

Psychologists have been quarreling over the Rorschach Inkblot Test for half a century. From 1950 to the present, most psychologists in clinical practice have treasured the test as one of their most precious tools. And for nearly that long, their scientific colleagues have been trying to persuade them that the test is well-nigh worthless, a pseudoscientific modern variant on tea-leaf reading and Tarot cards.

Introduced in 1921 by the Swiss psychiatrist Hermann Rorschach, the test bears a charming resemblance to a party game. A person is shown ten inkblots and asked to tell what each resembles. Like swirling images in a crystal ball, the ambiguous blots tell a different story to every person who gazes upon them. There are butterflies and bats, diaphanous dresses and bow ties, monkeys, monsters, and mountain-climbing bears. When scored and interpreted by an expert, people's responses to the blots are said to provide a full and penetrating portrait of their personalities.

The scientific evidence for the Rorschach has always been feeble. By

Reprinted with permission from *Skeptical Inquirer* (July/August 2003): 29–33, 61.

1965, research psychologists had concluded that the test was useless for most purposes for which it was used. The most popular modern version of the Rorschach, developed by psychologist John Exner, has been promoted as scientifically superior to earlier forms of the test. In 1997 the Board of Professional Affairs of the American Psychological Association bestowed an award on Exner for his "scientific contributions" and applauded his version of the Rorschach as "perhaps the single most powerful psychometric instrument ever envisioned."

Such bloated claims to the contrary, however, research has shown that Exner's approach is beset by the same problems that have always plagued the test. The Rorschach—including Exner's version—tends to mislabel most normal people as "sick." In addition, the test cannot detect most psychological disorders (with the exception of schizophrenia and related conditions marked by thinking disturbances), nor does it do an adequate job of detecting most personality traits (Lilienfeld 1999; Lilienfeld, Wood & Garb 2000).

Despite such shortcomings, the Rorschach is still administered hundreds of thousands of times each year in clinics, courts, and schools. Psychologists often use the test to help courts determine which parent should be granted custody of a child. It's used in schools to identify children's emotional problems and in prisons to evaluate felons for parole. Convicted murderers facing the death penalty, suspected victims of sexual abuse, airline pilots suspended from their jobs for alcohol abuse—all may be given the Rorschach by a psychologist who will use the test to make critical decisions about their lives.

In the 1940s and 1950s, the Rorschach was unblushingly promoted as a "psychological x-ray" that could penetrate the inner secrets of the psyche. Although it failed to live up to such promises, the test still possesses a powerful mystique.

# BLIND ANALYSES AND THE RORSCHACH MYSTIQUE

Why is such a scientifically dubious technique so revered among psychologists? The lasting popularity of the Rorschach has little to do with empirical validity. Certainly one secret of the Rorschach's success is clinicians' tendency to rely on striking anecdotes about its extraordinary powers—rather than on careful scientific studies—when assessing its value. Psychologists who treasure the Rorschach can recount colorful stories of how the test miraculously uncovered hidden facts about a patient that other tests failed to detect. Indeed, the test's rise to popularity was due mainly to the near-magical performances—known as "blind analyses"—that Rorschach experts exhibited to their amazed colleagues during the 1940s and 1950s.

In a blind analysis, the Rorschach expert was told a patient's age and gender and given the patient's responses to the blots. From this modest sample of information, the expert would then proceed to generate an amazing, in-depth description of the patient's personality. During the 1950s, the ability to make such astounding "blind diagnoses" came to be regarded among American psychologists as the mark of a true Rorschach genius.

Stunning performances by Rorschach "wizards" converted many psychologists of the era into true believers. For example, one highly respected psychologist has reported how, while still a student, he attended case conferences at which the famed Marguerite Hertz interpreted Rorschachs. Hertz's astute observations based on the test were "so detailed and exact" that at first he regarded them with great skepticism.

However, the young man's doubts dissolved the day that he and a fellow student presented the Rorschach results of a patient they both knew very well: "We fully expected Hertz to make errors in her interpretation. We were determined to point these out to the group. . . . We were shocked, however, when Hertz was able to describe this patient after reading only the first four or five responses. . . . Within 25 minutes Hertz not only told us what we already knew but began to tell us things we hadn't seen but which were obviously true once pointed out" (Kaplan & Saccuzzo 1982, 379).

Such astounding performances had a profound effect on many budding psychologists. As a leading clinical researcher observed, "Blind analysis is one of the spectacular aspects of the Rorschach technique and has probably been the most important factor in the acceptance of the Rorschach" (Zubin 1954, 305).

## RORSCHACH WIZARDS: A PUZZLE IN NEED OF AN EXPLANATION

The performances of Rorschach wizards bore more than a superficial resemblance to palm reading and crystal-ball gazing, although few psychologists of the 1950s were prepared to recognize this connection. By the early 1960s, however, the wizards' astonishing successes were beginning to turn into a puzzle in need of an explanation. Research revealed that Rorschach virtuosos didn't possess any miraculous powers. To the contrary, in several well-known studies, leading Rorschach experts failed miserably when they attempted to make predictions about patients (e.g., Little & Shneidman 1959; see discussion by Dawes 1994).

Such findings presented a striking paradox. If Rorschach wizards stumbled so badly in controlled studies, how could they produce such amazing performances in blind analyses? The answer to this question was understandable to anyone familiar with the wiles of palm readers.

## A FEW SIMPLE TRICKS

Two shrewd commentators of the late 1940s had already divined that at least some Rorschach wizards achieved their success by resorting to tricks. In a clever and sometimes humorous article, J. R. Wittenborn and Seymour Sarason of Yale identified three simple stratagems of

Rorschach interpreters that tended to create a false impression of infallibility (Wittenborn & Sarason 1949).

The first stratagem was as old as the Delphic Oracle of ancient Greece, whose notoriously ambiguous prophecies were crafted to turn out correct, no matter which direction events took. The Oracle once told a king that if he went to war, he'd destroy a great nation. Encouraged, he launched an attack and was disastrously defeated. The prophecy wasn't wrong, however. After all, the Oracle hadn't said *which* nation the king would destroy.

Wittenborn and Sarason noted that Rorschach interpreters resorted to a similar tactic, delivering "ambiguous phrases or esoteric Rorschach clichés which can be given almost any specific interpretation which subsequent developments may require."

Second, Wittenborn and Sarason observed, Rorschach adepts sometimes ensured their success by including several inconsistent or even contradictory statements in the same interpretation: "One or the other of these statements may be employed according to the requirements of the circumstances. Such resourcefulness on the part of the examiner is often ascribed to the test itself."

Third, Wittenborn and Sarason observed, Rorschach experts sometimes enhanced their reputations by giving impressive interpretations *after* they learned the facts of a case: "Some clinical psychologists, when told about some clinically important features of a patient, say, 'Ah, yes. We see indications of it here, and here, and here.'"

Despite the tricks described by Wittenborn and Saranson, however, it's difficult to believe that all Rorschach wizards of the 1940s and 1950s were conscious fakes. The explanation is almost certainly more complicated than that. But before proceeding further, we'll pause to discuss the psychology of astrology and palm reading.

# THE BARNUM EFFECT

In the late 1940s, psychologist Bertram Forer published an eye-opening study that he called a "demonstration of gullibility" (Forer 1949). After administering a questionnaire to his introductory psychology class, he prepared personality sketches. For example: "Disciplined and self-controlled outside, you tend to be worrisome and insecure inside. At times you have serious doubts as to whether you have made the right decision or done the right thing. You prefer a certain amount of change and variety and become dissatisfied when hemmed in by restrictions and limitations."

Forer asked the students to rate their own sketches for accuracy. The students gave an average rating of "very good." More than 40 percent said that their sketch provided a *perfect* fit to their personality.

The results seemed to show that Forer's personality questionnaire possessed a high degree of validity. However, there was a diabolical catch: Forer had given all the students the same personality sketch, which he manufactured using horoscopes from an astrology book. The students had gullibly accepted this boiler-plate personality description as if it applied to them uniquely as individuals.

Although the statements borrowed from the astrology book were seemingly precise, they applied to almost all people. Following the eminent researcher Paul Meehl, psychologists now call such personality statements "Barnum statements," after the great showman P. T. Barnum who said, "A circus should have a little something for everybody." (He's also credited with, "There's a sucker born every minute.")

As Forer had discovered, people tend to seriously overestimate the degree to which Barnum statements fit them *uniquely.* For example, students in one study who were given Barnum statements disguised as test results responded with glowing praise: "On the nose! Very good"; "Applies to me individually, as there are too many facets which fit me too well to be a generalization."

## ASTROLOGERS AND PALM READERS

Astrologers and palm readers have long used Barnum statements (along with a few other stratagems) to create a false impression that they know the personality, the past, and even the future of people they've never met. The name for such bogus psychic practices is "cold reading" (Hyman 1981; Rowland 2002). Skillful cold readers apply the Barnum principle in many ways, for example, by spicing their readings with statements like these: "You're working hard, but you have the feeling that your salary doesn't fully reflect your efforts"; and "You think that somewhere in the world you have a twin, someone who looks just like you." Such statements appear personal and individualized, but in fact are true of many American adults.

After being warmed up with Barnum statements, most clients relax and begin to respond with nonverbal feedback, such as nods and smiles. In most psychic readings, there arrives a moment when the client begins to "work" for the reader, actively supplying information and providing clarifications. It's at this critical juncture that a skillful cold reader puts new stratagems into action, such as the technique called the "push" (Rowland 2002). A psychic using the push begins by making a specific prediction (even though it may miss the mark), then allows feedback from the client to transform the prediction into something that appears astoundingly accurate:

> Psychic: I see a grandchild, a very sick grandchild, perhaps a premature baby. Has one of your grandchildren recently been very sick?
> Client: No. I. . . .
> Psychic: This may have happened in the past. Perhaps to someone very close to you.
> Client: My sister's daughter had a premature girl several years ago.
> Psychic: That's it. Many days in the hospital? Intensive care? Oxygen?
> Client: Yes.

By using the push, a cold reader can make a guess that's wildly off target appear uncannily accurate. The push and other techniques are effective because, by the time the cold reader begins using them, the client has abandoned any lingering skepticism and is in a cooperative frame of mind, thereby helping the psychic to "make things fit."

Intriguingly, scholars who have studied the psychology of palm reading and astrology agree that although some psychics are conscious frauds, many sincerely believe in their paranormal powers. For example, psychologist Ray Hyman, professor emeritus at the University of Oregon, published a classic article on cold reading in which he described his own saga as a palm reader (Hyman 1981). While in high school, Hyman was originally doubtful about the validity of palm reading. But after trying it himself, he became persuaded that it could work magic, particularly when he received a great deal of positive feedback from clients. He became a fervent believer in palm reading and made a "side" living from it for some time.

Then one day a friend suggested that Hyman provide his interpretations backwards, giving clients interpretations that were exactly the *opposite* of what the palm reading textbooks suggested. To Hyman's amazement, the "backwards" interpretations were received equally well (if not better) by clients. This sobering experience persuaded him that the "success" of palm reading had nothing to do with the correctness of the interpretations. As such cautionary tales illustrate, Barnum statements can fool both the client who believes them and the naive psychic who believes the client.

## RORSCHACH WIZARDS: THREE EXPLANATIONS

Having taken a detour into the realm of astrology and palm reading, we're ready to return to the land of Rorschach wizards. Let's begin by considering three plausible explanations for the spectacular performances of the Rorschach virtuosos of the 1950s.

First, it's possible that these Rorschach wizards possessed a special clinical insight, a heightened intuition, that allowed them to surpass ordinary human limitations. Drawing on their unique clinical talents and their experience with thousands of patients, they developed an uncanny skill that allowed them to extract unexpected insights from inkblots.

Of course, this is the view that Rorschach devotees have generally preferred. Even today, many psychologists exhibit an extraordinary faith in the powers of clinical intuition. However, belief in the intuitive powers of Rorschach wizards is difficult to reconcile with the revelations of research. As we mentioned earlier, when the supposedly extraordinary insight of Rorschach experts has been tested in rigorously controlled studies, results have been disappointing. Given such findings, it's implausible that the Rorschach wizards of the 1950s were possessed of extraordinary clinical insight. Thus, we have to consider a second explanation for their extraordinary performances: Maybe they were frauds.

Thanks to the shrewd article by J. R. Wittenborn and Seymour Sarason of Yale that we discussed earlier, there's little question that some Rorschachers of the 1940s and 1950s used tricks that lent the test a false impression of infallibility. However, it's extremely unlikely that all Rorschach wizards of the era were conscious frauds. Several prominent Rorschach experts, such as Marguerite Hertz (whose interpretive skills we described earlier), were known to be people of high integrity. Thus we're led to a third explanation: The uncanny Rorschach wizards of the 1950s were probably cold readers who, like the young palm reader Ray Hyman, were deceived by their own performances.

## THE RORSCHACH WIZARD AS COLD READER

If blind diagnosis with the Rorschach was really just cold reading, how could it have worked? A Rorschach wizard about to give a blind analysis usually has access to much more information than do most fortune tellers. First, Rorschach responses usually contain valuable clues regarding a patient's intellectual capacity and educational level. Furthermore, many responses provide hints regarding the patient's interests or occupation.

As an interesting example, the Rorschach analysis of Nobel Prize–winning molecular biologist Linus Pauling has recently been published (Gacono et al. 1997). Here are a few of his responses to the blots: "The two little central humps at the top suggest a sine curve. . . ." "This reminds me of blood and the black of ink, carbon and the structure of graphite. . . ." "I'm reminded of Dali's watches. . . ."

Even non-wizards can guess that the person who produced these Rorschach responses was well educated in mathematics ("sine curve") and chemistry ("the structure of graphite") and probably had broad cultural interests (the reference to artist Salvador Dali).

Besides such clues contained in the Rorschach responses, other sources of information are often available to a wizard. The fact that the test results come from a particular clinic or hospital can be informative. For example, if the test comes from an inpatient psychiatric unit, the chances are high that the patient is suicidal or out of touch with reality.

Thus, the Rorschach wizard who undertakes a "blind diagnosis" is often in possession of a wealth of information that would make a palm reader envious. In the early part of the diagnostic performance, this information can be fed back to the listeners in classic "cold-reading style." For example, with Linus Pauling's Rorschach, the reading might begin: "Hmmm. This is obviously a very bright individual. Well educated, a 'cerebral' type. Focuses on thoughts, probably avoids reacting to events in a purely emotional way. I have the impression of a scientist rather than a businessperson or artist, though I do see some artistic tendencies."

If the Rorschach comes from a particular source—for example, a therapist who works with moderately troubled clients—the wizard can use appropriate Barnum statements. For instance, here's a safe statement that fits virtually all clients one way or another: "This patient's emotions tend to be inconsistent in terms of their impact on thinking, problem solving, and decision-making behaviors. In one instance, thinking may be strongly influenced by feelings. In a second instance, even though similar to the first, emotions may be pushed aside and play only a peripheral role. . . ." This statement, based on a recent Rorschach text (Exner 2000, 87), might well have come from Bertram Forer's famous astrology book. Notice that the statement merely says that the client's thoughts sometimes control his feelings but that his feelings sometimes control his thoughts. Although the statement appears to be saying something important and specific, in fact it applies to virtually all therapy clients (and probably virtually all readers of this chapter!).

Such Barnum statements are apparently still taken seriously by many psychologists today, judging from the large number of Rorschach books that are purchased each year. Thus we can be fairly sure that when Rorschach wizards of the 1950s spouted similar phrases during blind analyses, their colleagues thought something important was being said.

Once the listeners were "warmed up" by such apparently profound insights, the Rorschach wizard's job became much easier. Abandoning any initial skepticism, listeners probably began giving subtle or not-so-subtle feedback by nodding or smiling. The wizard could use this feedback as a guide for making increasingly precise statements. In all likelihood, wizards probably used something like the push, described earlier. For instance, here's a hypothetical example of how the push could be used Rorschach-style:

> Wizard: There are signs of a very severe trauma. It could be recent. Perhaps a rape? Or a violent assault?
> Listener: No. She . . .
> Wizard: This trauma may have happened in her teen years or even earlier. She may be repressing it so she doesn't remember.
> Listener: She was in a severe car accident when she was only eight.
> Wizard: I think that may be it. She and people she loved were badly injured?
> Listener: Yes.

As this example shows, the push can place the Rorschach wizard in a "win-win" situation. If the long-shot guess is correct—for example, the patient has actually been raped or assaulted—then the wizard's prediction may seem miraculously accurate. In contrast, if the guess is incorrect, the wizard can reinterpret it so that it seems "close"—or claim that the trauma occurred but that the patient has repressed the experience!

As Ray Hyman pointed out, a cold reader can be entirely sincere. Professional cold readers even have a term, "shut eyes," to describe individuals who engage in psychic cold reading while sincerely believing in their own paranormal powers. Similarly, most Rorschach wizards of the 1950s who used cold-reading techniques probably genuinely believed in the test. When the wizards made certain statements about patients (for example, Barnum statements), they often met with the agreement and even astonishment of their listeners. When they made certain highly intuitive guesses about patients (actually, the push), they found that they were often "close" to the truth and that their listeners were highly impressed. Reinforced by positive feedback from their colleagues, the wizards gradually became skilled cold readers, believing that their remarkable insights had arisen from the Rorschach.

The era of the Rorschach wizards belongs mainly to the past. Although skilled clinicians still occasionally dazzle graduate students with their stunning Rorschach performances, only a few psychologists today engage in public blind diagnoses. But the legacy of the great wizards lives on. The aura of magic created in the 1940s and 1950s still lingers as the Rorschach mystique, the almost religious awe that many clinicians continue to display toward the test despite its tattered scientific status. Perhaps more important, the Rorschach wizards contributed to the belief—still strong among many clinical psychologists—that intuitions and clinical experience provide deeper insights than mere scientific knowledge can. Thus it is that clinicians still use the Rorschach for purposes for which it has no demonstrated usefulness, mistakenly believing that their supposed insights arise from the extraordinary powers of the test, rather than from their own unrecognized notions and preconceptions.

# REFERENCES

Dawes, Robyn M. 1994. *House of Cards: Psychology and Psychotherapy Built on Myth.* New York: Free Press.

Exner, John E. 2000. *A Primer for Rorschach Interpretation.* Asheville, NC: Rorschach Workshops.

Forer, Bertram R. 1949. The fallacy of personal validation: A classroom demonstration of gullibility. *Journal of Abnormal and Social Psychology* 44: 118–23.

Gacono, Carl. B., Clifford M. DeCato, Virginia Brabender, and Ted G. Goertzel. 1997. Vitamin C or Pure C: The Rorschach of Linus Pauling. In *Contemporary Rorschach Interpretation,* edited by J. Reid Meloy, Marvin W. Acklin, Carl B. Gacono, James E. Murray, and Charles A. Peterson. Mahwah, NJ: Lawrence Erlbaum.

Hyman, Ray. 1981. Cold reading: How to convince strangers that you know all about them. In *Paranormal Borderlands of Science,* edited by Kendrick Frazier. Amherst, NY: Prometheus Books.

Kaplan, Robert. M., and Dennis P. Saccuzzo. 1982. *Psychological Testing: Principles, Applications, and Issues.* Monterey, CA: Brooks/Cole.

Lilienfeld, Scott O. 1999. Projective measures of personality and psychopathology. How well do they work? *Skeptical Inquirer* 23 (May): 32–39.

Lilienfeld, Scott O., James M. Wood, and Howard N. Garb. 2000. The scientific status of projective techniques. *Psychological Science in the Public Interest* 1: 27–66.

Little, Kenneth B., and Earl S. Shneidman. 1959. Congruencies among interpretations of psychological test and anamnestic data. *Psychological Monographs* 73 (6, Whole No. 476).

Rowland, Ian. 2002. *The Full Facts Book of Cold Reading.* 3rd ed. London: Ian Rowland Limited.

Wittenborn, J. R., and Seymour B. Sarason. 1949. Exceptions to certain Rorschach criteria of pathology. *Journal of Consulting Psychology* 13: 21–27.

Zubin, Joseph. 1954. Failures of the Rorschach technique. *Journal of Projective Techniques* 18: 303–15.

# 8.

# CLINICAL INTUITION

## *David Myers*

*The real purpose of [the] scientific method is to make sure*
*Nature hasn't misled you into thinking you know something*
*that you actually don't.*

—Robert Pirsig, *Zen and the Art of*
*Motorcycle Maintenance*, 1974

A parole board meets with a convicted rapist and ponders whether to release him. A worker on a crisis intervention line judges whether a caller is suicidal. A physician notes a patient's symptoms and surmises the likelihood of cancer. A school social worker ponders whether a child's overheard threat was a macho joke, a one-time outburst, or a sign of potential violence.

Each of these professionals must decide how to weigh their subjective judgments against relative objective evidence. Should they follow their intuition? Should they listen to their experience-based instincts, their hunches, their inner wisdom? Or should they rely more on research-based wisdom sometimes embedded in formulas, statistical analyses, and computerized predictions?

Reprinted with permission from D. Myers, *Intuition: Its Powers and Perils* (New Haven, CT: Yale University Press, 2002), pp. 172–86. Copyright Yale University Press.

# INTUITIVE VERSUS STATISTICAL PREDICTION

In the contest between heart and head, clinicians often listen to whispers from their experience and vote with their hearts. They prefer not to let cold calculations decide the futures of warm human beings. Feelings trump formulas.

Yet when researchers pit intuition against statistical prediction (as when pitting an interviewer's predictions of academic achievement against a formula based on grades and aptitude scores), the stunning truth is that the formula usually wins. Statistical predictions are, as you would expect, fallible. But when it comes to predicting the future, human intuition—even professional intuition—is even more fallible. Three decades after demonstrating the superiority of statistical prediction over intuition, University of Minnesota clinical researcher Paul Meehl, in a retrospective essay on what he called "my disturbing little book," found the evidence more convincing than ever:

> There is no controversy in social science which shows [so many] studies coming out so uniformly in the same direction as this one. . . . When you are pushing 90 investigations, predicting everything from the outcome of football games to the diagnosis of liver disease and when you can hardly come up with a half dozen studies showing even a weak tendency in favor of the clinician, it is time to draw a practical conclusion.

The evidence continues to accumulate. In 1998 a Canadian Solicitor General research team combined data from sixty-four samples of more than twenty-five thousand mentally disordered criminal offenders. What best predicted risk of future offending? As in studies with other types of criminal offenders, it was the amount of past criminal activity (illustrating once again the maxim that the best predictor of future behavior is past behavior). And what was among the least accurate predictors of future criminality? A clinician's judgment.

A more recent review by a University of Minnesota research team combined data from 134 studies of clinical-intuitive versus statistical

predictions of human behavior, or of psychological or medical prog-
noses. Clinical intuition surpassed "mechanical" (statistical) prediction
in only eight studies. In sixty-three studies, statistical prediction fared
better. The rest were a draw.

Would clinicians fare differently when allowed to conduct a firsthand
clinical interview rather than just a file to read? Yes, reported the research
team: allowed interviews, the clinicians fared worse. Many of these
studies don't engage the everyday judgments commonly made by mental
health professionals. Moreover, the studies often lump judgments by
experienced and inexperienced clinicians. Nevertheless, "it is fair to say
that the 'ball is in the clinicians' court,'" the researchers concluded. "Given
the overall deficit in clinicians' accuracy relative to mechanical prediction,
the burden falls on advocates of clinical prediction to show that clinical
predictions are more [accurate or cost-effective]."

In some contexts, we do accept the superiority of statistical prediction. For life insurance executives, actuarial prediction is the name of the
game. Or imagine that someone says, "I just have a feeling about today's
presidential election. Something tells me X is going to win it." If you have
the same feeling, but then learn that "the final Gallup Poll is just out, and
Y is ahead," you probably know enough to switch your bet. Gallup Polls
taken just before US national elections over the past half century have
diverged from election results by an average of less than 2 percent. As a
few drops of blood speak for the body, so a random sample speaks for a
population.

But when it comes to judging individuals, intuitive confidence soars.
In 1983, the US Supreme Court ruled on a petition of murderer Thomas
Barefoot. The petition challenged the reliability of psychiatric predictions of his dangerousness. Justice Harry Blackmun expressed skepticism of the clinical intuitions of two psychiatrists who testified for the
prosecution. Although neither had examined Barefoot, one had testified
with "reasonable medical certainty" that Barefoot would constitute a
continuing threat to society. The other psychiatrist had concurred,
noting that his professional skill was "particular to the field of psychiatry
and not to the average layman" and that there was a "one hundred per-

cent and absolute" chance that Barefoot would constitute a continuing threat to society. Their clinical judgment carried the day, and on October 30, 1984, Texas officials executed Thomas Barefoot. Such testimony is junk science, argues experimental psychologist Margaret Hagen in *Whores of the Court*. Hagen grants a place for expert testimony about such things as the accuracy of eyewitness recall. But "psychobabble" by self-important experts is to psychological science what astrology is to astronomy, she says.

The limits of clinical intuition have also surfaced in false-memory experiments. In three different studies, psychiatrists, psychologists, social workers, attorneys, and judges have evaluated children's video-taped testimonies. Could they discern which children were reporting false memories formed during repeated suggestive questioning? The consistent finding: although often confident in their ability to winnow true from false memories, professionals actually did so at no better than chance levels. False memories feel and look like real memories.

What if we combined clinical intuition with statistical prediction? What if we gave professionals the statistical prediction of someone's future academic performance or risk of violence or suicide, and asked them to improve on the prediction? Alas, notes Carnegie-Mellon University psychologist Robyn Dawes, in the few studies where this has been done, prediction was better without the "improvements."

So what has been the effect of these studies on clinical practice? "The effect . . . can be summed up in a single word," says Dawes. "Zilch." Clinical researcher Paul Meehl, for example, was honored, elected to the American Psychological Association presidency at a very young age, elected to the National Academy of Sciences, and ignored.

Meehl himself attributed clinicians' continuing confidence in their intuitive predictions to a "mistaken conception of ethics":

> If I try to forecast something important about a college student, or a criminal, or a depressed patient by inefficient rather than efficient means, meanwhile charging this person or the taxpayer 10 times as much money as I would need to achieve greater predictive accuracy,

that is not a sound ethical practice. That it feels better, warmer, and cuddlier to me as predictor is a shabby excuse indeed. . . . It will not do to say "I don't care what the research shows, I am a *clinician*, so I rely on my clinical experience." Clinical experience may be invoked when it's all we have, when scientific evidence is insufficient (in quantity or quality) to tell us the answer. It is not a valid rebuttal when the research answer is negative. One who considers "My experience shows . . ." a valid reply to research studies is self-deceived, and must never have read the history of medicine, not to mention the psychology of superstitions. It is absurd, as well as arrogant, to pretend that acquiring a Ph.D. somehow immunized me from the errors of sampling, perception, recording, retention, retrieval, and inference to which the human mind is subject.

Given our capacity for social intuition and intuitive expertise, *why* does professional intuition fare so poorly?

### *Why Clinical Intuition Falters*

Consider what we as human judges must do to explain or predict behavior accurately. We must intuit correlations between different predictors and the criterion—academic achievement, violence, suicide, or whatever. Then we must appropriately weight each predictor. But as noted earlier, we're prone to err at such tasks. Expert intuition may allow us to excel at tasks ranging from chess to chicken sexing. But in grocery checkout lines—where the computations are comparatively simple—we need calculating machines.

In their pioneering experiments, Loren Chapman and Jean Chapman showed how illusory correlations can infect clinical interpretation. They invited professional clinicians to study some psychological test performances and some diagnoses. Clinicians who believed that suspicious people draw peculiar eyes on the Draw-a-Person test perceived what they expected to find. This was even so when they viewed cases in which suspicious people drew peculiar eyes *less* often than nonsuspicious people. Assume a relationship exists and we likely will notice confirming instances. To believe is to see.

Hindsight also boosts clinicians' sense that they could have predicted what they know to have happened. After the suicide of rock musician Kurt Cobain, Monday morning commentators thought they could see the depression leaking through his lyrics. David Rosenhan and seven associates provided a striking example of potential error in after-the-fact explanations. To test mental health workers' clinical insights, the study team members each made an appointment with a different mental hospital admissions office and complained of "hearing voices." Apart from giving false names and vocations, they reported their life histories and emotional states honestly and exhibited no further symptoms. Most got diagnosed with schizophrenia and remained hospitalized for two to three weeks. Hospital clinicians then searched for early incidents in the pseudo-patients' life histories and hospital behavior that "confirmed" and "explained" the diagnosis. Rosenhan tells of one pseudopatient who truthfully explained to the interviewer that he "had a close relationship with his mother but was rather remote from his father during his early childhood. During adolescence and beyond, however, his father became a close friend, while his relationship with his mother cooled. His present relationship with his wife was characteristically close and warm. Apart from occasional angry exchanges, friction was minimal. The children had rarely been spanked."

The interviewer, "knowing" the person suffered from schizophrenia, explained the problem this way:

> This white 39-year-old male . . . manifests a long history of considerable ambivalence in close relationships, which begins in early childhood. A warm relationship with his mother cools during his adolescence. A distant relationship to his father is described as becoming very intense. Affective stability is absent. His attempts to control emotionality with his wife and children are punctuated by angry outbursts and, in the case of the children, spankings. And while he says that he has several good friends, one senses considerable ambivalence embedded in those relationships also.

Rosenhan later told some staff members (who had heard about his controversial experiment but doubted such mistakes could occur in their hospital) that during the next three months, one or more pseudo-patients would seek admission to their hospital. After the three months, he invited the staff to use their clinical intuition to guess which of the 193 patients admitted during that time were really pseudopatients. Of the 193 new patients, 41 were accused by at least one staff member of being pseudopatients. Actually, there were none.

Once a clinician conjectures an explanation for a problem such as hearing voices, the explanation can take on a life of its own. In an early demonstration of belief perseverance, Stanford psychologist Lee Ross and his collaborators had people read some actual clinical case histories. Then they told some of them that a particular event, such as a suicide, later occurred and asked them to use the case history to explain it. Finally, they were told the truth—that the patient's later history was unknown. When the people then estimated the likelihood of this and other possible events, the event they had explained now seemed quite likely.

In another study, Ross led students to think that they had excellent clinical intuition. (He told them they had done well at distinguishing authentic from fictitious suicide notes.) After the students explained why they were so good at this, Ross and his co-workers let them know that he had fibbed. The positive feedback on their intuition was faked. Despite this revelation, the students retained their new belief in their clinical intuition, citing the reasons they had conjured up to explain their apparent success (their empathy, their insights from reading a novel about suicide, and so forth) and so maintained their new belief in their clinical intuition.

Clinical intuition is vulnerable to illusory correlations, hindsight biases, belief perseverance, and self-confirming diagnoses. In some clever experiments at the University of Minnesota, an epicenter of efforts to assess professional intuition and sharpen critical thinking, psychologist Mark Snyder and his colleagues gave interviewers some hypotheses to check out. To get a feel for their studies, imagine yourself meeting someone who has been told that you are an uninhibited, outgoing person. To see whether this is true, the person slips questions into the conversation, such as "Have you ever done anything crazy in front of other people?" As you answer such questions, will the person meet a different you than if probing for evidence that you're shy?

Snyder found that people indeed often test their hunches by looking for confirming information. If they are wondering whether someone is an extravert, they solicit instances of extraversion. ("What would you do if you wanted to liven things up at a party?") Testing for introversion, they are more likely to inquire, "What factors make it hard for you to really open up to people?" In response, those tested for extraversion seem more sociable, and those tested for introversion come off as shy.

Given a structured list of questions to choose from, even experienced psychotherapists prefer questions that trigger extraverted responses when testing for extraversion. Assuming they have definite preexisting ideas, the same is true when they make up their own questions. Strong beliefs generate their own confirmation.

To see whether he could get people to test a trait by seeking to disconfirm it, Snyder told interviewers in one experiment that "it is relevant and informative to find out ways in which the person . . . may not be like the stereotype." In another experiment, he offered $25 to the person who develops the set of questions that "tell the most about . . . the interviewee." Regardless, confirmation bias persisted: People resisted using "introverted" questions when testing for extraversion.

Snyder's experiments help us understand why the behaviors of psychotherapy clients so often seem to fit their therapists' theories. When Harold Renaud and Floyd Estess conducted life-history interviews of a hundred healthy, successful adult men, they were startled to discover that their subjects' childhood experiences were loaded with "traumatic events," tense relations with certain people, and parental miscues—the very factors often invoked to explain psychiatric problems. If someone is in a bad mood, such recollections get amplified. Ergo, when Freudian therapists go fishing for early childhood problems, they often find that their intuitions are confirmed. Robert Browning understood:

As is your sort of mind,
So is your sort of search:
You'll find
What you desire.

For clinicians the implications are easily stated (though less easily practiced): Monitor the predictive powers of your intuition. Beware the tendency to see associations you expect to see. Recognize the seductiveness of hindsight, which can lead you to feel overconfident (but sometimes also to judge yourself too harshly for not having foreseen and averted catastrophes). Recognize that theories, once formed, tend to persevere even if groundless. Guard against the tendency to ask questions that assume your ideas are correct; consider opposing ideas and test them, too. Remember Richard Feynman's cautionary words: "The first principle is that you must not fool yourself—and you are the easiest person to fool."

Better yet, harness the underappreciated power of statistical prediction. As college admissions officers use statistical predictors of college success, clinicians can use checklists such as the Violence Risk Appraisal Guide, which offers predictions of whether criminals being discharged from maximum-security hospitals will commit further violent acts. (In one study, 55 percent of those statistically predicted to be "high-risk" and 19 percent of "low-risk" offenders committed a new violent act.) Physicians now have similar statistical guides for predicting risk of breast and prostate cancer. All such guides are based on assembled objective data and do what our intuition cannot: systematically weight multiple factors. If I am a physician, what should I do if my own experience with prostate cancer patients indicates that PSA levels have not predicted mortality, though studies of thousands of other cases indicate otherwise? Well, I had better discount my own limited experience—or at least consider it as just a few more data points atop a mountain of other cases. If "medical intuitives" such as Caroline Myss—a former journalist who has demonstrated for an adoring *Oprah Winfrey Show* audience her supposed ability to "diagnose" people at a glance or after a brief conversation—can do better, they should welcome a chance to join the empirical competition.

Another research-based analysis enabled a guide for predicting school violence. (The guide scores eighteen student characteristics, ranging from discipline record to displays of cruelty toward animals.) Yet another predicts the likelihood of rearrest among sex offenders by adding up points from a simple list of predictors (never married? any victims who were strangers? age less than twenty-five? total number of prior sexual offenses? any violent offenses? total number of prior offenses?). The total score predicts risk of new offenses, which range from greater than 50 percent for the highest risk group to 10 percent for the lowest risk group. The moral: *actuarial science strengthens clinical judgment, or at least offers a second opinion.* Actuarial science also helps protect practitioners from malpractice suits, which might otherwise allege that the clinician made aberrant decisions without attending to relevant research.

Some fields don't hesitate to make smart use of actuarial prediction. For all the mockery that has been showered on them, weather forecasters have long been stars in the world of professional forecasting. Unlike clinicians, who may never learn whether their predictions of violence are fulfilled, forecasters receive repeated prompt feedback. With daily cycles of forecast and result, forecasters readily learn to gauge their shortcomings. Thus, even before the advent of modern computer forecasting, they became adept at calibrating the accuracy of their forecasts. If they said there was a 25 percent chance of rain, the odds of rain indeed were about 25 percent. Now, aided by satellites and computer programs that incorporate models of the association between barometric pressure, wind speeds, temperatures, and a host of other variables, their predictions are better than ever. And when local meteorologists take the computer "guidance" and tweak it with their own professional expertise, predictive accuracy increases still further.

Credit card companies also make sophisticated use of computers to monitor human behavior and to detect activity that departs from a user's normal behavior. Three times in recent memory, Visa has called my home because of questionable activity on my daughter's or wife's card. In one case, there was an aberrant but valid overseas use. In the two other instances, the company's artificial intelligence instantly detected fraudulent activity, triggering a Visa representative to call us and the card to be deactivated within minutes. In all three cases, I was staggered by the speed and power of this fraud detection, which human judges could never rival.

## THERAPEUTIC INTUITION

Amid the scathing critiques of clinical pretension, one does find glimmers of optimism. A Ball State University team led by Paul Spengler spent nearly six years tracking down more than a thousand studies of clinical decision making. In a sample of these studies that they examined, actuarial predictions had "only a slight edge" over clinical judgments on the sorts of judgments of risk and prognosis most commonly made by mental health professionals. Moreover, Spengler reports (and as we might expect from other research on learned expertise), clinicians become more accurate decision makers as they accumulate clinical experience.

Might accuracy also rise with clinicians' confidence? To find out, Dale McNiel and his colleagues invited seventy-eight psychiatrists to estimate the probability that 317 psychiatric inpatients would become violent in their first week of hospitalization. During that first week, 11 percent of the patients did behave violently, as reported by the nursing staff. When the psychiatrists' confidence was moderate or low, their predictions were no better than chance. But when the psychiatrists felt highly confident, three out of four patients they expected to behave violently did so, as did none of those expected to be nonviolent. So when actuarial prediction isn't available or when useful information goes beyond the actuarial guidelines, wise clinicians draw on their reservoir of experience if it speaks loud and clear.

Judging the effectiveness of various therapies is, however, a delicate task. Not only do clinicians benefit less than weather forecasters from prompt and frequent feedback, they're prone, like all of us, to misinterpret natural "regression to one's average" effects. People enter therapy at their darkest hours and usually leave when they're less unhappy. Thus, most clients and their therapists will readily testify to any therapy's success. "Treatments" have varied widely—from bloodletting to rebirthing, from chains to herbal remedies, from submersion chambers to systematic desensitization—but all have this in common: their practitioners have viewed them as effective and enlightened. Clients enter emphasizing their woes, justify leaving by emphasizing their well-being, and stay in touch only if satisfied. To be sure, therapists are aware of failures, but these are mostly the failures of *other* therapists, whose clients are now seeking a new therapist for a persisting or recurring problem.

To discern whether any particular therapy represents more than either a placebo effect or a natural regression from the unusual to the more usual, we must experiment. Psychology's most powerful tool for sorting reality from wishful intuition is the control group. For every would-be patient assigned to a new therapy, another is randomly assigned to an alternative. What matters, then, is not my intuition or yours, but simply this: does it work? When put to the test, can its predictions be confirmed?

For several forms of psychotherapy, the results are somewhat encouraging. With or without therapy, troubled people tend improve (to move from their worst times back toward normality). Nevertheless, as Mary Lee Smith and her colleagues exulted after conducting the first statistical digest of psychotherapy outcome studies, "psychotherapy benefits people of all ages as reliably as schooling educates them, medicine cures them, or business turns a profit." Follow-up synopses have mostly concurred: As one said, "Hundreds of studies have shown that psychotherapy works better than nothing." In one ambitious study, the National Institute of Mental Health compared three treatments for depression: cognitive therapy, interpersonal therapy, and a standard drug therapy. Twenty-eight experienced therapists at research sites in Norman, Oklahoma; Washington, DC; and Pittsburgh, Pennsylvania, were trained in one of the three methods and randomly assigned their share of the 239 people with depression who participated. Clients in all three groups improved more than did those in a control group, who received merely an inert medication and supportive attention, encouragement, and advice. Among clients who completed a full sixteen-week treatment program, the depression had lifted for slightly more than half of those in each treatment group—but for only 29 percent of those in the control group (Elkin). This verdict echoes the results of the earlier studies: those not undergoing therapy often improve, but those undergoing therapy are more likely to improve.

But what about the newer and much publicized alternative therapies? For most therapies, there is insufficient evidence, mostly because proponents and devotees feel no need for controlled research. Intuitively, they seem effective. Satisfied clients testify to this. Millions of people— Princess Diana reportedly was among them—haven't felt a need for controlled experiments before seeking out spiritualists, hypnotherapists, "anger-release" therapists, reflexologists, aroma-therapists, colonic irrigationists, and "mind-body" therapists. Some therapies, however, have commanded enough attention to demand scrutiny. Consider a quick synopsis of five counterintuitive therapies, three of which have been discounted and two which have been found surprisingly effective.

*Therapeutic touch.* Across the world, tens of thousands of therapeutic touch practitioners (many of them nurses) have been moving their hands a few inches from a patient's body, purportedly "pushing energy fields into balance." Advocates say these manipulations help heal everything from headaches to burns to cancer. Skeptics say the evidence shows no healing power beyond the placebo effect. But can we confirm the theory? Can healers actually intuit the supposed energy field when someone's hand is (unseen by them) placed over one of their hands? Experiments to date indicate that they cannot. Thus it appears that therapeutic touch (actually nontouch) does not work, nor is there any credible theory that predicts why it might.

*Eye movement desensitization and reprocessing (EMDR).* Walking in a park one day, Francine Shapiro observed that anxious thoughts vanished as her eyes spontaneously darted about. Thence was born a new therapy, for which twenty-two thousand mental health professionals have reportedly been trained. While clients imagine traumatic scenes, the therapist triggers eye movements by waving a finger in front of their eyes. Encouraged by some early reports of success with post-traumatic stress disorder clients, EMDR therapists have recently been applying the technique to anxiety disorders, pain, grief, schizophrenia, rage, and guilt. Alas, when others tested the therapy without the eye movements—with finger tapping, for example, or with eyes fixed straight ahead while the therapist's finger wagged—the therapeutic results were the same. The therapeutic effect, it seems, lies not in eye movements but in a combination of effective exposure therapy (from safely reliving the trauma) and a robust placebo effect.

*Subliminal self-help tapes.* Given that we process much information intuitively and outside conscious awareness, might commercial subliminal tapes with imperceptibly faint messages indeed "reprogram your unconscious mind for success and happiness"? Might procrastinators have their minds reprogrammed with unheard messages such as "I set my priorities. I get things done ahead of time!" To find out, Anthony Greenwald, a University of Washington researcher, ran sixteen experiments and found no therapeutic effect. In one, he gave a memory-boosting tape to some with memory problems and a self-esteem-boosting tape to some with self-esteem problems. For others, he played the merry prankster and switched the labels. Although neither tape had any effect on memory or self-esteem scores, those who *thought* they had heard a memory tape *believed* that their memories had improved. A similar result occurred for those who thought they had heard a self-esteem tape. Although the tapes were ineffective, the students perceived themselves receiving the benefits they expected.

*Light exposure therapy.* For some people, especially women and those living far from the equator, the wintertime blahs constitute a form of depression known as seasonal affective disorder (appropriately, SAD). To counteract these dark spirits, National Institute of Mental Health researchers in the early 1980s had a bright idea: give SAD sufferers a timed daily dose of intense light (via light boxes that can now be rented or purchased from health supply and lighting stores). After clinical experience confirmed that many SAD people became less sad after light exposure therapy, skeptics wondered: Is this another regression-to-the-mean or placebo effect? Experiments offered encouraging results. Some 50 to 60 percent of those given a daily half hour of light exposure found relief, as did fewer given evening exposure and fewer yet given a placebo treatment. Scientists have also identified a possible mechanism in the shifting of melatonin secretion to an earlier time. Thus the happy verdict: for many people, bright morning light does dim SAD symptoms.

*Electroconvulsive therapy.* When electroconvulsive therapy (ECT) was introduced in 1938, wide-awake patients were jolted into racking convulsions and rendered unconscious by a hundred volts of electricity. Not surprisingly, ECT acquired a Frankensteinlike, barbaric image. Today's kinder, gentler ECT administers general anesthesia, a muscle relaxant, and brief shock, often to only one side of the brain. But does this weird treatment work? To my astonishment, ECT is now widely regarded as the most effective therapy for severe depression that resists psychotherapy and medication. After three such sessions each week for two to four weeks, 80 percent or more of people receiving ECT improve markedly, showing memory loss for the treatment period but no discernible brain damage. Despite uncertainties about why it works, committees of the National Institutes of Health and the American Psychiatric Association have given ECT their stamp of approval.

So when put to the test, some crazy-sounding ideas find support, and scientific inquiry sometimes refutes the skeptics. Who would have guessed that bright light or an electrical buzz in the brain would prove therapeutic?

More often, however, scientific inquiry relegates crazy-sounding ideas to the mountain of forgotten claims of perpetual motion machines, out-of-body travels into centuries past, and miracle cancer cures. At the end of the day, soft-headed pseudoremedies can have wrong-headed effects. A heart of gold is no substitute for a head of feathers. To sift true intuitions from false, sense from nonsense, requires a scientific attitude: being skeptical but not cynical, open but not gullible. By testing clinical intuition—discerning its wisdom and fallibility, and learning when to undergird it with actuarial science—a hardheaded process promises to pay kindhearted dividends.

# 9.

# CUSTODY DISPUTED

## *Robert E. Emery, Randy K. Otto, and William O'Donohue*

Courts are overwhelmed with couples who are splitting up and disputing custody of their children. If parents cannot agree on their children's fates, a judge will decide who gets custody, and increasingly, psychologists are becoming involved as expert evaluators during legal wranglings. But do any of these professionals have proof that the bases for their life-determining decisions are empirically sound? It seems not, and it is the boys and girls who suffer.

Parents often think that judges possess some special wisdom that will allow them to determine a custody arrangement that is somehow better than what parents can devise themselves. They don't. Although the details vary, every state's law indicates that custody decisions are to be made according to the "best interests of the child." That rule of thumb sounds laudable, but it is so vague that the outcome of every case is unpredictable. The possibility of "winning" in court, paired with the emotional dynamics of divorce, encourages parents to enter into custody disputes, which only increases conflict between them—and conflict is a major cause of lasting psychological damage to children of separating spouses.

Furthermore, custody evaluators oftentimes administer to parents and children an array of tests to assess which custody arrangement might be best. Given the frequency, high cost, and social importance of custody evaluations, we might expect to find a large body of research on the tests' scientific validity. Yet only a few studies have been completed; more are needed, but the few do show that the tests are deeply flawed. Our own thorough evaluation of tests that purport to pick the "best parent," the "best interests of the child," or the "best custody arrangement" reveals that they are wholly inadequate. No studies examining their effectiveness have ever been published in a peer-reviewed journal. Because there is simply no psychological science to support them, the tests should not be used. And other, more general psychological tests that evaluators sometimes employ, such as IQ tests, have little or no relevance to custody decision making and should be dropped as well.

## CONFLICT, THE REAL BAROMETER

There is, however, one tremendously important conclusion about separation that has been proved by extensive, sophisticated, multidisciplinary research: the level of conflict between parents that children experience during separation, and the ongoing disagreements they may be exposed to thereafter, greatly influences the degree of psychological trouble the youngsters will have in the short and long term.

Research shows that most children are resilient despite a divorce, and it is quite possible for them to suffer no greater incidence of psychological maladjustment than kids whose conflicted parents remain married. Studies tell us that many of the problems observed among youths from divorced families are actually present before the separation. Parental fighting often precedes a separation or divorce, and various analyses demonstrate that children fare better psychologically if they live in a harmonious divorced family than in a conflict-ridden two-parent household.

The bottom line is that in any family situation, children do better if adult clashing is minimal or at least contained so children do not witness or become involved in it. The process of dissolution, and the nature of ongoing family relationships, is more important to a child's mental health than the structure of any particular arrangement, whether that be sole custody, joint physical custody, or liberal or limited visitation with the noncustodial parent. Researchers report that both boys and girls function equally well living primarily with either their mother or father. Other important factors in minimizing the trauma for offspring include having a good relationship with an authoritative resident parent (one who is loving but firm with discipline), economic security, and a good relationship with an authoritative nonresident parent.

The coupling of the vague "best interests of the child" standard with the American adversarial justice system puts judges in the position of trying to perform an impossible task: making decisions that are best for children using a procedure that is not. We appreciate the terrible dilemma that the best-interests standard creates for judges, custody evaluators, and, of course, parents and children. We also believe that a mental health professional may be in a better position to make sound recommendations about custody than a judge bound by rules of legal procedure. Nevertheless, we believe it is legally, morally, and scientifically wrong to make custody evaluators de facto decision makers, which they often are because judges typically accept an evaluator's recommendation.

## ENCOURAGE PARENTS TO DECIDE

Some straightforward policy changes would improve custody decisions. First, we urge judges, lawyers, and other advisers to encourage parents to reach custody agreements on their own through divorce mediation, collaborative law, good-faith attorney negotiations, or psychological counseling. Studies show that these efforts reduce conflict and encourage more cooperative, ongoing interactions between parents. Such arrangements facilitate positive relationships between children and their mothers and fathers. These practices also embrace the philosophy that, in the absence of abuse or neglect, parents should determine their own children's best interests after separation, just as they do when they are married or living together. Parents—not judges or mental health professionals—are the best experts on their own children.

One important reason to follow this approach from the outset is that parents ultimately must manage their own relationship and custody decisions. A cooperative approach, rather than adversarial litigation, will help achieve this outcome. Options include pro se divorce, in which parents manage legal matters without lawyers; divorce education, usually involving court-mandated classes on parenting; cooperative negotiations between parents and attorneys (including a new approach called collaborative law whereby lawyers agree not to go to court); family therapy; and the most firmly established of the options, divorce mediation, in which parents negotiate a settlement with the help of a neutral expert, usually a mental health professional or an attorney.

The second step for reducing conflict is for state legislatures to enact clearer guidelines for determining custody when parents cannot reach an agreement. A fair but less vague standard would reduce the number of contested cases that are brought to court in the first place. Too often one or both former partners seek litigation precisely because the best-interests approach encourages false hopes of "winning." Firmer rules would discourage litigation and reduce conflict between parents—the ultimate goal. We find particular merit in the proposed "approximation rule"—the suggestion that postdivorce arrangements should approximate parenting involvement in marriage. The most important advantage of this guideline is that parents and their attorneys would know what to expect of the courts, and this knowledge would promote earlier settlement.

No state has yet implemented the rule, so we have no evidence of its effectiveness; however, the American Law Institute, whose model statutes often become the basis for state laws, has endorsed the idea in its proposed reforms of divorce and custody law.

Finally, we recommend that custody evaluators offer only opinions that are clearly supported by psychological science. Until far stronger scientific support arises, this recommendation means that evaluators should abandon the use of all custody "tests" that purport to measure children's best interests directly or indirectly.

Our recommendation to limit expert testimony may seem radical, but we are simply urging the same rigor that is applied to expert testimony in all other legal proceedings. The American Psychological Association, the Association of Family and Conciliation Courts, and the American Academy of Child and Adolescent Psychiatry all have developed guidelines for professionals who conduct custody evaluations. Each group recommends an assessment of children's needs, parents' abilities to meet these needs, and parents' abilities to provide for future needs. Still, there is little agreement about how to assess these factors. We therefore urge professional organizations to develop clearer guidelines on which tests have a basis in science and to generate data on the appropriate inferences that can be drawn from responses children and parents provide in taking those tests.

# SECTION IV. HOW TO EVALUATE PSYCHIATRIC DIAGNOSES

# INTRODUCTION

We humans love to categorize. That's the way our brains work. Whites–African Americans, Fruits-Vegetables, Good Guys–Bad Guys, Baseball Fans–Football Fans, Liberals-Conservatives: the list goes on and on. We naturally sort people into discrete groups, even though the distinctions between these groups are actually often fuzzy.

The situation is no different in the arena of mental health. When we use a psychiatric classification system, we sort people into categories, called "diagnoses." Psychologists and psychiatrists acknowledge that the distinctions among diagnoses are typically imprecise, but they also recognize that some diagnoses are clinically useful.

How can we tell if a diagnosis, like major depression, schizophrenia, panic disorder, hypochondriasis, or antisocial personality disorder, is meaningful or bogus? The answer lies in *prediction*. If a diagnosis predicts new information that we did not already know, it is meaningful, or as psychologists like to say, valid (see also the introduction to section III). For example, the diagnosis of schizophrenia is, by and large, valid. That's because knowing that an individual bears a diagnosis of schizophrenia tells us many things that we did not previously know. For example, we now know that this individual is likely to (a) exhibit a chronic course over time (that is, the individual is likely to experience at least some symptoms of the disorder for many years); (b) respond well to certain types of medications (so-called typical or atypical neuroleptics), (c) perform abnormally on certain laboratory tasks, such as smooth pursuit eye-tracking tests; and (d) have close biological relatives with at least some symptoms of the disorder (like unusual thinking, suspiciousness, or suppressed outward emotions), if not outright schizophrenia. Similarly, many other psychiatric diagnoses, like major depression, bipolar disorder (known formerly as manic-depression), panic dis-order, and obsessive-compulsive disorder, are reasonably valid. They tell us things about the diagnosed person that we didn't already know. In some cases, they can also help us select an appropriate treatment.

Nevertheless, not all psychiatric diagnoses or proposed diagnoses pass the validity test. Some are little more than descriptive labels for behaviors that just happen to go together in some people. The past several decades have witnessed an explosion of controversial or unvalidated diagnostic labels, like sexual addiction, road rage disorder, Munchausen by proxy, codependency, post-traumatic slavery disorder, parental alienation syndrome, workaholism, and rape trauma syndrome. Many of these labels have infiltrated the world of popular psychology and are a staple of *Oprah* and other television talk shows. But they are not listed as formal diagnoses in the current "Bible" of psychiatric diagnoses, the *Diagnostic and Statistical Manual of Mental Disorders, 4th edition* (DSM-IV), published by the American Psychiatric Association. That is because researchers have yet to show convincingly that these labels predict much more than the behaviors they already describe. Nevertheless, some DSM-IV disorders, like attention-deficit hyperactivity disorder and post-traumatic disorder, are also highly controversial. Critics charge that these diagnoses "medicalize" essentially normal behaviors and thereby contribute to what Christina Hoff Somers and Sally Satel term "therapism"—the assumption that most or all distress must be resolved by formal psychological intervention rather than by good old-fashioned coping. Still others charge that these diagnoses cause harm by imposing stigma on their recipients.

Some critics of psychiatric diagnosis go further. They claim that the very process of psychiatric diagnosis is inherently stigmatizing. Labeling, the critics maintain, makes us perceive individuals ascribed these labels as ill. As a consequence, psychiatric labels become a self-fulfilling prophecy, generating psychological harm by leading people to treat labeled individuals poorly.

In the opening chapter in this section, James Herbert and his colleagues describe diagnostic and treatment controversies regarding autistic disorder, better known simply as autism. Autism appear to be becoming much more common in American society, although it is not clear whether this increase is attributable to a genuine change in its prevalence or to a more lenient threshold for diagnosing it. Herbert and colleagues examine widely publicized claims that the increase is due to vaccines, and find these claims waiting. As they also note, autism has been the object of a plethora of therapeutic fads, some of which may actually be dangerous to affected children. This chapter should be essential reading for parents and loved ones of children with autism, as it should help them steer clear of therapeutic land mines.

George Bonanno next examines common misconceptions regarding people's reactions to trauma and loss. As he notes, certain individuals unquestionably experience marked emotional reactions following overwhelming trauma and loss, and many require psychological help. Nevertheless, Bonanno argues that the field of psychology has greatly underestimated individuals' resilience in the face of stress and separation. Most individuals, although experiencing short-term stress reactions in the wake of anxiety-provoking events, regain their equilibrium on their own and manage to cope well.

In the final chapter in this section, August Piper evaluates the evidence for and against multiple personality disorder (now called dissociative identity disorder), a controversial diagnosis formally recognized by DSM-IV. The principal controversy centers around the role of psychotherapists. Are they discovering the supposed personalities ("alters") of this condition, or are they inadvertently creating them? This example of a controversial diagnostic label in modern psychology and psychiatry should help provide readers with a model of how to thoughtfully evaluate labels whose validity remains unclear.

## 10.

# Separating Fact from Fiction in the Etiology and Treatment of Autism: A Scientific Review of the Evidence

*James D. Herbert, Ian R. Sharp, and Brandon A. Gaudiano*
MCP Hahnemann University

Autistic-spectrum disorders are among the most enigmatic forms of developmental disability. Although the cause of autism is largely unknown, recent advances point to the importance of genetic factors and early environmental insults, and several promising behavioral, educational, and psychopharmacologic interventions have been developed. Nevertheless, several factors render autism especially vulnerable to pseudoscientific theories of etiology and to intervention approaches with grossly exaggerated claims of effectiveness. Despite scientific data to the contrary, popular theories of etiology focus on maternal rejection, candida infections, and childhood vaccinations. Likewise, a variety of popular treatments are promoted as producing dramatic results, despite scientific evidence suggesting that they are of little benefit and in some cases may actually be harmful. Even the most promising treatments for

Reprinted with permission from *Scientific Review of Mental Health Practice* 1, no. 1 (Spring/Summer 2002): 23–43.

autism rest on an insufficient research base and are sometimes inappropriately and irresponsibly promoted as "cures." We argue for the importance of healthy skepticism in considering etiological theories and treatments for autism.

Autism is a pervasive developmental disorder marked by profound deficits in social, language, and cognitive abilities. Prevalence rates range from 7 to 13 cases per 10,000 (Bryson 1997; Bryson, Clark & Smith 1988; Steffenberg & Gillberg 1986; Sugiyama & Abe 1989). It is not clear if the actual prevalence of autism is increasing, or if the increased frequency of diagnosis has resulted from wider recognition of the disorder and especially recognition of the full range of pervasive developmental disorders, often referred to as "autistic-spectrum disorders."[1] Either way, autism is no longer considered rare, occurring more commonly than Down's syndrome, cystic fibrosis, and several childhood cancers (Fombonne 1998; Gillberg 1996).

The degree of impairment associated with autism varies widely, with approximately 75 percent of autistic individuals also meeting criteria for mental retardation (American Psychiatric Association [APA] 1994). Autism occurs three to four times more frequently in males than females (Bryson et al. 1988; Steffenberg & Gillberg 1986; Volkmar, Szatmari & Sparrow 1993). Although recent advances have been made with respect to possible causal factors (Rodier 2000), the exact etiology of autism remains unknown. Moreover, although certain behavioral, educational, and pharmacological interventions have been demonstrated to be helpful for many individuals with autism, there is currently no cure for the disorder.

## WHY AUTISM IS FERTILE GROUND FOR PSEUDOSCIENCE

Several factors render autism especially vulnerable to etiological ideas and intervention approaches that make bold claims yet are inconsistent with established scientific theories and unsupported by research (Herbert & Sharp 2001). Despite their absence of grounding in science, such theories and techniques are often passionately promoted by their advocates. The diagnosis of autism is typically made during the preschool years and, quite understandably, is often devastating news for parents and families. Unlike most other physical or mental disabilities that affect a limited sphere of functioning while leaving other areas intact, the effects of autism are pervasive, generally affecting most domains of functioning. Parents are typically highly motivated to attempt any promising treatment, rendering them vulnerable to promising "cures." The unremarkable physical appearance of autistic children may contribute to the proliferation of pseudoscientific treatments and theories of etiology. Autistic children typically appear entirely normal; in fact, many of these children are strikingly attractive. This is in stark contrast to most conditions associated with mental retardation (e.g., Down's syndrome), which are typically accompanied by facially dysmorphic features or other superficially evident abnormalities. The normal appearance of autistic children may lead parents, caretakers, and teachers to become convinced that there must be a completely "normal" or "intact" child lurking inside the normal exterior. In addition, as discussed above, autism comprises a heterogeneous spectrum of disorders, and the course can vary considerably among individuals. This fact makes it difficult to identify potentially effective treatments for two reasons. First, there is a great deal of variability in response to treatments. A given psychotropic medication, for example, may improve certain symptoms in one individual, while actually exacerbating those same symptoms in another. Second, as with all other developmental problems and psychopathology, persons with autism sometimes show apparently spontaneous developmental gains or symptom improvement in a particular area for unidentified reasons. If any intervention has recently been implemented, such improvement can be erroneously attributed to the treatment, even when the treatment is actually ineffective. In sum, autism's pervasive impact on development and functioning, heterogeneity with respect to course and treatment response, and current lack of curative treatments render the disorder fertile ground for quackery.

A number of contemporary treatments for autism can be character-ized as pseudoscientific. Most scientists agree that there are no hard-and-fast criteria that distinguish science from pseudoscience; the differ-ences are in degree, rather than kind (Bunge 1984; Herbert et al. 2000; Lilienfeld 1998). Although a detailed treatment of pseudoscience in mental health is beyond the scope of this paper, a brief discussion of the features that distinguish it from legitimate science is important in order to provide a context for considering currently popular etiological theo-ries and treatments for autism. In general, pseudoscience is character-ized by claims presented as being scientifically verified even though in reality they lack empirical support (Shermer 1997). Pseudoscientific treatments tend to be associated with exaggerated claims of effectiveness that are well outside the range of established procedures. They are often based on implausible theories that cannot be proven false. They tend to rely on anecdotal evidence and testimonials, rather than controlled studies, for support. When quantitative data are considered, they are considered selectively. That is, confirmatory results are highlighted, whereas unsupportive results are either dismissed or ignored. They tend to be promoted through proprietary publications or Internet Web sites rather than refereed scientific journals, Finally, pseudoscientific treat-ments are often associated with individuals or organizations with a direct and substantial financial stake in the treatments. The more of these features that characterize a given theory or technique, the more sci-entifically suspect it becomes.

A number of popular etiological theories and treatment approaches to autism are characterized by many of the features of pseudoscience described above (Green 1996a; Green 2001; Herbert & Sharp 2001; Smith 1996). Still other treatments, although grounded on a sound the-oretical basis and supported by some research, are nonetheless subject to exaggerated claims of efficacy. What follows is a review of the most pop-ular dubious theories and questionable intervention approaches for autism. We also review promising etiologic theories and treatments. Some intervention programs are designed specifically for young chil-dren, whereas others are applied across a wider age range.

# THE ETIOLOGY OF AUTISM: SEPARATING FACT FROM FICTION

## *Psychoanalytic Explanations*

Although modern theories of autism posit the strong influence of biological factors in the etiology of the disorder, psychoanalytic theories have abounded traditionally. Kanner (1946) was the first to describe the parents of children with autism as interpersonally distant. For example, he concluded that the autistic children he observed were "kept neatly in refrigerators which did not defrost" (Kanner 1973, 61). However, Kanner also stressed that the disorder had a considerable biological component that produced disturbances in the formation of normal emotional contact. It was Bruno Bettelheim who was perhaps the most influential theorist promoting psychoanalytic interpretations of autism. Bettelheim rose to prominence as director of the University of Chicago's Orthogenic School for disturbed children from 1944 to 1978. He rejected Kanner's conclusions positing a biological role in the etiology in autism and was convinced that autism was caused by "refrigerator" mothers. According to Bettelheim, autistic symptoms are viewed as defensive reactions against cold and detached mothers. These unloving mothers were sometimes assumed to be harboring "murderous impulses" toward their children. For example, in his book *The Empty Fortress,* Bettelheim (1967) wrote that one autistic girl's obsession with the weather could be explained by dissecting the word to form "we/eat/her," indicating that she was convinced that her mother, and later others, would "devour her." Based on his conceptualization of autism, Bettelheim promoted a policy of "parentectomy" that entailed separation of children from their parents for extended periods of time (Gardner 2000). Other psychoanalytic therapists such as Mahler (1968) and Tustin (1981) promoted similar theories positing problems in the mother-child relationship as causing autism (see Roser 1996 for a review of psychoanalytic theories of autism).

After his suicide in 1990, stories began to emerge that tarnished Bettelheim's reputation (Darnton 1990). Several individuals claimed abuse at the hands of the famous doctor when they were at the Orthogenic School. Furthermore, information emerged that Bettelheim often lied about his background and training. For example, although he frequently claimed to have studied under Freud in Vienna, Bettelheim possessed no formal training in psychoanalysis whatsoever and instead held a degree in philosophy. Also, Bettelheim claimed that 85 percent of his patients at the Orthorgenic School were cured after treatment; however, most of the children were not autistic and the case reports he presented in his books were often fabrications (Pollak 1997). Despite the continued acceptance of Bettelheim's theories in some circles, no controlled research has been produced to support the refrigerator mother theory of autism. For example, Allen, DeMeyer, Norton, Pontus, and Yang (1971) did not find differences between parents of autistic and mentally retarded children and matched comparison children on personality measures. Despite the complete absence of controlled evidence, even today some psychoana- lytic theorists continue in the tradition of Bettelheim by highlighting the putative role of early mother-child attachment dysfunctions in causing autism (Roser 1996).

### Candida Infection

*Candida albicans* is a yeastlike fungus found naturally in humans that aids in the destruction of dangerous bacteria. Candidiasis is an infection caused by an overgrowth of candida in the body. Women often contract yeast infections during their childbearing years. In addition, antibiotic medication can disrupt the natural balance among microorganisms in the body, resulting in an overgrowth of candida (Adams & Conn 1997). In the 1980s, anecdotal reports began to emerge suggesting that some children with candidiasis later developed symptoms of autism. Sup- porters of this theory point to animal studies in which candida was shown to produce toxins that disrupted the immune system, leading to the possibility of brain damage (Rimland 1988). Furthermore, Rimland speculated that perhaps 5 to 10 percent of autistic children could show improved functioning if treated for candida infection. Proponents often recommend that Nystatin, a medication used to treat women with yeast infections, be given to children whose mothers had candidiasis during pregnancy, whether or not the children show signs of infection. However, there is no evidence that mothers of autistic children have a higher incidence of candidiasis than mothers in the general population, and only uncontrolled case reports are presented as evidence for the etiological role of candida infection in autism (Siegel 1996).

Adams and Conn (1997) presented the case study of a three-year-old autistic boy who reportedly showed improved functioning following a vitamin treatment for candida infection. However, the boy was never medically diagnosed with candidiasis and was only reported to meet criteria based on questionnaire data. In addition, reports of the child's functioning were mostly based on parental report (especially concerning functioning prior to the course of vitamin treatment) and not on standardized assessment instruments. Although interesting, such presentations provide no probative data on the possible role of candidiasis in causing autism. Without reliable and valid evidence to the contrary, case reports cannot rule out a host of confounding variables, including any natural remission or change in symptoms due to developmental maturation or even merely to the passage of time. It is important to remember that many people, especially women, contract candidia infections at different points in their lives, sometimes without even knowing that they are infected because the symptoms are so mild (Siegel 1996). However, there is no evidence that even severe candidiasis in humans can produce brain damage that leads to the profound deficits in functioning found in autism.

### MMR Vaccination

There has recently been much public concern that the mumps, measles, and rubella (MMR) vaccine is causing an increased incidence of autism. As evidence of the link between the MMR vaccine and autism, proponents point to the fact that reported cases of autism have increased dramatically over the past two decades, which appear to coincide with the widespread use of the MMR vaccine starting in 1979. In fact, Dales, Hammer, and Smith (2001) found in their analyses of California Department of Developmental Services records that the number of autistic disorder caseloads increased approximately 572 percent from 1980 to 1994. Indicating a similar trend in Europe, Kaye, Melero-Montes, and Jick (2001) reported that the yearly incidence of children diagnosed with autism increased sevenfold from 1988 to 1999 in the United Kingdom. Fears that the MMR vaccine may be responsible for this rise in the increasing incidence of autism have been picked up in the media, and some parents have decided to decline vaccinations for their children in an effort to protect them from developing autism (Manning 1999).

Rimland (2000) saw "medical overexuberance" as producing a tradeoff in which vaccinations protect children against acute diseases while simultaneously increasing their susceptibility to more chronic disorders, including autism, asthma, arthritis, allergies, learning disabilities, Crohn's disease, and attention deficit hyperactivity disorder. Pointing out that the average number of vaccines school-age children receive is now at thirty-three, Rimland blamed the "vaccine industry" for making products that have not been properly tested before their widespread usage. He concluded by stating that research on this problem should be of the "highest priority."

In fact, it was preliminary research findings that initially raised the possibility that the MMR vaccine might be related to the apparent increase in the incidence of autism. The British researcher Andrew Wakefield and colleagues (1998) reported twelve case studies of children who were diagnosed with particular forms of intestinal abnormalities (e.g., ileal-lymphoid-nodular hyperplasia). Eight out of the twelve children demonstrated behavioral disorders diagnosed as representing autism, which reportedly occurred after MMR vaccination. The authors concluded that "the uniformity of the intestinal pathological changes and the fact that previous studies have found intestinal dysfunction in children with autistic-spectrum disorders, suggests that the connection is real and reflects a unique disease process" (p. 639). However, Wakefield et al. made it clear in their report that they did not prove an actual causal connection between the MMR vaccine and autism.

Although the Wakefield et al. (1998) case reports suggested that the MMR vaccine may be associated with autism, recent epidemiological research has provided strong evidence against any such connection. Kaye et al. (2001) conducted a time trend analysis on data taken from the UK general practice research database. As discussed earlier, they found that the yearly incidence of diagnosed autism increased dramatically over the last decade (0.3 per 10,000 persons in 1988 to 2.1 per 10,000 persons in 1999). However, the prevalence of MMR vaccination among children remained virtually constant during the analyzed time period (97 percent of the sample). If the MMR vaccine were the major cause of the increased reported incidence of autism, then the risk of being diagnosed with autism would be expected to stop rising shortly after the vaccine was instated at its current usage. However, this was clearly not the case in the Kaye study, and therefore no time correlation existed between MMR vaccination and the incidence of autism in each birth order cohort from 1988 to 1993.

In an analogue study in the United States, Dales et al. (2001) found the same results when using California Department of Developmental Services autism caseload data from the period 1980 to 1994. Once again, the time trend analysis did not show a significant correlation between MMR vaccine usage and the number of autism cases. Although MMR vaccine usage remained fairly constant over the observed period, there was a steady increase of autism caseloads over the time studied. It is important to note that the increased incidence of autism found in these two studies most likely reflects an increased awareness of autism-spectrum disorders by professionals and the public in general, along with changes in diagnostic criteria, rather than a true increase in the incidence of the disorder (Kaye et al. 2001). Most recently, the US government's Institute of Medicine, in a comprehensive report co-sponsored by the National Institutes of Health and the Centers for Disease Control and Prevention, recently concluded that there exists no good evidence linking the MMR vaccine and autism (Stratton et al. 2001).

The MMR hypothesis reveals several important lessons for the student of autism. First, parents and professionals alike can easily misinterpret events that co-occur temporally as being causally related. The fact that the MMR vaccine is routinely given at around the same age that autism is first diagnosed reinforces the appearance of a link between the two. Second, the MMR-autism link reveals nicely the self-correcting nature of science. Like many hypotheses in science, the MMR-autism hypothesis, although reasonable when initially proposed, turned out to be incorrect or at best incomplete. Third, the issue illustrates the persistence of incorrect ideas concerning the etiology and treatment of autism even in the face of convincing evidence to the contrary. For example, Rimland (2000) purported to warn the public of the dangers of child vaccinations because of their link to autism and begins his article with the decree: "First, do no harm." However, recent research indicates that the MMR vaccine cannot be responsible for the sharp increases in diagnosed autism, and the real harm is the public health concern raised by encouraging parents to avoid vaccinating their children from serious diseases that can easily be prevented.

## CURRENT SCIENTIFIC FINDINGS

Research has implicated genetic factors, in utero insults, brain abnormalities, neurochemical imbalances, and immunological dysfunctions as contributing to autism. Siblings of individuals with autism have about a 3 percent chance of having the disorder, which is fifty times greater than the risk in the general population. In monozygotic twins, if one twin has autism, the second has a 36 percent chance of being diagnosed with the disorder and an 82 percent chance of developing some autistic symptoms (Trottier, Srivastava & Walker 1999). Although not definitive, the higher concordance rates in monozygotic twins relative to fraternal siblings suggests a genetic contribution to the etiology of autism. Nevertheless, the lack of 100 percent concordance for monozygotic twins suggests that the disorder probably develops as the result of combined effects of genetic and environmental factors.

Genetic disorders that have been identified as producing an

increased risk of developing autism or pervasive developmental disorders include tuberous sclerosis, phenylketonuria, neurofibromatosis, fragile X syndrome, and Rett syndrome (Folstein 1999; Trottier et al. 1999). Recent findings have also implicated a variation of the gene labeled HOXA1 on chromosome 7 as doubling the risk of autism, although this is only one of the many possible genes linked to the disorder (Rodier 2000). Nevertheless, although some gene variants may increase the risk of developing autism, other variants may act to decrease the risk, explaining the large variability in the expression of autism.

Rubella infection of the mother during pregnancy and birth defects resulting from ethanol, valproic acid, and thalidomide exposure are also known in utero risk factors (ibid.). However, these factors can only explain the development of autism in a small subset of individuals. Regarding time for increased vulnerability, evidence from individuals exposed to thalidomide now points to the conclusion that the in utero insults that increase the risk of the autism probably occur quite early, within the first trimester of gestation (Stromland et al. 1994). Other research that has compared individuals with autism with those without the disorder found differences in brain wave activity, brain (e.g., cerebellar) structures, and neurotransmitter levels (Trottier et al. 1999).

Scientific evidence supports the conclusion that autism is a behavioral manifestation of various brain abnormalities that likely develop as the result of a combination of genetic predispositions and early environmental (probably in utero) insults. Although recent scientific discoveries provide important clues to the development of the disorder, the etiology of autism is complex and the specific causes are still largely unknown.

## SUMMARY OF ETIOLOGIC THEORIES AND RESEARCH

There is currently no empirical support for theories that implicate unloving mothers, yeast infections, or childhood vaccinations as the cause of autism. The evidence invoked in support of these claims involves uncontrolled case studies and anecdotal reports. The confusion about the causes of autism appears to stem largely from illusory temporal correlations between the diagnosis of the disorder and normal events occurring in early childhood. No research has demonstrated a differential risk for autism due to maternal personality characteristics, the presence of candidiasis, or the use of the MMR vaccine. Scientific evidence points to genetic predispositions and various early environmental insults to the developing fetus as responsible for the development of the disorder.

## QUESTIONABLE TREATMENTS FOR AUTISM: BOLD CLAIMS, DUBIOUS THEORIES, AND LITTLE DATA

A number of interventions have been promoted as providing break-throughs in the treatment of autism. These treatments share many of the features of pseudoscience described earlier. Despite the absence of sup-portive data and even in the face of contradictory data, these treatments continue to be passionately promoted by their supporters.

### Sensory-Motor Therapies

Smith (1996) reported that over eighteen hundred variations of sensory-motor therapy have been developed to treat individuals with autism. The popularity of these approaches derives from the observation that many individuals with autism exhibit sensory-processing abnormalities, although these types of dysfunctions are neither universal nor specific to the condition (Dawson & Watling 2000). Furthermore, many individuals with autism exhibit a relatively high prevalence of fine and gross motor impairments. Nevertheless, little controlled research has examined the effectiveness of sensory-motor treatments for autism. We next briefly review the most commonly promoted treatments for autism that emphasize the importance of ameliorating the sensory-motor deficits often associated with the disorder.

## Facilitated Communication

Facilitated communication (FC) is a method designed to assist individuals with autism and related disabilities to communicate through the use of a typewriter, keyboard, or similar device.[2] The technique involves a trained "facilitator" holding the disabled person's hand, arm, or shoulder while the latter apparently types messages on the keyboard device. The basic rationale behind FC is that persons with autism suffer from a neurological impairment called *apraxia*, which interferes with purposeful motoric behavior. This neurological abnormality in motor functioning is often hypothesized to be unrelated to intellectual functioning. Thus, many if not all people with autism are believed to possess a "hidden literacy" that can be expressed by overcoming these motoric deficits (Green 1994).

FC was originally conceived in the early 1970s in Australia by Rosemary Crossley, a teacher at St. Nicholas Hospital in Melbourne. Crossley later cofounded and directed the Dignity Through Education and Language Center, which promoted the use of FC in Australia. Syracuse University education professor Douglas Biklen witnessed Crossley's use of FC in Australia and brought the technique to the United States. In 1992, Biklen formed the Facilitated Communication Institute at Syracuse University and began to promote its use for persons with autism. Biklen continues to maintain the Facilitated Communication Institute at Syracuse University and to be a vocal proponent of FC for autism (Gardner 2001; Jacobson, Mulick & Schwartz 1995).

FC initially inspired great hope in many family members (especially parents) of people with autism. Their heretofore largely uncommunicative son or daughter appeared to begin communicating via typed messages such as "I love you," presenting them with poems, or carrying on highly intellectual conversations. It is not surprising that FC went largely unquestioned by understandably desperate family members and even many professionals, despite several obvious causes for skepticism. For example, autistic individuals often did not even look at the keyboard while apparently typing with a single digit, yet expert typists were unable to type coherent sentences with one finger without looking at the keyboard (Gardner 2001). Such observations did not dampen the enthusiasm for FC by its proponents.

Despite this enthusiasm, the dramatic claims for FC have not survived scientific scrutiny. A number of scientifically rigorous studies have investigated FC, and the results of these studies clearly point to facilitators as the source of the typed information (Jacobson, Mullick & Schwartz 1995). For example, Wheeler, Jacobson, Paglieri, and Schwartz (1993) conducted a study in which autistic participants were asked to type the names of everyday objects that were shown to them on picture cards. The typing was done under three conditions: (a) the facilitators were not shown the picture; (b) the facilitators did not assist the typing; and (c) both the participants and the facilitators were shown pictures that were varied so that the participants and facilitators sometimes saw the same picture and sometimes saw different pictures. Not surprisingly, participants were unable to type the correct response in any of the conditions except when they were shown the same picture as the facilitators. Furthermore, in the condition in which the participants and the facilitators were shown different cards, the typed responses were of the pictures that were shown only to the facilitators. This study provided clear evidence that the facilitators were the source of the typed information.

Much of the controversy surrounding FC has stemmed from many facilitators' vehement denials of responsibility for the typed information. In one study, for example, Burgess et al. (1998) demonstrated that FC involves a form of "automatic writing" (i.e., writing without awareness that one is doing so), technically called an *ideomotor response,* on the part of the facilitator. Forty college students were trained to facilitate communication with a confederate in the role of a person with a developmental disability. Each participant was given different information about the confederate, who was then asked questions related to this information. Eighty-nine percent of the responses corresponded to the information provided to the facilitators, yet all but two reported that the information came from the confederate. In discussing the results of the Burgess et al. (1998) study, Kirsch and Lynn (1999) concluded that:

> the attribution of the response to the confederate was clearly an error. Just as clearly, participants were not aware of generating responses. Instead, their responses were automatic behaviors prepared by the intention to facilitate and their knowledge of the answers to the questions. (p. 510)

These are merely two of dozens of studies that have demonstrated conclusively that the source of messages in FC is the facilitator rather than the disabled individual, despite the absence of conscious intent or awareness on the part of facilitators. It is therefore not surprising that so many facilitators became ardent believers in FC.

The dangers of FC extend well beyond the disappointment of family members and the disillusionment of former facilitators who have acknowledged the actual origins of passages produced through the technique. Beginning in the late 1990s, facilitated messages describing vivid instances of sexual abuse at the hands of parents began to emerge. Such reports resulted in several cases of autistic individuals being removed from their homes and parents being arrested and jailed on charges of sexual abuse. Although such charges were eventually dismissed, some accused parents were forced to spend their family savings on legal defense fees (Gardner 2001; Jacobson et al. 1995).

### Auditory Integration Training

Auditory Integration Training (AIT) involves listening to filtered, modulated music that presents sounds of varying volumes and pitches. AIT was initially developed by French physician Guy Berard as a treatment for auditory disorders. In the late 1970s, Berard began promoting the use of AIT for autism. The technique gained larger recognition with the publication of the book *The Sound of a Miracle* (Stehli 1991), written by the mother of a child who was allegedly "cured" of autism through the use of AIT.

AIT is typically administered in two daily half-hour sessions for approximately ten days. Proponents theorize that a major factor in the problem behaviors of people with autism is hypersensitive hearing. The premise is that upon listening to the random variations in sounds, the individual's "auditory system" adjusts to the sounds and thus becomes more normal. Proponents of AIT claim that benefits include improvement in memory, comprehension, eye contact, articulation, independent living skills, appropriate social behavior, willingness to interact with others, and responsibility in school (Berard 1993; Stehli 1991).

Once again, scientific research casts serious doubt on the claims made for this innovative treatment for autism. One pilot study (Rimland & Edelson 1995), one uncontrolled study (Rimland & Edelson 1994), and one small controlled study (Edelson et al. 1999) suggested possible limited benefits of AIT. In the controlled study, Edelson et al. (ibid.) claimed to demonstrate that AIT produced significant improvements in aberrant behavior in a group of autistic children and adults relative to a placebo condition in which participants listened to unmodulated music. In addition to behavioral improvements, the authors further purported to demonstrate that AIT resulted in improved information processing as reflected in brain wave changes. In describing the results of this study, Edelson (2001) recently went so far as to claim that AIT produced "normalization of brain wave activity" in treated subjects.

Nevertheless, this study is plagued by methodological problems, and the actual results are in fact inconsistent with the authors' conclusions and interpretations. For example, Edelson et al. (1999) found a difference between the experimental and placebo groups on only one of three primary outcome measures and only at one of the four assessment periods. Given the number of analyses conducted and the absence of a statistical correction for multiple tests, this single finding may well be the result of chance rather than representing a legitimate effect of AIT. At other assessment periods the AIT-treated participants' scores on this measure actually returned to baseline, which the authors acknowledge reflects that one-third of the subjects in the experimental group actually became worse. The "normalization of brain wave activity" consisted of a putative increase in P300 event-related potential (ERP) amplitude in a tonal discrimination task. However, only five subjects (three from the experimental group and two from the placebo group) completed this task. No information is provided on how representative these five subjects were of the larger subject pool, much less the general population of autistic individuals. This small sample precluded statistical analyses of the data. Furthermore, inspection of the raw ERP data reported by the authors reveals apparently large baseline differences between the two groups, casting further doubt on their conclusions.

Four other well-controlled studies (Bettison 1996; Gillberg et al. 1997; Mudford et al. 2000; Zollweg et al. 1997) failed to find any specific benefit for AIT. In the most recent study, Mudford et al. (2000) compared AIT with a control condition in which children listened to ambient room music through nonfunctional headphones. No benefit of AIT over the control condition was found on measures of IQ, comprehension, or social adaptive behavior. Teacher-rated measures showed no differences between the groups and parent-rated measures of hyperactivity and direct observational measures of ear-occlusion actually nonsignificantly favored the control group. The authors concluded that "no individual child was identified as benefiting clinically or educationally from the treatment" (p. 118).

The American Academy of Pediatrics' Committee on Children with Disabilities published a statement in 1998 in the journal *Pediatrics* on the use of both AIT and FC for autism. The statement suggested that "currently available information does not support the claims of proponents that these treatments are efficacious," and further that "their use does not appear warranted at this time, except within research protocols" (American Academy of Pediatrics [AAP] 1998).

### Sensory Integration Therapy

A. Jean Ayres (1979), an occupational therapist, developed Sensory Integration Therapy (SIT) in the 1950s. The treatment is a form of sensory-motor therapy recommended for children with autism, learning disabil-

ities, mental retardation, cerebral palsy, and similar developmental disabilities. Ayres posited that the child with autism possesses deficits in
registering and modulating sensory input, and a deficit in the part of the
brain that initiates purposeful behavior, which she calls the "I want to do
it" system. SIT, typically delivered in individual sessions, purportedly
ameliorates these underlying deficits through sensory integration. In an
attempt to facilitate this integration, the treatment involves engaging the
child in full-body movements that are designed to provide vestibular,
proprioceptive, and tactile stimulation. Sensory integration activities
include swinging in a hammock, spinning in circles on a chair, applying
brushes to various parts of the body, and engaging in balance activities
(Smith 1996). These activities are hypothesized to correct the underlying
neurological deficits producing the perceptual-motor problems witnessed in many individuals with autism. In other words, SIT is not
designed to teach the child new physical/motor activities, but to correct
fundamental sensory-motor dysfunctions underlying the disorder in
order to increase the individual's capacity for learning new activities
(Hoehn & Baumesiter 1994).

Controlled studies have found little support for the efficacy of SIT
for treating children with various developmental disabilities. Mason
and Iwata (1990) found SIT ineffective for treating self-injurious
behaviors in three patients with mental retardation, although the problematic behaviors were later reduced through behavioral interventions.
Furthermore, self-injurious behaviors paradoxically increased in one
three-year-old patient when treated with SIT. Iwasaki and Holm (1989)
found no difference between the SIT and control condition (described
as informal talk and touch) in decreasing stereotypic behaviors in
young children and adults with mental retardation. Jenkins, Fewell, and
Harris (1983) found no differences between young children with mild-
to-moderate motor delays who received either SIT or small-group
therapy for seventeen weeks. Finally, Densem, Nuthall, Bushnell, and
Horn (1989) found no differences between SIT and no-treatment control conditions for children with learning disabilities. In fact, in their
review of the literature, Hoehn and Baumeister (1994) concluded that

controlled studies of SIT demonstrate no unique benefits for the treatment on any outcome areas in children with learning disabilities.

Dawson and Watling (2000) recently reviewed studies that used objective behavioral measures in investigating the efficacy of SIT for autism. Only one of the four studies had more than five participants, and no study included a comparison group. In the study with the largest sample size, Reilly, Nelson, and Bundy (1984) used a randomized, ABAB counterbalanced design to compare SIT with tabletop activities (e.g., puzzles and coloring). Eighteen children with autism received an hour of SIT and tabletop activities each. The authors reported that verbal behavior was superior in the tabletop as compared with the SIT condition because children spoke more during the fine motor activities. Nevertheless, the brevity of treatment, lack of specific training in SIT for the therapists, and failure of the researchers to assess verbal behavior outside the experimental condition limit the conclusions that can be drawn.

Other single-case studies comparing SIT with no-treatment baseline among autistic children have reported beneficial results (Case-Smith & Bryan 1999; Linderman & Stewart 1999). However, these designs cannot demonstrate that the benefits were produced specifically by SIT. As Reilly et al. (1984) demonstrated, simple tabletop activities actually appeared to result in benefits superior to SIT in their study. Green (1996a) pointed out that although children may find SIT activities enjoyable, this does not provide evidence of any significant, long-lasting benefits in the child's behavior or in any underlying neurological deficits. Furthermore, applying brushes of increasing firmness to the arms of autistic children, a common SIT activity, may help to desensitize them to certain tactile stimuli, but such benefits are most parsimoniously explained by well-known behavioral principles (e.g., habituation) rather than anything specific to SIT (Siegel 1996). In conclusion, the general null effects for SIT relative to control conditions in treating other developmental disabilities, combined with the results of the Reilly et al. (1984) study with autistic children, suggest little benefit of SIT for autism.

# PSYCHOTHERAPIES

Various forms of psychotherapy have been applied to autism, although there is a dearth of research on their effects. The American Academy of Child and Adolescent Psychiatry (AACAP) recently issued a statement of practice parameters for the assessment and treatment of autism and related developmental disorders. The AACAP work group concluded that "it now appears that the usefulness of psychotherapy in autism is very limited" (AACAP 1999). Nevertheless, various forms of psychotherapy continue to be used with autism. We briefly discuss three of the currently most popular psychotherapies: psychoanalytic psychotherapy, holding therapy, and options therapy.

## Psychoanalysis

As discussed earlier, psychoanalytic theories have long been applied to the etiology of autism despite considerable evidence that many of the basic tenets of these theories are inaccurate; nonetheless, psychoanalytic conceptualization and treatment of autism continues (Beratis 1994; Bromfield 2000). Far from being innocuous, psychoanalytic treatments for autism can be quite harmful. The focus on parental (and especially maternal) rejection in the etiology and treatment of autism can lead to a misplaced blame and a deep sense of guilt in parents. The highly unstructured nature of many psychoanalytic treatments, including granting autistic individuals wide latitude to pursue preferred activities in treatment and the lack of focus on contingencies between behaviors and their consequences, can lead to a worsening of problems (Smith 1996).

## Holding Therapy

Holding therapy has been promoted for numerous childhood problems, including autism (Welch 1988). Proponents of holding therapy theorize that autism results from a lack of appropriate attachment of child to mother. This deficit in mother-child bonding presumably causes the child to withdraw inward, thereby resulting in social and communicative deficits. It therefore follows that if the mother provides intense physical contact with the child, the previously deficient bond can be reestablished and the "normal" child can emerge. As is evident from this discussion, holding therapy is largely based on psychoanalytic theories of autism, and no researchers have examined its efficacy.

### Options Therapy

Options therapy grew out of the book *Son Rise* (Kaufman 1976), written by parents of an autistic child. The parents reported that they spent many hours every day mirroring the actions of their autistic child without placing demands on him. They theorized that they could enter the world of their son and, in turn, gradually draw him out. Following the reported success of this treatment with their son, the couple began charging fees to teach this method in workshops. Questions have been raised as to whether the boy was actually autistic (Siegel 1996). We could locate no published studies investigating the use of options therapy for autism.

## BIOLOGICAL TREATMENTS

Several factors have resulted in the increased popularity of biologically oriented treatments for autism. These include the increased consensus that autism is fundamentally a neurological condition, the increased popularity of psychotropic medications in psychiatry, and the increased popularity of homeopathic, herbal, vitamin, and other "alternative medicine" interventions. Several such treatments have been widely promoted as producing extraordinary benefits for autistic individuals, despite the absence of supportive data, or in some cases even in the face of disconfirming data.

## Secretin

Secretin is a hormone involved in the control of digestion that stimulates the secretion of pancreatic juices. It is used in a single dose to help diagnose such gastrointestinal problems as pancreatic disease or ulcers, and it is not approved by the Food and Drug Administration for other uses. Nevertheless, the use of secretin in the treatment of autism gained significant attention following a report in 1998 of a child who appeared to show significant improvement following a single dose (Horvath et al. 1998). Parents of thousands of autistic children began requesting and receiving injections of secretin for their children based solely on this single case.

In 1999, a study published in the *New England Journal of Medicine* reported the effects of a single dose of secretin on fifty-six children with autistic-spectrum disorders. The researchers found that a single dose of secretin had no effect on standard behavioral measures when compared with placebo (Sandler et al. 1999). Several other studies have since found similar results. For example, a study recently completed by researchers at the University of California, San Francisco, found no effects of secretin on standard measures of expressive or receptive language skills in twenty autistic children. Similarly, Chez et al. (2000) recently published a two-part study that found no clinically significant differences between secretin and placebo. Some parents reported improvements in their children's functioning following the initial open-label trial phase of the study after the children received an injection of secretin. However, in the second part of the study that was a double-blind trial, children given secretin did not show clinically meaningful improvements compared with those given placebo injections. Chez and Buchanan (2000) concluded that they "cannot rationalize the use of secretin at this point as a 'treatment' modality" (p. 97). Two additional studies likewise found no differences between secretin and placebo in autism (Dunn-Geier et al. 2000; Owley et al. 1999).

Despite these results, interest in secretin in the treatment of autism continues. In fact, in the face of disconfirming research, an influential psychologist and autism advocate, writing on the Internet site of the Autism Research Institute, described secretin as "the most promising treatment yet discovered for the treatment of autism" (Rimland 1999). Furthermore, likely due to the large consumer demand for secretin for autism, the biopharmaceutical company Repligen secured exclusive rights to a series of patent applications that cover the use of secretin for autism (New update 1999).

### Gluten- and Casein-Free Diets

Gluten is a mixture of proteins found in grain products such as wheat bread. Casein is a protein found in milk. Anecdotal reports have abounded that some persons with autism demonstrate increased negative behaviors following the consumption of milk, wheat bread, or similar products. There is some evidence that eliminating these proteins from the diet of some autistic individuals can lead to improvements in behavior (Kvinsberg et al. 1996; Whitely, Rodgers, Savery & Shattock 1999). Due to methodological weaknesses, however, these studies cannot rule out alternative explanations for any observed improvements following gluten- and casein-free diets. The vast majority of the evidence for the benefits of these diets derives from anecdotal reports or case studies (e.g., Adams & Conn 1997). More rigorous research is needed before the inclusion of these diets as part of a comprehensive treatment plan can be recommended.

### Vitamin B6 and Magnesium

Smith (1996) reported that there have been at least fifteen studies demonstrating that vitamin B6 with magnesium can be somewhat helpful for children with autism. However, the reports are mixed, with some studies showing no positive effects of high doses of pyroxidine and magnesium (HDPM) (Tolbert et al. 1993) or no difference between HDPM and placebo (Findling et al. 1997). Critics have argued that a major methodological weakness in most of the studies is that they rely on parent and staff reports instead of assessments from independent observers (Smith 1996). Also, there are some questions regarding the safety of megadoses of these substances. One potential risk is that high doses of B6 can cause nerve damage and high doses of magnesium can cause reduced heart rate and weakened reflexes (Deutsch & Morrill 1993). More research is needed to evaluate the safety and effectiveness of long-term use of B6 and magnesium before it can be considered as an efficacious treatment for autism.

### Dimethylglycine

Dimethylglycine (DMG) is an antioxidant that can be purchased over the counter as a dietary supplement. In addition to its purported usefulness in increasing energy and enhancing the immune system, DMG is often marketed as a treatment for autism. Some professionals claim that DMG increases eye contact and speech and decreases frustration levels among individuals with autism (Rimland 1996). In response to the proliferation of anecdotal reports for the effectiveness of DMG, Bolman and Richmond (1999) conducted a double-blind, placebo-controlled, crossover pilot study of DMG in eight males with autism. Similar to the results of the secretin studies, this study found no significant differences between DMG and placebo. DMG's proponents are undeterred, however, claiming that controlled studies are not needed to demonstrate DMG's effectiveness for autism (Rimland 1996).

## SUMMARY OF QUESTIONABLE TREATMENTS

A wide variety of treatments for autism abound, and families are often persuaded to try methods that are highly unorthodox and scientifically suspect. The observation that individuals with autism sometimes exhibit sensory and motor abnormalities has resulted in the promotion of treatments that claim either to unlock the hidden communicator trapped by the disorder (e.g., FC) or to correct the underlying neurological deficits that are thought responsible for the impairments (e.g., sensory and auditory integration therapies). Others, relying on scientifically untenable theories of the etiology of autism such as the causal role of dysfunctional infant attachment, seek to repair these relationships through intensive psychotherapies (e.g., holding therapy and psychoanalysis). Among the currently most popular treatments are biologically based interventions, including various diets, vitamins, or supplements (e.g., secretin). Even though these intervention approaches are extremely heterogeneous in theory and approach, they all share the characteristic of possessing little or no scientific evidence of effectiveness. What is even more distressing is that some of these treatments continue to be promoted even after controlled studies have clearly demonstrated that they are ineffective.

## PROMISING TREATMENTS FOR AUTISM: REVIEWING THE EVIDENCE AND REINING IN CLAIMS

The interventions reviewed thus far give little reason for hope in the treatment of autism. Fortunately, the situation is not so bleak. Several promising programs have been developed. Although some research has been conducted on these programs, none has been sufficiently evaluated using experimental research designs. In effect, no treatment currently meets the criteria established by the American Psychological Association's Committee on Science and Practice as an empirically supported treatment for autism (Gresham, Beebe-Frankenberger & MacMillan 1999; Rogers 1998). Nevertheless, the intervention programs reviewed in the following section are based on sound theories, are supported by at least some controlled research, and clearly warrant further investigation.

### Applied Behavior Analysis

Among the currently most popular interventions for autism are programs based on applied behavior analysis (ABA), an approach to behavior modification rooted in the experimental analysis of behavior, in which operant conditioning and other learning principles are used to change problematic behavior (Cooper, Heron & Heward 1989). Several intervention programs for autism based on ABA methods have been developed. Rogers (1998) noted that many studies of behavioral interventions for autism have focused on a single discrete symptom and that such interventions have often been shown to be quite effective for such limited targets. In contrast to the single-symptom approach, some programs have been designed to target the core deficits of autism and thereby improve the overall functioning of autistic individuals. By far the most popular of these programs are modeled after the Young Autism Project (YAP) developed at the University of California at Los Angeles by O. Ivar Lovaas and colleagues. Initiated in 1970, the YAP aims to improve the functioning of young children with autism through the use of an intensive, highly structured behavioral program delivered one-on-one by specially trained personnel. The program is designed to be implemented full-time during most of the child's waking hours, and family involvement is deemed to be critical. Treatment is initially delivered in the client's home, with eventual progression to community and school settings. The program is often referred to as "discrete trial training," reflecting the fact that each specific intervention utilizes a discrete stimulus-response-consequence sequence. For example, a child might be presented with three blocks of different colors and given the verbal stimulus "touch red." If the child touches the red block, a reward is provided (e.g., a small snack, verbal praise). Lovaas (1981) described the program in a treatment manual designed for parents and professionals.

The YAP was evaluated in a widely cited study by Lovaas (1987), with long-term follow-up data reported by McEachlin, Smith, and Lovaas (1993). Lovaas (1987) treated nineteen young children with the ABA program described above for forty or more hours per week for at least two years. Two control conditions were employed, one in which nineteen children received ten hours or less per week of the ABA program (minimal treatment condition), and another in which twenty-one children received unspecified community interventions but no ABA. Outcome measures were IQ and educational placement.

Lovaas (1987) reported dramatic results: After at least two years of intervention, almost half (47 percent) of the experimental group was found to have IQ scores in the normal range and were reported to be functioning in typical first grade classrooms without special support services. Lovaas described these children as having "recovered" from autism. Only one child from either of the two control groups demonstrated similar gains. In addition, there were large differences in IQ scores between the experimental group and the two control groups. McEachlin et al. (1993) followed up with participants from the experimental and minimal ABA treatment conditions several years later. The difference in IQ scores between the two groups was maintained. Of the nine children with the best outcomes from the original report, eight continued to function in regular education classrooms.

Not surprisingly, a great deal of enthusiasm was generated by these reports, and demand for ABA programs modeled after the YAP has grown rapidly since their publication. Unlike other treatment or educational programs, the YAP not only offered the possibility of significant improvement in functioning but also suggested that a substantial number of autistic youngsters could achieve completely normal functioning. Several commentators, however, raised serious concerns about the conclusions reached by Lovaas (1987) and McEachlin et al. (1993). Schopler, Short, and Mesibov (1989) noted that the outcome measures employed, IQ and school placement, might not reflect true overall functional changes. Increases in IQ scores, for example, could reflect increased compliance with testing rather than true changes in intellectual abilities, and school mainstreaming may be more a function of parental and therapist advocacy and changing school policies than increased educational functioning per se. In addition, Schopler et al. argued that the participants in the YAP study appeared to be relatively high-functioning individuals with good prognosis and were unrepresentative of the larger population of autistic children. Most importantly, they pointed out that the study design was not a true experiment, as subjects were not randomly assigned to the experimental and control groups. They suggested that the procedures for assigning subjects to groups likely resulted in important differences between the experimental and control conditions that may have contributed to the observed outcome differences. Schopler et al. (1989) concluded that "it is not possible to determine the effects of this intervention" from this study (p. 164).

Others subsequently raised similar criticisms. Gresham and MacMillan (1998) expanded on the threats to both internal and external validity raised by Schopler et al. (1989) and called for "healthy skepticism" in evaluating the claims of the YAP studies. Mesibov (1993) expressed concerns about pretreatment differences between the experimental and control groups and the many domains of functioning in which deficits commonly associated with autism (e.g., social interaction and conceptual abilities) that were not assessed. Mundy (1993) raised similar concerns, noting that many functioning autistic individuals achieve IQ levels in the normal range, thereby raising questions about the use of IQ scores to measure "recovery" from autism.

Although they uniformly take exception with claims of "recovery" from autism proffered by Lovaas and colleagues, even these critics concede that the study yielded promising results that merit further investigation. Although several studies of similar ABA interventions have now been published, two points about these studies are noteworthy. First, each is methodologically even weaker than the original YAP study. Second, the results of these studies, although generally promising, fall significantly short of those obtained by Lovaas (1987) and McEachlin et al. (1993). Birnbrauer and Leach (1993) reported on nine children who received nineteen hours per week of a one-on-one ABA program for two years and five control children who received no ABA. Four of the nine children in the experimental group made significant gains in IQ, relative to one of the five control children, although none of the participants achieved completely normal functioning. Sheinkopf and Siegel (1998) conducted a retrospective study of eleven children who received between twelve and forty-three hours per week of home-based ABA programs for between seven and twenty-four months, relative matched control group of children who received unspecified school-based treatment. Data were obtained through record reviews of an existing database. Relative to the control group, children in the experimental achieved higher gains in IQ, although few differences emerged between the groups in autistic symptoms. Finally, in an uncontrolled, pre-post-design study, Anderson, Avery, DiPietro, Edwards, and Christian (1987) reported on fourteen children who received between fifteen and twenty-five hours per week of home-based ABA for one year. Modest gains were reported in mental age scores and communication skills for most children, although those with the lowest baseline functioning made essentially no progress. In addition, no children were able to be integrated into regular educational settings.

All of these studies involved ABA programs modeled on Lovaas's YAP, in which services were delivered one-on-one in the child's home, although each study differed from the original YAP study in several respects (e.g., the number of hours per week of intervention, the duration of the program, the nature and training of the therapists). Two additional studies evaluated similar ABA interventions, in which services were delivered in school- or center-based programs. Fenske, Zalenski, Krantz, and McClannahan (1985) compared nine children who began receiving an ABA program through the Princeton Child Development Institute prior to the age of sixty months, relative to nine who enrolled after the age of sixty months. After at least two years of treatment, four of the nine children in the younger group were enrolled in regular school classes, relative to one of the nine children from the older group. No data were provided on autistic symptoms or functioning level. Harris and colleagues reported pre-post data on children treated with an ABA program through the Douglas Developmental Center of Rutgers University. Harris, Handleman, Gordon, Kristoff, and Fuentes (1991) reported average IQ gains of approximately nineteen points after ten to eleven months of intervention. It should be noted that this sample of children was relatively high functioning, with an average pretreatment IQ of 67.5 and with symptoms rated as "mild to moderate." Nevertheless, despite the observed gains in IQ, all children were described as having significant impairments after treatment.

Taken together, the literature on ABA programs for autism clearly suggest that such interventions are promising. Methodological weaknesses of the existing studies, however, severely limit the conclusions that can be drawn about their efficacy. Of particular note is the fact that no study to date has utilized a true experimental design, in which subjects were randomly assigned to treatment conditions. This fact limits the inferences that can be drawn about the effects of the programs studied. Moreover, these concerns are compounded by pretreatment differences between experimental and control conditions in each of the studies reviewed. Other methodological concerns include questions about the representativeness of the samples of autistic children, unknown fidelity to treatment procedures, limited outcome data for most studies, and problems inherent in relying on IQ scores and school placement as primary measures of autistic symptoms and functioning.

So what are we to make of the claims that ABA programs, and those modeled after the YAP in particular, can result in "recovery" from autism? After more than thirty years since its initiation and fourteen years since the first published outcome report, no study has replicated the results of the original YAP study and several critics have challenged its conclusions. Subsequent research has yielded more modest gains in functioning, casting further doubt on the claims that autistic youngsters can be "cured" through ABA programs. Nevertheless, these caveats have not tempered the enthusiasm of some proponents of ABA programs. Consider, for example, the following quotes from leading advocates of ABA intervention programs for autism:

> Several studies have now shown that one treatment approach—early, intensive instruction using the methods of Applied Behavior Analysis— can result in dramatic improvements for children with autism: successful integration in regular schools for many, *completely normal functioning* for some. . . . No other treatment for autism offers comparable evidence of effectiveness. (Green 1996b 29; emphasis in original)

> There is little doubt that early intervention based on the principles and practices of Applied Behavior Analysis can produce large, comprehen-

sive, lasting, and meaningful improvements in many important domains for a large proportion of children with autism. For some, those improvements can amount to achievement of completely normal intellectual, social, academic, communicative, and adaptive functioning. (ibid., 38)

Furthermore, we also now know that applying effective interventions when children are very young (e.g., under the age of 3–4 years) has the potential for achieving substantial and widespread gains and even normal functioning in a certain number of these youngsters. (Schreibman 2000, 374)

During the past 15 years research has begun to demonstrate that significant proportions of children with autism or PDD who participate in early intensive intervention based on the principles of applied behavior analysis (ABA) achieve normal or near-normal functioning. . . . (Jacobson, Mulick & Green 1998, 204)

It is difficult to justify such assertions in light of the extant scientific literature on ABA programs for autism. Ironically, many of these same authors have been highly critical of the exaggerated claims made for nonbehavioral interventions. Clearly, ABA programs do not possess most of the features of pseudoscience that typify many of the highly dubious treatments for autism. ABA programs are based on well-established theories of learning and emphasize the value of scientific methods in evaluating treatment effects. Nevertheless, given the current state of the science, claims of "cure" and "recovery" from autism produced by ABA are misleading and irresponsible.

## OTHER COMPREHENSIVE BEHAVIORAL PROGRAMS

Although ABA programs—the YAP in particular—are the best-known behavioral interventions for autism, other programs have been developed that draw to varying degrees on behavioral learning principles. One of the most significant ways in which these programs differ from the ABA programs described earlier is that they make no claims of "curing" autism. Rather, they strive to ameliorate the functioning of autistic individuals by utilizing a variety of educational and therapeutic strategies. Few studies have been conducted on these programs, and those that have utilize only pre-post research designs, thereby limiting the conclusions that can be drawn.

## *LEAP*

Hoyson, Jamieson, and Strain (1984) described the effects of a program known as Learning Experiences: An Alternative Program for Preschoolers and Parents (LEAP). The LEAP program is composed of an integrated preschool and a behavior-management skills training program for parents. The preschool program, which was one of the first to integrate normally developing children with those with autism, blends normal preschool curricula with activities designed specifically for children with autism. Peer modeling is encouraged in an effort to develop play and social skills. The parental skills-training component aims to teach parents effective behavior-management and educational skills in natural contexts (i.e., home and community). In a pre-post study, Hoyson et al. (1984) reported accelerated developmental rates in six "autistic-like" children over the course of their participation in the LEAP program. Strain, Kohler, and Goldstein (1996) reported that twenty-four out of fifty-one children were attending regular education classes, although no information was provided regarding functioning level or special school supports. Although certain aspects of the LEAP program appear promising, the paucity of the available research, and especially the absence of controlled research, preclude judgments about its usefulness.

## Denver Health Sciences Program

Developed by Sally Rogers and colleagues at the University of Colorado School of Medicine, the Denver Health Sciences Program is a developmentally oriented preschool program designed not only for children with autism-spectrum disorders, but varied other behavioral problems. Several pre-post studies have reported that autistic children participating in the program demonstrated accelerated developmental rates in several domains, including language, play skills, and social interactions with parents (Rogers & DiLalla 1991; Rogers et al. 1986; Rogers & Lewis 1989; Rogers, Lewis & Reis 1987). Once again, the lack of controlled research makes it impossible to draw firm conclusions about the effectiveness of this program.

## Project TEACCH

The program for the Treatment and Education of Autistic and Related Communication Handicapped Children (TEACCH) is a university-based project founded by Eric Schopler at the University of North Carolina at Chapel Hill (Schopler & Reichler 1971). TEACCH programs have become among the more widely used intervention programs for autism. Project TEACCH incorporates behavioral principles in treating children with autism, but differs from ABA in several fundamental ways. Most significantly, TEACCH focuses on maximizing the skills of children with autism while drawing on their relative strengths, rather than attempting "recovery" from the disorder. The program is designed around providing structured settings in which children with autism can develop their skills. Teachers establish individual workstations where each child can practice various tasks, for example, such visual-motor activities as sorting objects by color. Visual cues are often provided in an effort to compensate for the deficits in auditory processing often characteristic of autism. Like the YAP, LEAP, and Denver programs, TEACCH emphasizes a collaborative effort between treatment staff and parents. For example, parents are encouraged to establish routines and cues in the home similar to those provided in the classroom environment (Gresham, Beebe-Frankenberger & MacMillan 1999).

Only two treatment outcome studies to date have investigated the effectiveness of project TEACCH. Schopler, Mesibov, and Baker (1982) collected questionnaire data from 348 families whose children were currently or previously enrolled in the program. Individuals with autism who participated ranged in age from two to twenty-six and ranged cognitively from severe mental retardation to normal intellectual functioning. The majority of respondents indicated that the program was helpful. Also, the institutionalization rate of participants was 7 percent, as compared with the rates of 39 percent to 75 percent reported for individuals with autism in the general population based on data from the 1960s. Nevertheless, this study is marked by many serious methodological weaknesses. These include a highly heterogeneous sample (not all participants had autism), the absence of a meaningful control condition, and the lack of standardized and independent assessment measures. In addition, Schopler and colleagues' comparison of the institutionalization rate in their study with 1960s data is probably misleading. Changes in government policy during the 1960s and 1970s led to decreased institutionalization rates in general (Smith 1996).

More recently, Ozonoff and Cathcart (1998) tested the effectiveness of TEACCH home-based instruction for children with autism. Parents were taught interventions for preschool children with autism, focusing on the areas of cognitive, academic, and prevocational skills related to school success. The treatment group was composed of eleven preschool children with autism who received four months of home programming. The treatment group was assessed before and after treatment, with the Psychoeducational Profile–Revised (Schopler et al. 1990), and results were compared with those from a matched comparison group of children not in the TEACCH program who were similarly assessed. Results showed that the preschool children receiving TEACCH-based parent instruction improved significantly more in the areas of imitation, fine-motor, gross-motor, and nonverbal conceptual skills. Furthermore, the treatment group showed an average developmental gain of 9.6 months after the four-month intervention. Although this study provides some support for the TEACCH program, the conclusions are tempered by methodological limitations, including the lack of a randomized control condition and the absence of treatment fidelity ratings.

## SUMMARY OF BEHAVIORAL INTERVENTION PROGRAMS

Several programs utilizing various behavioral and developmental intervention strategies have been shown to yield promising results in the treatment of children with autism. Among the most promising are programs based on the intensive, one-on-one application of applied behavior analysis (ABA). Some proponents of ABA have made sweeping claims about the ability of such programs to "cure" autism that are not supported by the available literature. Other behaviorally based programs (e.g., LEAP, Denver Health Sciences Program, TEACCH) have been less prone to exaggerated claims. However, the available research on these programs is more akin to program evaluations than to traditional studies of treatment efficacy or effectiveness. For example, no studies have employed experimental designs, and none has used objective measures of the full range of symptoms and functional impairments associated with autism. Component analysis studies have not evaluated the specific mechanisms responsible for the programs' effects, and no research has compared the relative effectiveness of various behavioral programs.

Dawson and Osterling (1997) identified six features that are common to most comprehensive early-intervention programs for autism. They suggested that these "tried-and-true" features, rather than the specific methods emphasized by each program, may be responsible for the observed effects of early-intervention programs. These common features include (a) curriculum content emphasizing selective attention, imitation, language, toy play, and social skills; (b) highly supportive teaching environments with explicit attention to generalization of gains;

(c) an emphasis on predictability and routine; (d) a functional approach to problem behaviors; (e) a focus on transition from the preschool classroom to kindergarten, first grade, or other appropriate placements; and (f) parental involvement in treatment. Several of these features were incorporated into the treatment recommendations for autism made by the American Academy of Child and Adolescent Psychiatry (AACAP 1999). Further research is clearly indicated to assess the effects of each component, and to evaluate potential additive effects of the specific elements of various early intervention programs.

## PHARMACOTHERAPY

A detailed review of the psychopharmacologic treatment of autism is beyond the scope of this paper, and several excellent recent reviews are available (AACAP 1999; Aman & Langworthy 2000; Campbell et al. 1996; Gillberg 1996; King 2000). Although not curative, in open-label case reports, several medications appeared to improve various symptoms associated with autism, thereby increasing individuals' ability to benefit from educational and behavioral interventions. With a few noteworthy exceptions, few studies have utilized double-blind, placebo-controlled designs, especially with autistic children.

The most extensively studied agents are the dopamine antagonists, especially haloperidol (Haldol). Several well-controlled studies have shown haloperidol to be superior to placebo for a number of symptoms, including withdrawal, stereotypies, and hyperactivity (Anderson et al. 1984; Campbell et al. 1996; Locascio et al. 1991), although drug-related dyskinesias appear to be relatively common following long-term administration (Campbell et al. 1997). There is growing interest in the atypical neuroleptics, risperidone (Risperdal) in particular. In a double-blind, placebo-controlled trial with autistic adults, McDougle et al. (1998) found risperidone to be superior to placebo on several measures, and to be well tolerated.

Several studies suggest the usefulness of various selective serotonin reuptake inhibitors (SSRIs), including fluvoxamine (Luvox; McDougle et al. 1996), fluoxetine (Prozac; Cook et al. 1992; DeLong, Teague & Kamran 1998; Fatemi et al. 1998), and clomipramine (Anafranil; Gordon et al. 1992; 1993). However, SSRIs are often associated with intolerable adverse events. For example, recent open-label studies reveal significant rates of adverse side effects of clomipramine, including seizures, weight gain, constipation, and sedation (e.g., Brodkin et al. 1997). Moreover, there is a growing consensus that children appear to respond less well to SSRIs than do adolescents and adults (Brasic et al. 1994; McDougle, Kresch & Posey 2000; Sanchez et al. 1996). Tricyclic antidepressants are less frequently used relative to SSRIs, given the possibility of cardiovascular side effects and lowering of seizure threshold.

Although little research has examined anxiolytic agents in autism, what little research has been conducted suggests that they are of little benefit. In fact, Marrosu et al. (1987) found increases in hyperactivity and aggression following treatment with the benzodiazepine diazepam (Valium). More promising results have been obtained in open-label studies of buspirone (Buspar; McCormick 1997; Realmuto, August & Garfinkel 1989; Ratey, Mikkelsen & Chmielinski 1989).

## THE HARM IN PROMOTING UNPROVEN TREATMENTS

As the previous review illustrates, even the most promising treatments for autism are typically far from ideally effective, leaving the autistic individual with substantial impairments. It is therefore natural for parents, educators, and even mental health professionals to ask what the harm is in trying an unproven treatment. This is a difficult question for which there is no easy answer. On the one hand, we are not suggesting that parents and professionals not be allowed to explore a range of treatment options. What we are suggesting is that they do so with as much information as possible and armed with an attitude of healthy skepticism. For several reasons, such skepticism is particularly important in considering treatments for autism.

First, proponents of many treatments, both novel and established, often make impressive claims that are simply not supported by controlled research. Moreover, many mental health and educational professionals who work with autistic individuals have been reluctant to speak against pseudoscientific theories and practices. This silence places the burden directly on consumers to become educated about the empirical status of various treatment options. Unless they make efforts to become informed about the research literature themselves, consumers can be easily misled and given false hope.

Second, no treatment is without cost. Aside from the obvious financial burden, there are always other costs to consider when contemplating a new treatment. In particular, time and resources spent on an unproven therapy are time and resources that could have been spent on an intervention with a greater likelihood of success (what economists term "opportunity cost"). This point is especially critical with respect to early-intervention programs, as a growing literature suggests the importance of early intervention with specialized behavioral and educational programs (Fenske et al. 1985). The issue of cost is complicated by the tendency, in the absence of appropriate control conditions, to misattribute any positive changes that may be observed to an intervention and then expend even more resources on that intervention when the improvement may not be due to the treatment. Alternatively, repeated experience with treatments that are promoted with much fanfare but turn out to be ineffective might cause family members of autistic individuals to become unnecessarily cynical about even legitimate interventions.

Finally and perhaps most importantly, one must always be aware of the potential for harm. There are numerous examples in the history of pharmacotherapy of substances that were initially believed to be therapeutically useful and devoid of harmful side effects that turned out to be quite harmful (e.g., combined fenfluramine and dexfenfluramine, thalidomide). The effects of long-term use of substances like secretin and DMG have not investigated and are therefore unknown. The risk of is not limited to pharmacologic interventions, however. Consider, for example, the case of FC. The cases of family members being convicted of abuse and sent to prison based on alleged communications provides a sobering example of the harm that can arise from unvalidated interventions. Despite the wealth of scientific demonstrating that the "facilitator" is the source of messages, some courts still permit communications derived via FC to be used as evidence (Gorman 1999).

## CAVEAT EMPTOR

Autistic-spectrum disorders are associated with serious psychiatric symptoms, often profound developmental delays, and impairments in many areas of functioning. Although the etiology of autism remains largely unknown and there is currently no cure for the disorder, some promising interventions appear to be useful in helping persons with autism lead more productive lives. The nature of autism renders family members and other stakeholders vulnerable to highly dubious etiological theories and intervention strategies, many of which can be characterized as pseudoscientific. We believe that parents and professionals alike would do well to adopt the position of caveat emptor, or "let the buyer beware," when considering novel treatments for autism. If something sounds too good to be true, it often is.

## NOTES

1. We use the term "autism" throughout this paper to refer not only to classic autistic disorder (American Psychiatric Association 1994), but in some cases to the full range of autistic-spectrum disorders. The vast majority of the research reviewed in this paper does not distinguish among the various subtypes of autistic-spectrum disorders. It is therefore often impossible to judge the degree to which research findings are unique to autistic disorder per se or are generalizable to other pervasive developmental disorders.

2. It is important to distinguish facilitated communication from methods of augmentative and alternative communication (AAC), in which disabled persons independently utilize various keyboard devices to communicate. In legitimate AAC, the individual uses the keyboard independently, and there are therefore no questions about the origins of the resulting communications (Jacobson et al. 1995).

# REFERENCES

Adams, L., and S. Conn. 1997. Nutrition and its relationship to autism. *Focus on Autism & Other Developmental Disabilities* 12: 53–58.

Allen, J., M. K. DeMeyer, J. A. Norton, W. Pontus, and E. Yang. 1971. Intellectuality in parents of psychotic, subnormal, and normal children. *Journal of Autism & Childhood Schizophrenia* 3: 311–26.

Aman, M. G., and K. S. Langworthy. 2000. Pharmacotherapy for hyperactivity in children with autism and other pervasive developmental disorders. *Journal of Autism and Developmental Disorders* 30: 451–59.

American Academy of Child and Adolescent Psychiatry. 1999. Practice parameters for the assessment and treatment of children, adolescents, and adults with autism and other pervasive developmental disorders. *Journal of the American Academy of Child and Adolescent Psychiatry* 38: 32–54.

American Academy of Pediatrics. 1998. Auditory integration training and facilitated communication for autism. American Academy of Pediatrics committee on children with disabilities. *Pediatrics* 102: 431–33.

American Psychiatric Association. 1994. *Diagnostic and statistical manual of mental disorders.* 4th ed. Washington, DC: American Psychiatric Association.

Anderson, L. T., M. Campbell, D. M. Grega, R. Perry, A. M. Small, and W. H. Green. 1984. Haloperidol in the treatment of infantile autism: Effects on learning and behavioral symptoms. *American Journal of Psychiatry* 141: 1195–1202.

Anderson, S. R., D. L. Avery, E. K. DiPietro, G. L. Edwards, and W. P. Christian. 1987. Intensive home-based early intervention with autistic children. *Education and Treatment of Children* 10: 352–66.

Ayres, A. J. 1979. *Sensory integration and the child.* Los Angeles, CA: Western Psychological Services.

Berand, G. 1993. *Hearing equals behavior.* New Canaan, CT: Keats.

Beratis, S. 1994. A psychodynamic model for understanding pervasive developmental disorders. *European Journal of Psychiatry* 8: 209–14.

Bettelheim, B. 1967. *The empty fortress.* New York: Free Press.

Bettison, S. 1996. The long-term effects of auditory training on children with autism. *Journal of Autism & Developmental Disorders* 26: 361–74.

Birnbrauer, J., and D. Leach. 1993. The Murdoch early intervention program after 2 years. *Behavior Change* 10: 63–74.

Bolman, W. M., and J. A. Richmond. 1999. A double-blind, placebo-controlled, crossover pilot trial of low dose dimethylglycine in patients with autistic disorder. *Journal of Autism and Developmental Disorders* 29: 191–94.

Brasic, J. R., J. Y. Barnett, D. Kaplan, B. B. Sheitman, P. Aisemberg, R. T. Lafargue, S. Kowalik, A. Clark, M. O. Tsaltas, and J. G. Young. 1994. Clomipramine ameliorates adventitious movements and compulsions in prepubertal boys with autistic disorder and severe mental retardation. *Neurology* 44: 1309–12.

Brodkin, E. S., C. J. McDouble, S. T. Naylor, D. J. Cohen, and L. H. Price. 1997. Clomipramine in adults with pervasive developmental disorders: A prospective open-label investigation. *Journal of Child and Adolescent Psychopharmacology* 7: 109–21. Bromfield, R. 2000. It's the tortoise's race: Long-term psychodynamic psychotherapy with a high-functioning autistic adolescent. *Psychoanalytic Inquiry* 20: 732–45.

Bryson, S. 1997. Epidemiology of autism: Overview and issues outstanding. In *Handbook of autism and pervasive developmental disorders.* 2nd ed. Edited by D. J. Cohen and F. R. Volkmar. New York: Wiley, pp. 41–46.

Bryson, S. E., B. S. Clark, and I. M. Smith. 1988. First report of a Canadian epidemiological study of autistic syndromes. *Journal of Child Psychology and Psychiatry* 29: 433–45.

Bunge, M. 1984. What is pseudoscience? *Skeptical Inquirer* 9: 36–46.

Burgess, C. A., I. Kirsch, H. Shane, K. L. Niederauer, S. M. Graham, and A. Bacon. 1998. Facilitated communication as an ideomotor response. *Psychological Science* 9: 71–74.

Campbell, M., J. L. Armenteros, R. P. Malone, P. B. Adams, Z. W. Eisenberg, and J. E. Overall. 1997. Neuroleptic-related dyskinesias in autistic children: A prospective, longitudinal study. *Journal of the American Academy of Child and Adolescent Psychiatry* 36: 835–43.

Campbell, M., E. Schopler, J. E. Cueva, and A. Hallin. 1996. Treatment of autistic disorder. *Journal of the American Academy of Child and Adolescent Psychiatry* 35: 134–43.

Case-Smith, J., and T. Bryan. 1999. The effects of occupational therapy with sensory integration emphasis on preschool-age children with autism. *American Journal of Occupational Therapy* 53: 489–97.

Chez, M. G., and C. P. Buchanan. 2000. Reply to B. Rimland's "Comments on 'Secretin and autism: A two-part clinical investigation.'" *Journal of Autism &Developmental Disorders* 30: 97–98.

Chez, M. G., C. P. Buchanan, B. T. Bagan, M. S. Hammer, K. S. McCarthy, I. Ovrutskaya, C. V. Nowinski, and Z. S. Cohen. 2000. Secretin and autism: A two-part clinical investigation. *Journal of Autism & Developmental Disorders* 30: 87–94.

Cook, E. H., R. Rowlett, C. Jaselskis, and B. L. Leventhal. 1992. Fluoxetine treatment of children and adults with autistic disorder and mental retardation. *Journal of the American Academy of Child and Adolescent Psychiatry* 31: 739–45.

Cooper, J. O., T. Heron, and W. Heward. 1989. *Applied behavior analysis.* Columbus, OH: Merrill.

Dales, L., S. J. Hammer, and N. J. Smith. 2001. Time trends in autism and in MMR immunization coverage in California. *Journal of the American Medical Association*285: 1183–85.

Darnton, N. 1990. Beno Brutalheim? *Newsweek* 111, no.11 (September 10): 59–60.

Dawson, G., and J. Osterling. 1997. Early intervention in autism: Effectiveness and common elements of current approaches. In *The Effectiveness of Early Intervention*, edited by M. Guralnick. Baltimore: Brookes, pp. 307–26.

Dawson, G., and R. Watling. 2000. Interventions to facilitate auditory, visual, and motor integration in autism: A review of the evidence. *Journal of Autism & Developmental Disorders* 30: 415–21.

DeLong, G. R., L. A. Teague, and M. M. Kamran. 1998. Effects of fluoxetine treatment in young children with idiopathic autism. *Developmental Medicine and Child Neurology* 40: 551–62.

Denson, J. F., G. A. Nuthall, J. Bushnell, and J. Horn. 1989. Effectiveness of a sensory integrative therapy program for children with perceptual-motor deficits. *Journal of Learning Disabilities* 22: 221–29.

Deutsch, R. M., and J. S. Morrill. 1993. *Realities of nutrition.* Palo Alto, CA: Bull Publishing.

Dunn-Geier, J., H. H. Ho, E. Auersperg, D. Doyle, L. Eaves, C. Matsuba, E. Orr-bine, B. Pham, and S. Whiting. 2000. Effect of secretin on children with autism: A randomized controlled trial. *Developmental Medicine & Child Neurology* 42: 796–802.

Edelson, S. M. 2001. Disappointed [letter to the editor]. *Priorities for Health* 13, no. 1: 4–6.

Edelson, S. M., D. Arin, M. Bauman, S. E. Lukas, J. H. Rudy, M. Sholar, and B. Rimland. 1999. Auditory integration training: A double-blind study of behavioral and electrophysiological effects in people with autism. *Focus on Autism and Other Developmental Disabilities* 14: 73–81.

Fatemi, S. H., G. M. Realmuto, L. Khan, and P. Thuras. 1998. Fluoxetine in treatment of adolescent patients with autism: A longitudinal open trial. *Journal of Autism & Developmental Disorders* 28: 303–307.

Fenske, E. C., S. Zalenski, P. J. Krantz, and E. McClannah. 1985. Age at intervention and treatment outcome for autistic children in a comprehensive intervention program. *Analysis and Intervention in Developmental Disablities* 5: 49–58.

Findling, R. L., K. Maxwell, L. Scotese-Wojtila, and Hui. 1997. High-dose pyridoxine and magnesium administration in children with autistic disorder: An absence of salutary effects in a double-blind, placebo-controlled study. *Journal of Autism & Developmental Disorders* 27: 467–78.

Folstein, S. E. 1999. Autism. *International Review of Psychiatry* 11: 269–78.

Fombonne, E. 1998. Epidemiology of autism and related conditions. In *Autism and pervasive developmental disorders,* edited by F. R. Volkmar. New York: Cambridge University Press, pp. 32–63.

Gardner, M. 2000. The brutality of Dr. Bettelheim. *Skeptical Inquirer* 24, no. 6: 12–14.

———. 2001. Facilitated communication: A cruel farce. *Skeptical Inquirer* 25: 17–19.

Gillberg, C. 1996. The psychopharmacology of autism and related disorders. *Journal of Psychopharmacology* 10: 54–63.

Gillberg, C., M. Johansson, S. Steffenburg, and O. Berlin. 1997. Auditory integration training in children with autism: Brief report of an open pilot study. *Autism* 1: 97–100.

Gordon, C. T., J. L. Rapoport, S. D. Hamburger, R. State, and G. B. Mannheim. 1992. Differential response of subjects with autistic disorder to clomipramine and sipramine. *American Journal of Psychiatry*. 363–66.

Gordon, C. T., R. C. State, J. E. Nelson, S. D. Hamburger, and J. L. Rapoport. 1993. A double-blind comparison of clomipramine, desipramine, and placebo in the treatment of autistic disorder. *Archives of General Psychiatry* 50: 441–47.

Gorman, B. J. 1999. Facilitated communication: Rejected in science, accepted in court—A case study and analysis of the use of FC evidence under Frye and Daubert. *Behavioral Sciences and the Law* 17: 517–41.

Green, D. 1994. Facilitated communication: Mental miracle or sleight of hand? *Skeptic* 2: 68–76.

———. 1996a. Evaluating claims about treatments for autism. In *Behavioral intervention for young children with autism manual for parents and professionals*, edited by C. Maurice, G. Green, and S. C. Luce. Austin, TX: PRO-ED, pp. 15–28.

———. 1996b. Early behavioral intervention for autism: What does research tell us? In *Behavioral intervention for young children with autism: A manual for parents and professionals*, edited by C. Maurice, G. Green, and S. Luce. Austin, TX: PRO-ED, pp. 29–44.

———. 2001. Autism and "voodoo science" treatments. *Priorities for Health* 13, no. 1: 27–32, 69.

Gresham, F. M., M. E. Beebe-Frankenberger, and L. MacMillan. 1999. A selective review of treatments for children with autism: Description and methodological considerations. *School Psychology Review* 28: 559–76.

Gresham, F. M., and D. L. MacMillan. 1998. Early intervention project: Can its claims be substantiated and its effects replicated? *Journal of Autism & Developmental Disorders* 28: 5–13.

Harris, S. L., J. S. Handleman, R. Gordon, B. Kristoff, and F. Fuentes. 1991. Changes in cognitive and language functioning of preschool children with autism. *Journal of Autism and Developmental Disorders* 21: 281–90.

Herbert, J. D., S. O. Lilienfeld, J. M. Lohr, R. W. Montgomery, W. T. O'Donohue, R. M. Rosen, and D. F. Tolin. 2000. Science and pseudoscience in the development of eye movement desensitization and reprocessing: Implications for clinical psychology. *Clinical Psychology Review* 20: 945–71.

Herbert, J. D., and I. R. Sharp. 2001. Pseudoscientific treatments for autism. *Priorities for Health* 13, no. 1: 23–26, 59.

Hoehn, T. P., and A. A. Baumesiter. 1994. A critique of the application of sensory integration therapy to children with learning disabilities. *Journal of Learning Disabilities* 27: 338–51.

Horvath, K., G. Stefanatos, K. N. Sokolski, R. Wachtel, L. Nabors, and J. T. Tildon. 1998. Improved social and language skills after secretin administration in patients with autistic spectrum disorders. *Journal of the Association for Academic Minority Physicians* 9: 9–15.

Hoyson, M., B. Jamieson, and P. S. Strain. 1984. Individualized group instruction of normally developing and autistic-like children: The LEAP curriculum model. *Journal of the Division of Early Childhood* 8: 157–72.

Iwasaki, K., and M. B. Holm. 1989. Sensory treatment for the reduction of stereotypic behaviors in persons with severe multiple disabilities. *Occupational Therapy Journal of Research* 9: 170–83.

Jacobson, J. W., J. A. Mulick, and G. Green. 1998. Cost-benefit estimates for early intensive behavioral intervention for young children with autism—General model and single state case. *Behavioral Interventions* 13: 201–26.

Jacobson, J. W., J. A. Mulick, and A. A. Schwartz. 1995. A history of facilitated communication: Science, pseudo-science, and antiscience: Science working group on facilitated communication. *American Psychologist* 50: 750–65.

Jenkins, J. R., R. R. Fewell, and S. R. Harris. 1984. Comparison of sensory integrative therapy and motor programming. *American Journal of Mental Deficiency* 88: 221–24.

Kanner, L. 1946. Autistic disturbances of affective contact. *American Journal of Psychiatry* 103: 242–46.

———. 1973. *Childhood psychosis: Initial studies and new insights.* Washington, DC: V. H. Winston & Sons.

Kaufman, B. N. 1976. *Son rise.* New York: Harper & Row.

Kaye, J. A., M. Melero-Montes, and H. Jick. 2001. Mumps, measles, and rubella vaccine and the incidence of autism recorded by general practitioners: A time trend analysis. *British Medical Journal* 322: 460–63.

King, B. H. 2000. Pharmacological treatment of mood disturbances, aggression, and self-injury in persons with pervasive developmental disorders. *Journal of Autism & Developmental Disorders* 30: 439–45.

Kirsch, I., and S. J. Lynn. 1999. Automaticity in clinical psychology. *American Psychologist* 54: 504–15.

Kvinsberg, A. M., K. L. Reichelt, M. Nodland, and T. Hoien. 1996. Autistic syndromes and diet: A follow-up study. *Scandinavian Journal of Educational Research* 39: 223–36.

Lilienfeld, S. O. 1998. Pseudoscience in contemporary clinical psychology: What it is and what we can do about it. *Clinical Psychologist* 51: 3–9.

Linderman, T. M., and K. B. Stewart. 1999. Sensory integrative-based occupational therapy and functional outcomes in young children with pervasive developmental disorders: A single-subject study. *American Journal of Occupational Therapy* 53: 207–13.

Locascio, J. J., R. P. Malone, A. M. Small, V. Kafantaris, M. Ernst, N. S. Lynch, J. E. Overall, and M. Campbell. 1991. Factors related to haloperidol response and dyskinesias in autistic children. *Psychopharmacology Bulletin* 27: 119–26.

Lovaas, O. I. 1981. *Teaching developmentally disabled children: The me book.* Austin, TX: PRO-ED.

———. 1987. Behavioral treatment and normal educational and intellectual functioning in young autistic children. *Journal of Consulting and Clinical Psychology* 55: 3–9.

Mahler, M. 1968. *On human symbiosis and the vicissitudes of individuation.* New York: International Universities Press.

Manning, A. 1999. Vaccine-autism link feared. *USA Today,* August 16.

Marrosu, F., G. Marrosu, M. G. Rachel, and G. Biggio. 1987. Paradoxical reactions elicited by diazepam in children with classic autism. *Functional Neurology* 3: 355–61.

Mason, S. M., and B. A. Iwata. 1991. Artifactual effects of sensory-integrative therapy on self-injurious behavior. *Journal of Applied Behavior Analysis* 23: 361–70.

McCormick, L. H. 1997. Treatment with buspirone in a patient with autism. *Archives of Family Medicine* 6: 368–70.

McDougle, C. J., J. P. Holmes, D. C. Carlson, G. Pelton, D. J. Cohen, and L. H. Price. 1998. A double-blind, placebo-controlled study of risperidone in adults with autistic disorder and other pervasive developmental disorders. *Archives of General Psychiatry* 55: 633–41.

McDougle, C. J., L. E. Kresch, and D. J. Posey. 2000. Repetitive thoughts and behavior in pervasive developmental disorders: Treatment with serotonin reuptake inhibitors. *Journal of Autism & Developmental Disorders* 30: 427–35.

McDougle, C. J., S. T. Naylor, D. J. Cohen, F. R. Volkmar, G. R. Heninger, and L. H. Price. 1996. A double-blind, placebo-controlled study of fluvoxamine in adults with autistic disorder. *Archives of General Psychiatry* 53: 1001–1008.

McEachlin, J., T. Smith, and O. I. Lovaas. 1993. Long-term outcome for children with autism who received early intensive behavioral treatment. *American Journal on Mental Retardation* 97: 359–72.

Mesibov, G. B. 1993. Treatment outcome is encouraging. *American Journal on Mental Retardation* 97: 379–80.

Mudford, O. C. 1995. Review of the gentle teaching data. *American Journal on Mental Retardation* 99: 345–55.

Mudford, O. C., B. A. Cross, S. Breen, C. Cullen, D. Reeves, J. Gould, and J. Douglas. 2000. Auditory integration training for children with autism: No behavioral benefits detected. *American Journal on Mental Retardation* 105: 118–29.

Mundy, P. 1993. Normal versus high-functioning status in children with autism. *American Journal on Mental Retardation* 97: 381–84.

New update. 1999. *Psychopharmacology Update* 10, no. 2 (August).

Owley, T., E. Steele, C. Corsello, S. Risi, K. McKaig, C. Lord, B. L. Leventhal, and E. H. Cook. 1999. A double-blind placebo-controlled trial of secretin for the treatment of autistic disorder. *Medscape General Medicine* 1. http://www.medscape.com/medscape/GeneralMedicine/jounia1/1999/vOl.n10/mgm1006 .owle/mgm1006.owle-01.html. Accessed December 6, 2001.

Ozonoff, S., and K. Cathcart. 1998. Effectiveness of a home program intervention for young children with autism. *Journal of Autism & Developmental Disorders* 28: 25–32.

Pollak, R. 1997. *Creation of Dr. Bettelheim: A biography of Bruno Bettelheim.* New York: Simon & Schuster.

Ratey, J. J., E. Mikkelsen, and H. E. Chmielinski. 1989. Buspirone therapy for maladaptive behaviors and anxiety in developmentally disabled persons. *Journal of Clinical Psychiatry* 50: 382–84.

Realmuto, G. M., G. J. August, and B. D. Garfinkel. 1989. Clinical effect of buspirone in autistic children. *Journal of Clinical Psychopharmacology* 9: 122–25.

Reilly, C., D. L. Nelson, and A. C. Bundy. 1984. Sensorimotor versus fine motor activities in eliciting vocalizations in autistic children. *Occupational Therapy Journal of Research* 3: 199–212.

Rimland, B. 1988. Candida-caused autism? *Autism Research Review International Newsletter.* http://www.autism.com/ari/editorials/candida.html. Accessed December 6, 2001.

———. 1996. Dimethylglycine (DMG), a nontoxic metabolite, and autism. *Autism Research Review International.* http://www.autism.com/ari/ editorials/dmgl.html. Accessed December 6, 2001.

———. 1999. The use of secretin in autism: Some preliminary answers. *Autism Research Review International Newsletter.* http://www.autism.com/ari/ editorials/findings.html. Accessed December 6, 2001.

———. 2000. Do children's shots invite autism? *Los Angeles Times,* April 26.

Rimland, B., and S. M. Edelson. 1994. The effects of auditory integration training on autism. *American Journal Speech-Language Pathology* 5: 16–24.

———. 1995. Auditory integration training in autism: A pilot study. *Journal of Autism & Developmental Disorders* 25: 61–70.

Rodier, P. M. 2000. The early origins of autism. *Scientific American* 282: 56–63.

Rogers, S. J. 1998. Empirically supported comprehensive treatments for young children with autism. *Journal of Clinical Child Psychology* 27: 168–79.

Rogers, S. J., and D. DiLalla. 1991. A comparative study of developmentally based preschool curriculum on young children with autism and young children with other disorders of behavior and development. *Topics in Early Childhood Special Education* 11: 29–48.

Rogers, S. J., J. Herbison, H. Lewis, J. Pantone, and K. Reis. 1986. An approach for enhancing the symbolic, communicative, and interpersonal functioning of young children with autism and severe emotional handicaps. *Journal of the Division of Early Childhood* 10: 135–48.

Rogers, S. J., and H. Lewis. 1989. An effective day treatment model for young children with pervasive developmental disorders. *Journal of the American Academy of Child Adolescent Psychiatry* 28: 207–14.

Rogers, S. J., H. C. Lewis, and K. Reis. 1987. An effective procedure for training early special education teams to implement a model program. *Journal of the Division of Early Childhood* 11: 180–88.

Roser, K. 1996. A review of psychoanalytic theory and treatment of childhood autism. *Psychoanalytic Review* 83: 325–41.

Sanchez, L. E., M. Campbell, A. M. Small, J. E. Cueva, J. L. Armenteros, and P. B. Adams. 1996. A pilot study of clomipramine in young autistic children. *Journal of the American Academy of Child and Adolescent Psychiatry* 35: 537–44.

Sandler, A. D., K. A. Sutton, J. DeWeese, M. Girardi, V. Sheppard, and J. W. Bodfish. 1999. Lack of benefit of a single dose of synthetic human secretin in the treat of autism and pervasive developmental disorder. *New England Journal of Medicine* 341: 1801–1806.

Schopler, E., G. B. Mesibov, and A. Baker. 1982. Evaluation of treatment for autistic children and their parents. *Journal of the American Academy of Child Psychiatry* 21: 262–67.

Schopler, E., and R. J. Reichler. 1971. Parents as cotherapists in the treatment of psychotic children. *Journal of Autism and Childhood Schizophrenia* 1: 87–102.

Schopler, E., R. J. Reichler, A. Bashford, M. D. Lansing, and L. M. Marcus. 1990. *Individualized assessment and treatment for autistic and developmentally disabled children (Vol. 1): Psychoeducational profile revised.* Austin, TX: PRO-ED.

Schopler, E., A. Short, and G. Mesibov. 1989. Relation of behavioral treatment to "normal functioning": Comments on Lovaas. *Journal of Consulting and Clinical Psychology* 57: 162–64.

Schreibman, L. 2000. Intensive behavioral/psychoeducational treatments for autism: Research needs and future directions. *Journal of Autism & Developmental Disorders* 30: 373–78.

Sheinkopf, S., and B. Siegel. 1998. Home-based behavioral treatment of young children with autism. *Journal of Autism & Developmental Disorders* 28: 15–23.

Shermer, M. 1997. *Why people believe weird things: Pseudoscience, superstition, and other confusions of our time.* New York: W. H. Freeman.

Siegel, B. 1996. *The world of the autistic child: Understanding and treating autistic spectrum disorders.* New York: Oxford University Press.

Smith, T. 1996. Are other treatments effective? In *Behavioral intervention for young children with autism: A manual for parents and professionals,* edited by C. Maurice, G. Green, and S. C. Luce. Austin, TX: PRO-ED, pp. 45–59.

Steffenburg, S., and C. Gillberg. 1986. Autism and autistic-like conditions in Swedish rural and urban areas: A population study. *British Journal of Psychiatry* 149: 81–87.

Stehli, A. 1991. *The sound of a miracle: A child's triumph over autism*. New York: Doubleday.

Stratton, K., A. Gable, P. Shetty, and M. McCormick, eds. 2001. *Immunization safety review: Measles-mumpsrubella vaccine and autism*. Washington, DC: National Academy Press.

Stromland, K., V. Nordin, M. Miller, B. Akerstrom, and C. Gillberg. 1994. Autism in thalidomide embryopathy: A population study. *Developmental Medicine and Child Neurology* 36: 351–56.

Sugiyama, T., and T. Abe. 1989. The prevalence of autism in Nagoya, Japan: A total population study. *Journal of Autism & Developmental Disorders* 19: 87–96.

Tolbert, L. C., T. Haigler, M. M. Waits, and T. Dennis. 1993. Brief report: Lack of response in an autistic population to a low dose clinical trial of pyridoxine plus magnesium. *Journal of Autism & Developmental Disorders* 23: 193–99.

Trottier, G., L. Srivastava, and C. D. Walker. 1999. Etiology of infantile autism: A review of recent advancements in genetic and neurobiological research. *Journal of Psychiatry & Neuroscience* 24: 103–15.

Tustin, F. 1981. *Autistic states in children*. Boston: Routledge.

Volkmar, F. R., P. Szatmari, and S. S. Sparrow. 1993. Sex differences in pervasive developmental disorders. *Journal of Autism & Developmental Disorders* 23: 579–91.

Wakefield, A. J., S. H. Murch, A. Anthony, J. Linnell, D. M. Casson, M. Malik, M. Berelowitz, A. P. Dhillon, M. A. Thomson, P. Harvey, A. Valentine, S. E. Davies, and J. A. Walker-Smith. 1998. Ileal-lymphoid-nodular hyperplasia, non-specific colitis, and pervasive developmental disorder in children. *Lancet* 351: 637–41.

Welch, M. G. 1988. *Holding time: How to eliminate conflict, temper tantrums, and sibling rivalry and raise happy, loving, successful children*. New York: Simon & Schuster.

Wheeler, D. L., J. W. Jacobson, R. A. Paglieri, and A. A. Schwartz. 1993. An experimental assessment of facilitated communication. *Mental Retardation* 31: 49–59.

Whiteley, P., J. Rodgers, D. Savery, and P. Shattock. 1999. A gluten-free diet as an intervention for autism and associated spectrum disorders: Preliminary findings. *Autism* 3: 45–65.

Zollweg, W., D. Palm, and V. Vance. 1997. The efficacy of auditory integration training: A double blind study. *American Journal of Audiology* 6: 39–47.

Editors' Note: For a good update on the autism-vaccine controversy, see Roy Richard Grinker's *Unstrange Minds: Remapping the World of Autism* (New York: Basic Books, 2007).

## 11.

# RESILIENCE IN THE FACE OF POTENTIAL TRAUMA

### George A. Bonanno
Teachers College, Columbia University

Life is filled with peril. During the normal course of their lives, most adults face one or more potentially traumatic events (e.g., violent or life-threatening occurrences or the death of close friends or relatives). Following such events, many people find it difficult to concentrate; they may feel anxious, confused, and depressed; and they may not eat or sleep properly. Some people have such strong and enduring reactions that they are unable to function normally for years afterward. It should come as no surprise that these dramatic reactions have dominated the literatures on loss and trauma. Until recently, the opposite reaction—the maintenance of a relative stable trajectory of healthy functioning following exposure to a potential trauma—has received scant attention. When theorists have considered such a pattern, they have typically viewed it either as an aberration resulting from extreme denial or as a sign of exceptional emotional strength (e.g., McFarlane & Yehuda 1996).

Reprinted with permission from *Current Directions in Psychological Science* 14, no. 3 (June 2005): 135–38.

# RESILIENCE (NOT RECOVERY) IS THE MOST COMMON RESPONSE TO POTENTIAL TRAUMA

Over a decade ago, my colleagues and I began an ongoing investigation of this supposedly rare response and the means by which people might achieve such presumably superficial (or exemplary) functioning in the aftermath of a potentially traumatic event. The results of our research have consistently challenged the prevailing view on the subject. We took as our starting point the burgeoning developmental literature on resilience. Developmental researchers and theorists had for several decades highlighted various protective factors (e.g., ego-resiliency, the presence of supportive relationships) that promote healthy trajectories among children exposed to unfavorable life circumstances such as poverty (e.g., Garmezy 1991; Rutter 1987). We sought to adapt this body of research to the study of resilient outcomes among adults in otherwise normal circumstances who are exposed to isolated and potentially highly disruptive events.

Our research led to three primary conclusions, each mirroring but also extending the insights gained from developmental research. First, resilience following potentially traumatic events represents a distinct outcome trajectory from that typically associated with recovery from trauma. Historically, there have been few attempts to distinguish subgroups within the broad category of individuals exposed to potential trauma who do not develop post-traumatic stress disorder (PTSD). When resilience had been considered, it was often in terms of factors that "favor a path to recovery" (McFarlane & Yehuda 1996, 158). However, studies have now demonstrated that resilience and recovery are discrete and empirically separable outcome trajectories following a dramatic event such as the death of a spouse (e.g., Bonanno et al. 2002) or direct exposure to terrorist attack (e.g., Bonanno, Rennicke & Dekel 2005). The figure opposite depicts the prototypical resilience and recovery trajectories, as well as trajectories representing chronic and delayed symptom elevations (discussed later).

In this framework, recovery is defined by moderate to severe initial

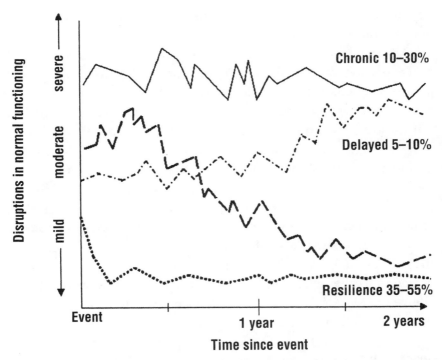

elevations in psychological symptoms that significantly disrupt normal functioning and that decline only gradually over the course of many months before returning to pre-trauma levels. In contrast, resilience is characterized by relatively mild and short-lived disruptions and a stable trajectory of healthy functioning across time. A key point is that even though resilient individuals may experience an initial, brief spike in distress (Bonanno, Moskowitz, Papa & Folkman 2005) or may struggle for a short period to maintain psychological equilibrium (e.g., several weeks of sporadic difficulty concentrating, intermittent sleeplessness, or daily variability in levels of well-being; Bisconti et al. 2006), they nonetheless manage to keep functioning effectively at or near their normal levels. For example, resilience has been linked to the continued fulfillment of personal and social responsibilities and the capacity for positive emotions and generative experiences (e.g., engaging in new creative activities or new relationships), both immediately and in the months following exposure to a potentially traumatic event (Bonanno & Keltner 1997;

Bonanno, Wortman, et al. 2002; Bonanno, Rennicke & Dekel 2005; Fredrickson et al. 2003).

A second conclusion that emerges from our research is that resilience is typically the most common outcome following exposure to a potentially traumatic event. It has been widely assumed in the literature that the most common response to such an occurrence is an initial but sizeable elevation in trauma symptoms followed by gradual resolution and recovery (McFarlane & Yehuda 1996). However, although symptom levels tend to vary for different potentially traumatic events, resilience has consistently emerged as the most common outcome trajectory. In one study, for example, over half of the people in a sample of middle-aged individuals who had lost their spouses showed a stable, low level of symptoms; and stable low symptoms were observed in more than a third of a group of gay men who were bereaved after providing care for a partner dying of AIDS, a considerably more stressful context (Bonanno, Moskowitz, et al. 2005). Resilience was also readily observed in a random phone-dialing survey of Manhattan residents following the September 11 terrorist attack (Bonanno, Galea, Bucciarelli & Vlahov 2005). Following conventions established in the study of subthreshold depression, we defined a mild to moderate trauma reaction as two or more PTSD symptoms and resilience as one or no PTSD symptoms in the first six months following the attack. Over 65 percent in the New York metropolitan area were resilient. Among people with more concentrated exposure (e.g., those who had either witnessed the attack in person or who were in the World Trade Center during the attack), the proportion showing resilience was still over 50 percent. Finally, even among people who were physically injured in the attack, a group for whom the estimated proportion of PTSD was extremely high (26.1 percent), one third (32.8 percent) of the individuals were resilient.

In establishing the validity of the resilient trajectory, it is imperative to distinguish stable, healthy functioning from denial or other forms of superficial adjustment. To this end, several studies have now documented links between resilience and generally high functioning prior to a potentially traumatic event (Bonanno, Wortman, et al. 2002; Bonanno,

Moskowitz, et al. 2005). Several studies have also documented resilient outcomes using relatively objective measures that go beyond participant self-report, including structured clinical interviews and anonymous ratings of functioning from participants' friends or relatives (e.g., Bonanno, Rennicke & Dekel 2005; Bonanno, Moskowitz, et al. 2005). For example, we (Bonanno, Rennicke & Dekel 2005) recruited the friends and relatives of high-exposure survivors of the World Trade Center terrorist attack and asked them to assign the survivors to either the resilience trajectory or one of the other outcome trajectories depicted in the graph on page 241. The assignments of friends and relatives closely matched the survivors' actual symptom levels over time, and thus provided important validation for the resilience trajectory.

## THE HETEROGENEITY OF RESILIENCE: FLEXIBLE AND PRAGMATIC COPING

A third conclusion to emerge from our research, again extending the conclusions of developmental researchers, is that there are multiple and sometimes unexpected factors that might promote a resilient outcome. At the most general level, many of the same characteristics that promote healthy development should also foster adult resilience. These would include both situational factors, such as supportive relationships, and individual factors, such as the capacity to adapt flexibly to challenges (Block & Block 1980). The capacity for adaptive flexibility was mirrored in a recent study associating resilience among New York City college students in the aftermath of September 11 with flexibility in emotion regulation, defined as the ability to effectively enhance or suppress emotional expression when instructed to do so (Bonanno, Papa, LaLande, Westphal & Coffman 2004).

In addition to these general health-promoting factors, however, our research also underscores a crucial point of departure from the developmental literature. Childhood resilience is typically understood in response to corrosive environments, such as poverty or enduring abuse.

By contrast, adult resilience is more often a matter of coping with an iso-lated and usually (but not always) brief potentially traumatic event. The key point is that whereas corrosive environments require longer-term adaptive solutions, isolated events often oblige a more pragmatic form of coping, a "whatever it takes" approach, which may involve behaviors and strategies that are less effective or even maladaptive in other con-texts. For instance, considerable research attests to the health benefits of expressing negative emotions. Although most resilient bereaved individ-uals express at least some negative emotion while talking about their loss, they nonetheless express relatively less negative emotion and greater positive emotion than other bereaved individuals (e.g., Bonanno & Keltner 1997), thereby minimizing the impact of the loss while "increasing continued contact with and support from important people in the social environment".

Another example of pragmatic coping is illustrated by trait self-enhancement, the tendency toward self-serving biases in perception and attribution (e.g., overestimating one's own positive qualities). People given to self-serving biases tend to be narcissistic and to evoke negative reactions in other people. However, they also have high self-esteem and cope well with isolated potential traumas. Our research team examined self-enhancement among people dealing with two powerful stressor events, the premature death of a spouse and exposure to urban combat during the recent civil war in Bosnia (Bonanno, Field, Kovacevic & Kaltman 2002). In both samples, trait self-enhancement was positively associated with ratings of functioning made by mental health experts. In the bereavement study, however, untrained observers rated self-enhancers relatively unfavorably (lower on positive traits, e.g., honest; and higher on negative traits, e.g., self-centered). Yet these negative impressions did not appear to interfere with self-enhancers' ability to maintain a high level of functioning after the loss.

This same pattern of findings was observed among high-exposure survivors of the September 11 attack (Bonanno, Rennicke & Dekel 2005). Trait self-enhancement was more prevalent among individuals exhibiting the resilient trajectory, whether established by self-reported symptoms or ratings from friends or relatives. Self-enhancers also had greater positive affect and were rated by their friends and relatives as having consistently higher levels of mental and physical health, goal accomplishment, and coping ability. However, self-enhancers' friends and relatives also rated them as decreasing in social adjustment over the eighteen months after September 11 and, among those with the highest levels of exposure, as less honest. This mixed pattern of findings suggests again that self-enhancers are able to maintain generally high levels of functioning in most areas except their social relations. Interestingly, however, self-enhancers themselves perceived their social relationships in relatively more positive terms than other participants, and this factor fully mediated their low levels of PTSD symptoms. In other words, self-enhancers appear to be blissfully unaware of the critical reactions they can evoke in others, and this type of self-serving bias evidently plays a crucial role in their ability to maintain stable levels of healthy functioning in other areas following a potentially traumatic event.

## DIRECTIONS FOR FUTURE RESEARCH

The study of adult resilience is nascent and there are myriad questions for future research. An obvious imperative is to learn how the various costs and benefits of resilience vary across different types and durations of potentially traumatic events. Is there a point, for example, when the long-term costs of a particular type of coping might outweigh whatever crucial short-term advantages it provides? Might such trade-offs vary by gender or culture? Western, independence-oriented societies, for example, tend to focus more heavily than collectivist societies on the personal experience of trauma. However, little is known about the extent that loss and trauma reactions vary across cultures. A recent comparative study showed that bereaved people in China recovered more quickly from loss than did bereaved Americans (Bonanno, Papa, et al. 2005). However, as is typical of Chinese culture, Chinese bereaved also reported more physical symptoms than Americans. These data raise the intriguing questions of whether resilience has different meanings in different cultural contexts and, perhaps even more important, whether different cultures may learn from each other about effective and not-so-effective ways of coping with extreme adversity.

These questions, in turn, raise multiple practical and philosophical uncertainties about whether resilience can or should be learned. On the one hand, the observed link between resilient outcomes and personality variables suggests that resilient traits may be relatively fixed and not easily inculcated in others. And given the social costs associated with some of the traits found in resilient people (e.g., self-enhancement), the advantage of simply imitating resilient individuals is questionable. On the other hand, a more promising avenue for training people to cope resiliently with trauma is suggested by the evidence linking resilience to flexible adaptation (Block & Block 1980; Bonanno et al. 2004). Because adaptive flexibility can be manipulated experimentally (e.g., people's ability to engage in various cognitive or emotional processes can be measured under different stressor conditions; Bonanno et al. 2004), it should be possible to systematically examine the stability of such a trait over time and the conditions under which it might be learned or enhanced.

A related question pertains to how resilient individuals might view their own effectiveness at coping with potential trauma. Although at least some resilient individuals are surprised at how well they cope (Bonanno, Wortman, et al. 2002), it seems likely that others (e.g., self-enhancers) might overestimate their own resilience. This issue is particularly intriguing in relation to the distinction between stable resilience and delayed reactions. Although delayed reactions are not typically observed during bereavement (e.g., Bonanno, Wortman, et al. 2002), a small subset of individuals exposed to potentially traumatic events (5–10 percent) typically exhibit delayed PTSD. Preliminary evidence indicates that delayed-PTSD responders have higher initial symptom levels than do resilient individuals (e.g., Bonanno, Rennicke & Dekel 2005). Further evidence of this distinction would hold potentially important diagnostic implications for early intervention.

Finally, another question pertains to how resilient individuals experience the crucial early weeks after an extreme stressor event. A recent study by Bisconti, Bergeman, and Boker (2006) shed some welcome light on this issue by examining daily well-being ratings in the early months after the death of a spouse. Although resilient bereaved typically show only mild and relatively short-lived overall decreases in well-being, examination of their daily ratings indicated marked variability across the first three weeks and then a more stable but still variable period that endured through the second month of bereavement. Perhaps similar research using larger samples and Internet methods might illuminate how resilient individuals manage to continue functioning and meeting the ongoing demands of their lives while nonetheless struggling, at least for a short period, to maintain self-regulatory equilibrium.

*Acknowledgments*—This research was supported by grants from the National Institutes of Health (R29-MH57274) and the National Science Foundation (BCS-0202772 and BCS-0337643).

# REFERENCES

Bisconti, T. L., C. S. Bergeman, and S. M. Boker. In press. Social support as a predictor of variability: An examination of recent widows' adjustment trajectories. *Psychology and Aging*.

Block, J. H., and J. Block. 1980. The role of ego-control and ego-resiliency in the organization of behavior. In *Development of cognition, Affect, and Social Relations*, edited by W. A. Collins. Hillsdale, NJ: Erlbaum.

Bonanno, G.A., N. P. Field, A. Kovacevic, and S. Kaltman. 2002. Self-enhancement as a buffer against extreme adversity: Civil war in Bosnia and traumatic loss in the United States. *Personality and Social Psychology Bulletin* 28: 184–96.

Bonanno, G. A., S. Galea, A. Bucciarelli, and D. Vlahov. 2005. Psychological resilience after disaster: New York City in the aftermath of the September 11th terrorist attack. Manuscript submitted for publication.

Bonanno, G. A., and D. Keltner. 1997. Facial expressions of emotion and the course of conjugal bereavement. *Journal of Abnormal Psychology* 106: 126–37.

Bonanno, G. A., J. T. Moskowitz, A. Papa, and S. Folkman. 2005. Resilience to loss in bereaved spouses, bereaved parents, and bereaved gay men. *Journal of Personality and Social Psychology* 88: 827–43.

Bonanno, G. A., A. Papa, K. Lalande, Z. Nanping, and J. G. Noll. 2005. Grief processing and deliberate grief avoidance: A prospective comparison of bereaved spouses and parents in the United States and China. *Journal of Consulting and Clinical Psychology* 73: 86–98.

Bonanno, G. A., A. Papa, K. LaLande, M. Westphal, and K. Coffman. 2004. The importance of being flexible: The ability to both enhance and suppress emotional expression predicts long-term adjustment. *Psychological Science* 15: 482–87.

Bonanno, G. A., C. Rennicke, and S. Dekel. In press. Self-enhancement among high-exposure survivors of the September 11th terrorist attack: Resilience or social maladjustment? *Journal of Personality and Social Psychology.*

Bonanno, G. A., C. B. Wortman, D. R. Lehman, R. G. Tweed, M. Haring, J. Sonnega, D. Carr, and R. M. Neese. 2002. Resilience to loss and chronic grief: A prospective study from pre-loss to 18 months post-loss. *Journal of Personality and Social Psychology* 83: 1150–64.

Fredrickson, B. L., M. M. Tugade, C. E. Waugh, and G. R. Larkin. 2003. What good are positive emotions in crisis? A prospective study of resilience and emotion following the terrorist attacks on the United States on September 11th, 2001. *Journal of Personality and Social Psychology* 84: 365–76.

Garmezy, N. 1991. Resilience and vulnerability to adverse developmental outcomes associated with poverty. *American Behavioral Scientist* 34: 416–30.

McFarlane, A. C., and R. Yehuda. 1996. Resilience, vulnerability, and the course of post-traumatic reactions. In *Traumatic stress,* ed. B. A. van der Kolk, A. C. McFarlane, and L. Weisaeth. New York: Guilford, pp. 155–81.

Rutter, M. 1987. Psychosocial resilience and protective mechanisms. *American Journal of Orthopsychiatry* 57: 316–31.

## 12.

# MULTIPLE PERSONALITY DISORDER: WITCHCRAFT SURVIVES IN THE TWENTIETH CENTURY

### August Piper Jr.

*Any people, given over to the power of contagious passion, may be swept by desolation, and plunged into ruin.*
—Charles W. Upham, 1867

An epidemic of psychiatric illness is sweeping through North America. Before 1980, a total of no more than about two hundred cases had ever been found in the entire world, throughout the entire recorded history of psychiatry. Yet today, some proponents of the condition claim that it afflicts at least a tenth of all Americans, and perhaps 30 percent of poor people—more than twenty-six million individuals. An industry involving significant sums of money, many specialty hospitals, and numerous self-described experts has rapidly grown up around the disorder.

The illness is multiple personality disorder (MPD), a condition that has always attracted a few wisps of controversy. Lately, these wisps have coalesced into clouds that, in drenching rainbursts, pour criticism on the disorder. An examination of the flawed reasoning, unsound claims, and logical inconsistencies of the MPD literature shows that well-founded concerns drive this storm of criticism.

Reprinted with permission from *Skeptical Inquirer* (May/June 1998): 44–50.

## WHAT IS MPD?

MPD is classified as a dissociative disorder. The term *dissociation* refers to disruption in one or more mental operations that constitute the central idea of "consciousness": forming and holding memories, assimilating sensory impressions and making sense of them, and maintaining a sense of one's own identity (American Psychiatric Association 1994, 477). The essence of dissociation is that material not in awareness influences behavior, mood, and thought (Spiegel & Schleflin 1994). Thus, the behavioral disturbances prominently manifested in dissociative disorders are considered to be unconscious: that is, resulting from forces beyond the patient's awareness, beyond voluntary control.

The king of dissociative disorders is MPD,[1] also called dissociative identity disorder. Afflicted people episodically fail to recall vital data about themselves, but what distinguishes MPD from all other psychiatric conditions is the putative cause for these memory failures. The condition's proponents claim the memory failures occur because patients are periodically taken over by one or more "alter personalities" (variously referred to as "identities," "ego states," "alters," or "personality states"). These guest personalities, submerged since being formed during childhood—more on this later—rise to the surface and impose their own memories, thoughts, and behaviors on patients.

The essential feature of MPD, it is said, is that an individual's behavior is controlled by two or more alters (Putnam et al. 1990); the separate identities are assumed involuntarily (Sarbin 1995; Watkins & Watkins 1984). One personality may feel "carried along in a panicked helpless state" as another endangers it or engages in behavior repugnant to it (Kluft 1983, 75). Patients are said to experience a sense of being made to misbehave or hurt themselves (Putnam 1991). Some theorists even claim the existence of "omnipotent alters," which can simply compel patients to do their bidding (Lewis & Bard 1991). As an example, C. A. Ross writes of alters that "force [the patient] to jump in front of a truck. [The alters] then go back inside just before impact, leaving the [patient] to experience the pain" (Ross 1989, 115).

The image of all this is of an invading army usurping a government, an operator taking control of a machine, or a parasite attacking another organism. For example, contributors to the MPD literature frequently make statements such as, "If [the patient] drops her guard, the alters take over" (Bliss 1980, 1393). Proponents describe the original personality as the "host"—again recalling notions of a parasite—and describe the change from host to alter, or from one alter to another, as "switching." Thus, a librarian may one minute be her forty-two-year-old true shy self, but behave in the next like a nine-year-old child; a deep-voiced, foul-mouthed logger; or a promiscuous woman who picks up men in bars (Putnam 1989, 111, 119–20).

These guest personalities, or "alters," are believed to have many truly remarkable capabilities and qualities. Some have the task of reproducing—of creating new alters. Others, it is claimed, determine which alter will take control of the body at any particular time (Kluft 1995, 364). There are alters of people of the opposite sex, of the treating therapist, of infants, television characters, and demons. Alters of Satan and God, of dogs, cats, lobsters, and stuffed animals—even of people thousands of years old or from another dimension—have been reported by MPD proponents *(Fifth Estate* 1993; Ganaway 1989; Hendrickson et al. 1990; Kluft 1991b, 166; Kluft 1995, 366; Ross 1989, 112; Ross et al. 1989).

MPD proponents assert that all manner of activities—creating a work of art, driving a car, fighting, doing schoolwork, engaging in prostitution, cleaning a bathtub, or even baking chocolate-chip cookies—are performed by alters (Braun 1988; Putnam 1989, 104; Ross 1989, 112).

Alters are often wily, secretive, and elusive. For instance, R. P. Kluft (1991a) says he has identified guest personalities whose role is to deny that the patient has MPD, thus obscuring the diagnosis. Personalities are also said to try to trick therapists by hiding and impersonating each other (Putnam 1989, 113). They are said to be plastic: "Alter A may be somewhat different when it has been preceded by alter B than when it follows alter C" (Kluft 1988, 49). They are said to multiply: each alter can undergo a cascade of splits, resulting in what is called "polyfragmented"

MPD (*Frontline* 1995; Ross 1994, 60). Or the opposite may occur: during therapy, several alters may coalesce into a kind of "superalter" (Kluft 1988). It is even claimed that they can permanently stop growing at some time or temporarily stop aging by going into "inner hibernation" and then emerging to resume growing older (Ross 1989, 112). Cases reported in the last few years have shown a median number of two alters at the time of diagnosis; however, during treatment, a further six or twelve usually appear (Putnam et al. 1986; Ross et al. 1989). Sometimes many more are found: as many as one quarter of cases have twenty-six or more alters (Kluft 1988). And the longer patients remain in treatment, the more guest personalities are discovered (ibid.; Kluft 1989): "It is the rule rather than the exception for previously unknown personalities to enter the treatment" (Kluft 1988, 54). Patients with three hundred and forty-five hundred personalities have now been reported (Kluft 1988; Ross 1989, 121; Ross et al. 1989). Kluft has been consulted "several times" on cases where therapists claim—wrongly, Kluft says—to have counted "upward of 10,000 alters" (Kluft 1995, 363).

Why this nearly endless flowering of personalities? According to MPD proponents, it occurs because each trauma or major life change experienced by an MPD patient causes some or all of the alters to be created anew (Kluft 1988).

## WHAT CAUSES MPD?

According to proponents, extraordinary childhood traumas—usually sexual or other abuse by adults—lead to MPD.

The theory is as follows. Because the child cannot physically escape the pain, its only option is to escape mentally: by dissociating. Dissociation is said to defend against pain by allowing the maltreatment to be experienced as if it were happening to someone else (Atchison & McFarlane 1994; Braun 1989; Kluft 1985a; Kluft 1987; Ross 1995). The distress of this childhood maltreatment is also endured by employing *repression*, a mental mechanism that supposedly allows the child to forget that the abuse happened at all (Lynn & Nash 1994): "Now, not only is the abuse not happening to me, [but] I don't even remember it" (Ross 1995, 67).

Eventually, MPD proponents claim, these defenses begin to be over-used—that is, enlisted more and more to cope with commonplace, everyday stressors (Braun 1986, 66; Putnam 1991). The abuse victim's "dissociated internal structures are slowly crystallized" until they become personalities (Atchison & McFarlane 1994; Putnam 1989, 53–54; Ross 1995a, 67). As mentioned earlier, this alter-building process is supposed to occur almost exclusively in early childhood (Greaves 1980; Vincent & Pickering 1988).

## WHAT'S WRONG HERE?

So stands the tottering house of MPD theory. Its foundation crumbles and termites gnaw; the storm beats upon it.

The house suffers from at least four serious ailments.

The first: What, exactly, is an "alter personality"?

One might believe that the disorder's proponents would long ago have taken the elementary step of answering this fundamental question. Such a belief would be mistaken. The MPD literature contains not one single plain, understandable definition that would allow an alter to be recognized if it were encountered on the street, in a person one has known intimately for years, or even in oneself.

The vagueness and imprecision of the alter concept are shown by the frequency with which even MPD experts contradict each other on the fundamental attributes of these entities. As an example, Ross (1990) says patients' minds are no more host to many distinct personalities than their bodies are to different people; another theorist believes that alter personalities are imaginary constructs (Bliss 1984). But in contradiction, *DSM-IV* and the writings of several MPD theorists repeatedly stress that alters are well developed, distinct from one another, complex, and well integrated (Kluft 1984b; Kluft 1987; Taylor & Martin 1944). Also, MPD-focused practitioners routinely report patients who have dozens or hundreds of personalities—yet Spiegel (1995) has recently claimed that because MPD patients cannot integrate various emotions and memories, such patients actually have less than one personality, not more than one.

Contradictions abound elsewhere, too. On the one hand, Bliss (1984) believes personalities have specific and limited functions and possess only a narrow range of moods. But on the other, Braun (1984) and other proponents (Putnam 1989, 104; Ross 1989, 81) say that *fragments* do not have a wide range of mood or affect. One proponent states that *fragments* "carry out a limited task in the person's life" (Ross 1989, 81) but then later in the same publication (111–18) argues that *personalities* may perform only one specific function, represent only a single mood or memory or exhibit only a narrow range of skills.

This failure to rigorously define the concept of a guest personality leads to all manner of excesses. For example, MPD proponents discover MPD in people whose close relatives, and others who have known those people for years, have never once seen any evidence of alters (Ganaway 1995). Kluft (1985b), for instance, diagnosed the disorder in a series of people—even though he himself acknowledged that almost half of them showed "no overt signs" of MPD. These proponents also find MPD even in people who lack any knowledge whatever of having the condition (Bliss 1980; Bliss 1984; Kluft 1985b), and at least one enthusiast recommends that people be treated for MPD even if they claim not to have the disorder (Putnam 1989, 139, 215).

The imprecision of the alter concept allows MPD adherents to claim that scores of patient behaviors should signal the possible presence of guest personalities. Thus, adherents claim that the following behaviors—and many others—are important diagnostic clues for MPD: glancing around the therapist's office; frequently blinking one's eyes; changing posture, or the voice's pitch or volume; rolling the eyes upward; laughing or showing anger suddenly; covering the mouth; allowing the hair to fall over one's face; developing a headache; scratching an itch; touching the face, or the chair in which one sits; changing hairstyles between sessions; or wearing a particular color of clothing or item of jewelry (Franklin 1990; Loewenstein 1991; Putnam

1989, 118–23; Ross 1989, 232). In one case known to the author, a leading MPD proponent claimed that the diagnosis was supported by behavior no more remarkable than the fact that the patient changed clothes several times daily and liked to wear sunglasses.

These beliefs about personalities raise some difficult questions that MPD enthusiasts fail to answer. First, how does alter-induced behavior differ from behavior people show every day—say, when they are angry or happy (Piper 1994a)? Do indwelling alters or fragments cause all feelings? If not, how does one determine which emotions result from the activities of alters, which from those of fragments, and which from neither? One proponent acknowledges the difficulty posed by these questions: he says alters may be indistinguishable from the original personality (Kluft 1991b).

Second, how do persons claiming they are overpowered by "irresistible alters" differ from those who attempt to avoid legal sanctions by claiming that, when they committed crimes, they couldn't control their behavior (Piper 1994c)?

Finally, one wonders how seriously to take MPD enthusiasts' claims that they can accurately keep track of fifteen or thirty invisible alters—or forty-five hundred—when those alters are deceiving the therapist, growing, splitting, ceasing to age, reproducing, coalescing, going into "inner hibernation," and changing their characteristics depending on which personality preceded or followed their appearance.

In summary, knowing how to test or prove an assertion that an individual has more than one personality, or how to clinically distinguish between personalities, ego states, identities, fragments, personality states, or the like, is impossible in the absence of agreement about what any of these terms means (Dinwiddie et al. 1993; Aldridge-Morris 1993, ch. 1). It follows, then, that few limits exist to the number of "personalities" one may unearth. The number is restrained only by the interviewer's energy and zeal in searching, and by his or her subjective—and perhaps idiosyncratic—sense of what constitutes an alter (Dinwiddie et al. 1993).

Enthusiasts thus expand the concept of personality beyond all bounds. If such a grandly expansive definition is employed, finding thousands of MPD "patients" becomes simple. Without clear behavioral criteria allowing the observer to know when a personality has been encountered, the term *personality* comes to mean anything and everything patient and clinician want it to. It thus comes to mean nothing.

The second affliction of the house of MPD is laid bare by one startling fact: the disorder's most dramatic signs appear after, not before, patients begin therapy with MPD proponents.

Those eventually given this diagnosis seek professional help because of many different kinds of psychiatric difficulties. When first presenting for treatment, these patients can exhibit signs or symptoms of each and every psychiatric condition (Coons et al. 1988; Putnam et al. 1986; Bliss 1984). One complaint, however, is conspicuously absent: evidence of separate alter personalities (Brick & Chu 1991; Franklin 1990; Kluft 1984a; Kluft 1985a; Ross 1989, 93).

But when the patients enter MPD-focused therapy, signs of alters' behaviors skyrocket. For instance, one patient's guest personalities created apparent grand mal seizures (Kluft 1995); another sold drugs when the host was supposed to be at work (the host would supposedly "come to" miles away) (Putnam 1989, 198). According to proponents, much of the behavior of MPD patients results from alters' "personified intrapsychic conflicts" (Putnam et al. 1986, 291); the personalities create crises in the patient's life by attempting to dominate, sabotage, and destroy one another (Kluft 1983; Kluft 1984c). As one example, an alter may lead the patient into compromising circumstances—say, a sexual encounter, an episode of firesetting, or an illegal drug purchase. This personality then vanishes, leaving the patient, who "wakes up" not knowing how he or she got into the situation, to handle the problem (Confer & Ables 1983; Kluft 1991b).

MPD patients often significantly deteriorate during treatment (Kluft 1984c; Ofshe & Watters 1994, ch. 10; Pendergrast 1995, ch. 6). One of the disorder's leading adherents acknowledges that MPD psychotherapy "causes significant disruption in a patient's life outside the treatment setting" and that suicide attempts may occur in the weeks following the diagnosis (Putnam 1989, 98, 299). As MPD psychotherapy progresses, patients may become more dissociative, more anxious, or more depressed (Braun 1989); the longer they remain in treatment, the more florid, elaborate, and unlikely their stories about their alleged childhood maltreatment tend to become (Ganaway 1995; Spanos 1996, ch. 20). This worsening contributes to the lengthy hospitalizations—some costing millions of dollars *(Frontline* 1995; Piper 1994b)—that often occur when MPD patients who are well insured are treated by the disorder's enthusiasts. Hospitalizations occur more frequently after the MPD diagnosis is made (Piper 1994b; Ross & Dua 1993).

MPD-focused therapists have struggled mightily to explain these rather embarrassing results of their interventions. (Examining these explanations is beyond the scope of this chapter: see Piper 1995; Piper 1997; Simpson 1995.) However, several recent malpractice juries have found the explanations unimpressive. The juries have preferred a simple and logical explanation for the worsening status of these patients: patients worsen after beginning MPD-focused therapy because therapists cause them to do so—by, among other things, encouraging evermore dramatic displays of "alters."

One important way in which therapists encourage such displays is to behave as if alter personalities were real. For example, leading authorities in this field routinely call alters out, hypnotize them, engage in "lengthy monologues" with them, name them, establish treatment alliances with them, talk to their stuffed animals, take them for walks to McDonald's ("The outside world often seems very big and frightening to child personalities"), engage in playful parody and sarcasm with them, allow them to work on age-appropriate children's projects in occupational therapy ("to show respect for the alter"), and recruit one alter to keep another from hurting still a third (Ross 1989, 227, 252–54; Ross & Gahan 1988). Other MPD adherents encourage alters to solve problems among themselves, to learn the Golden Rule, to participate in "internal group therapy," and even to decide whether or not the host should enter treatment (Caul 1984; Kluft 1993; Ross 1989, 209).

In 1988, Vincent and Pickering noted that in the published reviews of the literature, exactly *one* case presenting in childhood was reported in the 135 years prior to 1979. After reviewing the literature published since 1979, they were able to gather a mere twelve cases. (It seems, however, that Vincent and Pickering had to stretch a bit to find even those—four of the twelve were examples not of MPD, but rather of something the authors called "incipient MPD.") Nine additional cases were found by Peterson (1990).

These minuscule numbers, standing in stark contrast to the thousands of adult cases discovered in recent years, reveal the third weakness: if MPD results from child abuse, then why have so few cases been discovered in children?

The fourth and final weakness of the house is that it is built in a bog, namely, the belief that childhood maltreatment causes MPD. The literature strongly implies that childhood trauma has been unequivocally established as the primary cause of the disorder and that severe sexual abuse more or less directly leads to MPD (Braun 1989, 311; Ellason & Ross 1997; Putnam 1989, 47; Ross 1989, 101; Ross 1995, 505; Schafer 1986).

Several commentators have recently noted this formulation's deficiencies. Esman (1994) warns of the dangers of attempting to discover unitary causes of psychiatric disorders; he urges "measured skepticism" about assigning a role for sexual abuse, independently of other aspects of disturbed family function, in the genesis of later adult psychopathology. Numerous investigators, raising similar cautions, state that general family pathology in childhood better predicts adult dysfunction than does childhood sexual abuse alone (Bifulco et al. 1991; Fromuth 1986; Harter et al. 1988; Levitt & Pinnell 1995; Nash et al. 1993). Further, studies repeatedly note the difficulty of separating effects of abuse from the "matrix of disadvantage" giving rise to that abuse (Nash et al. 1993; Bushnell et al. 1992; Hussey & Singer 1993; Mullen et al. 1993). And finally, recent studies warn of the "very real uncertainties that surround evidence" concerning the relationship between childhood sexual abuse and psychiatric disorders (Fergusson et al. 1997) and conclude that available evidence to date does not support sweeping generalizations about childhood sexual abuse as an isolated cause of adult psychopathology (Beichtman et al. 1992; Finkelhor 1990; Levitt & Pinnell 1995).

The evidence for and against a relationship between trauma and dissociative pathology has also been examined. The data should "inspire skepticism, or at least serve to mute the grand conclusions about univariate cause and effect between trauma and dissociation that abound in the professional and lay literatures" (Tillman et al. 1994, 409).

Yet another weakness of this literature is inadequate verification of its child-abuse claims (Frankel 1993; Piper 1994a; Piper 1997). MPD patients very often report bizarre and extremely improbable experiences. For example, in a recent case familiar to the author, one patient claimed to have witnessed a baby being barbecued alive at a family picnic in a city park; another patient alleged repeated sexual assaults by a lion, a baboon, and other zoo animals in her parents' backyard—in broad daylight. (It should be mentioned that both therapists in these cases are prominent MPD adherents, and neither appeared to have any difficulty believing these allegations.) Despite the frequency of claims of this type, "repressed memory patients are seldom referred to medical doctors for examination and possible corroboration of past abuse [though one would assume that] the horrific physical abuse allegedly experienced . . . would require medical care at some point" (Parr 1996). (Space limitations limit discussion of this weakness; see Jones & McGraw 1987; Lindsay & Read 1994; Ofshe & Watters 1994; Pendergrast 1994, chs. 3–5; Spanos 1996, ch. 20; Wakefield & Underwager 1994, ch. 10).

The logic of the claim that childhood trauma causes MPD demonstrates a final serious flaw. If the claim were true, the abuse of millions of children over the years should have caused many cases of MPD. A case in point: children who endured unspeakable maltreatment in the ghettoes, boxcars, and concentration camps of Nazi Germany. However, no evidence exists that any developed MPD (Bower 1994; Des Pres 1976; Eitinger 1980; Krystal 1991; Sofsky 1997) or that any dissociated or repressed their traumatic memories (Eisen 1988; Wagenaar & Groeneweg 1990). Similarly, the same results hold in studies of children who saw a parent murdered (Eth & Pynoos 1994; Malmquist 1986), studies of kidnapped children (Terr 1979; Terr 1983), studies of children known to have been abused (Gold et al. 1994), and in several other investigations (Chodoff 1963; Pynoos & Nader 1989; Strom et al. 1962). Victims neither repressed the traumatic events, forgot about them, nor developed MPD.


## CONCLUDING COMMENTS

In the epigraph that begins this chapter, Upham speaks of the excesses of the seventeenth-century New England witchcraft craze. The story of Sarah Good exemplifies those excesses (Rosenthal 1993). In March of 1692, when thirty-eight years old and pregnant, she heard her husband denounce her to the witchcraft tribunal. He said that either she already was a witch, "or would be one very quickly" (ibid., 89). No one had produced evidence that she had engaged in witchcraft, no one had seen her do anything unusual, no one had come forward to say they had participated in satanic activities with her. But no matter.

On July 19, 1692, Sarah Good died on the gallows.

Three hundred years later, a woman in Chicago consulted a psychiatrist for depression (*Frontline* 1995). He concluded that she suffered from MPD, that she had abused her own children, and that she had gleefully participated in Satan-worshiping cult orgies where pregnant women were eviscerated and their babies eaten. Her failure to recall these events was attributed to alters that blocked her awareness. No one had produced any evidence for the truth of any of this, no one had seen her do anything unusual, no one had come forward to say they had participated in satanic activities with her. But no matter.

The doctor notified the state that the woman was a child molester. Then, after convincing her that she had killed several adults because she had been told to do so by satanists, he threatened to notify the police about these "criminal activities."

The woman's husband believed the doctor's claims. He divorced her. And, of course, because she was a "child molester," she lost custody of her children.

Charles Upham recognized the importance of erecting barricades against addlepated ideas blown by gales of illogic. The twentieth-century fad of multiple personality disorder indicates that even after a third of a millennium, such bulwarks have yet to be built.

# REFERENCES

Aldridge-Morris, R. 1993. *Multiple Personality: An Exercise in Deception.* Hove, UK: Erlbaum.

American Psychiatric Association. 1994. *Diagnostic and Statistical Manual of Mental Disorders.* 4th ed. Washington DC: American Psychiatric Association.

Atchison, M., and A. C. McFarlane. 1994. A review of dissociation and dissociative disorders. *Australian and New Zealand Journal of Psychiatry* 28: 591–99.

Beitchman, J. H., K. J. Zucker, J. E. Hood, G. A. DaCosta, D. Altman, and E. Cassavia. 1992. A review of the long-term effects of child sexual abuse. *Child Abuse and Neglect* 16: 101–18.

Bifulco, A., G. W Brown, and Z. Alder. 1991. Early sexual abuse and clinical depression in late life. *British Journal of Psychiatry* 159: 115–22.

Bliss, E. L. 1980. Multiple personalities: A report of 14 cases with implications for schizophrenia and hysteria. *Archives of General Psychiatry* 37: 1388–97.

———. 1984. Spontaneous self-hypnosis in multiple personality disorder. *Psychiatric Clinics of North America* 7: 135–48.

Bower, H. 1994. The concentration camp syndrome. *Australian and New Zealand Journal of Psychiatry* 28: 391–97.

Braun, B. G. 1984. Hypnosis creates multiple personality: Myth or reality? *International Journal of Clinical and Experimental Hypnosis* 32: 191–97.

———. 1986. *Treatment of Multiple Personality Disorder.* Washington, DC: American Psychiatric Press.

———. 1988. The BASK model of dissociation. *Dissociation* 1: 4–23.

———. 1989. Psychotherapy of the survivor of incest with a dissociative disorder. *Psychiatric Clinics of North America* 12: 307–24.

Brick, S. S., and J. A. Chu. 1991. The simulation of multiple personalities: A case report. *Psychotherapy* 28: 267–72.

Bushnell, J. A., J. E. Wells, and M. A. Oakley-Brown. 1992. Long-term effects of intrafamilial sexual abuse in childhood. *Acta Psychiatrica Scandinavica* 85: 136–42.

Caul, D. 1984. Group and videotape techniques for multiple personality disorder. *Psychiatric Annals* 14: 43–54.

Chodoff, P. 1963. Late effects of the concentration camp syndrome. *Archives of General Psychiatry* 8: 323–33.

Confer, W. N., and B. S. Ables. 1983. *Multiple Personality: Etiology, Diagnosis, and Treatment.* New York: Human Series Press.

Coons, P. M., E. S. Bowman, and V. Milstein. 1988. Multiple personality disorder: A clinical investigation of 50 cases. *Journal of Nervous and Mental Disease* 176: 519–27.

Des Pres, T. 1976. *The Survivor: An Anatomy of Life in the Death Camps.* New York: Washington Square Press.

Dinwiddie, S. H., C. S. North, and S. H. Yutzy. 1993. Multiple personality disorder: Scientific and medicolegal issues. *Bulletin of the American Academy of Psychiatry and Law* 21: 69–79.

Eisen, G. 1988. *Children and Play in the Holocaust: Games among the Shadows.* Amherst: University of Massachusetts Press.

Eitinger, L. 1980. The concentration camp syndrome and its late sequelae. In *Survivors, Victims, and Perpetrators: Essays on the Nazi Holocaust,* edited by J. E. Dimsdale. Washington, DC: Hemisphere Press.

Ellason, J. W., and C. A. Ross. 1997. Two-year follow-up of inpatients with dissociative identity disorder. *American Journal of Psychiatry* 154: 832–39.

Erh, S., and R. S. Pynoos. 1994. Children who witness the homicide of a parent. *Psychiatry* 57: 287–306.

Esman, A. H. 1994. "Sexual abuse," pathogenesis, and enlightened skepticism. *American Journal of Psychiatry* 151: 1101–1103.

Fergusson, D. M., M. T. Lynskey, and L. J. Horwood. 1997. Childhood sexual abuse and psychiatric disorder in young adulthood: II. Psychiatric outcomes of childhood sexual abuse. *Journal of the American Academy of Child and Adolescent Psychiatry,* 34: 1365–74.

*Fifth Estate.* 1993. *Multiple Personality Disorder.* Videotape shown on November 9. CTV, Canadian Television Network.

Finkelhor, D. 1990. Early and long-term effects of child sexual abuse: An update. *Professional Psychology: Research and Practice* 21: 325–30.

Frankel, E. H. 1993. Adult reconstruction of childhood events in the multiple personality literature. *American Journal of Psychiatry* 150: 954–58.

Franklin, J. 1990. The diagnosis of multiple personality disorder based on subtle dissociative signs. *Journal of Nervous and Mental Disease* 178: 4–14.

Fromuth, M. E. 1986. The relationship of childhood sexual abuse with later psychological and sexual adjustment in a sample of college women. *Child Abuse and Neglect* 10: 5–15.

Frontline. 1995. *Searching for Satan*. Videotape shown on October 24. PBS.

Ganaway, G. K. 1989. Historical versus narrative truth: Clarifying the role of exogenous trauma in the etiology of MPD and its variants. *Dissociation* 2: 205–20.

———. 1995. Hypnosis, childhood trauma, and dissociative identity disorder: Toward an integrative theory. *International Journal of Clinical and Experimental Hypnosis* 43: 127–44.

Gold, S. N., D. Hughes, and L. Hohnecker. 1994. Degrees of repression of sexual abuse memories. *American Psychologist* 49: 441–42.

Greaves, G. B. 1980. Multiple personality 165 years after Mary Reynolds. *Journal of Nervous and Mental Disease* 168: 577–95.

Harter, S., P. Alexander, and R. A. Neimeyer. 1988. Long-term effects of incestuous child abuse in college women: Social adjustment, social cognition, and family characteristics. *Journal of Consulting and Clinical Psychology* 56: 5–8.

Hendrickson, K. M., T. McCarty, and J. M. Goodwin. 1990. Animal alters: Case reports. *Dissociation* 3: 218–21.

Hussey, D. L., and M. Singer. 1993. Psychological distress, problem behaviors, and family functioning of sexually-abused adolescent inpatients. *Journal of the American Academy of Child and Adolescent Psychiatry* 32: 954–61.

Jones, D. P. H., and J. M. McGraw. 1987. Reliable and fictitious accounts of sexual abuse to children. *Journal of Interpersonal Violence* 2: 27–45.

Kluft, R. P. 1983. Hypnotherapeutic crisis intervention in multiple personality. *American Journal of Clinical Hypnosis* 26: 73–83.

———. 1984a. Treatment of multiple personality disorder: A study of 33 cases. *Psychiatric Clinics of North America* 7: 9–29.

———. 1984b. An introduction to multiple personality disorder. *Psychiatric Annals* 14: 19–24.

———. 1984c. Aspects of the treatment of multiple personality disorder. *Psychiatric Annals* 14: 51–55.

———. 1985a. *Childhood Antecedents of Multiple Personality*. Washington, DC: American Psychiatric Press.

———. 1985b. Making the diagnosis of multiple personality disorder. *Directions in Psychiatry* 5: 1–11.

————. 1987. An update on multiple personality disorder. *Hospital and Community Psychiatry* 38: 363–73.

————. 1988. The phenomenology and treatment of extremely complex multiple personality disorder. *Dissociation* 1: 47–58.

————. 1989. Iatrogenic creation of new alter personalities. *Dissociation* 2: 83–91.

————. 1991a. Multiple personality disorder. In *American Psychiatric Press Review of Psychiatry*. Washington, DC: American Psychiatric Press, vol. 10, pp. 161–88.

————. 1991b. Clinical presentations of multiple personality disorder. *Psychiatric Clinics of North America* 14: 741–56.

————. 1993. The initial stages of psychotherapy in the treatment of multiple personality disorder patients. *Dissociation* 6: 145–61.

————. 1995. Current controversies surrounding dissociative identity disorder. In *Dissociative Identity Disorder: Theoretical and Treatment Controversies,* edited by L. Cohen, J. Berzoff, and M. Elin. Northvale, NJ: Jason Aronson, pp. 347–77.

Krystal, H. 1991. Integration and self-healing in post-traumatic states: A ten-year retrospective. *American Imago* 48: 93–118.

Levitt, E. E., and C. M. Pinnell. 1995. Some additional light on the childhood sexual abuse-psychopathology axis. *International Journal of Clinical and Experimental Hypnosis* 43: 145–62.

Lewis, D. O., and J. S. Bard. 1991. Multiple personality and forensic issues. *Psychiatric Clinics of North America* 14: 741–56.

Lindsay, D. S., and J. D. Read. 1994. Psychotherapy and memories of childhood sexual abuse: A cognitive perspective. *Applied Cognitive Psychology* 8: 281–338.

Loewenstein, R. J. 1991. An office mental status examination for complex chronic dissociative symptoms and multiple personality disorder. *Psychiatric Clinics of North America* 14: 567–604.

Lynn, S. J., and M. R. Nash. 1994. Truth in memory: Ramifications for psychotherapy and hypnotherapy. *American Journal of Clinical Hypnosis* 36: 194–208.

Malmquist, C. P. 1986. Children who witness parental murder: Post-traumatic aspects. *Journal of the American Academy of Child and Adolescent Psychiatry* 25: 320–25.

Mullen, P. E., J. L. Martin, J. C. Anderson, S. E. Romans, and G. P. Herbison. 1993. Childhood sexual abuse and mental health in adult life. *British Journal of Psychiatry* 163: 721–32.

Nash, M. R., T. L. Hulsey, M. C. Sexton, T. L. Harralson, and W. Lambert. 1993. Long-term sequelae of childhood sexual abuse: Perceived family environment, psychopathology, and dissociation. *Journal of Consulting and Clinical Psychology* 61: 276–83.

Ofshe, R., and E. Watters. 1994. *Making Monsters: False Memories, Psychotherapy, and Sexual Hysteria.* New York: Scribners.

Parr, L. E. 1996. *Repressed Memory Claims in the Crime Victims Compensation Program.* Olympia, WA: Department of Labor and Industries Public Affairs.

Pendergrast, M. 1995. *Victims of Memory: Incest Accusations and Shattered Lives.* Hinesburg, V T.: Upper Access.

Peterson, G. 1990. Diagnosis of childhood multiple personality disorder. *Dissociation* 3: 3–9.

Piper, A. 1994a. Multiple personality disorder. *British Journal of Psychiatry* 164: 600–12.

———. 1994b. Treatment for multiple personality disorder: At what cost? *American Journal of Psychotherapy* 48: 392–400.

———. 1994c. Multiple personality disorder and criminal responsibility: Critique of a paper by Elyn Saks. *Journal of Psychiatry and Law* 22: 7–49.

———. 1995. A skeptical look at multiple personality disorder. In *Dissociative Identity Disorder: Theoretical and Treatment Controversies,* edited by L. Cohen, J. Berzoff, and M. Elfin. Northvale, NJ: Jason Aronson, pp. 135–73.

———. 1997. *Hoax and Reality: The Bizarre World of Multiple Personality Disorder.* Northvale, NJ: Jason Aronson.

Putnam, F. W. 1989. *Diagnosis and Treatment of Multiple Personality Disorder.* New York: Guilford.

———. 1991. Dissociative phenomena. In *American Psychiatric Press Review of Psychiatry,* vol. 10, edited by A. Tasman and S. M. Goldfinger. Washington, DC: American Psychatric Press, pp. 145–60.

Putnam, F. W., J. J. Guroff, E. K. Silberman, L. Barban, and R. M. Post. 1986. The clinical phenomenology of multiple personality disorder: Review of 100 recent cases. *Journal of Clinical Psychiatry* 47: 285–93.

Putnam, F. W., T. P. Zahn, and R. M. Post. 1990. Differential autonomic nervous system activity in multiple personality disorder. *Psychiatry Research* 31: 251–60.

Pynoos, R. S., and K. Nader. 1989. Children's memory and proximity to violence. *Journal of the American Academy of Child Psychiatry* 28: 236–41.

Rosenthal, B. 1993. *Salem Story: Reading the Witch Trials of 1692*. Cambridge, UK: Cambridge University Press.

Ross, C. A. 1989. *Multiple Personality Disorder: Diagnosis, Clinical Features, and Treatment*. New York: Wiley.

————. 1990. Twelve cognitive errors about multiple personality disorder. *American Journal of Psychotherapy* 44: 348–56.

————. 1994. *The Osiris Complex: Case Studies in Multiple Personality Disorder*. Toronto: University of Toronto Press.

————. 1995a. The validity and reliability of dissociative identity disorder. In *Dissociative Identity Disorder: Theoretical and Treatment Controversies*, edited by L. Cohen, J. Berzoff, and M. Elfin. Northvale, NJ: Jason Aronson, pp. 65–84.

————. 1995b. Current treatment of dissociative identity disorder. In *Dissociative Identity Disorder: Theoretical and Treatment Controversies*, edited by L. Cohen, J. Berzoff, and M. Elfin. Northvale, NJ: Jason Aronson, pp. 413–34.

Ross, C. A., and V. Dua. 1993. Psychiatric healthcare costs of multiple personality disorder. *American Journal of Psychotherapy* 47: 103–12.

Ross, C. A, and P. Gahan. 1988. Techniques in the treatment of multiple personality disorder. *American Journal of Psychotherapy* 42: 40–52.

Ross, C. A., G. R. Norton, and G. A. Fraser. 1989. Evidence against the iatrogenesis of multiple personality disorder. *Dissociation* 2: 61–65.

Sarbin, T. R. 1995. On the belief that one body may be host to two or more personalities. *International Journal of Clinical and Experimental Hypnosis* 33: 163–83.

Schafer, D. W. 1986. Recognizing multiple personality patients. *American Journal of Psychotherapy* 15: 500–10.

Simpson, M. 1995. Gullible's travels, or the importance of being multiple. In *Dissociative Identity Disorder: Theoretical and Treatment Controversies*, edited by L. Cohen, J. Berzoff, and M. Elfin. Northvale, NJ: Jason Aronson, pp. 87–134.

Sofsky, W. 1997. *The Order of Terror: The Concentration Camp*. Princeton: Princeton University Press.

Spanos, N. P. 1996. *Multiple Identities and False Memories: A Sociocognitive Perspective*. Washington, DC: American Psychological Association.

Spiegel, D. 1995. Psychiatry disabused. *Nature Medicine* 1: 490–91.

Spiegel, D., and A. W. Schleflin. 1994. Dissociated or fabricated? Psychiatric aspects of repressed memory in criminal and civil cases. *International Journal of Clinical and Experimental Hypnosis* 42: 411–32.

Strom, A., S. B. Refsum, and L. Eitinger. 1962. Examination of Norwegian ex-concentration camp prisoners. *Journal of Neuroprychiatry* 4: 43–62.

Taylor, W. S., and M. F. Martin. 1944. Multiple personality. *Journal of Abnormal and Social Psychology* 39: 281–300.

Terr, L. C. 1979. Children of Chowchilla. *Psychoanalytic Study of the Child* 34: 547–623.

———1983. Chowchilla revisited: The effects of psychic trauma four years after a school-bus kidnapping. *American Journal of Psychiatry* 140: 1543–50.

Tillman, J. G., M. R. Nash, and P. M. Lerner. 1994. Does trauma cause dissociative pathology? In *Dissociation: Clinical and Theoretical Perspectives*, edited by S. J. Lynn and J. W. Rhue. New York: Guilford, pp. 394–414.

Vincent, M., and M. R. Pickering. 1988. Multiple personality disorder in childhood. *Canadian Journal of Psychiatry* 33: 524–29.

Wagenaar, W. A., and J. Groeneweg. 1990. The memory of concentration camp survivors. *Applied Cognitive Psychology* 4: 77–87.

Wakefield, H., and R. Underwager. 1994. *Return of the Furies: An Investigation into Recovered-Memory Therapy*. Chicago: Open Court.

Watkins, J. G., and H. H. Watkins. 1984. Hazards to the therapist in the treatment of multiple personalities. *Psychiatric Clinics of North America* 7: 111–19.

# NOTE

1. In the fourth and latest edition of the American Psychiatric Association's *Diagnostic and Statistical Manual* the disorder has been renamed. Although the third edition called the condition MPD, the fourth calls it *dissociative identity disorder*. The differences between the two disorders' diagnostic criteria are slight and mainly cosmetic: in the newer criteria, terms such as *identities* or *personality states* are employed, rather than the older *personalities*. The newer definition also emphasizes the patient's inability to recall important personal information.

Whether the newer term will become popular has yet to be seen; because *MPD* has the distinct advantage of familiarity, it is used in this chapter.

# SECTION V. HOW TO EVALUATE MEMORY AND MEMORY RECOVERY TECHNIQUES

# INTRODUCTION

Most of us are quite certain we know how our memories work. But many of us are mistaken. Surveys show that a large percentage of people believe that our memories operate very much like video cameras, faithfully recording all events in a carefully preserved mental storage bin. Then, when we wish to recall an experience, we merely access the tape, press "rewind," and find out what happened. It's all simple—or so it seems.

Yet hundreds of studies, conducted by such pioneering psychologists as Elizabeth Loftus, Stephen Ceci, Maggie Bruck, Daniel Schacter, and Henry Roediger, have shattered this widespread belief in the infallibility of memory. We now know that our memories, although reasonably accurate much of the time, are quite malleable in many cases. We rarely, if ever, recall things precisely as they happened. Instead, remembering is largely a matter of retrieving our patchy recollections, along with piecing together our best guesses and hunches about what happened. As a consequence, we can be fooled into recalling things differently from how they actually occurred. In some cases, we may even recall nonexistent events.

The "reconstructive nature of memory," as psychologists like to call it, bears remarkably important implications for psychotherapy. Well-intentioned therapists who believe that a client was sexually abused in childhood may repeatedly prompt this client to recall early memories of abuse by using such suggestive techniques as leading questions, hypnosis, and guided imagery. As a consequence, at least some of these clients may come to "remember" imaginary traumatic events. They may develop psychological symptoms and even accuse family members of having abused them. In rare cases, clients may undergo basic alterations in identity, which is hardly surprising given that our sense of who we are

271

is shaped substantially by our memories. For example, following forceful prompting by well-meaning but misguided therapists, some clients may develop new "personalities" that were not present at the start of therapy.

In the first reading in this section, Elizabeth Loftus nicely lays out the scope of the problem, reviewing research evidence demonstrating that memory is fallible and, in many individuals, easily influenced by suggestion. As Loftus observes, studies demonstrate that it is possible to implant false memories of dramatic past events (e.g., being lost in a shopping mall as a child) in a substantial minority of participants. Moreover, merely imagining past events can make them seem more likely to have occurred.

Steven Jay Lynn and his coauthors then examine the manifold ways in which suggestive psychotherapeutic procedures can go dreadfully wrong. They describe a host of suggestive methods—such as hypnosis, leading questions, dream interpretation, and bogus personality interpretation—that can lead therapy clients to "recall" childhood events that never happened. As they note, these methods are especially persuasive when they provide clients with a plausible story that helps to explain the origin of their current psychological difficulties.

# 13.

# CREATING FALSE MEMORIES

## Elizabeth F. Loftus

In 1986 Nadean Cool, a nurse's aide in Wisconsin, sought therapy from a psychiatrist to help her cope with her reaction to a traumatic event experienced by her daughter. (See also chapter 14 in this volume.) During therapy, the psychiatrist used hypnosis and other suggestive techniques to dig out buried memories of abuse that Cool herself had allegedly experienced. In the process, Cool became convinced that she had repressed memories of having been in a satanic cult, of eating babies, of being raped, of having sex with animals and of being forced to watch the murder of her eight-year-old friend. She came to believe that she had more than 120 personalities—children, adults, angels, and even a duck—all because, Cool was told, she had experienced severe child-hood sexual and physical abuse. The psychiatrist also performed exor-cisms on her, one of which lasted for five hours and included the sprin-kling of holy water and screams for Satan to leave Cool's body.

When Cool finally realized that false memories had been planted, she sued the psychiatrist for malpractice. In March 1997, after five weeks of trial, her case was settled out of court for $2.4 million. Nadean Cool is not the only patient to develop false memories as a result of question-able therapy. In Missouri in 1992, a church counselor helped Beth Rutherford to remember during therapy that her father, a clergyman, had regularly raped her between the ages of seven and fourteen and that her mother sometimes helped him by holding her down. Under her therapist's guidance, Rutherford developed memories of her father twice

Reprinted with permission from *Scientific American* 277, no. 3 (September 1997): 70–75. Copyright © 1997 by Scientific American, Inc. All rights reserved.

impregnating her and forcing her to abort the fetus herself with a coat hanger. The father had to resign from his post as a clergyman when the allegations were made public. Later medical examination of the daughter revealed, however, that she was still a virgin at age twenty-two and had never been pregnant. The daughter sued the therapist and received a $1 million settlement in 1996.

About a year earlier, two juries returned verdicts against a Minnesota psychiatrist accused of planting false memories by former patients Vynnette Hamanne and Elizabeth Carlson, who under hypnosis and sodium amytal, and after being fed misinformation about the workings of memory, had come to remember horrific abuse by family members. The juries awarded Hamanne $2.67 million and Carlson $2.5 million for their ordeals.

In all four cases, the women developed memories about childhood abuse in therapy and then later denied their authenticity. How can we determine if memories of childhood abuse are true or false? Without corroboration, it is very difficult to differentiate between false memories and true ones. Also, in these cases, some memories were contrary to physical evidence, such as explicit and detailed recollections of rape and abortion when medical examination confirmed virginity. How is it possible for people to acquire elaborate and confident false memories? A growing number of investigations demonstrate that under the right circumstances false memories can be instilled rather easily in some people.

My own research into memory distortion goes back to the early 1970s, when I began studies of the "misinformation effect." These studies show that when people who witness an event are later exposed to new and misleading information about it, their recollections often become distorted. In one example, participants viewed a simulated automobile accident at an intersection with a stop sign. After the viewing, half the participants received a suggestion that the traffic sign was a yield sign. When asked later what traffic sign they remembered seeing at the intersection, those who had been given the suggestion tended to claim that they had seen a yield sign. Those who had not received the phony information were much more accurate in their recollection of the traffic sign.

My students and I have now conducted more than two hundred

experiments involving over twenty thousand individuals that document how exposure to misinformation induces memory distortion. In these studies, people "recalled" a conspicuous barn in a bucolic scene that contained no buildings at all, broken glass and tape recorders that were not in the scenes they viewed, a white instead of a blue vehicle in a crime scene, and Minnie Mouse when they actually saw Mickey Mouse. Taken together, these studies show that misinformation can change an individual's recollection in predictable and sometimes very powerful ways.

Misinformation has the potential for invading our memories when we talk to other people, when we are suggestively interrogated, or when we read or view media coverage about some event that we may have experienced ourselves. After more than two decades of exploring the power of misinformation, researchers have learned a great deal about the conditions that make people susceptible to memory modification. Memories are more easily modified, for instance, when the passage of time allows the original memory to fade.

## FALSE CHILDHOOD MEMORIES

It is one thing to change a detail or two in an otherwise intact memory but quite another to plant a false memory of an event that never happened. To study false memory, my students and I first had to find a way to plant a pseudomemory that would not cause our subjects undue emotional stress, either in the process of creating the false memory or when we revealed that they had been intentionally deceived. Yet we wanted to try to plant a memory that would be at least mildly traumatic, had the experience actually happened.

My research associate Jacqueline E. Pickrell and I settled on trying to plant a specific memory of being lost in a shopping mall or large department store at about the age of five. Here's how we did it. We asked our subjects, twenty-four individuals ranging in age from eighteen to fifty-three, to try to remember childhood events that had been recounted to us by a parent, an older sibling, or another close relative. We prepared a booklet for each participant containing one-paragraph stories about three events that had actually happened to him or her and one that had not. We constructed the false event using information about a plausible shopping trip provided by a relative, who also verified that the participant had not in fact been lost at about the age of five. The lost-in-the-mall scenario included the following elements: lost for an extended period, crying, aid and comfort by an elderly woman, and, finally, reunion with the family.

After reading each story in the booklet, the participants wrote what they remembered about the event. If they did not remember it, they were instructed to write, "I do not remember this." In two follow-up interviews, we told the participants that we were interested in examining how much detail they could remember and how their memories compared with those of their relative. The event paragraphs were not read to them verbatim, but rather parts were provided as retrieval cues. The participants recalled something about forty-nine of the seventy-two true events (68 percent) immediately after the initial reading of the booklet and also in each of the two follow-up interviews. After reading the booklet, seven of the twenty-four participants (29 percent) remembered either partially or fully the false event constructed for them, and in the two follow-up interviews, six participants (25 percent) continued to claim that they remembered the fictitious event. Statistically, there were some differences between the true memories and the false ones: participants used more words to describe the true memories, and they rated the true memories as being somewhat more clear. But if an onlooker were to observe many of our participants describe an event, it would be difficult indeed to tell whether the account was of a true or a false memory. Of course, being lost, however frightening, is not the same as being abused. But the lost-in-the-mall study is not about real experiences of being lost; it is about planting false memories of being lost. The paradigm shows a way of instilling false memories and takes a step toward allowing us to understand how this might happen in real-world settings. Moreover, the study provides evidence that people can be led to remember their past in different ways, and they can even be coaxed into "remembering" entire events that never happened.

Studies in other laboratories using a similar experimental procedure have produced similar results. For instance, Ira Hyman, Troy H. Husband and F. James Billing of Western Washington University asked college students to recall childhood experiences that had been recounted by their parents. The researchers told the students that the study was about how people remember shared experiences differently. In addition to actual events reported by parents, each participant was given one false event: either an overnight hospitalization for a high fever and a possible ear infection, or a birthday party with pizza and a clown that supposedly happened at about the age of five. The parents confirmed that neither of these events actually took place.

Hyman found that students fully or partially recalled 84 percent of the true events in the first interview and 88 percent in the second interview. None of the participants recalled the false event during the first interview, but 20 percent said they remembered something about the false event in the second interview. One participant who had been exposed to the emergency hospitalization story later remembered a male doctor, a female nurse, and a friend from church who came to visit at the hospital. In another study, along with true events, Hyman presented different false events, such as accidentally spilling a bowl of punch on the parents of the bride at a wedding reception or having to evacuate a grocery store when the overhead sprinkler systems erroneously activated. Again, none of the participants recalled the false event during the first interview, but 18 percent remembered something about it in the second interview. For example, during the first interview, one participant, when asked about the fictitious wedding event, stated, "I have no clue. I have never heard that one before." In the second interview, the participant said, "It was an outdoor wedding, and I think we were running around and knocked something over like the punch bowl or something and made a big mess and of course got yelled at for it."

# IMAGINATION INFLATION

The finding that an external suggestion can lead to the construction of false childhood memories helps us understand the process by which false memories arise. It is natural to wonder whether this research is applicable in real situations such as being interrogated by law officers or in psychotherapy. Although strong suggestion may not routinely occur in police questioning or therapy, suggestion in the form of an imagination exercise sometimes does. For instance, when trying to obtain a confession, law officers may ask a suspect to imagine having participated in a criminal act. Some mental health professionals encourage patients to imagine childhood events as a way of recovering supposedly hidden memories.

Surveys of clinical psychologists reveal that 11 percent instruct their clients to "let the imagination run wild," and 22 percent tell their clients to "give free rein to the imagination." Therapist Wendy Maltz, author of a popular book on childhood sexual abuse, advocates telling the patient: "Spend time imaging that you were sexually abused, without worrying about accuracy proving anything, or having your ideas make sense. . . . Ask yourself . . . these questions: What time of day is it? Where are you? Indoors or outdoors? What kind of things are happening? Is there one or more person with you?" Maltz further recommends that therapists continue to ask questions such as "Who would have been likely perpetrators? When were you most vulnerable to sexual abuse in your life?"

The increasing use of such imagination exercises led me and several colleagues to wonder about their consequences. What happens when people imagine childhood experiences that did not happen to them? Does imagining a childhood event increase confidence that it occurred? To explore this, we designed a three-stage procedure. We first asked individuals to indicate the likelihood that certain events happened to them during their childhood. The list contains forty events, each rated on a scale ranging from "definitely did not happen" to "definitely did happen." Two weeks later, we asked the participants to imagine that they had experienced some of these events. Different subjects were asked to imagine different events. Sometime later the participants again were asked to respond to the original list of forty childhood events, indicating how likely it was that these events actually happened to them. Consider one of the imagination exercises. Participants are told to imagine playing inside at home after school, hearing a strange noise outside, running toward the window, tripping, falling, reaching out and breaking the window with their hand. In addition, we asked participants questions such as "What did you trip on? How did you feel?" In one study, 24 percent of the participants who imagined the broken-window scenario later reported an increase in confidence that the event had occurred, whereas only 12 percent of those who were not asked to imagine the incident reported an increase in the likelihood that it had taken place. We found this "imagination inflation" effect in each of the eight events that participants were asked to imagine. A number of possible explanations come to mind. An obvious one is that an act of imagination simply makes the event seem more familiar and that familiarity is mistakenly related to childhood memories rather than to the act of imagination. Such source confusion when a person does not remember the source of information can be especially acute for the distant experiences of childhood.

Studies by Lyn Giff and Henry L. Roediger III of Washington University of recent rather than childhood experiences more directly connect imagined actions to the construction of false memory. During the initial session, the researchers instructed participants to perform the stated action, imagine doing it, or just listen to the statement and do nothing else. The actions were simple ones: knock on the table, lift the stapler, break the toothpick, cross your fingers, roll your eyes. During the second session, the participants were asked to imagine some of the actions that they had not previously performed. During the final session, they answered questions about what actions they actually performed during the initial session. The investigators found that the more times participants imagined an unperformed action, the more likely they were to remember having performed it.

## IMPOSSIBLE MEMORIES

It is highly unlikely that an adult can recall genuine episodic memories from the first year of life, in part because the hippocampus, which plays a key role in the creation of memories, has not matured enough to form and store long-lasting memories that can be retrieved in adulthood.

A procedure for planting "impossible" memories about experiences that occur shortly after birth has been developed by the late Nicholas Spanos and his collaborators at Carleton University. Individuals are led to believe that they have well-coordinated eye movements and visual exploration skills probably because they were born in hospitals that hung swinging, colored mobiles over infant cribs. To confirm whether they had such an experience, half the participants are hypnotized, age-regressed to the day after birth and asked what they remembered. The other half of the group participates in a "guided mnemonic restruc-turing" procedure that uses age regression as well as active encourage-ment to re-create the infant experiences by imagining them. Spanos and his co-workers found that the vast majority of their subjects were sus-ceptible to these memory-planting procedures. Both the hypnotic and guided participants reported infant memories. Surprisingly, the guided group did so somewhat more (95 versus 70 percent). Both groups remembered the colored mobile at a relatively high rate (56 percent of the guided group and 46 percent of the hypnotic subjects). Many partic-ipants who did not remember the mobile did recall other things, such as doctors, nurses, bright lights, cribs and masks. Also, in both groups, of those who reported memories of infancy, 49 percent felt that they were real memories, as opposed to 16 percent who claimed that they were merely fantasies. These findings confirm earlier studies that many indi-viduals can be led to construct complex, vivid and detailed false memo-ries via a rather simple procedure. Hypnosis clearly is not necessary.

# HOW FALSE MEMORIES FORM

In the lost-in-the-mall study, implantation of false memory occurred when another person, usually a family member, claimed that the incident happened. Corroboration of an event by another person can be a powerful technique for instilling a false memory. In fact, merely claiming to have seen a person do something can lead that person to make a false confession of wrongdoing.

This effect was demonstrated in a study by Saul M. Kassin and his colleagues then at Williams College, who investigated the reactions of individuals falsely accused of damaging a computer by pressing the wrong key. The innocent participants initially denied the charge, but when a confederate said that she had seen them perform the action, many participants signed a confession, internalized guilt for the act and went on to confabulate details that were consistent with that belief. These findings show that false incriminating evidence can induce people to accept guilt for a crime they did not commit and even to develop memories to support their guilty feelings.

Research is beginning to give us an understanding of how false memories of complete, emotional and self-participatory experiences are created in adults. First, there are social demands on individuals to remember; for instance, researchers exert some pressure on participants in a study to come up with memories. Second, memory construction by imagining events can be explicitly encouraged when people are having trouble remembering. And, finally, individuals can be encouraged not to think about whether their constructions are real or not. Creation of false memories is most likely to occur when these external factors are present, whether in an experimental setting, in a therapeutic setting or during everyday activities.

False memories are constructed by combining actual memories with the content of suggestions received from others. During the process, individuals may forget the source of the information. This is a classic example of source confusion, in which the content and the source become dissociated.

Of course, because we can implant false childhood memories in some individuals in no way implies that all memories that arise after suggestion are necessarily false. Put another way, although experimental work on the creation of false memories may raise doubts about the validity of long-buried memories, such as repeated trauma, it in no way disproves them. Without corroboration, there is little that can be done to help even the most experienced evaluator to differentiate true memories from ones that were suggestively planted.

The precise mechanisms by which such false memories are constructed await further research. We still have much to learn about the degree of confidence and the characteristics of false memories created in these ways, and we need to discover what types of individuals are particularly susceptible to these forms of suggestion and who is resistant.

As we continue this work, it is important to heed the cautionary tale in the data we have already obtained: mental health professionals and others must be aware of how greatly they can influence the recollection of events and of the urgent need for maintaining restraint in situations in which imagination is used as an aid in recovering presumably lost memories.

# 14.

# MEMORY RECOVERY TECHNIQUES IN PSYCHOTHERAPY: PROBLEMS AND PITFALLS

*Steven Jay Lynn, Elizabeth F. Loftus, Scott O. Lilienfeld, and Timothy Lock*

In 1997, Nadean Cool won a $2.4 million malpractice settlement against her therapist in which she alleged that he used a variety of suggestive memory recovery procedures to persuade her that she had suffered horrific abuse and harbored more than 130 personalities, including demons, angels, children, and a duck. (See also chapter 13 in this volume.) Prior to therapy, Nadean recounted problems typical of many women, including a history of bulimia, substance abuse, and mild depression. During her five-year treatment, Nadean's therapist allegedly maintained that she could not improve unless she uncovered repressed traumatic memories. To do so, Nadean participated in repeated hypnotic age regression and guided imagery sessions and was subjected to an exorcism and fifteen-hour marathon therapy sessions. Nadean recalled frightening images of participating in a satanic cult, eating babies, being raped, having sex with animals, and being forced to watch the murder of her eight-year-old friend after these interventions, and her psychological health deteriorated apace. Eventually Nadean came to doubt that the recovered memories were "real," terminated treatment with her therapist, and recouped much of the ground she had lost.

Although Nadean Cool's therapy strayed far beyond conventional

Reprinted with permission from *Skeptical Inquirer* (July/August 2003): 40–46.

practice, her therapist is in the company of many professionals who perform so-called memory work to help clients retrieve memories of ostensibly repressed abuse. Poole, Lindsay, Memon, and Bull (1995) reported that 25 percent of licensed doctoral-level psychologists surveyed in the United States and Great Britain indicated that they (a) use two or more techniques such as hypnosis and guided imagery to facilitate recall of repressed memories, (b) consider memory recovery an important part of treatment, and (c) can identify patients with repressed or otherwise unavailable memories as early as the first session (see Polusny and Follette 1996 for similar findings). In addition, over three-quarters of US doctoral-level psychotherapists reported using at least one memory recovery technique to "help clients remember childhood sexual abuse." In this chapter, we consider a number of widely used memory recovery procedures, and whether they can distort or create, rather than reveal, traumatic memories.

## CLINICAL TECHNIQUES

### Guided Imagery

One important class of techniques relies on guided imagery, in which patients imagine scenarios described by the therapist. So long as imagery techniques focus on current problems, as in visualizing pleasant scenes to develop relaxation skills, there is probably little cause for concern about false memory creation. However, the use of imagery to uncover allegedly repressed memories is controversial and warrants concern because people frequently confuse real and imagined memories, particularly when memories are initially hazy or unavailable. Roland (1993), for example, proposed using visualization to jog "blocked" memories of sexual abuse and a "reconstruction" technique for recovering repressed memories of abuse. According to Poole et al. (1995), 32 percent of US therapists report using "imagery related to the abuse."

## Suggesting False Memories

Memory errors are not random. What is recalled depends on current beliefs, inferences, guesses, expectancies, and suggestions. People can clearly be led by suggestions to integrate a fabricated event into their personal histories. In Loftus's research (Loftus, Coa & Pickrell 1996; Loftus & Pickrell 1995), twenty-four participants were asked by an older sibling to remember real and fictitious events (e.g., getting lost in a shopping mall). The older sibling initially provided a few details about the false event, such as where the event allegedly occurred, after which the subjects were interviewed one to two weeks apart. A quarter of the subjects claimed to remember the false event; some provided surprisingly detailed accounts of the event that they came to believe had actually occurred. Similar studies with college students have shown that approximately 20–25 percent report experiencing such fictitious events as (a) an overnight hospitalization for a high fever and a possible ear infection, accidentally spilling a bowl of punch on the parents of the bride at a wedding reception, and evacuating a grocery store when the overhead sprinkler systems erroneously activated (Hyman et al. 1995); and (b) a serious animal attack, serious indoor accident, serious outdoor accident, and serious medical procedure and being injured by another child (Porter, Yuille & Lehman 1998).

## Hypnosis

Many therapists endorse popular yet mistaken beliefs about hypnosis. Yapko's (1994) survey revealed that 47 percent of a sample composed of professionals had greater faith in the accuracy of hypnotic than non-hypnotic memories; 54 percent believed to some degree that hypnosis is effective for recovering memories as far back as birth; and 28 percent believed that hypnosis is an effective means of recovering past-life memories. If hypnosis were able to accurately retrieve forgotten memories, confidence in its use for recovering memories would be warranted. But this is not the case. The following conclusions are based on major reviews of the literature:[1]

(1) Hypnosis increases the sheer volume of recall, resulting in both more incorrect and correct information. When the number of responses is statistically controlled, hypnotic recall is no more accurate than nonhypnotic recall.

(2) Hypnosis produces more recall errors and higher levels of memories for false information.

(3) False memories are associated with subjects' levels of hypnotic suggestibility. However, even relatively non-suggestible participants report false memories.

(4) Hypnotized persons sometimes exhibit less accurate recall in response to misleading questions compared with nonhypnotized participants.

(5) In general, hypnotized individuals are more confident about their recall accuracy than are nonhypnotized individuals, and an association between hypnotizability and confidence has been well documented.

(6) Even when participants are warned about possible memory problems associated with hypnosis, they continue to report false memories during and after hypnosis, although some studies indicate that warnings decrease pseudomemories.

(7) Contrary to the claim that hypnosis facilitates the recall of emotional or traumatic memories, hypnosis does not improve recall of emotionally arousing events (e.g., films of shop accidents, depictions of fatal stabbings, a mock assassination, an actual murder videotaped serendipitously), and arousal level is not associated with hypnotic recall.

(8) Hypnosis does not necessarily produce more false memories or unwarranted confidence in memories than highly suggestive nonhypnotic procedures. However, simply asking participants to focus on the task at hand and to do their best to recall specific events yields accurate recall comparable to hypnosis, but with fewer or comparable recall errors.

Our dour assessment of hypnosis for recovering memories has been echoed by professional societies, including divisions and task forces of the American Psychological Association and the Canadian Psychiatric Association. The American Medical Association (1994) has asserted that hypnosis be used only for investigative purposes in forensic contexts. However, even when hypnosis is used solely for investigative purposes, there are attendant risks. Early in an investigation, the information obtained through hypnosis could lead investigators to pursue erroneous leads and even to interpret subsequent leads as consistent with initial and perhaps mistaken hypnotically generated evidence.

## SEARCHING FOR EARLY MEMORIES

According to Adler (1927), "The first memory will show the individual's fundamental view of life. . . . I would never investigate a personality without asking for the first memory (p. 75)." More recently, Olson (1979) articulated a belief shared by many therapists (Papanek 1979) that "[Early memories] when correctly interpreted often reveal very quickly the basic core of one's personality . . . and suggest . . . bedrock themes with which the therapist must currently deal in treating the client" (p. xvii).

Most adults' earliest reported memories date back to between thirty-six and sixty months of age. Virtually all contemporary memory researchers agree that accurate memory reports of events that occur before twenty-four months of age are extremely rare (see Malinoski, Lynn & Sivec 1998), due to developmental changes that influence how children process, retrieve, and share information. Adults' memory reports from twenty-four months of age or earlier are likely to represent confabulations, condensations, and constructions of early events, as well as current concerns and stories heard about early events (Spanos 1996). Although certain early memories might well have special significance,[2] such memories are highly malleable. Malinoski and Lynn (1999) examined early memories in a study in which interviewers probed for increasingly early memories until participants twice denied any earlier memories. Participants then received "memory recovery techniques" similar to those advocated by some therapists (e.g., Farmer 1989; Meiselman 1990). Interviewers asked participants to see themselves "in their mind's eye" as a toddler or an infant and "get in touch" with memories of long ago. Participants were informed that most young adults can retrieve memories of very early events—including their second birthday—if they "let themselves go" and try hard to visualize and concentrate. Interviewers then asked for subjects' memories of their second birthdays and reinforced increasingly early memory reports.

The average age of the initial reported memory was 3.7 years: Only 11 percent of individuals reported memories at or before age twenty-four months, and 3 percent reported a memory from age twelve months or younger. However, after receiving the visualization instructions, 59 percent of the participants reported a memory of their second birthday. After interviewers pressed for even earlier memories, the earliest memory reported was 1.6 years, on average. Fully 78.2 percent of the sample reported at least one memory that occurred at or earlier than two years, outside the boundary of infantile amnesia. More than half (56 percent) of the participants reported a memory between birth and eighteen months of life; a third (33 percent) reported a memory that occurred at age twelve months or earlier; and 18 percent reported memories dated from six months or earlier. Remarkably, 4 percent of the sample reported memories from the first week of life!

## AGE-REGRESSION

Age-regression involves "regressing" a person back through time to an earlier life period. Subjects are typically asked to mentally re-create events that occurred at successively earlier periods in life, or to focus on a particular event at a specific age, with suggestions to fully relive the event. A televised documentary (*Frontline* 1995) showed a group therapy session in which a woman was age-regressed through childhood, to the womb, and eventually to being trapped in her mother's Fallopian tube. The woman provided a convincing demonstration of the emotional and physical discomfort that one would experience if one were indeed stuck in such an uncomfortable position. Although the woman may have believed in the veracity of her experience, research indicates that her regression experiences were not memory-based. Instead, age-regressed subjects behave according to situational cues and their knowledge, beliefs, and assumptions about age-relevant behaviors. According to Nash (1987), age-regressed adults do not show the expected patterns on many indices of development, including brain activity (EEGs) and visual illusions. No matter how compelling, "age-regressed experiences" do not represent literal reinstatements of childhood experiences, behaviors, and feelings.

## HYPNOTIC AGE-REGRESSION

Although hypnosis is often used to facilitate the experience of age-regression, it can distort memories of early-life events. Nash, Drake, Wiley, Khalsa, and Lynn (1986) attempted to corroborate the memories of subjects who had participated in an earlier age-regression experiment. This experiment involved age-regressing hypnotized and role-playing (control) subjects to age three to a scene in which they were in the soothing presence of their mothers. During the experiment, subjects reported the identity of their transitional objects (e.g., blankets, teddy bears). Third-party verification (parent report) of the accuracy of recall was obtained for fourteen hypnotized subjects and ten control subjects. Hypnotic subjects were less able than were control subjects to identify the transitional objects actually used. Subjects' hypnotic recollections matched their parents' reports only 21 percent of the time, whereas control subjects' reports were corroborated by their parents 70 percent of the time.

Sivec, Lynn, and Malinoski (1997) age-regressed participants to the age of five and suggested that they played with a Cabbage Patch Doll (if a girl) or a He-Man toy (if a boy). These toys were not released until two or three years after the target time of the age-regression suggestion. Half of the subjects received hypnotic age-regression instructions, and half received suggestions to age-regress that were not administered in a hypnotic context. While none of the nonhypnotized persons was influenced by the suggestion, 20 percent of the hypnotized subjects rated the memory as real and were confident that the event occurred at the age to which they were regressed.

## PAST-LIFE REGRESSION

The search for traumatic memories can extend to well before birth (see Mills & Lynn 2000). "Past-life regression therapy" is based on the premise that traumas that occurred in previous lives contribute to current psychological and physical symptoms. For example, psychiatrist Brian Weiss (1988) published a widely publicized series of cases focusing on patients who were hypnotized and age-regressed to "go back to" the origin of a present-day problem. When patients were regressed, they reported events that Weiss interpreted as having their source in previous lives.

Vivid and realistic experiences during age-regression can seem very convincing to both patient and therapist. However, Spanos, Menary, Gabora, DuBreuil, and Dewhirst (1991) determined that the information participants provided about specific time periods during their hypnotic age-regression was almost "invariably incorrect" (p. 137). For example, one participant who was regressed to ancient times claimed to be Julius Caesar, emperor of Rome, in 50 B.C., even though the designations of B.C. and A.D. were not adopted until centuries later, and even though Julius Caesar died decades prior to the first Roman emperor. Spanos et al. (ibid.) informed some participants that past-life identities were likely to be of a different gender, culture, and race from that of the present personality, whereas other participants received no prehypnotic information about past-life identities. Participants' past-life experiences were elaborate, conformed to induced expectancies about past-life identities (e.g., gender, race), and varied in terms of the pre-hypnotic information participants received about the frequency of child abuse during past historical periods. In summary, hypnotically induced past-live experiences are fantasies constructed from available cultural narratives about past lives and known or surmised facts regarding specific historical periods, as well as cues present in the hypnotic situation (Spanos 1996).

## SYMPTOM INTERPRETATION

Therapists often inform suspected abuse victims that their symptoms suggest a history of abuse (Blume 1990; Fredrickson 1988). Examples of symptom interpretation can be found in many popular psychology and self-help sources (e.g., Bass & Davis 1992). Some popular self-help books on the topic of incest include lists of symptoms (e.g., "Do you use work or achievements to compensate for inadequate feelings in other parts of your life?") that are presented as possible or probable correlates of childhood incest. Blume's "Incest Survivors' Aftereffects Checklist" consists of thirty-four such correlates. The scale instructions read: "Do you find many characteristics of yourself on this list? If so, you could be a survivor of incest." Blume also indicates that "clusters" of these items predict childhood sexual abuse and that "the more items endorsed by an individual the more likely that there is a history of incest." Many of the characteristics on such checklists are vague and applicable to many non-abused individuals. Much of the seeming "accuracy" of such checklists could stem from "PT Barnum effects"—the tendency to believe that highly general statements true of many individuals in the population apply specifically to oneself (Emery 2002).

Although there may be numerous psychological correlates of sexual abuse (but see Rind, Tromovitch & Bauserman 1998, for a competing view), no known constellation of specific symptoms, let alone diagnosis, is indicative of a history of abuse. Some genuine victims of childhood incest experience many symptoms, others only some, and still others none. Moreover, nonvictims experience many of the same symptoms often associated with sexual abuse (Tavris 1993). Nevertheless, Poole et al. (1995) found that more than one-third of the US practitioners surveyed reported that they used symptom interpretation to recover suspected memories of abuse.

## BOGUS PERSONALITY INTERPRETATION

For ethical reasons, researchers have not directly tested the hypothesis that false memories of childhood abuse can be elicited by informing individuals that their personality characteristics are suggestive of such a history. However, studies have shown that personality interpretation can create highly implausible or false memories. Spanos and his colleagues (Spanos et al. 1999) informed participants that their personality indicated that they had a certain experience during the first week of life. After participants completed a questionnaire, they were told that a computer-generated personality profile based on their responses indicated they were "High Perceptual Cognitive Monitors" and that people with this profile had experienced special visual stimulation by a mobile within the first week of life. Participants were falsely told that the study was designed to recover memories to confirm the personality test scores. The participants were age-regressed to the crib; half of the participants were hypnotized and half received non-hypnotic age regression instructions. In the non-hypnotic group, 95 percent of the participants reported infant memories and 56 percent reported the target mobile. However, all these participants indicated that the memories were fantasy constructions or they were unsure if the memories were real. In the hypnotic group, 79 percent of the participants reported infant memories, and 46 percent reported the target mobile. Forty-nine percent of these participants believed the memories were real, and only 16 percent classified the memories as fantasies.

DuBreuil, Garry, and Loftus (1998) used the bogus personality interpretation paradigm and non-hypnotic age-regression to implant memories of the second day of life (crib group) or the first day of kindergarten (kindergarten group). College students were administered a test that purportedly measured personality and were told that, based on their scores, they were likely to have participated in a nationwide program designed to enhance the development of personality and cognitive abilities by means of red and green moving mobiles. The crib group was told that this enrichment occurred in the hospital immediately after birth, and the kindergarten group was told that the mobiles were placed in kindergarten classrooms. Participants were given the false information that memory functions "like a videotape recorder" and that age-regression can access otherwise inaccessible memories. Participants were age-regressed (non-hypnotically) to the appropriate time period and given suggestions to visualize themselves at the target age. Twenty-five percent of the kindergarten group and 55 percent of the crib group reported the target memory. All kindergarten participants believed that their memories corresponded to real events. In the crib group, 33 percent believed in the reality of their memories, 50 percent were unsure, and 17 percent of participants did not believe in the reality of their memories.

## DREAM INTERPRETATION

Viewed by Freud as the "royal road to the unconscious," dreams have been used to provide a window on past experiences, including repressed traumatic events. For example, van der Kolk, Britz, Burr, Sherry, and Hartmann (1984) claimed that dreams can represent "exact replicas" of traumatic experiences (p. 188), a view not unlike that propounded by Fredrickson (1992), who argued that dreams are a vehicle by which "Buried memories of abuse intrude into . . . consciousness" (p. 44).

The popularity of dream interpretation has waned in recent years. However, survey research indicates that at least a third of US psychotherapists (37–44 percent) still use this technique (see also Brenneis 1997; Polusny & Follette 1996). These statistics are noteworthy given that no data exist to support the idea that dreams can be interpreted as indicative of a history of child abuse (Lindsay & Read 1994). When dreams are interpreted in this manner by an authority figure such as a therapist, rather than as reflecting the residues of the day's events or as the day's concerns seeping into dreams, it can constitute a strong suggestion to the patient that abuse actually occurred.

Mazzoni and her colleagues simulated the effects of dream interpretation of stressful yet non-abuse-related life events. Mazzoni, Lombardo, Malvagia, and Loftus (1997) had participants report on their childhood experiences on two occasions, three to four weeks apart. Between sessions, some subjects were exposed to a brief (half-hour) therapy simulation in which an expert clinician analyzed a dream report that they had brought to the session. No matter what participants dreamed, they received the suggestion that their dream was indicative of having experienced certain events (e.g., being lost in a public place or abandoned by parents) before the age of three. Although subjects had indicated that they had not experienced these events before age three, many individuals revised their accounts of their past. Relative to controls who had not received the personalized suggestion, "therapy" participants were far more likely to develop false beliefs that before age three they had been lost in a public place, had felt lonely and lost in an unfamiliar place, and had been abandoned by their parents.

Mazzoni, Loftus, Seitz, and Lynn (1999) extended this paradigm to a memory of having been bullied as a child; dream interpretation increased participants' confidence that the event (being bullied or getting lost) had occurred, compared with control participants, who were given a brief lecture about dreams. Six of the twenty-two participants in the dream interpretation condition recalled the bullying event and four of the five participants in the dream interpretation condition recalled getting lost. In conclusion, it is possible to implant childhood memories using personality and dream interpretation.

## BIBLIOTHERAPY

Many therapists who treat patients with suspected abuse histories prescribe "survivor books" or self-help books written specifically for survivors of childhood abuse to provide "confirmation" that the individual's symptoms are due to past abuse and to provide a means of gaining access to memories. The books typically provide imaginative exercises and stories of other survivors' struggles, as well as potential support for actual abuse survivors. However, the fact that the writers interpret current symptoms as indicative of an abuse history and include suggestive stories of abuse survivors may increase the risk that readers will develop false memories of abuse. Some of the most influential popular books of this genre include Bass and Davis's (1988) *Courage to Heal,* Fredrickson's (1992) *Repressed Memories,* and Blume's (1990) *Secret Survivors: Uncovering Incest and Its Aftereffects in Women.*

Mazzoni, Loftus, and Kirsch (2001) provided a dramatic illustration of how reading material and psychological symptom interpretation can increase the plausibility of an initially implausible memory of witnessing a demonic possession. The study was conducted in Italy, where demonic possession is viewed as a more plausible occurrence than in America. However, in an initial testing session, all of the participants indicated that not only was demonic possession implausible, but that it was very unlikely that they had personally witnessed an occurrence of possession as children. A month after the first session, participants in one group read three short articles indicating that demonic possession is more common than is generally believed and that many children have witnessed such an event. Participants were compared with individuals who read three short articles about choking and with individuals who received no manipulation. Participants exposed to one of the manipulations returned the following week and, based on their responses to a fear questionnaire they completed, were informed (regardless of their actual responses) that their fear profile indicated that they had probably either witnessed a possession or had almost choked during early childhood.

When the original questionnaire was completed in a final session, 18 percent of the students indicated that they had probably witnessed possession. No changes in memories were evident in the control condition. In summary, events that were not experienced during childhood and initially thought to be highly implausible can, with sufficient credibility-enhancing information, come to be viewed as having occurred in real life.

## HYPOTHESIZED PATH OF FALSE MEMORY CREATION

Imaginative narratives of sexual abuse that never occurred and past life reports arise when patients come to believe that the narrative provides a plausible explanation for current life difficulties. The narrative can achieve a high degree of plausibility due to many factors: (1) the prevalent belief that abuse and psychopathology are associated; (2) the therapist's support or suggestion of this interpretation; (3) the failure to consider alternative explanations for everyday problems; (4) the search for confirmatory data; (5) the use of suggestive memory recovery techniques that increase the plausibility of abuse and yield remembrances consistent with the assumption that abuse occurred; (6) increasing commitment to the narrative on the part of the client and therapist, escalating dependence on the therapist, and anxiety reduction associated with ambiguity reduction; (7) the encouragement of a "conversion" or "coming out" experience by the therapist or supportive community (e.g., therapy group), which solidifies the role of "abuse victim," and which is accompanied by reinforcing feelings of empowerment; and (8) the narrative's provision of continuity to the past and the future, as well as a sense of comfort and identity.

People are not equally vulnerable to the potentially suggestive influences of memory recovery procedures. At the very least, it is necessary to believe that at least some memories remain intact indefinitely so that they can be retrieved and that memory recovery techniques can retrieve these stored memories. In addition, fantasy-prone, imaginative, compliant, as well as highly hypnotically suggestible people appear to be especially vulnerable to suggestive influences and to the development of false memories.

The evidence provides little support for the use of memory recovery techniques in psychotherapy. Contrary to the idea that people repress memories in the face of trauma, traumatic events are highly memorable (Shobe & Kihlstrom 1997). Even if a small percentage of accurate memories can be recovered in psychotherapy, there is no evidence for a causal connection between non-remembered abuse and psychopathology. In addition, the mere experience of painful emotions, when not tied to attempts to bolster positive coping and mastery, can be harmful (Littrell 1998). Indeed, there is no empirically supported psychotherapy that relies on the recovery of traumatic memories to achieve a positive therapeutic outcome. Adshead (1997) argued that if memory work with trauma patients is not effective, then "it would therefore be just as unethical to use memory work for patients who could not use it or benefit by it, as it would be to prescribe the wrong medication, or employ a useless surgical technique" (p. 437).

Before concluding, let us be clear about what the findings reviewed do not mean as well as what they do mean. First, all memory recovery techniques are not necessarily problematic. For example, the "cognitive interview" (Fisher & Geiselman 1992), which incorporates a variety of techniques derived from experimental research on memory (e.g., providing subjects with retrieval cues, searching for additional memorial details), holds promise as a method of enhancing memory in eyewitness contexts. Second, we do not wish to imply that all uses of hypnosis in psychotherapy are problematic. Controlled research evidence suggests that hypnosis may be useful in treating pain, medical conditions, and habit disorders (e.g., smoking cessation), and as an adjunct to cognitive-behavioral therapy (e.g., anxiety, obesity). Nevertheless, the extent to which hypnosis provides benefits above and beyond relaxation in such cases remains unclear (Lynn et al. 2000). The questionable scientific status of hypnosis as a memory recovery technique has no bearing on the therapeutic efficacy of hypnosis, which must ultimately be investigated and judged on its own merits. Finally, we do not wish to claim that all memories recovered after years or decades of forgetting are necessarily false. We remain open to the possibility that certain recovered childhood memories are veridical, although further research is needed to document their existence and possible prevalence. These important and unresolved issues notwithstanding, the conclusion that certain suggestive therapeutic practices can foster false memories in some clients appears indisputable.

## NOTES

1. The following reviews were used as sources: Erdelyi 1994; Lynn, Lock, Myers & Payne 1997; Lynn, Neuschatz, Fite & Rhue 2001; Nash 1987; Spanos 1996; Steblay & Bothwell 1994; Whitehouse, Dinges, Orne & Orne 1988.

2. Some therapists do not assume that early memories reports are necessarily accurate but posit that such memories nevertheless provide a window into clients' personalities; the claim of these therapists is not of concern to us here.

## REFERENCES

Adler, A. 1927. *Understanding Human Nature.* New York: Greenberg.

Adshead, G. 1997. Seekers after truth: Ethical issues raised by the discussion of "false" and "recovered" memories. In *Recollections of Trauma: Scientific Evidence and Clinical Practice,* edited by J. D. Read and D. S. Lindsay .New York: Plenum Press.

American Medical Association. 1994. Council on Scientific Affairs. *Memories of Childhood Abuse.* CSA Report 5-A-94.

American Psychological Association. 1995. *Psychotherapy guidelines for working with clients who may have an abuse or trauma history.* Division 17 Committee on Women, Division 42 Trauma and Gender Issues Committee.

Bass, E., and L. Davis. 1992. *The Courage to Heal.* New York: Harper & Row.

Blume, E. S. 1990. *Secret Survivors: Uncovering Incest and Its Aftereffects in Women.* New York: John Wiley and Sons.

Brenneis, C. B. (1997). Final Report of APA Working Group on Investigation of Memories of Childhood Abuse. *Psychoanalytic Psychology* 14: 531–47.

Canadian Psychiatric Association. 1996, March 25. Position statement: Adult recovered memories of childhood sexual abuse. *Canadian Journal of Psychiatry* 41: 305–306.

DuBreuil, S. C., M. Garry, and E. F. Loftus. 1998. Tales from the crib: Age-regression and the creation of unlikely memories. In *Truth in Memory*, edited by S. J. Lynn and K. M. McConkey. Washington, D.C.: American Psychological Association.

Emery, C. L. 2002. The validity of childhood sexual abuse victim checklists in popular psychology literature: A Barnum effect. Unpublished honors thesis, Emory University, Atlanta.

Erdelyi, M. 1994. Hypnotic hypermnesia: The empty set of hypermnesia. *International Journal of Clinical and Experimental Hypnosis* 42: 379–90.

Farmer, S. 1989. *Adult Children of Abusive Parents: A Healing Program for Those Who Have Been Physically, Sexually, or Emotionally Abused.* Los Angeles: Lowell House.

Fisher, R. P., and R. E. Geiselman. 1992. *Memory Enhancement Techniques for Investigative Interviewing.* Springfield, IL: Charles C. Thomas.

Frederickson, R. 1992. *Repressed Memories.* New York: Fireside/Parkside.

*Frontline.* 1995. Divided memories. Producer: Ofra Bikel.

Hyman, I. E., Jr., T. H. Husband, and F.J. Billings. 1995. False memories of childhood experiences. *Applied Cognitive Psychology* 9: 181–97.

Lindsay, D. S., and D. Read. 1994. Psychotherapy and memories of childhood sexual abuse: A cognitive perspective. *Applied Cognitive Psychology* 8: 281–338.

Littrell, J. 1998. Is the experience of painful emotion therapeutic? *Clinical Psychology Review* 18: 71–102.

Loftus, E. F. 1993. The reality of repressed memories. *American Psychologist* 48: 518–37.

Loftus, E. F., J. A. Coan, and J. E. Pickrell. 1996. Manufacturing false memories using bits of reality. In *Implicit Memory and Metacognition*, edited by L. M. Reder. Mahwah, NJ: Lawrence Erlbaum, pp. 195–220.

Loftus, E. F., and G. Mazzoni. 1998. Using imagination and personalized suggestion to change behavior. *Behavior Therapy* 29: 691–708.

Loftus, E. F., and J. E. Pickrell. 1995. The formation of false memories. *Psychiatric Annals* 25: 720–25.

Lynn, S. J., I. Kirsch, A. Barabasz, E. Cardena, and D. Patterson. 2000. Hypnosis as an empirically supported adjunctive technique: The state of the evidence. *International Journal of Clinical and Experimental Hypnosis* 48: 343–61.

Lynn, S. J., T. G. Lock, B. Myers, and D. G. Payne. 1997. Recalling the unrecallable: Should hypnosis be used to recover memories in psychotherapy? *Current Directions in Psychological Science* 6: 79–83.

Lynn, S. J., B. Myers, and P. Malinoski. 1997. Hypnosis, pseudomemories, and clinical guidelines: A sociocognitive perspective. In *Recollections of Trauma: Scientific Research and Clinical Practice*, edited by D. Read and S. Lindsay. New York: Plenum Press.

Lynn, S. J., J. Neuschatz, R. Fite, and J. W. Rhue. 2001. Hypnosis and memory: Implications for the courtroom and psychotherapy. In *Memory Suggestion, and the Forensic Interview*, edited by M. Eisen and G. Goodman. New York: Guilford.

Malinoski, P., and S. J. Lynn. 1999. The plasticity of very early memory reports: Social pressure, hypnotizability, compliance, and interrogative suggestibility. *International Journal of Clinical and Experimental Hypnosis* 47: 320–45.

Malinoski, P., S. J. Lynn, and H. Sivec. 1998. The assessment, validity, and determinants of early memory reports: A critical review. In *Truth in Memory*, edited by S. J. Lynn and K. McConkey. New York: Guilford.

Mazzoni, G. A., E. F. Loftus, and I. Kirsch. 2001. Changing beliefs about implausible autobiographical memories. *Journal of Experimental Psychology: Applied* 7: 51–59.

Mazzoni, G. A., E. F. Loftus, A. Seitz, and S.J. Lynn. 1999. Creating a new childhood: Changing beliefs and memories through dream interpretation. *Applied Cognitive Psychology* 13: 125–44.

Mazzoni, G. A., P. Lombardo, S. Malvagia, and E.F. Loftus. 1997. Dream Interpretation and False Beliefs. Unpublished manuscript, University of Florence and University of Washington.

Meiselman, K. 1990. *Resolving the Trauma of Incest: Reintegration Therapy with Survivors*. San Francisco: Jossey-Bass.

Mills, A., and S. J. Lynn. 2000. Past-life experiences. In *The Varieties of Anomalous Experience*, edited by E. Cardena, S.J. Lynn, and S. Krippner. New York: Guilford.

Nash, M. J., M. Drake, R. Wiley, S. Khalsa, and S. J. Lynn. 1986. The accuracy of recall of hypnotically age regressed subjects. *Journal of Abnormal Psychology* 95: 298–300.

Nash, M. R. 1987. What, if anything, is regressed about hypnotic age regression? A review of the empirical literature. *Psychological Bulletin* 102: 42–52.

Olson, H. A. 1979. The hypnotic retrieval of early recollections. In *Early Recollections: Their Use in Diagnosis and Psychotherapy*, edited by H. A. Olson. Springfield, IL: Charles C. Thomas.

Papanek, H. 1979. The use of early recollections in psychotherapy. In *Early Recollections: Their Use in Diagnosis and Psychotherapy*, edited by H. A. Olson. Springfield, IL: Charles C. Thomas.

Polusny, M. A., and V. M. Follette. 1996. Remembering childhood sexual abuse: A national survey of psychologists' clinical practices, beliefs, and personal experiences. *Professional Psychology: Research and Practice* 27: 41–52.

Poole, D. A., D. S. Lindsay, A. Memon, and R. Bull. 1995. Psychotherapists' opinions, practices, and experiences with recovery of memories of incestuous abuse. *Journal of Consulting and Clinical Psychology* 68: 426–37.

Porter, S., J. C. Yuille, and D. R. Lehman. 1999. The nature of real, implanted, and fabricated childhood emotional events: Implications for the recovered memory debate. *Law and Human Behavior* 23: 517–37.

Rind, B., P. Tromovitch, & R. Bauserman. 1998. A metal-analytic examination of assumed properties of child sexual abuse using college samples. *Psychological Bulletin* 124: 22–53.

Roland, C. B. 1993. Exploring childhood memories with adult survivors of sexual abuse: Concrete reconstruction and visualization techniques. *Journal of Mental Health Counseling* 15: 363–72.

Shobe, K. K., and J. F. Kihlstrom. 1997. Is traumatic memory special? *Current Directions in Psychological Science* 6: 70–74.

Sivec, H. J., S. J. Lynn, and P. T. Malinoski. 1997. Hypnosis in the cabbage patch: Age regression with verifiable events. Unpublished manuscript, State University of New York at Binghamton.

Spanos, N. P. 1996. *Multiple Identities and False Memories: A Sociocognitive Perspective*. Washington, DC: American Psychological Association

Spanos, N. P., C. A. Burgess, M. F. Burgess, C. Samuels, and W. O. Blois. 1999. Creating false memories of infancy with hypnotic and nonhypnotic procedures. *Applied Cognitive Psychology* 13: 201–18.

Spanos, N. P., E. Menary, M. J. Gabora, S. C. DuBreuil, and B. Dewhirst. 1991. Secondary identity enactments during hypnotic past-life regression: A sociocognitive perspective. *Journal of Personality and Social Psychology* 61: 308–20.

Steblay, N. M., and R. K. Bothwell. 1994. Evidence for hypnotically refreshed testimony: The view from the laboratory. *Law and Human Behavior* 18: 635–51.

Tavris, C. 1993. Beware the incest survivor machine. *New York Times Book Review,* January 3, pp. 1, 16–17.

Van der Kolk, B. A. 1994. The body keeps the score: Memory and the evolving psychobiology of posttraumatic stress. *Harvard Review of Psychiatry* 1: 253–65.

Van der Kolk, B., R. Britz, W. Burr, S. Sherry, & E. Hartmann. 1984. Nightmares and trauma: A comparison of nightmares after combat with lifelong nightmares in veterans. *American Journal of Psychiatry* 141: 187–90.

Weiss, B. L. 1988. *Many Lives, Many Masters.* New York: Simon & Schuster.

Whitehouse, W. G., D. F. Dinges, E. C. Orne, & M. T. Orne. 1988. Hypnotic hypermnesia: Enhanced memory accessibility or report bias? *Journal of Abnormal Psychology* 97: 289–95.

Yapko, M. D. 1994. Suggestibility and repressed memories of abuse: A survey of psychotherapists' beliefs. *American Journal of Clinical Hypnosis* 36: 163–71.

# SECTION VI. HOW TO EVALUATE PSYCHOTHERAPY

# INTRODUCTION

There are hundreds of brands of psychotherapy, with new ones added every year. Rebirthing, reparenting, eye movement desensitization and reprocessing, Thought Field Therapy (TFT), angel therapy, Buddha psychotherapy, music therapy, rage reduction therapy, Jungian sandplay therapy, calligraphy therapy, dolphin-assisted therapy, psychological theater therapy, vegetotherapy, and sensory-motor integration therapy—these are merely a handful of the bewildering therapeutic fads that populate the mental health *mind*field. Although some of these strange-sounding techniques may be helpful, most are untested. Still others have been tested and found to be largely or entirely ineffective— or even harmful.

Given this vast array of options, how can prospective psychotherapy clients sort out what's effective from what isn't? And how can they avoid treatments that might make them worse? Needless to say, the task is daunting.

Some psychotherapy researchers have argued, however, that prospective clients need not be all that concerned about their choice of therapy. In support of this position, these authors sometimes invoke the so-called Dodo Bird verdict, named after the Dodo Bird in Lewis Carroll's *Alice's Adventures in Wonderland*, who declared (following a race) that "All have won, and all must have prizes." According to the Dodo Bird verdict, all psychotherapies are about equally effective. Extending this logic, mental health consumers need not worry much about fad therapies, because most or all new treatments probably work about as well as existing treatments.

Some psychotherapy research conducted in the 1970s and 1980s offered support for the Dodo Bird verdict. Indeed, there is overwhelming evidence that many psychotherapies exert positive effects on depressed mood, anxiety, insomnia, sexual dysfunction, bulimia, and several other psychological problems. Moreover, for some disorders, like adult depression, a broad array of psychological treatments seem to work about equally well.

Nevertheless, recent findings call the Dodo Bird verdict into serious question. For example, studies of treatments for anxiety disorders show that behavioral and cognitive-behavioral therapies—those that focus on changing individuals' deeply ingrained patterns of avoiding feared stimuli and challenging their irrational beliefs concerning these stimuli—tend to be better than other therapies. Similarly, behavioral therapies tend to be better than nonbehavioral therapies for many childhood disorders, such as conduct disorder, a condition characterized by a history of antisocial and even criminal acts.

Moreover, evidence suggests that certain psychotherapies may make people worse rather than better. This evidence contradicts the Dodo Bird verdict. To consider just one example, take crisis debriefing, a popular technique that attempts to ward off post-traumatic stress disorder (PTSD) symptoms in trauma-exposed individuals by strongly encouraging them to "process" the emotions associated with the disturbing events they witnessed. Controlled studies show that crisis debriefing is at best ineffective; in several studies, it has actually been found to increase individuals' risk for post-traumatic stress symptoms.

Still other therapies aren't directly harmful but don't do much good either. These therapies can produce indirect harm by depriving clients of time, money, and resources. (As we noted earlier in the book, economists refer to these negative side effects as "opportunity costs.") Moreover, these therapies can lead people to forego effective treatments, thereby leading them to forfeit the opportunity for much-needed help. So the choice of a therapy does matter after all.

In this section, Robyn Dawes and Leonard Bickman take on common myths regarding mental health practice. Both note that there is little evidence for the widespread belief that amount of experience as a therapist is strongly associated with therapeutic efficacy, and Dawes describes findings from basic psychological research (such as the difficulty we all have in profiting from delayed and inconsistent feedback) that may explain this surprising finding. Bickman further outlines a number of other popularly held misconceptions concerning therapeutic practice. For example, he notes that there is scant support for claims that licensed therapists do better than nonlicensed therapists or that clinical supervision enhances the effectiveness of psychotherapy.

The next several chapters place a variety of widely used but largely unsubstantiated therapies under the research microscope. James Mulick and his colleagues examine the "craze" surrounding facilitated communication (FC), which became immensely popular in the early 1990s as a treatment for infantile autism and which appears to be staging a comeback in the early twenty-first century. The proponents of FC assert that it allows entirely mute autistic individuals to communicate with the aid of a facilitator, who offers resistance to their hands over a computer keyboard. Yet controlled research demonstrates overwhelmingly that the apparent effects of FC are due to inadvertent facilitator influence over individuals' hand movements. Disturbingly, FC has not merely falsely raised the hopes of thousands of parents of children with autism but also led to dozens of uncorroborated accusations of physical and sexual abuse against these parents.

Alan Dowd next briefly examines a myriad of treatments for attention-deficit/hyperactivity disorder (ADHD). He points out that despite widespread claims of easy "cures" for ADHD, the research literature offers no support for quick fixes. Dowd further describes several popular treatments for ADHD, including dietary interventions and homeopathy, that are largely devoid of scientific support.

Next, Scott Lilienfeld looks at the science of eye movement desensitization and reprocessing (EMDR), which gained fame in the 1990s as a popular treatment for PTSD. As Lilienfeld points out, there is little evidence that EMDR works better than standard behavioral treatments that rely on exposing individuals to feared stimuli. Nor is there much evidence that the back-and-forth eye movements that make EMDR distinctive contribute anything to its efficacy. Numerous studies conducted in the decade following the publication of Lilienfeld's article have only strengthened these conclusions. On the positive side, EMDR clearly works better than doing nothing, at least for PTSD. But on the negative side, there is no evidence that it represents an important innovation on the therapy scene, let alone a "miracle cure" or "paradigm shift," as claimed by some of its proponents.

Brandon Gaudiano and James Herbert examine yet another new approach to the treatment of PTSD and related conditions, namely, Thought Field Therapy (TFT). We can think of TFT as much like "psychological acupuncture": by tapping on certain points corresponding to individuals' invisible energy fields, TFT supposedly helps restore individuals' psychological balance. As Gaudiano and Herbert note, however, there is no good evidence that the apparent effects of TFT amount to anything more than a placebo.

Jean Mercer evaluates the theoretical rationale and scientific evidence underpinning a spectrum of treatments called attachment therapies, which include rebirthing, holding, and reparenting. Most of these treatments are premised on the dubious assumption that early separation from one's biological parents produces unprocessed rage, which needs to be "released." As Mercer points out, these treatments violate much of what is known about the science of human attachment. Moreover, she notes that the scientific evidence for these treatments is so sparse—and so methodologically flawed—as to render it impossible to draw any inferences concerning their efficacy. This striking absence of evidence is particularly problematic given that some variants of attachment therapy are physically dangerous. The late Margaret Singer and Janja Lalich draw similar conclusions in their review of these treatments and describe the flawed logic underpinning other therapies (e.g., regression therapies) that purport to solve present life conflicts by "reliving" past events.

The final chapter in this section examines debates surrounding antidepressant medication, an increasingly controversial area of treatment. In particular, Brandon Gaudiano and Gary Epstein-Lubow evaluate the raging scientific controversy regarding the extent to which the seeming efficacy of antidepressants is attributable to the placebo effect, and the authors discuss another recent controversy, namely, the question of whether antidepressants increase suicide risk in a subset of depressed individuals. As Gaudiano and Epstein-Lubow observe, there is reasonably clear evidence that antidepressants exacerbate suicidal behaviors in children and adolescents, although the magnitude of this effect is modest. In contrast, the evidence for adults is considerably murkier. Gaudiano and Epstein-Lubow demonstrate that media coverage of both scientific controversies has often been marked by a lack of context and scientific balance, contributing to understandable confusion on the part of mental health consumers.

## 15.

# PSYCHOTHERAPY: THE MYTH OF EXPERTISE

### Robyn M. Dawes

*I had therapy cases I just botched, and yet they got better. Other cases I did great, and yet the patient deteriorated. I wondered what was going on here.*

—Lee Sechrest[1]

Psychotherapy works overall in reducing psychologically painful and often debilitating symptoms. The reasons it works are unclear, because entirely different approaches may work equally well for the same problem or set of problems. Recovery is a *base rate* phenomenon. That is, in predicting the likelihood that a particular individual will recover, we can do little better than by predicting from the overall rate of recovery; we have no insight into exactly why some people get better while others don't. We do, however, know something about psychotherapist characteristics that make it work. Therapists in verbally oriented therapies, we know, should be "empathetic," while those using primarily behavioral techniques should have some knowledge of behavioral principles.

We also know that *the credentials and experience of the psychotherapists are unrelated to patient outcomes,* based on well over five hundred scientific studies of psychotherapy outcome. In fact, it is partly because psychotherapy in its multitude of forms is generally effective that I am writing this chapter. Having it more generally available is socially desirable.

## THE NEED FOR SCIENTIFIC STUDIES TO EVALUATE EFFICACY

The scientific evaluation of psychotherapy is a fairly recent activity. The profession's own resistance to evaluating itself stemmed partly from its psychoanalytic origins. Freud's basic idea was that distressing psychological symptoms result from "the return of the repressed" in a debilitating form (not from repression per se). Adults defend against unacceptable needs, wishes, and feelings—which in childhood may have been quite conscious—and keep them from consciousness by means of "defense mechanisms," which are themselves unconscious, specifically, an unconscious part of the "ego." If during childhood these defense mechanisms are not well constructed, or if certain experiences such as sexual seduction by an adult or persistent fantasies about it make it particularly difficult for the developing person to prevent these needs, thoughts, and wishes from impacting him or her, they may express themselves as psychiatric symptoms. For example, Freud's patient "Dora's" coughing fits were thought to express both her wish to engage in oral sex with her father (perhaps after observing him engaging in that activity with his mistress) and her revulsion at the wish.[2] (Freud, ever the Victorian moralist, believed that the father's engaging in oral sex provided conclusive proof that he was impotent, which supported Freud's further conclusion that some hereditary constitutional factors were involved in the development of neurotic symptoms.)

Only through prolonged psychoanalytic sessions leading to a "transference" to the therapist of the patient's childhood reactions to parents and other significant adults can the defense mechanisms, and the impulses they are attempting to keep from consciousness, be understood. The therapist is extremely passive during psychoanalytic sessions, both to encourage this transference and to avoid premature "interpretations" of either the defenses or the needs; premature interpretations would lead to a "resistance" from the patient that would discourage rather than encourage insight. With eventual insight comes an ability to "sublimate" the unacceptable impulses in socially constructive ways (sublimation itself being a type of defense mechanism). Such sublimation can occur without the help of a therapist or psychoanalyst; for example, when the modern psychiatrist George Vaillant[3] discussed the men whose lives he followed in terms of the "maturity" of their defense mechanisms, sublimation was considered the pinnacle. Unlike Freud, Vaillant concluded that defense mechanisms evolve throughout adult life as well as childhood and that final maturity cannot be well predicted from earlier life. An example of sublimation, according to Vaillant, was a man he studied who had channeled his rather intense anger into productive political activity and writing.

This psychoanalytic approach takes a long time ("interminable," according to some of its critics). Moreover, if a symptom is directly addressed before the patient is able to deal with it effectively, the theory runs, a new symptom will appear in its place, because the "basic issue" remains unresolved. The term used was "symptom substitution." Subsequently, studies indicated that contrary to Freudian theory, symptom substitution did not generally occur. Another claim was that only the therapist—and perhaps eventually the patient—could understand the true nature of the patient's problems and their possible resolution and evaluate the efficacy of the process.

Let me share an anecdote that illustrates this claim. In 1966 (when I had joint appointments at the Ann Arbor VA Hospital and in the psychology department at the University of Michigan), a former colleague at the hospital, Dr. Lawrence J. Bookbinder, was investigating the use of behavioral techniques to alleviate some of the more distressing psychological symptoms that the psychiatric patients suffered. One afternoon in the coffee shop of the psychology department, I discussed Bookbinder's work with two professors who were considered central to the department's clinical program. They agreed that there was no evidence of symptom substitution in these patients, but they made the remarkable assertion that the mere elimination of symptoms is irrelevant to the question of whether a patient is "cured." I argued that being freed of a really debilitating symptom would lead to an enhanced quality of life that, in turn, could alleviate other psychological problems. For example, many of the men at the hospital suffered from impotence, and the inability to have a good sex life was very painful to them. I was about to stress the importance of positive feedback among different symptoms, between symptoms and feelings, and so on. But my senior colleagues interrupted. It didn't matter whether a man was actually impotent or not, they said. What was important was the total meaning for that man of impotence as such. That meaning could be assessed only through prolonged therapy; the actual physical fact of regaining sexual potency would be important only if it resulted from the transference process and greater self-understanding. In fact, it didn't even matter whether the impotence went away at all, they said, as long as the transference was successful. Only a truly expert therapist could evaluate whether it had been successful.

It is indeed very difficult to "get inside" someone else to determine unambiguously whether that person has benefited from any form of psychotherapy. But eliminating a symptom that is of crucial concern to the client really does matter. I agree with Hans Strupp that "a global judgment of [psychotherapy] outcome, which is analogous to a still photograph of an object in motion, must always remain exceedingly difficult and elusive" and that outcome judgments are "contingent on *values* placed on human behavior."[4] But it is exactly a value-laden outcome for which the client (or insurance company, or government) is paying. Procedures—whether they are medical techniques or social programs—must be evaluated on the basis of certain indicators like blood pressure or infant mortality rate that nonetheless do not in and of themselves tell us the "whole story." A perfect one-to-one relationship between observable indicators and the global process in which we are interested is difficult to establish, but not having one available should not be used as an excuse to avoid evaluating what is happening by assessing these indicators. As Eugene Meehan points out, these indicators must be chosen wisely;

infant mortality rates cannot be used to evaluate the quality of nursing home care, to use his example.[5] But we must insist that a procedure such as psychotherapy be assessed in a way that allows the outside observer to reach a conclusion about its effectiveness. In psychotherapy, symptom remission is a prime candidate for such an indicator, as it is in medicine. What medical doctor would proclaim a patient "cured" without relief of painful symptoms? In fact, after my conversation in the coffee shop, the studies that have been conducted used symptom remission as the primary criterion of cure or improvement.

These studies are very important simply by virtue of the fact that they involve outside observers evaluating the efficacy of psychotherapy. The philosophy that only the individual therapist can tell whether improvement in a client has occurred is flawed. In the first place, the unsystematic judgment of a therapist is as subject to bias as is the unsystematic judgment of anyone else, including clients. The problems of unsystematic judgment are well documented, especially those of retrospective memory. Therapists, thoroughly committed to a profession—and perhaps to a particular technique—may well be "the last to know" when their efforts are ineffective. In the second place, evaluation without involving the patient's own feelings and behavior (that is, symptoms) ignores lessons from the history of mental health treatment. Mental patients were long treated in a cruel and unusual manner when practitioners disregarded their protestations that they did not want a "treatment" thrust on them; only later did the practitioners conclude in hindsight that many of these treatments were indeed poor or cruel. "Treatment" has included the use of chains, scalding baths, lobotomies, insulin shock, and now neuroleptics that can lead to tardive dyskinesia. Given this history, mental health professionals should be extremely careful before deciding that a treatment is "effective." The current approach is, as we know, much more enlightened—just as every previous generation knew that its approach was much more enlightened than previous ones. This conclusion is valid only when based on evidence.

It is even possible that treatments are biased by two attitudes that psychologists themselves hold but don't want to admit even to themselves: They don't like what the emotionally disturbed do and want to distance themselves from them. These attitudes could well bias psychologists' unsystematic evaluations of cures. Mental health professionals must reach their conclusions with extreme care, in a way that would convince a skeptic (again, a criterion implicit in almost all demonstrations that we term "scientific"). They owe that extreme care to people who seek professional help for themselves and alleviation of their problems, who trust those claiming to have expertise in mental health.

The question, then, is how to reach legitimate conclusions about the effectiveness of therapy. A number of deficient ways have certainly led to bad conclusions. One method that at first glance does not seem deficient is to search among therapy clients for examples of "success" and argue for the efficacy of therapy on the basis of this success. The problem with this method is that some people who experience distress will get over it whether or not they are in treatment. Having improved, these people will search for a reason for the improvement, as will their therapists. Not surprisingly, both client and therapist may well agree that the reason was psychotherapy. There is no way of evaluating that conclusion, because the client cannot compare what did happen with what would have happened if therapy had been unavailable. This simple objection illustrates an important logical fallacy. We do something in a particular situation, and something else follows. Was that something else caused or even influenced by what we did first? If we conclude that it was, we must have in mind a *hypothetical counterfactual,* or some idea of what would have happened if we had not done what we did. It is hypothetical because we can never be certain "what would have happened if." Nevertheless, we can evaluate the effect of what we did do only by comparing it with what we believe would have happened if we hadn't done it.

In most of our everyday functioning, we don't use hypothetical counterfactuals to confirm simple beliefs that we consider self-evident. Most of us believe that we know where our home is located, for example, because when we go there, it is there. We never check our belief by going to some other location—perhaps randomly chosen—when we wish to go home to verify that our home *isn't* at this other location. This absence of a check illustrates a "confirmation bias" in our everyday beliefs, a bias that generally serves us quite well. Most emotional disturbances are not fatal, and as our life situations change, we develop new ways of coping and thinking about them; our feelings of distress or happiness also vary. Where is the hypothetical counterfactual in the examples of "successful therapy"? Nowhere. Both therapists and clients nonetheless often cite such successes as "proof" of the effectiveness of therapy.[6]

Despite their uselessness, however, instances of success continue to be cited as "evidence" for the effectiveness of therapy, even by psychologists. For example, a writer maintains in *American Psychologist*: "Suppose you test artistic ability before and after therapy. Should you predict a difference between treatment and control [that is, no-treatment] groups? Not at all! Predict that your measure will increase only for the successful subgroup. After all, you do not want to predict an increase for the failure cases."[7] I leave it to the reader to figure out the validity of "predicting" success only for those cases later found to be successful.

A more common way to establish a claim for therapeutic effectiveness is to treat a group of people and find that in general they are better off after treatment than they were before. Here, the hypothetical counterfactual is that they would have remained the same without therapy. But there are serious flaws with this. For starters, we don't know that they would have remained the same. A much more subtle flaw is technically termed a *regression effect*. That is, processes appear to "regress" from less likely states to more likely ones simply because the more likely ones are likely to occur at later points in time. For example, people are not often extremely happy (or extremely unhappy). It follows that when they are, they are less likely to be as extremely unhappy (or happy) later—no matter what happens in the meantime. Because most people enter therapy when they are extremely unhappy, they are less likely to be as unhappy later, independent of the effects of therapy itself. Hence, this "regression effect" can create the illusion that the therapy has helped to alleviate their unhappiness, whether or not it has. In fact, even if the therapy has been downright harmful, people are less likely to be as unhappy later as when they entered it.[8]

To understand regression effects in general, suppose we toss a coin twice, and it falls heads both times. We toss it two more times. We expect fewer heads on these second two tosses; specifically, we expect that the probability that we will get two heads again is only 1 in 4; we will get one head and one tail (in either order) with a probability of 1 in 2, and two tails with a probability of 1 in 4; thus, our expected number of heads on the second two tosses is only one. Does that mean that coins "catch up to themselves" (a belief termed "the gamblers' fallacy")? No. It simply means that when we get an unusual result one time in a random process, we are unlikely to repeat it. This regression to 50 percent heads is, of course, probabilistic, because the probability is only 1 in 4 that the two heads will be repeated in the second two trials, but they can be. Similarly, if a fair coin has landed heads 9 times in 10 trials, the probability that there will be fewer than 9 heads in the next 10 trials is 99 in 100, but there is still a chance of roughly 1 in 1000 that it will land heads all 10 times in this subsequent set of 10 trials.

I am not claiming that life is a toss of a coin (any more than it is a river). The point of the example is that when there is any random component whatsoever, and we pick a group on the basis of being unusual in some way or other, we get a regression effect. It is, moreover, not even necessary to hypothesize a random component in what is being observed. All that is necessary is that the variables studied are not perfectly correlated. Not everyone realizes that illusions can result from regression effects. The best way to receive an award for "noted improvement" in academic work in some grade and high schools is to do terribly the previous semester; for example, an Israeli fight instructor has protested to psychologist trainers[9] that he "knows" punishment works better than reward, because: "I've often praised people warmly for beautifully executed maneuvers, and the next time they almost always do worse. And I've screamed at people for badly executed maneuvers, and by and large, the next time they improve."

The direct relevance of regression effects to evaluating psychotherapy is that people often enter therapy at times when they are particularly unhappy and distressed. But if their problem is one that varies over time rather than having a consistently downward course, regression effects alone could result in "improvement"—and an illusion that the improvement is due to psychotherapy: "If treated, a cold will go away in seven days, whereas if left alone, it will last a week." Emotional distress is certainly more serious than a cold, but even serious emotional distress will vary over time. Since such variability implies an imperfect relationship between outcomes at two different points in time, regression effects are to be expected. In fact, they occur even within a condition: "Of particular significance was the fact that those scoring highest on symptom reduction after SD (*systematic desensitization*) were those whose symptoms were initially more severe, and who were less promising candidates for conventional types of therapy."[10] Of course.

The best way to evaluate the efficacy of therapy, however, is to compare a group of people who receive therapy with a group who don't. That is to say, as in any such scientific experiment, there must be an *experimental* group and a *control* group. The two groups must be equivalent when they begin therapy, moreover, so the comparison cannot be between people who seek out therapy and others who don't seek it out but who all have the same symptoms. People who seek out therapy will likely be more motivated to get over their problems than those who don't, which will skew the results. Even a highly sophisticated statistical control cannot establish equivalence on this most important characteristic—whether individuals seek out therapy. The result is a *self-selection bias*.

That bias occurs in other domains as well. For example, there was considerable concern in 1989 about whether abortion may have bad psychological effects. C. Everett Koop, the surgeon general, testified in Congress that the studies attempting to assess this possibility were not done well enough to reach any type of firm conclusion. As some critics pointed out,[11] such studies *cannot* reach a firm conclusion in a society in which women are free to choose to have abortions or not—because having one is confounded with a desire to have one, and not having one is confounded with a desire to carry the pregnancy through to birth. (I'm not claiming that all women who want one necessarily obtain one, or that all who desire to have a baby necessarily do not have one; the point is that the two groups of women in general are not equivalent on the basis of this crucial factor of choice.)

The effects of self-selection can be quite subtle, and they often occur in contexts in which they would not "reasonably" be expected. In medicine, for example, a late 1970s study of the drug Clofibrate, which is used to lower mortality from coronary heart disease, found that those who took the prescribed dose of Clofibrate 80 percent or more of the time had a 15 percent mortality rate within the next five years, as opposed to a 25 percent mortality rate for those who took the prescribed dose of Clofibrate less than 80 percent of the time. But people who took a placebo 80 percent or more of the time also had a 15 percent mortality rate, while those who took the placebo less than 80 percent of the time had a 25 percent rate.[12] It is unlikely that a placebo effect could influence a five-year mortality rate; more likely, those who adhered to the recommended medical treatment by taking the pill consistently took better care of themselves in other ways than those who didn't. In studies evaluating psychotherapy, the possibility of self-selection among subjects is quite prominent. People who are highly motivated to get better will not only seek out therapy but will engage in other activities that will help their condition more than those who aren't highly motivated. Thus, studies may well reveal nothing when they conclude that those seeking psychotherapy do better than those who do not.

The solution to this problem of self-selection is to evaluate psychotherapy in the same manner that drugs are evaluated. Volunteers for a study are randomly divided into an experimental group, which is given the treatment, and a control group, which is not; the outcomes for these two groups are then compared. Such random assignment of individuals to groups does not guarantee that the two groups will not differ in ways relevant to the outcome. It merely creates a statistical expectation that the two groups will not differ. Larger sample sizes produce more likelihood that the experimental and control groups will be alike. This approach is called a *randomized* experiment in the social science literature and a *randomized trials* experiment in the medical literature, where

it is most commonly used. What happens is that the control group provides the hypothetical counterfactual against which the outcome for the
experimental group can be compared. The logic is explained well in Sinclair Lewis's novel *Arrowsmith*; the most widely publicized randomized
trials experiment was that on the Salk polio vaccine in 1954.[13]

In psychotherapy, randomized experiments often involve randomly
selecting people for a control group and promising them that they will
receive treatment after a specified period of time—a "wait list control."
Classical medical randomized control experiments do not do this.
Another difference is that many medical experiments involve a *placebo
control*, in which subjects in the control group are given a placebo and
neither group is told whether they are the experimental or the control
group. Such experiments are termed double-blind experiments because
both the people in them and the people evaluating them are "blind" to
whether they are in the experimental group or in the control group.

It is hard to develop a double-blind experiment in psychotherapy.
Both the subjects and those examining the subjects are generally
aware of whether they have received therapy. In psychotherapy, moreover, many of the criteria used to assess the success of treatment rely
on the self-report of the subject, for the simple reason that much
treatment is aimed to alleviate the emotional distress that the subject
has experienced. Such self-reports could easily be biased by subjects'
knowledge that they had or had not received psychotherapy. For this
reason, self-reports are rarely used without considering other outcome criteria as well.

Such randomized experiments are very necessary in evaluating
treatments for emotional disorders. Studies that did not conform to the
principles of randomized experiments have had dubious results. In one
study the investigator concluded that of 136 people given a promising
new treatment, 98 improved, 23 were somewhat improved, and only 12
failed to improve.[14] In a second study, 228 people given the same treatment were dichotomized into two groups: "improved" versus "the same
or worse." One hundred and fifty-one could be classified in the first
group, only 73 in the second.[15] (The numbers do not add up for reasons

we'll see presently.) Let me describe the promising new technique that was being studied:

> After drilling a small hole in the temple on each side of the skull, the surgeon then inserts a dull knife into the brain, makes a fan-shaped incision through the prefrontal lobe, then downward a few minutes later. He then repeats the incision on the other side of the brain. . . . The patient is given only local anesthetic at the temples—the brain itself is insensitive—and the doctors encourage him [sic] to talk, sing, recite poems or prayers. When his replies to questions show that his mind is thoroughly disoriented, the doctors know that they have cut deep enough into his brain.[16]

How was "improvement" determined? By the lobotomists themselves casually talking to the patients at some later time. "I am a sensitive observer," one said, "and my conclusion is that a vast majority of my patients get better as opposed to worse after my treatment." The reason the numbers didn't add up was that the other patients had died on the operating table—three in the first study mentioned, four in the second. Where was the control group? Nowhere. Every patient who was believed "eligible" for the horror of being lobotomized underwent the operation. In fact, without doing anything even remotely close to a scientific examination of the procedure, the doctors performing it advocated its widespread use. After performing more than twelve hundred lobotomies, one doctor stated that while he had previously maintained that he "wouldn't touch them unless they are faced with disability or suicide," he had come to believe that "it is safer to operate than to wait" and that lobotomy "would be considered in a mental patient who fails to improve after six months of consecutive failure."[17] Moreover, the technique itself was "improved." The description quoted above refers to prefrontal lobotomy. It was later replaced with transorbital lobotomy, a safer operation that involved gently lifting the patient's eyeball from its socket, sticking in a thick needle behind it, and then as before manipulating it to destroy the same brain tissue until the patient becomes incoherent—the "ice-pick operation." More such "improvements" were envisioned before the

American Medical Association put a stop to it. The more the doctors performed this treatment, however, the more confident they became. Their main concern was to find a new—better—variant of the treatment, rather than determine the efficacy of the basic treatment itself. The last to know!

The effects of such lobotomies are well illustrated in the movies *Francis* and *One Flew Over the Cuckoo's Nest*. I myself have observed their devastating results. The first patient with whom I attempted psychotherapy had taken off all her clothes one day and run around the streets of her home town screaming, "My father is the handsomest goddamn drunk in [X], Pennsylvania!" She was subsequently hospitalized and then was lobotomized within six *weeks*. She often continued to shout, "My father is the handsomest goddamn drunk in [X], Pennsylvania," but she would not take off her clothes or otherwise express her clearly ambivalent and partially sexual feelings toward her father, because she would immediately forget what she was shouting about. Unable to concentrate for more than ten seconds at a time, she was unable to obtain a job outside the hospital or live with relatives. She had, in effect, been sentenced to life imprisonment for having expressed her feelings in a socially inappropriate way. Although lobotomies are now greatly reduced, destructive techniques are far from ancient history.[18] I direct the reader to Jeffrey Masson's description of the "direct therapy" techniques of John Rosen. These techniques included harassment, and in some cases imprisonment, of clients in order to force them to "air out their problems"; Rosen didn't lose his license to pursue them until 1983.[19]

My point is that mental health professionals can all too easily do what was done to my patient if they don't subject their cherished techniques to the type of scientific scrutiny found in randomized experiments. And the less they use such scrutiny, the more confident they will become that they are doing good. All mental health practitioners are susceptible to an overinflated belief in their own position, and they should constantly subject themselves to the discipline of testing their ideas empirically or reading about others' tests of them. Medicine learned that lesson well when the widespread practice of removing children's tonsils in the late 1930s and early 1940s was subject to scrutiny by Harry Bakwin.[20] He found that although a majority (61 percent) of children in the New York school system in the 1930s and early 1940s had had their tonsils removed, there was no correlation whatsoever between the estimate of one physician and that of another regarding the advisability of tonsillectomy when a sample of the remaining 39 percent of the children were examined,[21] of whom 45 percent were said to be in need of having their tonsils removed (as were 46 percent in a later screening of those children who passed *this* screening). Eighty children had died each year as a result of the anesthesia administered for tonsillectomies. Findings such as these have led medicine, especially medical school professors, to appreciate the importance of systematically checking clinical judgment, for example, through employing randomized clinical trials. Mental health professionals would be well advised to follow medicine's example.

## STUDIES THAT EVALUATE EFFICACY

Randomized experiments evaluating the efficacy of psychotherapy began appearing occasionally in the scientific journals during the 1960s. One impetus for them came from psychologists' increased use of behavioral techniques, in which specific behaviors were targeted for change through the use of reinforcement principles. Since the whole point was to change these behaviors, the efficacy of the techniques was easily evaluated, and randomly selected (usually wait-list) control groups could be easily evaluated as well. As professional psychologists proliferated—and their fees soared—the "only the therapist knows" philosophy became increasingly difficult to maintain.

In 1977, Mary L. Smith and Gene V. Glass published a famous article in *American Psychologist* that concluded that psychotherapy is very effective. They summarized the results of 375 studies of psychotherapy effectiveness that had purported to use random assignment to experimental and control groups.[22] The summary technique they used, termed *meta-analysis,* first determined the average difference in each study between the experimental and control groups on some outcome variable that the therapy attempted to address (like behavior, self-report of anxiety or depression, or assessment of psychological functioning by "blind" observers). These differences were measured in terms such as subjects' well-being or reduction of symptoms. Each difference was assessed after therapy had ended for the people in the experimental group and at the same time for those in the control group. Smith and Glass treated the overall differences found in each single study as single units, computed their means (averages), and then analyzed these means.

One of their concerns was whether the average difference between the means for the experimental group and the means for the control group on the measures of well-being or symptom reduction were positive. These mean differences were computed separately for each study. In general, they were positive. In fact, the average of the means for the experimental groups on the various measures examined was at the seventy-fifth percentile of the control group distribution. Making standard statistical assumptions,[23] Smith and Glass found that someone chosen at random from the experimental group after therapy had a two-to-one chance of being better off on the measure examined than someone chosen at random from the control group. That is a very strong finding—stronger, in fact, than findings for most medical procedures and for comparisons of healthy versus deleterious lifestyles.[24]

Smith and Glass's critics soon weighed in. Meta-analysis, they argued, compares apples and oranges. The various problems of clients seeking therapy differ across various studies. Some are acutely anxious, some are depressed, and some are even schizophrenic. The outcome measures differ. The therapeutic techniques employed differ. The therapists differ. The measures used to evaluate outcomes differ. Consequently, meta-analysis was criticized as sloppy. But the forms of the overall phenomenon being evaluated—psychotherapy—differ in all these respects as well. In order to generalize about fruit, it is perfectly appropriate to combine apples and oranges. In order to generalize about psychotherapy, it is perfectly appropriate to combine different measures of improvement that assess changes important in overcoming different psychological problems. Moreover, the particular contexts of the experiments may be more important in psychology than in medicine. The functioning of the human body seems less subject to specific temporal, social, and chance factors than is psychological well-being. It may then be quite reasonable to treat each study rather than each subject as the unit about which to generalize, even though standard statistical theory is less applicable to sampling diverse and ill-defined studies than to sampling people (or other units) from a homogeneous and well-defined population.[25] In fact, the same diversity that makes statistical generalization dubious may well be a necessity in psychology and the allied social sciences.

Smith and Glass's meta-analysis not only presented impressive evidence about the efficacy of psychotherapy; it concluded that three factors that most psychologists believed influenced this efficacy actually did not influence it.

First, they discovered that the therapists' credentials—PhD, MD, or no advanced degree—and experience were *un*related to the effectiveness of therapy.

Second, they discovered that the *type* of therapy given was unrelated to its effectiveness, with the possible exception of behavioral techniques, which seemed superior for well-circumscribed behavioral problems.[26] They also discovered that length of therapy was unrelated to its success.

The professional psychology community hailed Smith and Glass's overall finding but not the three subsidiary findings. A series of studies was thereafter conducted to indicate that at least the first finding was inaccurate. But these studies failed to refute Smith and Glass.

I became involved in the field of meta-analysis after reading Smith and Glass's paper. At the time I was skeptical of it because while the authors of the studies they had reviewed claimed to have used random assignment, I found that many of them didn't. As we have seen, the subjects of a scientific study must be assigned randomly to experimental and control groups to avoid the self-selection problem. In fact, however, several experimenters who purported to have done random assignment actually chose the control group members randomly from people who were *similar* to those seeking therapy, but not on the basis of seeking therapy itself.

One experimental group, for example, consisted of students with poor grades seeking help to improve their study habits and attitudes toward academic work through group therapy. The control group in this study consisted of randomly selected students with equally poor records—but who, for all the experimenters knew, might have given up or even left college altogether. Self-selection can be much more subtle than this. For example, in one study comparing a group therapy approach to juvenile delinquency with the standard probation officer "treatment," the experimenter randomly assigned subjects to the experimental (group therapy) group and the control (probation) group. Any of those assigned to the group therapy group who stopped attending the group therapy sessions would be returned to having to see their probation officers. These subjects soon discovered that their absence from group therapy sessions would not necessarily be officially noted, and many dropped out. When the experimenter compared the overall success rates (lack of subsequent arrests), of the two approaches, he found little differences between the experimental and control groups. But, he concluded, group therapy can meaningfully be evaluated only for those who attend group sessions. When he compared only those who had good attendance records with the control group, he did find a difference in favor of the group therapy treatment. The problem with this comparison is that we don't know who in the control group *would* have attended sessions regularly *if* they had been assigned to the experimental group. Thus, there is no hypothetical counterfactual. Moreover, it is reasonable to hypothesize that the more motivated people in the experimental group were the regular attendees, so that the latter comparison involves self-selection. The situation is exactly analogous to the Clofibrate study. The Smith and Glass analysis, however, involved only a single overall measure of study quality, in which violations of truly random assignment were just one component. I thought it possible that the overall average effects were due to the inclusion of studies that didn't have true random assignment, an effect that Smith and Glass's single measure would have obscured.

When I was on sabbatical leave at the University of Michigan in the academic year 1978–79, Janet Landman (then a graduate student) and I collaborated on a project to check out self-selection in the studies Smith and Glass summarized. We obtained the list of studies from Smith and Glass, which had since been augmented to include 435. We omitted all unpublished studies, such as doctoral dissertations, on the grounds that they had not been subjected to the scrutiny by presumably disinterested peers that is required for publication. We sampled every fifth study on the remaining list, for a total of sixty-five. We read each study independently to judge whether there had been random assignment to the experimental and control groups. We never discussed studies with each other before making our independent judgments about them. When we compared our judgments, we found that our agreement rate was high; we disagreed on only three of the studies. (While that constitutes 95 percent agreement, a better statistic for evaluating agreement is the "phi-coefficient," which was .90.) After resolving these disagreements through discussion, we concluded that only 42 of the 65 studies (about two-thirds) had used the true random assignment that the authors claimed.

The studies we examined were remarkably diverse. One studied a "country club" for alcoholics that didn't serve liquor. Another studied a "general resource person" in an intensive care unit serving people who had experienced heart attacks. This person randomly selected one of each two patients admitted, explained to them in detail the literature given on their bedside table about successful living following a heart attack, and offered to work as a liaison with their families, to explain the consequences and challenges to them as well. (No "depth" therapy was involved.) The differences between the experimental and the control groups on physiological measures indicating recovery were impressive. The most common conditions being treated in the studies were behavioral anxiety and phobias (which some critics, not being chronically anxious or phobic themselves, dismiss as trivial), but depression and even chronic schizophrenia were treated in others. Measures of success varied according to the problem, but the results were similar.

Landman and I analyzed these studies in the same way Smith and Glass had analyzed the studies in their original article, and we compared our results with the results we would have obtained had we analyzed all sixty-five studies. Much to our surprise, our results were virtually identical to those of Smith and Glass based on their whole sample of 435. That is, it didn't matter whether the studies had had true random assignment.[27] As I later told the Oregon Psychological Association, I had become a "reformed sinner"—someone who had originally been ready to ascribe the apparent effectiveness of psychotherapy to methodological flaws in the studies supporting it but who had now become a "true believer."

## WHAT THE STUDIES SHOW ABOUT THERAPIST EFFECTIVENESS

The results of such analyses, however, also imply that the credentials and experience of the therapist don't matter. This result is rather unpleasant for professionals who require years of postgraduate training and post-doctoral experience for licensing to perform therapy, and who would like to restrict practice to those who are licensed. In the years after the Smith and Glass article was published, many attempts were made to disprove their finding that the training, credentials, and experience of therapists are irrelevant. These attempts failed. The abstract of a review by Jeffrey S. Berman and Nicholas C. Norton summarized such results:

[A recent review] concluded that patients treated by paraprofessionals [people minimally trained] improved more than those treated by professionals. However, this provocative conclusion is based on inappropriate studies and statistical analyses. The present review omitted problematic studies and organized the data to permit valid statistical inference. Unlike [earlier authors listed] we found that professional and paraprofessional therapists were generally equal in effectiveness. Our analyses also indicated that professionals may be better for brief treatments and older patients, but these differences were slight. Current research evidence does not indicate that paraprofessionals are more effective, but neither does it reveal any substantial superiority for the professionally trained therapist.[28]

In other words, the professionals are no different from the paraprofessionals in the effectiveness of their treatment. Furthermore, consistent with earlier summaries of studies they and other authors had examined:

In a first set of analyses, we examined whether the relative effectiveness of professionals and paraprofessionals might vary for different types of problems and treatments. When we classified studies according to the four most commonly occurring categories of patient complaint (social adjustment, phobia, psychosis and obesity), we found no reliable differences [between professionals and paraprofessionals] among the separate effect sizes. . . . We also failed to detect any systematic differences when we divided the studies into five forms of treatment (behavioral, cognitive-behavioral, humanistic, crisis intervention, and undifferentiated counseling).

And:

Similarly, there were no statistically significant differences [again, between professionals and paraprofessionals, not between experimental and control groups] between four different sources of outcome (patient, therapist, independent observer, and behavioral indicator).

Perhaps the most famous study supporting this conclusion was performed by Hans Strupp and Suzanne Hadley.[29] They recruited as therapists university professors who had no background in psychology and randomly assigned clients either to them or to professionally trained and credentialed psychologists. In all, they assigned fifteen clients to the professionals and fifteen to the professors. The clients were those whose problems, as Strupp and Hadley put it, "would be classified as neurotic depression or anxiety reactions. Obsessional trends and borderline personalities were common." The professionals charged higher fees, but they were no more effective as therapists than the professors. The only slight difference was that after therapy the clients of the professionals tended to be a bit more optimistic about life than those of the untrained professors, but they didn't function any better on any of the multiple measures the investigators evaluated. While this difference may result from the current professional belief that optimism is an important criterion in mental health (perhaps *the* criterion), it could also have arisen on a chance basis.

Other reviews indicate that the level of experience of professional therapists is unrelated to their efficacy.[30] Consistent with such "it doesn't matter" findings, William Miller and Reid Hester published a highly influential review indicating that the intensity of professional treatment does not matter even for people with the problem of alcoholism.[31] Miller and Hester summarized all the studies in which alcoholics were randomly assigned to inpatient or outpatient treatment. Some of the inpatient programs involved prolonged stays in institutions devoted to radical changes in lifestyle, beliefs, and attitudes. But there were no differences in outcomes between inpatients and outpatients. Nor did Miller and Hester find any relationship between the length of treatment and outcome. In fact, nothing worked better for alcoholics than a minimal treatment involving detoxification and one hour of counseling!

This result contradicts results of studies or other types of therapy, in which a "dose-effect" relationship between length of psychotherapy and outcome has been established; approximately 50 percent of clients are measurably improved after eight sessions and 75 percent after twenty-nine.[32] The disturbing possibility also remains, however, that *few or none of the programs Miller and Hester studied did any good at all.* That possibility would be consistent with the results of the first randomly controlled experiment on alcoholism treatment, published in 1967 by Keith Ditman and his colleagues.[33] In that study, chronic drunk-driving offenders were randomly assigned to a psychiatric treatment clinic, to an Alcoholics Anonymous program, or to a no-treatment control group. In the subsequent year, 68 percent of those who had been assigned to the clinic were arrested again, as were 69 percent of those who had been assigned to Alcoholics Anonymous, but "only" 56 percent of those who had been assigned to no treatment were arrested again. (Most probably, these were statistical variations reflecting no stable difference in outcome.)

Our society now views alcoholism, especially drunk driving, as sufficiently serious that we do not consider assigning people to a no-treatment control. We take a similar approach to juvenile delinquency, which may be a mistake.

Believers in professional training, credentials, and experience for psychologists have responded to these study results in basically three ways. First, they combine an attack on the studies themselves with an appeal to hypothetical studies that have not been conducted. Even Strupp and Hadley used this familiar argument-from-a-vacuum at the conclusion of their paper about the equal effectiveness of untrained university professors: "Professional psychologists, by virtue of their training and clinical experience, are clearly much better equipped to deal with the vagaries and vicissitudes encountered in interactions with most patients."[34] There, "most patients" means the ones Strupp and Hadley didn't study. There is no support for that statement among the patients they did study.

Michael Lambert, David Shapiro, and Allen Bergin make the same argument in a broader form in the 1986 *Handbook of Psychotherapy and Behavior Change:* "Although the failures in this literature generally to show unique therapeutic effectiveness for trained professionals are sobering, these studies are flawed in several respects."[35] But *all* studies are "flawed in several respects." Psychology is a difficult field in which to conduct a good study, let alone one without any flaws at all. Are we to ignore what all these admittedly flawed studies indicate in common? Ignoring them would make sense only if they were all generally flawed in the same respect, but they aren't. Without such common flaws, it is extremely improbable that all the separate and unrelated flaws would lead to the same conclusion. No specific common flaw has been found or even proposed that would systematically bias the results against the professional. This absence poses the biggest problem for those attempting to ignore their implications: namely, that there is no *positive* evidence supporting the efficacy of professional psychology. There are anecdotes, there is plausibility, there are common beliefs, yes—but there is no good evidence. The reader wishing details about the studies is referred to the Lambert, Shapiro, and Bergin article.

A second, related defense of professionalism in psychology has been to postulate "interaction effects"—that is, that the outcomes for the professionals might be different from those of the paraprofessionals depending on the types of clients they treated or the types of techniques they used, while simultaneously there is no difference overall. The expertise of professionally trained therapists, for example, is said to be required for more seriously disturbed clients, who were in a minority in the studies conducted. One critic of Miller and Hester's analysis of the alcohol program studies suggested that inpatient and prolonged treatments may be required for more severe alcoholics, whereas Miller and Hester analyzed only programs that serviced a high proportion of less severe alcoholics.[36] This critic then presented an argument about why more intensive treatments would be good for the more severe alcoholics.

The problem with his suggestion, however, is that he fails to make a simultaneous argument about why the more intensive programs would be *bad* for the *less* severe alcoholics. If one treatment program is better for one class of patients, then—to be equally effective for all patients combined—it must be worse for some other class of patients. That's simple arithmetic. If the average of one set of numbers is zero and some of the numbers are positive, then some of the other numbers in the set must be negative. The presence of less severe alcoholics in the more intensive programs could obscure these programs' superiority for the more severe alcoholics, but it would not wipe out their overall superiority—unless these programs were simultaneously inferior for the other, less severe alcoholics. The one exception to the Berman and Norton finding quoted earlier was that "professionals were somewhat more effective in studies using short term treatments."[37] Logically, however, given no difference overall, they had to balance this with the finding that "paraprofessionals were somewhat more effective in studies involving longer therapies, as was found."

The type of interaction that would lead to a zero effect overall is technically termed *disordinal*, or *crossed*.[38] If one type of treatment or therapist, say, an experienced professional, is better for one type of client, while another is better for another type, this has severe implications: it implies that a professional therapist is worse for some clients than other types of therapists.[39] If so, it is extraordinarily important to discover who those clients are before employing professional therapists rather than paraprofessional ones. No such attempt has been made.

Occasionally, therapists may be more effective when they are using a technique that they believe to be superior than when they are using one in which they have less faith but that they have adopted for experimental purposes.[40] Reid Hester and his colleagues compared the efficacy of two treatments for alcoholism: Alcoholics Anonymous (AA), with its traditional "disease" model and emphasis on spiritual recovery, and traditional counseling.[41] They randomly assigned clients to these two treatments. They found that the treatments had equivalent effects overall. Six months after treatment was over, however, those clients who *before* entering treatment had expressed the view that alcoholism was a disease rather than a bad habit were much more likely to be abstinent if they had received the AA treatment rather than traditional counseling; conversely, those clients who had expressed the view that alcoholism was a bad, addictive habit were much more likely to be abstinent if they had received traditional counseling rather than AA. (Since there was no no-treatment control group, it is not possible to determine whether the clients were actually harmed by receiving a treatment incompatible with their pretreatment views.)

Some theorists have taken the negative findings on therapist credentials quite seriously. Advocates like Jerome Frank and Hans Strupp propose that psychotherapy works due to "nonspecific effects."[42] Nonspecific effects are those that result from "the quality of the relationship" between client and therapist. This idea is supported by the finding that good psychotherapists tend to be empathetic, trustworthy, and warm.[43] In one study, William Miller, Cheryl Taylor and JoAnne West found that therapists' "accurate empathy," as they assessed it, accounted for 67 percent of the variability in their success with problem drinkers, while therapists' years of experience accounted for only one percent.[44] Unfortunately, some studies that support the importance of empathy, unlike this one, do not assess empathy independently of client outcome. For example, one investigator chose above- or below-average therapists by assessing client success and then concluded that the above-average therapists were more empathetic because their clients, who were successful, rated them as higher on empathy than the unsuccessful clients rated their therapists. That is about like predicting success on the basis of observing who is successful. (This study will not be referenced here.)

Even the existence of the correlation between empathy and success, however, does not explain the process of success or failure, and given that some therapies that are not based on relationship variables (like some behavior modification techniques) are successful, the interpretation that their success, too, must be based on some unevaluated quality of relationship remains speculative. My own favorite speculation, in contrast, in based on Hamlet, who in his famous soliloquy speaks of "taking arms against a sea of troubles." (That's a wonderfully mixed metaphor, because "taking arms" literally means putting on armor, and armor leads to quick drowning, as demonstrated when the Dutch once destroyed an invading Spanish army by luring it into the lowlands and opening up the dikes. But futility is not the point here.) The implicit message is that taking up arms against troubles does some good psychologically even if it does not fully "by opposing end them." When people enter therapy, they are making a choice to deal with their problems rather than simply feel overwhelmed by them.[45] Being placed in a waitlist control group may deprive people of that opportunity, temporarily at least. (Again, such people may choose to deal with their problems in other ways, as do people in medical randomized trials experiments. These are meant to evaluate the superiority of the experimental treatment, not to prevent those not given it from attempting to get better in other ways.) If only the *motive* to enter therapy were important, then experimental groups and wait-list control groups would do equally well. If only the quality of the client-therapist relationship were important, then we would not expect behavioral techniques to do so well. I suggest it may be the actions of the clients themselves in "taking up arms"—that is, in doing something about the problems addressed in therapy—that result in a change in life itself that has a "therapeutic" effect. In other words, while therapy generally succeeds, the same success might be obtained by other means as well.

There are three additional factors that might contribute to therapist efficacy. First, the therapist is an "outsider" to the client's life and therefore may be less apt to take certain attitudes, procedures, and constraints or possibilities for granted. The therapist will also feel less bound to justify the client's past behavior than the client does (a sunk cost)[46]—and hence is less likely than the client to wish it repeated (to prove that it really was wise, despite its lack of success). Second, any change that breaks or stops self-defeating or socially pernicious positive feedback (a "vicious circle," often between behavior and feelings) may be a therapeutic one, and entering therapy may provide the "initial kick" to break an ongoing loop.[47] Thoughts, behaviors, and feelings are interrelated, and any technique that leads to a positive change in one of them (or in the body itself) may (*may*) lead to positive changes in the others as well.[48] If, for example, I act less uptight and hostile than I previously did as a result of establishing good rapport with a therapist, others may shun me less than they previously did. The pleasant and even close relationships I go on to establish may not only improve my "mental health" themselves, but they may also encourage me to be more relaxed about facing up to my problems and more energetic in attempting to overcome them. (Note that this model does *not* postulate that one must "work through one's problems" first and begin changing only later.) Third, therapy may begin a process of seeking out changes in one's environment or lifestyle that can be helpful (although conservative psychoanalysts "require" that clients not make radical changes in their lives—like getting married, having children, getting divorced, or changing vocations—while they are in analysis).

But I myself am arguing from a vacuum here, because I have no direct measure of the therapeutic effect of actively dealing with problems, or evidence of its efficacy. The most defensible answer to the question of why therapy works is, *We don't know.* We should do research to find out, and indeed many people are devoting careers to just such research. But we do know that the training, credentials, and experience of psychotherapists are irrelevant, or at least that is what all the evidence indicates. The horrible irony is that by supporting licensing, income, and status for credentialed practitioners, the mental health professions have treated variables that really don't matter as if they did matter. Much greater good could come from finding out what does matter, then from supporting the professional and social clout of those who can provide it.

The discussion in this chapter has been limited in two ways. First, it concerns the efficacy of only psychotherapy, not drug therapy. Research findings about the qualifications of effective psychotherapists do not address the question of who is better or worse at prescribing drugs. Outcome studies assessing the efficacy of various drugs generally treat the drugs themselves as the phenomenon to be evaluated, such as lithium for manic depression. To my knowledge, there have been no studies on how the effects of drugs are related to the qualifications, experience, or personal characteristics of the doctors who prescribe them and presumably monitor their effects—perhaps an interesting area.

The second limitation of this discussion is that most, although not all, studies involve treatments that clients freely choose. The clear exception is chronic patients in mental facilities. Gordon L. Paul and Anthony A. Menditto summarize what is known at this writing: "We do know what works best for chronically disabled patients with excesses in maladaptive and psychotic behavior, deficits in adaptive functioning, or both (a comprehensive social-learning program). We do not yet really know what works best for less extensively disabled, acutely admitted, or revolving-door patients, particularly in inpatient programs involving short to intermediate stays."[49] . . .

## CONCLUSIONS AND IMPLICATIONS

Psychotherapy works. The magnitude of its positive effects is greater than the magnitude of many physical treatments, deleterious lifestyles, and changes in those lifestyles. Those who believe they have problems are encouraged to try it—especially if they have been unable to change their behavior by simply "willing" a change.

There is no reason, however, to seek out a highly paid, experienced therapist with a lot of credentials. If verbal therapy is sought, paraprofessionals are equally effective, especially empathetic ones. If the problems appear to require behavioral modification, as do phobias and lack of impulse control, a paraprofessional who understands behavioral principles is as effective as a highly credentialed professional. But success in therapy is far from assured, even though it works overall in a statistical sense. Someone who is dissatisfied with their current progress in therapy should not be inhibited about changing therapists or mode of treatment. (The therapist that is abandoned may attribute this decision to the depth of the client's pathology, but so what.) In particular, the results of the Hester et al. study of alcoholism treatment should be kept in mind. These results provide evidence that compatibility of a treatment approach with the client's views and beliefs before entering therapy may be an important factor in its success; clients may often be in a better position than the professional to choose a treatment modality and therapist. (For myself, in choosing a professional psychologist, I would want one of the 30 percent of APA members who reads one or more of its scientific journals.)[50] Statements from professionals that they "know" much better than the client what is "needed" may often best be politely ignored—especially when these statements are made after minimal contact, followed by a standard diagnostic label. If verbal therapy is sought, find someone empathetic. Unfortunately, I have no good advice about how to judge whether someone is empathetic before getting to know that person.

# CAVEAT EMPTOR

It takes a long time to do a study of the effectiveness of a particular type of psychotherapy or of psychotherapy in general. It requires examining many clients and many therapists, often over a period of years. Most of the studies on which I have based my conclusions were initiated years ago, even when the results have been published only recently. But the quality of the training of clinical psychologists, a major group of therapists studied, has deteriorated rapidly in the past several years. That might not mean much, given that training and credentials don't predict therapeutic effectiveness; but along with the decreased quality of training has come an explosion in numbers that assures that there will be more poor therapists around in the coming years than at the time when the studies were initiated. A greater concern is that many new ideas and therapies have been initiated that are at best characterized as ideologically based or faddish. There are therefore more therapists who base their practice on such ideologies and fads, of which the reader should beware.

# NOTES

1. S. C. Hayes, "An Interview with Lee Sechrest: The Courage to Say 'We Do Not Know How,'" *APS Observer* 2, no. 4 (1989): 8.

2. S. Freud, *An Analysis of a Case of Hysteria* (New York: Collier Books, 1963).

3. G. E. Vaillant, *Adaptation to Life* (Boston: Little, Brown and Co., 1977).

4. H. H. Strupp, "Psychotherapy: Research, Practice, and Public Policy (How to Avoid Dead Ends)," *American Psychologist* 41 (1986): 123.

5. E. Meehan, "Social Indicators: Policies and Inventories," paper presented at the meeting of the Public Choice Society, New Haven, March 1974. Or see E. J. Meehan, *The Thinking Game: A Guide to Effective Study* (Chatham, NJ: Chatham House, 1988).

6. Pointing out examples of success constitutes such flawed evidence for the efficacy of therapy that the APA Ethics Code when I was a member of its

national ethics committee specifically forbade "testimonials" about successful therapy as a way for a therapist to advertise her or his effectiveness. Principle 4, dealing with public statements, has since been revised. Compare, for example, the principle about public statements (number 4) in the 1981 Ethics Code, in *American Psychologist* 36 (1981): 533–638, with that same principle in American Psychological Association, Ethical Principles of Psychologists, amended June 2, 1989, *American Psychologist* 45 (1989): 390–95. During my service on that committee, however, the Federal Trade Commission (FTC) came to the conclusion that such a prohibition constituted restraint of trade and information. The public, the FTC contended, had a right to decide for itself that such testimonials were worthless, or—if the APA felt so strongly that they were worthless and misleading—it could educate the public about its reasons for reaching this conclusion. It never did. The prohibition had to be dropped. (I personally am on the side of the FTC *and* of education.)

7. E. T. Gendlin, "What Comes After Traditional Psychotherapy Research?" *American Psychologist* 41 (1986): 131–36.

8. See R. M. Dawes, *Rational Choice in an Uncertain World* (San Diego: Harcourt Brace Jovanovich, 1988), pp. 84–89. For an excellent journal article, see L. Furby, "Interpreting Regression toward the Mean in Developmental Research," *Developmental Psychology* 8 (1973): 172–79.

9. K. McKean, "Decisions: Two Eminent Psychologists Disclose the Mental Pitfalls in Which Rational People Find Themselves When They Try to Arrive at Logical Conclusions," *Discover*, June 1985, pp. 22–31.

10. *Behavior Today* 3 (May 16, 1977). There are some statistical ways to attempt to understand whether change over time after an intervention such as psychotherapy is simply due to regression effects or to the intervention. See D. T. Campbell and J. C. Stanley, *Experimental and Quasi-experimental Design for Research* (Chicago: Rand McNally and Co., 1963). One of these ways is to predict functioning at a subsequent time from functioning at the initial time that therapy was begun and then look at the *discrepancy* between the predicted later functioning and the actual functioning. For example, in assessing whether an educational program has an effect on people who have scored particularly badly (or well) on a test of achievement at one point in time, their scores at the second point can be predicted from those at the first point and then an assessment can be made of whether their scores in general are higher than this predicted value. Technically, such a discrepancy is termed a *residual* score, as opposed to a *discrep-*

*ancy* score. (Thus, doing *as well* may indicate effectiveness for a high-scoring group, because the prediction is that in general they will do less well at the second point in time.) Another method is to use an entire set of variables to predict functioning at the second point in time and again look at discrepancies. See R. W. Mee and T. C. Chau, "Regression toward the Mean and the Paired Sample T Test," *American Statistician* 45 (1991): 39–42. Here, the statistical model predicting what *would* have happened without the intervention provides the hypothetical counterfactual. Both these and other methods, however, rely on strong statistical assumptions, and all that can be done is to demonstrate that the results do not "significantly" violate these assumptions (see chapter 1), not that the assumptions are necessarily met. It is, moreover, always possible that even though no significant violations are found examining one set of assumptions, additional tests of other assumptions would find such violations.

11. E. J. Posavac and T. Q. Miller, "Some Conceptual Problems Caused by Not Having a Conceptual Foundation for Health Research: An Illustration from Studies of the Psychological Effects of Abortion," *Psychology and Health* 5 (1990): 13–23. See also R. M. Dawes, letter to the editor, *Chronicle of Higher Education*, February 28, 1990, p. B4.

12. Coronary Drug Project Research Group, "Influence of Adherence to Treatment and Response to Cholesterol on Mortality in the Coronary Drug Project," *New England Journal of Medicine* 303 (1980): 1038–41.

13. P. Meier, "The Biggest Public Health Experiment Ever: 1954 Field Trials of the Salk Poliomyelitis Vaccine," in *Statistics: A Guide to the Unknown*, ed. J. Tanur, F. Mosteller, W. H. Kruskel, R. F. Link, R. S. Pieters, and G. R. Rising (San Francisco: Holden Day, 1972).

14. "Psychosurgery," *Time*, November 30, 1942, p. 42.

15. "Mass Lobotomies," *Time*, October 15, 1952, p. 86.

16. "Psychosurgery," 1942, p. 42.

17. Ibid., p. 100.

18. "Mass Lobotomies," p. 86. Lobotomies on a smaller scale and other forms of psychosurgery have nevertheless continued. The commonly accepted definition of *psychosurgery* is the destruction of brain tissue for the *primary* purpose of achieving behavioral or psychological change—not of alleviating pain or reducing seizures, even though success in such an endeavor would yield behavioral and psychological changes as well. A National Commission for the Protection of Human Subjects report published in 1977 was able to report on psychosurgery (to treat such problems as obesity) conducted after 1970. As ear-

lier, the evaluation of the results of such surgery were inadequate. As the commission noted in its tables reporting the results of these studies, "In the vast majority of instances, results of surgery were summarized by neurosurgeons and/or associated psychiatrists and are based on subjective (or poorly defined) criteria." See K. J. Ryan, *Psychosurgery: The National Commission for the Protection of Human Subjects of Biomedical and Behavioral Research*, DHEW Publication No. 105J 77–0002 (Washington, DC: US Department of Health, Education, and Welfare, 1977), tables 19 (I-76) and 20 (I-79) of the appendix.

19. J. M. Masson, *Against Therapy: Emotional Tyranny and the Myth of Psychological Healing* (New York: Atheneum, 1988), chap. 5.

20. H. Bakwin, "Pseudodoxia Pediatrics," *New England Journal of Medicine* 232 (1945): 691–97.

21. Ibid., p. 692.

22. M. L. Smith and G. V. Glass, "Meta-analysis of Psychotherapy Outcome Studies," *American Psychologist* 32 (1977): 752–60.

23. That the two groups are normally distributed on the outcome measures (the standard "bell-shaped" distribution) and that sampling is independent.

24. For some striking comparisons, see, for example, R. Rosenthal, "How Are We Doing in Soft Psychology?" *American Psychologist* 45 (1990): 775–76.

25. R. M. Dawes, "Comment: Quandary: Correlation Coefficient and Contexts," in *Life Crises and Experiences of Loss in Adulthood*, ed. L. Montada, S. H. Filipp, and M. J. Lerner (Hillsdale, NJ: Erlbaum, 1992), pp. 521–29.

26. A. A. Lazarus, "If This Be Research," *American Psychologist* 45 (1990): 670–71.

27. J. T. Landman and R. M. Dawes, "Psychotherapy Outcome: Smith and Glass' Conclusions Stand Up to Scrutiny," *American Psychologist* 37 (1982): 504–16.

28. J. S. Berman and N. C. Norton, "Does Professional Training Make a Therapist More Effective?" *Psychological Bulletin* 98 (1985): 401–407.

29. H. H. Strupp and S. W. Hadley, "Specific versus Nonspecific Factors in Psychotherapy," *Archives of General Psychiatry* 36 (1979): 1125–36.

30. D. M. Stein and M. J. Lambert, "On the Relationship between Therapist Experience and Psychotherapy Outcome," *Clinical Psychology Review* 4 (1984): 127–42; and B. Smith and L. Sechrest, "The Treatment of Aptitude X Treatment Interactions," *Journal of Consulting and Clinical Psychology* 59 (1991): 233–44.

31. W. R. Miller and R. K. Hester, "Inpatient Alchoholism Treatment: Who Benefits?" *American Psychologist* 41 (1986): 794–805.

32. K. L. Howard, S. M. Kopta, M. S. Krause, and D. E. Orlinsky, "The Dose-Effect Relationship in Psychotherapy," *American Psychologist* 41 (1986): 159–64.

33. K. S. Ditman, G. G. Crawford, E. W. Forgy, H. Moskowitz, and C. Madandrew, "A Controlled Experiment on the Use of Court Probation for Drunk Arrests," *American Journal of Psychiatry* 124 (1967): 64–67.

34. Strupp and Hadley "Specific versus Nonspecific Factors," p. 1136.

35. M. J. Lambert, D. A. Shapiro, and A. E. Bergin, "The Effectiveness of Psychotherapy," in *Handbook of Psychotherapy and Behavior Change*, 3rd ed., ed. S. L. Garfield and A. E. Bergin (New York: John Wiley, 1986), p. 175.

36. D. Mazza, "Comment on Miller and Hester's 'Inpatient Achoholism Treatment: Who Benefits?'" *American Psychologist* 43 (1988): 199–200.

37. Berman and Norton, "Does Professional Training Make a Therapist More Effective?" p. 404.

38. See R. M. Dawes, "Monotone Interactions: It's Even Simpler Than That," *Behavior and Brain Sciences* 13 (1990): 128–29; and W. F. Chaplin and R. M. Dawes, "The Interpretation and Evaluation of Statistical Interactions in Psychotherapy Outcomes," in preparation.

39. Smith and Sechrest, "Aptitude X Treatment Interactions" (in preparation).

40. P. Lafferty, L. E. Beutler, and M. Crago, "Differences between More and Less Effective Psychotherapists: A Study of Select Therapist Variables," *Journal of Consulting and Clinical Psychology* 57 (1989): 76–80. See also J. S. Berman, R. C. Miller, and P. J. Massman, "Cognitive Therapy versus Systematic Desensitization: Is One Treatment Superior?" *Psychological Bulletin* 97 (1985): 451–61.

41. R. K. Hester, W. R. Miller, H. D. Delaney, and R. J. Meyers, "Effectiveness of the Community Reinforcement Approach," paper presented at the twenty-fourth annual meeting of the Association for the Advancement of Behavior Therapy, San Francisco, November 2, 1990.

42. J. D. Frank, *Persuasion and Healing*, 2nd ed. (Baltimore, MD: Johns Hopkins University Press, 1973); and H. H. Strupp, "Psychotherapy: Can the Practitioner Learn from the Researcher?" *American Psychologist* 44 (1989): 717–24. Others such as Otto Rank and Sandor Ferenczi have previously stressed the importance of the relationship.

43. For a critique of such vague assertions, see N. D. Schaffer, "Multidimensional Measures of Therapist Behavior as Predictors of Outcome," *Psychological Bulletin* 92 (1982): 670–81.

44. W. R. Miller, C. A. Taylor, and J. C. West, "Focused versus Broad-Based

Behavior Therapy for Problem Drinkers," *Journal of Consulting and Clinical Psychology* 48 (1980): 590–601.

45. This idea is neither original nor recent. For example, Otto Rank wrote in 1929: "The modern neurotic has thus completed the human process of internalization which reaches its peak in psychological self-knowledge, but also is reduced to an absurdity. He [*sic*] needs no more knowing *only experience and the capacity for it may yet be able to save him*" (italics added). In O. Rank, *Will Therapy and Truth and Reality* (New York: Alfred A. Knopf, 1964), p. 94.

46. For an explanation of "sunk costs" and their potential power in leading to irrational decisions, see Dawes, *Rational Choice*, chap. 2.

47. For an excellent description of such positive feedback, see the award-winning paper of M. Maruyama, "The Second Cybernetics: Deviation-Amplifying Mutual Causal Processes," *American Scientist* 51 (1963): 164–79.

48. P. M. Lewinsohn, D. O. Antonuccio, J. L. Steinmetz, and L. Teri, *The Coping with Depression Course* (Eugene, OR: Castalia Press, 1984).

49. G. L. Paul and A. A. Menditto, "Effectiveness of Inpatient Treatment Programs for Mentally Ill Adults in Public Psychiatric Facilities," *Applied and Preventive Psychology* 1 (1992): 41–63, quote on p. 56.

50. According to a communication from the APA publication board on February 14, 1991, approximately 30 percent of APA members subscribe to one or more scientific journals. That figure includes research and academic members as well as professional practice members. Since that time, dues have been raised and one journal of the member's choosing is provided along with the increased dues.

# 16.

# PRACTICE MAKES PERFECT AND OTHER MYTHS ABOUT MENTAL HEALTH SERVICES

## *Leonard Bickman*
Vanderbilt University

Expenditures for mental health services, as a proportion of healthcare expenditures, plummeted during the 1990s. Concurrently psychologists have been unable to muster scientific evidence for the effectiveness of typical services. The clinical world failed to collect such evidence, while the academic world focused on laboratory studies. Beliefs in the mechanisms thought to assure the quality and effectiveness of typical services may have created complacency. Psychologists seem confident that effective services are assured by (a) more experienced clinicians, (b) degree programs, (c) continuing education, (d) licensing, (e) accreditation, and (f) clinical supervision. After reviewing relevant scientific literature, the author concludes that these are myths with little or no evidence to support them. The author suggests four ways to improve the quality and effectiveness of services.

There is growing pressure to reform mental health services. The forces for change include managed care, evidence-based medicine, consumerism, and accountability for outcomes and costs (Bickman & Salzer 1997; Salzer 1999). Failure to respond to these forces may have serious

Reprinted from *American Psychologist* (November 1999): 965–78. Copyright 1999 by the American Psychological Association. Reproduced with permission.

consequences. For example, in the past eleven years, behavioral health expenditures, as a percentage of the total healthcare benefit, dropped 50 percent, and significantly more health plans have placed limits on all types of mental healthcare benefits (Hay Group, 1999). These changes may indicate that society is losing confidence in the mental health industry. How are psychologists to respond to these societal forces for change? Do we continue business as usual, or are more fundamental changes called for? Why has the mental health service sector found itself besieged?

I will first review the forces motivating reform in mental health services, provide some reasons for why service providers have found themselves in this position, and suggest alternatives to the status quo. In particular, I will argue that mental health practitioners and researchers have been overly protective of their autonomy and unresponsive to societal needs. Moreover, both practitioners and researchers have relied on traditional and apparently unsuccessful methods to assure the quality and effectiveness of services. I label these beliefs as myths because they follow the Webster's dictionary definition of a myth as "a belief given uncritical acceptance by the members of a group especially in support of existing or traditional practices and institutions" (Gove 1967, 1497). Thus, I am not attempting to prove that these beliefs are wrong, just that there is little or no scientific support for them. Finally, I suggest that insufficient communication and collaboration between the research and services communities has resulted in both communities being harmed.

My concern for the field of psychology and for what I see as its insufficient response to societal needs motivates this chapter. This concern grew out of over a decade of research and evaluation on mental health services for children and adolescents. My experience from this research convinced me that something was wrong with the way the mental health industry has been delivering services and that research on mental health often was not focused on approaches that help the consumer. I felt that we were neither adequately addressing the assumptions that underlie our services nor sufficiently questioning the usefulness of much academic research. However, I do not doubt the motives and good intentions of either the research or the clinician communities. I am suggesting that we need to consider other directions for the worlds of both research and practice. To illustrate this, I want to tell a little story, not a concrete history of psychology, but a tale that represents my beliefs about how psychology got to where it is today.

## THE TWO WORLDS OF PSYCHOLOGY

Once upon a time, there were two worlds in psychology. One world was composed of researchers. They generally resided in cloistered academic venues. They published their articles in academic journals read by other academics. The quality of their work was judged by their fellow academics, usually using narrow scientific standards. They tended not to get involved with policy issues or funding agencies other than the National Institutes of Health (NIH) and the National Science Foundation. They were generally a happy lot because they had the most cherished of academic freedoms, the freedom to do what they wanted.

The other world of psychology was the world of clinical practice. Here psychologists practiced their craft with pride and without interference from others. They were judged by their peers according to vague standards of reputation. They, too, were generally a happy lot because, like the academics, they had the most cherished clinical freedom—the freedom to do what they wanted.

These two worlds existed in blissful indifference to each other. The clinicians were happy to ignore what they saw as irrelevant research conducted in university clinics or laboratories using specially selected clients and specially trained therapists. This type of research is known as *efficacy research* because it tests interventions in highly controlled environments and with high levels of support. This type of research has many legitimate and valuable functions, but these environments rarely exist in the practice world. In contrast, *effectiveness research* studies services in the natural environment with typical clinicians and ordinary, unselected clients (Hoagwood et al. 1995). Although I draw out the contrast between these two research environments as if they were discrete categories, they are most likely complex continuums that vary over several dimensions.

The clinicians' attitude appeared to be that as long as the academics did not interfere with their practice of their profession, the academics could do whatever they wanted. The researchers could continue to publish their research on what ideal treatment should look like—but that really did not matter because few clinicians read scientific journals. The researchers appeared happy to rule their kingdom where subjects behaved as they should and the researchers did not have to deal with the practicing clinicians in their complex environment.

## THE INTERDEPENDENCE OF THE TWO WORLDS

In the 1990s, four forces started to affect mental health practice. First, the most obvious influence was the emergence of managed healthcare (DeLeon, VandenBos & Bulatao 1991; Government Accounting Office 1993). A major effect of managed care was the direct attack on the clinicians' autonomy or ability to decide what care a client should receive. Managed care companies greatly constricted clinicians' behavior. Clinicians were at a great disadvantage in responding to these restrictions because they had few data about the effectiveness of the services they delivered (Zimet 1989).

The second movement that affected healthcare and impinged on mental health services was evidence-based medicine (Anderson 1997; Goldner & Bilsker 1995). All healthcare providers became concerned with demonstrating that the services they provided were effective and based on sound scientific evidence. After many years of conducting little research on their own services, practitioners were eager to find supporting research. The academics, at first, may have been indifferent to what was happening to clinical services. After all, their university laboratories were rarely affected by managed care. As for evidence-based medicine, well, weren't they providing the evidence with their research?

Third, consumers also raised their voices about services. Consumers could be the most important constituency for the support of reform if they insisted not just on greater access, but on more effective services. Traditionally, consumers did not have much to say about academic research. However, this academic stance above the fray was not to last. More careful examination of academic clinical research began to raise significant questions about the external validity or generalizability of their work.

Finally, there has been worldwide pressure on governments to be accountable for the cost-effectiveness of the services they fund. For example, in the United States, the Government Performance and Results Act required agencies to demonstrate that their expenditure of funds had an effect on the public (NIMH 1999c). Major research funding agencies were becoming more sensitive about the public funds they were spending. There was some realization that publication of efficacy studies in scientific journals was not affecting clinical practice or consumer outcomes. Finally, consumers began to have a real voice about the funding of research because of the NIMH policy that placed consumers on some panels that review research (NIMH 1999b).

One of the first inroads into a move away from efficacy research and toward effectiveness research was the congressional mandate for three NIH institutes (NIMH, the National Institute of Alcohol Abuse and Alcoholism, and the National Institute on Drug Abuse) to spend at least 15 percent of their funds on services research. Although this policy is no longer in effect, it did move resources away from basic and efficacy research and toward services research. More recent policy shifts called for a new emphasis to be placed on what is being called effectiveness and practice research. A recent council report to NIMH, entitled "Bridging Science and Service" (NIMH 1998) called for NIMH to increase relevance, development, and use of research for both routine clinical practice and policies. A recent meeting of experts on research in children and adolescent mental health services produced a report (the Belmont Report) that also emphasized the importance of designing research that is more directly relevant to clinical practice and policy (NIMH 1999a).

It is my impression that a significant portion of the academic research community has not welcomed this movement. As funds are shifted away from efficacy research, the traditional academics are becoming concerned about their loss of funding (Klein & Smith 1999). However, academic researchers can be very flexible and inventive when it comes to funding research. I anticipate that researchers who had little to do with clinical practice will form alliances with this sector to support their research.

In summary, external forces are beginning to encourage both the academic research community and the practitioner community to collaborate in producing more cost-effective services. But weren't the services already cost effective? Do we just need to fine tune what we have, or are more fundamental changes necessary?

## CURRENT EVIDENCE ON THE EFFECTIVENESS OF TYPICAL SERVICES

For many years, psychotherapy and medication efficacy studies were assumed to demonstrate the effectiveness of treatments in the practice world. Several meta-analyses and reviews of these studies have shown medium to large effects of psychotherapy and medication (Antonuccio, Danton & DeNelsky 1995; Weisz & Jensen 1999). The research community had confidence in the treatments they studied because these reviews were consistent in finding positive effects. Many practitioners, on the other hand, relied on their own observations to evaluate the effectiveness of their services. Clearly, as they saw it, consumers got better under their care so what they were doing must be working.

However, both worlds may have been asking the wrong questions. The researchers had no strong interest in or incentive to study the usual treatments provided in the community. The issue of the generalizability of efficacy research was not a priority question. The practice community was not collecting systematic information, and no scientifically valid conclusions could be drawn from the anecdotal experiences of its clinicians.

It appeared that clinicians and funders assumed that services were effective. Although there was a suspicion that services could be improved, the major culprit of poor client outcomes was identified as the fragmentation and the lack of coordination of services and not ineffectiveness of the services themselves. The major reform efforts in the past decade operated at the systems level, not at the service or treatment levels. The Fort Bragg evaluation (Bickman 1996; Bickman et al. 1995) for children and adolescents and the Robert Wood Johnson Foundation (RWJF) program on chronic mental illness (Goldman, Morrissey & Ridgely 1994; Morrissey et al. 1994; Shore & Cohen 1990) were initiated at about the same time in the late 1980s. Both were major and expensive studies based on similar principles. The developers believed that better integration and management of services would yield superior client outcomes and lower costs. The Fort Bragg study was based on the continuum-of-care model (Stroul & Friedman 1986), and the RWJF program focused more on the intensive-case-management model. Neither study found better client outcomes as a result of the intervention. The Fort Bragg study was followed by the Stark County Study (Bickman, Noser & Summerfelt 1999; Bickman, Summerfelt & Noser 1997), with similar results, while the RWJF research was followed by several studies on case management that showed the same null effect on client outcomes (Burns et al. 1999). Systems-level reforms are not the answer to improving clients' outcomes. These reforms are very successful in affecting systems-level variables, such as access, cost, and location of treatment (e.g., hospital vs. outpatient), but did not successfully affect consumer outcomes such as symptom reduction or improvement in functioning.

The system-of-care studies and other studies of typical care raised questions about why services did not seem to be effective (Weiss et al. 1999; Weiss & Weisz 1995; Weisz et al. 1995; Weisz & Jensen 1999). Judgment in this area has to be tentative because there are not many effectiveness studies in the literature and because very few studies randomly assigned consumers to control groups that received no services. Moreover, as Shadish et al. (1997) pointed out, very few studies have replicated typical clinical practice.

We must also depend on more indirect evidence, such as dose-response evidence, to examine effectiveness in the real world. My colleagues and I recently conducted two studies (Andrade, Lambert & Bickman 2000; Salzer, Bickman & Lambert 1999) that found no relationship between the amount of treatment and outcomes. We argued that these results suggest that the treatment provided was not effective. Clearly, additional studies are needed to be certain of this conclusion. I am not concluding that services are ineffective—only that there is no systematic evidence that services are effective. Moreover, I believe that there is sufficient evidence to question psychologists' beliefs about the traditional ways of assuring the effectiveness of mental health services.

## SIX MYTHS ABOUT MENTAL HEALTH SERVICES

How did psychologists begin believing that typical services were effective without adequate research support? I think that we were seduced into believing this by the procedures we ourselves put into place for assuring effective services. I have identified six beliefs that are routinely used to bolster our confidence in the effectiveness of mental health services and yet have very little scientific support. Many of the practices derived from these beliefs have legitimate functions other than improving clinical outcomes. For example, licensing may help assure the safety of clients and the public. In addition, I am focusing on clinical outcomes, such as reductions in symptoms and improvements in functioning, and am not considering other client outcomes, such as satisfaction and personal safety. I am focusing on what I label clinical outcomes because I think they are the primary objectives of treatment and because most mental health services do not consider them in a systematic manner. Finally, I acknowledge that the research cited is often very limited in scope and quality. However, that the field has not invested in research and evaluation of these areas is itself an important statement.

## Myth 1: We Can Depend on Experienced Clinicians to Deliver Effective Services

One of the major assumptions psychologists make is that practitioners get better with experience. This is reflected in part of the title of this article: "Practice Makes Perfect." We require practicums and internships for novice clinicians, and we recommend others to clinicians who are more experienced. But what assumptions do we make when we posit experience to have this power? Questioning the value of experience in psychotherapy practice is not new (Sechrest, Gallimore & Hersch 1967). Dawes (1994), in particular, devoted a chapter in his book to debunking this role of experience. I focus more on this myth than on other myths because it provides an opportunity to clarify the linkage between clinical practice and clients' outcomes.

After over thirty years of study on the role of experience, there is no consensus that experience affects outcomes. One set of studies and meta-analyses indicates that the role of experience has almost no effect on clients' outcomes (e.g., Luborsky et al. 1980; Smith & Glass 1977; Stein & Lambert 1984; Strupp & Hadley 1979), whereas the other set reports that therapists' level of experience has a strong, positive, linear relationship to outcome (e.g., Dush, Hirt & Schroeder 1989; Lyons & Woods 1991; Stein & Lambert 1995).

There are at least three important criteria for evaluating research relevant to the question of whether the amount of clinical experience improves the effectiveness of clinicians. First, does the study take place in the natural environment, with bona fide clients, rather than under special laboratory training settings? Second, was the study designed to examine the experience question as the explicit empirical focus, or was the question addressed as a secondary, post hoc analysis? In the latter instance, it may be that the data are insufficient to address the issue. Third, do the outcomes studied directly relate to consumer mental health outcomes (e.g., symptoms, functioning) and not to outcomes such as client satisfaction (Lambert, Salzer & Bickman 1998)? Applying these criteria to these studies resolves the apparently discrepant conclusions.

Lyons and Woods's (1991) review of rational-emotive therapy does not meet the first two criteria. Approximately 60 percent of the "clients" receiving treatment in the studies they reviewed were students rather than typically referred therapy clients. In nearly 13 percent of the cases, Lyons and Woods categorized participants' diagnoses as normal or unknown/ unclassifiable. Furthermore, the review draws its conclusions about therapists' experience entirely through cross-study comparisons that do not control for potential confounds. Finally, the number of therapists in each study was typically small.

Dush et al.'s (1989) review fares better in terms of examining studies in typical clinical settings; however, most of the studies reviewed involved special training programs that were delivered under highly controlled and supervised situations that were not analogous to typical clinical services. Moreover, Dush et al.'s review did not provide any data with which to make within-study comparisons of how therapists' experience related to outcome.

Finally, Stein and Lambert (1995) have provided one of the best analyses to date that was directly designed to investigate whether experience translates into better outcomes. Their review included only studies that were conducted in typical clinical settings, and each study reviewed had therapists with varying levels of experience, which provided for a better estimate of the effects of therapists' experience levels on clients' outcomes. However, the vast majority of the outcome measures used in these studies were satisfaction ratings or ratings of improvement by the clinicians, rather than measures of clients' mental health. When these criteria were applied to the remaining fourteen studies, only one of their studies found a positive relationship between experience and outcomes (Burlingame et al. 1989).

The evidence indicates no substantial systematic relationship between clinicians' experience and clients' outcomes. Why is this the case? The cognitive learning literature is relevant here, especially literature devoted to expertise and its acquisition (Bransford et al. 1989; Cimino 1999; Johnson 1988). However, a feedback learning model is probably the most relevant (Sperry et al. 1996). In this deceptively simple model, a clinician receives feedback on successes and failures of treatment and improves on the basis of that feedback. For this model to work for psychotherapeutic treatment, clinicians have to be able to accomplish the following seven steps. Without any one of them, they would have difficulty in learning from experience. Clinicians must (a) know outcomes, (b) receive feedback, (c) know their own treatment strategies, (d) connect process with outcome, (e) fit knowledge to individuals, (f) generalize, and (g) apply their knowledge. I now review these requirements in detail.

*Know the outcomes of treatment.* For clinicians to be able to learn from experience, they need to have knowledge of the outcomes of therapy. How valid are clinicians' judgments about clients' outcomes? Some data from the Fort Bragg study (Bickman 1996) have addressed what clinicians know about these immediate outcomes (Bickman & Lambert 1999). Bickman and Lambert (ibid.) asked clinicians to rate how much improvement there had been in their clients over the past six months and compared this with the improvement shown on baseline and follow-up data collected six months apart using several standardized instruments. In a multi-trait, multi-method analytic approach, we found no relationship between the clinicians' ratings of improvement and the changes shown in the standardized instruments. In fact, the data suggest that clinicians' perceptions of improvement are similar to client-satisfaction data; clinicians' ratings correlated with ratings of treatment compliance and not with the change scores on the standardized instruments. I was unable to find any published studies that addressed this question.

A possible explanation for poor clinician awareness of outcomes is that clinicians do not receive *systematic* follow-up information about clients' outcomes either during or after treatment. Moreover, clinicians may be judging success by focusing on those clients they perceive as having successfully completed treatment, because consumers who leave services are usually not followed up. It is difficult for clinicians to gain an unbiased view of clients' outcomes because they rarely know the fate of people who drop out of therapy, and it may be easy to attribute outcomes erroneously (e.g., Harding, Zubin & Strauss 1987). The only out-comes that clinicians can possibly know are those of clients who "com-plete therapy" from the clinicians' perspective. In other words, they are more likely to learn from their successes than from their potential fail-ures, but even completion of therapy does not mean it was successful.

*Receive quick, continuous, and correct feedback.* Clients generally give feedback in an informal and unsystematic manner. However, it appears that clinician "experts," as opposed to experts in other fields, have a dif-ficult time becoming better practitioners through this type of feedback (Dawes 1994). In psychotherapy, unlike physics or chess, there is not a right answer in decision making under uncertainty, and there is not a clear way to determine the validity of decision rules based on feedback from individual cases (Johnson 1988).

The feedback that clinicians receive can also be erroneous. Although there are no studies on the effects of client-to-clinician feedback on out-comes, feedback received from clients about clinicians' diagnostic accu-racy can often be misleading. There are several studies that suggest that clients will often endorse the accuracy of diagnostic tests even if the con-clusions are general enough to include most people (Logue, Sher & Frensch 1992; Snyder, Shenkel & Lowery 1977).

*Be aware of the processes, tactics, or strategies of treatment.* For clini-cians to be able to learn from their actions, they must be capable of recalling their particular behaviors in therapy sessions. This can be established by measuring the concordance between therapists' recollec-tions of behavior and the observations of independent raters. Surpris-ingly, there has been little research devoted to studying how accurately clinicians remember their specific behaviors in therapy sessions (Carroll, Nich & Rounsaville 1998). Most studies of the psychotherapy process have used only independent raters and have not compared the reports of raters with clinicians' self-reports.

However, the research that has been conducted indicates little sup-port for the ability of clinicians to accurately recall their behaviors. Inde-pendent raters achieved acceptable interrater reliability in evaluating the responses by psychodynamic therapists, but the reliability between rater and therapist was unacceptably low for most of the behaviors (Xenakis et al. 1983). Similar findings occurred in a manual-guided-treatment study (Carroll et al. 1998). Few studies have examined clinicians' knowledge of their own behaviors. The evidence that is available suggests that clinicians cannot accurately recall their behaviors when compared with a group of trained independent raters.

*Know the relationships between processes and outcomes.* Because there is not much evidence to suggest that clinicians have knowledge of either their own behaviors or clients' outcomes, it is reasonable to suggest that they will not know the relationships between these constructs. There is some evidence to suggest that it is difficult to link processes and outcomes even with the intensive training provided in efficacy research (Calhoun et al. 1998). If clinicians experience difficulty in learning to adhere to a program consistently and quickly on the basis of feedback consequences (i.e., outcomes) of their behaviors (i.e., processes), it is hard to defend their ability to make these important linkages in the absence of specific training and feedback. Finally, Garb (1989) and Dawes (1994) have been instrumental in showing that many of the linkages that clinicians could potentially make are hampered by cognitive biases. These biases include primacy effect (making quick judgments based on first observations), confirmatory bias (selectively remembering evidence that confirms the hypothesis), representative heuristic (basing observations on categories or stereotypes), and not attending to base rates. Thus, there appears to be no scientific evidence that clinicians can successfully perceive these linkages between their clinical processes and clients' outcomes.

*Be able to contextualize knowledge to fit individuals.* Another ability that clinicians must have to effectively learn from experience is the ability to contextualize their general knowledge to fit the needs of individuals. That is, they have to be able to take general principles and correctly adapt them to individuals. Although there is no specific evidence of this in the clinical literature, there is much evidence in the cognitive literature to suggest that it is difficult to apply this information to new settings. Bransford et al. (1989) outlined several studies that indicated the difficulty of contextualizing "inert" knowledge. Literature on problem solving shows that students who have knowledge of a problem-solving strategy (i.e., they can explain it and generate examples of its utility) tend not to think in terms of the model (Bransford, Nitsch & Franks 1977) or to think with the model (Broudy 1977). Other research indicates that feedback that is didactic or that is gained through experience can often stay inert, even if it could be useful.

*Be able to generalize from individual cases to establish principles.* To learn from experience, it is paramount to begin developing principles of behavior and decision making from individual cases. However, this is nearly impossible to do for many of the reasons cited already. The lack of sources of valid, unbiased feedback (Garb 1989) and the presence of cognitive heuristics that increase the confidence of our past predictions or facilitate erroneous conclusions (Dawes 1993) prevent clinicians from truly benefiting from past experiences. Without objective outside observers, clinicians are subject to these cognitive traps. Thus, it is difficult to learn new principles.

*Be able to apply knowledge.* Finally, for clinicians to learn from experience, they must be able to apply what they learn. However, evidence suggests that even if clinicians have acquired the knowledge of specific skills, applying these skills in appropriate situations is very difficult to learn. In a review (Holloway & Neufeldt 1995) of the supervision literature, there is evidence that although skills can be learned by trainees, it is difficult for supervisors to teach them when to use these skills (Bootzin & Ruggill 1988; Shaw 1984). If clinicians cannot learn how to apply their knowledge easily with direct feedback from trainers, the ability of practitioners to apply their knowledge in the comfort of their unsupervised offices is even more suspect.

In summary, the empirical evidence of several studies does not support the belief that clinicians get better at producing client outcomes with more experience. The seven points noted above provide some of the reasons why it is difficult for clinicians to improve from practice alone.

## Myth 2: Advanced-Degree Programs Produce More-Effective Clinicians

A key way psychologists assure that effective clinical services are provided to consumers is by training clinicians in advanced-degree programs. For example, to be called a psychologist in the United States, a practitioner must have a doctor's degree (Nixon 1990). What is the evidence that a practitioner with an advanced degree in psychology or one of the other health disciplines (e.g., psychiatry, social work, nursing) is more effective than a person without an advanced degree?

As you might expect, this is a sensitive question for professional associations and the institutions of higher education. It is also a difficult question to research. However, there have been several studies that have attempted to address this issue. One of the first studies was by my colleague Hans Strupp (Strupp & Hadley 1979). Investigators found that professional psychologists with doctoral degrees had no better outcomes with distressed students than liberal arts college professors who had no clinical training. This study generated a great deal of controversy because of design problems and because it questioned the importance of training and education in the helping professions.

However, over the past twenty years, the role of formal education has been examined several times in numerous studies and meta-analyses (Berman & Norton 1985; Durlak 1979; Hattie, Sharpley & Rogers 1984; Lyons & Woods 1991; Stein & Lambert 1984, 1995; Weisz et al. 1987; Wierbicki & Pekarik 1993). These studies sometimes found that the professional therapists were better, and other times they favored the paraprofessional therapists. Reviews of this research motivated a cycle of methodological criticisms, followed by analytic improvements and rebuttals (for reviews, see Christensen & Jacobson 1994; Stein & Lambert 1995).

In a review that addressed the question of whether graduate training makes a difference in therapy outcomes, Stein and Lambert (1995) excluded studies that investigated only more trained versus less trained therapists, and they included studies involving the effects of psychotherapy in actual clinical settings. When considering clients' functioning and symptoms before and after therapy in forty-seven studies, effect sizes were reported to range between .17 and .55 in favor of professionally trained therapists over paraprofessionals.

However, when I applied even more relevant but stringent criteria to Stein and Lambert's (1984, 1995) studies, I found that eleven of the forty-seven studies measured outcome by using eight assessments, which may be biased. Of the remaining studies, only eight involved consumers' mental health outcomes (as opposed to their satisfaction ratings), along with clear distinctions between degreed and nondegreed therapists. Only one of these eight studies had effect sizes significantly different from zero (Burlingame et al. 1989).

One of the most rigorous analyses to date examined the effects of family and marital psychotherapies through a meta-analysis of 163 studies, including many unpublished dissertations (Shadish et al. 1993). Once again, in this review the presence or absence of a degree among therapists did not moderate therapy treatment effects. Thus, even many years after the publication of Strupp and Hadley's (1979) controversial study, it appears that whatever improvements are made, whatever studies are included or excluded, findings still indicate no clear differences in outcome between professionals and paraprofessionals who lack an advanced degree. Until additional research demonstrates consistent results, we should consider the belief that degree programs produce better clinicians a myth.

### Myth 3:  Continuing Education Improves the Effectiveness of Clinicians

Professional associations and licensing authorities believe clinicians' formal and informal education must continue throughout their professional lifetimes: "The goal of most continuing education activities is to improve proficiency" (Knox 1990, 261). A large continuing education industry has developed to service this need. I could not find any estimate of the cost of continuing education, but even a superficial examination of the back pages of the *APA Monitor* shows that there is a lot of activity in this area. Does continuing education change clinician behavior and lead to better outcomes for consumers?

The medical literature (not including psychiatry) contains an extensive collection of empirical evaluations of continuing education's effectiveness. Although the evaluations provide conflicting results, evidence suggests that some types of continuing education in medicine can improve clinician knowledge and behavior and client outcomes (Beaudry 1989; Davis 1998; Davis et al. 1992; Haynes et al. 1984).

The evidence supporting the effectiveness of continuing education for postgraduate mental health providers (e.g., psychologists, social workers, counselors, nurses, and psychiatrists) is limited to a few empirical evaluations using experimental designs. In a database search through PsycINFO, Medline, Healthstar, the Educational Resources Information Center (ERIC), and GPO Access (a service of the US Government Printing Office [GPO]), I found over a thousand titles relevant to continuing education and mental health providers, but found very few studies that evaluated continuing education. Although there are three studies indicating continuing education can change clinicians' knowledge, they do not evaluate whether that knowledge affects providers' clinical behavior or clients' outcomes (Hawkins & Sinha 1998; O'Hara, Gorman & Wright 1996; Webb et al. 1981). One experimental study found no significant differences in clients' outcomes, even though the clinicians in the experimental group reported greater improvements for their clients (Pekarik 1994). In conclusion, although the medical literature suggests that continuing education improves clinician proficiency and client outcomes, the mental health literature offers little evidence of continuing education's effectiveness.

### Myth 4: Licensing Helps Assure That Clinicians Will Be Effective

All US states, Guam, the District of Columbia, and nine provinces of Canada require licensing for practitioners who offer psychological services to the public for a fee (Bass et al. 1996). The stated purpose of this mechanism is to protect the public from ineffective clinicians. State licensing boards develop complex requirements, including supervised experience and oral and written examinations. Another industry has developed to teach people how to pass these examinations. Is there evidence that licensing helps select the professionals who are effective?

A literature search using the keywords *professional licensing* and *psychology* identified 173 publications in PsycINFO from 1967 to 1999 and identified 175 journal articles in the current APA full-text database. None of these articles investigated the association between licensure and quality of professional services. Although some analysis has been done on the relations between scores on the Examination for the Professional Practice of Psychology and psychology training programs (e.g., Kupfersmid & Fiala 1991), researchers have yet to determine whether examination scores or licensure predict practitioner effectiveness. The role of licensing in affecting client outcomes is, to date, mythical.

### Myth 5: *Accreditation of Health Delivery Organizations Improves Outcomes for Consumers*

To ensure that our institutions, in contrast to individuals, are delivering safe and effective services, several accreditation or quality-assurance organizations have been established. Some of these organizations, such as the Joint Commission on Accreditation of Healthcare Organizations (JCAHO), have long and distinguished histories in the health field, whereas others, such as the National Committee for Quality Assurance (NCQA), are more recent. For some organizations (e.g., NCQA and JCAHO), mental health is a very small part of their responsibilities, whereas others (e.g., the Commission on Accreditation of Rehabilitation Facilities [CARF]) offer more specialized accreditation pertinent to mental healthcare providers. For example, CARF provides accreditation for programs related to disabilities, rehabilitation, vocational services, and mental health.

The accreditation industry is big business. Hospitals have voiced concerns about the costs of accreditation review, but I could not find a source that would provide the total costs associated with accreditation. I did find, for instance, one published estimate of the total cost of preparing for and undergoing a JCAHO survey in a university neuropsychiatric hospital that suggested the expense was just over 1 percent of the hospital's operating budget in the year of the survey (Rockwell, Pelletier & Donnelly 1993). However, I could not locate any source of the total costs of accreditation for mental health facilities. Is there any evidence that this activity produces better outcomes for consumers?

Systematic research on accreditation is sparse. However, existing studies comparing data between accredited and nonaccredited hospitals have reported relationships between accreditation or certification and indicators of quality of care that are weak (e.g., Hadley & McGurrin, 1988) or nonsignificant (e.g., Bravo et al. 1999). Thus, the relationship of accreditation to client outcomes must await additional research before it moves out of the myth column.

## Myth 6: Clinical Supervision Results in More-Effective Clinicians

One of the traditional mechanisms for assuring that consumers receive effective services is clinical supervision. APA requires pre- and postdoctoral supervision for accreditation and for licensing in most states. There are detailed procedures for documenting the amount of supervision and the qualifications of the supervisors (Holloway & Neufeldt 1995). A great deal has been written about clinical supervision and how to do it. I found over twelve hundred articles, chapters, and books on clinical supervision. However, very little research has been done on the effects of clinical supervision on the clinician and the consumer. A comprehensive review could cite only one study that attempted to measure outcomes other than satisfaction or ratings by the supervisor (ibid.). One relevant study found no relationship between the amount of supervision and clients' outcomes (Steinhelber et al. 1984). The dearth of valid studies that address this issue was noted previously in the literature (Ellis et al. 1996).

# RECOMMENDATIONS

Psychologists depend on several procedures, mechanisms, and organizations to assure that mental health services are effective. Some of these approaches have been with us for countless years, whereas others are more recent.

Regardless of the age of these approaches, research evidence that they accomplish what they are supposed to is sparse at best and is often totally lacking. Psychologists and other mental health professionals have not critically examined the assumptions they have made in trusting these approaches to help produce effective services. Research has failed to produce sufficiently applicable knowledge. Research does not provide the necessary tools practitioners need to make valid clinical decisions, such as decisions about diagnoses, treatment planning, and treatment termination. However, if mental health services are to survive as a specialty, we need to explore alternatives to these approaches. There are four alternatives that I suggest. None of these recommendations is a panacea, and all will require evaluation.

## Conduct Research and Training on Manualized Treatments and Practice Guidelines

It is now virtually impossible to know what treatment is being delivered in typical mental healthcare settings. I know of no instrument that can describe what clinicians do in usual care settings. We may know the location (e.g., inpatient, outpatient, in home) and the cost, but we rarely know, except in the case of medication, what treatment is delivered.

Treatment in the clinical world is a "black box" that needs to be understood. In contrast, we do know the content of treatment delivered in manualized treatments done under laboratory conditions. Many have identified the need to test these efficacious treatments in typical treatment settings to determine if they are feasible, generalizable, and effective in those contexts (Hoagwood et al. 1995; Shadish et al. 1997). Psychologists need to discover if the manualized approach is useful in the typical clinical setting. Can and will practitioners adopt these approaches? Another major movement to change practice is the emergence of practice guidelines developed by several professional associations. Similar priorities need to be placed on determining if the practice guidelines developed are used in practice and if they affect clients' outcomes.

## Conduct Research and Training on Mediating Factors

In addition to the diagnostic-specific approach represented by the practice guidelines and manualized treatments, a more generic approach to interventions should also be attempted (Bickman 1996). In this method, factors thought to mediate outcomes that apply across most therapeutic modalities and theories are identified. The therapist behaviors associated with these factors are also identified. Therapists are then taught to use these behaviors in their treatment.

One factor that appears to mediate treatment outcomes is the therapeutic alliance between the therapist and the consumer (Eltz, Shirk & Sarlin 1995; Hartley & Strupp 1983; Horvath & Symonds 1991; Tryon & Kane 1993). Research needs to be conducted on alliance and other putative mediators of treatment following the generic approach. The diagnostically oriented manualized treatment approach should not carry the full weight of improving treatment outcomes. Although we do not know how to enhance the therapeutic alliance, or even if it can be changed, investigating the potential role of mediators should be a priority.

## Develop and Implement Comprehensive Measurement Systems

Without comprehensive data systems in place, it will be very difficult to learn which treatments and therapists are most effective with different types of problems and consumers. The future growth of knowledge about mental health services cannot come from just the universities. This knowledge also needs to be developed by service organizations and by providers themselves. The amount of applied research that needs to be done cannot be accomplished solely by academically based researchers. Service organizations need to become learning organizations (Kofman & Senge 1993; Senge 1993, 1998). The effectiveness of services is most reliably assessed by the use of standardized measures. However, to be optimally used, measurement systems should be integrated into clinical services and policy decisions.

Service organizations would benefit from a measurement system in which data are systematically collected, recorded, scored, interpreted, and fed back in a timely fashion and in an appropriate form to consumers, clinicians, managers, administrators, and policymakers. A measurement system of this type is the basis for continuous quality improvement and for rational decisions concerning resource allocation. In a report to the Australian government (Bickman et al. 1998), my colleagues and I developed a plan for such a system. A measurement system should lead to better outcomes, but like my other recommendations, it would need to be carefully evaluated so it does not just become another myth.

### Use and Study Continuous Quality Improvement

Continuous quality improvement (CQI) requires that psychologists understand the linkages between the processes and the outcomes of care, that they systematically collect data on these linkages, and that they create an atmosphere at all levels of organizations that supports the implementation of changes in treatment based on observed linkages (Bickman & Noser 1999; Deming 1982, 1986; Dickens 1994).

A CQI strategy relies on the continuous evaluation of processes and outcomes. CQI involves a dynamic interplay of assessment, feedback, and application of information. Although many support the application of CQI in healthcare settings (Dickens 1994), there have been very few demonstrations of its implementation, much less its success, in other human service fields. Dickens (ibid.) has noted the popularity of CQI in education (Edwards 1991; Ivancevitch & Ivancevitch 1992), government (Swiss 1992), and healthcare (Fried 1992; Graham 1995) but not in mental healthcare. Although the potential for outcomes monitoring and feedback to improve the quality of mental health services is recognized, there is little empirical evidence that this type of feedback improves quality of care. Thus, this approach needs to be introduced with careful evaluation.

## CONCLUSIONS

There are several major barriers to the improvement of services that must be dealt with if we are going to achieve progress in the delivery of quality mental health services. Testing the effectiveness of our current approaches to assuring quality and effectiveness is one step. We need to develop scientific support for the mechanisms that I have labeled myths and to explore better alternatives. In addition, we need to have standardized treatments that have been shown to work in the real world. This will require more research on identifying effective treatments in community settings. We need to establish valid and reliable measurement of both processes and outcomes in service settings, and we need research on practice to understand the factors that affect the delivery of services. However, we have to be on guard not to corrupt good science in the service of some new ideology driven by the sense of urgency often found in service organizations and government agencies. With the proper resources, commitment, and training, service organizations should be able to lead this movement, in partnership with academic researchers, to create truly effective mental health services.

## REFERENCES

Anderson, I. 1997. Psychiatry: Evidence-based but still value-laden. *British Journal of Psychiatry* 171: 226.

Andrade, A. R., E. W. Lambert, and L. Bickman. In press. Dose effect in child psychotherapy: Outcomes associated with negligible treatment. *Journal of the American Academy of Child and Adolescent Psychiatry.*

Antonuccio, D. O., W. G. Danton, and G. Y. DeNelsky. 1995. Psychotherapy versus medication for depression: Challenging the conventional wisdom with data. *Professional Psychology: Research and Practice* 26: 574–85.

Bass, L. J., S. T. DeMers, J. P. R. Ogloff, C. Peterson, J. L. Pettifor, R. P. Reaves, T. Retfalvi, N. P. Simon, C. Sinclair, and R. M. Tipton. 1996. *Professional conduct and discipline in psychology.* Washington, DC: American Psychological Association.

Beaudry, J. S. 1989. The effectiveness of continuing medical education: A qualitative synthesis. *Journal of Continuing Education and Health Professions* 9: 285–307.

Berman, J. S., and N. C. Norton. 1985. Does professional training make a therapist more effective? *Psychological Bulletin* 98: 401–406.

Bickman, L. 1996. A continuum of care: More is not always better. *American Psychologist* 51: 689–701.

Bickman, L., P. R. Guthrie, E. M. Foster, E. W. Lambert, W. T. Summerfelt, C. S. Breda, and C. A. Heflinger. 1995. *Evaluating managed mental health services: The Fort Bragg experiment.* New York: Plenum Press.

Bickman, L., and E. W. Lambert. 1999. *Challenges to the development of a mental health measurement system for children and youth.* Paper presented at the Fifth Annual National Health Outcomes Conference, Canberra, Australian Capital Territory, Australia, July.

Bickman, L., and K. Noser. 1999. Meeting the challenges in the delivery of child and adolescent mental health services in the next millennium: The continuous quality improvement approach. *Applied and Preventive Psychology* 8: 247–55.

Bickman, L., K. Noser, and W. T. Summerfelt. 1999. Long-term effects of a system of care on children and adolescents. *Journal of Behavioral Health Services Research* 26: 185–202.

Bickman, L., B. Nurcombe, C. Townsend, M. Belle, J. L. Schut, and M. Karver. 1998. *Consumer measurement systems for child and adolescent mental health.* Brisbane, Queensland, Australia: University of Queensland and Nashville, TN: Vanderbilt University Press.

Bickman, L., and M. S. Salzer. 1997. Introduction: Measuring quality in mental health services. *Evaluation Review* 21: 285–91.

Bickman, L., W. T. Summerfelt, and K. Noser. 1997. Comparative outcomes of emotionally disturbed children and adolescents in a system of services and usual care. *Psychiatric Services* 48: 1543–48.

Bootzin, R. R., and J. S. Ruggill. 1988. Training issues in behavior therapy. *Journal of Consulting and Clinical Psychology* 56: 703–706.

Bransford, J. D., J. J. Franks, N. J. Vye, and R. D. Sherwood. 1989. New approaches to instruction: Because wisdom can't be told. In *Similarity and analogical reasoning*, edited by S. Vosniadou and A. Ortony. New York: Cambridge University Press, pp. 470–97.

Bransford, J. D., K. E. Nitsch, and J. J. Franks. 1977. Schooling and the facilitation of knowing. In *Schooling and the acquisition of knowledge*, edited by R. C. Anderson, R. J. Spiro, and W. E. Montague. Hillsdale, NJ: Erlbaum, pp. 31–55.

Bravo, G., M. Dubois, M. Charpentier, P. De Wals, and A. Emond. 1999. Quality of care in unlicensed homes for the aged in the eastern townships of Quebec. *Canadian Medical Association Journal* 160: 1441–45.

Broudy, H. S. 1977. Types of knowledge and purposes of education. In *Schooling and the acquisition of knowledge*, edited by R. C. Anderson, R. J. Spiro, and W. E. Montague. Hillsdale, NJ: Erlbaum, pp. 1–17.

Burlingame, G. M., A. Fuhriman, S. Paul, and B. M. Ogles. 1989. Implementing a time-limited therapy program: Differential effects of training and experience. *Psychotherapy* 26: 303–13.

Burns, T., F. Creed, T. Fahy, S. Thompson, P. Tyrer, I. White, C. Issakidis, K. Sanderson, M. Teesson, S. Johnston, and N. Buhrich. 1999. Intensive versus standard case management for severe psychotic illness: A randomized trial. *Lancet* 353: 2185–89.

Calhoun, K. S., K. Moras, P. A. Pilkonis, and L. P. Rehm. 1998. Empirically supported treatments: Implications for training. *Journal of Consulting and Clinical Psychology* 66: 151–62.

Carroll, K. M., C. Nich, and B. J. Rounsaville. 1998. Utility of therapist session checklists to monitor delivery of coping skills treatment for cocaine abusers. *Psychotherapy Research* 8: 307–20.

Christensen, A., and N. S. Jacobson. 1994. Who (or what) can do psychotherapy: The status and challenge of nonprofessional therapies. *Psychological Science* 5: 8–14.

Cimino, J. J. 1999. Development of expertise in medical practice. In *Tacit knowledge in professional practice*, edited by R. J. Sternberg and J. A. Horvath. Mahwah, NJ: Erlbaum, pp. 101–20.

Davis, D. 1998. Does CME work? An analysis of the effect of educational activities on physician performance or health care outcomes. *International Journal of Psychiatry in Medicine* 28: 21–39.

Davis, D. A., M. A. Thomson, A. D. Oxman, and R. B. Haynes. 1992. Evidence for the effectiveness of CME. A review of 50 randomized controlled trials. *Journal of the American Medical Association* 268: 1111–17.

Dawes, R. M. 1993. Cognitive bases of clinicians' overconfidence. Paper presented at the meeting of the Nevada Psychological Association, Squaw Valley, Nevada, May.

———. 1994. *House of cards: Psychology and psychotherapy built on myth.* New York: Free Press.

DeLeon, P. H., G. R. VandenBos, and E. Q. Bulatao. 1991. Managed mental health care: A history of the Federal Policy Initiative. *Professional Psychology: Research and Practice* 22: 15–25.

Deming, W. E. 1982. *Quality, productivity, and competitive position.* Cambridge, MA: MIT Center for Advanced Engineering Study.

———. 1986. *Out of the crisis.* Cambridge, MA: MIT Center for Advanced Engineering Study.

Dickens, P. 1994. *Quality and excellence in human services.* Chichester, UK: Wiley.

Durlak, J. 1979. Comparative effectiveness of paraprofessional and professional helpers. *Psychological Bulletin* 86: 80–92.

Dush, D. M., M. L. Hirt, and H. E. Schroeder. 1989. Self-statement modification in the treatment of child behavior disorders: A meta-analysis. *Psychological Bulletin* 106: 97–106.

Edwards, E. 1991. Total quality management in higher education. *Management Services* 35, no. 12: 18–20.

Ellis, M. V., N. Ladany, M. Krengel, and D. Schult. 1996. Clinical supervision research from 1981 to 1993: A methodological critique. *Journal of Counseling Psychology* 43: 35–50.

Eltz, M., S. Shirk, and N. Sarlin. 1995. Alliance formation and treatment outcome among maltreated adolescents. *Child Abuse and Neglect* 19: 419–31.

Fried, R. A. 1992. A crisis in health care. *Quality Progress* 24, no. 4: 67–69.

Garb, H. 1989. Clinical judgment, clinical training, and professional experience. *Psychological Bulletin* 105: 387–96.

Goldman, H. H., J. P. Morrissey, and S. M. Ridgely. 1994. Evaluating the Robert Wood Johnson Foundation program on chronic mental illness. *Milbank Quarterly* 72: 37–48.

Goldner, E. M., and D. Bilsker. 1995. Evidence-based psychiatry. *Canadian Journal of Psychiatry* 40: 97–101.

Gove, G. 1967. *Webster's third international dictionary of the English language unabridged.* Springfield, MA: Merriam.Government Accounting Office. 1993. *Managed health care: Effect on employers' costs difficult to measure* (GAO/HRD Rep. No. 94-3). Washington, DC: Author.

Graham, N. O. 1995. *Quality in health care, theory, application and evolution.* Gaithersburg, MD: Aspen.

Hadley, T. R., and M. C. McGurrin. 1988. Accreditation, certification, and the quality of care in state hospitals. *Hospital and Community Psychiatry* 39: 739–42.

Harding, C., J. Zubin, and J. Strauss. 1987. Chronicity in schizophrenia: Fact, partial fact, or artifact. *Hospital and Community Psychiatry* 38: 477–86.

Hartley, D. E., and H. H. Strupp. 1983. The therapeutic alliance: Its relationship to outcome in brief psychotherapy. *Empirical studies of psychoanalytical theories,* vol. 1, edited by J. Masling. Hillsdale, NJ: Analytic Press, pp. 1–37.

Hattie, J. A., C. F. Sharpley, and H. J. Rogers. 1984. Comparative effectiveness of professional and paraprofessional helpers. *Psychological Bulletin* 95: 534–41.

Hawkins, K., and R. Sinha. 1998. Can line clinicians master the conceptual complexities of dialectical behavior therapy? An evaluation of State Department of Mental Health training programs. *Journal of Psychiatric Research* 32: 379–84.

Hay Group. 1999. *Health care plan design and cost trends—1988 through 1998.* Arlington, VA: National Association of Psychiatric Health Systems and Association of Behavioral Group Practices.

Haynes, R. B., D. A. Davis, A. McKibbon, and P. Tugwell. 1984. A critical appraisal of the efficacy of continuing medical education. *Journal of the American Medical Association* 251: 61–64.

Hoagwood, K., E. Hibbs, D. Brent, and P. Jensen. 1995. Introduction to the special section: Efficacy and effectiveness in studies of child and adolescent psychotherapy. *Journal of Consulting and Clinical Psychology* 63: 683–87.

Holloway, E. L., and S. A. Neufeldt. 1995. Supervision: Its contributions to treatment efficacy. *Journal of Consulting and Clinical Psychology* 63: 207–13.

Horvath, A. O., and B. D. Symonds. 1991. Relation between working alliance and outcome in psychotherapy: A meta-analysis. *Journal of Consulting Psychology* 38: 139–49.

Ivancevitch, D. M., and S. H. Ivancevitch. 1992. TQM in the classroom. *Management Accounting* 74, no. 4: 14–15.

Johnson, E. J. 1988. Expertise and decision under uncertainty: Performance and process. In *The nature of expertise*, edited by M. T. H. Chi and R. Glaser. Hillsdale, NJ: Erlbaum, pp. 209–28.

Klein, D. E, and L. B. Smith. 1999. Organizational requirements for effective clinical effectiveness studies. *Prevention and Treatment* 2, article 0002a. http//journals.apa.org/prevention/volume2/pre0020002a.html. Accessed July 4, 1999.

Knox, A. B. 1990. Influences on participation in continuing education. *Journal of Continuing Education in Health Professions* 10: 261–74.

Kofman, F, and P. M. Senge. 1993. Communities of commitment: The heart of learning organizations. *Organizational Dynamics* 22, no. 2: 5–23.

Kupfersmid, J., and M. Fiala. 1991. Comparison of EPPP scores among graduates of varying psychology programs. *American Psychologist* 46: 534–35.

Lambert, E., M. Salzer, and L. Bickman. 1998. Clinical outcome, consumer satisfaction, and ad hoc ratings of improvement. *Journal of Consulting and Clinical Psychology* 66: 270–79.

Logue, M. B., K. J. Sher, and P. A. Frensch. 1992. Purported characteristics of adult children of alcoholics: A possible "Barnum effect." *Professional Psychology: Research and Practice* 23: 226–32.

Luborsky, L., J. Mintz, A. Auerbach, P. Christoph, H. Bachrach, T. Todd, M. Johnson, M. Cohen, and C. P. O'Brien. 1980. Predicting the outcome of psychotherapy: Findings from the Penn Psychotherapy Project. *Archives of General Psychiatry* 37: 471–81.

Lyons, L. C., and P. J. Woods. 1991. The efficacy of rational-emotive therapy: A quantitative review of the outcome research. *Clinical Psychology Review* 11: 357–69.

Morrissey, J., M. Calloway, W. Bartko, M. Ridgely, H. Goldman, and R. Paulson. 1994. Local mental health authorities and service system change: Evidence from the Robert Wood Johnson Foundation program on chronic mental illness. *Milbank Quarterly* 72: 49–80.

NIMH. 1998. *Bridging science and service: A report of the National Advisory Mental Health Council's Clinical Treatment and Services Research Workshop.* Bethesda, MD: NIH and NIMH.

———. 1999a. *Child and Adolescent Services Research Strategic Planning Meeting* (Belmont Conference Center Draft Report). Elkridge, MD: NIMH Division of Services and Intervention Research.

————. 1999b. *Developing an NIMH strategic plan.* http://www.nimh.nih
.gov/strategic/strategicplan.htm#plan. Accessed July 11, 1999.

————. 1999c. *Overview of the Government Performance and Results Act.*
http://www.nimh.nih.gov/grants/pubpartl.htm. Accessed July 11, 1999.

Nixon, M. 1990. Professional training in psychology: Quest for international
standards. *American Psychologist* 45: 1257–62.

O'Hara, M. W., L. L. Gorman, and E. J. Wright. 1996. Description and evaluation of the Iowa Depression Awareness, Recognition, and Treatment Program. *American Journal of Psychiatry* 153: 645–49.

Pekarik, G. 1994. Effects of brief therapy training on practicing psychotherapists and their clients. *Community Mental Health Journal* 30, no. 2: 135–44.

Rockwell, D. A., L. R. Pelletier, and W. Donnelly. 1993. The cost of accreditation: One hospital's experience. *Hospital and Community Psychiatry* 44, no.
2: 151–55.

Salzer, M. S. 1999. United States mental health policy in the 1990s: An era of
cost-effectiveness, research, and consumerism. *Policy and Politics* 27, no. 1:
75–84.

Salzer, M. S., L. Bickman, and E. W. Lambert. 1999. Dose-effect relationship in
children's psychotherapy services. *Journal of Consulting and Clinical Psychology* 66: 270–79.

Sechrest, L., R. Gallimore, and P. D. Hersch. 1967. Feedback and accuracy of
clinical predictions. *Journal of Consulting and Clinical Psychology* 31: 1–11.

Senge, P. M. 1993. Transforming the practice of management. *Human Resource
Development Quarterly* 4, no. 1: 5–32.

————. 1998. The leader's new work: Building learning organizations. In
*Leading organizations: Perspectives for a new era*, edited by G. R. Hickman.
Thousand Oaks, CA: Sage, pp. 439–57.

Shadish, W. R., G. E. Matt, A. M. Novaro, G. Siegle, P. Crits-Christoph, M.
Hazelrigg, A. Jorm, L. S. Lyons, M. T. Nietzel, H. T. Prout, L. Robinson, M.
L. Smith, M. Svartberg, and B. Weiss. 1997. Evidence that therapy works in
clinically representative conditions. *Journal of Consulting and Clinical Psychology* 65: 355–65.

Shadish, W. R., L. M. Montgomery, P. Wilson, M. R. Wilson, I. Bright, and T.
Okwumabua. 1993. Effects of family and marital psychotherapies: A meta-
analysis. *Consulting and Clinical Psychology* 61: 992–1002.

Shaw, B. E. 1984. Specification of the training and evaluation of cognitive therapists for outcome studies. In *Psychotherapy research: Where are we and*

*where should we go?* edited by J. B. W. Williams and R. L. Spitzer. New York: Guilford Press, pp. 173–88.

Shore, M. F., and M. D. Cohen. 1990. The Robert Wood Johnson Foundation program on chronic mental illness: An overview. *Hospital and Community Psychiatry* 41: 1212–16.

Smith, M. L., and G. V. Glass. 1977. Meta-analysis of psychotherapy outcome studies. *American Psychologist* 32: 752–60.

Sperry, L., P. L. Brill, K. I. Howard, and G. R. Grissom. 1996. *Treatment outcomes in psychotherapy and psychiatric interventions.* New York: Brunner/Mazel.

Stein, D. M., and M. J. Lambert. 1984. On the relationship between therapist experience and psychotherapy outcome. *Clinical Psychology Review* 4: 127–42.

———. 1995. Graduate training in psychotherapy: Are therapy outcomes enhanced? *Journal of Consulting and Clinical Psychology* 63: 182–96.

Steinhelber, J., V. Patterson, K. Cliffe, and M. LeGoullon. 1984. An investigation of some relationships between psychotherapy, supervision, and patient change. *Journal of Clinical Psychology* 40: 1346–53.

Stroul, B., and R. Friedman. 1986. A *system of care for severely emotionally disturbed children and youth.* Rev. ed. Washington, DC: Child and Adolescent Service System Program Technical Assistance Center.

Strupp, H. H., and S. W. Hadley. 1979. Specific versus nonspecific factors in psychotherapy: A controlled study of outcome. *Archives of General Psychiatry* 36: 1125–36.

Swiss, J. E. 1992. Adapting total quality management to government. *Public Administration Review* 52: 356–62.

Synder, C. R., R. J. Shenkel, and C. R. Lowery. 1977. Acceptance of personality interpretations: The "Barnum effect" and beyond. *Journal of Consulting and Clinical Psychology* 45: 104–14.

Tryon, G. S., and A. S. Kane. 1993. Relationship of working alliance to mutual and unilateral termination. *Journal of Counseling Psychology* 40: 33–36.

Webb, L. J., R. S. Gold, E. E. Johnstone, and C. C. Diclemente. 1981. Accuracy of *DSM—III* diagnoses following a training program. American Journal of Psychiatry 138: 376–78.

Weiss, B., T. Catron, V. Harris, and T. M. Phung. 1999. The effectiveness of traditional child psychotherapy. *Journal of Consulting and Clinical Psychology* 67: 82–94.

Weiss, B., and J. R. Weisz. 1995. Effectiveness of psychotherapy. *Journal of the American Academy of Child and Adolescent Psychiatry* 34: 971–72.

Weisz, J. R., G. R. Donenberg, S. S. Han, and D. Kauneckis. 1995. Child and adolescent psychotherapy outcomes in experiments versus clinics: Why the disparity? *Journal of Abnormal Child Psychology* 23: 83–105.

Weisz, J. R., and P. S. Jensen. 1999. Efficacy and effectiveness of psychotherapy and pharmacotherapy with children and adolescents. *Mental Health Services Research* 1, no. 3: 125–57.

Weisz, I. R., B. Weiss, M. D. Alicke, and M. L. Klotz. 1987. Effectiveness of psychotherapy with children and adolescents: A meta-analysis for clinicians. *Journal of Consulting and Clinical Psychology* 55: 542–49.

Wierbicki, M., and G. Pekarik. 1993. A meta-analysis of psychotherapy dropout. *Professional Psychology: Research and Practice* 24: 190–95.

Xenakis, S. N., M. F. Hoyt, C. R. Marmar, and M. J. Horowitz. 1983. Reliability of self-reports by therapists using the Therapist Action Scale. *Psychotherapy: Theory, Research, and Practice* 20: 314–20.

Zimet, C. N. 1989. The mental health care revolution: Will psychology survive? *American Psychologist* 44: 703–708.

# 17.

# ANGUISHED SILENCE AND HELPING HANDS: AUTISM AND FACILITATED COMMUNICATION

*James A. Mulick, John W. Jacobson, and Frank H. Kobe*

The vulnerability of parents of handicapped children to offers of easy or miraculous cures is legendary among health professionals. Like most legends, this one has some truth to it. Parents are, in fact, astute critics of the professionals who work with their children. They react strongly to signs of professional aloofness or apparent disinterest or dislike and become understandably fearful at signs of indecision. They want intensely for their children to overcome the handicap, to grow out of it, to get some swift and effective treatment. They can forgive and forget aloofness or vague reasoning as long as help and hope are forthcoming. This transformation of distrust into trust can happen in the space of a single breath.

This is not abnormal. All parents want the little boy or girl they see before them to have a world full of promise and happiness, to grow into the kind of adult they can so vividly and lovingly imagine. Indeed, they begin nurturing dreams of the person their child will become from the time of their first knowledge of conception. Imagined details change with the passage of time and as experiences unfold, especially for parents of handicapped children as facts about the handicap and resulting limitations become evident; but hope, like the child, is seldom abandoned. It keeps people going.

Reprinted with permission from *Skeptical Inquirer* (Spring 1993): 270–80.

Parents of handicapped children spend much time visiting and listening to a bewildering variety of professional people who sometimes present conflicting information. Despite literature designed to improve parent-professional collaboration (Mulick & Pueschel 1983; Pueschel, Bernier & Weidenman 1988), misunderstanding is commonplace, and ever-present stress increases miscommunication. Stress affects both parent and professional. Nothing can lessen the emotional shock for the parents who hear that their child has a significant disability likely to result in lifelong limitations. The anguish is profound and tends to be rekindled by everyday events, especially when hoped-for improvements are slow or fail to occur (Simons 1987). Professionals empathize easily at such times and may experience similar emotional reactions.

The destruction of what have been termed "highly valued dreams" by dismal facts produces predictable emotional results (Moses 1983). These include guilt, denial, and anger. Of these, only anger, and the aggression or hostility that can occur, has been adequately studied scientifically and understood in terms of its underpinnings in biologically based defensive reactions (e.g., Bandura 1973; Flannelly, Blanchard & Blanchard 1984). The others, guilt and denial, are essentially cognitive phenomena. While less well understood, they represent highly reliable emotional effects of bad experiences, which also may have adaptive functions. Guilt may motivate problem solving and independent action. Denial seems to work as a cognitive barrier to the perception of incapacitating or troubling thoughts that might impede an ability to get on with essentials of day-to-day living (Meichenbaum 1985, 7475); it allows people time to revise their priorities.

Selectively screening out bad news through denial allows people to carry on with plans and relationships that would otherwise have to be abandoned, but which may serve other valued functions. Not believing something that is true also has a darker side. It allows people to go on doing things that could be, in part, bad for someone (including oneself). This is especially problematic when some aspects of continuing a course of action in the face of contradictory information are good for the denier but bad for someone else. When this is the case, harm can continue for as long as the person doing the denying derives benefit from the thoughts and actions the erroneous beliefs permit.

Denial, a form of avoidant coping, is recognized as a common reaction to the diagnosis of a serious illness or disability in oneself or a loved one. Margalit, Raviv, and Ankonina (1992) demonstrated that parents with disabled children requiring continuous special education differed from demographically similar parents in their increased use of avoidant coping and that they exhibited lower confidence in being able to control and understand their world. Interestingly, a greater tendency to adopt avoidant coping strategies did not appear to prevent them from using active coping strategies (i.e., more direct problem-solving). Rather, families with disabled children used a greater mix of the two problem-solving strategies. Further, families whose disabled children had more socially disruptive behavior seemed to use more avoidant coping than families whose disabled children exhibited fewer socially disruptive acts. These findings also are consistent with the effects of chronic stress on the selection of coping styles.

## AUTISM

Autism is a severe developmental disability, fortunately uncommon, but prevalent enough to merit specialized educational and habilitative services for affected individuals in even medium-sized communities. According to some authors, it occurs in four to five of every ten thousand children (Kiely et al. 1989; Pueschel et al. 1988). It is normally a life-long disability, associated with mental retardation in about 60 to 80 percent of cases, defined by seriously delayed and often qualitatively abnormal language and communication, and strongly associated with frequent behavioral abnormalities. Common abnormal behaviors include social withdrawal; ritualistic, self-injurious, or odd repetitive acts; and higher rates of asocial or aggressive types of disruptive behavior. A single neurophysiological cause has not been identified for the syndrome.

An additional tragic fact is that affected children are often otherwise

quite normal in appearance, bearing none of the physical deformities associated with many other developmental disabilities. Hence autistic children
are sometimes described as "beautiful," probably a poignant reminder that
except for their decreased ability to learn many types of things, to communicate, and to interact socially, they are initially as likely to evoke positive
emotional commitment from adults as any other children.

There have been a few signs of improved scientific understanding of
how to help autistic children learn to behave and communicate more
normally (Lovaas 1987), but the necessary techniques are costly and
demanding and not always effective. There is an active international
research effort. Great strides have been made providing needed educational and medical services to these and all handicapped children in the
United States (Pueschel et al. 1988). Still, there is no denying that anyone
who works or lives with autistic children, especially when they are
young, has the sense and the hope that with just the right nudge—or
drug or treatment or environment or *something*—they will snap out of
the syndrome and act as appealing and as normal as they look. Parents
of autistic children must harbor such thoughts even more often than
most of us; unfortunately, most autistic children simply do not snap out
of it, or even improve, without much expense, training, and effort.

Parents of autistic children may be expected to employ avoidant
coping styles more than most parents (Margalit et al. 1992) and to be
highly motivated to obtain services that seem to help their children. For
better or worse, these hopes are fueled by the implicit promise of our
technological society and its cultural preference for hyping the amazing,
the simple, and the ever more dramatic benefits of "discoveries" and
"breakthroughs." This sets the stage for increased vulnerability to early
adoption of untested and poorly conceived interventions and services.

## RESCUERS FROM DOWN UNDER

Enter Professor Douglas Biklen of Syracuse University with an imported
miracle cure from Australia for the often utter failure of autistic children

to learn to speak normally, a technique referred to as Facilitated Communication (FC). FC is "communication by a person in which the response of that person is expressed through the use of equipment and is dependent on the assistance of another person" (Intellectual Disability Review Panel 1988, iv). FC procedures involve using graduated physical (manual) prompting, in an initial least-to-most-effort hierarchy, with gradual reduction of guidance, to help a person point to or strike the keys of a typewriter, a computer keyboard, or a paper facsimile. The intent is to support a person's hand sufficiently to make it more feasible to strike the keys he or she wishes to strike, without affecting the key selection. In practice, the manual guidance is maintained indefinitely, suggesting an opportunity for the facilitator to exert continuing influence influence on key or picture selection by the person being facilitated.

Biklen has justified and advocated the use of this technique in the United States (Biklen 1991, 1992; Biklen et al. 1992), an amazingly effective effort. FC has been given wide and relatively uncritical recognition in the popular press (e.g., Spake 1992; Whittemore 1992; in contrast to more skeptical treatment by Shapiro 1992) and scandalously credulous treatment in nationally televised news programs.

This "therapy" is currently used nationally with thousands of handicapped people each day at a likely direct cost of millions of dollars each month. Biklen has bolstered his arguments by developing a novel theory of autism based in reframing its root cause as a form of developmental apraxia (i.e., a disorder of voluntary control of movement). Scientific evidence for developmental apraxia in autism is lacking. Autistic youngsters are often characterized by better-developed motor than verbal skills, even real nonverbal problem-solving talent. This presents little conceptual difficulty for Biklen. He also appears to imagine that people with no prior evidence of acquiring letter-recognition skills can quickly begin typing out sentences of fairly complex grammatical structure, albeit with a little help from their facilitator, and indeed have had hidden literacy all along despite previous classification as severely mentally retarded.

# A FEEBLE PROFESSIONAL RESPONSE

Speech pathologists are prominent in the clinical promotion of FC, especially via fee-for-service introduction of the basic procedures to parents and paraprofessionals directly involved in day-to-day care of people with handicaps. Two of the present authors (Mulick and Kobe) attended a presentation by a speech pathologist at a 1992 state autism meeting in Ohio. The speaker (Veale 1992) stressed that facilitators must enter the FC situation with complete trust and *belief* in the autistic person's communicative competence, with the intention that *together you can show others.*

Veale did not describe the FC training procedure in any detail. Apparently, you prop the keyboard up on an easel and hold the child's hand near the keys while having a verbal or typed conversation. In fact, procedural detail was specifically characterized as unnecessary for such a "simple" procedure. Additional points made: (*a*) Clients might not seem to be looking at the keyboard. (*b*) Interfering behaviors for problems might need to be opposed with just-right amounts of *physical force* to prevent movement of the learner's hand away from the keyboard. (It was implied that eventually, through FC, patients will thank you for doing so, as one of Veale's own patients communicated even while apparently trying vigorously to escape her grip.) (*c*) Because true communication is not composed of factual questions and answers but, rather, of open-ended alternating comments, one shouldn't ask factual questions in FC training; instead, one should just be receptive to what is produced by the handicapped individual.

Veale did not caution the audience about possible facilitator influence. She used testimonial evidence in the form of transcripts of FC conversations and a guest appearance by a grateful parent. Although statements made in conference papers are relatively ephemeral, they can have an inordinate impact on the practices of paraprofessionals and parents who may not be skeptical of obtaining unexpected literacy (especially when they are led to expect it by conference presenters). These features have little resemblance to the valid training in instruction for handicapped people that we have seen (Matson & Mulick 1991).

Novice FC trainees may not be well informed about how to teach or modify behavior. When the advice given is inconsistent, it will surely induce different practices by different trainers. Whereas these vague instructions encourage trainees to believe they need not require clients to look directly at the keyboard, Rosemary Crossley (1992a), the originator of FC in Australia, states that looking at the keyboard is absolutely necessary. Whereas the foregoing descriptions of benefit suggest that substantial progress can be obtained rather quickly, Crossley (1992b), Crossley and Remington-Gurney (1992), and Biklen et al. (1992) state that basic competence (e.g., some understandable content) may require up to six months. DEAL (1992) states that six years may be needed to attain communicative competence.

Unfortunately, no measurable definition of "basic competence" is provided. All sources reviewed by us that favor the use of FC mention some person with autism who demonstrated unexpected literacy upon the first try with FC. Transcripts of apparent conversational content are the only evidence provided (e.g., Biklen et al. 1991). We feel that the perceived unexpected literacy and sudden communicative competence is likely due to facilitator influence in most, if not all, such cases.

## SCIENTIFIC EVIDENCE AND FC

There has been no adequate controlled veridical support for any of the crucial claims made by FC proponents. We are aware of no demonstration that complex and meaningful linguistic performance, independent of possible facilitator influence, has been obtained from people who had been diagnosed severely or profoundly mentally retarded using valid methods by qualified diagnosticians. Complex linguistic performance is highly correlated with IQ and level of functioning in people with mental retardation and autism. We are aware of no evidence for rapid emergence of linguistic competence in individuals for whom a clear history of learning cannot be documented. We are aware of little support for a motor-impairment theory of autism. There is scientific evidence relevant to each point.

Because its claimed effects were so marked, so unexpected in the context of existing scientific knowledge, FC provoked academic research interest, first by the government and others in Australia and recently by a few behavioral scientists in the United States. Studies in Australia used message-passing (giving information to a nonverbal person while the "facilitator" was out of the room, and subsequently attempting to verify the nonverbal person's comprehension via the typed content of FC) or question-asking directed to the disabled person with masking of facilitator hearing by white noise. While there were isolated instances of apparent valid communication through FC, a review by Cummins and Prior (1992) concluded that the responses of all people tested in these studies were contaminated by influence over content by the facilitators.

Another message-passing evaluation study in the United States (involving twenty-three people) reported that the validity of communications could be confirmed for *none* of the participants, despite the fact that all were believed to be conversing with some degree of ability by facilitators and therapists (Szempruch & Jacobson 1992).

A controlled study involving twelve clients (believed by their caregivers to have been routinely communicating via FC for some time) and nine facilitators, by Wheeler, Jacobson, Paglieri, and Schwartz (1993); was more explicitly revealing. In a procedure where two stimulus pictures were employed, Wheeler et al. (ibid.) show that clients responded accurately with labels of the pictures only when the same pictures were seen by the facilitators. Sometimes clients were shown the same pictures as the facilitators; sometimes the pictures were different. Clients responded "accurately" with labels of some pictures even when the pictures were seen by the facilitators but *not* by the clients, revealing that the typing was controlled by the facilitators.

In yet another study, the recommended training sequence for FC was used over forty sessions with twenty-one young people with autism (Eberlin et al. 1992); the technique produced no unexpected literacy, and no client was able to better his or her measured expressive language skills using FC over the level that was obtained using controlled testing of these abilities verbally. At present, there are no scientifically controlled studies that unambiguously support benefits in expressive language function from taking part in FC for people with mental retardation or autism.

There have been controlled research studies of very successful communication training in toddlers and preschool-age children with autism using conventional methods (e.g. Lovaas 1987), more limited but still successful reports of speech improvement in older children with autism (Schreibman, Koegel & Koegel 1989), and growing recognition of effective nonspeech communication approaches. The use of computers with adapted input devices and electronic, printed, or synthesized speech output is well established with motor impaired people (e.g., Cory, Viall & Walder 1984; Demasco & Foulds 1982; Mulick et al. 1983). Appropriately configured and adapted computers have long been useful as instructional devices communication tools, environmental control systems, and game platforms with special populations (Vanderheiden 1982), just as they are for everyone else. Other communication systems successfully used by people with autism include manual sign language and picture or idiogram-based systems. Clearly, the issue is not how communication is mediated, but whether or not it is controlled by someone else, whether or not there are at least two independent participants in a communicative transaction.

## MOTOR APRAXIA IN AUTISM

The FC perspective directly challenges neuropsychological and linguistic perspectives, founded in a large body of scientific research, about the language of autistic people. Language is complex and involves elaborate neurological substrata. The speech and language of autistic people differs greatly from that of other people, presumably as a result of neurological impairment. While understanding of the spoken word by autistic people is consistent with their general intelligence, they tend to retain and use the meaning of what is said to them differently, without some of the social information that normally accompanies language and that occurs without much effort for the average person. For example, people with autism who can talk have difficulty sharing nuances of meaning that involve taking another person's perspective. They also have difficulty expressing their emotions and accurately attributing emotions to others. These features greatly affect what autistic people say, how they say things, and in some ways, what they mean by what they say. The language of people with autism who have normal intelligence (and quite a few do) is more concrete, sometimes esoteric, and more oblique compared to the average person. The language of autistic people previously diagnosed with severe mental retardation, but now using FC and cited as examples of success, in contrast, is often rich in interpersonal subtleties well beyond the aspirations of many college English majors (but perhaps not beyond those of philosophically inclined teachers or therapists with master's degrees who promote FC).

How is all this viewed by FC proponents? The motor-impairment perspective on language function set forth in writings on FC is based on the concept of motor apraxia. Apraxia refers to the neurologically determined inability to voluntarily initiate behavior or movement (because one cannot "figure out" how to move). In contrast, the term *aphasia*, which was once the term used for problems in language, now is reserved for more strictly cognitive or conceptual problems in using language. Champions of FC believe that people who have autism are not affected by aphasia but, rather, by apraxia, which involves the neurological substrate of the movement system for organizing or performing speech. At the same time, they argue that autistic people have problems "finding" the words (especially nouns), which should be called dysphasia, and speaking the words, dyspraxia.

Neurological terms have specific meanings. What is described by FC proponents refers to difficulties, rather than inabilities, of people who are considered autistic, in using words in certain ways. The quandary in trying to understanding the propositions that proponents offer, in a largely post hoc fashion, to explain the disorder and why FC is needed is complicated by the fact that they seem to confuse terminological distinctions. The prefix properly related to "difficulty" is *dys-*, not *a-*. If neuroscientists were to offer the same arguments that are set forth in articles advocating FC, they would consistently use the terms *dysphasia* and *dyspraxia*.

There is a great deal of evidence that what autistic people say intrinsically reflects the social character of much of their unusual behavior, how they seem to regard other people, and some features that might accurately be described as specific dysphasia(s) and specific vocal dyspraxia(s). Nevertheless, neurophysiological research has not yet demonstrated even a firm basis for a specific dysphasic disorder. However, aside from using terms that, as they are normally used, do not apply to the effects of autism on how people speak, FC proponents further suppose "global apraxia" characterizes autism: that affected people cannot voluntarily initiate movement. The usage error, again, is that they mean autistic people only experience difficulty. Further, there is no research evidence at all to support the position that people with autism experience such global problems. The usual clinical finding, familiar to any psychologist who routinely works in this area, is that motor impairment and delay is much less prominent than communication disorder and delay (Jacobson & Ackerman 1990). In fact, when playing quietly, or simply walking or using a climbing toy, their relatively smooth and coordinated movement and lack of physical deformity is part of the reason autistic children look so appealingly normal and kindle such general interest and hope.

Surprisingly, although the media and disability advocacy groups have greatly promoted FC, little fundamental opposition by professionals to FC has emerged. Very little criticism has been voiced within developmental disability service agencies or regulatory bodies. Many seem to view FC as the greatest breakthrough of all time, the very breakthrough for which advocates interested in full integration of all handicapped people have been waiting so that no one will, by virtue of inability to express themselves, be deprived of a place in society. Many in disability services who might be critical understandably hesitate to be, probably for fear of rejection by those involved with FC every day at their place of work.

Why, at the same time, there has not been an aggressive and visible reaction by professional and scientific societies in medicine, psychology, and neuroscience is more difficult to explain. There are numerous pressing issues facing professionals and scientists in their own fields, many involving funding and competition for resources. It may also be that large portions of these professional and scientific groups have abandoned issues related to people with chronic disabilities, whom they cannot cure, to the human service organizations and government agencies that vocally and confidently present themselves meeting all disability needs. At the same time, toleration of marginal standards for care and quality by the learned professions serving disabled people does everyone a serious disservice. Ineffective services can be costly, unnecessarily increasing the strain on the nation's health budget. Further, it represents indirect support for the prevalent belief among growing segments of the public that health professionals and scientists are not to be trusted.

## CONCLUSION

There is good reason to be skeptical of extravagant claims made for FC. Our impression is that, at best, it represents a false ray of hope for many families. Many parents and empathic, concerned paraprofessionals might be especially vulnerable to the appeal of FC because of avoidant coping styles or the action of cognitive denial mechanisms that reduce perception of some features of severe disability in others.

The promotion of FC diverts effort and funding from more plausible long-term strategies that have empirical support. The theoretical confusion gratuitously injected into the research and professional literature by FC proponents is damaging to accumulation of knowledge about handicapping conditions and their causes and detracts from the credibility of sincere efforts to integrate findings about abnormal development. The popular confusion of FC with other nonspeech communication systems that have been used successfully with disabled people will discourage public support for these tried-and-true strategies when the FC bubble bursts. And burst, it will. In the end, regret will provide small solace. The irony of FC is perhaps best revealed by a poem reproduced in the Fall 1992 issue of the *Advocate, a* newsletter of the Autism Society of America (p. 16), a poem that won recognition for its author, identified as a twenty-six-year-old youth with autism. The poem (despite its spooky resemblance to an old Beatles song) was said to have been produced via FC. Two lines in particular stand out; it begins, "I am you, and you are me . . .", and goes on, "We are each other as we are what we can be."

The professional and scientific communities, as well as government human service and regulatory agencies, should not allow people with handicaps and their families to be used by a few professors and therapists who stoke their hopes with empty promises, regardless of their sincerity, while reaping personal or political rewards and working hard to prevent systematic verification of their claims. Such practices should always be called into question. In our experience, people with handicaps can be valued members of their families and communities without resorting to appeals to miracle cures. There is effective help available, help that makes scientific sense. The genuine efforts of scientifically trained and compassionate professionals surpass all fad treatments, and always will. Advances in treatment and understanding come at the price of rigorous training, dedication to accuracy and scientific standards, and objective verification of all treatment claims.

# REFERENCES

Bandura, A. 1973. *Aggression: A Social Learning Analysis.* Englewood Cliffs, NJ: Prentice-Hall.

Biklen, D. 1991. Communication unbound: Autism and praxis. *Harvard Educational Review* 60: 291–314.

——. 1992. Typing to talk: Facilitated communication. *American Journal of Speech and Language Pathology.* January: 15–17, 21–22.

Biklen, D., M. W. Morton, D. Gold, C. Berrigan, and S. Swaminanthan. 1992. Facilitated communication: Implications for individuals with autism. *Topics in Language Disorders* 12: 1–28.

Biklen, D., M. W. Morton, S. N. Saha, J. Duncan, D. Gold, M. Hardardottir, E. Karna, S. O'Connor, and S. Rao. 1991. "I AMN NOT A UTISTIVC OH THJE TYP" (I'm not autistic on the typewriter). *Disability, Handicap & Society* 6: 161–80.

Cory, L. W., P. H. Viall, and R. Walder. 1984. "Computer Assisted Communication Devices." In *Transitions in Mental Retardation, Vol. 1: Advocacy, Technology, and Science,* edited by J. A. Mulick and B. L. Mallory, pp. 151–73. Norwood, NJ: Ablex.

Crossley, R. 1992a. Facilitated communication. Invited address at the Annual Conference of the Northeast Region X American Association on Mental Retardation, Albany, NY, October 5.

———. 1992b. Getting the words out: Case studies in facilitated communication training. *Topics in Language Disorders* 12: 46–59.

Crossley, R., and J. Remington-Gurney. 1992. Getting the words out: Facilitated communication training. *Topics in Language Disorders* 12: 29–45.

Cummins, R. A., and M. P. Prior. 1992. Autism and facilitated communication: A reply to Biklen. *Harvard Educational Review* 62: 228–41.

DEAL (Dignity Through Education and Language) Communication Centre. 1992. *Facilitated Communication Training.* Caulfield, Victoria, Australia: DEAL.

Demasco, P., and R. Foulds. 1982. A new horizon for nonvocal communication devices. *Byte* (September): 166–82.

Eberlin, M., G. McConnachie, S. Ibel, and L. Volpe. 1992. A systematic investigation of "facilitated communication": Is there efficacy or utility with children and adolescents with autism? Paper presented at the Annual Conference of Northeast Region X of the American Association on Mental Retardation, Albany, NY, October 5.

Flannelly, K. J., R. J. Blanchard, and D. C. Blanchard, eds. 1984. *Biological Perspectives on Aggression.* New York: Alan R. Liss.

Intellectual Disability Review Panel. 1988. *Report to the Director-General on the Validity and Reliability of Assisted Communication.* Melbourne, Victoria, Australia: Victoria Community Services.

Jacobson, J. W., and L. J. Ackerman. 1990. Differences in adaptive functioning among people with autism or mental retardation. *Journal of Autism and Developmental Disorders* 20: 205–19.

Kiely, M., J. W. Jacobson, N. Schupf, W. B. Zigman, and W. P. Silverman. 1989. *Prevalence of Developmental Disabilities* (Project Report). Staten Island, NY: New York State Institute for Basic Research in Developmental Disabilities.

Lovaas, O. I. 1987. Behavioral treatment and normal education and intellectual functioning in young autistic children. *Journal of Consulting and Clinical Psychology* 55: 3–9.

Margalit, M., A. Raviv, and D. B. Ankonina. 1992. Coping and coherence among parents with disabled children. *Journal of Clinical Child Psychology* 21: 202–209.

Matson, J. L., and J. A. Mulick, eds. 1991. *Handbook of Mental Retardation.* New York: Pergamon.

Meichenbaum, D. 1985. *Stress Inoculation Training.* New York: Pergamon.

Moses, K. 1983. "The Impact of Initial Diagnosis: Mobilizing Family Resources." In *Parent-Professional Partnerships in Developmental Disability Services,* edited by J. A. Mulick and S. M. Pueschel, pp. 11–34. Cambridge, MA: Academic Guild Publishers.

Mulick, J. A., and S. M. Pueschel, eds. 1983. *Parent-Professional Partnerships in Developmental Disability Services.* Cambridge, MA: Academic Guild Publishers.

Mulick, J. A., F. D. Scott, R. F. Gaines, and B. M. Campbell. 1983. "Devices and Instrumentation in Skill Development and Behavior Change." In *Treatment Issues and Innovations in Mental Retardation,* edited by J. L. Matson and F. Andrasik, pp. 515–80. New York: Plenum.

Pueschel, S. M., J. C. Bernier, and L. E. Weidenman. 1988. *The Special Child: A Source Book for Parents of Children with Developmental Disabilities.* Baltimore, MD: Paul H. Brookes.

Schreibman, L., L. K. Koegel, and R. L. Koegel. 1989. "Autism." In *Innovations in Child Behavior Therapy,* edited by M. Hersen, pp. 395–428. New York: Springer.

Shapiro, J. P. 1992. See me, hear me, touch me. *U.S. News & World Report,* July 27, pp. 63–64, .

Simons, R. 1987. *After the Tears: Parents Talk about Raising a Child with a Disability:* San Diego: Harcourt Brace Jovanovich.

Spake, A. 1992. "In Classroom 210 . . ." *Washington Post Magazine*, May 31, pp. 17–22.

Szempruch, J., and J. W. Jacobson. 1992. *Evaluating the Facilitated Communication of People with Developmental Disabilities* (TR #92–TA2). Rome, NY: Rome DDSO.

Vanderheiden, G. 1982. Computers can play a dual role for disabled individuals. *Byte* 7: (September) 136–62.

Veale, T. K. 1992. Facilitated communication. Presentation at the 4th Annual State Conference of the Austism Society Ohio, Toledo, October 23–24.

Wheeler, D. L., J. W. Jacobson, R. A. Paglieri, and A. A. Schwartz. 1993. An experimental assessment of facilitated communication. *Mental Retardation* 31: 49–60.

Whittemore, H. 1992. He broke the silence. *Parade: The Sunday Newspaper Magazine*, September 20, pp. 8, 25.

Editors' Note: Despite convincing debunking, FC continues to be used in many quarters in 2008.

## 18.

# "CURING" ADHD

### Alan D. Bowd

*I have a son who has just turned nine, and his teacher thinks he has ADHD. I don't want him taking drugs every day. Is there some natural way to treat it?*

*My seventeen-year-old was diagnosed with ADHD in grade six. I was told he would grow out of it by now, but he hasn't. His medication helps but I worry. Is there an alternative?*

These are fairly typical of the calls and e-mails we receive at our Centre of Excellence for Children and Adolescents with Special Needs from parents concerned about their children who have Attention Deficit Hyperactivity Disorder (ADHD). We explain that psychostimulant medications such as Ritalin (methylphenidate) are helpful in about 70 percent of cases, that they help control symptoms, but that there is no cure and the disorder does not end with high school graduation. We sometimes point out that the traditional classroom is an especially restrictive environment for children with ADHD and that in adulthood they often find employment where their work is not hampered, or may even be enhanced, by their levels of activity. Finally, we add that no link has been established to sugar, food coloring, or diet and that there is no cure for the disorder.

Reprinted with permission from *Skeptical Inquirer* (May/June 2006): 50–53.

## ADHD: WHY THE CONTROVERSY?

ADHD is defined in the American Psychiatric Association's *Diagnostic and Statistical Manual of Mental Disorders—IV, Text Revision (DSM IV-TR)* (APA 2000). It describes the behavior of persons who have a chronic level of inattention, impulsive hyperactivity, or both, to such an extent as to compromise daily functioning. There are three types: Predominantly Inattentive, Predominantly Hyperactive–Impulsive, and Combined. The diagnostic criteria are spelled out in considerable detail and emphasize that developmental level, social setting, and cultural environment need to be taken into account when identifying the disorder. Three to seven percent of children have ADHD, and approximately three times more boys than girls are affected. Recent findings clearly indicate that the disorder is a lifelong, neurologically based condition (Weyandt 2001).

However, the diagnosis and treatment—even the existence—of ADHD are subjects of very real controversy. The National Institutes of Health (NIH) found it necessary to release a consensus statement confirming the scientific validity of the diagnosis and treatment of ADHD, including "the literal existence of the disorder" (NIH 2000). Critics have argued that ADHD should not be regarded as a distinct diagnostic entity, because its symptoms are ill defined, unreliably differentiated from those of other conduct disorders, and not supported by sufficient empirical data (Hallahan & Kauffman 2003). While it is true that the identification of individuals with ADHD includes a substantial element of subjectivity, each objection has been dismissed, not only by the APA but also by the US Surgeon General, the American Medical Association, the American Psychological Association, and the American Academy of Pediatrics (International Consensus Statement on ADHD 2002). Many of the critics have come from educational backgrounds where there is ongoing concern about misidentification and inappropriate prescription of medication for students who may be difficult to manage in school but who do not have a mental disorder.

The controversy about ADHD receives much attention in the mass media. Hundreds of "cures" and treatments of no demonstrated worth are promoted by individuals with questionable qualifications, as well as by outright hucksters. Most share a financial interest in persuading the public that treatment with psycho-stimulant drugs is ineffective and even dangerous or life-threatening. Not only do they raise false hope by making promises that cannot be met, they encourage parents to avoid or discontinue medical treatment and educational/behavioral interventions of proven value.

## CAUSES, CURES, REMEDIES, AND HEALING— FOR A PRICE

Given the abundance of products and services advertised online, I will review here only a small selection, chosen to reflect the diversity of claims for cures and to illustrate the outright misinformation that often accompanies them. Although offering treatments they claim to be superior to the best medical science has to offer, most of these Web sites play it safe by including disclaimers. Ironically, these frequently include the statement that their advice should not to be construed as a substitute for that of physicians or other healthcare professionals!

### Diet

The most widely promoted myth regarding ADHD is that it is caused by a poor diet. Sugar, artificial food coloring, preservatives, additives, refined carbohydrates, and dairy products are most frequently targeted, despite evidence to the contrary, much of it published as early as two decades ago and based on dozens of scientific studies (e.g., Conners 1980; Kavale & Forness 1983; Weyandt 2001; Wolraich, Wilson & White 1995).

The ADHD Information Library Web site advertises Vaxa products (Cowan 2005). It tells parents what their children should *not* eat for the first two weeks of their "ADHD diet eating program for ADD and ADHD kids." These restrictions are: (1) No dairy products (cow's milk is "the single most important restriction"); it is further suggested that because "the brain is about 80 percent water," seven to ten glasses a day might be "helpful all by itself"! (2) No yellow foods—but the author points out that bananas are, in point of fact, white—"just don't eat the peel." (3) No junk foods ("if it comes in a cellophane wrapper, don't eat it," presumably referring to both the wrapper and the contents). (4) No fruit juices (too much of the dreaded sugar). (5) Cut sugar intake by 90 percent. (6) Cut chocolate by 90 percent. (These reductions are suggested with no account being taken of the amount originally ingested.) (7) No aspartame. "None. Period." (8) No processed meats and no MSG—"if the meat has chemicals listed that you can't pronounce, don't buy it." (9) Cut fried foods by 90 percent. (10) Avoid food colorings whenever possible. The author concludes with the sage advice: "Just eat foods that God made for a while"! (Cowan 2005).

The Web site includes a disclaimer stating in part that the information on ADHD is presented for educational purposes only and that "products mentioned herein are not intended to diagnose, treat, cure, or prevent any disease." However, the reader is encouraged to purchase a homeopathic remedy priced at $36.95 per bottle, with three varieties suggested for a month's supply. "Millions of people are being placed on activity modifying drugs for their ADHD/ADD but many of these drugs can have dangerous side effects. Attend is a safe, all-natural alternative to these ADHD/ADD drugs. . . . Attend is not just for children and teens. Attend also works great for adult ADD . . ." (GotSupplements.com 2005).

No evidence is offered in support of these claims; the words "safe" and "all-natural" are key in persuading the hopeful.

### Cleansing

CureZone.com (2005), whose motto is "Education Instead of Medicating," explains that ADHD (which it describes as a learning disability) is typically the result of one of three factors: a blow to the head; "chemical trauma" manifesting as allergies and food intolerances, often as a consequence of maternal drug ingestion (e.g., birth control pills or antibiotics) before, or during, pregnancy and delivery (if this were true, few mothers would be exempt from placing their babies at risk); and heredity ("better diet can even correct that one"). This Web site recommends "eliminating sugars (fruits, juices, milk products, and refined, simple carbohydrates) from the children's diet," and claims Dr. Atkins found that this "can correct most ADHD." While advocating the adoption of an "Attention Deficit Disorder diet" as the first step in the "Prevention and Curing Protocol," CureZone.com recommends "Body cleansing for kids," noting it is an "extremely important part of every prevention and curing program." This bizarre step in the protocol has three parts: parasite cleanse (recommended without reference to any clinical evidence of infection), dental cleanup (for children older than eight, because of supposedly toxic amalgam fillings), and liver cleanse/flush (to remove stones and impurities). The protocol prescribes physical activity for Attention Deficit Disorder because "it helps cleansing, it brings balance and relieves stress." In fact, noncompetitive activities such as in-line skating or skateboarding, in which a child with ADHD experiences success, can help build self-esteem (Weill 1995). Sweating for ADD is described as a powerful way to clear accumulated toxins: "It is known that some modern industrial toxins and pesticides can leave your body only through sweat glands."[1]

Considerable space is devoted to parasites, along with more than sixty pages of graphic photographs, just to show how repulsive these little animals look, and perhaps to create some anxiety in potential clients. Herbs are recommended to eliminate parasites, and a specific brand, Clarkia, comes highly recommended. This is a formulation produced by Hulda Regehr Clark, whose books include *The Cure for HIV and AIDS, The Cure for All Advanced Cancers,* and surely her magnum opus, *The Cure for All Diseases.* CureZone.com receives a percentage of all sales of books and products when clients link to the relevant purchase site from the CureZone.com host site. Clark, incidentally, has been the subject of several court cases and now spends most of her time at the Century Nutrition Clinic in Mexico (Clark 2005).

## Homeopathy/Naturopathy

While many sites claiming cures for ADHD emphasize diet, nearly all that I visited create and capitalize on a fear of physician-prescribed medications to help peddle their untested remedies. An example follows (the boldface is in the original):

> Rather than **prescribing strong** and sometimes **addictive psychiatric drugs**, (Ritalin, Concerta, Adderall) naturopathic approaches to the treatment of ADHD and ADD take a more holistic look at the individual and take into account diet, lifestyle, personality type, surroundings, and emotional factors.
>
> Natural remedies are used to **gently and effectively** treat the symptoms, while at the same time helping the person to **heal** and to reach a state of balance and health.
>
> The natural approach is less harmful and more thorough and has a **greater chance** of curing the problem altogether, instead of keeping the individual on psychiatric drugs for many years.
>
> This is very important, **especially** in the case of children, because of the frequent side effects of prescription drugs and the risk of addiction (NativeRemedies.com 2005).

Note the weasel words: *strong, addictive,* and *psychiatric* with reference to prescription medication; *gently, effectively,* and *heal* applied to the product being promoted. Following that is a pitch for Focus, a product containing six plant extracts, with no evidence for its effectiveness or mention of possible side effects. There is, of course, the usual selection of testimonials that so frequently accompanies advertising for products of this kind. A bottle of Focus will last twenty-five to thirty days at a cost of $26.95 plus shipping. For children as young as three, Focus may be combined with BrightSpark, a homeopathic ADHD "remedy."

It is outrageous that the purveyors of these unproven treatments are taking money from vulnerable parents desperately seeking help for their children. But of equal concern is their deliberate—and often successful—ploy of creating unreasonable fears and anxiety about the use of prescription medications of proven efficacy. According to the American Academy of Pediatrics (2005), methylphenidate (Ritalin, Concerta) and other stimulant medications are both safe and effective. When combined with cognitive-behavioral therapy, "about 80 percent of children with ADHD who are treated with stimulants improve a great deal" (American Academy of Pediatrics 2005). This advice is supported by an extensive scientific literature involving double-blind controlled studies (see Spencer et al. 1996 for a review). It is important that the correct dosage and most appropriate medication be determined individually, a process that usually takes several weeks. Side effects, which are not common, are mild and short-lived and usually occur early in the treatment. The most prevalent include decreased appetite, weight loss, sleep problems, headaches, jitteriness, social withdrawal, and stomach aches (American Academy of Pediatrics 2005; Greenhill, Halperin & Abikoff 1999).

## THE TIP OF THE ICEBERG

CureZone.com was founded in 1997, and by the end of 2001, it had become one of the three most visited "natural-health" Web sites. It claims to openly welcome information, to be not for profit, and thus forced to solicit donations. Thousands of individuals have submitted their stories and articles for publication on the site, and CureZone promotes more than sixty e-mail "support groups" with over fifty thousand members (CureZone.com 2005). Yet it is only one among a multitude of similarly dedicated sites clamoring to advocate cures and treatments for ADHD, along with other mental-health conditions and disabilities. Besides the few described in this chapter, "cures" and "effective treatment" of ADHD are to be found at Web sites representing behavioral optometry (vision therapy), acupressure and acupuncture, chiropractic, megavitamins and mineral supplements, EEG biofeedback, and applied kinesiology—and this is only a partial listing.

The proclamation "At Cure Zone, we do not recognize word *incurable* [*sic*]" (CureZone.com 2005) is insidiously tempting, especially for vulnerable parents. It is, unfortunately, less dramatic to honestly and openly state, as does the Web site of the American Academy of Pediatrics: "You may have heard media reports or seen advertisement for 'miracle cures' for ADHD. . . . At this time, there is no scientifically proven cure for this condition."

Unfortunately, as many readers must be well aware, reason speaks with a measured voice; flim-flam's is shrill and, for many, enticing.

## NOTE

1. I could find no evidence for this statement. It may stem from an "urban myth" apparently begun by an anonymous e-mail in 1999. This claimed that using antiperspirants can cause cancer by preventing the sweat glands from excreting toxins. Mervyn Elgart, a professor emeritus of dermatology at George Washington University, has referred to the claim as "a bunch of crap" (Urbanlegends 2005).

## REFERENCES

American Academy of Pediatrics. 2005. Modern Medical Library, ADHD treatment with medication. Available at www.medem.com/MedLB/article _detaillb.cfm?article_ID=ZZZ98TFTXSC&sub_cat=0; accessed July 9, 2005.

American Psychiatric Association. 2000. *Diagnostic and Statistical Manual of Mental Disorders, Fourth Edition, Text Revision.* Washington, DC.

Clark, H. 2005. Dr. Clark's home page. Available at www.huldaclark.net/; accessed July 8, 2005.

Conners, C. K. 1980. *Food Additives and Hyperactive Children.* New York: Plenum Press.

Cowan, D. L. 2005. The ADHD diet for your Attention Deficit Disorder. Available at www.newideas.net/adddiethtin; April 11, 2005.

CureZone.com. 2005. About CureZone.com. Available at http://curezone.com/ about.asp; accessed July 8, 2005.

GotSupplements.com. 2005. Vaxa attend. Available at www.gotsupplements .com/dispProduct.asp?ProductID=186439; accessed June 30, 2005.

Greenhill, L. L., J. M. Halperin, and H. Abikoff. 1999. Stimulant medications. *Journal of the American Academy of Child and Adolescent Psychiatry* 38, no. 5: 503–12.

Hallahan, D. P., and J. M. Kauffman. 2003. *Exceptional Learners: Introduction to Special Education.* 9th ed. Boston: Allyn & Bacon.

International Consensus Statement on ADHD. 2002. *Clinical Child and Family Psychology Review* 5, no. 2 (January): 89–111.

Kavale, N. A., and S. R. Forness. 1983. Hyperactivity and diet treatment: A meta-analysis of the Feingold hypothesis. *Journal of Learning Disabilities* 16: 324–30.

National Institutes of Health. 2000. Consensus and development conference statement: Diagnosis and treatment of Attention-Deficit/Hyperactivity Disorder. *Journal of the American Academy of Child and Adolescent Psychiatry* 39, no. 2: 182–93.

NativeRemedies.com. 2005. Focus ADHD formula. Available at www.native remedies.com/focus_for_adhd.shtml; accessed April 11, 2005.

Spencer, T., J. Biederman, T. Wilens, M. Harding, B. A. O'Donnell, and S. Griffin. 1996. Pharmacotherapy of Attention Deficit/Hyperactivity Disorder across the life cycle. *Journal of the Anterimn Academy of Child and Adolescent Psychiatry* 35: 409–32.

Urbanlegends. 2005. False rumor links antiperspirants to breast cancer. Available at http://urbanlegends.about.com/cs/healthmedical/a/antiperspirants .htm; accessed July 10, 2005.

Weill, M. 1995. Helping children with attention problems: Strategies for parents (insert). *National Association of School Psychologists Communique* (November).

Weyandt, L. L. 2001. *An ADHD Primer.* Boston: Allyn & Bacon.

Wolraich, M. L., D. B. Wilson, and J. W. White 1995. The effect of sugar on behavior or cognition in children. *Journal of the American Medical Association* 274: 1617–21.

Editors' Note: For a comprehensive review of effective and ineffective treatments for ADHD, see D. A. Waschbusch and G. P. Hill (2003). Empirically supported, promising, and unsupported treatments for children with attention-deficit/hyperactivity disorder. In S.O. Lilienfeld, S. J. Lynn and J. M. Lohr, *Science and Pseudoscience in Clinical Psychology*, New York: Guilford.

# 19.

# EMDR TREATMENT: LESS THAN MEETS THE EYE?

## Scott O. Lilienfeld

"Quick fixes" for emotional maladies have long struck a responsive chord in the general public, as biopsychologist B. L. Beyerstein (1990) has noted. Because these interventions often hold out the hope of alleviating long-standing and previously intractable problems with a minimum of time and effort, they are understandably appealing to both victims of psychological disorders and their would-be healers.

More often than not, however, the initial enthusiasm generated by such treatments has fizzled as soon as their proponents' claims have been subjected to intensive scrutiny. In the case of certain highly touted techniques such as neurolinguistic programming (Druckman & Swets 1988), subliminal self-help tapes (Moore 1992; Pratkanis 1992), and facilitated communication for autism (Mulick, Jacobson & Kobe 1993), controlled studies overwhelmingly indicate that early reports of their effectiveness were illusory. In other cases, such as biofeedback for psychosomatic disorders, there is some limited evidence for efficacy, but scant evidence that this efficacy exceeds that of less expensive and less technologically sophisticated treatments (Druckman & Swets 1988). The benefits of biofeedback, for example, are not demonstrably greater than those of relaxation training (Silver & Blanchard 1978).

In the past few years, a novel and highly controversial treatment known as "eye movement desensitization and reprocessing" (EMDR)

Reprinted with permission from *Skeptical Inquirer* (January/February 1996): 25–31.

has burst onto the psychotherapy scene. EMDR has been proclaimed by its advocates as an extremely effective and efficient treatment for Post-Traumatic Stress Disorder (PTSD) and related anxiety disorders. These assertions warrant close examination because PTSD is a chronic and debilitating condition that tends to respond poorly to most interventions.

Although PTSD was not formally recognized as a mental disorder until 1980, descriptions of "shell shock," "battle fatigue," and similar reactions to wartime trauma date back at least to the late nineteenth century (Barlow 1988). PTSD is defined by the American Psychiatric Association (1994, 427) as an anxiety disorder resulting from exposure to "an event . . . that involved actual or threatened death or serious injury, or a threat to the physical integrity of self or others." Among the most frequent precipitants of PTSD are military combat, rape, physical assault, motor vehicle accidents, natural disasters, and the witnessing of a murder or an accidental death. The primary symptoms of PTSD fall into three categories: (1) psychological reexperiencing of the traumatic event (e.g., recurrent and disturbing flashbacks and dreams of the event); (2) avoidance of stimuli (e.g., television programs, conversations) that remind the individual of the event; and (3) heightened arousal (e.g., sleep disturbances, increased startle responses).

Although PTSD is difficult to treat, there is accumulating evidence that "exposure treatments," which involve confronting clients with memories and images of the traumatic event, are effective for many cases of PTSD (Frueh, Turner & Beidel 1995). One of the best known of such interventions is "flooding," in which clients are exposed to trauma-related stimuli for prolonged time periods (often two hours or more) until their anxiety subsides. Flooding can be performed using either real-life stimuli or visual imagery, although the inability to re-create the actual details of the traumatic scene typically means that the treatment must be conducted imaginally. The mechanisms underlying the success of exposure techniques are still a subject of debate, but many psychologists believe that the effective ingredient in such treatments is "extinction"—the process by which a response dissipates when the stimulus triggering this response is presented without the original emotional concomitants.

Despite their advantages, exposure treatments for PTSD tend to provoke extreme anxiety and consume much time. Often twenty sessions are required for maximal efficacy (Frueh et al. 1995). As a result, many clients with PTSD are reluctant to undergo such treatments, leading some practitioners to search for less stressful and more time-efficient interventions. Enter EMDR.

## EMDR: METHOD, RATIONALE, AND CLAIMS

Francine Shapiro, the psychologist who originated EMDR, recalls having fortuitously "discovered" this technique when she found that rapid back-and-forth eye movements reduced her own anxiety (Shapiro 1989b). Shapiro thereafter applied this procedure to her own clients with anxiety disorders and claims to have met with remarkable success. Since the initial published report of its use in 1989, EMDR has skyrocketed in popularity among practitioners. As of mid-1995, approximately fourteen thousand therapists were licensed to perform EMDR in the United States and other countries (Bower 1995), and this number is growing. EMDR is also attracting international attention. For example, a team of American psychologists recently trained forty European therapists to administer EMDR to victims of war trauma in Bosnia (Cavaliere 1995).

Although EMDR is alleged to be a complicated technique that requires extensive training (Shapiro 1992), the treatment's key elements can be summarized briefly. Clients are first asked to visualize the traumatic event as vividly as possible. While retaining this image in mind, they are told to supply a statement that epitomizes their reaction to it (e.g., "I am about to die"). Clients are then asked to rate their anxiety on a Subjective Units of Distress (SUDs) scale, which ranges from 0 to 10, with 0 being no anxiety and 10 being extreme terror. In addition, they are told to provide a competing positive statement that epitomizes their desired reaction to the image (e.g., "I can make it"), and to rate their degree of belief in this statement on a 0 to 8 Validity of Cognition scale.

Following these initial steps, clients are asked to visually track the therapist's finger as it sweeps rhythmically from right to left in sets of 12 to 24 strokes, alternated at a speed of two strokes per second. The finger motion is carried out 12 to 14 inches in front of the client's eyes. Following each set of 12 to 24 strokes, clients are asked to "blank out" the visual image and inhale deeply and are then asked for a revised SUDs rating. This process is repeated until clients' SUDs ratings fall to 2 or lower and their Validity of Cognition ratings rise to 6 or higher.

Although EMDR technically requires the use of eye movements, Shapiro (1994a) claimed that she has successfully used the technique with blind clients by substituting auditory tones for movements of the therapist's finger. Recently I attended a presentation on EMDR given by a clinician who reported that, when working with children, he uses alternating hand-taps on the knees in lieu of back-and-forth finger movements.

Since its development, EMDR has been extended to many problems other than PTSD, including phobias, generalized anxiety, paranoid schizophrenia, learning disabilities, eating disorders, substance abuse, and even pathological jealousy (Beere 1992; Marquis 1991; Shapiro 1989b). Moreover, Shapiro (1991, 135) asserted that "EMDR treatment is equally effective with a variety of 'dysfunctional' emotions such as excessive grief, rage, guilt, etc." The theoretical rationale for EMDR has not been clearly explicated by either Shapiro or others. Indeed, an attempt by Shapiro (1994b, 153) to elaborate on EMDR's mechanism of action may mystify even those familiar with the technique: "The system may become unbalanced due to a trauma or through stress engendered during a developmental window, but once appropriately catalyzed and maintained in a dynamic state by EMDR, it transmutes information to a state of therapeutically appropriate resolution." Shapiro has further conjectured that the eye movements of EMDR are similar to those of rapid eye movement (REM) sleep. Because there is evidence from animal studies that REM sleep is associated with the processing of memories (Vinson 1990), Shapiro has suggested that the eye movements of EMDR may similarly facilitate the processing of partially "blocked" memories. Because there is no evidence that EMDR produces brain changes resembling those occurring during REM sleep, however, the analogy between the eye movements of EMDR and those of REM sleep may be more superficial than real.

EMDR has been hailed by its advocates as a novel treatment that produces much faster and more dramatic improvements than alternative treatments. Shapiro (1989b), for example, asserted that EMDR can successfully treat many or most cases of PTSD in a single fifty-minute session, although especially severe cases may require several sessions. Moreover, claims for EMDR's efficacy have not been limited to Shapiro. Psychologist Roger Solomon (1991, cited in Herbert & Mueser 1992) described EMDR as "a powerful tool that rapidly and effectively reduces the emotional impact of traumatic or anxiety evoking situations." Beere (1992, 180) reported "spectacular" results after using EMDR on a client with multiple personality disorder.

Similar reports of EMDR's sensational effectiveness have appeared in the media. On July 29, 1994, ABC's *20/20* newsmagazine show aired a segment on EMDR. Host Hugh Downs introduced EMDR as "an exciting breakthrough . . . a way for people to free themselves from destructive memories, and it seems to work even in cases where years of conventional therapy have failed." Downs stated, "No one understands exactly why this method succeeds, only that it does." The program featured an excerpt from an interview with Stephen Silver, a psychologist who averred, "It (EMDR) leads immediately to a decrease in nightmares, intrusive memories, and flashback phenomena. It is one of most powerful tools I've encountered for treating post-traumatic stress" (ABC News 1994).

Although based largely on unsystematic and anecdotal observations, such glowing testimonials merit careful consideration. Are the widespread claims for EMDR's efficacy substantiated by research?

## UNCONTROLLED CASE REPORTS

Many uncontrolled case reports appear to attest to the efficacy of EMDR (e.g., Forbes, Creamer & Rycroft 1994; Lipke & Botkin 1992; Marquis

1991; Oswalt et al. 1993; Pellicer 1993; Puk 1991; Spates & Burnette 1995; Wolpe & Abrams 1991). All of these case reports utilize a "pre-post design" in which clients are treated with EMDR and subsequently reassessed for indications of improvement. These case reports, although seemingly supportive of EMDR, are for several reasons seriously flawed as persuasive evidence for its effectiveness.

First, case reports, probably even more than large controlled investigations, are susceptible to the "file drawer problem" (Rosenthal 1979)—the selective tendency for negative findings to remain unpublished. It is impossible to determine the extent to which the published cases of EMDR treatment, which are almost all successful, are representative of all cases treated with this procedure.

Second, in virtually all of the published case reports, EMDR was combined with other interventions, such as relaxation training and real-life exposure (Acierno, Hersen, et al. 1994). As a result, one cannot determine whether the apparent improvement reported in such cases is attributable to EMDR, the ancillary treatments, or both.

Third, and most important, these case reports cannot provide information regarding cause-and-effect relations because they lack a control group of individuals who did not receive EMDR. The ostensible improvement resulting from EMDR in these reports may be due to numerous variables other than EMDR itself (Gastright 1995), such as placebo effects (improvement resulting from the expectation of improvement), spontaneous remission (natural improvement occurring in the absence of treatment), and regression to the mean (the statistical tendency of extreme scores at an initial testing to become less extreme upon retesting). Consumers of uncontrolled case reports thus must be chary of falling prey to the logical fallacy of post hoc, ergo propter hoc (after this, therefore because of this): Only in adequately controlled studies can improvement following EMDR treatment be unequivocably attributed to the treatment itself.

# CONTROLLED STUDIES

Despite abundant claims for EMDR's efficacy, few controlled outcome studies on EMDR have been conducted. They are of two major types: (1) between-subject designs, in which subjects are randomly assigned to either a treatment or a control group; and (2) within-subject designs, in which subjects serve as their own control.

# BETWEEN-SUBJECT DESIGNS

In the first controlled investigation of EMDR, Shapiro (1989a) randomly assigned twenty-two individuals who had experienced a traumatic event to either an EMDR treatment group or an exposure control group. In the latter condition, subjects were provided with imaginal exposure to the trauma, but without the eye movements involved in EMDR. Shapiro reported that after only one session, EMDR subjects exhibited significantly lower SUDs levels and significantly higher Validity of Cognition ratings than subjects in the control group. The control group subjects showed essentially no improvement on either measure.

Superficially, these findings seem to provide impressive support for the effectiveness of EMDR. Even a casual inspection of the study's methodology, however, reveals serious deficiencies in experimental design (Acierno et al. 1994; Herbert & Mueser 1992). First, Shapiro herself conducted both treatments and elicited the SUDs and Validity of Cognition ratings from subjects in both groups. Because Shapiro knew the subjects' treatment condition, her findings are potentially attributable to the well-documented experimenter expectancy effect (Rosenthal 1967)—the tendency for researchers to unintentionally bias the results of their investigations in accord with their hypotheses. Specifically, Shapiro might have unwittingly delivered treatment more effectively or convincingly to the EMDR group, or subtly influenced subjects in this group to report greater improvement. Second, the cessation of traumatic imagery was contingent on low SUDs ratings in the EMDR group, but not in the imaginal exposure group (Lohr et al. 1992). It is therefore possible that subjects in the EMDR group reported low SUDs ratings in order to terminate this aversive imagery. Moreover, the total amount of exposure in the two groups may have differed (ibid.). These methodological shortcomings render the results of Shapiro's study (Shapiro 1989a) virtually uninterpretable.

Since this initial report, a number of investigators have attempted to replicate Shapiro's methodology of comparing EMDR with an imaginal exposure control condition for clients with PTSD or other anxiety disorders. Several of these researchers used a "dismantling" design in which EMDR was compared with an otherwise identical procedure minus the eye movements; in this design certain components of the treatment that are purported to be effective (in this case, eye movements) are removed from the full treatment package to determine if their omission decreases therapeutic effectiveness. Renfrey and Spates (1994), for example, compared EMDR with an imaginal exposure condition in which subjects stared at a stationary object.

In virtually all of these investigations, EMDR was not consistently more effective than the exposure control condition, although both conditions appeared to produce improvements on some measures. In one study (Boudewyns et al. 1993), EMDR was found to be more effective than the control condition, but only when within-session SUDs ratings were used. In this investigation, however, as in Shapiro's study (1989a), cessation of the traumatic scene was contingent on low SUDs ratings in the EMDR condition only, so this finding may again reflect the subjects' desire to terminate exposure to unpleasant imagery. Interestingly, SUDs ratings obtained outside of sessions in response to audiotaped depictions of clients' traumatic experiences indicated no differences between conditions. Moreover, physiological reactions (e.g., heart rate increases) to these depictions showed no improvement in either condition.

Sanderson and Carpenter (1992), who administered EMDR and imaginal exposure in counterbalanced order, found that EMDR and imaginal exposure yielded equivalent improvements (using SUDs ratings taken outside of treatment sessions) but that EMDR was effective only when preceded by imaginal exposure. Renfrey and Spates (1994, 238) reported that EMDR was no more effective than a control procedure involving fixed visual attention, leading them to conclude that "eye movements are not an essential component of the intervention."

Only one published study has directly compared EMDR with a no-treatment control group. Jensen (1994) randomly assigned Vietnam veterans with PTSD to either an EMDR group or a control group that was promised delayed treatment. EMDR produced lower within-session SUDs ratings compared with the control condition, but did not differ from the control condition in its effect on PTSD symptoms. In fact, the level of interviewer-rated PTSD symptoms *increased* in the EMDR group following treatment.

## WITHIN-SUBJECT DESIGNS

Three teams of investigators have used within-subject designs to examine the efficacy of EMDR. Acierno, Tremont, Last, and Montgomery (1994) treated a client with phobias of dead bodies and the dark using both EMDR and "Eye-Focus Desensitization," the latter identical to EMDR except that the therapist's finger remained stationary. In the case of the client's fear of dead bodies, EMDR was administered first; in the case of the client's fear of the dark, Eye-Focus Desensitization was administered first. EMDR showed little or no advantage over the control procedure on self-report, physiological, or behavioral measures, the last of which involved assessments of the client's willingness to approach feared stimuli.

In contrast, Montgomery and Ayllon (1994a) reported that EMDR yielded significant decreases in SUDs levels and client reports of PTSD symptoms, whereas a control procedure consisting of EMDR minus eye movements did not. These two procedures were not, however, administered in counterbalanced order; the control procedure was always presented first. Consequently, the improvements following EMDR may have been due to a delayed effect of the control procedure. Alternatively, they might have resulted from the cumulative effect of the exposure provided by both procedures, regression to the mean effects, or to other factors unrelated to EMDR. EMDR did not produce improvements on physiological indices (heart rate and systolic blood pressure).

Finally, Montgomery and Ayllon (1994b) treated a client with PTSD who had experienced two distinct traumatic events (a car accident and an assault at knifepoint). EMDR was applied separately to the memories of each event. EMDR appeared to show beneficial effects on subjective distress, although the degree of improvement was much less than that reported by Shapiro (1989a). Because EMDR was not compared with a control procedure involving imaginal exposure, its unique effects cannot be ascertained.

## THE VERDICT

Because of the paucity of adequately controlled studies on EMDR, it would be premature to proffer any definitive conclusions regarding its effectiveness. Nevertheless, the following assertions are warranted on the basis of the evidence.

1. Although a multitude of uncontrolled case reports seemingly demonstrate that EMDR produces high success rates, these reports are open to numerous alternative explanations and thus do not provide compelling evidence for EMDR's effectiveness.

2. Controlled studies provide mixed support for the efficacy of EMDR. Most of the evidence for EMDR's effectiveness derives from clients' within-session ratings (which in some cases may be influenced by the desire to terminate exposure), but not from more objective measures of improvement. There is no evidence that EMDR eliminates many or most of the symptoms of PTSD in one session.

3. There is no convincing evidence that EMDR is more effective for

post-traumatic anxiety than standard exposure treatments. If EMDR works at all, it may be because it contains an exposure component (Steketee & Goldstein 1994). The proponents of EMDR have yet to demonstrate that EMDR represents a new advance in the treatment of anxiety disorders, or that the eye movements purportedly critical to this technique constitute anything more than pseudoscientific window dressing.

Thus, the most justified conclusion concerning EMDR's effectiveness is: Not proven. Nonetheless, many proponents of EMDR remain convinced that the treatment utility of EMDR will ultimately be demonstrated. Shapiro (1992, 114), for example, opined, "When the efficacy of EMDR is fully established, I would like to see it taught in the universities. When that happens, three-hour workshops on specialized applications of EMDR will undoubtedly be offered. . . ." These statements, which were made after approximately twelve hundred licensed therapists had already received formal training in EMDR (Shapiro 1992), raise troubling questions. Should not the efficacy of a therapeutic technique be established *before* it is taught to clinicians for the express purpose of administering it to their clients? Moreover, does not the spirit of open scientific inquiry demand that the proponents of a novel technique remain agnostic regarding its efficacy pending appropriate data, and that the two sentences quoted above should therefore begin with "if" rather than "when?"

## CONCLUDING COMMENTS

Dawes (1994) has argued that assertions about the utility and validity of psychological techniques, like assertions in all areas of science, must answer to a commonsense demand: "Show me." EMDR has thus far failed to convincingly pass the "Show me" test. Claims for its efficacy have greatly outstripped its empirical support. Although Shapiro has suggested that "there is more to EMDR than meets the eye" (1994b, 155), a skeptical consumer of the literature might well be tempted to draw the opposite conclusion.

Moreover, because EMDR has not been clearly shown to be beneficial for the condition for which it was originally developed, namely, PTSD, its extension as a treatment for schizophrenia, eating disorders, and other conditions is even more premature and ethically problematic. Furthermore, both scientific and logical considerations dictate that the developers of a treatment should specify the boundary conditions under which this technique is and is not effective. Because EMDR purportedly facilitates the processing of traumatic memories, one would not expect it to be useful for conditions (e.g., schizophrenia) in which severe emotional trauma has not been found to play a major causal role. Indeed, claims that EMDR is helpful for such conditions (Marquis 1991) actually call into question the presumed mechanisms underlying EMDR's mode of action. So far, however, the proponents of EMDR have made little or no effort to delineate the boundary conditions of their method's effectiveness. Moreover, the assertion that EMDR works equally well with auditory tones and hand-taps as with eye movements (Shapiro 1994a) runs counter to Shapiro's theoretical conjectures regarding EMDR's commonalities with REM sleep.

Although further research on EMDR is warranted, such research will likely be impeded by the prohibitions placed on the open distribution of EMDR training materials (Acierno, Hersen, et al. 1994). For example, participants in EMDR workshops must agree not to audiotape any portion of the workshop, train others in the technique without formal approval, or disseminate EMDR training information to colleagues (Rosen 1993). It seems difficult to quarrel with Herbert and Mueser's (1992, 173) contention that although "this procedure is justified to maintain 'quality control,' such a restriction of information runs counter to the principle of open and free exchange of ideas among scientists and professionals." (Editors' Note: Such prohibitions have since been lifted.)

Because of the limited number of controlled studies on EMDR, both practitioners and scientists should remain open to the possibility of its effectiveness. Nevertheless, the standard of proof required to use a new procedure clinically should be considerably higher than the standard of proof required to conduct research on its efficacy. This is particularly true in the case of such conditions as PTSD, for which existing treatments have already been shown to be effective. The continued widespread use of EMDR for therapeutic purposes in the absence of adequate evidence can be seen as only another example of the human mind's willingness to sacrifice critical thinking for wishful thinking.

## REFERENCES

ABC News. 1994. "When All Else Fails." *20/20* transcript, July 29.

Acierno, R., M. Hersen, V. B. Van Hasselt, G. Tremont, and K. T. Mueser. 1994. Review of the validation and dissemination of eye-movement desensitization and reprocessing: A scientific and ethical dilemma. *Clinical Psychology Review* 14: 287–99.

Acierno, R., G. Tremont, C. Last, and D. Montgomery. 1994. Tripartite assessment of the efficacy of eye-movement desensitization in a multi-phobic patient. *Journal of Anxiety Disorders* 8: 259–76.

American Psychiatric Association. 1994. *Diagnostic and Statistical Manual of Mental Disorders*. 4th ed. Washington, DC: American Psychiatric Association.

Bandler, R., and J. Grinder. 1975. *The Structure of Magic*. Palo Alto, CA: Science and Behavior Books.

Barlow, D. H. 1988. *Anxiety and Its Disorders*. New York: Guilford Press.

Beere, D. B. 1992. More on EMDR. *Behavior Therapist* 15: 179–80.

Beyerstein, B. L. 1990. Brainscams: Neuromythologies of the New Age. *International Journal of Mental Health* 19: 27–36.

Boudewyns, P. A., L. A. Stwertka, J. W. Hyer, X. Albrecht, and E. G. Sperr. 1993. Eye movement desensitization for PTSD of combat: A treatment outcome pilot study. *Behavior Therapist* 16: 29–33.

Bower, B. 1995. Promise and dissent. *Science News* 148: 270–71.

Cavaliere, F. 1995. Team works to quell stress in Bosnia. *American Psychological Association Monitor* 26, no. 8: 8.

Dawes, R. M. 1994. *House of Cards: Psychology and Psychotherapy Built on Myth.* New York: Free Press.

Druckman, D., and J. A. Swets, eds. 1988. *Enhancing Human Performance: Issues, Theories, and Techniques.* Washington, DC: National Academy Press.

Forbes, D., M. Creamer., and P. Rycroft. 1994. Eye movement desensitization and reprocessing in post-traumatic stress disorder: A pilot study using assessment measures. *Journal of Behavior Therapy and Experimental Psychiatry* 25: 113–20.

Frank, J. D. 1973. *Persuasion and Healing: A Comparative Analysis of Psychotherapy.* Baltimore: John Hopkins University Press.

Frueh, B. C., S. M. Turner, and D.C. Beidel. 1995. Exposure Therapy for PTSD: A Critical Review. Unpublished manuscript.

Gastright, J. 1995. EMDR works! Is that enough? *Cincinnati Skeptic* 4, no. 3: 1–3.

Herbert, J. D., and K. T. Mueser. 1992. Eye movement desensitization: A critique of the evidence. *Journal of Behavior Therapy and Experimental Psychiatry* 23: 169–74.

Jensen, J. A. 1994. An investigation of eye movement desensitization and reprocessing (EMD/R) as a treatment for post-traumatic stress disorder (PTSD) symptoms of Vietnam combat veterans. *Behavior Therapy* 25: 311–25.

Lipke, H. J., and A. L. Botkin. 1992. Case studies of eye movement desensitization and reprocessing (EMDR) with chronic posttraumatic stress disorder. *Psychotherapy* 29: 591–95.

Lohr, J. M., R. A. Kleinknecht, A. T. Conley, S. Dal Cerro, J. Schmidt, and M. E. Sonntag. 1992. A methodological critique of the current status of eye movement desensitization (EMDR). *Journal of Behavior Therapy and Experimental Psychiatry* 23: 159–67.

Marquis, J. N. 1991. A report on seventy-eight cases treated by eye movement desensitization. *Journal of Behavior Therapy and Experimental Psychiatry* 22: 187–92.

Montgomery, R.W., and T. Ayllon. 1994a. Eye movement desensitization across images: A single case design. *Journal of Behavior Therapy and Experimental Psychiatry* 25: 23–28.

———. 1994b. Eye movement desensitization across subjects: Subjective and physiological measures of treatment efficacy. *Journal of Behavior Therapy and Experimental Psychiatry* 25: 217–30.

Moore, T. E. 1992. Subliminal perception: Facts and fallacies. *Skeptical Inquirer* 16: 273–81.

Mulick, J. A., J. W. Jacobson, and F. H. Kobe. 1993. Anguished silence and helping hands: Autism and facilitated communication. *Skeptical Inquirer* 17, no. 3 (Spring): 270–80.

Oswalt, R., M. Anderson, K. Hagstrom, and B. Berkowitz. 1993. Evaluation of the one-session eye-movement desensitization reprocessing procedure for eliminating traumatic memories. *Psychological Reports* 27: 99.

Pellicer, X. 1993. Eye movement desensitization of a child's nightmares: A case report. *Journal of Behavior Therapy and Experimental Psychiatry* 24: 73–75.

Pratkanis, A. R. 1992. The cargo-cult science of subliminal persuasion. *Skeptical Inquirer* 16, no. 3 (Spring): 260–72.

Puk, G. 1991. Treating traumatic memories: A case report on the eye movement desensitization procedure. *Journal of Behavior Therapy and Experimental Psychiatry* 22: 149–51.

Renfrey, G., and C. R. Spates, 1994. Eye movement desensitization: A partial dismantling study. *Journal of Behavior Therapy and Experimental Psychiatry* 25: 231–39.

Rosen, G. M. 1993. A note to EMDR critics: What you didn't see is only part of what you don't get. *Behavior Therapist* 16: 216.

Rosenthal, R. 1967. Covert communication in the psychological experiment. *Psychological Bulletin* 67: 356–67.

———. 1979. The "file drawer problem" and tolerance for null results. *Psychological Bulletin* 86: 638–41.

Rowley, D. T. 1986. *Hypnosis and Hypnotherapy.* London: Croom Helm.

Sanderson, A., and R. Carpenter. 1992. Eye movement desensitization versus image confrontation: A single session crossover study of 58 phobic subjects. *Journal of Behavior Therapy and Experimental Psychiatry* 23: 269–75.

Shapiro, E 1989a. Eye movement desensitization: A new treatment for posttraumatic stress disorder. *Journal of Behavior Therapy and Experimental Psychiatry* 20: 211–17.

———. 1989b. Efficacy of the eye movement desensitization procedure in the treatment of traumatic memories. *Journal of Traumatic Stress* 2: 199–223.

———. 1991. Eye movement desensitization and reprocessing procedure: From EMD to EMD/R—A new treatment model for anxiety and related traumata. *Behavior Therapist* 14: 133–35.

————. 1992. Dr. Francine Shapiro responds. *Behavior Therapist* 15: 111–14.

————. 1994a. Alternative stimuli in the use of EMD(R). *Journal of Behaviour Therapy and Experimental Psychiatry* 25: 89–91.

————. 1994b. EMDR: In the eye of a paradigm shift. *Behavior Therapist* 17: 153–56.

Silver, B. V., and E. B. Blanchard. 1978. Biofeedback and relaxation training in the treatment of psychophysiological disorders: Or are the machines really necessary? *Journal of Behavioral Medicine* 1: 217–38.

Spates, C. R., and M. M. Burnett. 1995. Eye movement desensitization: Three unusual cases. *Journal of Behavior Therapy and Experimental Psychiatry* 26: 51–55.

Steketee, G., and A. J. Goldstein. 1994. Reflections on Shapiro's reflections: Testing EMDR within *a theoretical* context. *Behavior Therapist,* 17: 156–57.

Winson, J. 1990. The meaning of dreams. *Scientific American* 263: 86–96.

Wolpe, J., and J. Abrams. 1991. Post-traumatic stress disorder overcome by eye-movement desensitization: A case report. *Journal of Behavior Therapy and Experimental Psychiatry* 22: 39–43.

Editors' Note: The research base for EMDR has expanded considerably since this article appeared, although the central conclusions still stand. See, e.g., P. R. Davison & K. C. Parker (2001): Eye movement desensitization and reprocessing (EMDR): A meta-analysis. *Journal of Consulting and Clinical Psychology* 6a, 305–16.

# 20.

# CAN WE REALLY TAP OUR PROBLEMS AWAY? A CRITICAL ANALYSIS OF THOUGHT FIELD THERAPY

## Brandon A. Gaudiano and James D. Herbert

I t is nothing new to find enterprising entrepreneurs seeking to profit from their novel inventions, which are often claimed to produce miraculous results for their users. The field of mental health is no exception. In fact, there has recently been a surge of putatively revolutionary treatments for various psychological problems that claim to be far superior to standard treatments in both effectiveness and efficiency. Known as "power" or "energy" therapies (Gist, Woodall & Magenheimer 1999; Herbert et al. 2003; Swenson 1999), these treatments are gaining widespread acceptance among mental health practitioners, despite their frankly bizarre theories and techniques, extraordinary claims, and absence of scientific support. One of the most popular of these power therapies, known as Eye Movement Desensitization and Reprocessing (EMDR), involves a therapist waving his or her fingers in front of the patient's eyes while the client imagines various disturbing scenes that are thought to be related to the patient's problems. In fact, EMDR, a "power therapy" that alludes to neural networks instead of energy fields for its theoretical basis, has been described as a prototypical case of pseudoscience within mental health (Herbert et al. 2000; Lohr, Montgomery, et al. 1999; Lilienfeld 1996).

Reprinted with permission from *Skeptical Inquirer* (July/August 2000): 29–33, 36.

There is another treatment approach on the rise that threatens to overtake EMDR as the premiere power therapy for the twenty-first century: Thought Field Therapy (TFT; Callahan 1985). Roger Callahan, TFT's inventor, claims that he can train therapists to be over 97 percent effective using his "revolutionary" procedures in treating a variety of common psychological problems, including anxiety and depression. Since the history of psychotherapy is replete with treatments that failed to live up to their initial hype, it seems prudent to take a closer look at TFT.

## ORIGINS AND METHODS

Callahan (1997) states that he accidentally discovered TFT while treating a client named Mary, who had a severe fear of water. Inspired by an acupuncture class he was taking at the time, Callahan instructed Mary to firmly tap the area under her eye with her fingers, leading to a miraculous and immediate resolution of Mary's phobia. Callahan subsequently developed the comprehensive set of techniques and theory that is now known as TFT. The therapy is based on the idea that invisible energy fields called "thought fields" exist within the body (Callahan & Callahan 1997). Environmental traumas and inherited predispositions are theorized to cause blockages, or what Callahan terms "perturbations," in the flow of energy in these thought fields. Callahan theorizes that the commonly observed neurochemical, behavioral, and cognitive indicators of disorders such as depression are the result of these perturbations. In other words, the root cause of all psychological problems is blockages in energy fields.

In order to correct these perturbations, clients are directed by the TFT therapist to tap on the body's "energy meridians" in specific sequences, called "algorithms," which vary based on the particular problem being treated (ibid.). For example, the client may be instructed to tap at the corner of the eyebrow five times and then continue tapping on other parts of the body in a specific sequence as instructed by the therapist. In addition, the clients are told to roll their eyes, count, and hum a few bars of a song at various points during the treatment. Callahan states that when the thought field is "attuned," that is, when the person is thinking about the distressing event or image, perturbations are able to be located and corrected. The tapping is theorized to add energy to the system, which then re-balances the overall energy flow, thereby eliminating the distress at the source.

## THEORETICAL UNDERPINNINGS

The theory behind TFT is a hodgepodge of concepts derived from a variety of sources. Foremost among these is the ancient Chinese philosophy of *chi*, which is thought to be the "life force" that flows throughout the body. Beyerstein and Sampson (1996) argue that *chi* is more accurately conceptualized as a philosophy, not a science, and its existence is not empirically supported. In addition, they note that while acupuncture, a procedure used to correct the flow of *chi*, has been shown to provide some minor analgesic effects, its utility has not been demonstrated for treating illnesses or diseases. TFT also borrows techniques from a procedure known as Applied Kinesiology that is used to test muscles for "weaknesses" caused by certain food or chemical pathogens (Sampson & Beyerstein 1996). Applied Kinesiology is a scientifically discredited procedure. For example, Kenny, Clemens, and Forsythe (1988) found that those using the techniques did no better than chance in determining nutritional status using muscle testing. Finally, TFT even borrows some of its concepts from quantum physics. For instance, the idea of active information, in which small amounts of energy can affect large systems, is used to support the existence of perturbations (Bohm & Hiley 1993). There are obvious problems with the theoretical basis for TFT, not the least of which is the complete lack of scientific evidence for the existence of "thought fields."

TFT, as with other new "energy" therapies, is based on misconceptions or outright distortions of the concept of energy as it is used by scientists (Saravi 1999). In physics, energy is defined simply as the capacity to do work, and energy exchanges are observable and measurable. Energy therapists, in contrast, use the term to describe a kind of universal life force that influences health, but they provide no direct data to document the presence of such a force. Saravi concludes that "New Agers' and psychobabblers' 'energy' has only a remote relationship with its physical, scientific counterpart. For them, it is just a word conveniently invoked to explain phenomena whose very existence is far from certain" (47).

## EXTRAORDINARY CLAIMS OF SUCCESS

TFT is marketed primarily through the Internet. To attract potential therapists to take TFT courses and to persuade prospective clients to pay for this therapeutic approach, amazing claims are presented on several TFT-related Web sites. For example, Callahan's primary Web site[1] claims that TFT allows individuals "to eliminate most negative emotions within minutes." In addition, Callahan asserts that TFT's effectiveness increases with higher levels of training. For example, another Web site[2] publicizes that therapists can achieve an 80 percent effectiveness rate from learning to use specific algorithms, a 90–95 percent effectiveness rate from using "Causal Diagnostic" techniques, and an over 97 percent effectiveness rate using a technique mysteriously termed "Voice Technology." Yet another Web site,[3] this one based in the United Kingdom, states that TFT is the only psychotherapy that can "genuinely claim to offer a cure." TFT claims to be able to "cure" people of a variety of psychological problems, including phobias, panic, post-traumatic stress disorder, addictions, sexual problems, pain, depression, anger, general distress, and even other less serious problems such as fingernail biting (Hooke 1998a). One noted TFT therapist even claims to have cured her dog of a fear of heights using the trauma algorithm (Danzig 1998).

Despite these miraculous assertions, no controlled studies have been published in peer-reviewed scientific journals to provide evidence for TFT's claims. Instead, testimonials and uncontrolled case studies are offered to support these astonishing declarations of success (Callahan 1995). The vast majority of these claims are made via Internet postings (Lohr, Montgomery et al. 1999). Such anecdotes, however, do not constitute probative data on the question of TFT's efficacy. Callahan often claims that his public demonstrations of TFT on television shows such as *The Leeza Gibbons Show* (aired October 12, 1996) provide dramatic proof of success, thereby circumventing the need for empirical research. However, such vivid but uncontrolled presentations are not evidential, given the extraordinary demand characteristics (i.e., the implicit pressures engendered by the situation for clients to behave in accordance with their beliefs about what is expected of them) inherent in such settings, not to mention the lack of objective, standardized assessments of improvement in symptoms (Hooke 1998b). Given that Callahan claims to have been using his techniques for over twenty years, it is curious why no controlled studies have been conducted. It should be quite easy to demonstrate the effects of a treatment with a 97 percent effectiveness rate using accepted methods of clinical science.

## THE LIMITED RESEARCH FINDINGS

TFT has recently attracted the attention of two Florida State University researchers. In considering their work, it is important to note that none of their findings have been published in peer-reviewed journals; instead, they report their results in one of the researcher's self-published Internet "journal." Carbonell and Figley (1999) tested four controversial treatments for trauma, including TFT. Thirty-nine individuals who reported distress from having experienced a traumatic event were given one of the four treatments for up to one week. Overall, Carbonell and Figley reported that participants demonstrated some improvement in self-rated distress and on questionnaire measures from pre-treatment to six-month follow-up. This study is so seriously flawed, however, that the results are completely uninterpretable. The most critical flaw is the absence of any control for the passage of time. In the absence of a no-treatment or a placebo control group, there is no way to know if any observed improvement was a function of factors such as the natural remission of symptoms over time, statistical regression to the mean (i.e., the tendency for extreme scores on a measure to be less extreme upon retest), or placebo effects. This concern is heightened by the absence of measures taken immediately following treatment, as the only outcome measures were reported six months following treatment. Also, subjects were not diagnosed with post-traumatic stress disorder using standard diagnostic criteria, and it is not clear how much subjects were impaired by their traumatic experiences. Moreover, daily diaries and recordings of distress revealed that subjects appeared to have difficulty distinguishing distress associated with the normal ups and downs of life from distress associated with their trauma. For example, a participant who had suffered childhood abuse reported high distress, but upon query disclosed that this distress was due to her car getting a flat tire rather than her trauma, raising questions about the reliability of these subjective distress ratings (Huber 1997).

Furthermore, the authors did not report subjecting their data to statistical analysis, instead relying on their visual inspection of the data for interpretation. Interestingly, even these data do not support the large effect sizes claimed by TFT supporters. On the contrary, mean scores on the self-report questionnaires showed only relatively paltry changes in symptoms, far below the claims of miraculous improvement that Callahan and others have consistently claimed. Thus, Carbonell and Figley's (1999) study, which is the most serious research attempt to date, does not support the effectiveness of TFT. Nevertheless, the results of this study, originally presented at a 1995 symposium, are frequently cited by Callahan and others as providing evidence of TFT's efficacy (Callahan & Callahan 1997). The only other "research" on TFT is presented either in internally circulated publications such as Callahan's newsletter the *Thought Field*, nonscientific magazine reports (e.g., Shamis 1996), or on Web sites (e.g., Carbonell 1996; see Swenson 1999 for a review).

## ALTERNATE EXPLANATIONS

Occam's Razor is a principle often applied in science, indicating that, all things being equal, the most parsimonious explanation for a phenomenon is the preferred one. Applying this principle to TFT, there is little need for concepts such as energy fields and perturbations to explain any effects that TFT might show. TFT highlights specific tapping sequences as its proposed mechanism of action; however, other components of the treatment protocol may be responsible for any observed benefits. In addition to the absence of controls for spontaneous remission, no research has ruled out factors that are common—to greater or lesser degrees—in all psychotherapies. These include placebo effects resulting from the mere expectation of improvement, demand characteristics, therapist enthusiasm and support, therapist-client alliance, and effort justification (i.e., the tendency to report positive changes in order to justify the effort exerted; Lohr, Lilienfeld, et al. 1999). Thus, despite the absence of empirical evidence to support TFT's claims of tremendous effectiveness, it would not be surprising to find that the procedure sometimes produces benefits for some individuals owing to these common mechanisms shared by all forms of psychotherapy. Serious psychotherapy innovators go to great lengths to conduct studies to demonstrate that the hypothesized active ingredients of their procedures outperform these so-called nonspecific effects. No such effort has been made by the promoters of TFT.

Callahan, however, dismisses the possibility that TFT could be explained by such mechanisms. He asserts that "clinical evidence" has ruled out the possibility of nonspecific or placebo effects accounting for TFT's results, but fails to support this claim (Callahan & Callahan 1997). He frequently states that placebo effects cannot be operative in TFT because some clients express skepticism that the tapping will work (Hooke 1998a). This argument demonstrates a misunderstanding of the placebo concept, which does not necessarily require the individual to fully believe in the practitioner's explanation for why a procedure works (Bootzin 1985; Dodes 1997). Callahan (1999) also reports case studies in which he claims to have observed a "re-balancing" of the autonomic nervous system after treatment with TFT and that this somehow refutes the placebo explanation. In fact, it is well accepted that the autonomic nervous system, including phenomena such as pulse, blood pressure, and electrocardiogram changes, can be influenced by various psychological events, including placebos (Ross & Buckalew 1985).

In addition to nonspecific and placebo effects, TFT appears to incorporate procedures from existing, well-established therapies. TFT therapists instruct clients to focus repeatedly on distressing thoughts and images during the tapping sequences. Such repeated exposure to distressing cognitions is a well-known behavior therapy technique called imaginary exposure (Foa & Meadows 1997). Furthermore, TFT therapists utilize cognitive coping statements throughout treatment (e.g., "I accept and forgive them for what they did"), which represent another established cognitive therapy technique. In short, any effects that TFT might show can be readily explained by known mechanisms, without invoking unfounded concepts such as "perturbations" and "thought fields" (Hooke 1998a).

## TFT AND EFT

Since the emergence of TFT, several therapists have recently developed offshoot therapies based on treating the body's energy fields. The most successful of these TFT derivatives was developed by Gary Craig. Craig (1997), who has a degree in engineering and formerly studied under Callahan, created what he calls Emotional Freedom Techniques (EFT). EFT is very similar to TFT, except that it employs one simplified and ubiquitous tapping procedure instead of applying different algorithms to treat different problems. On his Web site,[4] Craig asserts that Callahan's reliance on differing algorithms is unnecessary because he has witnessed TFT therapists tap in the wrong order or apply the wrong algorithm to the particular problem and still obtain improvements. Craig's anecdotal evidence appears to contradict Callahan's anecdotal evidence. Furthermore, Craig extends his tapping therapy far beyond the realm of mental health, reporting testimonials from individuals who claim to have successfully used EFT to treat everything from autism to warts and various other medical problems with positive results. In the latest developments, Craig has reported on the positive effects of "surrogate tapping," in which therapists tap on themselves to treat the problems of others.

A scientifically minded investigator would have then taken Craig's observations a step further and tested a completely "placebo" algorithm which did not tap on any supposed energy meridians to see if it produced similar results. However, Craig reports that he has never carried out this simple experiment, nor does he know of anyone who has (Craig, personal communication, January 14, 2000). Furthermore, Craig speculates that a placebo algorithm may be impossible because tapping anywhere on the body will affect the body's energy meridians. This position conveniently renders Craig's theory unfalsifiable and therefore outside the realm of science.

## PSEUDOSCIENCE IN PSYCHOTHERAPY

Lilienfeld (1998) argues that the proliferation of pseudoscience in psychotherapy is threatening the public welfare and damaging the reputation of psychology. Lohr, Montgomery et al. (1999) assert that the contemporary commercial promotion of treatments for the sequelae of trauma, such as EMDR and TFT, are commonly characterized by a host of pseudoscientific practices. In general, pseudoscience can be identified as consisting of "claims presented so that they appear scientific even though they lack supporting evidence and plausibility" (Shermer 1997, 33). For example, TFT incorporates scientific-sounding terminology by speaking of "bioenergies" and taking concepts from quantum physics out of context in an attempt to gain credibility. No empirical evidence is provided for the existence of central concepts such thought fields or perturbations, which are instead inferred through ad hoc, circular reasoning. For example, Callahan and Callahan (1997) state that perturbations are ultimately demonstrated through their effects, meaning that a perturbation in the thought field must have existed because after treatment the person no longer experiences distress.

The hallmark of a science is falsifiability (Popper 1965). A scientific proposition must specify, a priori, predictions that can be refuted, at least in principle. Callahan has not provided a framework by which his theory could be brought under scientific investigation. As is characteristic of pseudoscience, only confirming evidence of TFT is sought out and presented by advocates (Lohr, Montgomery et al. 1999). Neither Callahan nor other proponents, including Carbonell and Figley (1999), have subjected TFT to controlled evaluation using accepted scientific methods and published results in peer-reviewed journals.

The objective of a pseudoscience is often persuasion and promotion, in lieu of responsible investigation of claims (Bunge 1967). Web sites advertise courses and multilevel training in TFT techniques for thousands of dollars. The highest level of training in TFT is called Voice Technology (VT), which supposedly allows the therapist to diagnosis perturbations and treat clients entirely over the telephone by analyzing their voices. The effectiveness of VT is said to approach 100 percent (Callahan 1998). Callahan sells this technique for $100,000, and trainees must sign nondisclosure contracts that forbid them from discussing or revealing any aspects of the technique. Recently, the Arizona Board of Psychologist Examiners put a psychologist on probation for refusing to provide specific information about VT to back up his assertion of its high degree of effectiveness (Foxhall 1999; Lilienfeld & Lohr 2000). Interestingly, on his Web site,[5] Gary Craig, who was trained in the method, stresses that the putative "secret" behind VT is readily available "in the public domain and can be learned at a weekend workshop for a few hundred dollars." The mystery surrounding VT only has the effect of obfuscating independent examination and investigation.

Finally, pseudosciences explain away or reinterpret failures as actually providing confirmatory evidence (Lakatos 1978). Callahan proposes the existence of a phenomenon termed "psychological reversal" to explain instances in which TFT fails to work. Psychological reversal is claimed to result in self-sabotaging attitudes and behaviors and is manifested in the reversed flow of energy that blocks the effects of the treatment (Callahan 1998). The prescribed treatment for such a condition involves reciting more cognitive coping statements (e.g., "I accept myself, even though I have this problem") that may alleviate distress independent of tapping. In addition, "energy toxins" are claimed to be substances that negatively affect the thought field, even if the person is not physically allergic to these supposed pathogens. These substances are proposed to cause a previously eliminated symptom to return (Joslin 1999). Using "muscle testing" procedures and VT, the offending pathogen can allegedly be identified, then removed until the treatment works again. Both psychological reversal and energy toxins are prime examples of post hoc reasoning and attempts to ignore disconfirming evidence by creating uncorroborated explanations of TFT failures.

## CONCLUSION AND IMPLICATIONS

Despite extraordinary claims to the contrary, TFT is not supported by scientific evidence. The theoretical basis of TFT is grounded in unsupported and discredited concepts, including the Chinese philosophy of *chi* and Applied Kinesiology. Many of the practices of TFT proponents are much more consistent with pseudoscience than science. Controlled studies evaluating the efficacy of TFT will be required for the treatment to be taken seriously by the scientific community.

TFT is only now beginning to garner negative press, and critiques are starting to appear in the popular literature. For example, Swenson (1999) recently reviewed the extraordinary claims for TFT made by Callahan and others, and noted the absence of controlled research to support these claims. Recently in the *Skeptical Inquirer*, Lilienfeld and Lohr (2000) reported on the American Psychological Association's decision in late 1999 to prohibit its sponsors of continuing education programs for psychologists from offering credits for training in TFT, as well as the sanctioning of an Arizona psychologist for using TFT and Voice Technology within the practice of psychology.

Nevertheless, thousands of therapists from various professional disciplines continue to pay for TFT training courses. Much of TFT's marketing success can be attributed to the prevalence of pro-TFT Web sites that promote strong claims of its effectiveness. TFT therapists, some of whom have no traditional training in psychology or psychotherapy, appear to be satisfied with TFT's vivid anecdotal stories of success and are not aware of or not bothered by the overwhelming lack of empirical support for the procedure. Englebretsen (1995), among others, points to the alarming rise of postmodernist attitudes currently permeating the mental health field, exemplified by the willingness of some clinicians to value compelling anecdotal stories over controlled empirical data. This postmodernist mind-set promotes the notion that all truth is relative and contextual; science is only one of many modes of thinking, each of which is equally valid. Such attitudes render the mental health field fertile breeding ground for pseudoscientific therapies such as TFT and its derivatives. Healthy skepticism competes head-to-head with extraordinary claims and, as is often the case, many mental health clinicians choose to ignore the facts in favor of miraculous possibilities.

## NOTES

1. http://www.tftrx.com.
2. http://www.thoughtfield.com.
3. http://homepages.enterprise.net/ig/.
4. http://www.emofree.com/scien-i.htm.
5. http://www.emofree.com/about.htm.

## REFERENCES

Beyerstein, B. L., and W. Sampson. 1996. Traditional medicine and pseudo-science in China: A report of the second CSICOP delegation (part 1). *Skeptical Inquirer* 20, no. 4: 18–27.

Bohm, D., and B. Hiley. 1993. *The Undivided Universe: An Ontological Interpretation of Quantum Theory.* New York: Roudedge.

Bootzin, R. R. 1985. The sole of expectancy in behaviors change. In *Placebo: Theory, Research, and Mechanisms,* edited by L. White, B. Tursky, and G. Schwartz. New York: Guilford, pp. 196–210.

Bunge, M. 1967. *Scientific Research.* New York: Springer.

Callahan, R. 1985. *Five Minute Phobia Cure.* Wilmington, DE: Enterprise.

———. 1995. Thought Field Therapy (TFT) algorithm for trauma: A reproducible experiment in psychotherapy. Paper delivered at the Annual Meeting of the American Psychological Association.

———. 1997. Thought Field Therapy: The case of Mary. *Electronic Journal of Traumatology* 3, no. 1. Available: http://www.fsu.edu/~trauma/T039.html.

———. 1998. Response to Hooke's review of TFT. *Electronic Journal of Traumatology* 3, no. 2. Available: http://www.fsu.edu/-trauma/v3i2art4.html.

———. 1999. TFT and Heart Rate Variability. *Thought Field Newsletter* 5(2).

Callahan, R. J., and J. Callahan. 1997. Thought Field Therapy: Aiding the bereavement process. In *Death and Trauma: The Traumatology of Grieving,* edited by C. Figley, B. Bride, and N. Mazza. Washington, DC: Taylor & Francis, pp. 249–67.

Carbonell, J. L. 1996. An experimental study of TFT and acsophobia. Available: http://www.tftrx.com/ref articles/6heights.html.

Carbonell, J. L., and C. Figley. 1999. A systematic clinical demonstration of promising PTSD treatment approaches. *Electronic Journal of Traumatology* 5, no. 1. Available: http://www.fsu.edu/~trauma/promising.html.

Craig, G. 1997. *Six days at the VA: Using Emotional Freedom Therapy.* Produced by Gary Craig. Videocassette.

Danzig, V. 1998. CT-TFT changes Karma. *Thought Field Newsletter* 4, no. 2.

Dodes, J. E. 1997. The mysterious placebo. *Skeptical Inquirer* 21, no. 1: 44–46.

Englebretsen, G. 1995. The filling of scholarly vacuums. *Skeptical Inquirer* 21, no. 4: 57–59.

Foa, E. B., and E. A. Meadows. 1997. Psychosocial treatments for post-traumatic stress disorder: A critical review. *Annual Review of Psychology* 48: 449–80.

Foxhall, K. 1999. Arizona board sanctions psychologist for use of Thought Field Therapy. *American Psychological Association Monitor* 30, no. 8: 8.

Gist, R., S. J. Woodall, and L. K. Magenheimer. 1999. "And then you do the Hokey-Pokey and you turn yourself around . . ." In *Response to Disaster:*

*Psychosocial Community and Ecological Approaches,* edited by R. Gist and B. Lubin. Philadelphia: Brunner/Mazel, pp. 269–90.

Herbert, J. D., S. O. Lilienfeld, J. M. Lohr, R .W. Montgomery, W. T. O'Donohue, G. M. Rosen, and D. F. Tolin. 2008. Science and pseudo-science in the development of Eye Movement Desensitization and Reprocessing: Implications for clinical psychology. *Clinical Psychology Review* 20: 945–71.

Hooke, W. 1998a. A review of Thought Field Therapy. *Electronic Journal of Traumatology* 3, no. 2. Available: http://www.fsu.edu/~trauma/v3i2art3 .html.

———. 1998b. Wayne Hooke's reply to Roger Callahan. *Electronic Journal of Traumatology* 3, no. 2. Available: http://www.fsu.edu/~trauma/v3i2art5 .html.

Huber, C. H. 1997. PTSD: A search for "active ingredients." *Family Journal* 5, no. 2: 144–48.

Joslin, G. 1999. A follow-up toxin treatment for a previously treated multiple personality patient. *Thought Field Newsletter* 5, no. 2.

Kenny J. J., R. Clemens, K. D. Forsythe. 1988. Applied kinesiology unreliable for assessing nutrient status. *Journal of the American Dietetic Association* 88, no. 6: 698–704.

Lakatos, I. 1978. Introduction: Science and pseudoscience. In *The Methodology of Scientific Research Programs: Philosophical Papers,* edited by J. Worrall and G. Currie. Cambridge, UK: Cambridge University Press.

Leonoff, G. 1995. The successful treatment of phobias and anxiety by telephone and radio: A replication of Callahan's 1987 study. *Thought Field Newsletter* 1, no. 2.

Lilienfeld, S. O. 1996. EMDR treatment: Less than meets the eye? *Skeptical Inquirer* 20, no. 1: 25–31.

———. 1998. Pseudoscience in contemporary clinical psychology: What it is and what we can do about it. *Clinical Psychologist* 51, no. 4: 3–9.

Lilienfeld, S. O., and J. M. Lohr. 2000. Thought Field Therapy practitioners and educators sanctioned. *Skeptical Inquirer* 24, no. 2: 5.

Lohr, J. M., S. O. Lilienfeld, D. F. Tolin, and J. D. Herbert. 1999. Eye Movement Desensitization and Reprocessing: An analysis of specific versus nonspecific treatment factors. *Journal of Anxiety Disorders* 13, nos. 1–2: 185–207.

Lohr, J. M., R. W. Montgomery, S. O. Lilienfeld, and D. F. Tolin. 1999. Pseudoscience and the commercial promotion of trauma treatments. In *Response to Disaster: Psychosocial Community, and Ecological Approaches,* edited by R. Gist and R Lubin. Philadelphia: Brunner/Mazel, pp. 291–326.

Popper, K. 1965. *The Logic of Scientific Discovery.* New York: Harper.

Ross, S., and L. W. Buckalew. 1985. Placebo agentry: Assessment of drug and placebo effects. In *Placebo: Theory, Research, and Mechanism,* edited by L. White, B. Tursky, and G. Schwartz. New York: Guilford, pp. 67–82.

Sampson, W., and B. L. Beyerstein. 1996. Traditional medicine and pseudoscience in China: A report of the second CSICOP delegation (part 2). *Skeptical Inquirer* 20, no. 5: 27–36.

Saravi, E. D. 1999. Energy and the brain: Facts and fantasies. In *Mind Myths: Exploring Popular Assumptions about the Mind and Brain,* edited by S. Della Sala. New York: Wiley & Sons, pp. 43–58.

Shamis, B. 1996. Thought Field Therapy. *Visions Magazine* 8 (November): 8–9, 32–33.

Shermer, M. 1997. *Why People Believe Weird Things: Pseudoscience, Superstition, and Other Confusions of Our Time.* New York: W. H. Freeman.

Swenson, D. X. 1999. Thought Field Therapy: Still searching for the quick fix. *Skeptic* 7, no. 4: 60–65.

# 21

# ATTACHMENT THERAPY:
# A TREATMENT WITHOUT
# EMPIRICAL SUPPORT

*Jean Mercer*
Richard Stockton College

Attachment therapy (AT) is a mental health intervention for children that involves physical restraint and discomfort. Practitioners base its use on the assumption that rage resulting from early frustration and mistreatment must be provoked and released in order for the child to form an emotional attachment and become affectionate and obedient. Death and injury have resulted from AT, which has nevertheless been supported by some state agencies. AT practitioners have claimed that research evidence supports the effectiveness of their techniques. In the present paper, the research evidence is examined with respect to research design and statistical analysis, and it is concluded that AT remains without empirical validation.

Few events have raised so many questions about the validity of a mental health intervention as the death of ten-year-old Candace Newmaker during a therapy session in April 2000 (Crowder 2000). The conviction in a Colorado court of the two principal therapists in the case made national news a year later. Connell Watkins and Julie Ponder were each sentenced to sixteen years' imprisonment on charges related to Candace's death (Lowe 2001).

Reprinted with permission from *Scientific Review of Mental Health Practice* 1, no. 2 (Fall/Winter 2002): 105–12.

Watkins and Ponder were carrying out an exercise called "rebirthing" as part of their practice of attachment therapy. Candace's adoptive mother, Jeane Newmaker, had brought Candace to Colorado on the advice of therapists in North Carolina, seeking treatment for symptoms she believed to be caused by an attachment disorder. According to testimony at the Watkins-Ponder trial, a therapist in North Carolina had diagnosed Candace with Reactive Attachment Disorder (RAD) on the basis of a questionnaire filled out by Jeane Newmaker.

At the trial, as well as in published material and on associated Web sites (Randolph 1997a), practitioners and advocates of AT asserted that research evidence existed supporting the treatment. Some government agencies and insurance companies have apparently agreed with this claim. States have appropriated funds for the practice and teaching of AT (New Hampshire Executive Council Minutes 1999), and testimony at the trial referred to payment for treatment through health insurance. There has been little formal opposition to AT. Only a few clinicians (Hanson & Spratt 2000; James 1994; Lieberman & Zeanah 1999) have published criticisms of AT; legislation attempting to control the practice has been passed in only one state, Colorado, and, as of this writing, has been proposed in Utah.

The present paper will (a) present a brief description of the practice and theoretical rationale of AT, (b) note some inherent problems AT presents with respect to empirical validation, (c) summarize the research evidence offered by AT advocates, and (d) argue that AT should be identified as an unvalidated treatment (Mercer 2001) as well as a potentially dangerous one.

## ATTACHMENT THERAPY: ITS PURPOSE, PRACTICE, AND RATIONALE

AT (also known as holding therapy, rage-reduction therapy, and Z-process therapy, among other terms) was initially presented as a treatment for autistic children, although some practitioners claimed success with a variety of conditions, including acne (Zaslow & Menta 1975). Currently, AT is used for children who are considered to be emotionally disturbed as a consequence of early difficulties with attachment experiences, which AT practitioners believe include premature birth. Many of the children are adopted; AT therapists consider all adopted children to need AT (Levy & Orlans 2000). The children have most often been diagnosed with RAD, for which there are *DSM-IV* criteria, but some practitioners believe that there is a more severe and different form of attachment disorder (AD, in their terms), involving a combination of RAD and other features such as Oppositional Defiant Disorder (Randolph 2000). Descriptions of the children often include details that imply severe disturbance. Fire setting and such acts of cruelty as tearing the heads off puppies are frequently mentioned (although, as we will see later, few if any complete case histories have been reported). Some proponents of AT have predicted that without this treatment, affected children will become serial killers, like Ted Bundy (Thomas 2000).

## AT PRACTICES

### Holding Therapy

The actual practice of AT differs among practitioners, but certain features appear to be consistently present. One is holding therapy, in which the child is restrained in the arms of one or more therapists, who attempt to trigger the expression of rage. As this was shown in a therapy videotape during the Watkins-Ponder trial, the child's face was grabbed, her head was shaken and bounced, and a therapist shouted into the child's face and demanded that she shout back. The therapist was provocative and insulting, calling the child a "twerp" and a liar and threatening her with abandonment by her adoptive mother. Each of these sessions lasted an hour or more.

Although holding therapy is an important feature of AT, practitioners vary greatly in their opinions about details of the treatment.

Some, like Welch (1989), have held that holding should be done every day by parents of normal children as well as for therapeutic purposes. Others, such as Delaney and Kunstal (1993), have regarded holding as a treatment of last resort and have cautioned practitioners to check on legal and insurance guidelines and never to threaten a child with abandonment or use other excessive provocation.

### Therapeutic Foster Parenting

A second consistent component of AT is therapeutic foster parenting (Thomas 2000). Children undergoing this aspect of the treatment are separated from their parents and live in foster homes, where foster parents drill them in compliance to orders and in such practices as "strong sitting," which involves sitting tailor-fashion on the floor, without moving, for up to two hours or longer. Withholding of food, performance of heavy chores, and other "boot camp" practices form part of the child's experience.

### Rebirthing

Rebirthing, the practice during which Candace Newmaker died, is not invariably used in AT. In Candace's case, rebirthing involved being wrapped in a flannel sheet while lying on the floor, having pillows placed on her, and being leaned on by four or five adults. She was to emerge from the sheet by her own efforts and thus "experience a rebirth" as the child of the adoptive mother, who was present and participating. Candace could not escape and was not released despite her screams and pleas for help. Her efforts were apparently blocked in some way, for the enveloping sheet sustained a long tear as a result of her struggles. When she was unwrapped after seventy minutes, the last thirty without a sound or movement, she was found to have suffocated. (According to courtroom testimony, other children given this treatment had been kept wrapped for only about five minutes.)

# AT THEORY

Despite frequent assertions of AT writers and their use of certain vocabulary, there is no demonstrable connection between AT and the attachment theory of John Bowlby (1982). The theory underlying attachment therapy has connections with the ideas of Wilhelm Reich (1945), who stressed eye contact and physical manipulation of the patient, as well as with some of the later Transactional Analysts (Schiff 1970) and other advocates of New Age thinking (Emerson 1996). As described by such AT writers as Foster Cline (1992), this approach assumes that the emotional attachment of a child to a parent begins before birth and is continued postnatally by a lengthy cycle of experienced frustrations followed by gratification when the parent feeds or cares for the baby and makes eye contact at the same time. Prenatal rejection or postnatal lack of gratification are thought to cause affectional attachment to be blocked by a buildup of unexpressed rage (see Tavris 1989 for a better-supported opposing view of anger). Not only the child's lack of affection for the parent, but many problems (disobedience, poor language development, school failure, writing reversals, Candace's inability to emerge from the sheet) are attributed to blocked rage; that is also associated with failure to make eye contact when the parent wants it (Cline 1992; Welch 1989; Zaslow 1966; Zaslow & Menta 1975). The pain and terror experienced during holding are thought to trigger the catharsis of rage and to unblock the capacity for attachment, after which the child will be affectionate, cheerful, grateful, and obedient. If the child resists, complains, cries, coughs, or vomits during treatment, these behaviors are regarded as aspects of resistance and are believed to demonstrate the need to maintain or increase the discomfort until catharsis occurs (Reber 1996).

# CONCEPTUAL PROBLEMS FOR EMPIRICAL VALIDATION

There are several barriers to empirical validation inherent in the theory and practice of AT. For example, the generally accepted requirement that older children as well as their parents provide informed consent before research is fundable or publishable conflicts with AT thinking.

# INFORMATION AND CONSENT

An important theme of AT is that children are helped to recognize adult authority and form an attachment when knowledge is withheld from them (Thomas 2000). Children as young as preschool age are not told when they are to be separated from their parents and taken to a foster home. Second, children are said not to have a right to stay sick; the idea that a child has the right to refuse holding is considered as unwarranted as the idea that chemotherapy can be refused (Hage 1997). Third, a child's refusal would be simply considered resistance and additional evidence of the need for holding therapy.

# PUBLIC VERIFIABILITY

A second conceptual issue involves the usual assumption that data should be capable of communication to others and verifiable by confirmatory measurement. This is generally considered one of the foundations of scientific method, but it is rejected by AT writers who assert that the only valid measure of the symptoms of an attachment disorder is the mother's report. The signature of these disorders is said to be the child's ability to conceal emotional problems from the most experienced observers, but to behave with vicious hostility when alone with the mother (Randolph 2000; it is considered rare for the child's anger to be directed toward the father, although the possibility of cruelty to animals or younger children is stressed). In the absence of a concealed recording system or hidden observer, which never seem to be used in AT practice, there is no public verifiability of the mother's report.

This problem with verifiability has become exacerbated over the years. For example, one symptom of attachment disorders was initially defined as "failure to make eye contact"; now it is trouble "making eye contact when adults want him/her to" (Randolph 2000). Presumably, only the adults themselves can know whether they wanted the child to make eye contact at a given moment.

## OUTCOME MEASURES

A third conceptual issue, related to the second, involves the need for a reliable and valid outcome measure to be used in evaluation of the treatment (Chambless & Hollon 1998). If the primary outcome measure is the mother's unsupported report, independent testing of its validity is difficult. It would be possible to establish predictive validity, especially in light of the fact that some easily measured behaviors such as serial killing are predicted for untreated AD children, but this has not been done. The establishment of concurrent validity is complicated by the claim that the disorder is unrecognized by most therapists. As we will see in the next section, AT writers have attempted to establish the reliability of a questionnaire measure of the mother's report, but this does not solve the problem of an independent measure against which to gauge validity. Serious limitations for the establishment of the questionnaire's reliability and validity thus emerge from the test's reliance on the mothers' judgments.

## RESEARCH ON AT

Most of the research discussed here was carried out by the staff of the Attachment Center at Evergreen (ACE) in Colorado. This organization is also the source of the major book discussing AT (Levy & Orlans 2000). Connell Watkins was at one time affiliated with ACE, but the organization's Web site was quick to repudiate her techniques after Candace's death.

# QUESTIONNAIRE DEVELOPMENT

As commercial ventures, AT clinics can benefit from the use of a checklist that demonstrates to parents their children's need for treatment. AT writers began with such a checklist and have attempted to develop a questionnaire that could be described as reliable and valid.

### Checklist

Efforts toward questionnaire development began with an Attachment Disorder Symptom Checklist, which is still posted on some AT Web sites (for example, www.attachment-ga.com/html/ADSX2.html). This checklist shows a remarkable overlap with similar checklists presented in the past as indicators of sexual abuse (Dawes 1994; Underwager & Wakefield 1990). A peculiarity of the checklist is its inclusion of statements about the parent's feelings toward the child as well as statements about the child's behavior. For example, parental feelings are evaluated through responses to such statements as "Parent feels used" and "is wary of the child's motives if affection is expressed," and "Parents feel more angry and frustrated with this child than with other children." The child's behavior is referred to in such statements as "Child has a grandiose sense of self-importance" and "Child 'forgets' parental instructions or directives."

### RADQ

The 30-item Randolph Attachment Disorder Questionnaire (RADQ) (Randolph 2000) was developed from the Attachment Disorder

Symptom Checklist. The RADQ is presented not as an assessment of RAD but rather of attachment disorder (AD), a diagnosis not "yet" in the DSM. This posited condition involves both RAD and either Conduct Disorder or many symptoms of Oppositional Defiant Disorder.

The RADQ manual emphasizes that the RADQ score alone should not be used to make the AD diagnosis. The test is always to be completed by the adult female who knows the child best and has been living continuously with the child, but she should be carefully guided by an AD expert to provide accurate answers (Randolph 2000).

The RADQ is at the fifth grade reading level. Only one form appears to exist, although repeated measures are used. The mother ranks her responses to statements from 1 (rarely) to 5 (usually) and is instructed that these ranks are to be linked to specific frequencies with which the behaviors occur. All items are set up with 5 on the reader's left and 1 on the right. Positive statements are never converted to negative forms as a check for an acquiescence or a counteracquiescence response set. Some statements are cast in unusually dramatic or emotional ways: "My child has a *tremendous* need to have control . . ."; "My child acts *amazingly* innocent . . ." (emphasis in original).

Randolph (2000) reported data based on the completion of the RADQ by 350 parents. She noted high reliability, reporting correlation coefficients of over .80 for test-retest stability and internal consistency (as measured by odd-even correlations, which are rarely used today by psychometricians).

### Validity Issues

As noted earlier, validity is inherently the more serious problem with the RADQ. Randolph claimed content validity because the RADQ items were based on the Attachment Disorder Symptom Checklist mentioned earlier. She also presented significant correlations with two of six selected subscales from the Personality Inventory for Children (Lachar 1979) and two of eight subscales of the Child Behavior Checklist (Achenbach 1991). There was a significant correlation with one of twelve subscales of the Millon Adolescent Personality Inventory (Millon, 1982). Randolph also noted the importance of Rorschach information for increased validity in the assessment of certain types of children (but see Wood & Lilienfeld 1999 for a critique). There was no discussion of any direct measure of behavior independent of the mother's report, although such items as stealing, fire setting, cruelty, and frequent injuries should be amenable to independent corroboration.

Randolph (2000) reported that the RADQ clearly distinguished, with nonoverlapping distributions ($N = 186$), between children who have an AD diagnosis and groups who (a) had been maltreated, (b) had disruptive behavior disorders, and (c) were classed with other disorders, primarily anxiety and depression. There were large differences among the groups in living situations (birth home, foster home, adoptive home, group home) and therefore presumably differences in the types of persons responding to the RADQ. The groups also differed, sometimes dramatically, in the children's ethnicity and gender.

### RADQ Subscales

Randolph also presented a division of the RADQ into subscales that she considered associated with four posited subtypes of AD. These four subtypes were given names associated with categories of toddler attachment behavior seen in the Strange Situation (Main & Solomon 1990), but Randolph specifically noted that she did not mean to imply any connection between the two; she had, she said, been unable to think of any other names (Randolph 2000, 52). Randolph's attempts to present the subscale scores as linked to subtypes, based on measures from 160 children, were weakened by the fact that she herself apparently assigned the children to subtype groups and did not seek an independent evaluation.

Randolph's extensive work on the RADQ suggests that this test should be the instrument of choice in the evaluation of AT outcomes, but, as we will soon see, this has not been the case.

# EMPIRICAL EVALUATION OF AT

In written material and in testimony at the Watkins-Ponder trial, AT practitioners have repeatedly asserted that AT not only is effective but should be considered "best practice" for a disorder that other treatments do not ameliorate. This claim would be difficult to substantiate using the APA Task Force criteria for empirically supported treatments, because of the absence of a clearly valid outcome measure. In addition, however, there are no reported studies of the effect of AT on children using random assignment to groups, viz., the Class I evidence (in terms of the evidence-based approach [Patrick, Mozzoni & Patrick 2000]) that allows best practice to be determined. The absence of randomized trials is not surprising, because AT appears to be performed in poorly organized, commercially oriented clinic arrangements rather than in the institutional settings in which randomized trials are commonly planned and overseen.

These methodological limitations notwithstanding, we should examine the less stringent approaches that some practitioners have adopted for the evaluation of AT. Preliminary steps in research can be valuable guides to the development of randomized, controlled studies. To think in terms of evidence-based care, such work may not tell us about best practice, but it can sometimes provide treatment guidelines or options (ibid.).

In the following section, I review what appears to be all of the available evidence regarding the efficacy of AT. Two dissertations mentioned by AT writers do not appear in *Dissertation Abstracts International* and were not located. (One dissertation whose title refers to AT is, in fact, on a different topic.)[1] The material discussed here amounts to a dissertation, a journal article based on this dissertation, a Web site article apparently taken from an organization's newsletter, and other materials from the ACE Web site.

Considering the entirely clinical emphasis of AT practitioners, we might expect some carefully described case histories or similar clinical reports. The practice of videotaping therapy sessions, shown at the Watkins-Ponder trial, lends itself to detailed descriptions. However, although many brief anecdotes are presented, there seem to be no complete case reports. A detailed case report in one book on AT (Cline 1992) is in fact the work of Erickson (1962), whose thinking was not generally based on AT principles.

## QUASI-EXPERIMENTAL STUDIES

Three quasi-experimental studies have investigated the efficacy of AT. The first of these, the only one not associated with ACE, is a simple study whose interpretation does not outstrip the data. Lester (1997) examined twelve families whose adopted children received AT. The children, whose age range was broad, experienced different levels of treatment, many with three-hour sessions daily for weeks. The parents responded to the Devereux Scale of Mental Disorders, a rating scale for which evidence of reliability has been published, as well as another scale in the process of development, on four occasions (before the child's initial assessment, at the time of the initial assessment, after the assessment but before therapy began, and at least four weeks after therapy began). Average scores were presented, but there were no statistical analyses. Lester reported that all scores improved over time but that the greatest improvement occurred before therapy had begun. She noted that the parents might simply have felt better after talking to a sympathetic person. Like other AT writers, Lester apparently did not consider regression to the mean as a possible source of improvement, although it is likely that the parents sought treatment when the children's symptoms were at their worst and that some degree of spontaneous remission was likely.

A more elaborate quasi-experimental study, presented on the ACE Web site, was apparently carried out by Elizabeth Randolph and other ACE staff members (Randolph 1997a). The Web site report lacks a number of details that would normally be found in published material, such as measures of variability to accompany means or complete analysis of variance tables. This study examined Child Behavior Checklist data from twenty-five children, seven to twelve years old, on three occasions. Parents or foster parents completed the checklist (a) before treatment began, (b) following a two-week intensive treatment period and between three and six months of long-term treatment in a therapeutic foster home, and (c) following an additional six months. No untreated comparison group was included to establish the effects of factors such as maturation that could cause change over such a time period. (AT practitioners have asserted that the disorder they treat is so intractable that it does not change over time without treatment, so they would probably argue that maturation was a negligible factor in improvement; Randolph, 1997b.)

The Web site report noted mean scores on the eight subscales of the checklist, but no measures of variability. The statistical analysis was described as a simple analysis of variance (ANOVA), although presumably a repeated measures ANOVA would have been appropriate. One of the eight subscales showed no change, and five showed significant changes over the twelve-month period.

A dissertation by Myeroff (1997) at the Union Institute of Ohio, which was subsequently published (Myeroff, Mertlich & Gross 1999), was the third quasi-experiment that attempted to evaluate AT. This study included an untreated comparison group. Myeroff and her colleagues collected parents' responses to the Child Behavior Checklist for twenty-three families who contacted ACE to seek AT for their adopted children. The treatment group was composed of twelve children who were brought for treatment, and the untreated comparison group was composed of eleven children whose parents made contact but were unable to bring them to ACE.

Both groups of parents completed reports on two subscales of the checklist, after their initial contact and again after a four-week interval. For the treatment group, a two-week "intensive" occurred midway between the two reports. Myeroff et al. (1999) reported significant differences between the two groups, with the treatment group showing significant improvement on both the aggression and delinquency subscales.

According to Myeroff et al. (ibid.), the failure of the untreated children to attend the clinic was not due to the condition of either parent or child.

Family income, gender, race, and pre-adoption placement did not differ significantly across the two groups. Whether these groups were also matched statistically on initial checklist scores was not mentioned. Myeroff et al. noted that differences in finances might have been responsible for the failure to attend. Such differences could also influence the developmental outcome for an adopted child. Similarly, marital disagreements, number of siblings, physical or mental problems of family members, educational needs of siblings, and job situations of parents could all affect both development of adopted children and the decision of parents to bring a child to the clinic. Myeroff et al.'s claim that the groups were appropriately matched is thus unwarranted, and the differences reported between the groups may well be due to the numerous factors that determined the families' self-selection. This conclusion is in agreement with the briefer critique offered by Wilson (2001) on some of the weaknesses of AT research.

## STATISTICAL ANALYSIS

Many of the statistical analyses performed by AT researchers have been problematic. The substitution of a simple ANOVA for the appropriate repeated measures ANOVA in Randolph's (1997a) work increased the possibility of a Type I error (Ferguson 1959). In Randolph's (2000) reports on the RADQ, she noted what appear to be large standard deviations in comparison with reported ranges but did not comment on the normality of the distributions.

Myeroff et al.'s (1999) published work reported significant $t$ comparisons for both pre-treatment and post-treatment aggression scores and pre- and post-delinquency scores for the treatment group, but non-significant $t$s on both measures for the nontreatment group. She also compared pre- and post-difference scores for the treatment and non-treatment groups on the aggression and the delinquency subscales, with significant $t$s in both cases. The latter two comparisons are the appropriate ones to conduct rather than the first four, and the use of six rather than two $t$ calculations increases the chances of a Type I error.

# DISCUSSION

Claims for AT's efficacy have not been supported by the sparse research evidence presented by AT advocates. Because this intervention is not only without validation but has been associated with injury and death, insurance companies and state agencies appear to have used poor judgment in supporting it.

AT remains an important topic of study for professional psychology in spite of the absence of empirical support, or perhaps even because of it. AT and similar therapies offer a window into the folk beliefs that cause people to reject conventional psychotherapy in favor of unvalidated mental health interventions. Practitioners of AT may share, or at least speak to, some assumptions about human nature that are foreign to many professional psychologists but that are embedded in American popular culture. An example would be the belief that personality transformations can be produced by such ritual acts as baptism or exorcism. Such a sacramental view of personality change is greatly at odds with cognitive and behavioral approaches to therapy.

Examination of AT theory and research also reveals a tendency toward certain basic cognitive errors that are characteristic of adolescents (Demetriou et al. 1993). For example, our earlier discussion of AT research showed researchers' difficulty in isolating variables. The theory and practice of AT involve the *dependent variable error*, a tendency to assume that if manipulation of the independent variable causes changes in the dependent variable, the opposite should also be true. For instance, AT theory assumes that lack of eye contact (the dependent variable) is caused by failure of attachment (the independent variable); treatment involves the forcing of eye contact, which is expected to correct attachment. This immature thinking on the part of the AT practitioner may seem comfortable to parents, whereas the reasoning inherent in conventional psychotherapy may be resisted because of its unfamiliar sophistication. Many adults continue to make this type of error, broadly known in logic as "affirming the consequent," and may be reassured by the familiar thought pattern as they try to cope with the diagnosis given to their child and the concern that they may be blamed.

A final point about the importance of attending to AT is the possible connection of this treatment to other dangerous forms of "wild" therapy (see Singer & Lalich 1996). For example, some deaths of adolescents in wilderness camps may be attributable to a belief system shared with AT. The American director of a camp in Samoa in which severe physical abuse and fraud have been alleged has been quoted as saying, "Kids come in with all sorts of little ways to manipulate, with a lot of anger. We physically stress them out and that breaks down the facades to get to their heart" (Janofsky 2001, A14); this man was acquitted of charges related to the death of a girl in another camp some years ago. An assumption shared by a number of these "crazy therapies" (Singer & Lalich 1996) involves *recapitulation,* the notion that it is possible to rework a developmental sequence by mimicking at a later time the factors that the practitioners believe cause normal developmental change in early life.

It would seem desirable for legislation to regulate treatments that are unvalidated and potentially harmful, but a legislative approach brings up First Amendment issues and may be resisted by professional groups wishing to retain the privilege of self-policing. Legislation can also drive undesirable treatments underground and decrease the extent to which they can be controlled. More effective approaches may involve public education. As a first effort in this direction, I suggest withdrawal of the continuing education units currently given by some institutions for AT workshops and seminars.

# NOTE

1. G. G. Williams. Attachment therapy as a method for altering significantly family cohesion and adaptability. *Dissertation Abstracts International* 51 (5-A) (1990): 1795. (UMI NO. 9026811)

# REFERENCES

Achenbach, T. M. 1991. *Manual for the Child Behavior Checklist and 1991 Profile*. Burlington: University of Vermont Press.

Bowlby, J. 1982. *Attachment*. New York: Basic.

Chambless, D. L., and S. D. Hollon, 1998. Defining empirically supported therapies. *Journal of Consulting and Clinical Psychology* 66: 7–18.

Cline, F. W. 1992. *Hope for High Risk and Rage Filled Children*. Evergreen, CO: EC Publications.

Crowder, C. 2000. Prosecutors add charges for rebirthing therapist. *Rocky Mountain News*, July 29. Retrieved July 29, 2000, from http://insidedenver .com/news/0729char0.shtml.

Dawes, R. M. 1994. *House of cards: Psychology and Psychotherapy Built upon Myth*. New York: Free Press.

Delaney, R. J., and F. R. Kunstal. 1993. *Troubled Transplants*. Fort Collins, CO: Horsetooth Press.

Demetriou, A., A. Efklides, M. Papadaki, G. Papantoniou, and A. Economou. 1993. Structure and development of causal-experimental though from early adolescence to youth. *Developmental Psychology* 29: 480–97.

Emerson, W. R. 1996. Points of view: The vulnerable prenate. *Pre- and Perinatal Psychology Journal* 10, no. 3: 125–42.

Erickson, M. H. 1962. The identification of a secure reality. *Family Process* 1, no. 2: 294–303.

Ferguson, G. A. 1959. *Statistical Analysis in Psychology and Education*. New York: McGraw-Hill.

Hage, D. 1997. Holding therapy: Harmful? . . . or rather beneficial. *Roots and Wings Adoption Magazine* 9, no. 1: 46–49. Retrieved June 15, 2000, from http://debrahage.com/pwp.

Hanson, R. F., and E. G. Spratt. 2000. Reactive Attachment Disorder: What we know about the disorder and implications for treatment. *Child Maltreatment* 5, no. 2: 137–51.

James, B. 1994. *Handbook for Treatment of Attachment-Trauma Problems in Children*. New York: Lexington.

Janofsky, M. 2001. Boot camps proponent becomes focus of critics. *New York Times*, August 9, p. A14.

Lachar, D. 1979. *Manual for the Personality Inventory for Children*. Minneapolis, MN: National Computer Systems.

Lester, V. S. 1997. Behavior change as reported by caregivers of children receiving holding therapy. Retrieved August 4, 2000, from the Association for Treatment and Training in the Attachment of Children Web site: http://www.attach.org/lester.htm.

Levy, T. M., and M. Orlans. 2000. Attachment disorder and the adoptive family. In *Handbook of Attachment Interventions*, edited by T. M. Levy, pp. 244–60. San Diego, CA: Academic.

Lieberman, A., and C. H. Zeanah. 1999. Contributions of attachment theory to infant-parent psychotherapy and other interventions with infants and young children. In *Handbook of Attachment*, edited by J. Cassidy and P. Shaver, pp. 555–74. New York: Guilford.

Lowe, P. 2001. Therapists get 16 years. *Rocky Mountain News*, June 19. Retrieved June 19, 2001, from http://rockymountainnews.com/drmn/0,1299,DRMN_15_6750 52,00.html.

Main, M. B., and J. A. Solomon. 1990. Procedures for identifying infants as disorganized/disoriented during the Ainsworth Strange Situation. In *Attachment in the Preschool Years*, edited by M. Greenberg, D. Cicchetti, and E. M. Cummings, pp. 121–60. Chicago: University of Chicago Press.

Mercer, J. 2001. Attachment therapy using deliberate restraint: An object lesson in the identification of unvalidated treatments. *Journal of Child and Adolescent Psychiatric Nursing* 14, no. 3: 105–114.

Millon, T. 1982. *Millon Adolescent Personality Inventory Manual*. Minneapolis, MN: National Computer Systems.

Myeroff, R. L. 1997. Comparative effectiveness of attachment therapy with the special needs adoptive population. *Dissertation Abstracts International* 586–B, 3323. UMI No. AAM9736716

Myeroff, R. L., G. Mertlich, and G. Gross. 1999. Comparative effectiveness of holding therapy with aggressive children. *Child Psychiatry and Human Development* 29, no. 4: 303–13.

New Hampshire Executive Council Minutes. 1999. Item #85A. Retrieved August 19, 2000, from the New Hampshire State Government Web site: http://www.state.nh.us/ council/min/092899.

Patrick, P. D., M.Mozzoni, and S. T. Patrick. 2000. Evidence-based care and the single-subject design. *Infants and Young Children* 13, no. 1: 60–73.

Randolph, E. 1997a. Attachment therapy does work! Retrieved January 20, 2001, from the Attachment Center Evergreen Web site: http://www.attach mentcenter.org.

————. 1997b. Is attachment therapy necessary? *Connections* (August): 45. Retrieved January 20, 2001 from the Attachment Center at Evergreen Web site: http attachment center.org/articles/article029.htm.

————. 2000. *Manual for the Randolph Attachment Disorder Questionnaire.* Evergreen, CO: Attachment Center Press.

Reber, K. 1996. Children at risk for reactive attachment disorder: Assessment, diagnosis, and treatment. *Progress Family Systems Research and Therapy* 5: 83–98.

Reich, W. 1945. *Character Analysis.* Rangely, ME: Orgone Institute Press.

Schiff, J. L. 1970. *All My Children.* New York: M. Evans.

Singer, M. T., and J. A. Lalich. 1996. *Crazy therapies.* San Francisco: Jossey-Bass.

Tavris, C. 1989. *Anger: The Misunderstood Emotion.* New York: Simon and Schuster.

Thomas, N. L. 2000. Parenting children with attachment disorders. In *Handbook of Attachment Interventions*, edited by T. Levy, pp. 67–111. San Diego, CA: Academic.

Underwager, R. C., and H. Wakefield. 1990. *The Real World Child Interrogations.* Springfield, IL: C. C. Thomas.

Welch, M. G. 1989. *Holding Time.* New York: Fireside.

Wilson, S. L. 2001. Attachment disorders: Review and currrent status. *Journal of Psychology* 135, no. 1: 37–51.

Wood, J. M., and S. O. Lilienfeld. 1999. The Rorschach Inkblot Test: A case of overstatement? *Assessment* 341–49.

Zaslow, R. W. 1966. Reversals in children as a result of midline body orientation. *Journal of Educational Psychology* 57, no. 3: 133–39.

Zaslow, R. W., and M. Menta. 1975. *The psychology of the Z-Process: Attachment and Activity.* San Jose, CA: San Jose State University Press.

# 22.

# BACK TO THE BEGINNING: REGRESSION, REPARENTING, AND REBIRTHING

## Margaret Singer and Janja Lalich

"Rose," thirty-seven, married with two teenage daughters, saw a psychologist's poster advertising that patients would attain dramatic personal transformation, learn long-forgotten events, and achieve emotional intensity that would revitalize their lives. "Women—Prepare for the New Century Through Rebirthing and Reparenting," the poster proclaimed. Rose was intrigued and called for an appointment.

During the first session, the female psychologist asked Rose some questions about her personal and emotional history, but seemed to have little interest in what Rose was recounting. The therapist spent a great deal of the time explaining how her groups worked and the requirements. Rose was told that future sessions would be in the evening in a group setting. "Others of my children will be rebirthed that night," the therapist softly murmured. Rose was to wear old clothes and bring along a blanket, pillow, and baby bottle.

The group met in a large conference room without chairs or furniture of any kind. Large pillows, many blankets, and lightweight cotton rugs were stacked against the walls. Rose learned that she was one of four new "children" to be rebirthed that night. Four other advanced patients would assume the role of the "primary mother" of each of the new women.

The psychologist instructed each newcomer to lie on a spread-out cotton throw rug. Each primary mother showed her assigned new-

Reprinted from Margaret Thaler Singer and Janja Lalich, *Crazy Therapies: What Are They? Do They Work?* (San Francisco: Jossey-Bass, 1996), pp. 23–45. Copyright 1996 Jossey-Bass. Reproduced with permission of John Wiley & Sons, Ltd.

comer how to get into the "birthing position": on her side, fetal position, chin tucked toward chest, arms against torso, legs drawn up. Each primary mother rolled her rebirthing candidate into the rug so that it formed a cocoon. Meanwhile the psychologist was telling them in the background that she would use guided imagery to regress them back to birth and that they should visualize being in a dark, tight place that was squeezing in on them. They were to fight and wriggle their way out of the birth canal, just like at their first birth. She assured them that this time they would be birthed the right way, received with unconditional love. "I will receive you as my children," she intoned. "I will release you to your new primary mother who, one step at a time, will help you grow up right." Much squealing, wriggling, and crying out ensued as the primary mothers tugged at the wrapped women until each was "rebirthed." Eventually Rose was dragged over to a large pillow against the wall. Her primary mother lifted Rose's torso, and while cradling her fed her milk from the baby bottle.

The eight women met four times a week for a month. Rose's husband, "Fred," noticed that she was regressing rapidly in her daily behaviors. Soon she would not get up in the morning until he brought her milk in a cup and fed her. She lost the will to do the most simple self-care tasks, letting her hair become unwashed and unkempt, not showering, and rarely getting dressed. Fred and the daughters had no home life with Rose gone to the reparenting group four nights a week, where she wore diapers, crawled on her hands and knees, and babbled baby talk.

Finally, Fred called the psychologist, telling her that he felt that Rose had disintegrated into a regressed, depressed, enfeebled human who stayed in bed most of the day. The psychologist replied, "Everyone has to get worse before they get better." She suggested that Fred join one of her men's rebirthing groups so that he could understand and share with Rose. Before slamming down the phone, Fred yelled in anger, "But who is going to take care of all of us then if she and I both are lying in bed expecting to be fed!"

Over time, Fred began to fear that Rose had gone crazy. He convinced her to cancel further reparenting and got her mother up from another part of the state to take care of Rose and the teenage daughters.

After a few days, Rose, Fred, the mother, and the two girls met with a psychiatrist for an evaluation. A person meeting Rose for the first time who didn't know she had formerly been a sprightly, bright woman would have wondered if she were mentally retarded, severely depressed, or in some way demented. It took some months for Rose to recover, and she felt particularly bad when she saw the impact her regressed, stuporous behavior had had on her two teenage daughters, who like their father had been worried that their mother had "lost her mind."

S tories like these are plentiful, and practitioners of various forms of regression therapy combined with the use of mind-altering techniques are rampant in the United States and abroad. As of 1992, one "corrective parenting association" formed in the mid-1980s reportedly had 350 member therapists. This figure represents but a handful of the therapists and counselors who believe in these unfounded theories and use potentially harmful methods.

Leonard Orr, said by some to be the founder of rebirthing, claims to have talked to ten million "energy-breathing students." Energy breathing is the goal of rebirthing, and Orr writes on his Internet home page, "People who have mastered their ability to breathe energy as well as air, report that they can breathe away physical and emotional pain, and long standing [sic] diseases." At his new location in Staunton, Virginia, Orr offers five-day Rebirther's Training sessions *every week of the year.* And who knows how many others get trained by these graduates?

Another well-known rebirther and early cohort of Orr is Sondra Ray. Information from her organization lists "qualified" rebirthers in New York, Georgia, Massachusetts, Connecticut (the location of Ray's center), Florida, Nevada, Michigan, New Jersey, North Carolina, Nebraska, Missouri, Tennessee, Virginia, Puerto Rico, and Manitoba—so don't think that only people in "flaky" California get involved with these weird goings-on. (Ray's list of rebirthers and their seminars includes only one contact in Los Angeles.) As readers will soon discover, unscientific therapies are a national, and in some cases an international, phenomenon.

In the pages to follow, we examine the use of regression as it relates specifically to rebirthing and reparenting, but the techniques have been adopted, adapted, and promoted in countless therapies by numerous practitioners, as will be evident in the chapters that follow. Proponents of regression therapies often refer to their work by a variety of names, sometimes making them hard to detect at first glance, especially for the uninformed potential client. In general, these therapists combine suggestion, guided imagery, and hypnosis to reinforce their encouragement of marked regression—a method that can be psychologically disastrous to many persons, as it was to Rose.

Because objective research on regression techniques is limited, the assumptions about regression remain merely myths based on anecdotal reports from enthusiastic proponents. In fact, Sondra Ray states several times in one of her books that there is no research and there are no accurate records or statistics; she even claims that this isn't her job: "Rebirthers consider themselves to be spiritual guides, not scientists." So much for reality checking or scientific verification.

Rather than helping clients to become stronger and more independent, most regression therapies, and in particular the rebirthing-reparenting sort, induce in the client an abdication of responsibility and a state of sickly dependence on the therapist. This is a blatant abuse and misuse of the power relationship inherent in the therapeutic process; it is in effect the exploitation of the client's emotional vulnerability. The "Mommy" or "Daddy" therapist who is supposed to parent the client correctly is in fact playing with fire, potentially entrapping and crippling their "children," and causing undue suffering and in some cases long-lasting damage.

Regression techniques continue to be used throughout the United States today—from San Diego to Seattle to Kansas City—as well as in Germany, India, England, Sweden, Canada, Belgium, and Holland, having been successfully spread via weekend seminars sold around the world by traveling trainers. On the whole, professional associations in the mental health field have ignored the practice, although there has been the occasional mild reprimand to practitioners of these therapies.

Generally, it is only when enough damaged patients and their families have sought legal redress in the courts that the public has learned through the media about the egregious behavior and the sometimes disastrous consequences.

## WHERE DO THESE IDEAS COME FROM?

Most schools of psychotherapy believe that childhood and the early years of life have formative influences on the adult personality. But some therapies—regression, direct analysis, reparenting, corrective parenting, and rebirthing—are based on the untested assumption that a therapist can regress patients to infancy in order to reparent them, even rebirth them, and then bring them up correctly. Believers claim that these therapies are able to alter, repair, and even reverse the alleged negative impact of someone's early life experiences, simply by making babies out of clients and having them relive the experiences—only this time, supposedly, the therapist is going to carry out the parenting in the right way.

The underlying assumption is that an adult patient first needs to be regressed in order to act like and be treated as a small infant; then, through "corrective parenting" by the therapist, the patient will emerge as a more ideal person. As we have seen in the case of Rose and others, some therapists who engage in rebirthing and reparenting techniques feed adult patients from baby bottles; have patients suck on therapists' breasts, thumbs, and penises; instruct patients to wear diapers and to engage in such behaviors as being cuddled as an infant, being made to stand in the corner, and even being physically restrained and beaten, sometimes brutally, by the reparenting therapist. This type of therapy may go on for varying lengths of time. Some we've heard of lasted as long as seven to ten years.

This unfortunate and dangerous theory is grounded in a widespread tendency in our society toward "parent bashing," in which parents are blamed for not producing totally happy, satisfied, creative, wonderful offspring. For several decades, some professionals have ignored the fact that there are other significant influences on human personality—

namely, genes, illnesses, physical conditions, and social and political conditions such as wars, poverty, crime, and natural disasters. Parents have been blamed for every misery their offspring have suffered: being fat, thin, sickly, depressed, or schizophrenic or just plain dissatisfied with their lot in life.

We can trace this tendency back to Freud, who readily blamed parents for his patients' supposed problems. The belief reached its zenith in the 1940s and 1950s within the ranks of traditional psychoanalysts. A primary wave of attack was on mothers. Some were labeled "schizophrenogenic" and accused of causing schizophrenia in their children, while other mothers were called "homosexual-inducing." By the late 1940s, some therapists were proclaiming that their patients' parents were unloving, mean, intrusive, and controlling and had in effect harmed, if not ruined, their offspring. From there, some therapists deduced the solution that the all-loving therapist would restore the patients by bringing them up properly.

## PIONEERS IN REGRESSION AND REPARENTING

Two therapists in particular, Marguerite Sechehaye and John Rosen, received considerable attention as forerunners in the use of regression and reparenting therapy in their work with schizophrenic patients. Colleagues in the field readily praised Sechehaye and Rosen for their innovative methods.

Sechehaye and Rosen began by claiming that their massive regression techniques, coupled with authoritarian control, would cure schizophrenia. Fortunately for them, the post–World War II period was an era when people were willing to justify extreme forms of therapy in an effort to "cure" schizophrenia. Because it was also a time when parents, especially mothers, were being vilified in the world of therapy, the severing of family ties and the regression techniques were tolerated, even lauded, by other therapists. They accepted the "logic" of thinking that perhaps rough treatment and separation from families would cure a major mental illness. But soon not only schizophrenics (who almost never have a constituency looking out for their welfare) were subjected to this treatment; almost anyone who went into certain therapists' offices was open game for being regressed and reparented to cure *any* ill.

Sechehaye was an academic psychologist and psychoanalyst in Geneva, Switzerland. She developed a method called "symbolic realization," with which she treated a twenty-one-year-old schizophrenic woman for more than ten years. Sechehaye had the woman live with her; she fed her and in general parented her in a warm way. For about seven of those years, the patient was acutely psychotic and cared for as a baby would be. Sechehaye had concluded that the woman's problems grew from a lack of maternal love.

Renee, the patient, referred to Sechehaye as "Mama." Holding an apple against her breast, Mama would then feed the girl by cutting a piece of the apple and having the girl lie against Mama's breast to eat. The raw apple was to be "breast milk" for Renee. Sechehaye's treatment was far more symbolic than the reparenting therapies developed by others, which became more and more overt, and sometimes even sinister, in their "mothering" practices.

John Rosen, a physician who had been analyzed but never trained as a psychoanalyst, originally professed in 1947 that his new method, which he called "direct analysis," led to schizophrenic patients "recovering" and having their "psychosis resolved." Claiming that his patients had not been loved during childhood, Rosen reported spending sometimes as much as ten hours a day with one patient. What was eventually revealed about what went on in those sessions is almost too horrific to imagine. Some of these techniques were tantamount to extreme violence and torture.

As a young psychologist in the late 1940s, I (coauthor Singer) had the opportunity to observe Rosen work with schizophrenic patients when he was a guest faculty member at the university medical school where I was working. I recall seeing Rosen do his direct analysis on some seriously ill patients. He yelled at them, threatened them, and verbally badgered and insulted them. This, as we all were later to learn, was only the half of it.

The selected patients were presented before hospital staff, medical students, and faculty. A nurse brought patients down from the wards, and one at a time Rosen began his direct analysis of their remarks. In front of such an awesome group of strangers, most patients looked frightened and puzzled and became even more so as Rosen proceeded. Rosen's conduct was nothing like the expected demeanor of a physician speaking with patients, and he was far from polite. With little knowledge of the individual patient, Rosen began to ask questions. He responded to whatever the patient said with insult and bluster, including the use of profanities and scatological terms. The patients appeared stunned, but Rosen's manner conveyed that they must stay and take what he was dishing out.

I recall sitting in wonderment as I watched Rosen's onslaughts on patients during his demonstrations at the hospital. I kept asking myself, "What could be his rationale for what he's doing?" He claimed he was talking the language of the id, the language of the primary process, and that he was showing them he cared for them. But what logical connections were there between the diagnosis of schizophrenia, Rosen's conduct, and his assumptions that it cured patients? He wrote, "Sometimes, when I have the patient pinned to the floor, I say, 'I can castrate you. I can kill you, I can eat you. I can do whatever I want to you, but I am not going to do it.'" He went on: "The patient gets the feeling of having met a master who could do anything he wanted to him by virtue of his physical strength but will not do it because he loves him."

Later in the day I saw these same patients on the wards. Rosen's treatment had indeed produced regression. There they were, either sitting rocking in a mute, stunned manner with a staring gaze, or lying in various parts of the ward quietly sobbing. Prior to these sessions with Rosen, the patients had been up and about on the wards interacting with other patients and the staff.

The senior staff at the university medical school all seemed to endorse what Rosen was doing. Most of us underlings were appalled and spoke to each other about how cruel and demeaning the "treatment" was, but we dared not speak out, I'm sorry to say. In fact, Rosen was extolled in the literature and at professional meetings where he demonstrated his approach as heroic and dedicated. In 1971 he even won the American Academy of Psychotherapy Man of the Year award.

An article by Rosen in a 1947 *Psychiatric Quarterly* reported on thirty-seven of his cases. Rosen claimed that all thirty-seven individuals recovered. Six years later in his book *Direct Analysis*, Rosen reported that thirty-one of the original sample were no longer psychotic and were doing well. Yet, in a follow-up study in 1958, nineteen of the former patients from Rosen's report were located by researchers at the New York Psychiatric Institute. They found that seven of the nineteen were not schizophrenic at that time, nor had they ever been; instead, six were evaluated as neurotic and one as manic-depressive. These independent researchers concluded that "the claim that direct analytic therapy results in a high degree of recovery remains unproven."

Finally, in March of 1983, thanks to the courage of a number of Rosen's former patients who came forward to speak out and expose the abuses they suffered, Rosen surrendered his medical license. He had been charged with "sixty-seven violations of the Pennsylvania Medical Practices Act and thirty-five violations of the rules and regulations of the Medical Board, [which included] the commission of acts involving moral turpitude, dishonesty, or corruption, as well as misconduct in the practice of medicine, practicing medicine fraudulently, beyond its authorized scope, with incompetence, or with negligence." In fact, unbeknownst to many, as far back as 1960 Rosen had lost a case in New York in which he had been accused of beating a female patient. From investigations, depositions, and testimonies given regarding the various charges against Rosen, information came forth about the kind of care patients were getting at Rosen's facilities. Striking, stripping, and beating patients were a regular occurrence. Patients were kept locked in security rooms without toilets, and at least two patients died. Both male and female patients were sexually abused by Rosen and forced to engage in the most atrocious acts with him and sometimes with other patients.

John Rosen had been highly regarded for years throughout the psychiatric community. To this day, some still uphold Rosen's work, when in fact Rosen and his direct analysis led to some serious abuses of patients and legal suits. Rosen may have lost his license, but the confrontational techniques that he professed live on, as we will see.

# BABY BOTTLES, BERATING, AND BEATINGS

Many of Rosen's methods have filtered into the profession and are alive and well today in various therapies that regress and infantilize clients to the point of having them drink from baby bottles and be humiliated and punished in other ways. When asked by author and researcher Jeffrey Masson in an interview in 1986 if he still used the methods he learned from Rosen, a doctor replied that he used "physical methods that included shaking patients, sitting on them, and wrestling with them." Because there is more awareness and concern today about abuse and patients' rights, the doctor qualified his comments by saying that "he would use something like the cattle prod only experimentally."

Some regression therapists like to call what they do "little work." You know, making patients little again. Much of this "little work," as seen in Missouri, Minnesota, Washington, California, Colorado, Oklahoma, and elsewhere, can be linked to another controversial name in this field—Jacqui Schiff, once a social worker in Virginia.

## Jacqui Schiff and Cathexis

In 1967 Jacqui Schiff turned her home into a care facility for severely disturbed young adults. A few years later she wrote a bestselling book—*All My Children.* In it, she chronicled how a young adult named Dennis became her adopted son, Aaron. Schiff had been seeing the young man in group and individual therapy for some time. One day he seemed very upset. Schiff's husband was present, and in the book Schiff describes what happened.

"Without another word, Dennis very quietly assumed a fetal position, cuddled into my lap, and attempted to nurse. We stared at him in astonishment. Both of us had been prepared for an outbreak of terrible anger. But Dennis's face was serene. Despite the beard, it was clearly the face of a baby of about nine months of age, a nursing infant." This event became a turning point for Schiff and her work.

Schiff's establishment grew as she took in more young adults to be reparented in this way, incorporating regression techniques into the setting. She referred to these young adults as "our babies." She wrote, "Now we put all our babies in diapers and feed them from bottles and let them sleep as much as they like."

Virginia authorities closed the place down in 1971 because the home was unlicensed and "endangered the health, safety, welfare, and lives of the patients." The Schiff facility moved to Alamo, California, where in 1972 an eighteen-year-old schizophrenic resident died after being placed in a bathtub of scalding water. He had been stripped naked, bound hand and foot, lowered into a very hot bath, and fatally burned.

Schiff's adopted son Aaron, who had become a therapist at the facility, pleaded guilty to a reduced charge of involuntary manslaughter, which was reduced even further to misdemeanor child abuse. One resident testified that she had been kept tied to a chair for six days and five nights. "They let me out twice to go to the bathroom," she said. She eventually managed to escape. When authorities refused to renew the license on the Alamo facility, Schiff moved to Oakland and set up the Cathexis Institute.

Jacqui Schiff was a member of the International Transactional Analysis Association (ITAA); to the dismay of some, within a few years her reparenting ideas had become accepted by the ITAA. In fact, in 1974, only two years after the scalding death just described, Jacqui and her son Aaron were given the Eric Berne Scientific Memorial Award. Before long, Schiff's reparenting theories became extremely popular among those who practice Transactional Analysis (TA), and study of the techniques was incorporated into TA training.

According to Alan Jacobs, a scholar and prominent ITAA member, "Schiff apparently believed that she had reached the point in her experience and knowledge about reparenting that her views and her judgment were unassailable." He quoted Schiff as having written, "My professional advisors offered no help; I was already beyond the range of their imagination."

However, all did not flow smoothly for Schiff, and eventually ITAA received an ethics complaint against her, after which she withdrew from the association. She went next to Bangalore, India, where she continued her reparenting practice, and later relocated in Great Britain. Through Cathexis-Europe, Schiff served as a consultant to reparenting programs in England, Germany, and the Netherlands.

Recently, the Schiffian method of reparenting gained notoriety in England. The local paper in Birmingham reported finding patients tied by lengths of rope to their therapists, crawling around on all fours making baby sounds; having to stand for hours, even overnight, in a corner; changing their names; and being denied telephone calls and mail. Patients were seen wearing disposable diapers, sucking their thumbs, and drinking from baby bottles, with some on a regime called "living room" in which the patient is kept in a room with another person until they have solved a "problem." In order to leave the room, a patient was required to be accompanied by another person no more than three feet away. Patients were encouraged to regard their therapists "as new and better parents, and to make open displays of physical affection towards them."

Reparenting techniques, despite this controversial history, are still widely used today. As recently as July 1995, Jacqui Schiff made an appearance at the ITAA conference in San Francisco, where she was given a warm reception and more than one hundred people waited in line to greet her and wish her well.

Not long ago, a California psychologist surveyed 267 reparenting therapists whose names were obtained from Cathexis Institute, New Directions in Education and Psychotherapy, and the ITAA newsletter. Eighty-six percent of the 267 reported using regressive work in their practices. Patients were being regressed to target ages of prenatal to thirteen years. The survey responses added up to some rather startling results, highlighted, in the table that follows.

**Regression Therapy at Work**

98  percent held their regressed clients

98  percent played with their regressed clients

88  percent fed their "young child" client

22  percent spanked their regressed clients

82  percent punished clients by having them stand in a corner

46  percent bathed them

48  percent admitted to doing "toileting work" with them

7  percent breast-fed clients

26  percent said sessions may be used inappropriately by the patient; in other words, some patients may become addicted to the process as an escape from adult problems, a place to hide rather than to grow

16  percent said patients' lowering their adult defenses and experiencing their younger child can lead to difficulty in their grown-up lives

15  percent reported patients developed unrealistic expectations about what their therapists can provide, including the illusion that the therapist will be the parent they never had, among other transference problems

34  percent were concerned about liability and the therapist's use of authority

16  percent were concerned about the use of physical restraint or confrontation

Few respondents mentioned the need for adequate training (a mere 3 percent), and only 1 percent mentioned the need for consultation or supervision.

# MATRIX IN MISSOURI

Matrix (also known as the Mid-America Training and Reparenting Institute, Inc.), a Kansas City psychotherapy institute, took up the reparenting-regression techniques popularized by Schiff. During lawsuits against the clinic, it was revealed that the clinic had a supply closet with stacks of adult diapers, a kitchen with baskets of bottle nipples, and a pantry full of baby food and Zwieback toast. Wherever one turned, there were bottle warmers, buckets of baby wipes, baby silverware, even a changing table! Handcuffs, ropes, and other physical restraints are also not uncommon sights in reparenting centers here and around the world.

Journalist Tom Jackman exposed Matrix in a series of articles in 1988. He described adult patients in the Kansas City facility sucking on pacifiers, eating baby food, and drinking from baby bottles, with therapists coddling patients as if they were babies. Much of the therapy was done by unlicensed psychotherapists. Not only schizophrenic patients were treated there.

Between 1988 and 1994 at least four legal cases were settled by the organization—all in favor of the former patients who were mistreated and abused. The cases and the allegations against the Matrix therapists were as follows:

1. *Charges: Negligence; breach of contract to provide competent profes-sional services; intentional or reckless infliction of emotional dis-tress. Settled out of court in 1994.* In this case, a woman in her freshman year of college away from home became depressed and had suicidal ideation. She sought therapy at Martix. Allegedly the therapists had regressed and hypnotized the patient "to the mind of an infant, bottle-feeding, breast-feeding her and becoming her surrogate mother with the effect of replacing her biological mother." The patient said she was induced to suck on the thera-pist's nipple and on nursing bottles, to change her name, to address one therapist as "Mommy" and another as "Aunt Gail," and to buy a teddy bear that the therapist sprayed with her per-fume as a reminder of her for the patient.

Among other charges were that the patient's "body was pinned to the floor and she was coerced to scream anger against her parents." On another occasion, the patient fractured her thumb when she was pushed to the floor by the therapist.

After several months of this regression therapy, the young woman was admitted to a hospital for being suicidal. She was returned to the therapy, and in about three months was rehospitalized for cutting herself on the arms, legs, and stomach with razors and scissors and beating herself with a belt. Further therapy ensued for a little under one year, at which point the therapists negligently terminated their relationship with the patient in violation of professional ethical principles, thereby allegedly triggering the patient's attempt to kill herself with a drug overdose.

> 2. *Charges: Fraudulent misrepresentation; intentional infliction of emotional distress; negligence; malpractice; negligent hiring and supervision. Settled out of court in 1989.* A couple sought consultation at Matrix about their teenage daughter. It was later determined that she was an ordinary teenager, not in need of psychotherapy, but by that time all four family members (the parents and their two daughters) had been induced to engage in reparenting therapy based on the diagnoses given them by an unlicensed therapist who repeatedly and falsely represented himself as licensed and as someone experienced in working with adolescents.

At one point the therapist falsely told the wife that her daughter's psychological problems were so serious that she may have to be "put into a group home." Later, the daughter was "wrongfully and with inadequate evaluation hospitalized for a so-called suicidal condition." The daughter was also encouraged and instructed by the therapists to move out of the family home.

The parents were wrongfully hypnotized on various occasions, were counseled to "distrust their own mental processes and to place their trust, belief, and reliance in direction and judgment of the defendants," and were subjected to "Game" therapy, "a form of physical, emotional and verbally abusive and demeaning interaction." The husband was told that he would suffer lifelong serious psychological problems unless he continued counseling with Matrix. Over time, the family had paid more than $12,000 to Matrix. (Matrix, by the way, was incorporated as a tax-exempt organization.)

3. *Charges: Negligent acts, errors, or omissions in professional services provided to plaintiffs; intentional or reckless infliction of emotional distress; negligent infliction of* mental *distress. Settled out of court in 1989.* The lead therapist in this case was an unlicensed practitioner who had been denied licensure in three states and, in a prior legal case, had been banned from holding himself out as a psychologist. His degree was in education, not psychology. He is also one of the four persons charged in the case just described.

A couple married twenty-seven years entered family therapy with their two teenage children. During the course of four years in therapy at Matrix, the family members received 1,051 therapy treatments, for which they paid close to $55,000. Divided equally, that would mean each family member went for therapy sixty-five times each year, more than once a week.

Each was subjected to hypnosis, reparenting, and regression, including being made to swing a batlike instrument against cushions. There was also improper touching by the therapist. Shortly after the first year, the wife was hospitalized for "increasing depression, erratic behavior, and suicidal thinking." She was put on antidepressants for the first time in her life and within days took an overdose of the pills because she felt betrayed by her therapist. During that year the wife lost twenty-eight pounds, her weight dropping to ninety-nine pounds. The therapist, who was counseling both husband and wife, directed the husband to file for divorce. As a result, the wife and two children lived in a motel. Meanwhile, the therapist instructed the wife to hospitalize the daughter for "not going to school and crying." During the course of therapy, the daughter, who'd originally been a B-average student, began doing less and less well, until she finally dropped out of high school.

Eventually, family members were alienated from one another, and the marriage and family broke up. Prior to going to Matrix, the family had not sought out therapy, nor had anyone experienced mental problems or emotional illness.

4. *Charges: Negligent acts, errors, or omissions in professional services provided to plaintiff; intentional or reckless infliction of emotional distress; negligent infliction of mental distress. Settled out of court in 1988.* A woman received a flier announcing an art workshop. When she called to inquire, she learned that the workshop was taught at Matrix and cost fifteen hundred dollars. Enrolled as a student training to be an art therapist, she was told that seventy-five sessions of psychotherapy were required. For this, she personally was billed nine thousand dollars and was seen by nine different people, six of whom were unlicensed. Additional claims were sent by Matrix to her insurance company for collection.

The young woman was "hypnotized, mesmerized, and regressed to the mind of a baby"; she was told that she was a paranoid schizophrenic. The male therapist had her suckle his nipples, and he had sexual contact with her, including fellatio, masturbation, and sexual intercourse.

The lawyer handling some of the Kansas City cases wrote us the following: "My lawsuits have shown it takes about six reparenting sessions to begin to bring about profound and pervasive changes in self-image, affect, cognition and behavior." These changes have been shown to be for the worse.

### The Case of Paul Lozano

Harvard medical student Paul Lozano committed suicide in April 1991 after being subjected to the regression-reparenting treatment of a Harvard psychiatrist, Dr. Margaret Bean-Bayog. At the end of his second year of medical school, Lozano sought treatment for depression and was seen by Bean-Bayog almost daily for the next four years.

Bean-Bayog had never before used regression therapy with any patient, but she set about regressing Lozano to the age of three: "We invented a baby version of him." At Bean-Bayog's suggestion, she and Lozano role-played during his therapy sessions: she would be the mother, he the three-year-old baby. With no proof, but latching onto another popular trend, Bean-Bayog concluded that Lozano must have been sexually abused by his mother as a child.

According to the records, Lozano had no history of abuse or mental illness before he entered Harvard Medical School. He said at one point that his so-called memories were brought forth by him "as a means of retaining Dr. Bean-Bayog's interest and affection."

After his death, two books and numerous articles on the case appeared. The dead student's family sued the psychiatrist and accused her of seducing Paul and driving him to suicide. Documentation of what transpired in the therapy was never wanting, as Bean-Bayog kept copious notes, written right after each session with Lozano also spoke with other psychiatrists after the reparenting therapy, and volumes of testimony were accumulated during the preparation for the lawsuit and for the license revocation hearing (which was aborted when Bean-Bayog relinquished her medical license). Additionally, fifty-five pages "describing the most graphic fantasies in Bean-Bayog's own handwriting were introduced as evidence."

There was some question about the kind and amount of sexual contact that had occurred between Bean-Bayog and Lozano. Dr. Willam Gault of the Newton-Wellesley Hospital, who was Paul Lozano's therapist subsequent to Paul's treatment with Bean-Bayog, was the first professional to be shown documentation of the reparenting therapy and the sexualized behavior that had occurred. Gault, referring to his talks with Paul, said: "Neither of us spelled out what we meant by sexual relations. . . . And if they did have sexual contact, I wouldn't think of that as having been one of the harmful things that happened. . . . The harm was in the therapy itself."

Gault wrote to the Massachusetts Board of Registration in Medicine: "[Bean-Bayog] told him [Lozano] not to communicate with family, and told and wrote him over and over that she was his mother, and that he was an infant. She sent him many children's books as gifts, as well as numerous cards and letters on which she said was his 'mom' and he was her little boy. He says she openly masturbated during some of the therapy sessions. . . . His course of treatment was improper. During the past five years his life and professional education have been severely disrupted."

Not only Gault but other therapists who saw Lozano during his hospitalizations were unanimous in saying that medication and sensible, supportive therapy were indicated in light of the depressive states Lozano experienced when he first sought therapy. They believed that the kind of emotional, intense, and off-beat treatment he was given was not in his interest.

## BORN-AGAIN THERAPY

A variation—some might consider it an offshoot—of reparenting is the idea of rebirthing. These therapeutic schemes are organized around the birth process itself. Rebirthing therapists offer clients the idea that in ordinary human birth there is trauma, especially trauma around breathing. Some of these therapists have concocted rebirthing, which is a method of teaching patients to imagine going through the birth process in order to learn "proper breathing." Patients are told that the traumas of ordinary birth, suffered by us all, can be cured in this manner.

### The Origins of Rebirthing

Leonard Orr, generally regarded as the founder of modern-day rebirthing, developed his theories by spending considerable time in a bathtub having "revelations." In 1974 he began to suspend friends in a redwood hot tub with snorkels and nose plugs. During these immersions, many of them began to get in touch with (as they said back then) certain of their own destructive behavioral patterns. A number of them said they experienced their own birth during the process. As

Orr and his friends introduced it to others, rebirthing as a therapy began to spread.

After a time, Orr apparently came to realize that his very presence was an important part of the rebirthing event. He attributed this to the belief that he had released enough of his own birth trauma that other people felt safe to experience theirs with him in the hot tub. About a year later, Orr began working with the breathing pattern he felt happened at birth, but this time without using a hot tub. It then became apparent to him that it was the "rebirther" (that is, the person leading the session) and the method of breathing that were important, not so much the warm water.

Here's the theory in a nutshell: damage is done to the breathing mechanism at birth because the child is cut off from its supply of oxygen through the premature cutting of the umbilical cord. This initial panic ("breathe or die") remains in the person's subconscious as a nameless fear. The goal of the rebirthing process is to get the person to release this long-held tension and learn to take advantage of the fully functioning breathing mechanism. Once accomplished, the person can lead a full, happy, breathy life.

Rebirthing takes an average of three to ten two-hour sessions. Initially, rebirthees were promised both dramatic life changes and subtle feelings of contentment. Later, rebirthing was purported to bring on "permanent changes. . . . [It] releases deep body tension and thought patterns . . . [causes] spontaneous remission of diseases, and just about every disease, from chronic lower back pain to cancer, has been released." Psychic abilities are supposed to increase and expand, not to mention that rebirthing wards off common colds and allergy attacks.

People have been rebirthed in ordinary home tubs in blue bubble-bath solutions, and in outdoor redwood hot tubs under starry skies. Others, like Rose at the beginning of this chapter, have succumbed to "dry rebirths," being rolled into a carpet on the floor and made to struggle to free themselves in order to "reexperience the birth process." Some have been wrapped in a series of blankets and rebirthed on an office couch.

One certified hypnotherapist who advertises on the Internet describes rebirthing as a form of hypnotherapy and as a "patterned breathing process which allows you to access and resolve blocks that are held in the body." Without qualifiers, she asserts that hypnotherapy is safe, and a trance state is a natural and familiar state, and that it can benefit you. She states that the technique of rebirthing combined with hypnotherapy will work for dealing with compulsive behavior, weight problems, anxiety, and phobias; that it will heal the child within related to abuse, abandonment, self-esteem, and improved relationships; that it will reduce stress and improve concentration; that it will improve health, pain, cancer, and chronic illnesses; that it will elevate performance in selling, communication skills, sports, dance, and art.

As far as we can tell, rebirthing is magic.

## MAJOR LEADERS IN REBIRTHING

Sondra Ray and Bob Mandel are two big names in the rebirthing field. Their organization, previously called Loving Relationships Training, has recently taken on the new name Association of Rebirth Trainings International. Weekend sessions described as "educational and experiential" cost between $275 and $300. Participants are told that not only will they experience two rebirths during the weekend, but also "you will be helped to locate and release any negative decisions you may have made at your birth and which are still affecting your current life."

Sondra Ray, once a student of Leonard Orr, describes her own birth in this way: "When I was in the womb, I tried to communicate to my mother that I wanted to be born at home." She had also tried to communicate to her delivery team. Her mother heard her, she says, and she was born at home. The only problem was that Sondra was born on the kitchen table, to which she attributes her lifelong neurosis about food.

Bob Mandel, Ray's coauthor, describes his birth, too. His birth was "normal," he writes, but he mentions having been born in a Jewish hospital with Father Divine nurses assisting: "This might explain some of my religious confusion later in life, and my unending quest for my personal divinity."

In Ray and Mandel's book, a chapter is devoted to every imaginable type of birth: premature or late, unwanted, fast or held back, cesarean, wrong sex, induced, breech, forceps—you get the picture. The authors enumerate what they view as typical traits of those who were birthed in a particular way. For example, in the chapter on unwanted, unplanned, and illegitimate births, they suggest that if that's how you were born, then you may be addicted to rejection, or you may reject everyone who wants to be with you, or you may work to avoid being rejected by making yourself indispensable.

Stereotyping people and giving them all the same simple solutions seems to be a major characteristic of many of the odd therapies that have emerged over the years. Regression, reparenting, and rebirthing therapies fall on a narrow path. The innovators found themselves doing something: sitting in a hot tub, berating patients, or feeding them out of baby bottles. It felt good or worked for the therapists, so they made some assumptions in order to create an ideology that would support practicing the method on others. Without much thought, and little or no proof, the technique was expanded to become a "cure-all" for all people.

An additional factor that tends to make a risky situation worse is that some forms of therapy—which initially might gain support as "a breakthrough," "creative," or "innovative"—are not inspected critically by the professional community. Instead, these therapies are allowed to harm a number of patients until the courts are asked to evaluate the conduct of the therapists, the rationality of the therapy, and the extent of the damage done. Sometimes public inspection or legal redress never occurs, and the therapies continue to be promoted for decades, as we've seen here, with the ongoing potential for outlandish or disastrous consequences.

Despite the widespread continuing use of regression techniques over the years, there are still only anecdotal tales to support any of the massive regressions described here (with the one exception of the outside study of the Rosen sample, which showed that the actual patient outcomes were contrary to what Rosen claimed).

Age regression, reparenting, and rebirthing are not proven helpful techniques. There is no scientifically established or objective clinical evidence showing them to be beneficial. So be careful! Think twice before going backwards.

## 23.

# Controversies about Antidepressants and the Promotion of Evidence-Based Treatment Alternatives for Depression

*Brandon A. Gaudiano, PhD*
*Gary Epstein-Lubow, MD*
Brown Medical School & Butler Hospital

The selective serotonin reuptake inhibitors (SSRIs) are a class of antidepressant medications that emerged onto the psychiatric scene in the 1990s. Their arrival was heralded as a modern drug miracle due to their putative efficacy and safety relative to earlier medications. Initial unbridled enthusiasm and aggressive industry marketing have made SSRIs among the most widely prescribed medications today—psychiatric or otherwise (IMS 2003). In fact, antidepressant prescribing in relation to a diagnosis of depression increased 147.5 percent in the United States from 1990 to 1998, an effect driven mainly by the SSRIs (Skaer et al. 2000). Over the past several years, the media increasingly have highlighted controversial data suggesting that SSRIs are not as efficacious as once hoped (Gaudiano & Herbert 2003) and that they may carry their own potentially lethal safety risks (Sharp & Chapman 2004). In addition, there has been a dramatic rise in public interest in and use of

Reprinted with permission from *Scientific Review of Mental Health Practice* (May 2005).

unconventional medical practices for depression since the 1990s (Bongiorno 2005; Eisenberg et al. 1998). The current heightened media coverage about the dangers of SSRIs is potentially confusing to the public and leaves them vulnerable to nontraditional medicine and mental health practitioners who promote scientifically questionable and potentially harmful treatments. It is unfortunate that evidence-based treatment alternatives for depression, such as effective psychotherapies, frequently have been given short shrift in the debate. In this chapter, we will review the research behind the antidepressant efficacy and safety concerns, analyze the media's coverage of these controversies, and discuss the implications for evidence-based treatment alternatives for depression.

## CONTROVERSIES SURROUNDING ANTIDEPRESSANT EFFICACY

Increasing evidence suggests that the placebo response in clinical trials of antidepressant medications is substantial and has been growing over the past two decades (Walsh et al. 2002). Such data have led to much debate within the psychiatric community regarding the development and implementation of improved methodologies to ascertain the specific efficacy of antidepressants (Gaudiano & Herbert 2005; Klein et al. 2002; Moncrieff 2001). In order to examine the complex issues involved in evaluating antidepressant effects, however, the placebo concept itself first must be clearly understood.

## THE PLACEBO AND ITS EFFECTS

The term *placebo* comes from the Latin phrase meaning "I shall please" (Shapiro & Shapiro 1997). Its use in medicine began in the nineteenth century, when "placebo" referred to practices offered merely to placate patients and not cure them. By the mid-twentieth century, the double-blind randomized controlled trial became the "gold standard" for evaluating the efficacy of investigational drugs. In this context, "placebos" began referring to the inert substances used to separate the active biochemical effects of medications from those produced by expectancy and other extraneous factors (Leber 2000). Although various definitions of medical placebos have been offered over the years, Shapiro and Shapiro provided a useful description:

> A placebo is any therapy (or that component of any therapy) that is intentionally or knowingly used for its nonspecific, psychological, or psychophysiological, therapeutic effect, or that is used for a presumed specific therapeutic effect on a patient, symptom, or illness but is without specific activity for the condition being treated. (p. 41)

In other words, a placebo can refer to an intentionally or unintentionally inert treatment provided by a practitioner. A placebo treatment is differentiated from the *placebo effect*, which refers to the "nonspecific psychological or psychophysiological therapeutic effect produced by a placebo" (ibid.). Although the placebo effect can be conceptualized more broadly or narrowly, general factors thought to be related to improvement after administration of a placebo include patients' and physicians' expectancies for improvement and the general benefits proffered by a supportive relationship and therapeutic setting (Frank & Frank 1993; Shapiro & Shapiro 1997).

In his classic paper "The Powerful Placebo," Beecher (1955) estimated that placebos benefit approximately 30–40 percent of patients. Although the subject of some recent debate (Hróbjartsson & Gøtzsche 2001), a convergence of evidence suggests the benefits of placebo treatments for a wide range of medical conditions, including asthma, pain, postoperative wound recovery, headache, nausea, and even surgical procedures such as arthroscopic knee surgery (Benedetti, Maggi & Lopiano 2003; Kirsch & Scoboria 2001; Moseley et al. 2002; Wampold et al. 2005). Furthermore, placebo response rates vary as a function of the expectancy produced by the treatment, with known brand names, administration via injection, larger pill sizes, and higher "doses" producing increased effects (see for a review, Kirsch 2005).

# ANTIDEPRESSANTS VERSUS INERT PILL PLACEBOS

In recent years, perhaps nowhere has the placebo response attracted more scrutiny than in antidepressant trials. Some critics have questioned the assumption that antidepressants are specifically efficacious for the conditions they are being used to treat (Antonuccio et al. 1999; Fava et al. 2003; Gaudiano & Herbert 2005; R. P. Greenberg et al. 1992; Moncrieff 2001). For example, Kirsch and Sapirstein (1998) conducted a meta-analysis of nineteen antidepressant trials with adult patients and found that inert pill placebos reproduced 75 percent of the improvement associated with the active medication. Furthermore, the study found a high correlation between drug and placebo response rates, and a substantial therapeutic effect from active drugs that are not typically considered antidepressants. These results support the argument that expectancy plays a key role in improvement associated with antidepressant treatment.

Although heavily criticized on methodological and conceptual grounds (see for a detailed critique Klein 1998), Kirsch, Moore, Scoboria, and Nicholls (2002) later published a replication of earlier results using the Food and Drug Administration database of antidepressant trials that includes unpublished studies. Results of this meta-analysis showed an even less robust drug effect, with placebo accounting for approximately 82 percent of the improvement. More specifically, the drug effect represented only an approximately two-point improvement on the commonly used Hamilton Rating Scale for Depression. Although a statistically significant difference, Kirsch et al. questioned its clinical relevance. Other meta-analyses examining different sets of studies have shown similar results (e.g., R. P. Greenberg et al. 1994). Although the exact placebo-antidepressant difference varies from study to study, most researchers today agree that the placebo effect is associated with a substantial proportion of the improvement observed in antidepressant trials, often making it exceedingly difficult to demonstrate the efficacy of antidepressants (Charney et al. 2002).

Findings have been even less sanguine in antidepressant trials with depressed children and adolescents. Early trials of tricyclic antidepressants with this population showed poor response rates coupled with potentially lethal health risks (Gadow 1992). Recently, the American College of Neuropsychopharmacology (ACNP 2004) reviewed both published and unpublished data from fifteen randomized controlled trials of SSRIs in the treatment of childhood depression and concluded that fluoxetine, sertraline, paraoxetine, citalopram, and nefazodone are efficacious for children under age eighteen. However, these conclusions were based on the finding that the aforementioned medications had at least one positive clinical trial, regardless of whether or not other trials failed replicate the effects. It is sometimes argued by antidepressant proponents that trials failing to replicate drug-placebo differences contain "assay sensitivity" problems, such that methodological weaknesses produce an inability to demonstrate superiority over placebo (Klein 2000). However, such arguments have been criticized as representing a fundamental derailment of the scientific process, as it is assumed that there is a drug-placebo difference prior to the study even being conducted (Gaudiano & Herbert 2005; Otto & Nierenberg 2002). Other independent reviews of SSRI trials using child samples have reached conclusions different from those of the ACNP report (e.g., Whittington et al. 2004). In general, meta-analyses have suggested weak and inconsistent benefits for SSRIs over placebo for children and adolescents, with only fluoxetine showing reasonable support of efficacy at this time (see for a review, Kendall, Pilling & Whittington 2005).

One explanation for the superiority of antidepressants over inert placebos shown in some clinical trials is that these drugs are specifically efficacious in treating depression due to their unique biochemical properties. However, some critics assert that even when a reliable antidepressant-placebo difference is found, factors other than the drugs' chemical constituents are likely to be playing a substantial, if not complete, role in the results (Kirsch & Sapirstein 1998; Moncrieff & Kirsch 2005). The amount of improvement shown in patients treated with antidepressants is influenced by a number of methodological and statistical factors, including attrition rate, type of statistical analysis employed (e.g., intent to treat versus completer analyses), choice of outcome measure (e.g., categorical versus continuous), and sample size (Fava et al. 2003; Gaudiano & Herbert 2005; Klein et al. 2002; Moncrieff 2001). In addition, problems with financial conflicts of interest have led some to suspect the influence of "allegiance effects," referring to the observation that results of clinical trials often conform to the preexisting beliefs of the investigators (Luborsky et al. 1999). For example, research has demonstrated that industry funding and competing financial interests predict favorable study results (independent of methodological quality) (Kjaergard & Als-Nielsen 2002), with effects demonstrated specifically in antidepressant research (Baker et al. 2003). Also, it is an underappreciated fact that antidepressant trials often fail to demonstrate the superiority of the investigational agent, even for FDA-approved medications (Khan, Khan & Brown 2002). The commonly found null results in these clinical trials contribute to the "file-drawer problem," or the tendency for nonsignificant findings to be left unpublished and therefore hidden from public knowledge (Rosenthal 1979). This phenomenon can result in an incomplete knowledge database for evaluating medication efficacy in systematic reviews (Melander et al. 2003). Thus, any meta-analytic review of antidepressant trials is likely to be an *overestimate* of efficacy if it does not include methodologically sound but unpublished data as well.

## ANTIDEPRESSANT SIDE EFFECTS, UNBLINDING IN CLINICAL TRIALS, AND "ACTIVE" PLACEBOS

Another potentially confounding factor in antidepressant trials is related to the underlying theoretical assumptions of such investigations. The logic of the placebo-controlled trial is one of an additive model, at least in theory (Kirsch 2000; Wampold et al. 2005). Although natural recovery may account for some improvement, no treatment conditions in clinical trials are inadequate controls, because they do not eliminate factors associated with a placebo response (e.g., expectancy). Therefore, clinical trials require that the active medication be shown to produce an additive effect above and beyond the improvement produced by the administration of an intentional placebo treatment. In other words, the medication's effect is calculated by subtracting it from the placebo treatment's effect. This additive model relies on an important assumption—that the double-blind is never broken and, therefore, that neither the patient nor the physician can distinguish between the treatment conditions. The experimental manipulation in antidepressant trial is assumed to be the specific chemical constituents of the investigational agent. However, if the double-blind in antidepressant trials is broken, then the effects may no longer conceptually be additive, as the placebo condition will cease to control for all nonbiochemical factors related to improvement. Knowledge of treatment assignment could result in the medication and placebo treatments producing their effects through different mechanisms of action, as attributions for improvement would likely be dissimilar.

Antidepressants such as the tricyclics are associated with anticholinergic side effects, including dry mouth, constipation, blurred vision, urinary retention, and even delirium. Several authors have argued that unblinding is a major concern in antidepressant trials due to the telltale side effects produced by all antidepressants (R. P. Greenberg et al. 1992; Kirsch et al. 2002; Moncrieff 2001). A variety of evidence supports the notion that detectable side effects represent a genuine methodological concern in antidepressant trials. Research has found that patients and clinicians often can guess the randomized condition above chance accuracy (Bystritsky & Waikar 1994; White et al. 1992). Furthermore, detectable side effects have been shown to be an issue not only with older classes of antidepressants, but with the newer SSRIs as well (Piasecki et al. 2002). Although some have questioned whether correct guessing of treatment condition is in actuality an artifact of clinical improvement rather than side effects, research has shown that unblinding is at least partially independent of therapeutic effect (Basoglu et al. 1997). Unfortunately, most antidepressant trials do not report the integrity of the blind or even assess it in the first place (Petkova et al. 2000).

A further piece of evidence suggesting problems with unblinding comes from early research done using "active" placebos. An active placebo is a therapeutically inert substance that contains active agents that mimic the side effects of antidepressants. For example, the drug atropine, a muscarinic antagonist, has been used as an active placebo due to its ability to produce the anticholinergic side effects found with tricyclics (Moncrieff 2001). As part of a Cochrane Review report, Moncrieff, Wessely, and Hardy (2001) conducted a meta-analysis of nine early active placebo-controlled antidepressant trials. They found that only two out of nine of the trials reported superiority of the antidepressant. Further, the pooled effect size difference between active placebo and antidepressant was small and not significantly different from zero. As these early antidepressant trials often possessed methodological limitations (e.g., small sample sizes), Moncrieff et al. also examined the association between the effect size difference and the quality of the study. Interestingly, study quality was inversely correlated with outcome, such that methodologically superior trials tended to show the smallest differences between active placebo and drug. These data suggest that less of an antidepressant effect is shown in studies using active versus inert placebos, further supporting the notion that unblinding may result in differing placebo response rates due to expectancy effects. However, as the quality and number of such studies is limited, only new data from well-designed active placebo trials will be able to clarify these issues. Unfortunately, we are not aware that any such studies are being conducted or planned.

## CONTROVERSIES SURROUNDING ANTIDEPRESSANT SAFETY

Questions surrounding the efficacy of antidepressants are not necessarily new, but neither are concerns over their safety. As is the case with any medication, antidepressants are associated with potentially lethal side effects, requiring their use to be closely supervised by a medical professional. Although systematic reviews have not suggested that SSRIs are more efficacious than their historical counterparts (Geddes et al. 2000), one oft-promoted advantage of SSRIs is their safety relative to earlier medications (Kasper, Fuger & Moller 1992). However, over the years there have been many reports of underappreciated side effects that have raised concerns about the safety of SSRIs, some of which are well supported (e.g., discontinuation syndrome, Lejoyeux & Ades 1997) and others debatable (e.g., safety in pregnancy/breastfeeding, Gentile 2005). A concern about a possible suicidality "side effect" of antidepressants has become one of the most hotly contested issues recently.

### Antidepressant-Suicidality Link in Adults

Fears of a suicide effect emerged in 1990, when Teicher and colleagues (1990) reported that six patients without a prior history of suicidality developed intense suicidal preoccupation after beginning treatment with fluoxetine. The authors suggested that akathisia (i.e., an agitation syndrome that is sometimes produced by SSRIs) was related to the emergence of suicidal ideation in these patients. Other case reports later emerged describing a similar phenomenon.

However, antidepressant proponents largely dismissed these early published reports due to their small sample sizes and the uncontrolled nature of the data. In addition, they argued that epidemiological studies failed to show an association between increased antidepressant use and a rise in suicide rates (Healy 2003). Earlier meta-analyses of antidepressant trials did not provide much cause for concern either. For example, Kahn and colleagues (2000) conducted a meta-analysis of the FDA database of adult antidepressant trials to investigate rates of suicide risk relative to placebo. Results failed to show a statistically significant difference between placebo, antidepressant, and active comparator conditions.

David Healy has been one of the most controversial and outspoken critics of antidepressants. Using somewhat different methodology than Kahn et al. (2000) by separating suicidal acts occurring during placebo treatment from those during the placebo washout phase, Healy (2003) reported that the rates of suicide attempt or completion were significantly higher with SSRIs compared to placebo. Odds ratios suggested that suicidal behavior was over twice as likely to occur in those receiving antidepressants. More recently, Fergusson and colleagues (2005) conducted a meta-analysis of antidepressant trials for depression, anxiety, and neurosis from the Medline and Cochrane Collaboration registries. Results, which were based on analyses of over eighty-seven thousand patients, showed a twofold greater risk of attempted suicide in the antidepressant group, which the authors concluded poses a significant public health concern even though the absolute risk remained relatively low. Still, conclusions in adult samples remain tentative at this point as other meta-analyses using different datasets have found equivocal or contradictory findings (e.g., Gunnell, Saperia & Ashby 2005). The FDA recently has undertaken a systematic study of this topic and will issue a full report after their investigation is completed.

### Antidepressant-Suicidality Link in Children and Adolescents

Although conclusions regarding an antidepressant-suicidality effect in adult clinical trials remain debatable, this effect has been much more widely acknowledged in child and adolescent studies since the emergence of compelling data. In December of 2003, the United Kingdom's Medicines and Healthcare Products Regulatory Agency (MHRA) issued a report warning that the SSRIs citalopram, escitalopram, paroxetine, and sertraline and the related drug venlafaxine were contraindicated in the treatment of depression in children under the age of eighteen due to unfavorable risk-benefit ratios (Duff 2003). Fluoxetine was excluded from this warning, although some have criticized this decision (see Kendall et al. 2005). The MHRA's conclusions were based on a systematic review of randomized controlled trials (RCTs) of these antidepressants in child and adolescent samples. Results of the MHRA's internal regulatory review showed that the SSRIs generally were not efficacious for this population, and further were associated with an increased risk of suicidal thinking and behavior in the studies.

In the United States, the FDA undertook a similar study to investigate the efficacy and safety of SSRIs and atypical antidepressants in individuals under eighteen (FDA 2004b). Although the FDA also concluded that there was little support for the efficacy of the antidepressants studied, their conclusions were more tentative than those of the MHRA's report, citing insufficient data. After conducting a blinded reclassification of suicidal events in the RTCs, results showed a 71 percent increased risk of suicidality (i.e., ideation/self-harm) and a 134 percent increased risk of hostility and agitation relative to placebo in these trials. Other independent systematic reviews have reached similar conclusions (Jureidini et al. 2004; Whittington et al. 2004). These findings led the FDA to issue "blackbox" warnings for SSRIs that now describe the possibility of increased suicidality in juveniles (FDA 2004a).

One question arises from the findings of serious adverse events in antidepressant trials: Why are such data coming to light only now? Several factors may have contributed to this problem. First, RCTs typically are designed to detect drug-placebo differences, and they are known to underestimate the likelihood of serious adverse events (Lasser et al. 2002). It is important to consider that absolute rates of completed suicide and self-harm in antidepressants trials are quite low, requiring the examination of datasets that include large numbers of patients in order for sufficient statistical power to be available to detect differences between conditions. Similar problems have been widely publicized recently regarding newly discovered adverse events associated with hormone replacement therapy for postmenopausal women and certain anti-inflammatory drugs for arthritis.

A second factor contributing to a delay in identifying increased suicidality with antidepressants relative to placebo is that the specific mechanism of action has been unclear. As discussed, many have suggested that the SSRIs produce agitation in some patients that has been linked to suicidality (Healy 2003). However, as antidepressant trials were not designed to examine a suicidality effect, further data are needed to rule out other potential moderators or mediators, such as methodological flaws in the studies themselves, incomplete recording of adverse events, unknown patient characteristics, early symptomatic improvement, differential expectancy, or some combination of these variables that could contribute to the adverse events observed.

Finally, a further cause for the delayed warning of a suicidality concern may be industry bias and financial disincentives. Based on their meta-analysis of antidepressant trials for childhood depression, Jureidini et al. (2004) asserted that: "In discussing their own data, the authors of all of the four larger [antidepressant] studies have exaggerated the benefits, downplayed the harms, or both" (p. 881). These critics point out that the authors of several of the large childhood antidepressant trials have been inconsistent in reporting their results, sometimes changing the primary outcome measure after failing to find an effect as originally hypothesized. Increasing recognition of how industry bias is affecting the validity of data has led to recent changes in the reporting and publishing of clinical trials, such as the policy requiring that only pre-registered clinical trials will be published by certain medical journals (Fontanarosa, Flanagin & DeAngelis 2005).

## SUMMARY OF FINDINGS

To briefly review the evidence presented thus far, pooled data from numerous clinical trials suggest that there is a small but detectable difference between antidepressants and inert pill placebos. The exact magnitude of this effect varies from study to study due to methodological differences. Furthermore, evidence from trials using "active" placebos suggests that at least a proportion of this drug-placebo difference may be explained by discrepancies in patient expectancy, possibly due to unblinding in relation to side effects. In addition to questions of efficacy, antidepressants have been shown to be associated with increased suicidality relative to placebo in clinical trials. At this time, a suicidality effect has conclusively been demonstrated only in studies involving children and adolescents. Although many postulate that a drug-produced agitation syndrome is to blame, there currently is no clear explanation. However, observed effects on suicidal behavior are relatively small, and therefore were not fully appreciated until data from numerous trials were combined. Nevertheless, such findings suggest that regulatory agencies must consider the potential negative influence of industry bias in drug trials and develop tougher scrutiny and tighter control.

# MEDIA COVERAGE: HELPING OR HYPING?

It is clear from the preceding discussion that the controversies involving antidepressants are complex and nuanced, often requiring sophisticated knowledge of psychopharmacology, clinical trial methodology, inferential statistics, psychopathology, and the placebo effect, to name just a few areas. As questions concerning antidepressant efficacy and safety are quite provocative and of high public health significance, it should come as no surprise that these issues have garnered their fair share of mass media coverage (i.e., print, television, radio, Internet) over the past few years. Unfortunately, the quality of this media coverage has been quite variable. Poor-quality media coverage of the antidepressant controversies poses significant challenges for efforts aimed at informing the public of concerns, while simultaneously acknowledging the tentative nature of the conclusions.

## Media Coverage of the Antidepressant Controversies

The media can act as an incredibly useful and powerful source of information for consumers, and many medical journalists provide reports that are a public service. Nevertheless, medical reporting frequently has been plagued by inaccuracies and sensationalism. For example, research suggests that the media exaggerate the benefits and downplay the potential harms of medications (Moynihan et al. 2000), fail to adequately report conflicts of interest and bias (Zuckerman 2003), sensationalize health risks (Rowe, Frewer & Sjoberg 2000), overemphasize preliminary and pilot data (Schwartz, Woloshin & Baczek 2002), possess inadequate training in science and research issues (Entwistle 1995), and fail to adequately publicize retracted or invalid findings previously reported (Rada 2005). Frequently cited obstacles to accurate journalism include lack of time to properly investigate the topic, space to explain the issues involved, and knowledge of science and medicine (Larsson et al. 2003).

Over the past few years, the media have been widely publicizing controversies about antidepressant medications. Sharp and Chapman (2004) reported that a LexisNexis (www.lexisnexis.com) search of major news sources showed a 252 percent increase in stories discussing antidepressants and suicide between 2002 and 2003, with a similarly large increase during the beginning of 2004 (when the review was conducted). We conducted an expanded LexisNexis search for articles in major newspapers and magazines that contained the words "suicide" and "antidepressants" from 1995 through August 2005. Results show a 458 percent increase in news coverage from 2003 to 2004, the approximate time that the MRHA and FDA issued their SSRI-suicidality warnings.

Sharp and Chapman (2004) also conducted a qualitative review of a randomly selected sample of 48 percent ($n = 10$) of the major news articles identified between January and March of 2004. They evaluated several criteria to assess the quality of the reporting. Most articles showed evidence of bias and sensationalism when reporting the potential antidepressant-suicide link. Although half of the articles acknowledged the tentative nature of the conclusions and discussed contradictory viewpoints, the information absent from the articles was perhaps more important. Only one article provided specific information about monitoring for warning signs in those taking antidepressants. Furthermore, none of the articles reviewed provided a discussion of evidence-based nonpharmacologic treatments for depression. These findings suggest that media coverage has largely focused on safety concerns, but then has failed to provide adequate information about safe and effective treatment alternatives.

## Media Influence and the Potential for a Nocebo Effect?

One important question is whether this heightened media coverage of antidepressant concerns is likely to affect the public's perceptions and behaviors. In general, research suggests that the media can have a substantial influence on health behaviors. For example, a Cochrane review of five relevant studies by Grilli, Ramsay, and Minozzi (2002) showed that mass-media campaigns have a significant influence on healthcare utilization, clinical practice, and research interest in the direction of the position taken (favorable or unfavorable). In what Zuckerman (2003) calls "checkbook science," drug industry claims about antidepressant efficacy historically have been accepted at face value without a proper examination of the quality of the data supplied to support their claims. For years, early media presentations of antidepressants have touted their "wonder drug" status and ability to improve everything from one's personality to emotional problems in a pet (Montagne 2001). However, media coverage is a type of "double-edged sword," and it can easily influence public perception negatively as well as positively. For example, Einarson and colleagues (2005) conducted interviews of callers at a women's information center following public health advisories warning of potential adverse events related to antidepressant use during pregnancy. They found that the media messages caused high levels of anxiety in the women. In addition, misunderstandings about the recommendations from the advisories resulted in some women discontinuing their medications inappropriately.

Most recent coverage of the antidepressants has been characterized by decidedly negative and overly alarmist copy. In fact, a sea change can be witnessed in media representations of antidepressants relative to the early stories touting antidepressants' benefits. Examples of recent provocative headlines concerning antidepressant-suicidality links in major newspapers include "Student, 19, in Trial of New Antidepressant Commits Suicide," "A Suicide Effect? What Parents Aren't Being Told about Their Kids' Antidepressants," "Seroxat and Prozac 'Can Make People Homicidal,'" and "Antidepressant Makers Withhold Data on Children." The current barrage of media coverage on antidepressants has probably played a role in the current sharp downtrend in antidepressant prescribing for children (Vendantam 2005).

In addition, media descriptions of placebo response rates with antidepressant frequently convey an inaccurate impression to the public suggesting that placebos and the drugs are equivalent in efficacy (Gaudiano & Herbert 2003). In a *Washington Post* article, Vedantam (2002) writes: "After thousands of studies, hundreds of millions of prescriptions and tens of billions of dollars in sales, two things are certain about pills that treat depression: Antidepressants like Prozac, Paxil and Zoloft work. And so do sugar pills" (p. A01). As noted earlier, although the effects are smaller than many might expect, pooled data show that antidepressants are often more effective than inert pill placebos. Furthermore, it is unlikely that the placebo effect would be as strong if not for the power of expectancies produced in these trials.

It is well known that positive expectancies can produce improvements in the absence of an efficacious treatment, but less attention has been given to when treatments produce iatrogenic or harmful effects. The *nocebo* (Latin meaning "I will harm") *effect* occurs when an inert substance or procedure produces a negative outcome (Barsky et al. 2002). On average, 20 percent of patients receiving a medical placebo report adverse side effects (Rosenzweig, Brohier & Zipfel 1993). The mass media have been implicated as an important source of erroneous public beliefs about medications that foster negative expectancies (Barsky et al. 2002). Such phenomena raise the disquieting possibility that a nocebo response could result from media coverage overhyping antidepressants as ineffective or unsafe (Gaudiano & Herbert 2003). An interesting example of a nocebo response due to changing treatment expectancies can be found in a recent antidepressant trial investigating brain changes related to improvement (Leuchter et al. 2002). The lead investigator reported that the majority of placebo responders in the trial relapsed almost immediately after being unblinded upon study completion (Reid 2002; Vendantam 2002). Physicians must consider that media coverage sensationalizing the problems with antidepressants may provoke negative reactions in some patients currently being treated successfully with medications for their depression.

# WHERE HAVE ALL THE EMPIRICALLY SUPPORTED TREATMENTS FOR DEPRESSION GONE?

Although there are examples of credible reporting, health information presented in the mass media often is deficient. Critics have argued that media representations of antidepressant controversies frequently raise concerns but then fail to provide adequate guidance as to what individuals suffering from depression can or should do (Gaudiano & Herbert 2003; Sharp & Chapman 2004). We would argue that biased and sensationalistic media coverage of antidepressant controversies has the potential to create a "treatment vacuum" by fostering public confusion and ignorance. What will fill the void? Will practitioners and the public gravitate toward empirically informed treatment alternatives for depression in the wake of the antidepressant controversies, or will the ineffective and potentially harmful interventions being aggressively promoted by some be the true beneficiaries?

## The Landscape of Medicine and Public Interest in Nontraditional Treatments

Prior to describing the alternatives to antidepressant medications and the most recommended options, it is important to consider the social context in which treatments for depression have been developed and used in medicine. For centuries, the manner in which to provide medical care has been a topic of much debate. In the modern era, beginning in the middle of the nineteenth century, the American Medical Association (AMA) has lobbied for empirically based treatments and strict guidelines to delineate the requirements for medical education and the parameters within which clinicians should practice. In the early 1900s, the AMA supported Abraham Flexner in his production of "The Flexner Report" (Flexner 1910), a detailed document of all US medical schools in existence at that time. Flexner's report examined the entrance requirements and resources, including endowment, faculty, and facilities, at each medical school and made specific recommendations regarding the continuation of only those medical schools meeting the highest standards. By the 1930s, this report was generally supported by governmental agencies and major medical institutions, encouraging the development of science-based medical training programs. Of course, the report also negatively affected some individuals in medical disciplines. For example, programs in rural areas and medical schools dedicated primarily to the training of African American physicians suffered and were forced to close. In addition, the AMA's lobbying and the widespread acceptance of the Flexner Report had deleterious effects on "non-scientific" training programs in homeopathy and botanical medicine (A. H. Beck, 2004). Nonetheless, the momentum toward increased rigor in medical training and practice led to an increasingly evidence-based and scientific practice of contemporary medicine.

The same social forces that promoted modern medicine may also have contributed to some of its shortcomings, with psychiatry's overreliance on antidepressant medication being one example. An explanation of some factors driving modern psychiatric treatments may be found in the academic field of medical anthropology, which has spent over forty years working to elucidate the effects of social forces on the practice of medicine. In a recent review, Hemmings (2005) identified several shortcomings of modern medical practices, some of which are directly relevant to contemporary debate about the treatment of depression. For instance, "scientific medicine emphasizes technological fixes rather than psychosocial interventions" (ibid.), suggesting a bias toward the use of medication despite established efficacious non-pharmacological treatments. Further, Hemmings suggests that "medicine has lost focus on the person and their experience of illness . . . [and medicine] responds inadequately to patients' need to find meaning" (ibid.).

It is becoming increasingly apparent that treatments for depression be aimed at bolstering patients' sense of meaning and purpose, decreasing hopelessness, and improving the relationship between patients, families, and clinicians (Schulz & Patterson 2004). Efforts toward these goals in contemporary medicine, including psychiatry, may be less than adequate. There are multiple barriers to effective depression treatment, including public stigma about mental illness, the failure of the primary care medical system to recognize and to provide effective treatment for depressed patients, and the lack of financial incentives to provide services other than medication in the current reimbursement climate (Pincus et al. 2003). Although the evidence base for specific psychotherapies and some health behaviors continues to grow, primary care clinicians and contemporary psychiatrists do not receive education and information about non-pharmacological treatments for depression on par with antidepressant medications (Luhrmann 2000; Pincus & McQueen 1996). Emphasis on teaching psychotherapy to psychiatrists has been increasing, but it is unrealistic to expect trainees to develop competency in the practice of diverse psychotherapies (Yager & Bienenfeld 2003). It is clear that physicians must be competent to diagnose, prescribe medication, and develop a comprehensive treatment plan that incorporates evidence-based interventions. However, treatment providers often fall short of this mark. Based on the results of a large-scale study examining physician-patient communication and treatment outcome in recurrent depression, the authors concluded: "Our main findings are that these patients were not being treated to full remission, complete wellness, and full function" (Schwenk et al. 2004, 1899).

Dissatisfaction with the routine treatment for depression that a patient might receive in a primary care physician or psychiatrist's office may be one explanation for the increasing public interest in "non-traditional" or complementary and alternative medicine (CAM) interventions for depression (Gordon 1990). In a prominent series of reports, the use of CAM for any medical condition increased between 1990 and 1997 and then remained notably high between 1997 to 2002, during which time approximately one in three survey respondents reported use of one or more CAM therapies, representing approximately 72 million American adults (Tindle et al. 2005). Although some question the overly broad classification of what is considered "CAM" in this epidemiological research (Gorski, 1999), public and professional interest in CAM has prompted much discussion regarding the training of physicians (Wetzel et al. 2003), the credentialing of CAM practitioners (Cohen, Hrbek, et al. 2005), and policies regarding the use of CAM in academic medical centers (Cohen, Sandler, et al. 2005). Regarding the use of CAM for depression, Kessler and colleagues (2001) reported rates of 53.6 percent over a twelve-month period in the United States. In a survey of nearly nine thousand consecutive visits to CAM practitioners in four states, it was noted that 7 to 11 percent of visits to acupuncturists, massage therapists, and naturopathic physicians were for mental health complaints (Simon et al. 2004). Also, up to 50 percent of the patients in this study had previously sought treatment from a conventional practitioner, and only a small minority (1–5 percent) of patients was referred to conventional practitioners. This suggests that some patients with major depression may be receiving CAM treatments for depression prior to exhausting options that are known from clinical trials to be efficacious.

Depression is a complex and heterogeneous phenomenon. It has taken considerable effort to transform public opinion away from the idea that mood symptoms are "all in one's head." However, the substituted contemporary catchphrase, "a chemical imbalance," also does not adequately convey the complexity of depressive syndromes. Modern conceptualizations of depression recognize it as a biopsychosocial syndrome requiring continued translational research. This research must seek to bridge understandings of genetics, environmental influence on gene expression, the relationship between neurophysiology and specific neuropsychiatric symptoms, and the social and cultural context in which depression occurs (Blazer 2003; Nemeroff & Vale 2005). Depression clearly has genetic underpinnings as evidenced by increased concordance in monozygotic (identical) versus dizygotic (fraternal) twins. Candidate genes that may contribute to the heritability of depression include those that code for the structure of the serotonin transporter, although this process may operate indirectly via the serotonergic modulation of more general "stress" reactions (Hamet & Tremblay 2005). Contemporary investigations of how environment may impact depression have focused on exposure to stress, particularly in early life (Wurtman 2005). Although these investigations will clearly help elucidate how environment and genes may interact to produce depressive syndromes, they do little to speak to a patient's day-to-day experience of depression. This task has been left to psychological interventions and the few remaining psychoanalytic psychiatrists (Gabbard 2000). In addition, some alternative therapies, particularly those with roots in Eastern traditions, may have appeal to some patients' first-person experiences of depression for at least two reasons. First, some CAM treatments may produce pronounced positive expectancy and hopefulness by proposing interventions for those who have negative opinions about medication and psychotherapy. Second, CAM practitioners may be felt by patients to be more attentive to promoting wellness behavior rather than treating "illness" (Bongiorno 2005; Gordon 1996).

Patient preference for treatment is another important consideration in depression treatment, especially given the fact that several different types of treatment have been shown to be about equally effective. The majority of studies show that most patients clearly prefer psychotherapy over antidepressant treatment, but they are much more likely to receive antidepressants in certain settings (e.g., primary care) (van Schaik et al. 2004). Patients' preferences can affect treatment compliance, and there is some evidence that preferences affect treatment outcome. If credible treatment alternatives for depression exist, then patients should be provided with options, especially as several treatments have been shown to be cost-effective and justifiable in comparison to antidepressant treatment. However, patients' preferences must ultimately be weighted against the evidential warrant supporting the use of the particular treatment.

### Evidence-Based Treatment Options for Depression

*Treatment guidelines.* There are legitimate arguments against reliance on a narrow medical model that views depression largely or exclusively as a medical illness (e.g., diabetes) that (a) is related directly to a neurotransmitter dysregulation and (b) requires pharmacological treatment.

Further, consumers appear to be quite interested in and motivated to explore nonpharmacologic approaches. However, we would argue that the answer is not in "alternative" medicine, per se, but in evidence-based treatment alternatives. Nonpharmacologic treatments should not be dismissed out of hand simply because they fail to superficially resemble conventional medical treatment. To the contrary, there is a need for expanded research on non-antidepressant treatments for depression, which may require a very different approach to treating the syndrome (e.g., deep brain stimulation). However, the assessment of the validity of such treatment alternatives should always rely on firm scientific data.

Evidence-based medicine (EBM) is defined as "the conscientious, explicit, and judicious use of current best evidence in making decisions about the care of individual patients" (Sackett et al. 1996, 71). In addition to the emphasis of EBM in psychiatry, there is an emerging movement within psychology to specify practice guidelines for treating psychological problems (Herbert & Gaudiano 2005). EBM relies on hierarchical levels of evidential warrant. Evidence of efficacy and safety from methodologically sound RCTs are considered the best scientific evidence and therefore given the most weight in the decision-making process. However, in addition, EBM provides specific recommendations for choosing treatments based on the quality and amount of the evidence, as well as an analysis of risk-benefit ratios. One advantage of EBM is that clear direction is provided based on state-of-the-art scientific data meant to provide optimal treatment selection. We believe that this general framework should be utilized when evaluating evidence-based treatment options for depression.

Certain scientific groups have provided specific guidelines for the treatment of depression, including the UK's National Institute for Clinical Excellence (NICE). After a systematic review of available data on treatments for depression and based on consensus from an expert panel, NICE guidelines (2004) recommend a stepped care model based on depression severity (summarized in table 1).

**Table 1: National Institute for Clinical Excellence's (NICE's) Guidelines for the Treatment of Depression in Primary and Secondary Care**

|        | Treatment Provider | Target of Intervention | Evidence-Based Treatment Recommendations |
|--------|--------------------|------------------------|------------------------------------------|
| *Step 1* | General practitioner | Recognition | Assessment |
| *Step 2* | Primary care team, primary care mental health worker | Mild depression | Monitoring, guided self-help (e.g., CBT), exercise, brief psychological treatments (e.g., PST) |
| *Step 3* | Primary care team, primary care mental health worker | Moderate to severe depression | Medication, psychological treatments (e.g., CBT, IPT) |
| *Step 4* | Mental health specialists | Treatment-resistant, recurrent, atypical, psychotic depression and those at significant risk | Medication, complex psychological treatments, combined treatments |
| *Step 5* | Inpatient teams | Safety risk, severe neglect | Medication, combined treatments, ECT |

CBT = cognitive behavior therapy; IPT = interpersonal psychotherapy; PST = problem-solving therapy; ECT = electroconvulsive therapy.
Adapted from National Institute for Clinical Excellence. 2004. *Depression: Management of Depression in Primary and Secondary Care (National Clinical Practice Guideline Number 23)*. London: NICE. Retrieved from: http://www.nice.orgJuk/pdf/cg023fullguideline.pdf.

In addition to medication, psychological interventions play a key role as evidence-based treatments for depression. They form the primary intervention for more mild forms of depression and are legitimate treatment alternatives to antidepressants for moderate to severe depression, depending on patient preferences and risk-benefit assessments. Further, for more severe depression, psychological treatments are particularly useful when combined with medication for certain patients. Although the use of psychological treatments during all strategies of depression treatment is consistently recommended in evidence-based guidelines, such treatments are often unavailable or when available still underutilized (Williams et al. 1999). The lack of evidence-based practice guidelines in psychology is probably a contributing factor to the underutilization of evidence-based psychotherapy, as psychiatric guidelines are often biased toward medication treatments (Herbert & Gaudiano 2005).

*Evidence-based psychotherapies.* Several types of psychotherapy represent credible alternatives to antidepressant medication when it is contraindicated (e.g., children, elderly, pregnancy, noncompliance, comorbid medical conditions, suicidality risk). *Cognitive behavior therapy* (CBT) is one of the most known efficacious treatments for depression. CBT approaches are typically skills-based and focus on efforts to modify the negative cognitions and maladaptive behaviors characteristic of depression. Common examples of CBT approaches include cognitive therapy (Beck et al. 1979), behavioral activation (Martell, Addis & Jacobson 2001), problem-solving therapy (Nezu, Nezu & Perri 1989), and couples-focused approaches (Beach & Jones 2002). A strong body of research has demonstrated that CBT is as effective as antidepressants in clinical trials, even for those with more severe forms of depression (DeRubeis et al. 2005). Furthermore, CBT has been shown to be superior to antidepressants at preventing relapse, is cost-efficient, and is easily adaptable to various formats and settings (see for a review by Hollon, Haman & Brown 2002). For example, research has supported the use of guided self-help versions of CBT for mildly depressed primary care patients (Richards et al. 2003). There also is emerging evidence that CBT is safe and effective for juvenile depression and should be recommended as the frontline treatment (Bostic et al. 2005). At this point, cognitive-behavioral interventions are the most empirically supported psychological treatments for depression.

Another credible psychotherapy option for depression is *interpersonal psychotherapy* (IPT), which focuses more on psychosocial and relationship problems, including grief, role disputes, role transitions, and interpersonal deficits. Numerous clinical trials have documented its efficacy for treatment of depression (see for a review Weissman & Markowitz 2002). For example, a large multisite National Institute of Mental Health Treatment of Depression Collaborative Research Program study found that IPT showed efficacy similar to CBT and antidepressant medication and superiority over pill placebo (Elkin et al. 1989). However, current availability of IPT providers in the community is more limited than CBT.

In addition, there is emerging evidence to suggest that *combined treatment with pharmacotherapy plus psychotherapy* may be more efficacious for some patients than either treatment alone. Recent meta-analyses show that combined treatments (typically including CBT) tend to show modest effect size gains over monotherapies, particularly for more severely depressed patients (Friedman et al. 2004). Similar findings are beginning to emerge in studies of childhood depression. For example, a recent large clinical trial comparing fluoxetine, CBT, or their combination relative to placebo found that patients improved most in the combined treatment condition (March et al. 2004). However, it is important to emphasize that patients in this condition were not blinded as to antidepressant treatment, rendering conclusions tentative. One potential advantage of combined treatment is that patients can be monitored more regularly for medication side effects and emergent suicidality and be provided with psychotherapy that better addresses symptom-related distress, quality of life, and social support needs. Perhaps most importantly in the current discussion, research is beginning to suggest that combined treatments may ameliorate the antidepressant-suicidality risk found in patients taking antidepressants alone (Kendall et al. 2005).

It is important to note that, although psychological treatments such as CBT have a substantial base of outcome research to support their use, the mechanisms of actions producing their effects remain elusive, similar to the situation with antidepressants. For example, some research suggests that CBT, IPT, and antidepressants are generally equivalent in efficacy (Elkin et al. 1989). Further, dismantling studies have failed to convincingly demonstrate that multi-component CBT interventions are any more efficacious than "stripped down" interventions that focus on basic behavioral strategies (Jacobson et al. 1996). The question arises as to whether it is necessary to establish that the improvements from psychotherapy are beyond those produced by a placebo effect, as is the case with drug research. Attempts have been made to study specific psychological treatments for depression compared with experimentally designed "placebo" psychotherapies, but conceptual and practical issues make such efforts virtually impossible (Herbert & Gaudiano 2005). As Kirsch (2005) noted, attempting to categorize the effects produced by psychological treatments as "real" versus "placebo" demonstrates a fundamental misunderstanding of the concept. He argued: "A placebo is something that is sham, fake, false, inert, and empty. [Effective] Psychotherapy is none of these. In this sense, it is different from medical placebos, and it does not deserve the pejorative connotations associated with the term" (p. 7). Although some have attempted to rely on the distinction between "specific" and "nonspecific" factors in defining placebo psychotherapy, such classifications are necessarily arbitrary and contingent upon the particular theoretical orientation of the discussant. For example, the therapeutic alliance is conceptualized as a nonspecific factor in CBT, but as a specific factor in many psychodynamic treatments (Herbert & Gaudiano 2005).

Psychotherapy is by definition a psychological treatment, meaning that it operates mainly as a verbal or experiential process in the absence of direct physical (or chemical) manipulation. Therefore, it is conceptually misguided to attempt to prove psychotherapy efficacy beyond "placebo effects." Such is not the case in drug research, where it is meaningful to separate the effects produced by the biochemical properties of the agents themselves from all extraneous factors, including any and all psychological effects such as expectancy. If a specific drug effect is not demonstrated, then the evidence suggests that the mechanisms of action include important psychological factors such as expectancies, the specific domain of psychotherapies. In psychotherapy research, the proper focus of attention should be on defining the precise psychological mechanisms associated with effective treatments for depression (including antidepressants) that may be responsible for the majority of improvement witnessed (e.g., expectancies, behavioral activation). This is not to say that the quality of research on psychotherapies should be any less rigorous than drug research, only that the interpretations and aims of such research necessarily differ. This goal can be achieved using RCT methodologies adapted for psychotherapy research, including dismantling studies, comparison trials, and process research (ibid.).

*Other alternatives to antidepressant treatment.* Treatment options other than antidepressants and psychotherapy for depression may be considered by patients based upon the severity of their depressive symptoms and patient preferences. For those patients with severe depression who have not adequately responded to medication and psychotherapy, practice guidelines typically recommend the use of *electroconvulsive therapy* (ECT), based on a long history of efficacy and increasing understanding of the mechanisms of action (Greenberg & Kellner 2005). Other novel neurostimulatory treatments for resistant severe depression under investigation have show some promise, including vagus nerve stimulation (VNS), repetitive transcranial magnetic stimulation, magnetic seizure therapy, electroencephalogram biofeedback, and deep brain stimulation (George et al. 2002; Trivedi 2003). However, more research on the safety and efficacy of these procedures is needed before promoting their widespread use.

For those with depression that is not severe and treatment resistant, there are alternatives to medication and psychotherapy that may be seen as compatible with both "traditional" and CAM approaches. Although there are fewer controlled studies to support its use at this time, the prescription of *mild exercise* has been found to be a useful intervention for treating less severe forms of depression (Lawlor & Hopker 2001) and is recommended in the NICE guidelines (NICE 2004). In addition, based on results from several placebo-controlled studies, *light therapy* is an interesting environmental intervention that may be effective for depressive syndromes with or without a seasonal pattern (Tuunainen, Kripke & Endo 2004).

Furthermore, there are a variety of nutritional supplements or medicinal herbs that may have antidepressant effects, of which the most investigated and the most commonly known in the United States is *Hypericum peiforatum*, or St. John's Wort (Linde et al. 2005; Walsh et al. 2002). Use of this herb may produce a beneficial effect for people with mild or moderate depression; however, as with any medicinal, its use requires careful assessment of the associated risks and benefits. Nevertheless, many trials have failed to show its superiority to placebos, as is the case with traditional antidepressant medications. Other popularly promoted agents include Gingko biloba, Lavendula angustifolium, chromium, melatonin, fish oil (containing omega-3 fatty acids), folic acid, S-adenosyl-L-methionine (SAMe), L-tryptophan, vitamin E, and zinc (Bongiorno 2005; Walsh et al. 2002). However, there is little support for the efficacy of these agents, and this fact, combined with potential contraindications and side effects, may make them poor alternatives for some patients.

Finally, it is important to note that concerns over antidepressant safety raise intriguing questions about the adequacy of our knowledge about other treatments for depression. First, known severe side effects are associated with nutritional or herbal treatments of depression. Of particular concern is the potential risk of serotonin syndrome when St. John's Wort is used in combination with another serotonergic antidepressant (Zhou et al. 2004). Also, Kava, a medicinal herb considered for use as an anxiolytic, has been associated with acute toxicity and liver failure (Perez & Holmes 2005). Further, controversy has surrounded the recent FDA approval of VNS for treatment-resistant depression, as some have questioned its efficacy and safety (Rosack 2004). There are even warnings that light therapy should be used cautiously due to concerns that it may provoke hypomanic states in some patients (Tuunainen et al. 2004).

Although currently there is little information to suggest an increase in suicidality in efficacious psychotherapies, the possibility cannot be completely ruled out. It is only because of the systematic collection of adverse events required in drug trials with thousands of patients accumulated over many decades with antidepressants that has allowed us to identify a possible suicidality effect in some patients. In fact, studies of psychotherapies rarely report isolated adverse events, and there is no database established to systematically collect such data. The potential problems emerging with antidepressants suggest the need for closer scrutiny of the safety of nonpharmacological treatments for depression as well. Ultimately, treatment decisions for depression must be based on assessments of risk-benefits ratios for particular patient groups (e.g., children and adolescents), as well as patient preferences based on the best available data.

## CONCLUSION

Much confusion can be witnessed today among researchers, practitioners, and the public alike related to concerns surrounding antidepressant efficacy and safety. Proposals being offered in light of the antidepressant controversies tend to emphasize the need for more costly and time-consuming research to be conducted to investigate pharmacologic treatments further. However, we hope that the current spotlight being placed on antidepressants will not leave nonpharmacologic treatments for depression in the dark. In addition to better research on antidepressants, current concerns about pharmacologic treatments for depression should underscore the need for the development and testing of evidence-based treatment alternatives. Fortunately, psychotherapies such as

CBT have enough support to reasonably promote their use today. Nevertheless, the newly appreciated problems with antidepressants should highlight the need for improvements in our conceptualization of depression, including the biological underpinnings, relevant psychological constructs, and psychosocial context in which it occurs. Further, much more research is needed into the safety of these nonpharmacologic treatments for depression, including psychotherapy.

Efforts to develop and test nonpharmacologic treatments such as psychotherapy face an uphill battle in the current economic climate. It is clear that no "psychotherapy industry" exists to fund research on psychological treatments for depression as exists for drugs. Psychotherapy researchers currently must rely almost entirely on federal funding, which increasingly is limited. This has created an urgent need for additional funding to test nonpharmacologic treatments for depression, to train practitioners in their use, and to disseminate this information to the media and public. It is unlikely that such changes will occur overnight, but increased public awareness and promotion of evidence-based treatments for depression, including but not limited to antidepressants, is essential. Unfortunately, contemporary medicine is not well versed in health and wellness promotion, and there may be economic disincentives toward providing health education during physician visits (e.g., these are more time-consuming and less easily billed as services). Therefore, the media may be a useful resource in these endeavors, as they represent a powerful vehicle for increasing public awareness of legitimate treatment options and the urgent need for additional research in these areas.

A common complaint among journalists is that it is difficult to find credible researchers willing to be interviewed (Larsson et al. 2003). However, researchers should view such interviews as part of their public health duty. Media interviews can be used to provide information on credible alternatives to antidepressants, to warn against the use of unvalidated treatments, and to emphasize the need for increased governmental funding in these areas. Researchers and treatment providers who speak to the media should spend more time educating journalists as to the full complexity of the issues surrounding antidepressant concerns, so as not to inadvertently foster nocebo expectations. Any discussion should include clear recommendations about how patients should handle concerns about taking antidepressants. In addition, knowledge-able researchers should make themselves readily available to the media not only to discuss antidepressant controversies but also to provide information concerning other valid treatment options. Finally, the use of formal workshops provided to inform journalists about controversial medical findings has been used successfully in the past (Arnold 2003) and should be explored in the case of the antidepressant controversies.

A positive example of media coverage of the antidepressant-suicidality controversy can be found in a recent article in the *Washington Post* (McMillen 2004). The piece discussed the emerging evidence for using CBT or IPT for juvenile depression based on preliminary studies. Further, the article emphasized the need for increased research efforts to assure that these psychotherapies are truly safe and efficacious. Unfortunately, such coverage tends to be the exception rather than the rule. Perhaps Steven Sharfstein (2005), the current American Psychiatric Association president, put it best:

> As we address these Big Pharma issues, we must examine the fact that as a profession, we have allowed the biopsychosocial model to become the bio-bio-bio model. In a time of economic constraint, a "pill and an appointment" has dominated treatment. We must work hard to end this situation and get involved in advocacy to reform our healthcare system from the bottom up. (p. 3)

Ultimately, it will take a concerted effort among researchers, practitioners, the media, and consumers to promote evidence-based treatments for depression in light of the current antidepressant controversies.

## REFERENCES

ACNP. 2004. *Executive Summary: Preliminary Report of the Task Force on SSRIs and Suicide Behaviour in Youth.* Retrieved from www.acnp.org/execsummary .pdf.

Antonuccio, D. O., W. G. Danton, G. Y. DeNelsky, R. P. Greenberg, and J. S. Gordon. 1999. Raising questions about antidepressants. *Psychotherapy and Psychosomatics* 68: 3–14.

Arnold, K. M. 2003. Medicine in the Media: Symposium Addresses Challenge of Reporting on Medical Research. *Science Editor* 26: 17–18.

Baker, C. B., M. T. Johnsrud, M. L. Crismon, R. A. Rosenheck, and S. W. Woods. 2003. Quantitative analysis of sponsorship bias in economic studies of antidepressants. *British Journal of Psychiatry* 183: 498–506.

Barsky, A. J., R. Saintfort, M. P. Rogers, and J. F. Borus. 2002. Nonspecific medication side effects and the nocebo phenomenon. *Journal of the American Medical Association* 287: 622–27.

Basoglu, M., I. Marks, M. Livanou, and R. Swinson. 1997. Double-blindness procedures, rater blindness, and ratings of outcome. Observations from a controlled trial. *Archives of General Psychiatry* 54: 744–48.

Beach, S. R. H., and D. J. Jones. 2002. Marital and family therapy for depression in adults. In *Handbook of Depression*, edited by I. H. Gotlib and C. L. Hammen. New York: Guilford, pp. 422–40.

Beck, A. H. 2004. STUDENTJAMA. The Flexner report and the standardization of American medical education. *Journal of the American Medical Association* 291: 2139–40.

Beck, A. T., A. J. Rush, B. F. Shaw, and G. Emery. 1979. *Cognitive Therapy of Depression*. New York: Guilford.

Beecher, H. K. 1955. The powerful placebo. *Journal of the American Medical Association* 159: 1602–1606.

Benedetti, F., G. Maggi, and L. Lopiano. 2003. Open versus hidden medical treatments: The patient's knowledge about a therapy affects the therapy outcome. *Prevention and Treatment* 6: Article 1. Retrieved from http://journals.apa.org/prevention/volume6/pre0060001a.html.

Blazer, D. G. 2003. Depression in late life: Review and commentary. *Journal of Gerongology Series A: The Biological Sciences and Medical Sciences* 58: 249–65.

Bongiorno, P. B. 2005. Complementary and alternative medical treatment for depression. In *Biology of Depression: From Novel Insights to Therapeutic Strategies*, edited by J. Licinio and M.-L. Wong. New York: Wiley, pp. 995–1022.

Bostic, J. Q., D. H. Rubin, J. Prince, and S. Schlozman. 2005. Treatment of depression in children and adolescents. *Journal of Psychiatric Practice* 11: 141–54.

Bystritsky, A., and S. V. Waikar. 1994. Inert placebo versus active medication. Patient blindability in clinical pharmacological trials. *Journal of Nervous and Mental Disease* 182: 485–87.

Charney, D. S., et al. 2002. National Depressive and Manic-Depressive Association consensus statement on the use of placebo in clinical trials of mood disorders. *Archives of General Psychiatry* 59: 262–70.

Cohen, M. H., A. Hrbek, R. B. Davis, S. C. Schachter, K. J. Kemper, E. W. Boyer, and D. M. Eisenberg. 2005. Emerging credentialing practices, malpractice liability policies, and guidelines governing complementary and alternative medical practices and dietary supplement recommendations: A descriptive study of 19 integrative healthcare centers in the United States. *Archives of Internal Medicine* 165: 289–95.

Cohen, M. H., L. Sandler, A. Hrbek, R. B. Davis, and D. M. Eisenberg. 2005. Policies pertaining to complementary and alternative medical therapies in a random sample of 39 academic health centers. *Alternative Therapies in Health and Medicine* 11: 36–40.

DeRubeis, R. J., S. D. Hollon, J. D. Amsterdam, R. C. Shelton, P. R. Young, R. M. Salomon, J. P. O'Reardon, M. L. Lovett, M. M. Gladis, L. L. Brown, and R. Gallop. 2005. Cognitive therapy vs medications in the treatment of moderate to severe depression. *Archives of General Psychiatry* 62: 409–16.

Duff, G. 2003. Selective serotonin reuptake inhibitors: Use in children and adolescents with major depressive disorder. Retrieved from http://medicines.mhra.gov/uk/ourwork/monitorsafequalmed/safetymessages/cemssri101203.pdf.

Einarson, A., A. K. Schachtschneider, R. Halil, E. Bollano, and G. Koren. 2005. SSRIs and other antidepressant use during pregnancy and potential neonatal adverse effects: Impact of a public health advisory and subsequent reports in the news media. *BMC Pregnancy and Childbirth* 5: 11. Retrieved from http://www.biomedcentral.com/1471-2393/1475/1411.

Eisenberg, D. M., R. B. Davis, S. L. Ettner, S. Appel, S. Wilkey, M. Van Rompay, and R. C. Kessler. 1998. Trends in alternative medicine use in the United States, 1990–1997: Results of a follow-up national survey. *Journal of the American Medical Association* 280: 1569–75.

Elkin, I., et al. 1989. National Institute of Mental Health Treatment of Depression Collaborative Research Program. General effectiveness of treatments. *Archives of General Psychiatry* 46: 971–82.

Entwistle, V. 1995. Reporting research in medical journals and newspapers. *British Medical Journal* 310: 920–23.

Fava, M., A. E. Evins, D. J. Dorer, and D. A. Schoenfeld. 2003. The problem of the placebo response in clinical trials for psychiatric disorders: Culprits, possible remedies, and a novel study design approach. *Psychotherapy and Psychosomatics* 72: 115–27.

FDA. 2004a. Labeling change request letter for antidepressant medications. Retrieved from http://www.fda.gov/cder/drug/antidepressants/SSRIlabel Change.htm.

———. 2004b. Public health advisory: Suicidality in children and adolescents being treated with antidepressant medications. Retrieved from http://www .fda.gov/cder/drug/antidepressants/SSRIPHA200410.htm.

Fergusson, D., S. Doucette, K. C. Glass, S. Shapiro, D. Healy, P. Hebert, and B. Hutton. 2005. Association between suicide attempts and selective serotonin reuptake inhibitors: systematic review of randomised controlled trials. *British Medical Journal* 330: 396.

Flexner, A. 1910. *Medical Education in the United States and Canada.* New York: Carnegie Foundation for the Advancement of Teaching.

Fontanarosa, P. B., A. Flanagin, and C. D. DeAngelis. 2005. Reporting conflicts of interest, financial aspects of research, and role of sponsors in funded studies. *Journal of the American Medical Association* 294: 110–11.

Frank, J. D., and J. B. Frank. 1993. *Persuasion and Healing: A Comparative Study of Psychotherapy.* 3rd ed. Baltimore: Johns Hopkins University Press.

Friedman, M., J. Detweiler-Bedell, H. Leventhal, R. Home, G. Keitner, and I. Miller. 2004. Combined psychotherapy and pharmacotherapy for the treatment of major depressive disorder. *Clinical Psychology: Science and Practice* 11: 47–68.

Gabbard, G. O. 2000. *Psychodynamic Psychiatry in Clinical Practice.* 3rd ed. Washington, DC: American Psychiatric Press.

Gadow, K. D. 1992. Pediatric psychopharmacotherapy: A review of recent research. *Journal of Child Psychology and Psychiatry* 33: 153–95.

Gaudiano, B. A., and J. D. Herbert. 2003. Antidepressant-placebo debate in the media: Balanced coverage or placebo hype? *Scientific Review of Mental Health Practice* 2: 74–77.

———. 2005. Methodological issues in clinical trials of antidepressant medications: Perspectives from psychotherapy outcome research. *Psychotherapy and Psychosomatics* 74: 17–25.

Geddes, J. R., N. Freemantle, J. Mason, M. P. Eccles, and J. Boynton. 2000. SSRIs versus other antidepressants for depressive disorder. *Cochrane Database Systematic Review*, CD001851.

Gentile, S. 2005. The safety of newer antidepressants in pregnancy and breast-feeding. *Drug Safety* 28: 137–52.

George, M. S., Z. Nahas, X. Li, F. A. Kozel, B. Anderson, K. Yamanaka, J. H. Chae, and M. J. Foust. 2002. Novel treatments of mood disorders based on brain circuitry ECT, MST, TMS, VNS, DBS. *Seminars in Clinical Neuropsychiatry* 7: 293–304.

Gordon, J. S. 1990. Holistic medicine and mental health practice: Toward a new synthesis. *American Journal of Orthopsychiatry* 60: 357–70.

———. 1996. *Manifesto for a New Medicine*. Reading, MA: Addison-Wesley.

Gorski, T. 1999. Do the Eisenberg data hold up? *Scientific Review of Alternative Medicine* 3.

Greenberg, R. M., and C. H. Kellner. 2005. Electroconvulsive therapy: A selected review. *American Journal of Geriatric Psychiatry* 13: 268–81.

Greenberg, R. P., R. F. Bornstein, M. D. Greenberg, and S. Fisher. 1992. A meta-analysis of antidepressant outcome under "blinder" conditions. *Journal of Consulting and Clinical Psychology* 60: 664–69; discussion, 670–67.

Greenberg, R. P., R. F. Bornstein, M. J. Zborowski, S. Fisher, and M. D. Greenberg. 1994. A meta-analysis of fluoxetine outcome in the treatment of depression. *Journal of Nervous and Mental Disease* 182: 547–51.

Grilli, R., C. Ramsay, and S. Minozzi. 2002. Mass media interventions: Effects on health services utilisation. *Cochrane Database Systematic Review*, CD000389.

Gunnell, D., J. Saperia, and D. Ashby. 2005. Selective serotonin reuptake inhibitors (SSRIs) and suicide in adults: Meta-analysis of drug company data from placebo controlled, randomised controlled trials submitted to the MHRA's safety review. *British Medical Journal* 330: 385.

Hamet, P., and J. Tremblay. 2005. Genetics and genomics of depression. *Metabolism* 54: 10–15.

Healy, D. 2003. Lines of evidence on the risks of suicide with selective serotonin reuptake inhibitors. *Psychotherapy and Psychosomatics* 72: 71–79.

Hemmings, C. P. 2005. Rethinking medical anthropology: How anthropology is failing medicine. *Anthropology and Medicine* 12: 91–103.

Herbert, J. D., and B. A. Gaudiano. 2005. Moving from empirically supported treatment lists to practice guidelines in psychotherapy: The role of the placebo concept. *Journal of Clinical Psychology* 61: 893–908.

Hollon, S. D., K. L. Haman, and L. L. Brown. 2002. Cognitive-behavioral treatment of depression. In *Handbook of Depression*, edited by I. H. Gotlib and C. L. Hammen. New York: Guilford, pp. 383–403.

Hrobjartsson, A., and P. C. Gotzsche. 2001. Is the placebo powerless? An analysis of clinical trials comparing placebo with no treatment. *New England Journal of Medicine* 344: 1594–602.

IMS. 2003. IMS reports 8 percent constant dollar growth in 2002 audited global pharmaceutical sales to $400.6 billion. Retrieved from http://www .imshealt.com/ims/portal/front/articleC/0,2777,6319_3665_41336931,00. html.

Jacobson, N. S., K. S. Dobson, P. A. Truax, M. E. Addis, K. Koerner, J. K. Gollan, E. Gortner, and S. E. Prince. 1996. A component analysis of cognitive-behavioral treatment for depression. *Journal of Consulting and Clinical Psychology* 64: 295–304.

Jureidini, J. N., C. J. Doecke, P. R. Mansfield, M. M. Haby, D. B. Menkes, and A. L. Tonkin. 2004. Efficacy and safety of antidepressants for children and adolescents. *British Medical Journal* 328: 879–83.

Kasper, S., J. Fuger, and H. J. Moller. 1992. Comparative efficacy of antidepressants. *Drugs* 43, suppl. 2: 11–22.

Kendall, T., S. Pilling, and C. J. Whittington. 2005. Are the SSRIs and atypical antidepressants safe and effective for children and adolescents? *Current Opinion in Psychiatry* 18, no. 1: 21–25.

Kessler, R. C., J. Soukup, R. B. Davis, D. F. Foster, S. A. Wilkey, M. M. Van Rompay, and D. M. Eisenberg. 2001. The use of complementary and alternative therapies to treat anxiety and depression in the United States. *American Journal of Psychiatry* 158: 289–94.

Khan, A., S. Khan, and W. A. Brown. 2002. Are placebo controls necessary to test new antidepressants and anxiolytics? *International Journal of Neuropsychopharmacology* 5: 193–97.

Khan, A., H. A. Warner, and W. A. Brown. 2000. Symptom reduction and suicide risk in patients treated with placebo in antidepressant clinical trials: An analysis of the Food and Drug Administration database. *Archives of General Psychiatry* 57: 311–17.

Kirsch, I. 2000. Are drug and placebo effects in depression additive? *Biological Psychiatry* 47: 733–35.

———. 2005. Placebo psychotherapy: Synonym or oxymoron? *Journal Clinical Psychology* 61: 791–803.

Kirsch, I., T. Moore, A. Scoboria, and S. Nicholls. 2002. The emperor's new drugs: An analysis of antidepressant medication data submitted to the U.S. Food and Drug Administration. *Prevention and Treatment* 5: Article 23. Retrieved from http://journals.apa.org/prevention/volume25/pre0050023a.

Kirsch, I., and G. Sapirstein. 1998. Listening to Prozac but hearing placebo: A meta-analysis of antidepressant medication. *Prevention and Treatment* 1: Article 0002a. Retrieved from http://journals.apa.org/prevention/volume0001/pre0010002a.html.

Kirsch, I., and A. Scoboria. 2001. Apples, oranges, and placebos: Heterogeneity in a meta-analysis of placebo effects. *Advances in Mind-Body Medicine* 17: 307–309.

Kjaergard, L. L., and B. Als-Nielsen. 2002. Association between competing interests and authors' conclusions: Epidemiological study of randomised clinical trials published in the BMJ. *British Medical Journal* 325: 249.

Klein, D. F. 1998. Listening to meta-analysis but hearing bias. *Prevention and Treatment* 1: Article 0006c. Retrieved from http://journals.apa.org/prevention/volume0001/pre0010006c.html.

———. 2000. Flawed meta-analyses comparing psychotherapy with pharmacotherapy. *American Journal of Psychiatry* 157: 1204–11.

Klein, D. F., M. E. Thase, J. Endicott, L. Adler, I. Glick, A. Kalali, S. Leventer, J. Mattes, P. Ross, and A. Bystritsky. 2002. Improving clinical trials: American Society of Clinical Psychopharmacology recommendations. *Archives of General Psychiatry* 59: 272–78.

Larsson, A., A. D. Oxman, C. Carling, and J. Herrin. 2003. Medical messages in the media—Barriers and solutions to improving medical journalism. *Health Expectations* 6: 323–31.

Lasser, K. E., P. D. Allen, S. J. Woolhandler, D. U. Himmelstein, S. M. Wolfe, and D. H. Bor. 2002. Timing of new black box warnings and withdrawals for prescription medications. *Journal of the American Medical Association* 287: 2215–20.

Lawlor, D. A., and S. W. Hopker. 2001. The effectiveness of exercise as an intervention in the management of depression: Systematic review and meta-regression analysis of randomised controlled trials. *British Medical Journal* 322: 763–67.

Leber, P. 2000. The use of placebo control groups in the assessment of psychiatric drugs: An historical context. *Biological Psychiatry* 47: 699–706.

Lejoyeux, M., and J. Ades. 1997. Antidepressant discontinuation: A review of the literature. *Journal of Clinical Psychiatry* 58, suppl. 7: 11–15.

Leuchter, A. F., I. A. Cook, E. A. Witte, M. Morgan, and M. Abrams. 2002. Changes in brain function of depressed subjects during treatment with placebo. *American Journal of Psychiatry* 159: 122–29.

Linde, K., C. D. Mulrow, M. Berner, and M. Egger. 2005. St John's wort for depression. *Cochrane Database Systematic Review*, CD000448.

Luborsky, L., L. Diguer, D. A. Seligman, R. Rosenthal, E. D. Krause, S. Johnson, G. Halperin, M. Bishop, and E. Schweizer. 1999. The researcher's own therapeutic allegiances—A "wild card" in comparisons of treatment efficacy. *Clinical Psychology: Science and Practice* 6: 95–106.

Luhrmann, T. M. 2000. *Of Two Minds: The Growing Disorder in American Psychiatry.* New York: Knopf.

March, J., S. Silva, S. Petrycki, J. Curry, K. Wells, J. Fairbank, B. Burns, M. Domino, S. McNulty, B. Vitiello, and J. Severe. 2004. Fluoxetine, cognitive-behavioral therapy, and their combination for adolescents with depression: Treatment for Adolescents with Depression Study (TADS) randomized controlled trial. *Journal of the American Medical Association* 292: 807–20.

Martell, C. R., M. E. Addis, and N. S. Jacobson. 2001. *Depression in Context: Strategies for Guided Action.* New York: Norton.

McMillen, M. 2004. If not pills, what? *Washington Post,* April, p. HE01.

Melander, H., J. Ahlqvist-Rastad, G. Meijer, and B. Beermann. 2003. Evidence b(i)ased medicine—Selective reporting from studies sponsored by pharmaceutical industry: Review of studies in new drug applications. *British Medical Journal* 326: 1171–73.

Moncrieff, J. 2001. Are antidepressants overrated? A review of methodological problems in antidepressant trials. *Journal of Nervous and Mental Disease* 189: 288–95.

Moncrieff, J., and I. Kirsch. 2005. Efficacy of antidepressants in adults. *British Medical Journal* 331: 155–57.

Moncrieff, J., S. Wessely, and R. Hardy. 2001. Antidepressants using active placebos. *Cochrane Database Systematic Review*, CD0030I2.

Montagne, M. 2001. Mass media representations as drug information for patients: The Prozac phenomenon. *Substance Use and Misuse* 36: 1261–74.

Moseley, J. B., K. O'Malley, N. J. Petersen, T. J. Menke, B. A. Brody, D. H. Kuykendall, J. C. Hollingsworth, C. M. Ashton, and N. P. Wray. 2002. A controlled trial of arthroscopic surgery for osteoarthritis of the knee. *New England Journal of Medicine* 347: 81–88.

Moynihan, R., L. Bero, D. Ross-Degnan, D. Henry, K. Lee, J. Watkins, C. Mah, and S. B. Soumerai. 2000. Coverage by the news media of the benefits and risks of medications. *New England Journal of Medicine* 342: 1645–50.

Nemeroff, C. B., and W. W. Vale. 2005. The neurobiology of depression: Inroads to treatment and new drug discovery. *Journal of Clinical Psychiatry* 66, suppl. 7: 5–13.

Nezu, A. M., C. M. Nezu, and M. G. Perri. 1989. *Problem solving therapy for depression: Theory, research, and clinical guidelines.* New York: Wiley.

NICE. 2004. *Depression: Management of depression in primary and secondary care, National Clinical Practice Guideline Number 23.* London: NICE. Retrieved from http://www.nice.org/uk/pdf/cg023fullguideline.pdf.

Otto, M. W., and A. A. Nierenberg. 2002. Assay sensitivity, failed clinical trials, and the conduct of science. *Psychotherapy and Psychosomatics* 71: 241–43.

Perez, J., and J. F. Holmes. 2005. Altered mental status and ataxia secondary to acute Kava ingestion. *Journal of Emergency Medicine* 28: 49–51.

Petkova, E., F. M. Quitkin, P. J. McGrath, J. W. Stewart, and D. F. Klein. 2000. A method to quantify rater bias in antidepressant trials. *Neuropsychopharmacology* 22: 559–65.

Piasecki, M. P., D. O. Antonuccio, G. M. Steinagel, B. S. Kohlenberg, and K. Kapadar. 2002. Penetrating the blind in a study of an SSRI. *Journal of Behavior Therapy and Experimental Psychiatry* 33: 67–71.

Pincus, H. A., L. Hough, J. K. Houtsinger, B. L. Rollman, and R. G. Frank. 2003. Emerging models of depression care: Multi-level ('6 P') strategies. *International Journal of Methods in Psychiatric Research* 12: 54–63.

Pincus, H. A., and L. S. McQueen. 1996. US primary care training in mental health and the role of the DSM-IV primary care version DSM-IV-PC. *Primary Care Psychiatry* 2: 139–54.

Rada, R. 2005. A case study of a retracted systematic review on interactive health communication applications: Impact on media, scientists, and patients. *Journal of Medical and Internet Research* 7: e18. Retrieved from http://www.jmir.org/2005/2002/e2018.

Reid, B. 2002. The nocebo effect: Placebo's evil twin. *Washington Post*, April, p. HE01.

Richards, A., M. Barkham, J. Cahill, D. Richards, C. Williams, and P. Heywood. 2003. PHASE: A randomised, controlled trial of supervised self-help cognitive behavioural therapy in primary care. *British Journal of General Practice* 53: 764–70.

Rosack, J. 2004. Vagus nerve stimulation device approved with multiple cautions. *Psychiatric News* 40: 14.

Rosenthal, R. 1979. The "file drawer problem" and tolerance for null results. *Psychological Bulletin* 86: 638–41.

Rosenzweig, P., S. Brohier, and A. Zipfel. 1993. The placebo effect in healthy volunteers: Influence of experimental conditions on the adverse events profile during phase I studies. *Clinical Pharmacology and Therapeutics* 54: 578–83.

Rowe, G., L. Frewer, and L. Sjoberg. 2000. Newspaper reporting of hazards in the UK and Sweden. *Public Understanding of Science* 9: 59–78.

Sackett, D. L., W. M. Rosenberg, J. A. Gray, R. B. Haynes, and W. S. Richardson. 1996. Evidence based medicine: What it is and what it isn't. *British Medical Journal* 312: 71–72.

Schulz, R., and T. L. Patterson. 2004. Caregiving in geriatric psychiatry. *American Journal of Geriatric Psychiatry* 12: 234–37.

Schwartz, L. M., S. Woloshin, and L. Baczek. 2002. Media coverage of scientific meetings: Too much, too soon? *Journal of the American Medical Association* 287: 2859–63.

Schwenk, T. L., D. L. Evans, S. K. Laden, and L. Lewis. 2004. Treatment outcome and physician-patient communication in primary care patients with chronic, recurrent depression. *American Journal of Psychiatry* 161: 1892–901.

Shapiro, A. K., and E. Shapiro. 1997. *The powerful placebo: From ancient priest to modern physician.* Baltimore: Johns Hopkins University Press.

Sharfstein, S. S. 2005. Big Pharma and American psychiatry: The good, the bad, and the ugly. *Psychiatric News* 40: 3.

Sharp, I. R., and J. E. Chapman. 2004. Antidepressants and increased suicidality: The media portrayal of controversy. *Scientific Review of Mental Health Practice* 3: 71–75.

Simon, G. E., D. C. Cherkin, K. J. Sherman, D. M. Eisenberg, R. A. Deyo, and R. B. Davis. 2004. Mental health visits to complementary and alternative medicine providers. *General Hospital Psychiatry* 26: 171–77.

Skaer, T. L., D. A. Sclar, L. M. Robison, and R. S. Galin. 2000. Trend in the use of antidepressant pharmacotherapy and diagnosis of depression in the US: An assessment of office-based visits 1990–1998. *CNS Drugs* 14: 473–81.

Teicher, M. H., C. Glod, and J. O. Cole. 1990. Emergence of intense suicidal preoccupation during fluoxetine treatment. *American Journal of Psychiatry* 147: 207–10.

Tindle, H. A., R. B. Davis, R. S. Phillips, and D. M. Eisenberg. 2005. Trends in use of complementary and alternative medicine by US adults: 1997–2002. *Alternative Therapies in Health and Medicine* 11: 42–49.

Trivedi, M. H. 2003. Treatment-resistant depression: New therapies on the horizon. *Annals of Clinical Psychiatry* 15: 59–70.

Tuunainen, A., D. F. Kripke, and T. Endo. 2004. Light therapy for non-seasonal depression. *Cochrane Database Systematic Review*, CD004050.

van Schaik, D. J., A. F. Klijn, H. P. van Hout, H. W. van Marwijk, A. T. Beekman, M. de Haan, and R. van Dyck. 2004. Patients' preferences in the treatment of depressive disorder in primary care. *General Hospital Psychiatry* 26: 184–89.

Vendantam, S. 2002. Against depression, a sugar pill is hard to beat. *Washington Post*, May, p. A01.

———. 2005. Fewer kids prescribed drugs for depression. *Washington Post*, February, p. A08.

Walsh, B. T., S. N. Seidman, R. Sysko, and M. Gould. 2002. Placebo response in studies of major depression: Variable, substantial, and growing. *Journal of the American Medical Association* 287: 1840–47.

Wampold, B. E., T. Minami, S. C. Tierney, T. W. Baskin, and K. S. Bhati. 2005. The placebo is powerful: Estimating placebo effects in medicine and psychotherapy from randomized clinical trials. *Journal Clinical Psychology* 61: 835–54.

Weissman, M. M., and J. C. Markowitz. 2002. Interpersonal psychotherapy for depression. In *Handbook of Depression*, edited by I. H. Gotlib and C. L. Hammen. New York: Guilford, pp. 404–21.

Wetzel, M. S., T. J. Kaptchuk, A. Haramati, and D. M. Eisenberg. 2003. Complementary and alternative medical therapies: Implications for medical education. *Annals of Internal Medicine* 138: 191–96.

White, K., J. Kando, T. Park, C. Waternaux, and W. A. Brown. 1992. Side effects and the "blindability" of clinical drug trials. *American Journal of Psychiatry* 149: 1730–31.

Whittington, C. J., T. Kendall, P. Fonagy, D. Cottrell, A. Cotgrove, and E. Boddington. 2004. Selective serotonin reuptake inhibitors in childhood depression: Systematic review of published versus unpublished data. *Lancet* 363: 1341–45.

Williams, J. W., Jr., K. Rost, A. J. Dietrich, M. C. Ciotti, S. J. Zyzanski, and J. Cornell. 1999. Primary care physicians' approach to depressive disorders. Effects of physician specialty and practice structure. *Archives of Family Medicine* 8: 58–67.

Wurtman, R. J. 2005. Genes, stress, and depression. *Metabolism* 54: 16–19.

Yager, J., and D. Bienenfeld. 2003. How competent are we to assess psychotherapeutic competence in psychiatric residents? *Academic Psychiatry* 27: 174–81.

Zhou, S., E. Chan, S. Q. Pan, M. Huang, and E. J. Lee. 2004. Pharmacokinetic interactions of drugs with St John's wort. *Journal of Psychopharmacology* 18: 262–76.

Zuckerman, D. 2003. Hype in health reporting: "Checkbook science" buys distortion of medical news. *International Journal of Health Services* 33: 383–89.

# SECTION VII.
# THE POPULARIZATION OF
# POPULAR PSYCHOLOGY

# INTRODUCTION

As should be clear by this point in the book, popular psychology is a decidedly mixed bag. Many widespread beliefs, such as the claims that our memories work like a video camera, that expressing anger is almost always good for us, or that we must "process" trauma to get over it, turn out to be false. Moreover, many self-proclaimed media self-help "experts," such as Dr. Phillip McGraw ("Dr. Phil") and Tony Robbins, have often offered advice that is not consonant with high-quality psychological evidence. For example, on his popular television show, Dr. Phil has promoted the polygraph test as a reliable means of indicating whether partners in a relationship are lying or telling the truth. Yet decades of published research indicate that the polygraph test is a highly fallible detector of lies.

Still, there is no intrinsic reason why popular psychology need be unscientific. Fortunately, not all of it is. For example, as we'll discover in this section, some self-help books derived from solid scientific principles have been shown to be helpful for certain psychological problems, including depression and anxiety. Moreover, some well-known mental health experts have offered helpful advice concerning the merits of accepting personal responsibility for one's problems, although this advice may not differ all that much from that we obtained from our grandmothers—or what social psychologist Leon Festinger termed "bubba psychology." ("Bubba" is Yiddish for "grandmother.")

Yet how can we determine which aspects of pop psychology to ignore and which to accept? In this section, we will offer some user-friendly tips.

The late Neil Jacobson issues some cautions regarding the overpromotion of psychotherapy. Jacobson, a well-known psychotherapy pioneer himself, notes that many psychological treatments are efficacious. Nevertheless, he urges us to distinguish *statistical significance* (whether a treatment works better than chance) from *clinical significance* (whether a treatment produces practically meaningful effects). To paraphrase Gertrude Stein, a clinically significant difference is a difference that makes a difference. In Jacobson's discerning eyes, most efficacious psychological treatments are only modestly effective, and therapy practitioners must take pains not to promise more than they can deliver. Jacobson also points out the importance of full informed consent in psychotherapy and notes sagely that psychotherapy should never be interminable. If a client is not improving despite years of therapy, it is typically time to request a referral and move on.

In the next two chapters, Eileen Gambrill and Gerald Rosen discuss the perils and promises of self-help books. Both authors acknowledge that such books can be helpful in some circumstances, but both also discuss cases in which untested self-help programs may be harmful. Rosen in particular offers a number of dramatic examples in which self-help programs have been hyped in the absence of adequate scientific evidence. Gambrill provides a helpful "checklist" of points to bear in mind when evaluating the advice offered by self-help books.

Roy Baumeister and his colleagues then examine the hazards of the ever-popular "self-esteem movement," which posits that adequate self-esteem is essential for mental health. As they observe, there is precious little research evidence for this claim. Moreover, Baumeister and his co-authors maintain, high self-esteem, especially when associated with narcissism, may actually be related to aggression and violence following provocation. As they note, widespread attempts to increase schoolchildren's self-esteem may be misguided and perhaps dangerous.

In the final chapter in this section, Timothy Moore evaluates "brainscams," techniques designed to enhance mental functioning by stimulating various brain areas. Moore examines the science and pseudoscience underlying subliminal perception and persuasion. As he notes, there is good evidence that we can be influenced in subtle ways by stimuli outside of our conscious awareness. This finding does not, however, imply that we can be persuaded to purchase products that we would otherwise pass over, as claimed by advocates of subliminal self-help tapes. Indeed, as Moore points out, controlled studies have repeatedly demonstrated that such tapes are essentially useless for enhancing self-esteem, memory, or just about anything else.

# 24.

# THE OVERSELLING OF THERAPY

## *Neil Jacobson*

When Monique, a first-year law student, began psychoanalysis with a prominent analyst in 1982, she complained of pervasive sadness, hopelessness, fatigue, difficulty concentrating and loss of appetite. She regularly woke up in the middle of the night, unable to go back to sleep. She had been plagued by these problems for most of her adult life and met the diagnostic criteria for "major depression." During the entire eight years that Monique was in psychoanalysis, she remained depressed. Despite her lack of improvement, Monique's psychoanalyst never changed treatments, never suggested alternative approaches and never consulted with colleagues about her case.

While shopping at a pharmacy one day, Monique noticed a self-help book about cognitive therapy. After reading it and doing some investigating, she discovered that there were a number of brief psychotherapies that had some success in helping people with depression.

Monique also learned of several antidepressant medications that were often effective. Needless to say, she was disturbed that her analyst had never told her about these options, let alone offered them to her. For all Monique knew when she began treatment, psychoanalysis was the treatment of choice, indeed the only viable treatment, for major depression.

Monique found a cognitive therapist, started taking an antidepressant and recovered from her depression within six weeks of terminating her analysis. By now a practicing attorney, she considered it unconscionable that her analyst had allowed her to suffer for eight years while

Reprinted from *Psychotherapy Networker* (March/April 1995): 41–47. © Psychotherapy Networker, Inc. Used by permission, http://www.psychotherapynetworker.org.

continuing unsuccessfully with psychoanalysis. Drawing an analogy to physicians who are expected to provide clients with all available treatment options and to outline their costs and benefits, she was astonished to find that it was not common practice among psychotherapists to do the same. Monique believed that her analyst was guilty of malpractice, but, in the end, she was so delighted to be feeling better that she didn't pursue litigation.

There are aspects of this case that are all too familiar to most mental health professionals. It is not uncommon for therapists to keep clients in therapy long after it is obvious that little or no progress is being made. Nor is it unusual to encounter therapists who are either unaware of or do not present their clients with a range of treatment options or discuss the existing scientific knowledge of their relative efficacy. Indeed, numerous surveys of mental health professionals indicate that even those trained in research do not keep up with the research literature, which itself seems to have little influence on clinical practice. Instead, the practice of psychotherapy seems to be influenced primarily by tradition, current fads and fashions, and the persuasiveness of charismatic workshop leaders and book writers.

As a clinical scientist, a psychotherapy researcher and the former director of a doctoral program in clinical psychology, I have been training therapists and practicing psychotherapy since 1972. It is clear to me that, as an instrument of human change, psychotherapists have been overselling their product since the days of Freud. If the media and even some of our social science colleagues are beginning to criticize psychotherapy, it may be in part because the culture is beginning to come to this same realization. How bad is the problem? Is there anything that can be done?

While lobbying hard for a piece of the healthcare reform pie, advocates for the mental health professions have presented psychotherapies (and pharmacotherapy) as proven treatments for a variety of mental health problems, citing positive research findings, whenever possible, to support their claims. Where research findings don't exist, they cite opinions, which often amount to nothing more than an endorsement of long-established, unsubstantiated clinical traditions. For example, one

common unsubstantiated assumption is that brief therapy may be sufficient for relatively circumscribed problems, such as phobias or panic
attacks, but long-term psychotherapy is necessary for lifelong, serious
problems, such as personality disorders. This position is not based on
any evidence of efficacy, but simply on the *belief* that brief therapies do
not work with certain problems. Some proposals by state psychological
associations have actually requested insurance reimbursement for up to
150 therapy sessions per year for serious problems, even though there is
no empirical basis that would justify such coverage.

Of course, advocates for psychotherapy are no different from advocates for other healthcare providers, who also practice many unproven
techniques with impunity and receive reimbursement for them from
insurance companies. In some respects, healthcare reimbursement has
been based on the professional qualifications of the *provider* rather than
on the efficacy of their chosen *treatment*. Physicians are prone to practicing unsubstantiated techniques and requesting that the government
pay for them, as are mental health lobbyists. For example, until recently,
ulcers were treated as psycho-physiological disorders, without any empirical basis for this assumption. It has since been discovered that ulcers are
infectious diseases that have little or nothing to do with stress and can be
treated quite effectively with antibiotics if discovered early enough. Still,
at least some medical treatments offered by physicians make a clinically
significant difference in the quality of life of the patients even if they do
not "cure" the condition. Can the same be said of psychotherapy?

There is substantial research apparently demonstrating that psychotherapy actually does work. The increasing sophistication of research
methodology has made it possible to pool together large numbers of
therapy outcome studies and, through a statistical technique called
meta-analysis, come to general conclusions about therapy's efficacy. *The
Benefits of Psychotherapy,* by Mary Lee Smith, Gene V. Glass, and Thomas
I. Miller, perhaps the most extensive meta-analysis of therapy research,
has been widely cited as providing incontrovertible evidence that psychotherapy helps people. Indeed, the authors conclude, "Psychotherapy
is beneficial, consistently so and in many different ways. Its benefits are

on a par with other expensive and ambitious interventions such as schooling and medicine. . . . The evidence overwhelmingly supports the efficacy of psychotherapy. . . . Indeed, its efficacy has been established with monotonous regularity."

In the widely used textbook on psychotherapy research, *Handbook of Psychotherapy and Behavior Change,* edited by Sol Garfield and Allen Bergin, the chapters are filled with explicit and implicit conclusions that the outcome question has been resolved. Even RobynDawes, in his muckraking critique of professional psychology, *House of Cards: Psychology and Psychotherapy Built on Myth,* concludes that "Psychotherapy works overall in reducing psychologically painful and often debilitating symptoms. . . . In fact, it is partly because psychotherapy in its multitude of forms *is* generally effective that I am writing this book."

Unfortunately, these conclusions are premature. For one thing, critics point out that such generalized assertions about psychotherapy's efficacy are meaningless, because they provide no information about what treatments provided by which therapists work for what problems. In other words, just because psychotherapy in general has a positive effect, we cannot infer that a particular treatment will work for a particular type of client treated by a particular therapist. For example, is psychotherapy of any value in the treatment of depression and, if so, what types of treatments are likely to work? Are certain types of therapists more likely than others to be effective with depressives? This sort of question tends not to be addressed in reviews that examine hundreds of studies with diverse client populations, diverse modalities of treatment and diverse types of therapists.

There is, however, a more fundamental problem with any conclusions about psychotherapy efficacy based on statistical comparisons between treatment groups. Suppose you are comparing an experimental treatment for obesity with a control treatment. If the average weight loss in the experimental treatment is ten pounds and the average weight loss in the control treatment is zero, the size of the statistical effect could be immense. Yet if the clients entered treatment weighing three hundred pounds, an average weight loss of ten pounds would not make a clinically significant difference in their lives. In other words, the size of a statistical effect tells you little or nothing about its clinical significance.

Statistical comparisons bear no necessary relationship to the clinical significance of the treatment under consideration. Clinical significance refers to the extent to which clients feel that therapy has given them something approximating what they came for or has made a meaningful difference in their lives. But what does this mean in terms that can somehow be measured? Although the concept of clinical significance has taken on increased importance among psychotherapy researchers, there is little consensus as to how it should be defined. My colleagues Dirk Revenstorf, William C. Follette, and I have developed a set of statistical techniques that provide a definition of clinical significance in terms of recovery. We reasoned that if clients make clinically significant changes during the course of therapy, by the end of therapy, they should resemble their "functional" counterparts more than their "dysfunctional" cohorts on whatever problem they entered therapy to solve.

For example, if clients enter therapy complaining of depression, by the end of therapy they should score within the normal range on measures of depression in order for their improvement to be clinically significant. Thus, a client who leaves therapy less depressed than when he or she entered, but who still has significant depressive symptoms, would be considered to be improved but not recovered. We have developed statistical techniques to determine whether the magnitude of change is substantial enough to place the client within the normal range by the end of therapy. Generally, consumers of therapy expect that the problem they came in with will be resolved. It is of considerable interest to know how often clients get what they came for, and it is important to recognize that clients enter therapy with little regard for statistically significant improvement—they simply want to feel better, which they believe will happen as soon as therapy eliminates the problem as they define it, whether or not the therapist deems that belief realistic.

Using these statistical techniques, we have discovered that when psychotherapy outcome is examined under the microscope of clinical significance, its effects appear to be quite modest, even for disorders that are thought to be easily treated and even when so-called established techniques are used. For example, it is often said that there are many effective treatments for major depression. Biological psychiatrists consider it proven that various forms of antidepressant medication work. A number of brief psychotherapies—most notably Aaron T. Beck's cognitive therapy and Gerald Klerman and Myrna Weissman's interpersonal psychotherapy—have ostensibly received considerable empirical support.

Yet when the actual outcomes of these treatments are examined in terms of their clinical significance, the results are disturbing. Consider the federally funded, multisite investigation conducted in the 1980s known as the Treatment of Depression Collaborative Research Program (TDCRP), designed to compare the effectiveness of psychotherapies versus antidepressant medication. It is difficult to study depression because it tends to be episodic; that is, most depressives recover within a year even without therapy, and most who recover eventually have another episode of depression. Thus, it is relatively easy to attribute to therapy what may have transpired even without therapy. The TDCRP is widely considered to have achieved the highest degree of methodological rigor of any large-scale outcome study yet conducted, and thus has produced results that are more believable than those from many other trials of dubious design quality.

From the standpoint of clinical significance, the question is, "What percentage of clients stay in treatment, recover from their depressive episode and stay recovered for a reasonable period following termination?" In this particular study, where expert therapists were used and millions of dollars were spent to ensure quality control, the proportion of clients who completed the twelve-week, twenty-session treatment, recovered from their depressive episode, and stayed nondepressed for eighteen months ranged from 19 to 32 percent across the three active treatments (imipramine, cognitive therapy and interpersonal psychotherapy). Thus, only a minority of patients recovered and stayed recovered for more than a year. Even the placebo treatment did as well (20 percent). Neither pharmacotherapy nor psychotherapy led to lasting recovery for the great majority of cases.

These findings are not atypical, either for major depression or for other mental health problems. In a series of studies of clinical significance, our research group has examined conduct disorders in adolescents, couples seeking therapy for marital distress and people with anxiety disorders. We have found the recovered patient (the one who shows few or no signs or symptoms of the initial complaint and believes him- or herself to be "cured") to be the exception rather than the rule for every type of disorder examined and for every type of therapy that we have looked at—psychodynamic, behavioral, cognitive and family therapy. When one considers even more intractable problems, such as addictive behaviors, schizophrenia and personality disorders, the clinical significance data are even more bleak. The only exception we have found thus far to these modest recovery rates is the cognitive behavioral treatment of panic disorder, developed by David Clark at Oxford University and David Barlow then at the State University of New York in Albany.

This is not to say that psychotherapy never produces recovery or that some therapies are not more effective at inducing recovery rates than others. Rather, it simply attests to the relatively modest average recovery rates shown by psychotherapy when examined under the microscope of clinical significance.

It is important to note that there are numerous psychotherapy researchers who dispute my gloomy interpretation of the psychotherapy research literature, arguing that "statistical significance" is a sufficient criterion for determining that a form of psychotherapy is effective. If a treatment works better than nothing, exceeds the outcome of a placebo, or adds to the effectiveness of alternative treatments, they argue, then the effect is worth talking about, however modest it might be. These critics point out that even small changes can enhance the quality of a client's life. They may be right. However, I do think it is important to maintain the distinction between statistical and clinical significance to make sure clients are not misled into expecting the latter when, in all likelihood, they must settle for the former.

Other critics argue that the measures outcome researchers use are too crude to adequately evaluate the changes occurring in psychotherapy. For example, measures of depressive symptoms may not reflect the full impact of therapy on a client's overall sense of well-being, self-confidence and the like. It is hard to know how to answer these critics. If a depressed person *still* feels depressed after therapy, what is the significance to him or her of being able to sleep through the night? What is the meaning of "overall well-being"? At the very least, we know that by currently available measures, the average outcomes of most psychotherapies are modest. Whether outcomes will look better with improved measures remains to be seen. I actually believe that there are a variety of excellent measures of psychotherapy outcome. Asking someone how they feel, which is essentially the basis of most self-report measures of change, is about as direct as one can get. If anything, clients are prone to exaggerate how much better they feel rather than to minimize their improvement, since the desire to please the therapist is a well-established psychological phenomenon.

There are other researchers who criticize randomized clinical trials because they inevitably involve samples of clients who are unrepresentative of those seen in clinical practice. Nobody in their right mind would volunteer for a randomized clinical trial, these critics assert, where they may end up in a control group, especially when they could see a therapist who will focus on their individual needs rather than on the requirements of an experimental design. Yet there is good reason to believe that the effects of psychotherapy found in randomized clinical trials *overestimate* the positive effects found in the world of clinical practice, because patients who are selected typically have discrete, encapsulated problems, and complicated cases involving, for example, dual diagnoses, are typically excluded. Also, therapists are scrutinized much more carefully during a clinical trial than they are when left to their own devices in private practice: the sessions are taped and rated and regular supervision meetings are held. In fact, there is actually some empirical support for the notion that the psychotherapy works better in efficacy studies than it does in clinical practice. In a landmark study published in the *American Psychologist*, John Weisz reported that child psychotherapy shows a statistical advantage over no treatment only when conducted in research settings. In naturalistic practice settings, child psychotherapies appear to be ineffective, not just from the standpoint of clinical significance, but of statistical significance as well. They apparently are not better than no therapy at all!

But perhaps the toughest challenge for those who believe that research underestimates the effectiveness of psychotherapy is the overwhelming evidence that, on the average, psychotherapy outcome is not improved by either years of clinical experience or by professional training. In a famous 1979 study, in which Hans Strupp and his colleagues compared psychodynamic therapists with an average of twenty-five years of experience to college professors with no therapy training, experience or supervision. In the treatment of anxious and depressed college students, the professors did as well as the experienced therapists. The question of whether experience or training enhances outcome has been studied extensively, reviewed exhaustively and meta-analyzed to death. Skeptics have looked at the data in all sorts of ways, trying to find a way to challenge the devastating conclusions of these hundreds of studies. No matter how determined the advocate, no matter how the data are analyzed, no one has been able to find that either the amount of clinical experience or the degree of professional training enhances outcome. In one of my studies, I found that novice clinical psychology graduate students with no prior experience outperformed licensed psychologists in doing marital therapy.

Much as we would like to believe that we are better therapists now than we were before we started our training, the research literature tells us that, on the average, we aren't. The only advantage that experienced therapists have over inexperienced ones is that they have a lower dropout rate, an accomplishment that may be of dubious value given the modest effects of psychotherapy, showing that clients valiantly hang in there even when it's not doing them any reasonable good. A substantial body of research tells us that sometimes people recover during the course of therapy, but, more often, they do not. Neither the level of experience nor the degree of training influences the likelihood of change.

To make matters even more troubling, it is not even clear that contact with a live therapist is necessary for a positive outcome. Although the research on self-administered treatments (self-help books, inspirational tapes, meditation, adult education courses) and peer support groups is not definitive, the studies completed so far show no advantage for clinical work with a therapist over a self-administered treatment. Moreover, when peer support groups have been examined rigorously (for example, in the treatment of obesity), they appear to perform as well as psychotherapy conducted by a professional.

There is no particular school or modality that is uniquely subject to the criticism that therapy has a limited impact. Cognitive and behavior therapies, as well as specific forms of psychotropic medication, have received more attention in clinical trials than other approaches, and thus can claim at least some support, whereas the same cannot be said of the vast majority of approaches to psychotherapy. However, with few exceptions, the therapies examined all seem to be wanting in terms of clinical significance. Therefore, "empirical validation" too often means only that a form of treatment has been studied in a controlled setting and has been shown to have some positive effects, however weak they may be.

While family therapy has been shown to do about as well as individual psychotherapy, it is not demonstrably superior to individual psychotherapy for any clinical problem (with the possible exception of schizophrenia). My own research shows that, on the average, when marital discord coexists with major depression, couples therapy does as well as—but no better than—individual psychotherapy. Moreover, this research investigated behavioral marital therapy, not exactly a popular theoretical approach within a field dominated by general systems theory.

Family therapy began with, and continues to be fertilized by, an exceptionally creative group of clinicians who have generated a great many viable and still untested hypotheses about family functioning and how it can be harnessed to generate change. Much of what family therapists write about constitutes an important phase—perhaps the most important phase—of the research process: the generation of hypotheses. The field is ripe with ideas waiting to be validated, confirmed, replicated, or disconfirmed. Thus, it is all the more disappointing that family therapy is so guilty of making unsubstantiated claims of success. "This works, trust me!" has become the standard of proof on the family therapy workshop circuit, and the popularity of various approaches becomes a question of who is most persuasive, whose teaching tapes are most pristine, or even whose name is best known. The claims of astoundingly high success in an astoundingly few number of sessions made by some solution-focused therapists are particularly disturbing. Despite the assertion that these success rates are substantiated by research findings, nothing cited in the literature could conceivably be thought of as empirically valid clinical research.

False prophets are easy to recognize and need to be exposed. They expect you to trust their clinical judgment, while showing no signs of humility or doubts about the wisdom of what they are proselytizing. They show an indifference to independent tests of their ideas and sidestep the issue of research evidence. We have to ask our plenary speakers, theorists and workshop leaders questions such as, "How do you know this works?" We have to pin down 90 percent success claims with questions like, "How did you measure success?" "Was the *measurement* process independent of the *therapy* process, to ensure that it was not contaminated by the client's desire to make the therapist feel good?" Family therapists must face the challenge of building a knowledge base if we are to respond effectively to the criticism leveled at other forms of psychotherapy.

Today our field faces the challenge of making sure that therapy promises nothing it can't deliver and delivers the best, most honestly presented care of which clinicians are capable. Therapists can no longer afford to ignore the scientific foundations of their profession for, as Jay Efran and Mitchell Greene recently pointed out in the *Networker*, in the long run, science is all "that presumably distinguishes [therapists] from the expanding cadre of self-proclaimed psychics, new-age healers, religious gurus, talk-show hosts and self-help book authors." From a therapy researcher's viewpoint, a number of changes need to be made in how our field operates.

First, therapists must treat only clients who have given truly informed consent, and must stop treatment when it is apparent that it is not working. Psychotherapists are obligated to be familiar with the research literature on whatever disorders they are treating, to present to their clients the full range of treatment options along with their costs and benefits—based on currently available information—and to refrain from overselling the brand they happen to be providing. In most cases, therapists should openly acknowledge that their treatments are "experimental," since the success rates of most commonly practiced models for most disorders are unknown. Where outcome evidence *is* available, it should be presented. Clients should be given the information they need to make informed choices before being asked to consent to treatment.

Therapy should never be interminable, as Freud once referred to psychoanalysis. Progress should be expected to occur in a timely manner, or alternatives should be discussed. Criteria for determining progress should be part of a dialogue initiated by the therapist and regularly assessed by both therapist and client. When therapy isn't working, the therapist has an ethical obligation to try something else—another form of therapy, a referral to another therapist, a psychotropic drug, a self-help book, meditation, yoga, gardening, exercise or something else. A disgruntled ex-client once said to me, "In retrospect, after spending $5,000 on unsuccessful psychotherapy, with no suggestion from the therapist that there was any alternative, it occurred to me that it would have been much more therapeutic to use that money to hire babysitters, a maid service, even a butler." Alternatives to psychotherapy may often be the best solution when timely progress is not evident.

Researchers themselves have been negligent in not focusing on the questions of most interest to psychotherapists. One primary reason that psychotherapists so often operate in an empirical vacuum is that there is no alternative. Until recently, for example, there was no basic research on childhood sexual abuse, and there is still very little on repressed memories. Thus, when faced with these issues, psychotherapists have little scientific support in formulating their treatment approaches. Responding to this need for information, many organizations and interest groups have already developed "clinical digests" that summarize and disseminate research findings for practicing therapists, and these efforts should be applauded and expanded. Until research training receives more attention in all clinical training programs, psychotherapists cannot be expected to rely on primary sources for their information. Meanwhile, agencies that fund clinical research have to become more flexible in their definition of good science. Setting the rigors of randomized clinical trials as the gold standard for research discourages many investigators from exploring the questions most relevant to clinicians.

Managed care services are frequently criticized by psychotherapy advocates for denying coverage for adequate treatment. In fact, managed care providers are placing the burden of proof where it belongs: in the hands of psychotherapists. It is frustrating that we cannot justify long-term treatment, nor can we justify the choice of hiring an MD or a PhD to provide services when master's- and bachelor's-level providers would, on the average, perform just as well. We may resent having to talk to case managers, request additional treatment sessions, and lower our fees, but the demands made by managed care bureaucrats follow from the psychotherapy research literature with a great deal more logic than do the criticisms directed at them by psychotherapy lobbyists.

This chapter has highlighted research findings that should make clinicians squirm. Carried away with our popular acceptance, we have promised far more than we can deliver. We need to take a close look at our excesses and our often tenuous relationship to scientific principles. But while research can tell us a lot about the impact of therapy, conclusions about its ultimate merits and its role in the culture cannot be made solely from outcome data. While the existing empirical evidence raises serious questions about the transformative power of the therapy experience, people clearly get *something* from it or they would not keep coming back for more. Consumer satisfaction measures are virtually always higher than outcomes based on measures of psychiatric symptoms. How are we to understand this?

It may be that for many people, the process of being in therapy is the whole point. The collaboration between therapist and client creates an experience of hope and optimistic possibility that many clients prize whether or not their specific presenting problems disappear. Not only does the process of being in such a relationship feel good to many clients, it may also have outcome benefits that have thus far eluded easy measurement. Even when the outcomes are not clinically significant, many clients are satisfied and feel they have derived great benefit from the experience. They may not resolve their problem with one therapist, enter therapy with another, still not resolve the original issue, but nonetheless feel satisfied with both experiences of therapy! For many people, the process of treatment itself seems to provide some subtle but significant and meaningful benefits that have so far eclipsed our efforts to measure or even define them. The power of the therapeutic alliance and the availability of a person who, at the very least, is present and caring should never be underestimated.

For all our society's much-vaunted attention to the pursuit of happiness, the mass shuffle of a society dominated by vast, impersonal forces of consolidated power and privilege makes it harder and harder for many people to experience that happiness. In large part, that accounts for the mushrooming popularity of psychotherapy over the last twenty-five years. Where else, in an age that has seen the decline of family, church, school and community, and the widespread, creeping anxiety fueled by social violence and economic insecurity, can people find an authentic and personal experience of human connection and compassionate challenge to their own best possibilities? What other professional field has devoted so much intelligence, systematic study and toilsome labor to doing humane work in an inhumane world, trying to instill in people a vision of optimistic realism about their own lives that avoids false sentimentality on the one hand and deadening cynicism on the other? With all its flaws, for all its bumblings and stumblings, psychotherapy keeps some vital spirit alive in a culture that would be much the poorer and more desperate without it.

# 25.

# SELF-HELP BOOKS: PSEUDOSCIENCE IN THE GUISE OF SCIENCE?

## *Eileen Gambrill*

Self-help books are a tradition in the United States (Starker 1989), and they have long been recognized as sources of moral guidance. As Starker (1989, 15) describes, they "became increasingly established in the eighteenth century as a repository of useful and practical knowledge. [They] offered readers advancement in skill, wealth, and social status under the tutelage of successful and respected figures while remaining within the framework of the Protestant ethic." Benjamin Franklin's writings encouraged people to advance socially through their own efforts. He himself kept track of seventeen virtues, such as temperance ("Eat not to dullness") and tranquility ("Be not disturbed by trifles"), in an effort to alter his own behavior (Silverman 1986). Self-improvement books provided religious leaders a format for diffusing prescriptive guidelines; and, indeed, self-help books "emerged from a religious context" (Starker 1989, 37).

In his book *Oracle at the Supermarket* (1989, 10), Starker writes that the self-help book in America "appears to occupy a social niche roughly on a par with that of the legendary oracle at Delphi. Offering wisdom and enlightenment at discount prices, it has the ability to speak with a vast audience on a variety of topics and provides specific directions for achieving love, health, money, peace of mind, and any number of prac-

Reprinted with permission from *Skeptical Inquirer* (Summer 1992): 389–99.

tical skills." Social historians have suggested that *self* is a modern-day term for "soul" and that there has been a progression from the use of "the soul" to "the mind" and now to "the self." If this is true, then indeed Starker (1989) is correct in viewing self-help books as a modern-day oracle replacing older sources of guidance, such as organized religion. A belief in mind power (the power to change through changing what we think) is a key part of the "American myth of success" (Weiss 1969; see also Wyllie 1954).

In the broadest sense, a self-help book could be any book that helps people in some way, whether or not the author expresses an intent to help. For example, in this broad sense the Bible could probably be described as the most popular self-help book. My concern here is with self-help books related to self-change (not those that describe how to build a bookcase or how to repair a television set). Rosen (1981, 190) defines a self-help book by "the claims and contents of the book itself. This leaves responsibility for labeling a book as 'treatment' where it belongs, namely, in the hands of the one who writes the book"—and, it could be added, in the hands of the publishers who prepare bookjackets and other promotional materials.

Sales of self-help books are increasing (Rosen 1987). About two thousand are published each year (Doheny 1988). Audio cassettes and videotapes have also entered the self-help market. A recent study found that 60 percent of psychologists prescribe self-help books to supplement their treatment (see Starker 1988). Some of these books do seem to offer readers what they promise (see, for example, DeAngelis 1991). I will first review potential benefits and dangers of self-help books and then present guidelines potential consumers can use in selecting self-help material.

## POTENTIAL DANGERS AND BENEFITS OF SELF-HELP BOOKS

It could be argued that guidelines to help consumers select self-help books that deliver what they promise are not appropriate because people read such books for entertainment. But do they? Research into why people read self-help books indicates that, when they spend their money and time on them, people indeed seek certain promised outcomes. As Starker (1989, 10) notes: "Inasmuch as self-help books are dispensing advice to millions on matters physical, psychological, and spiritual, they cannot responsibly be ignored by social scientists and healthcare professionals. Questions regarding their relative merits and potential dangers deserve careful attention."

What are the possible benefits? They include the attainment of desired outcomes with little expenditure of time, money, and effort and access to accurate information about particular outcomes or problems of interest (e.g., social anxiety, depression) as well as about the conditions required for self-change. Other possible benefits include enhancing self-change skills and decreasing beliefs that get in the way of self-change.

Dangers of ineffective self-help materials have been described by Rosen (1981). These include an increase in hopelessness and helplessness when desired outcomes do not occur, neglect of other methods that might be successful—such as consulting a clinician—and a worsening of problems. Additional dangers include the fostering of superstitious beliefs and the suppression of real sources of influence over valued outcomes. This may make attainment of desired goals less likely. Self-help books may increase rather than decrease incorrect views about self-change and how it can be accomplished. They may encourage a dysfunctional focus on the self and on one's problems or encourage the unrealistic view that life should be without problems (see, for example, Barsky 1988; Kayne & Alloy 1988) and may foster dysfunctional attributions (see Taylor & Brown 1988 for a discussion of the value of positive illusions).

# THE SUPPRESSION AND MYSTIFICATION OF REAL SOURCES OF INFLUENCE

Self-help focuses on the individual who is attempting to alter his or her own behavior, thoughts, or feelings to attain specific goals. Individual change, however, is but one level of intervention. Many other levels may be required to attain valued outcomes like losing weight or becoming less anxious, less depressed, or happier. The focus on self-help obscures the role of political, social, and economic factors that influence most of the behaviors that individuals try to alter through self-change. This focus also often exaggerates the potential a person has to alter his or her environment and self (Gambrill 1990). It's like using only a few of the keys on a piano to play a polonaise.

Let's take a look at stress, for example. Many factors related to stress are environmental—high noise levels, hours spent on crowded smoggy highways commuting from home to office, pressure to make more money to buy discretionary consumer items, and so on.

The fundamental attribution error (that of overlooking environmental causes of problems and focusing on dispositional causes) is common and is likely to be encouraged by a focus on the self (Nisbett & Ross 1980; Miller & Porter 1988). Encouraging a focus on the self may increase depression in people who already tend to focus extensively on themselves (Kayne & Alloy 1988). Self-help books may encourage unhelpful views of "the self" (for example, they may support a search for the "true self"). I have already noted the continuity of the terms *soul, mind,* and *self.* Thus the term *self* is a heavily loaded, almost sacrosanct concept, and writers and publishers of self-help books often take advantage (sometimes to the detriment of their readers) of this heavily value-laden term and the ideology that accompanies it—that there are no limits to what can be accomplished through self-change.

Rosen (1981) has for some time pointed out the dangers of self-help books written by psychologists (see also Becvar 1978; Barrera, Rosen & Glasgow 1981). Have these warnings been taken to heart? Hardly. As he points out, even psychologists who argue against publication of untested material themselves often go on to publish self-help books with exaggerated, untested claims (Rosen 1990). As Rosen (1990, 3) writes, consumers are being "flooded with new untested do-it-yourself therapies."

## WHAT DO WE KNOW ABOUT SELF-CHANGE?

Self-help books usually promise great changes with little effort. Is that possible? If so, under what conditions? Are there limits to self-help? If so, what are they? Under what conditions do they arise? We know a great deal about the potential for and limitations of self-change. (See, for example, Agran & Martella 1991; Kanfer & Schefft 1988; Mahalik & Kivlighan 1988; Peterson 1983; Prochaska et al. 1985; Scogin et al. 1990; Stuart 1977; Watson & Tharp 1989.) The potential is impressive. For example, comparison of self-exposure instruction from a psychiatrist, a self-help book, or a computer showed that phobic individuals assigned to any one of these three groups improved (Ghesh & Marks 1987). The book used in this program included detailed instructions. It is difficult for people to clearly identify what they did to achieve change. They often attribute changes in their behavior (such as stopping smoking) to "will power." It is often difficult to persuade readers to comply with suggested procedures for self-change. Certain kinds of individuals are more likely than others to profit from self-help formats (see, for example, Kivlighan & Shapiro 1987). We know that there are different kinds of self-change goals; some are given a higher status than others (Carver & Scheier 1986). People differ in their repertoire of self-change skills and in their history of using them to attain valued outcomes. Research on self-management and self-instruction suggests that some methods and formats are more likely than others to facilitate self-help. To what extent do self-help books build on this knowledge about self-management?

# QUESTIONS TO ASK

## *Are expected outcomes clearly described?*

Vague descriptions of outcomes (e.g., increased self-actualization) have a number of disadvantages, including difficulty in planning how to attain them and in evaluating progress (see table 1).

---

**TABLE 1: A Consumer's Checklist**
**Questions to Ask about Self-Help Books**

---

- Are expected outcomes clearly described (what/where/how long will they last)?
- What evidence is there that the book is helpful for people like me? How credible is this information? (Are the results of experimental studies reported?) What is the success rate? What is the failure rate? Are there any potential negative effects of the program? What are they? How long will gains be maintained?
- Will this book help me develop accurate beliefs about self-change?
- Will this book help me acquire accurate information about outcomes or problems of interest?
- Will this book help me accurately identify problems?
- Will this book help me clearly define my goals and identify changes required to achieve these goals?
- Are guidelines provided to help me assess my current knowledge and skills?
- Will this book help me select effective self-change methods?
- Are guidelines for evaluating progress provided?
- Are the instruction formats used the most likely to be effective?
- Are effective methods described that will help me carry out needed tasks (that will "motivate me")?
- Does the book describe how I can generalize and maintain positive outcomes?
- Are troubleshooting aids included to help me if I get stuck?

### Who is (and who is not) likely to benefit? Who may be harmed?

Readers should ask: Is this book likely to help me? What evidence is given that it will help me? Have any experimental studies been conducted in which people are randomly assigned to different groups, including a control group composed of individuals who do not have access to the self-help material? If so, what are the results? Do all people benefit, or just some? How long do gains last? Who is most likely to benefit? Has anyone been harmed? Was the book itself tested under the same conditions readers will be using it? Often only testimonials are offered or the presumed expertise of the author is used to buttress claims made. Views about what has been helpful may not reflect what is actually the case. Research in psychotherapy as well as in social psychology indicates that we do not necessarily accurately perceive or report the degree of change (see, for example, Nisbett & Ross 1980; Schnelle 1974). Consumer satisfaction ratings are often quite high (Lebow 1983) whether or not people gained what they originally sought from counseling (Zilbergeld 1983).

Many people do not understand what science is and what it is not (Miller 1987) and do not have the critical-thinking skills required to accurately assess claims. They will accept claims based on pseudoscience as readily as those based on science (Bunge 1984).

### Will this book help me develop accurate beliefs about self-change?

People have beliefs about self-change—what it is, what it requires, and what ethical and moral prescriptions relate to it in terms of responsibility. Many people believe that they can change by using will power. Belief in will power for overcoming common problems, such as shyness, smoking, and fear of flying, is widespread (Knapp & Delprato 1980). (For a review of lay theories, see Furnham 1987.) Does the book discuss personal beliefs about self-change and help readers to acquire accurate beliefs based on research about self-change?

## Will this book increase (or decrease) accurate information about topics addressed?

Does the book offer accurate information about an outcome or problem area of concern? Not all books offer accurate, up-to-date information. Rosenthal and Yalem (1985), for example, found that suicide-prevention information presented in self-help books was not always accurate.

## Will this book help me accurately identify problems?

Errors in problem definition are one of the main sources of failure of all kinds of programs. The histories of medicine and psychiatry are replete with instances of inaccurate identification of problems and their causes, with resultant ineffective or iatrogenic results (e.g., Morgan 1983). Consider the example of someone with low self-worth who inaccurately believes that excess weight is the reason for this low self-worth. The entire focus of self-change in such a case would be misdirected. When weight is lost but the self is still viewed as unworthy, the person may feel even worse than before. Or consider people who believe that their difficulty in meeting others is due to poor personal appearance, when in fact it is because they are not actively seeking out promising social situations and initiating conversations. Here, too, the focus of change may be misdirected.

Rosen (1981, 190) emphasized the importance of "self-diagnosis." One of the seven guidelines he has proposed for reviewers of self-help books is this: "Does the book provide a basis for self-diagnosis . . . and have the methods for self-diagnosis been evaluated to establish rates of false positives and false negatives." He points out that "there is not a single published study concerning the ability of individuals to self-diagnose a problem." Selection of specific behaviors to focus on may not become clear until further information is gathered, as described in the next sections.

### Will this book help me clearly define my goals and identify the changes required to achieve them?

Readers approach self-help books with different goals. Some wish to alter a specific behavior, such as to stop smoking. Others have vague goals, such as becoming a better person. If clear rather than vague goals are pursued, attaining desired outcomes is more likely and progress can be carefully followed. Although readers may say that they received help from a particular book, unless outcomes are clearly described and progress monitored, the results are really unknown. A feeling of being helped may not be accompanied by a real change in behavior. People may feel better but not *be* better. In some cases, this might be satisfactory (if nothing can be done to achieve desired outcomes). But what if desired outcomes could be attained? What if readers could have more than just a feeling (or belief) that desired outcomes have been achieved?

Another step in behavior change is identifying factors related to desired outcomes. Let's say that a woman reads a self-help book designed to increase enjoyable social contacts. Does it give guidelines that help her clearly understand why her current contacts are not satisfactory? Possible reasons include a lack of skills, a fear of negative evaluation, social anxiety, unrealistic expectations, poor self-management, and environmental obstacles. Errors often occur when making judgments about the causes of behavior. These include mistaking correlation for causation and overlooking environmental causes (Nisbett & Ross 1980). Other sources of error are noted in table 2.

**TABLE 2**
**Sources of Error in Making Judgments**

### Acquiring Information

- Attending to vivid (but uninformative or misleading) data.
- Seeking data that confirm expectations.
- Ignoring conflicting data.
- Mistaking correlation for causation.
- Overlooking environmental causes and focusing on dispositional (personal) characteristics (the fundamental attribution error).

### Output

- Influence of choice of format.
- Wishful thinking (our preferences influence our view of events).
- The illusion of control (a feeling that one has control over events that are in fact uncertain).

### Feedback

- Misperception of chance fluctuation.
- Attributing success to skill and failure to change.
- Hindsight bias

Sources: Nisbett & Ross 1980; Hogarth 1987.

*Are guidelines provided to help me assess my current knowledge and skills?*

People differ in their repertoires of self-change skills. For example, some readers may know how to set clear goals. Some may already know how to rearrange consequences related to changes of interest. To what extent does a book help each reader to take advantage of skills he or she already has?

### Will this book help me select effective self-change methods?

The data gathered during assessment or "self-diagnosis" are used to plan intervention programs. According to the extent to which data are informative (reduce uncertainty about how to attain valued outcomes) and assumptions about causes are sound, wise decisions are likely to be made. Inaccurate data and assumptions may result in incorrect choices.

What self-management skills are required? There are two major kinds of self-management. One involves the rearrangement of antecedents related to behaviors of interest. This is known as stimulus control. For example, environmental stimuli that encourage unwanted behavior can be removed or reduced in vividness, and those that encourage desired behaviors can be increased. Stimulus control is used to achieve a wide variety of outcomes (see, for example, Stuart 1977; Kanfer & Schefft 1988; Meyer & Evans 1989; Watson & Tharp 1989). A second kind of self-management involves rearrangement of consequences. Positive consequences are provided for behaviors we would like to encourage, and punishing consequences are removed. Negative consequences may be provided for unwanted behaviors, and positive consequences that usually follow such behaviors may be withheld.

### Are guidelines for evaluating progress provided?

Feedback about progress can help maintain change. Some desired outcomes are clear: stopping smoking, for example. Others are vague, such as communicating better with others. What would people do if they did communicate better? It could be argued that fuzzy goals have an advantage in that any positive change will be of value. For example, Zilbergeld (1983) points out that many people are glad they have seen a counselor and feel better even though they didn't get what they came for. Perhaps this is the reason consumer satisfaction is so high in outpatient mental-health agencies (Lebow 1983). However, perhaps these clients would be even more satisfied if their original complaints were also removed. Does a self-help book help readers to identify clear, personally relevant progress indicators, motivate readers to track these on an ongoing basis, and provide effective instructions about what to do depending on progress found?

### Are the instructional formats used the most likely to result in success?

A good deal of research is available that has investigated the effectiveness of different kinds of instructional formats. This indicates that some are more effective than others (Gagne 1987). Instructional formats that include clear description of desired outcomes, intermediate steps, and entering repertoires (knowledge and skills initially available) and use model presentation, coaching, and rehearsal are more likely to be effective compared with programs that do not have these characteristics. Successful self-help programs for anxiety reduction include a detailed manual and a specially designed diary to record tasks completed and progress made (see Marks 1987). Detailed instructions are given about how to (1) identify target problems, (2) practice self-exposure to anxiety-provoking events, (3) keep records of tasks performed and track reduction in anxiety in diaries, (4) anticipate and deal with setbacks, and (5) involve significant others if feasible.

### Are motivational guidelines presented?

Although prescriptive advice offers guidelines (which may be more or less clear) about what to do, it does not provide the motivation to act on this advice. For example, knowledge about helpful rules does not provide the motivation to act on these rules (Hayes 1989; Skinner 1987). It would be quite a different world if this were the case. Not carrying out instructions is a common problem in self-change programs (Rosen 1981). Review of self-exposure treatment for anxiety indicates that brief initial contact with a counselor is an important motivator for some individuals (Marks 1987).

Motivation is largely a matter of arranging cues and contingencies of reinforcement to support desired changes. A contingency is a relationship between behavior and the environment. Smoking cigarettes may be followed by pleasurable feelings of relaxation. Altering contingencies involves rearranging the environment. Questions here are (1) Are consequences of concern under a client's control? (2) Does the client have the skills required to rearrange these? (3) Are there competing contingencies that will interfere with success? and (4) Can these be removed or muted? Many self-help books rely on exhortation to motivate readers; that is, they encourage them to "do it." Exhortation is notoriously ineffective.

### Are guidelines presented for generalizing and maintaining gains?

To what extent will new behaviors occur in different situations? Will gains be durable? Generalization and maintenance are major problems in change programs—both self-help and counselor-based (Marlatt & Gordon 1985; Stokes & Osnes 1989).

### Are troubleshooting guidelines included?

Self-help books require readers to use material "on their own." Errors may occur at many points and may compromise hoped-for results. Troubleshooting guidelines should be included at relevant points to address obstacles that may arise.

## SUMMING UP

The popularity of self-help books cannot be understood without a historical understanding of the transformation of the term *soul* into *mind* and now into *self*. The self is thus almost a holy concept, a reverential one. This is one reason that efforts to point out the limits of self-change and self-management are strenuously resisted even though they would increase understanding of real sources of influence and consequent potential to exert counter-control against unwanted influences (e.g.,

Skinner 1971). Self-help books should take advantage of what is known about self-change. Research that bears on self-change does not so much question the possibility of self-change, but points to a different set of factors that will help in the attainment of desired outcomes.

Limitations of self-help books include inadequate or misleading guidelines for self-assessment, lack of guidelines on how to monitor the degree of compliance with programs and to increase compliance as needed, and lack of guidelines for selecting intervention programs uniquely suited for each reader and for monitoring progress. Few guidelines are described for "troubleshooting" (what to do if there is no progress/no compliance, etc.). Few, if any, guidelines are provided to encourage generalization and maintenance. One of the greatest deficiencies of self-help books is their ignoring environmental variables that influence behavior and not providing guidelines to readers about how to alter the environment to achieve desired outcomes.

Many people benefit from advocating self-help as a panacea for physical and psychological maladies. Millions of dollars are made by publishing companies and bookstores each year from the sale of self-help books. Only if earlier books are not successful in fulfilling readers' goals will new books be purchased that promise greater success. The change process and the factors related to it remain mystified as readers turn to the self-help book displays in search of the latest self-help guide—*this* one is bound to work.

## REFERENCES

Agran, M., and R. C. Martella. 1991. "Teaching Self-Instruction Skills to Persons with Mental Retardation: A Descriptive and Exploratory Analysis." In *Progress in Behavior Modification*, vol. 27, edited by M. Hersen, R. M. Eisler, and P. M. Miller. Newbury Park, CA: Sage.

Barrera, M., G. M. Rosen, and R. E. Glasgow. 1981. "Rights, Risks and Responsibilities in the Use of Self-Help Psychotherapy." In *Preservation of Client Rights*, edited by G. Hannah, W. Christian, and H. Clark. New York: Free Press.

Barsky, A. J. 1988. *Worried Sick: Our Troubled Quest for Wellness.* Boston: Little, Brown.

Becvar, R. J. 1978. Self-help books: Some ethical questions. *Personnel and Guidance Journal* 57: 160–62.

Bunge, M. 1984. What is pseudoscience? *Skeptical Inquirer* 9: 36–47.

Carver, C. S., and M. F. Scheier. 1986. "Self and the Control of Behavior." In *Perceptions of Self in Emotional Disorder and Psychotherapy: Advances in the Study of Communication and Affect,* vol. 11, edited by L. Hartman and K. Blankstein. New York: Plenum.

DeAngelis, T. 1991. Self-help books, no joke in easing panic disorder. *APA Monitor* 22, no. 6: 16.

Doheny, K. 1988. Self-help. *Los Angeles Times,* October 2, part VI, p. 1.

Furnham, A. F. 1987. *Lay Theories: Everyday Understanding of Problems in the Social Sciences.* New York: Pergamon.

Gagne, P. M. 1987. *Instructional Technology: Foundations.* Hillsdale, NJ: Erlbaum.

Gambrill, E. D. 1990. *Critical Thinking in Clinical Practice.* San Francisco: Jossey-Bass.

Ghesh, A., and E. M. Marks. 1987. Self-treatment of agoraphobia by exposure. *Behavior Therapy* 18: 3–16.

Hayes, S. C. 1989. *Rule-Governed Behavior: Cognitions, Contingencies, and Instructional Control.* New York: Plenum.

Hogarth, R. M. 1987. *Judgement and Choice: The Psychology of Decisions.* 2nd ed. New York: Wiley.

Kanfer, F. H., and B. K. Schefft. 1988. *Guiding the Process of Therapeutic Change.* Champaign, IL: Research Press.

Kayne, N. T., and L. B. Alloy. 1988. "Clinician and Patient as Aberrant Actuaries: Expectation-Based Distortions in Assessment of Covariation." In *Social Cognition and Clinical Psychology: A Synthesis,* edited by L. Y. Abramson. New York: Guilford Press.

Kivlighan, D. M., and R. M. Shapiro. 1987. Holland type as a predictor of benefit from self-help career counseling. *Journal of Counseling Psychology* 34: 326–29.

Knapp, J., and D. Delprato. 1980. Willpower, behavior therapy and the public. *Psychological Record* 30: 477–82.

Lebow, J. 1983. Research assessing consumer satisfaction with mental health treatment: A review of findings. *Evaluation and Program Planning* 6: 211–36.

Mahalik, J. R., and D. M. Kivlighan. 1988. Self-help treatment for depression: Who succeeds? *Journal of Counseling Psychology* 35: 237–42.

Marks, I. M. 1987. *Fears, Phobias, and Rituals: Panic, Anxiety, and Their Disorders.* New York: Oxford University Press.

Marlatt, G. A., and J. R. Gordon. 1985. *Relapse Prevention: Maintenance Strategies in the Treatment of Addiction.* New York: Guilford.

Meyer, L. H., and I. M. Evans. 1989. *Nonaversive Intervention for Behavior Problems: A Manual for Home and Community.* Baltimore, MD: Paul H. Brooks.

Miller, D. T., and C. A. Porter. 1988. "Errors and Biases in the Attribution Process." In *Social Cognition and Clinical Psychology: A Synthesis,* edited by L. Y. Abramson. New York: Guilford.

Miller, J. D. 1987. The scientifically illiterate. *American Demographics* 9: 26–31.

Morgan, R. F. 1983. *The Iatrogenics Handbook.* Toronto: IPI Publishers.

Nisbett, L., and L. Ross. 1980. *Human Inference: Strategies and Shortcomings of Social Judgment.* Englewood Cliffs, NJ: Prentice-Hall.

Peterson, L. 1983. "Failures in Self-control." In *Failures in Behavior Therapy,* edited by E. B. Foa and P. M. G. Emmelkamp. New York: Wiley.

Prochaska, J. O., C. C. DiClemente, W. F. Velicer, S. Ginpil, and J. C. Norcross. 1985. Predicting change in smoking status for self-changers. *Addictive Behaviors* 10: 395–406.

Rosen. G. M. 1981. Guidelines for the review of do-it-yourself treatment books. *Contemporary Psychology* 26: 189–91.

———. 1987. Self-help treatment books and the commercialization of psychotherapy. *American Psychologist* 42: 46–51.

———. 1990. "Psychology: Ability to Advance Self-Care." Paper presented at the 98th annual convention of the American Psychological Association, August 10.

Rosenthal, H. G., and P. J. Yalem. 1985. Suicide prevention information and self-help books. *Crisis Intervention* 14: 122–31.

Schnelle, J. F. 1974. A brief report on invalidity of parent evaluations of behavior change. *Journal of Applied Behavior Analysis* 7: 341–43.

Scogin, F., J. Bynum, G. Stephens, and S. Calhoon. 1990. Efficacy of self-administered treatment programs: Meta-analytic review. *Professional Psychology: Research and Practice* 21: 42–47.

Silverman, K. 1986. *Benjamin Franklin: The Autobiography and Other Writings.* New York: Penguin.

Skinner, B. F. 1953. *Science and Human Behavior*. New York: Macmillan.

———. 1971. *Beyond Freedom and Dignity*. New York: Knopf.

———. 1987. *Upon Further Reflection*. Englewood Cliffs, NJ: Prentice-Hall.

Starker, S. 1988. Do-it-yourself therapy: The prescription of self-help books by psychologists. *Psychotherapy* 25: 142–46.

———. 1989. *Oracle at the Supermarket: The American Preoccupation with Self-Help Books*. New Brunswick, NJ: Transactions.

Stokes, T. F., and P. G. Osnes. 1989. An operant pursuit of generalization. *Behavior Therapy* 20: 337–56.

Stuart, R. B., ed. 1977. *Behavioral Self-Management*. New York: Brunner/Mazel.

Taylor, S. E., and J. D. Brown. 1988. Illusion and well-being: A social psychological perspective on mental health. *Psychological Bulletin* 103: 193–210.

Watson, D. L., and R. G. Tharp. 1989. *Self-Directed Behavior: Self-modification for Personal Adjustment*. 5th ed. Monterey, CA: Brooks/Cole.

Weiss, R. 1969. *The American Myth of Success: From Horatio Alger to Norman Vincent Peale*. New York: Basic Books.

Wyllie, I. G. 1954. *The Self-Made Man in America*. New Brunswick, NJ: Rutgers University Press.

Zilbergeld, B. 1983. *The Shrinking of America: Myths of Psychological Change*. Boston: Little, Brown.

# 26.

# SELF-HELP OR HYPE?
# COMMENTS ON PSYCHOLOGY'S
# FAILURE TO ADVANCE SELF-CARE

## Gerald M. Rosen

Jacobs and Goodman (1989) used the term *self-care* to discuss self-help groups, do-it-yourself therapies, and other self-change efforts that do not involve direct contact with a professional. Jacobs and Goodman discussed the boundaries of self-care and envisioned a future in which self-help groups and do-it-yourself therapies play a more critical role in mental healthcare than traditional psychotherapy. They envisioned a corporate-controlled healthcare industry motivated by cost-containment factors and impressed with the effectiveness and cost-efficiency of self-help groups and do-it-yourself therapies. They saw powerful employee assistance programs and health maintenance organizations promoting self-help groups, prevention educational programs, and libraries of tested self-care books. Jacobs and Goodman further suggested that this vision of the future is already taking place, and new models of healthcare will be developed with or without the help of psychologists. They urged psychologists to meaningfully contribute to self-care methods and warned that "failure to seize the opportunity would amount to a failure in expanding the relevance of our profession" (p. 544).

This idea—that psychologists can use their skills to advance self-care—echoes the sentiments of the American Psychological Association's

Reprinted from *Professional Psychology: Research and Practice* 24, no. 3 (1993): 340–45. Copyright 1993 by the American Psychological Association. Reproduced with permission.

(APA's) past president George Miller, who encouraged his colleagues to give psychology away by teaching people how to help themselves (Miller 1969). Miller was suggesting that psychologists could translate their knowledge for the public well-being and empower individuals with self-change programs. A 1978 APA task force on self-help therapies similarly noted that psychologists, by virtue of their training, are in a unique position to contribute to the self-help movement (APA 1978). More than any other professional group, psychologists are trained to evaluate the clinical efficacy of self-care methods, to assess people's ability to self-diagnose problems, to compare various instructional formats and identify those that are most effective, and to clarify when self-care efforts should be supplemented by therapist-assisted or therapist-directed programs. Psychologists can systematically investigate, clarify, and possibly answer all of these questions, thereby contributing to self-care.

Starker (1988, 1989) showed that professional psychologists frequently use self-help as adjuncts to their clinical practice. In one survey (Starker, 1988), clinicians positively evaluated do-it-yourself therapies and frequently "prescribed" them to patients. In the present chapter, I consider whether there is a basis for this general acceptance of self-help by both the public and psychologists. I also discuss how psychologists have, or have not, contributed to the development of effective do-it-yourself therapies. A similar review could be made for self-help groups and other self-care methods, but such a discussion is not within the scope of this chapter. Do-it-yourself therapies refer to self-help books, self-help audiocassettes, and any other informational modality that individuals may use on their own to change behavioral, relationship, or emotional problems.

## SELF-HELP IS BIG BUSINESS

When discussing do-it-yourself treatment programs, the first point to be made is that their quantity and scope are growing beyond imagination. Simply put, self-change is big business. One publisher estimated for a reporter of the *Los Angeles Times* that more than two thousand self-help books are published each year (Doheny 1988). The explosive growth of do-it-yourself books that dominated the self-help industry in the 1970s and early 1980s is now matched by the development of self-help audio-cassettes. A 1988 *New York Times* article reported that one company, Mind Communications Inc., sold more than 6 million dollars' worth of subliminal tapes in that year, a tenfold increase in sales in just two years (Lofflin 1988). The APA even was in the business of developing, marketing, and promoting self-help audiocassettes when it owned *Psychology Today*.

In addition to the proliferation of do-it-yourself books and self-help audiocassettes, video and computer self-change programs are available. An article in *Health* magazine entitled "Off-the-Shelf Salvation" mentions software companies with names such as Psycomp, Psychological Software, and Mindware (Stark 1989). In a recent catalog from Mindware, the consumer is told, "So if you ever get the blues, a new day is dawning. The era of computer-assisted self-therapy for your PC has arrived" (Mindware 1990).

The self-help industry has seen not only a growth in numbers and instructional modalities but also an increase in the scope of issues it addresses. Nowhere is this better illustrated than in the area of programs for children. Once, there were standard books on parenting techniques. Now there are audiotapes parents can play to children before bedtime to rid them of fears, bed-wetting problems, and low self-esteem. There is a book to help infants with colic (Ayllon & Freed 1989). If a parent wants to intervene even earlier, there are audiotapes mothers can play to their unborn, developing fetus. These tapes claim to give the fetus a distinct learning advantage that will carry into adulthood. The company manufacturing these audiotapes (Pre-learning Inc., Redmond, Washington) even offers a diploma when the developing fetus is born.

It should go without saying that not all self-help programs are developed by psychologists, and some financial estimates reported by news media may be exaggerated. However, a visit to any local bookstore will reveal the abundance of self-help materials available for purchase. Furthermore, Rosen (1976a, 1987) documented the increased involvement of prominent academically based psychologists in the development of self-help programs beginning in the 1970s. There can be little doubt that self-help is big business and psychologists are significantly involved.

## Do Self-Help Therapies Really Help?

The explosive growth of self-help programs might seem amusing if it were not for serious issues that are raised for the public and our profession. Barrera, Rosen, and Glasgow (1981) suggested that the benefits of self-help materials may be great, but a number of risks exist as well. For example, it remains unclear whether do-it-yourself programs allow for accurate self-diagnosis. Self-help treatments typically lack provisions for monitoring compliance with instructions or providing for follow-up. Consequently, do-it-yourself therapies can be self-administered inappropriately; instructions can be misapplied; and, in the event of treatment failure, there may be risks of negative self-attributions, of anger toward self or others, and of reduced belief in the efficacy of today's therapeutic techniques (Barrera et al. 1981). Given these risks, it is important to assess the clinical efficacy of self-help materials.

There is no question that some self-help programs are helpful. Glasgow and Rosen (1978, 1982) reviewed 117 studies or case support for the efficacy of some programs. A recent meta-analytic review has found that tested self-help programs are about as helpful as other therapeutic conditions (Scogin et al. 1990). At the same time, some tested programs have not been effective (Glasgow & Rosen 1978, 1982). In addition, and perhaps most important, the majority of do-it-yourself treatments have never been assessed. In fact, there appears to be an increasing trend to not test these programs. In the two reviews conducted by Glasgow and Rosen (1978, 1982), which focused on programs developed by academically based psychologists with a behavioral orientation, the overall ratio of studies to books decreased in a two-year period from .86 to .59.

Psychologists should be credited for conducting research that has helped define the uses and limits of self-help therapies. Unfortunately, some psychologists have not heeded the results of their own studies or studies conducted by colleagues. Take, for example, a study that demonstrates quite clearly that techniques applied successfully by a therapist are not always self-administered successfully (Matson & Ollendick 1977). The study evaluated a book entitled *Toilet Training in Less Than a Day* (Azrin & Foxx 1974) and found that four of five mothers in a therapist-administered condition successfully toilet trained their children, whereas only one of five mothers who used the book in a self-administered condition was successful. This study also observed that unsuccessful self-administered interventions were associated with an increase in children's problem behaviors and negative emotional side effects between mothers and children. In other words, highly successful interventions based in a clinic or supervised by a therapist do not necessarily translate into helpful do-it-yourself programs. Despite these findings, the book's publisher independently contracted with a toy manufacturer of musical toilet seats to produce a combination program entitled *Less Than a Day Toilet Trainer.* In addition, one of the authors proceeded to publish a new and untested book, *Habit Control in a Day* (Azrin & Nunn 1977).

The importance of this finding is not diminished by a treatment's effectiveness in a clinic setting, or by the real possibility that some people are helped by a low-cost book. Imagine, for example, that a hundred thousand copies of *Toilet Training in Less Than a Day* were sold. If Matson and Ollendick's (1977) findings are generalized to this situation, it would mean that twenty thousand children may have been helped, an impressive number at extremely low cost. If only 5 percent of those who benefited were to take the time to write a letter and thank the authors, this would result in a thousand letters attesting to the benefits of the self-administered treatment. With a program effective in clinic settings and a thousand testimonial letters, a psychologist could feel proud of his or her contribution to the public well-being. Unfortunately, this says nothing about the eighty thousand parents who might be frustrated, if not angry, because their children did not comply with a program touted to work with any cooperating youngster.

The importance of Matson and Ollendick's (1977) finding also is not diminished by research that demonstrates that a particular book is helpful or that self-help therapies are effective in general (Scogin et al. 1990). It is still the case that the value of a particular program can be known only by studying that particular program. This point has been demonstrated most dramatically by two studies on self-administered desensitization. In the first of these studies, Rosen, Glasgow & Barrera (1976) found that highly fearful snake phobia subjects who used a totally self-administered written program were able to significantly reduce their anxiety reactions, but 50 percent of subjects failed to comply with the program. On the basis of these findings, an attempt was made to increase compliance by adding a pleasant events self-reward contracting supplement (Barrera & Rosen 1977). Phobic subjects were randomly as-signed to the original self-administered program (Draft 1) or to the revised program with self-reward contracting (Draft 2). As in the first study, 50 percent of subjects completed Draft 1 and substantially reduced their fears. However, in the revised program, in which self-con-tracting had been added, compliance went from 50 percent to 0 percent. In other words, no one completed the new and "improved" second draft. The importance of this unanticipated finding cannot be overemphasized for it clearly demonstrates the following significant point:

> Well-intentioned changes in instructional materials can have a signif-icant and negative impact on treatment outcome. Accordingly, the therapeutic value of a self-help book can only be determined by testing the specific instructions to be published under the conditions in which they are to be given. (Rosen 1987, 47)

## BETTER PROGRAMS OR MORE EFFECTIVE MARKETING?

The position advanced here is that some psychologists have rushed to market with untested programs in the face of research that calls for greater caution. Take, for example, the previously discussed research suggesting major compliance issues in the development of an effective fear-reduction program. Despite these findings, the author of Drafts 1 and 2 revised his program yet another time and published Draft 3 under the title *Don't Be Afraid* (Rosen 1976b). The actual utility of this program is unknown because the first draft had helped 50 percent of snake phobia subjects in two studies, the second draft had helped 0 percent of snake phobics in a single study, and the third draft was totally untested.

To fully appreciate these findings within a historical perspective, it should be noted that an earlier text entitled *Don't Be Afraid* was published by Edward Cowles in 1941. This older *Don't Be Afraid* does not share identical or even similar content with the *Don't Be Afraid* of 1976, and "modern" desensitization may be more effective than "older" methods based on nerve fatigue theories. However, without appropriate research, psychologists and consumers do not know if any advance in the self-treatment of phobic disorders has occurred in the past half century. The 1941 *Don't Be Afraid* may be as effective, less effective, or more effective than any of the well-intentioned drafts developed by Rosen in the 1970s.

In addition to rushing untested programs to market, some psychologists have allowed their programs to be accompanied by exaggerated claims. Take, for example, the 1976 *Don't Be Afraid*, which stated on its book jacket: "In as little as six to eight weeks, without the expense of professional counseling, and in the privacy of your own home, you can learn to master those situations that now make you nervous or afraid" (Rosen 1976b). Notice that research findings are not mentioned that suggest that, at best, 50 percent of people succeed at self-administered treatment, and the true value of the published program is totally unknown.[1]

The claims made by publishers for the efficacy of do-it-yourself treatments can be even more extreme. Consider, for example, a self-help text by the noted psychologist Arnold Lazarus. His book, *In the Mind's Eye* (1977), presents a variety of cognitive behavioral strategies. The publisher of this totally untested book tells the reader that the instructions will "enhance your creative powers, stop smoking, drinking or overeating, overcome sadness and despondence, build self-confidence and skill, overcome fears and anxiety."[2] Only three years later, Jerome Singer, director of the clinical program at Yale University, published *Mind Play: The Creative Uses of Fantasy* (Singer & Switzer 1980), another book presenting cognitive behavioral techniques. This time, according to the book jacket, a reader can learn to "relax, overcome fears and bad habits, cope with pain, improve your decision-making and planning, perfect your skill at sports and enhance your sex life." More recently, a book of similar genre has been published entitled *Mind Power* (Zilbergeld & Lazarus 1987). Because this book illustrates a number of important issues, it is considered in some detail.

*Mind Power*, like its predecessors *In the Mind's Eye* and *Mind Play*, is marketed with a number of bold claims. On the inside jacket of the original hardcover edition, the consumer is told, "In this remarkable book, two internationally acclaimed clinical psychologists have combined their professional expertise to provide clear strategies and nuts and bolts techniques that can give you new power over your life." It further states that "*Mind Power* is the first book to show you how easy it can be to use these techniques to set goals, reduce stress, and increase performance, creativity, and productivity—in other words, to help you shape your life into what you wish it to be." These claims are backed up with testimonials. Consider the report by psychologist Lonnie Barbach, herself an author of self-help books: "I've used many of the techniques in *Mind Power* and can guarantee they work." The paperback version makes claims of equal magnitude: "In this remarkable book, you will learn, step by freeing step, how to unlock your mind's vast potential, turning your negative thoughts into positive action, your limitations into strengths, your gloom into brightly lit horizons, and your hopes and dreams into reality." Both Zilbergeld and Lazarus (1987) are reported to have acknowledged that there was no systematic testing of the book itself (Rosen 1988). Accordingly, there is no real basis for the stated claims, and it remains unknown what percentage of well-intentioned and motivated consumers can use *Mind Power* effectively on their own.

Furthermore, the claim that *Mind Power* is the first of its type is not justified. The techniques it presents have been used many times before. They involve the application of relaxation techniques, during which time the reader is encouraged to imagine the successful achievement of goals while making positive autosuggestions. In its earlier forms, this framework was presented in Wood's *Ideal Suggestion Through Mental Photography,* first published in 1893. Other similar books include Sadler's *Worry and Nervousness or the Science of Self-Mastery* published in 1914 and Crane's *Right and Wrong Thinking and Their Results* published in 1905. There has even been an earlier *Mind Power* by Albert Olston with a copyright of 1903. In addition, there existed in the 1940s or 1950s a Mind Power Company that marketed a series of records with relaxing music and positive imagery statements. So the claim that *Mind Power* is the first of its kind is unfounded as regards both content and name. Like the *Don't Be Afraid*s of 1976 and 1941, it is unknown if the 1987 *Mind Power* is any more effective than the 1903 *Mind Power.*

What does distinguish the recent *Mind Power* from earlier books of a similar name and genre is the linking of its text with a set of audiocassettes that can be purchased separately. At this point, it is helpful to clarify how the *Mind Power* program is carried out. The reader of the book learns relaxation techniques and then is instructed to make his or her own audiotapes. These audiotapes contain suggestions to successfully complete imaged goals. Sample scripts are provided that the reader can record directly or modify for personal needs. For example, here is a sample script for a person who wants to lose weight: "Can you imagine the new, thin you lying on the beach in an absolutely smashing bikini, bright red and very skimpy? You deserve it, so imagine it as vividly as you can. . . . Can you imagine being in bed with Nick, very proud of your body, showing it off at every opportunity, with no more fear. . . . Imagine the new, svelte you, imagine him appreciating and approving" (pp. 139–40).

If a reader is dissatisfied with the homemade audiotapes, he or she can purchase professionally made audiotapes through the Mind Power Project. These audiotapes are actively promoted throughout the book. On page 56 of the text, the reader is told, "If you find that you have trouble understanding the methods or putting them into practice, or that you're not achieving the desired results, you may want to consider ordering the prerecorded audiotapes that we have prepared." On pages 85 and 86, the reader is told "[You can] order the pre-recorded exercise tape we've prepared (follow the instructions on the last page of this book). This tape offers a number of enhancements over homemade products by incorporating the latest in psychological and audiotechnologies. It is designed to be used in your own mental training program and will guide you through the important exercises." On page 87, the reader is told, "Some people have trouble with their own tapes because they are self-conscious about their voices. 'My God, do I sound like that?' is a fairly common reaction. Yes, you do sound like that, and it's fine. This self-consciousness typically disappears after a few minutes of listening. If it doesn't, or if you can't even think about listening to a recording of your own voice, you may want to order the tapes we've prepared." On page 89, the reader is told, "When making recordings, don't expect the impossible. It's true that the ideal would be a recording with no slurred words, no wrong words, and no distracting noises such as coughs and those that result from turning the machine off and on. If you listen to the tapes we offer for sale, you'll find they come close to this ideal." On a page in the back of the book providing instructions for ordering materials, the authors tell the reader that Tape No. 1 is "a 90-minute cassette of the exercises in *Mind Power* that makes full use of the audio medium, including music, multiple voices, and multi-track recording. The enhancements bring a greater efficacy to the exercises than is possible with simpler reproduction techniques."

I contacted Zilbergeld and Lazarus to ascertain whether the claims of greater efficacy for the *Mind Power* tapes had been substantiated (Rosen 1988). Lazarus indicated that he had nothing to do with the tapes, and Zilbergeld confirmed there had been no systematic evaluation to support the stated claims. Accordingly, *Mind Power* appears to be an untested self-help book linked to a set of equally untested cassettes. As such, it represents a new level of product development: Cassette tapes, videotapes, computer programs, and self-help books can now be linked to each other in a total product line. Unfortunately, we do not know whether this development makes for a better and more effective treatment program or whether it simply represents an advance in the packaging and marketing of consumer self-help products.

## HAS THE APA BEEN INVOLVED?

Psychology as a profession is diminished when some of its leading academic figures promote untested self-help programs accompanied with exaggerated claims.[3] A reviewer (personal communication 1991) of the original draft of this article stated, "With the exception of those . . . engaged in training psychologists in diploma mills . . . there is no larger group of our membership engaged in questionable activities than those generating media 'help' of all kinds for the lay public." Hans Strupp (personal communication October 14, 1988) responded to a review of *Mind Power* in *Contemporary Psychology* (Rosen 1988) and said: "Products of this kind impress me as a disgrace to our field and the height of irresponsibility. It often troubles me that our field does not command greater respect from the public. The subject book may be evidence that we get what we deserve unless we do a better job of putting our house in order." Allen Bergin (personal communication September 22, 1987), in response to an article on self-help books and the commercialization of psychotherapy (Rosen 1987) commented: "I suppose you've had some negative responses from some of the commercializers, but you have every reason to stick firmly with your position. The materialism of the current scene seems to be sweeping our moral sensibilities aside."

There are substantial grounds for suggesting that some elected representatives who have voluntarily served in the governance system of the APA (American Psychological Association) have done little to improve the situation. For example, members of the APA Board of Professional Affairs have failed to endorse a single recommendation made by task forces reporting to them in 1978 and again in 1990. Perhaps more significantly, the membership of APA has itself been identified with the development, marketing, and promotion of untested self-help materials. This came about through APA's 1983 purchase of *Psychology Today* and the companion *Psychology Today Tape Series.*[4] By 1985, psychologists on the staff of *Psychology Today* were contracting for new audiotapes to be added to the series. The criteria used to determine which audiotapes should be used were the prominence or credibility of the author and the face validity of the instructions. No attempt was made actually to test the ability of consumers to use the audiotapes.

In the context of this history, the reader of this chapter can now consider what was offered to the public. First, consumers who purchased the audiotapes received a brochure with the name of the APA right on the front cover. On the back of the brochure, it stated, "Backed by the expert resources of the eighty-seventy thousand members of the American Psychological Association, The Psychology Today Tape Program provides a vital link between psychology and you."

Then there are the untested audiotapes themselves. These covered a variety of issues. There was a tape entitled *Personal Impact* in which "clinical psychologist Cooper helps listeners become aware of and enhance their self-presentation to improve the impact they make on others." Under the section "Becoming More Self-Reliant," the potential consumer was told "You [can] become a more attractive, appealing person." Under the section "Expanding Awareness," the consumer was told that "Daniel Goldman leads you to a deep relaxation procedure that you can learn and do on your own." Under "Mental Imagery," developed by Lazarus, the consumer was told: "Harness the powers of your mind! A noted psychologist explains how to use mental imagery to increase self-confidence, develop more energy and stamina, improve performance and proficiency, cope more effectively, overcome fears, and lose weight."

By 1986 there was a special section within the advertisements entitled "New Releases." In *A Guide to Self-Understanding,* the consumer was told the cassette will "help you make better decisions, improve interpersonal communication, and aid in problem solving at home and at work!" A tape by Pelletier provided imaging exercises that would "stimulate creative, original thinking." Psychologist Moyne shows you "how to get your way the nice way." In yet another cassette, "a clinical psychologist teaches listeners to identify and to reverse self-defeating body images." Still other audiotapes were added by 1987. Pomerleau "outlines step-by-step instructions for quitting smoking!" Berglas in the *Success Syndrome* "gives guidelines on how to enjoy the rewards of success!" Miller, in *A Slimmer You*, "explains how his methods condition your body to burn more calories so that as you reach your desired weight you can resume eating satisfying meals without regaining unwanted pounds."

By 1988, the APA Board of Directors had disengaged from *Psychology Today* and sold the magazine to another publisher. This means that for at least three years our professional organization actively sought, produced, and promoted untested self-help materials accompanied by unsubstantiated claims that were purported to be backed (without membership approval) by the then eighty-seven thousand members.

Jonas Robitscher, in a text entitled *The Powers of Psychiatry*, wrote a passage that applies to the present discussion. Whenever the terms *psychiatry* or *psychiatrist* appear, the reader should substitute or add the appropriate term for our profession.

> Every commercial exploitation of psychiatry, large or small, detracts from an integrity that psychiatry needs if it is to have meaning. . . . When it becomes commercial, psychiatry dwindles down to a treatment of symptoms and exploitation of techniques, a pretense of interpersonality that achieves only impersonality, a pretense of helping another that helps only the self. Many psychiatrists do not approve the commercialism of psychiatry. They follow a code that prohibits fraud and personal publicity and the other concomitants of the new materialistic psychiatry. But almost no psychiatrists speak out against it. They turn their eyes away to avoid the sight of the money tree being shaken, and if they become aware of it, they hold their tongues. In the absence of a protest from the psychiatrists who do not exploit psychiatry, those who do, flourish. (p. 456)

It can be said that the APA has not only turned its eyes away from the money tree but, for a period of time, was itself trying to harvest the tree's fruits. By developing and marketing untested self-help tapes, the APA failed to provide a model or higher standard for its members, some of whom were publishing their own untested programs.

The failure of the APA to set a standard also occurs in subtle ways. Consider, for example, the organization's annual conventions, at which untested self-help programs accompanied with exaggerated claims are hawked at numerous booths. At the 1991 conference, I was able to find dozens of untested self-help books and audiocassettes with exaggerated claims, self-treatment biofeedback programs with incredible claims, and expensive "alpha chambers" whose very name refers to a refuted notion (Beyerstein 1985, 1990).

## CAN PSYCHOLOGISTS MEET THE CHALLENGE?

This chapter has attempted to demonstrate that self-help programs are experiencing explosive growth; that psychologists are to be credited with a substantial body of research dating back to the 1970s; that this research demonstrates the potential and real effectiveness of self-help programs as well as their limits; that some psychologists have failed to heed the results of their own studies by rushing to market with exaggerated product claims; and that the APA has itself set a poor example for the profession and failed to advance clear standards. It is critically important to emphasize that these points are not a criticism of self-help. Rather, the points serve as an observation of psychology's failure to advance self-care.

Professional psychologists who recommend the use of self-help programs are not discouraged from doing so. As indicated earlier here, psychologists are to be credited with conducting more than a hundred studies that clearly show the benefits of some self-help programs. The use of these programs to benefit patients and the general public is clearly indicated. At the same time, professional psychologists should make an effort to counter extravagant claims and the exaggerated outcome expectancies that may result. In this way, professional psychologists can advance the responsible use of self-help while waiting for their colleagues to develop and market these programs responsibly.

As regards the responsible development and marketing of do-it-yourself treatments, it is not the purpose of this chapter to detail corrective actions or to recommend future research directions. The first of these goals was accomplished in an article by Rosen (1987) and in a report to APA's Board of Professional Affairs submitted by the 1978 Task Force on Self-Help Therapies.[5] The second of these goals has been met in earlier published reviews (Glasgow & Rosen 1978, 1982).

The purpose of the present chapter is to put psychologists on notice, to make them aware, and, if successful in its intent, to make them concerned. Concern is warranted because *Mind Power, Don't Be Afraid,* and other programs written by psychologists illustrate the failure of our profession to contribute meaningfully to self-care. The challenge facing our profession, the challenge given to us by Miller in 1969, is not to sell psychology but to use our research and clinical skills to advance our understanding and the effectiveness of self-care interventions. Only by meeting this challenge will the next *Mind Power,* published perhaps in the year 2010, be more effective then the *Mind Powers* of 1987 and 1903. Only then will the next *Don't Be Afraid* be more effective then the *Don't Be Afraids* of 1976 and 1941. Only then will psychology fulfill its ability to advance self-care.

## NOTES

1. One reviewer of this article argued that psychologists do not control the advertising copy or they have not known to try to do so. Ellis (1977) reported that he demanded many years ago to have such previewing rights, and the Task Force Report on Self-Help Therapies of 1978 urged the APA to assist psychologists with sample contracts. This point is returned to later in this article. For purposes of the present discussion, suffice it to say that some psychologists have gained this control, and all psychologists could have known about the issue if the APA's Board of Professional Affairs had responded to its task force's recommendation in 1978.

2. Lazarus clarified that these claims were made by the publisher without his knowledge and that, subsequent to this experience, he insisted that "all advertising and promotional materials must receive my approval prior to pub-

lication" (Lazarus 1988, 600). This appears similar to the position advanced by Ellis (1977) as discussed in note 1.

3. This portion of the article cites several correspondences that are not in the public domain. In each case, the veracity of these correspondences has been confirmed by the editor of this journal. Copies of the correspondences can be obtained by writing Gerald M. Rosen.

4. The history of APA's involvement with *Psychology Today* was provided by VandenBos through telephone conversations and correspondences. His assistance is greatly appreciated but in no way connotes that VandenBos was himself involved or associated with APA's ownership and direction of *Psychology Today*.

5. Copies of the task force report should be on file with the Board of Professional Affairs of the APA.

# REFERENCES

American Psychological Association Task Force on Self-Help Therapies. 1978. *Task force report on self-help therapies.* Washington, DC: American Psychological Association.

Ayllon, T., and M. Freed. 1989. *Stopping baby's colic.* New York: Putnam.

Azrin, N. H., and R. M. Foxx. *Toilet training in less than a day.* New York: Simon and Schuster.

Azrin, N. H., and R. G. Nunn. 1977. *Habit control in a day.* New York: Simon and Schuster.

Barrera, M., Jr., and G. M. Rosen. 1977. Detrimental effects of a self-reward contracting program on subjects' involvement in self-administered desensitization. *Journal of Consulting and Clinical Psychology* 45: 1180–81.

Barrera, M., Jr., G. M. Rosen, and R. E. Glasgow. 1981. Rights, risks, and responsibilities in the use of self-help psychotherapy. In *Preservation of client rights*, edited by J. T. Hannah, R. Clark, and P. Christian. New York: Free Press, pp. 204–20.

Beyerstein, B. 1985. The myth of alpha consciousness. *Skeptical Inquirer* 10: 45–59.

———. 1990. Brainscams: Neuromythologies of the new age. *International Journal of Mental Health* 19: 27–36.

Cowles, E. S. 1941. *Don't be afraid!* New York: McGraw-Hill.

Crane, A. M. 1905. *Right and wrong thinking and their results.* Boston: Lothrop, Lee, and Shepard.

Doheny, K. 1988. Self-help. *Los Angeles Times,* October 2, part VI, p. 1.

Ellis, A. 1977. Rational-emotive therapy and self-help therapy. In *Non-prescription psychotherapies: A symposium on do-it-yourself treatments.* Symposium conducted at the 85th Annual Convention of the American Psychological Association, San Francisco, chaired by G. M. Rosen, August.

Glasgow, R. E., and G. M. Rosen. 1978. Behavioral bibliotherapy: A review of self-help behavior therapy manuals. *Psychological Bulletin* 85: 1–23.

———. 1982. Self-help behavior therapy manuals: Recent developments and clinical usage. *Clinical Behavior Therapy Review* 1: 1–20.

Jacobs, M. K., and G. Goodman 1989. Psychology and self-help groups: Predictions on a partnership. *American Psychologist* 44: 536–44.

Lazarus, A. 1977. *In the mind's eye.* New York: Rawson.

———. 1988. Right aim, wrong target. *American Psychologist* 43: 600.

Lofflin, J. 1988. Help from the hidden persuaders. *New York Times,* March 20.

Matson, J. L., and T. H. Hendick. 1977. Issues in toilet training normal children. *Behavior Therapy* 8: 549–53.

Miller, G. A. 1969. Psychology as a means of protecting human welfare. *American Psychologist* 24: 1063–75.

Mindware. 1990. *Mindware catalog.* Santa Cruz, CA: Author.

Olston, A. B. 1903. *Mind power.* Boston: Rockwell and Churchill.

Robitscher, J. 1980. *The powers of psychiatry.* Boston: Houghton Mifflin.

Rosen, G. M. 1976a. The development and use of nonprescription behavior therapies. *American Psychologist* 31: 139–41.

———. 1976b. *Don't be afraid.* Englewood Cliffs, NJ: Prentice-Hall.

———. 1987. Self-help treatment books and the commercialization of psychotherapy. *American Psychologist* 42: 46–51.

———. 1988. Multi-modal marketing: The selling of mind power. *Contemporary Psychology* 33: 861–63.

Rosen, G. M., R. E. Glasgow, and M. Barrera Jr. 1976. A controlled study to assess the clinical efficacy of totally self-administered systematic desensitization. *Journal of Consulting and Clinical Psychology* 44: 208–17.

Sadler, W. S. 1914. *Worry and nervousness or the science of self-mastery.* Chicago: A. C. McClurg.

Scogin, F., J. Bynum, G. Stephens, and S. Calhoon. 1990. Efficacy of self-administered treatment programs: Meta-analytic review. *Professional Psychology: Research and Practice* 21: 42–47.

Singer, J. L., and E. Switzer. 1980. *Mind play: The creative uses of fantasy.* Englewood Cliffs, NJ: Prentice-Hall.

Stark, E. 1989. Off-the-shelf salvation. *Health*, July, pp. 28–30.

Starker, S. 1988. Do-it-yourself therapy: The prescription of self-help books by psychologists. *Psychotherapy* 25: 142–46.

———. 1989. *Oracle at the supermarket: The American preoccupation with self-help books.* New Brunswick, NJ: Transaction.

Wood, H. 1893. *Ideal suggestion through mental photography.* Boston: Lee and Shepard.

Zilbergeld, B., and A. A. Lazarus. 1987. *Mind power.* Boston: Little, Brown.

## 27.

# EXPLODING THE SELF-ESTEEM MYTH

### Roy F. Baumeister, Jennifer D. Campbell, Joachim I. Krueger, and Kathleen D. Vohs

People intuitively recognize the importance of self-esteem to their psychological health, so it isn't particularly remarkable that most of us try to protect and enhance it in ourselves whenever possible. What is remarkable is that attention to self-esteem has become a communal concern, at least for Americans, who see a favorable opinion of oneself as the central psychological source from which all manner of positive outcomes spring. The corollary, that low self-esteem lies at the root of individual and thus societal problems, has sustained an ambitious social agenda for decades. Indeed, campaigns to raise people's sense of self-worth abound.

Consider what transpired in California in the late 1980s. Prodded by State Assemblyman John Vasconcellos, Governor George Deukmejian set up a task force on self-esteem and personal and social responsibility. Vasconcellos argued that raising self-esteem in young people would reduce crime, teen pregnancy, drug abuse, school underachievement and pollution, and even help to balance the state budget, a prospect predicated on the observation that people with high self-regard earn more than others and thus pay more in taxes. Along with its other activities, the task force assembled a team of scholars to survey the relevant literature. The results appeared in a 1989 volume titled *The Social Importance of Self-Esteem* (University of California Press, 1989), which stated that "many, if not most, of the major problems plaguing society have roots in the low self-esteem of many of the people who make up society." In reality, the report contained little to support that assertion. The California task force disbanded in 1995, but a nonprofit organization called the National Association for Self-Esteem (NASE) has picked up its mantle. Vasconcellos, until recently a California state senator, is on the advisory board.

Was it reasonable for leaders in California to start fashioning therapies and social policies without supportive data? Perhaps, given that they had problems to address. But one can draw on many more studies now than was the case fifteen years ago, enough to assess the value of self-esteem in several spheres. Regrettably, those who have been pursuing self-esteem-boosting programs, including the leaders of NASE, have not shown a desire to examine the new work, which is why the four of us recently came together under the aegis of the Association for Psychological Science to review the scientific literature.

## IN THE EYE OF THE BEHOLDER

Gauging the value of self-esteem requires, first of all, a sensible way to measure it. Most investigators just ask people what they think of themselves. Naturally enough, the answers are often colored by the common tendency to want to make oneself look good. Unfortunately, psychologists lack good methods to judge self-esteem.

Consider, for instance, research on the relation between self-esteem and physical attractiveness. Several studies have generally found clear positive links when people rate themselves on both properties. It seems plausible that physically attractive people would end up with high self-esteem because they are treated more favorably than unattractive ones—being more popular, more sought after, more valued by lovers and friends, and so forth. But it could just as well be that those who score highly on self-esteem scales by claiming to be wonderful people all around also boast of being physically attractive.

In 1995 Edward F. Diener and Brian Wolsic of the University of Illinois and Frank Fujita of Indiana University South Bend examined this possibility. They obtained self-esteem scores from a broad sample of the population and then photographed everybody, presenting these pictures to a panel of judges, who evaluated the subjects for attractiveness. Ratings based on full-length photographs showed no significant correlation with self-esteem. When the judges were shown pictures of just the participants' unadorned faces, the correlation between attractiveness and self-esteem was once again zero. In that same investigation, however, self-reported physical attractiveness was found to have a strong correlation with self-esteem. Apparently, those with high self-esteem are gorgeous in their own eyes but not necessarily to others.

This discrepancy should be sobering. What seemed at first to be a strong link between physical good looks and high self-esteem turned out to be nothing more than a pattern of consistency in how favorably people rate themselves. A parallel phenomenon affects those with low self-esteem, who are prone to floccinaucinihilipilification, a highfalutin word (among the longest in the *Oxford English Dictionary*) but one that we can't resist using here, it being defined as "the action or habit of estimating as worthless." That is, people with low self-esteem are not merely down on themselves; they are negative about everything.

This tendency has certainly distorted some assessments. For example, psychologists once thought that people with low self-esteem were especially prejudiced. But thoughtful scholars, such as Jennifer Crocker of the University of Michigan at Ann Arbor, questioned this conclusion. After all, if people rate themselves negatively, it is hard to label them as prejudiced for rating people not like themselves similarly. When one uses the difference between the subjects' assessments of their own group and their ratings of other groups as the yardstick for bias, the findings are reversed: people with *high* self-esteem appear to be more prejudiced. Floccinaucinihilipilification also raises the danger that those who describe themselves disparagingly may describe their lives similarly, thus furnishing the appearance that low self-esteem has unpleasant outcomes.

Given the often misleading nature of self-reports, we set up our

review to emphasize objective measures wherever possible—a requirement that greatly reduced the number of relevant studies (from more
than fifteen thousand to about two hundred). We were also mindful to
avoid another fallacy: the assumption that a correlation between self-
esteem and some desired behavior establishes causality. Indeed, the
question of causality goes to the heart of the debate. If high self-esteem
brings about certain positive outcomes, it may well be worth the effort
and expense of trying to instill this feeling. But if the correlations mean
simply that a positive self-image is a result of success or good behavior—
which is certainly plausible—there is little to be gained by raising self-
esteem alone. We began our two-year effort by reviewing studies relating
self-esteem to academic performance.

## SCHOOL DAZE

At the outset, we had every reason to hope that boosting self-esteem would
be a potent tool for helping students. Logic suggests that having a good
dollop of self-esteem would enhance striving and persistence in school,
while making a student less likely to succumb to paralyzing feelings of incompetence or self-doubt. Modern studies have, however, cast doubt on
the idea that higher self-esteem actually induces students to do better.

Such inferences about causality are possible when the subjects are
examined at two different times, as was the case in 1986 when Sheila M.
Pottebaum and her colleagues at the University of Iowa tested more than
twenty-three thousand high school students, first in the 10th and again
in the 12th grade. They found that self-esteem in 10th grade is only
weakly predictive of academic achievement in 12th grade. Academic
achievement in 10th grade correlates with self-esteem in 12th grade only
trivially better. Such results, which are now available from multiple
studies, certainly do not indicate that raising self-esteem offers students
much benefit. Some findings even suggest that artificially boosting self-
esteem may lower subsequent performance.

Even if raising self-esteem does not foster academic progress, might it serve some purpose later, say, on the job? Apparently not. Studies of possible links between workers' self-regard and job performance echo what has been found with schoolwork: the simple search for correlations yields some suggestive results, but these do not show whether a good self-image leads to occupational success, or vice versa. In any case, the link is not particularly strong.

The failure to contribute significantly at school or at the office would be easily offset if a heightened sense of self-worth helped someone to get along better with others. Having a good self-image might make someone more likable insofar as people prefer to associate with confident, positive individuals and generally avoid those who suffer from self-doubts and insecurities.

## GOOD FEELINGS, GOOD GRADES?

In an attempt to gauge whether high self-esteem leads to good academic performance, researchers surveyed thousands of high school students in their sophomore and senior years. The correlation between self-esteem sophomore year and academic performance senior year proved to be about the same as the correlation between academic performance sophomore year and self-esteem senior year. Thus, it is hard to say that either trait helps the other or whether some third factor gives rise to both high self-esteem and superior achievement.

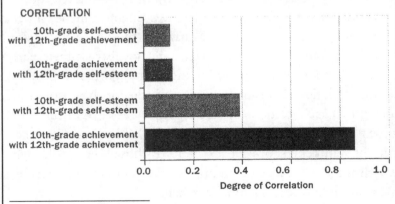

SOURCE: S. M. Pottebaum, T. Z. Keith, and S. W. Ehly in *Educational Research* (1986):140–44.

People who regard themselves highly generally state that they are popular and rate their friendships as being of superior quality to those described by people with low self-esteem, who report more negative interactions and less social support. But as Julia Bishop and Heidi M. Inderbitzen-Nolan of the University of Nebraska–Lincoln showed in 1995, these assertions do not reflect reality. The investigators asked 542 ninth grade students to nominate their most liked and least liked peers, and the resulting rankings displayed no correlation whatsoever with self-esteem scores.

A few other sound studies have found that the same is true for adults. In one of these investigations, conducted in the late 1980s, Duane P. Buhrmester, now at the University of Texas at Dallas, reported that college students with high levels of self-regard claimed to be substantially better at initiating relationships, disclosing things about themselves, asserting themselves in response to objectionable behaviors by others, providing emotional support and even managing interpersonal conflicts. Their roommates' ratings, however, told a different story. For four of the five interpersonal skills surveyed, the correlation with self-esteem dropped to near zero. The only one that remained statistically significant was with the subjects' ability to initiate new social contacts and friendships. This does seem to be one sphere in which confidence indeed matters: people who think that they are desirable and attractive should be adept at striking up conversations with strangers, whereas those with low self-esteem presumably shy away, fearing rejection.

One can imagine that such differences might influence a person's love life, too. In 2002 Sandra L. Murray of the University at Buffalo found that people low in self-esteem tend to distrust their partners' expressions of love and support, acting as though they are constantly expecting rejection. Thus far, however, investigators have not produced evidence that such relationships are especially prone to dissolve. In fact, high self-esteem may be the bigger threat: as Caryl E. Rusbult of the University of Kentucky showed back in 1987, those who think highly of themselves are more likely than others to respond to problems by severing relations and seeking other partners.

## Initiating Relationships

A study of college students revealed strong links between self-esteem and various interpersonal skills—when the subjects rated themselves. Ratings by their roommates provided a different picture: for four of the five skills surveyed, the correlations with self-esteem fell to levels that were not significant (NS) statistically. Nevertheless, the connection between self-esteem and prowess in initiating relationships stayed reasonably robust, as one might expect.

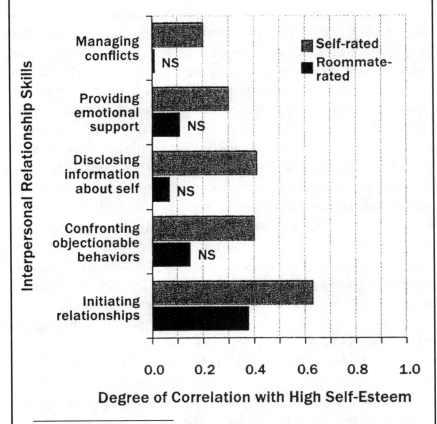

SOURCE: D. Buhrmesterp, W. Furmanp, M. T. Wettenberg, and H. T. Reis in *Journal of Personality and Social Psychology* (1988): 991–1008.

## SEX, DRUGS, AND ROCK 'N' ROLL

How about teenagers? How does self-esteem, or the lack thereof, influence their love life, in particular their sexual activity? Investigators have examined this subject extensively. All in all, the results do not support the idea that low self-esteem predisposes young people to more or earlier sexual activity. If anything, those with high self-esteem are less inhibited, more willing to disregard risks and more prone to engage in sex. At the same time, bad sexual experiences and unwanted pregnancies appear to lower self-esteem.

If not sex, then how about alcohol or illicit drugs? Abuse of these substances is one of the most worrisome behaviors among young people, and many psychologists once believed that boosting self-esteem would prevent such problems. The thought was that people with low self-esteem turn to drinking or drugs for solace. The data, however, do not consistently show that low adolescent self-esteem causes or even correlates with the abuse of alcohol or other drugs. In particular, in a large-scale study in 2000, Rob McGee and Sheila M. Williams of the Dunedin School of Medicine at the University of Otago in New Zealand found no correlation between self-esteem measured between ages nine and thirteen and drinking or drug use at age fifteen. Even when findings do show links between alcohol use and self-esteem, they are mixed and inconclusive. We did find, however, some evidence that low self-esteem contributes to illicit drug use. In particular, Judy A. Andrews and Susan C. Duncan of the Oregon Research Institute found in 1997 that declining levels of academic motivation (the main focus of their study) caused self-esteem to drop, which, in turn, led to marijuana use, although the connection was weak.

Interpretation of the findings on drinking and drug abuse is probably complicated by the fact that some people approach the experience out of curiosity or thrill seeking, whereas others may use it to cope with or escape from chronic unhappiness. The overall result is that no categorical statements can be made. The same is true for tobacco use, where our study-by-study review uncovered a preponderance of results that show no influence. The few positive findings we unearthed could conceivably reflect nothing more than self-report bias.

Another complication that also clouds these studies is that the category of people with high self-esteem contains individuals whose self-opinions differ in important ways. Yet in most analyses, people with a healthy sense of self-respect are, for example, lumped with those feigning higher self-esteem than they really feel or who are narcissistic. Not surprisingly, the results of such investigations may produce weak or contradictory findings.

## MIXED MESSAGES

A 1999 study by Donelson R. Forsyth and Natalie A. Kerr, both then at Virginia Commonwealth University, suggests that attempts to boost self-esteem among struggling students may backfire. College students getting grades of D or F in a psychology course were divided into two groups, arranged initially to have the same grade-point average. Each week students in the first group received an e-mail message designed to boost their self-esteem (*example at left*). Those in the second group received a message intended to instill a sense of personal responsibility for their academic performance (*right*).

By the end of the course, the average grade in the first group dropped below 50 percent—a failing grade. The average for students in the second group was 62 percent—a D minus, which is poor but still passing.

### Self-Esteem and Happiness

A person's overall satisfaction with life tends to go hand in hand with his or her level of self-esteem, as shown by the high degree of correlation between the two. In most countries overall life satisfaction correlates better with self-esteem than with financial satisfaction. Exceptions tend to be countries with low per capita GDP (*bracketed values, US dollars.*)

## WHAT CAUSES GOOD AND BAD GRADES?

Research suggests that when students get back their tests, they tend to lose confidence: they say things like "I can't do this," or "I'm worthless," or "I'm not as good as other people in college."

Other studies suggest, though, that students who have high self-esteem not only get better grades, but they remain self-confident and assured.

In fact, in one study researchers had students write down what "went through their minds" when they were trying to get better grades. Students who improved with each test were thinking:

*"I can be proud of myself."*

*"I can do this."*

*"I am better than most of the other people in this school."*

*"I am satisfied with myself."*

Students who did not improve were thinking:

*"I'm ashamed of myself."*

*"I don't deserve to be in college."*

*"I'm worthless."*

BOTTOM LINE: Hold your head—and your self-esteem—high.

## WHAT CAUSES GOOD AND BAD GRADES?

Research suggests that when students get back their tests, they tend to blame poor scores on external factors: they say things like "the test was too hard," or "the prof didn't explain that," or "the questions are too picky."

Other studies suggest, though, that students who take responsibility for their grades not only get better grades, but they also learn that they, personally, can control the grades they get.

In fact, in one study researchers had students write down what "went through their minds" when they were trying to get better grades. Students who improved with each test were thinking:

*"I need to work harder."*

*"I can learn this material if I apply myself."*

*"I can control what happens to me in this class."*

*"I have what it takes to do this."*

Students who did not improve were thinking:

*"It's not my fault."*

*"This test was too hard."*

*"I'm not good at this."*

BOTTOM LINE: Take personal control of your performance.

# Self-Esteem and Happiness

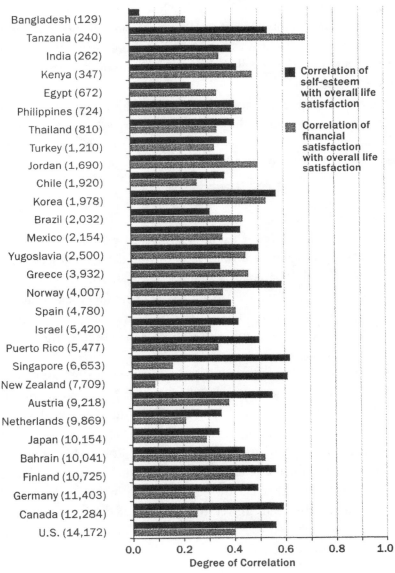

SOURCE: E. Diener and M. Diener, in *Journal of Personality and Social Psychology* (1995): 653–63.

# BULLY FOR YOU

For decades, psychologists believed that low self-esteem was an important cause of aggression. One of us (Baumeister) challenged that notion in 1996, when he reviewed assorted studies and concluded that perpetrators of aggression generally hold favorable and perhaps even inflated views of themselves.

Take the bullying that goes on among children, a common form of aggression. Dan Olweus of the University of Bergen was one of the first to dispute the notion that under their tough exteriors, bullies suffer from insecurities and self-doubts. Although Olweus did not measure self-esteem directly, he showed that bullies reported less anxiety and were more sure of themselves than other children. Apparently the same applies to violent adults.

After coming to the conclusion that high self-esteem does not lessen a tendency toward violence; that it does not deter adolescents from turning to alcohol, tobacco, drugs, and sex; and that it fails to improve academic or job performance, we got a boost when we looked into how self-esteem relates to happiness. The consistent finding is that people with high self-esteem are significantly happier than others. They are also less likely to be depressed.

One especially compelling study was published in 1995, after Diener and his daughter Marissa, now a psychologist at the University of Utah, surveyed more than thirteen thousand college students, and high self-esteem emerged as the strongest factor in overall life satisfaction. In 2004 Sonja Lyubomirsky, Christopher Tkach and M. Robin DiMatteo of the University of California, Riverside, reported data from more than six hundred adults ranging in age from fifty-one to ninety-five. Once again, happiness and self-esteem proved to be closely tied. Before it is safe to conclude that high self-esteem leads to happiness, however, further research must address the shortcomings of the work that has been done so far.

First, causation needs to be established. It seems possible that high self-esteem brings about happiness, but no research has shown this outcome. The strong correlation between self-esteem and happiness is just that—a correlation. It is plausible that occupational, academic or interpersonal successes cause both happiness and high self-esteem and that corresponding failures cause both unhappiness and low self-esteem. It is even possible that happiness, in the sense of a temperament or disposition to feel good, induces high self-esteem.

Second, it must be recognized that happiness and its opposite, depression, have been studied mainly by means of self-report, and the tendency of some people toward negativity may produce both their low opinions of themselves and unfavorable evaluations of other aspects of life. Yet it is not clear what could replace such assessments. An investigator would indeed be hard-pressed to demonstrate convincingly that a person was less (or more) happy than he or she supposed. Clearly, objective measures of happiness and depression are going to be difficult if not impossible to obtain, but that does not mean self-reports should be accepted uncritically.

What then should we do? Should parents, teachers and therapists seek to boost self-esteem wherever possible? In the course of our literature review, we found some indications that self-esteem is a helpful attribute. It improves persistence in the face of failure. And individuals with high self-esteem sometimes perform better in groups than do those with low self-esteem. Also, a poor self-image is a risk factor for certain eating disorders, especially bulimia—a connection one of us (Vohs) and her colleagues documented in 1999. Other effects are harder to demonstrate with objective evidence, although we are inclined to accept the subjective evidence that self-esteem goes hand in hand with happiness.

So we can certainly understand how an injection of self-esteem might be valuable to the individual. But imagine if a heightened sense of self-worth prompted some people to demand preferential treatment or to exploit their fellows. Such tendencies would entail considerable social costs. And we have found little to indicate that indiscriminately promoting self-esteem in today's children or adults, just for being themselves, offers society any compensatory benefits beyond the seductive pleasure it brings to those engaged in the exercise.

# 28.

# SUBLIMINAL PERCEPTION: FACTS AND FALLACIES

## Timothy E. Moore

Can the meaning of a stimulus affect the behavior of observers in some way in the absence of their awareness of the stimulus? In a word, *yes*. While there is some controversy, there is also respectable scientific evidence that observers' responses can be shown to be affected by stimuli they claim not to have seen. To a cognitive psychologist, this is not particularly earthshaking, but the media and the public have often responded to the notion of subliminal perception with trepidation.

What is subliminal perception? Should we be worried (or perhaps enthused) about covert manipulation of thoughts, attitudes, and behaviors? My reviews (Moore 1982; 1988) have dealt primarily with the validity of the more dramatic claims made on behalf of subliminal techniques and devices. Such an appraisal requires a working definition of "subliminal perception." Then we need to determine whether the conditions under which it occurs and the means by which it is achieved are reflected in the products on the market.

How should "awareness" be defined? One way is simply to ask observers whether or not they are "aware" of a stimulus. If the observer denies any awareness, then the stimulus, is, by definition, below an awareness threshold. Using this approach, unconscious perception consists of demonstrating that observers can be affected by stimuli *whose presence they do not report*. Another way to define "awareness" involves requiring observers to distinguish between two or more stimuli that are

Reprinted with permission from *Skeptical Inquirer* (Spring 1992): 273–81.

presented successively. With fast exposure durations, observers may be unable to distinguish between stimuli or between a stimulus's presence or absence. This method was advocated by Eriksen (1960) and defines consciousness as the observer's ability to discriminate between two or more alternative stimuli in a forced-choice task. In this context, unconscious perception consists of a demonstration that observers are affected by stimuli *whose presence they cannot detect.* The approaches are different and involve different sorts of evidence. In the former case, the stimuli are not reported; in the latter instance, the stimuli cannot be detected.

These two methods of defining consciousness have been referred to as "subjective" and "objective," respectively, by Merikle and his coworkers (Cheesman & Merikle 1986). Higher levels of visibility are typically associated with subjective thresholds. The disadvantage of a subjective definition is that a failure to report a stimulus's presence may result from response bias (i.e., the observer is ambivalent about the stimulus's presence and elects to report its absence). As Merikle (1984) has argued, the use of subjective thresholds implies that each participant provides his or her own idiosyncratic definition of "awareness." Consequently, awareness thresholds could (and would) vary greatly from subject to subject.

Some recent studies (e.g., Cheesman & Merikle 1986) have looked at performance when both subjective *and* objective thresholds have been assessed. Such studies indicate that subliminal perception is most appropriately viewed as perception in the absence of concurrent phenomenal experience. We sometimes receive information when subjectively we feel that nothing useful has been "seen." Investigators can establish that perception has occurred in the face of disavowals from participants by forcing them to guess. Respondents may object that they have no basis for making a decision, but by using a forced-choice task, we can see that their guesses are more accurate than they would be if they were guessing at random. Clearly, some information is being utilized.

When respondents' guesses *are* at chance in a detection task, there is no well-established evidence for perception. Thus, subliminal perception is not perception in the absence of a detectable signal. Rather, it occurs under conditions where subjects can detect a signal on at least some proportion of trials. Subjects may claim to be guessing without realizing that their guesses are better than chance. According to Merikle, the dissociation between these two indicators of perception (signal detection vs. introspective reports) defines the necessary empirical conditions for demonstrating subliminal perception. There is an inconsistency between what observers know and what "they know they know."

Recent reviews of research findings in subliminal perception have provided very little evidence that stimuli below observers' subjective thresholds influence motives, attitudes, beliefs, or choices (Moore 1988; 1991b; Pratkanis & Greenwald 1988; Greenwald 1992). In most studies, the stimuli do not consist of directives, commands, or imperatives, and there is no reliable evidence that subliminal stimuli have any pragmatic impact or effects on intentions. Studies that do purport to find such effects are either unreplicated or methodologically flawed in one or more ways (Pratkanis, Spring 1992 issue of *Skeptical Inquirer*). There is very little evidence for any perceptual processing *at all* (let alone any pragmatic consequences) when perceptual awareness is equated with an objective threshold.

How do the dramatic claims regarding undetectable stimuli stack up against the preceding review? What are these claims and what is their status? I shall confine my comments to claims involving advertising applications and self-help auditory tapes.

## ADVERTISING

Many people believe that most advertisements contain hidden sexual images or words that affect our susceptibility to the ads. This belief is widespread even though there is no evidence for such practices, let alone evidence for such effects. "Embedded" stimuli are difficult to characterize in terms of signal-detection theory or threshold-determination procedures because most of them remain unidentifiable even when focal attention is directed to them. Nevertheless, the use of the term *sublim-*

*inal* is a fait accompli, and belief in such an influence is primarily the consequence of the writings and lectures of just one person—Wilson Bryan Key (1973; 1976; 1980; 1990). Key offers no scientific evidence to support the existence of subliminal images, nor does he provide any empirical documentation of their imputed effects (Creed 1987; see also Vokey & Read 1985).

In a review of Key's 1990 book, John O'Toole, president of the American Association of Advertising Agencies, wondered: "Why is there a market for yet another re-run of this troubled man's paranoid nightmares?" (O'Toole 1989, 26). Part of the reason that Key's books sell so well may be that they are not what they appear to be. The information is not presented as the subjective fantasies of one person. Instead, it is presented as scientific, empirical fact. Science is respectable. Consequently, if claims are cloaked in scientific jargon, and if propositions are asserted to be scientifically valid, people can be fooled. Key knows this and uses it to his advantage. His intent is to persuade, and if he can do so by misrepresenting scientific data and findings, he is apparently prepared to do so.

Key provided pretrial testimony at the Judas Priest trial in Reno, Nevada, in the summer of 1990. Two teenagers had committed suicide. Their parents sued Judas Priest and CBS Records Inc., alleging that subliminal messages in Judas Priest's music contributed to the suicides. Key was testifying on behalf of the plaintiffs, and at the trial he responded to a question about scientific methodology by saying: "Science is pretty much what you can get away [with] at any particular point in history and you can get away with a great deal" (*Vance/Roberson v. CBS/Judas Priest* 1990, 60). This unabashed disdain for anything approaching scientific integrity has not endeared him to the scientific community.

Attempting to apply scientific criteria to propositions for which there is no pretense at scientific foundation is a relatively futile exercise. Key's only interest in science seems to be in the persuasive power of adopting a scientific posture or style. The use of scientific jargon does not necessarily reflect scientific attitudes or methods. Under these circumstances, even to apply the term *pseudoscience* seems unwarranted.

Extravagant claims notwithstanding, advertising may affect us in subtle and indirect ways. While there is no scientific evidence for the existence of "embedded" figures or words, let alone effects from them, the images and themes contained in advertisements may well influence viewers' attitudes and values without their awareness. In other words, the viewer may be well aware of the stimulus, but not necessarily aware of the connection between the stimulus and responses or reactions to it. For example, there was a television commercial a few years ago for skin cream in which a mother and daughter were portrayed. The viewer was challenged to distinguish mother from daughter. According to Postman (1988), the unstated message is that in our culture it is desirable that a mother not look older than her daughter. A number of social scientists believe that advertising may play a role in the development of personal identity and social values (Leiss, Klein & Jhally 1986; Schudson 1984; Wachtel 1983). It is difficult, however, to isolate advertising's role from the many other social forces at work. Moreover, most research on advertising effects consists of content analyses of the ads themselves. Such studies leave many unanswered questions about the impact of that content on the viewing public.

## SUBLIMINAL AUDITORY SELF-HELP TAPES

When claims about covert advertising were raised in September 1957, the *New Yorker* lamented that "minds had been broken and entered" (Moore 1982). More than three decades later, claims of covert subliminal manipulation persist. Television commercials, magazine ads, and bookstores promote subliminal tapes that promise to induce dramatic improvements in mental and psychological health. These devices are ostensibly capable of producing many desirable effects, including weight loss, breast enlargement, improvement of sexual function, and relief from constipation.

Subliminal tapes represent a change in modality from visual to auditory, and now subliminal stimulation is supposedly being harnessed for a more noble purpose—psychotherapy, clearly a less crass objective than that of covert advertising. However, the scientific grounds for substantiating the utility of today's self-help tapes is as poor as was the documentation for advertising effects thirty years ago. Proponents seem to have assumed that for obtaining subliminal effects one modality is as good as another. Claims about the utility of subliminal tapes are essentially claims about the subliminal perception of speech—a phenomenon for which there is very little evidence (Moore 1988). The basic problem is that the few studies that purport to have demonstrated effects of subliminal speech used such crude methods for defining subliminality that the findings are quite uninteresting (e.g., Henley 1975; Borgeat et al. 1985).

It is not obvious what the analogue to visual masking is for a speech signal. Masking, in the visual domain, is procedurally defined with relative precision. The mask does not mutilate or change the target stimulus—it simply limits the time available for perceiving the preceding target. In the absence of the mask, the target is easily perceived. In the auditory domain, the target signal is reduced in volume and further attenuated by the superimposition of other supraliminal material. Often the subliminal "message" is accelerated or compressed to such a degree that the message is unintelligible, even when supraliminal. It is an extraordinary claim that an undetectable speech signal engages our nervous system and is perceived—consciously or not. Signal detection is an implicit sine qua non of most theories of speech perception (Massaro 1987). To assert that "subliminal speech" is unconsciously perceived appears to call into question some very fundamental principles of sensory physiology. What is the nature of the signal that arrives at the basilar membrane? If the critical signal is washed out or drowned out by other sounds, then on what basis are we to suppose that the weaker of the two signals becomes disentangled and comprehensible?

The tapes also have a dubious conceptual rationale in their assumed therapeutic impact. Even if the message could achieve semantic representation, how or why should it affect motivation? Answering the question "How?" is important, because it provides the theoretical justification for the practice.

## "Neither Theoretical Foundation Nor Experimental Evidence"

The committee's review of the available research literature leads to our conclusion that, at this time, there is neither theoretical foundation nor experimental evidence to support claims that subliminal self-help tapes enhance human performance . . .

Several sociopsychological phenomena, including effort justification and expectancy or placebo effects, may contribute to an erroneous judgment that self-help products are effective, even in the absence of any actual improvements in emotion, appearance, attitude, or any other physical or psychological quality.

—*In the Mind's Eye*, Committee on Techniques for the Enhancement of Human Performance, National Research Council (Washington, DC: National Academy Press, 1991), pp. 15–16.

There are subliminally embedded messages at work. You won't be able to hear them consciously. But your subconscious will. And it will obey. [Zygon]

To gain control, it is necessary to speak to the subconscious mind in a language that it comprehends—we have to speak to it subliminally. [Mind Communications Inc.]

Is there a pipeline to the id? Can we sneak directives into the unconscious through the back door? There may be a fundamental misconception at work here, consisting of equating unconscious perceptual processes with the psychodynamic unconscious (Eagle 1987; Marcel 1988). Cognitive psychologists use the term *unconscious* to refer to perceptual processes and effects of which we have no phenomenal awareness. Induced movement is an example of an unconscious perceptual process. Tacit knowledge of and conformity to grammatical rules is another example of unconscious processing. No one would want to argue, however, that either of these domains of activity have anything to do with the psychodynamic unconscious. Psychodynamic theorists use the term *unconscious* as a noun with a capital U, to refer to, for lack of a better term, the id—"a cauldron full of seething excitations," as Freud expressed it. Because semantic activation without conscious awareness can be demonstrated, some observers have jumped to the conclusion that subliminal stimulation provides relatively direct access to the id. This assumption has neither theoretical nor empirical support.

While tape distributors often claim that their products have been scientifically validated, there is no evidence of therapeutic effectiveness (e.g., Auday et al. 1991; Greenwald et al. 1991; Merikle & Skanes 1992; Russell et al. 1991). In addition, both Merikle (1988) and Moore (1991a) have conducted studies that showed that many tapes do not appear to contain the sort of signal that could, in principle, allow subliminal perception to occur.

Quite apart from the lack of empirical support, there is little or no theoretical motivation for expecting therapeutic effects from such stimuli. The "explanation" consists of attributing to the systemic unconscious whatever mechanisms or processes would be logically necessary in order for the effects to occur. Because there is no independent evidence for such "unconscious" perceptual processes, it is not surprising that there is no evidence for the imputed effects (see Eich & Hyman 1991; Moore 1991b). Furthermore, Greenwald (1992) has recently queried the conventional psychoanalytic conception of a sophisticated unconscious processor, arguing that it is neither theoretically necessary nor empirically substantiated.

The burden of proof of the viability of these materials is on those who are promoting their use. There is no such proof, and therefore the possibility of health fraud could be raised. These tapes sometimes sell for as much as $400 a set. Of even greater concern is the fact that legitimate forms of therapy may go untried in the quest for a fast, cheap "cure."

According to William Jarvis, president of the National Coalition Against Health Fraud, a quack is "anyone who promotes, for financial gain, a remedy known to be false, unsafe, or unproven" (Jarvis 1989, 4).

Fraud, on the other hand, implies intentional deception. Consequently, not all quackery is fraud, nor is fraud synonymous with quackery. As Jarvis has pointed out, in some ways quacks may be *worse* than frauds. "The most dangerous quacks are the zealots who will take the poison themselves in their enthusiasm for their nostrums. Sincerity may make quacks more socially tolerable, but it goes far in enhancing their danger to the public" (ibid.).

## SCIENTISTS, THE MEDIA, AND THE POPULARIZATION OF SCIENCE

The popularity and interest in the topic of subliminal influences—both inside and outside academic circles—can be attributed, in part, to media coverage. Conspiracy theories make good copy, and in subliminal advertising we have a large-scale technological conspiracy to control people's minds with invisible stimuli. With subliminal tapes you can allegedly change your behavior and your personality in profound and important ways—effortlessly and painlessly. The quick fix of psychotherapy is an intriguing notion. It is therefore small wonder that it continues to be a popular topic for writers.

Carl Sagan (1987) has suggested that pseudoscience flourishes because the scientific community does a poor job of communicating its findings. To propose that we can be influenced in dramatic ways by undetectable stimuli is a remarkable claim with little scientific support, but blaming journalists for promulgating the claim absolves the scientific community from any responsibility in the educational process. Relations between scientists and the press could be improved if scientists communicated more clearly. Researchers take such great pains to avoid making absolute pronouncements that they often err in the opposite direction. We sometimes speak with a tentativeness that belies the facts, understating our confidence that some propositions are true and that others are false (Rothman 1989). When we talk to the press, we need to speak plainly. For example, Phil Merikle recently observed that "there's unanimous opinion that subliminal tapes are a complete sham and a fraud" (Rae 1991). Merikle is correct, but such candor is relatively rare. Who will distinguish science from pseudoscience if not the scientists?

Paradoxically, while negative scientific evidence continues to accumulate, the subliminal-tape industry—fueled by aggressive advertising campaigns—thrives. As Burnham (1987) has noted, advertising's authority often derives from the use of scientific regalia. Advertising's purpose is, however, antithetical to that of science: "Advertisers [are] engaged in remystifying the world, not demystifying it" (Burnham 1987, 247). Extraordinary claims, if they are repeated often enough, can perpetuate extraordinary beliefs. When nonsense masquerades as science and magic is diguised as therapy, the result is not always laughable. Consider the self-help tape for survivors of sexual abuse; the user is informed that lasting relief from the trauma of abuse is contingent upon the victim's acknowledgment of their own role in causing the abuse in the first place (Moore 1991b).

## CONCLUSION

Subliminal advertising and psychotherapeutic effects from subliminal tapes are ideas whose scientific status appears to be on a par with wearing copper bracelets to cure arthritis. Not even the most liberal speculations regarding the use of subliminal techniques for "practical" purposes impute any potential utility to these practices (Bornstein 1989). The interesting question to ask is not "Do subliminal advertising techniques or subliminal auditory tapes work?" but, rather, "How did these implausible ideas ever acquire such an undeserved mantle of scientific respectability?" The answer involves a complex interplay of public attitudes toward science, how social science is popularized in the mass media, and how the scientific community communicates to those outside the scientific community. Carl Sagan may be right—pseudoscience *will* flourish if scientists don't take more responsibility for the accurate dissemination of scientific information.

According to Burnham (1987), superstition has triumphed over rationalism and skepticism partly because scientists no longer engage in the popularization of science—summarizing, simplifying, and translating scientific findings for lay audiences. The function of popularizing science and health is now carried out by journalists and educators. Consequently, many topics, including this one, receive coverage that is, at best, deficient in background information and meaningful context, and at worst, fragmented and misleading. Further confusion is caused by the tendency among journalists to manufacture controversies where none exists by juxtaposing the pronouncements of "authorities" who contradict one another. If all authorities (including those with financial stakes in their positions) are equally admissible, controversies abound.

# REFERENCES

Auday, B. C., J. L. Mellett, and P. M. Williams. 1991. "Self-Improvement Using Subliminal Self-help Audiotapes: Consumer Benefit or Consumer Fraud?" Paper presented at the meeting of the Western Psychological Association, San Francisco, April.

Borgeat, F., R. Elie, L. Chaloult, and R. Chabot. 1985. Psychophysiological responses to masked auditory stimuli. *Canadian Journal of Psychiatry* 30: 22–27.

Bornstein, R. F. 1989. Subliminal techniques as propaganda tools: Review and critique. *Journal of Mind and Behavior* 10: 231–62.

Burnham, J. C. 1987. *How Superstition Won and Science Lost: Popularizing Science and Health in the United States.* New Brunswick, NJ: Rutgers University Press.

Cheesman, J., and P. M. Merikle. 1986. Distinguishing conscious from unconscious perceptual processes. *Canadian Journal of Psychology* 40: 343–67.

Creed, T. L. 1987. Subliminal deception: Pseudoscience on the college lecture circuit. *Skeptical Inquirer* 11: 358–66.

Eagle, M. 1987. "The Psychoanalytic and the Cognitive Unconscious." In *Theories of the Unconscious and Theories of the Self,* edited by R. Stern. Hillsdale, NJ: Analytic Press.

Eich, E., and R. Hyman. 1991. Subliminal self-help. In *In the Mind's Eye: Enhancing Human Performance*, edited by D. Druckman and R. Bjork. Washington, DC: National Academy Press.

Eriksen, C. W. 1960. Discrimination and learning without awareness: A methodological survey and evaluation. *Psychological Review* 67: 279–300.

Greenwald, A. G. 1992. New look 3: Reclaiming unconscious cognition. *American Psychologist* 47: 766–79.

Greenwald, A. G., E. R. Spangenberg, and J. Eskenazi. 1991. Double-blind tests of subliminal self-help audiotapes. *Psychological Science* 2: 119–22.

Henley, S. 1975. Cross-modal effects of subliminal verbal stimuli. *Scandinavian Journal of Psychology* 16: 30–36.

Jarvis, W. 1989. What constitutes quackery? *NCAHF Newsletter* 12, no. 4: 4–5.

Key, W. B. 1973. *Subliminal Seduction*. Englewood Cliffs, NJ: Signet.

———. 1976. *Media Sexploitation*. Englewood Cliffs, NJ: Prentice-Hall.

———. 1980. *The Clam-Plate Orgy*. Englewood Cliffs, NJ: Prentice-Hall.

———. 1990. *The Age of Manipulation: The Con in Confidence, the Sin in Sincere*. Englewood Cliffs, NJ: Prentice-Hall.

Leiss, W., S. Kline, and S. Jhally. 1986. *Social Communication in Advertising*. Toronto: Methuen.

Marcel, A. J. 1988. Electrophysiology and Meaning in Cognitive Science and Dynamic Psychology—Comments on "Unconscious Conflict: A Convergent Psychodynamic and Electrophysical Approach." In *Psychodynamics and Cognition*, edited by M. J. Horowitz. Chicago: University of Chicago Press.

Massaro, D. W. 1987. *Speech Perception by Ear and Eye: A Paradigm for Psychological Inquiry*. Hillsdale, NJ: Erlbaum.

Merikle, P. M. 1984. Toward a definition of awareness. *Bulletin of the Psychonomic Society* 22: 449–50.

———. 1988. Subliminal auditory tapes: An evaluation. *Psychology & Marketing* 46: 355–72.

Merikle, P., and H. E. Skanes. 1992. Subliminal Self-Help Audio Tapes: A Search for Placebo Effects. *Journal of Applied Psychology* 77: 772–76.

Moore, T. E. 1982. Subliminal advertising: What you see is what you get. *Journal of Marketing* 46: 38–47.

———. 1988. The case against subliminal manipulation. *Psychology & Marketing* 46: 297–316.

————. 1991a. "Evaluating Subliminal Auditory Tapes: Is There Any Evidence for Subliminal Perception?" Unpublished manuscript, Glendon College, York University, Toronto.

————. 1991b. "Subliminal Auditory Self-Help Tapes." In *Self-Care: A Symposium on Self-Help Therapies.* Symposium conducted at the 99th convention of the American Psychological Association, San Francisco, August.

O'Toole, P. 1989. Those sexy ice cubes are back. *Advertising Age,* October 2, p. 26.

Postman, N. 1988. *Conscientious Objections.* New York: Knopf.

Pratkanis, A. R., and A. G. Greenwald. 1988. Recent perspectives on unconscious processing: Still no marketing applications. *Psychology & Marketing* 5: 337–53.

Rae, S. 1991. Brain waves: Subliminal self-help messages while you sleep? *Elle,* April, pp. 118–19.

Rothman, M. 1989. Myths about science . . . and belief in the paranormal. *Skeptical Inquirer* 14: 25–34.

Russell, T. G., W. Rowe, and A. Smouse. 1991. Subliminal self-help tapes and academic achievement: An evaluation. *Journal of Counselling & Development* 69: 359–62.

Sagan, C. 1987. The burden of skepticism. *Skeptical Inquirer* 12: 38–46.

Schudson, M. 1984. *Advertising, the Uneasy Persuasion.* New York: Basic Books.

*Vance/Roberson v. CBS Inc./Judas Priest.* 1990. No. 86-5844 and 86-3939 (Washoe County, 2nd Judicial District Court of Nevada, Motion for Summary Judgment, June 3, 1989).

Vokey, J. R., and J. D. Read. 1985. Subliminal messages: Between the devil and the media. *American Psychologist* 40: 1231–39.

Wachtel, P. 1983. *The Poverty of Affluence.* New York: Macmillan.

# SECTION VIII:
# SOLUTIONS AND REMEDIES

# INTRODUCTION

A s we have seen, the field of mental health practice has a great deal to offer to prospective psychotherapy clients. A number of therapies are at least moderately helpful for a broad array of mental health problems, and some self-help programs derived from well-validated scientific principles appear to work reasonably well.

At the same time, it is painfully clear that serious problems remain in the mammoth world of mental health. Sizable minorities of practitioners continue to rely heavily on assessment instruments of questionable reliability and validity, as well as to administer dubious psychotherapies that are either untested or ineffective. Moreover, the growing industry of self-help books and self-help experts continues to propagate many claims of doubtful scientific validity.

So what can clinical psychologists, psychiatrists, psychiatric nurses, social workers, counselors, and other mental health professionals do about these problems? In this final section of the book, we propose some constructive solutions and remedies for the ailments afflicting the field of mental health.

First, Scott Lilienfeld and his colleagues offer a five-point prescription for the field of clinical psychology. They recommend that (1) clinical psychology training programs require formal education in critical-thinking skills, (2) the field of clinical psychology focus on identifying potentially harmful treatments in addition to efficacious treatments, (3) professional psychological organizations play a more active role in maintaining quality control in continuing education offerings for practitioners, (4) these organizations play a more active role in combating misleading media and popular psychology claims regarding unsubstantiated psychological techniques, and (5) these organizations impose sanctions on practitioners who offer services that are clearly ineffective or potentially harmful.

In the book's concluding selection, Margaret Singer and Jana Lalich offer an invaluable set of mental health consumers' guidelines for avoiding therapeutic land mines. For example, they urge therapy clients to be skeptical of practitioners who attempt to indoctrinate them into a "mythology" of human behavior, who arrive at diagnoses and interpretations quickly, and who begin to take control of increasing spheres of their personal lives. Singer and Lalich also lay out a set of "common traits of bad therapy," including inadequate psychological history-taking, failure to provide a diagnosis, absence of clear goals or treatment plans, fostering of excessive dependency on the therapist, and lack of monitoring of clients' ongoing progress. By heeding Singer and Lalich's sage warnings, readers will emerge better prepared to navigate the *mind*field while avoiding potentially hazardous missteps.

## 29.

# SCIENCE AND PSEUDOSCIENCE IN CLINICAL PSYCHOLOGY: CONCLUDING THOUGHTS AND CONSTRUCTIVE REMEDIES

*Scott O. Lilienfeld, Steven Jay Lynn, and Jeffrey M. Lohr*

We believe that the preceding chapters have made clear that the scientific underpinnings of the field of clinical psychology are threatened by the increasing proliferation of unsubstantiated and untested psychotherapeutic, assessment, and diagnostic techniques. In this concluding section of the book, we propose five remedies that we believe will go a substantial way toward healing the ills presently afflicting the field of clinical psychology. We are reasonably confident that if these remedies are followed, the problem of pseudoscience in clinical psychology may ultimately prove amenable to a cure.

Here is our five-point prescription for the field of clinical psychology:

1. All clinical psychology training programs must require formal training in critical-thinking skills, particularly those needed to distinguish scientific from pseudoscientific methods of inquiry (see Lilienfeld, Lohr, & Morier, 2001, for helpful resources). In particular, clinical training programs must emphasize such

Reprinted from Scott O. Lilienfeld, Steven Jay Lynn, and Jeffrey M. Lohr, eds., *Science and Pseudoscience in Clinical Psychology* (New York: Guilford Press, 2003), pp. 461–64. Copyright 2003 Guilford Press.

issues as (1) clinical judgment and prediction, and the factors (e.g., confirmatory bias, overconfidence, illusory correlation; Garb 1998) that can lead clinicians astray when evaluating assessment information (see Grove 2000 for similar recommendations); (2) fundamental issues in the philosophy of science, particularly the distinctions between scientific and nonscientific epistemologies; (3) research methodologies required to evaluate the validity of assessment instruments and the efficacy and effectiveness of psychotherapies; and (4) issues in the psychology of human memory, particularly the reconstructive nature of memory and the impact of suggestive therapeutic procedures on memory. Moreover, the American Psychological Association (APA) must be willing to withhold accreditation from clinical PhD and PsyD programs that do not place substantial emphasis on these and related topics, which should be mandatory in the education and training of all clinical psychologists.

2. The field of clinical psychology must focus on identifying not only empirically supported treatments (ESTs; see Chambless & Ollendick 2001), but also treatments that are clearly devoid of empirical support. We regard the effort to produce explicit lists of ESTs as laudable, although we share some authors' concerns regarding the criteria used to identify these techniques.

Nevertheless, the battle against pseudoscience is too substantial to be waged on only a single front. Although the identification of efficacious therapeutic techniques is an important long-term goal, we must also work toward identifying techniques that are either clearly inefficacious or harmful. The development of a formal list of "psychotherapies to avoid" would be an important start in that direction, both for practitioners and would-be consumers of psychotherapy. We would suggest that such techniques as facilitated communication for infantile autism, rebirthing and reparenting, and critical-incident stress debriefing be among the first entries on this list.

3. The APA and other psychological organizations must play a more

active role in ensuring that the continuing education of practitioners is grounded in solid scientific evidence. A perusal of recent editions of the *APA Monitor on Psychology,* an in-house publication of the APA that is sent to all its members, reveals that the APA has been accepting advertisements for a plethora of unvalidated psychological treatments, including Thought Field Therapy and Imago Relationship Therapy, two techniques for which essentially no published controlled research exists. Among the workshops for which the APA has recently provided continuing education (CE) credits to practicing clinicians are courses in calligraphy therapy, neurofeedback, Jungian sandplay therapy, and the use of psychological theater to "catalyze critical consciousness" (see Lilienfeld 1998). The APA has also recently offered CE credits for critical-incident stress debriefing, a technique that has been shown in several controlled studies to be harmful. Some state psychological associations have not done much better. Very recently, the Minnesota Board of Psychology approved workshops in rock climbing, canoeing, sandplay therapy, and drumming meditation for CE credits (Lilienfeld 2001).

If professional organizations intend to assist practitioners in the critical task of distinguishing techniques with and without adequate scientific support, they must insist on providing continuing education that serves this goal. Moreover, academics and clinicians who possess expertise in the differences between scientifically supported and unsupported assessment and therapeutic techniques must play a more active role in the development and dissemination of CE courses and workshops. To facilitate this process, academic clinical psychology programs must encourage their faculty members to participate in the construction and design of scientifically oriented CE courses.

4. The APA and other psychological organizations must play a more visible public role in combating erroneous claims in the popular press and elsewhere (e.g., the Internet) regarding psychotherapeutic and assessment techniques. These organizations have tra-

ditionally been reluctant to play the role of media "watchdogs" in the battle against unsubstantiated mental health methods and claims. In an era in which unsubstantiated mental health techniques are thriving with unabated vigor, such reluctance is becoming increasingly difficult to defend. The airwaves are increasingly dominated by talk show and media psychologists who dispense advice and information that is often not supported by research evidence, rather than by scientifically informed mental health professionals with the expertise necessary to provide the public with scientifically based information. As George Miller reminded us many years ago, "popular" psychology need not be a nonscientific psychology (Lilienfeld 1998).

We therefore strongly recommend that the APA and other psychological organizations, including the Association for Psychological Science (APS), create coordinated networks of media contacts (ideally consisting of experts who possess expertise regarding questionable or untested techniques in clinical psychology) who can respond to problematic or unsubstantiated mental health claims whenever they are presented in the media, as well as to media inquiries regarding such claims.

5. Finally, the APA and other psychological organizations must be willing to impose stiff sanctions on practitioners who engage in assessment and therapeutic practices that are not grounded in adequate science or that have been shown to be potentially harmful. The APA Ethics Code clearly indicates that the use of unsubstantiated assessment techniques constitutes ethically inappropriate behavior. For example, APA Ethics Code Rule 2.01(b) mandates that "Psychologists' assessments, recommendations, reports, and psychological diagnostic or evaluative statements are based on information and techniques (including personal interviews of the individual when appropriate) sufficient to provide appropriate substantiation for their findings," and APA Ethics Code Rule 2.01(a) mandates that "Psychologists do not base their assessment or intervention decisions or recommen-

dations on data or test results that are outdated for the current purpose." The APA Ethics Code (Rule 1.14) is similarly unambiguous in the case of potentially harmful psychotherapeutic methods: "Psychologists take reasonable steps to avoid harming their patients or clients, research participants, students, and others with whom they work, and to minimize harm where it is foreseeable and unavoidable."

Clinical psychologists who violate these codes of professional conduct must suffer appropriate consequences and must be prevented from harming the general public. Appropriate sanctions on the part of the APA and other professional organizations are a prerequisite for safeguarding the integrity of the profession and ensuring the safety of clients. *Primum non nocere* (first, do no harm).

Editors' Note: For a formal list of potentially harmful treatments, see Lilienfeld, S. O. 2007. Psychological treatments that cause harm. *Perspectives on Psychological Science* 2: 53–70.

# REFERENCES

Chambless, D. L., and T. H. Ollendick 2001. Empirically supported psychological interventions: Controversies and evidence. *Annual Review of Psychology* 52: 685–716.

Garb, H. N. 1998. *Studying the clinician: Judgment research and psychological assessment.* Washington, DC: American Psychological Association.

Grove, W. M. (Chair). 2000. *APA Division 12 (Clinical) Presidential Task Force "Assessment for the year 2000": Report of the task force.* Washington, DC: American Psychological Association, Division 12 (Clinical Psychology).

Lilienfeld, S. O. 1998. Pseudoscience in contemporary clinical psychology: What it is and what we can do about it. *Clinical Psychologist* 51: 3–9.

———. 2001. Fringe psychotherapies: Scientific and ethical implications for clinical psychology. In S. O. Lilienfeld (Chair), *Fringe psychotherapies: What lessons can we learn?* Presentation at invited symposium conducted at the

Annual Meeting of the American Psychological Association, San Francisco, August 25.

Lilienfeld, S. O., J. M. Lohr, and D. Morier. 2001. The teaching of courses in the science and pseudoscience of psychology: Useful resources. *Teaching of Psychology* 28: 182–91.

## 30.

# HOW DID THIS HAPPEN? AND WHAT CAN YOU DO?

## *Margaret Singer and Janja Lalich*

Going to see a therapist or counselor can be a weighty decision, especially now that therapies and treatments are being offered in such diversity. We believe in good therapy, and much good psychotherapy is provided by thousands of mental health professionals to many more thousands of patients. A recently published study showed that in 1987 nearly eighty million psychotherapy visits were made at a total cost of $4.2 billion. And according to a 1994 survey, a great portion of clients are satisfied with their psychotherapy.

The difficulty for the consumer is that the therapy smorgasbord is offered as if all treatment methods were equal and all were beneficial and free of harm. But we have shown they are not. We hope that from reading this book you will have understood not only the vast array of therapies available but also the possible risks involved in getting into a crazy therapy.

In this chapter, we present our understanding of how and why crazy therapies have been allowed to proliferate, we review the characteristics of some of these therapies, and we offer guidelines for selecting and evaluating a therapy or a therapist so you can avoid wasting your time and money or risking psychological harm.

Reprinted from Margaret Thaler Singer and Janja Lalich, *Crazy Therapies: What Are They? Do They Work?* (San Francisco: Jossey-Bass, 1996), pp. 197–216. Copyright 1996 Jossey-Bass. Reproduced with permission of John Wiley & Sons, Ltd.

## HOW DID THIS HAPPEN?

There is no one simple answer to the question of how and why we find ourselves in a society riddled with bizarre mental health offerings. Nevertheless, we can identify three factors that have had a crucial influence: (1) the special nature of the relationship between client and therapist, (2) the emergence of the blame-and-change approach in the field of psychotherapy, and (3) the flight from rational thought in our society as a whole.

( 1 ) *The Therapeutic Relationship*

The relationship between patient and therapist is unique in important ways when compared to relationships between clients and other professionals, such as physicians, dentists, attorneys, and accountants. The key difference is present from first contact: *it is not clearly understood exactly what will transpire.* There is no other professional relationship in which consumers are more in the dark than when they first go to see a therapist.

In other fields, the public is fairly well informed about what the professional does. Tradition, the media, and general experience have provided consumers with a baseline by which to judge what transpires. If you break your arm, the orthopedist explains that she will take an x-ray and set the bone; she tells you something about how long the healing will take if all goes well and gives you an estimate of the cost. When you go to a dentist, you expect him to look at your teeth, take a history, explain what was noted, and recommend a course of treatment with an estimate of time and cost. Your accountant will focus on bookkeeping, tax reports, and finances and help you deal with regulatory agencies.

Consumers enter these relationships expecting that the training, expertise, and ethical obligations of the professional will keep the client's best interests foremost. Both the consumer and the professional are aware of each person's role, and it is generally expected that the professional will stick to doing what he or she is trained to do. The consumer does not expect his accountant to lure him into accepting a new cosmology of how the world works or to "channel" financial information from "entities" who lived thousands of years ago; or for his dentist to induce him to believe that the status of his teeth was affected by an extraterrestrial experimenting on him. Nor does the patient expect the orthopedist to lead him to think the reason he fell and broke his arm was because he was under the influence of a secret Satanic cult.

But seeing a therapist is a far different situation for the consumer. In the field of psychotherapy, there is no relatively agreed upon body of knowledge, no standard procedures that a client can expect. There are no national regulatory bodies, and not every state has governing boards or licensing agencies. There are many types and levels of practitioners. Often the client knows little or nothing at all about what type of therapy a particular therapist "believes in" or what the therapist is really going to be doing in the relationship with the client.

In meeting a therapist for the first time, most consumers are almost as blind as a bat about what will transpire between the two of them. At most, they might think they will talk to the therapist and perhaps get some feedback or suggestions for treatment. What clients might not be aware of is the gamut of training, the idiosyncratic notions, and the odd practices they may be exposed to by certain practitioners.

Consumers are a vulnerable and trusting lot. And because of the special, unpredictable nature of the therapeutic relationship, it is easy for them to be taken advantage of. This makes it all the more incumbent on therapists to be especially ethical and aware of the power their role carries in our society. The misuse and abuse of power is one of the central factors in what goes wrong. B.V.R.

## ( 2) Blame and Change

Parent bashing is a main theme that has permeated psychotherapy since Freud's day. This development has for the most part gone unchallenged as a core feature of much psychotherapy. Underlying this approach is a heavy reliance on one of two notions: one, that getting insight will automatically change conduct; the other, that emotional catharsis will make you a more perfect being. The perpetuation of these three ideas has helped bring us to where we are today.

The attack on the family began with Freud and was mounted in earnest after World War II when psychotherapy became available and popular in the United States. Eventually, a full onslaught against parents took hold within mental health circles. With this emphasis on parent blaming, most therapists were trained to teach their clients to "blame" as a way of finding change. Clients are led to inspect their childhood and blame their parents or those who cared for them as the causes of their present-day distress, lack of comfort, and so forth.

Using a blame-and-change approach, the therapist never has to have cognitive, behavioral, or psychoeducational methods to assist clients to learn new behaviors. Essentially, blame-and-change therapies imply to the client that if you find whom to blame for your miseries, you will automatically get well and feel better.

Best of all, blame-and-change therapists rarely or never have to confront clients about their characterological problems. These therapists are spared from hearing stories of conduct that might suggest a real lack of sympathy on the clients' part toward their partner, family, and fellow humans. Traits such as a sense of entitlement, self-centeredness, lack of compassion, greediness, lack of responsibility, and lying require real skill on the part of therapists to handle and help. But if the therapist is just doing blame and change, she doesn't have to worry about these other sticky wickets.

Not to be left unmentioned, many therapists feel economically dependent. Therapists may shy away from even subtly bringing up how a client's behavior elicits the responses it does from others, out of fear that the client will get mad and not come back.

Looking for someone, or something, to blame became a big part of therapy. The philosophy seeped into the thinking of many mental health professionals and other types of counselors. Interwoven were the other two main threads we have discussed: (1) search your soul or memory for that one key insight that will suddenly make everything clear and better, or (2) enact, reenact, and feel and emote to purge yourself of the bad feelings, and that will suddenly make everything clear and better. Each of these three points of view presumes that there is one way and one answer: single cause–single cure.

Gone unchecked, these therapeutic trends—blame and change, insight, and catharsis—have had a direct influence on the development of many problematic therapies, some of which we've disucssed in this book. The result has been that certain therapists tend to skip over the reality of the client's problems, because they do not have methods for realistically helping and can apply only one method of therapy. One size fits all.

## (3) Flight from Rational Thought

For the past several decades, there has been a trend in our society away from science and rational thought and toward magical thinking. Much of this is a result of trends that began in the 1960s with antiestablishment and antiauthoritarian movements and came to be known as the New Age. Concurrently there has been a growing interest in self-improvement and self-awareness. Much of this took shape during the 1960s and 1970s and came to be known as the human potential movement. Combined, we have the potential for both expanded awareness and disaster.

A cursory glance at today's best-seller lists or television program guides alerts us to the prevalence of New Age thinking, usually couched in psychological or spiritual jargon. For prime-time viewing, we have angels on baseball fields, alien autopsies, and mystical messages from everyone from Jesus and Mary to a hodgepodge of self-styled philosophers and soothsayers. *The Celestine Prophecy,* a fable about one man's search for a mysterious manuscript holding the keys to life, was at the top of the book sales charts for more than two years. Considered by many to be a New Age healer, Deepak Chopra, MD, had two books on the best-seller lists. There are also *Women Who Run with Wolves* and *Men from Mars* and *Chicken Soup for the Soul. Bringers of the Dawn,* a popular book "channeled" to the author by a mass of collective energy from the star cluster Pleiades, has sold more than two hundred thousand copies. Academic John Mack may have studied ET encounters for his hit book *Abduction*, but academic Hank Wesselman went one step further. *Spiritwalker* describes the anthropologist's personal shamanic journey in the spirit world via twelve episodes while in an altered state.

Happy-go-lucky Trekkies have been superseded by *X-Files* aficionados. Once one of the most popular shows on TV—on Friday night, no less—its two main characters get involved in frightening paranormal mysteries: we've had "firestarters, alien threats to mankind, UFOs, genetically warped serial killers who ate human livers, evil clone children, and alien abduction galore." Documentary versions of similar subject matter can be found on *Sightings* and *Encounters*. Another show, *Mysteries, Magic and Miracles,* was rated number one on the SciFi cable channel. Commenting on this trend, a writer for *Omni* magazine said, "Not since the advent of spiritualism and H. P. Blavatsky in the nineteenth century have so many Americans been so interested in the possibility that the bizarre is real." During hard times in his tenure, even President Clinton met with firewalker and self-development guru Anthony Robbins.

As lighthearted and good-natured as much of this may be, there is a lurking danger. With the popularity of these ideas, we have been nurtured over the years to reduce our thinking to the lowest common denominator. We are expected to accept the most outlandish claims on blind faith. Bubbling enthusiasm has replaced serious thought processes. Convoluted gibberish has often been substituted for logic and reason.

In June 1995, the New York Academy of Sciences held a meeting of two hundred doctors, scientists, philosophers, and thinkers from around the country who expressed great concern over this very matter of the "flight from science and reason," as they called it. These worried scientists were hoping to organize a call to arms, urging all to defend scientific methodologies and to "counterattack faith healing, astrology, religious fundamentalism, and paranormal charlatanism." They also called attention to the current trend of exploiting scientific ideas to enhance magical thinking. Some New Age critics of science will, for example, distort the physics of relativity and quantum mechanics to argue that nothing in science is certain, or that mystery and magic are as valid as science.

Riding on this wave of interest in the self and this thrust toward magical thinking, some inadequately trained and unmonitored therapists and "healers"—reinforced by praise from colleagues, celebratory media appearances, and mass-market book sales—are influencing their clients, their students, and the general public. The odd and sometimes harmful techniques used by some of these practitioners tend to perpetuate unhealthy, irrational, and in some cases unethical ways of living, working, and relating socially—to which the rest of us are reluctantly subjected.

## CONSUMER GUIDELINES

In this final section, we offer four sets of guidelines to help consumers wend their way through the mental health maze and avoid crazy therapies. These guidelines will cover questions to ask a new therapist, ways to evaluate your current therapy, the "Procrustean Bed Test," and common traits of bad therapy.

### Questions to Ask Your Prospective Therapist

Ultimately, a therapist is a provider who sells a service. A prospective client should feel free to ask enough questions to be able to make an informed decision about whether to hire a particular therapist.

We have provided a general list of questions to ask a prospective therapist, but feel free to ask whatever you need to know in order to make a proper evaluation. Consider interviewing several therapists before settling on one, just as you might in purchasing any product.

Draw up your list of questions before phoning or going in for your first appointment. We recommend that you ask these questions in a phone interview first, so that you can weed out unlikely candidates and save yourself the time and expense of initial visits that don't go anywhere.

If during this process a therapist continues to ask you, "Why do you ask?" or acts as though your questioning reflects some defect in you, think carefully before signing up. Those types of responses tell you a lot about the entire attitude this person will express toward you—that is, that you are one down and he is one up and that furthermore you are quaint to even ask the "great one" to explain himself.

If you are treated with disdain for asking about what you are buying, think ahead: how could this person lead you to feel better, plan better, or have more self-esteem if he begins by putting you down for being an alert consumer? Remember, you may be feeling bad and even desperate, but there are thousands of mental health professionals, so if this one is not right, keep on phoning and searching.

1. How long is the therapy session?
2. How often should I see you?
3. How much do you charge? Do you have a sliding scale?
4. Do you accept insurance?
5. If I have to miss an appointment, will I be billed?
6. If I am late, or if you are late, what happens?
7. Tell me something about your educational background, your degrees. Are you licensed?
8. Tell me about your experience and your theoretical orientation. What types of clients have you seen? Are there areas you specialize in?
9. Do you use hypnosis or other types of trance-inducing techniques?
10. Do you have a strong belief in the supernatural? Do you believe in UFOs, past lives, or paranormal events? Do you have any kind of personal philosophy that guides your work with all your clients?
11. Do you value scientific research? How do you keep up with research and developments in your field?
12. Do you believe that it's okay to touch your clients or be intimate with them?

13. Do you usually set treatment goals with a client? How are these determined? How long do you think I will need therapy?
14. Will you see my partner, spouse, or child with me if necessary in the future?
15. Are you reachable in a crisis? How are such consultations billed?

After the interview, ask yourself:

1. Overall, does this person appear to be a competent, ethical professional?
2. Do I feel comfortable with this person?
3. Am I satisfied with the answers I got to my questions?
4. Are there areas I'm still uncertain about that make me wonder whether this is the right therapist for me?

Remember, you are about to allow this person to meddle with your mind, your emotional well-being, and your life. You will be telling her very personal things and entrusting her with intimate information about yourself and other people in your life. Take seriously the decision to select a therapist, and if you feel you made a mistake, stop working with that one and try someone else.

### How to Evaluate Your Current Therapy

What if you have been in treatment a while? What do you ask or consider in order to help evaluate what is going on? The issues discussed here may assist you.

1. *Do you feel worse and more worried and discouraged than when you began the therapy?* Sometimes having to assess one's current life can be a bit of a downer, but remember, you went for help. You may feel you are not getting what you need. Most important, watch out if you call this to your therapist's attention and he says, "You have to get worse in order to get better." That's an old saw

used as an exculpatory excuse. Instead of discussing the real issues, which a competent therapist would, this response puts all the blame on you, the client. The therapist one-ups you, telling you he knows the path you have to travel. It's an evasion that allows the therapist to avoid discussing how troubled you are and that his treatment or lack of skill may be causing or, at the very least, contributing to your state.

2. *Is your therapist professional?* Does she seem to know what she is doing? Or do features such as the following characterize your therapy:

The therapist arrives late, takes phone calls, forgets appointments, looks harassed and unkempt, smells of alcohol, has two clients arrive at one time, or otherwise appears not to have her act together at a basic level.

The therapist seems to lack overall direction, has no plans about what you two are doing.

The therapist seems as puzzled or at sea as you do about your problems.

The therapist repeats and seems to rely on sympathetic platitudes such as "Trust me," or "Things will get better. Just keep coming in."

The therapy hour is without direction and seems more like amiable chitchat with a friend.

The therapy hour just rambles on. Does the therapist provide direction or simply respond to what you say? Does she rarely connect one session with another, just starting anew each time?

The therapist implies that just seeing her is what is going to cure you.

The therapist tells you about herself, her feelings, her history, implying that hers is the proper way to live.

The therapist avoids confronting you, always sides with you, tries to stay your friend, or seems fearful that you will leave therapy if she questions or challenges behavior that you describe. Do you think the fact that you pay her causes her to avoid challenging you because she doesn't want to lose a customer?

3. *Does your therapist seem to be controlling you, sequestering you from family, friends, and other advisers?*

Does the therapist insist that you not talk about anything from your therapy with anyone else, thus cutting off the help that such talk normally brings to an individual, and making you seem secretive and weird about your therapy?

Does the therapist insist that your therapy is much more important in your life than it really is?

Does the therapist make himself a major figure in your life, keeping you focusing on your relationship with him?

Does the therapist insist that you postpone decisions such as changing jobs, becoming engaged, getting married, having a child, or moving, implying or openly stating that your condition has to be cured and his imprimatur given before you act on your own?

Does the therapist mainly interpret your behavior as sick, immature, unstable? Does he fail to tell you that many of your reactions are normal, everyday responses to situations?

Does the therapist keep you looking only at the bad side of your life?

Does the therapist tell you that your family is the sole cause of any distress you have in your life?

Does the therapist attribute malevolent motives to others in your life—your family, friends, spouse, children, fellow workers—and, in the end, seem to cause you to be even more dependent on him as he alienates you from them?

Do you feel torn between what your therapist wants or supports and what someone else very close suggests might be beneficial for you? Do you feel unable to talk with the therapist about this apparent conflict of interests?

Do most of the therapist's interpretations of your behavior make you feel that he does not trust you or regards you as inadequate, incompetent, and pathological? Does he tell you that you appear to be sabotaging yourself, driven to ruining yourself, when you don't get that kind of feedback elsewhere in your life?

4. Does your therapist try to touch you? Handshakes at the beginning and end of a session can be routine. Anything beyond that is not acceptable. Some clients do allow their therapist to hug them when they leave, but this should be done only after you've been asked and have given your approval. If you are getting the impression that the touching is becoming or is blatantly sexualized, quit the therapy immediately.

   Are you noticing what we call "the rolling chair syndrome"? Some therapists who begin to touch and encroach on the bodies of their clients have chairs that roll, and as time goes by they roll closer and closer. Before you realize what's happened, your therapist might have rolled his chair over and clasped your knees between his opened legs. He may at first fake this as a comforting gesture. Don't buy it!

   Remember: *sex is never part of therapy.* Thus no matter how flattering it may seem at first that an older, professional person finds you attractive, when that happens, therapy has gone out the window. You are merely being used by a law-violating, impaired, self-gratifying, incompetent, and narcissistic therapist. Both male and female therapists violate personal boundaries with improper touching and by sexualizing the therapy.

5. *Does your therapist seem to have only one interpretation for everything? Does she lead you to the same conclusion about your troubles, no matter what you tell her?* You might have sought help with a crisis in your family, a seemingly irresolvable dilemma at your job, some personal situation, a mild depressed state after a death of a

loved one, or any number of reasons. But before you were able to give sufficient history so that the therapist could grasp why you were there and what you wanted to work on, the therapist began to fit you into a mold. You find that, for example, the therapist insists on focusing on your childhood, telling you your present demeanor suggests that you were ritually abused or subjected to incest, or that you may be a multiple personality—currently three very faddish diagnoses. If the therapist has her agenda and set belief about what is bothering you, it is unlikely that what you brought in to work on will ever get dealt with.

### The Procrustean Bed Test—One Size Fits All

As you may recall, Procrustes was the villain in Greek mythology who forced travelers to fit into his bed by stretching their bodies or cutting off their legs. The term is now used to characterize someone who has ruthless disregard for individual differences or special circumstances. For our purposes, this refers to a therapist who believes in single cause–single cure or who imposes his agenda on you, rather than taking into consideration your concerns and needs as a client.

From the nearly four hundred interviews done by coauthor Singer in the past decade and from other studies of individuals who had bad results from therapy, we can summarize some general patterns found in therapists who have been inadequately and poorly trained, who are considered to be "impaired professionals," and who harm, control, or apply untested, unscientific methods, some of which are personally devised theories and techniques. Being able to recognize these therapist behaviors will allow you, the client, to check whether or not you are being put in a Procrustean bed—that is, whether you are the subject of one-size-fits-all therapy. Notice whether the following are occurring or have happened:

1. *The therapist teaches you a mythology about human behavior.* It might be any one of the following, which is by no means meant to be an all-inclusive list of the possible theories or belief systems thrust upon clients:

- Humans have lived past lives, and so have you.
- Space aliens are kidnapping people, and you are one of those who've been abducted.
- A symptom checklist will reveal whether you were molested as an infant.
- There is a massive secret conspiracy of worldwide Satanic cults, and your parents were or are part of it.
- All those conflicting feelings you have are actually a sign that you have multiple personality disorder.
- Reexperiencing the birth trauma will rid you of your troubling symptoms.
- Through hypnosis you can retrieve memories of everything that ever happened to you.

2. *You are taught and encouraged to use the language and jargon the therapist uses as part of this mythology or pet theory.* Much as a cult leader teaches followers to use certain jargon and accept the myths he wants them to accept, so do many therapists. Jargon is adopted in order to reinforce the myth, and you find that you are speaking a kind of code language in your sessions and elsewhere. For example:

- You have to learn what a primal is, how to locate and cuddle your inner child, how to fall into trance and create a past life, how to assume the warrior role, how to become a survivor, how to become an "experiencer," or how to "let it all out."
- You refer to your feelings, vexations, or moments of poor behavior as examples of your "alters" or explain them by saying, "The children are acting up."
- You must learn such expressions as "I am in resistance," "I am in denial," "I am a survivor," "I came from a dysfunctional family," and so on.

3. *The therapist arrived at your diagnosis all too swiftly and seems unwilling to consider any interpretations and meanings other than the ones*

*he assigns.* He turns everything back on you if you don't accept his point of view. He abuses his power by making you feel that you just don't understand or are not working hard enough. For example:

- If you say you don't agree with the therapist's conclusions, he tells you that you are "resisting" and that you will never get well until you fully accept his reasoning.
- If you disagree with the therapist's interpretation of what's going on with you, you are told you are "in denial."
- If you protest that something was nice and good about your family, the therapist again insists you are "in denial."

4. *The therapist tries to get you to believe that she can tell what happened to you in your past even if you have no memory of it at all.* For example:

- Because you have come to be dependent on the therapist and are feeling very needy, and because you've been indoctrinated into being "a good patient," you begin to revise your past.
- You no longer trust your own memory and you find that you fill in what the therapist is asking about with what she seems to want to hear.

5. *The therapist is taking control over more and more of your life.* For example:

- He may tell you not to have children because "multiples abandon their children." The therapist of course has no factual or scientific support for this; it is just a myth of the trade that he may have heard at the last weekend seminar, or something he made up in his head.
- You are told not to see your family anymore. The therapist tells you that your family is the cause of all your problems, and being around them is dangerous to your mental health.

- The therapist starts limiting your friendships and tells you to socialize only with other people in groups run by the therapist or groups where his particular belief system is promoted.

Why are these practices frowned on by well-trained, conscientious therapists who practice within the ethical bounds of their profession? Because therapists are trained to promote autonomy in patients, to help patients become more independent, make their own decisions, and be responsible to themselves and to society. Inducing dependency and forcing you to fit into the therapist's Procrustean bed is doing you no good.

### Common Traits of Bad Therapy

1. Inadequate history taken at the outset
2. No diagnosis or ill-formed, incorrect diagnosis
3. Lack of formulation or conceptualization of the problem and how to proceed
4. No goals, no treatment plan, or inappropriate treatment plan
5. Unclear roles or boundaries, including self-revelations and seductive or sexual remarks
6. No appreciation of discrepancy in power
7. Dependency and regression fostered
8. Therapeutic techniques mismanaged or inappropriate techniques used, including placing client in group too soon, misuse or overuse of hypnosis and/or medications
9. Overriding adherence to paranormal theories or New Age philosophies that cannot be rationally or scientifically proven and that are covertly or overtly foisted on clients, requiring them to make tremendous leaps of faith in order to go along with the therapist's interpretations and treatment
10. No rational theoretical connection between the practices and the goal of rehabilitation
11. Transference mismanaged, including failure to recognize, interpret, and understand its impact on the therapeutic relationship

12. Confidentiality violated, including telling client about others and/or telling others about client
13. Objectivity and professionalism lost, including becoming sexually or otherwise involved
14. Failure to monitor progress
15. Failure to treat or deal with presenting problems
16. Precipitous abandonment of client

## AVOIDING MYTHS AND MAYHEM

Engaging in therapy with a practitioner who upholds unfounded theories or glorifies bizarre techniques involves too many risks. We see that all too often basic human and social instincts for a better life and a better world are being corrupted by lazy theories and cockeyed procedures by which some persons are making a name and fortune while their patients are being used, abused, and made to feel worse instead of better.

Crazy therapies promulgate myths and perpetuate mayhem. Keeping this in mind, consumers would do well to heed the advice of writer Charlotte Brontë, "Look twice before you leap."

# APPENDIX I

## Recommended Books for Distinguishing Effective from Ineffective Psychological Treatments

Anthony, M. M., and D. H. Barlow, eds. 2002. *Handbook of Assessment and Treatment Planning for Psychological Disorders*. New York: Guilford Press. Intended primarily for mental health professionals, this book is an invaluable guide to the scientifically grounded assessment and treatment of a broad spectrum of psychological problems, including depression, anxiety, insomnia, schizophrenia, personality disorders, sexual dysfunction, and insomnia.

Dawes, R. M. 1994. *House of Cards: Psychology and Psychotherapy Built on Myth*. New York: Free Press. A classic exposé of the questionable and unscientific bases of some of today's psychotherapeutic and diagnostic practices. Polemical and sharp-tongued, but very much worth reading.

Della Salla, S., ed. 1999. *Mind Myths: Exploring Popular Assumptions about the Mind and Brain*. New York: Wiley. Engaging, although slightly uneven, volume examining a variety of widespread misconceptions concerning psychology and neuroscience, including self-improvement devices for enhancing mental functioning.

Gambrill, E. 2006. *Critical Thinking in Clinical Practice: Improving the Quality of Judgments and Decisions*. 2nd edition. New York: Wiley. A remarkably comprehensive and immensely useful guide to thinking critically about clinical judgments and predictions, to commonplace errors in clinical settings, and to scientifically supported methods for overcoming them.

Jacobson, J. W., R. M. Foxx, and J. A. Mulick, eds. 2005. *Controversial Therapies for Developmental Disabilities: Fad, Fashion, and Science in Professional Practice*. Hillsdale, NJ: Lawrence Erlbaum Associates. An outstanding resource for those hoping to sort fiction from fact in the treatment of autism and related conditions.

Lilienfeld, S. O., S. J. Lynn, and J. M. Lohr, eds. 2003. *Science and Pseudoscience in Clinical Psychology*. New York: Guilford Press. This book lays out criteria for distinguishing science from pseudoscience in mental health, examines

631

a broad spectrum of diagnostic and assessment fads, and provides a comprehensive evaluation of unsubstantiated and substantiated treatments for childhood disorders (e.g., autism, attention-deficit/hyperactivity disorder) and adult disorders (e.g., PTSD, depression).

Nathan, P. E., and J. M. Gorman. 2002. *A Guide to Treatments That Work.* 2nd edition. New York: Oxford University Press. An excellent guide to empirically supported treatments for major mental disorders. Although intended primarily for mental health professionals, it is accessible to the educated layperson.

Roth, A., and P. Fonagy. 2004. *What Works for Whom?* 2nd edition. New York: Guilford Press. Another terrific resource for up-to-date knowledge regarding the efficacy of psychotherapy for different psychological problems.

Ruscio, J. 2006. *Critical Thinking in Psychology: Separating Sense from Nonsense.* 2nd edition. Pacific Grove, CA: Wadsworth. A superb guide for the layperson and undergraduate for critically evaluating controversial and questionable claims in a wide variety of areas, including mental health and medical practice.

Salerno, S. 2005. *SHAM: How the Self-Help Movement Made America Helpless.* New York: Crown. A provocative examination of the modern self-help movement and its dual emphases on victimization and empowerment, this book challenges the claims and approaches of well-known figures in the realm of popular psychology.

Seligman, M. E. P. 1995. *What You Can Change and What You Can't: The Complete Guide to Self-Improvement.* New York: Ballantine Books. A useful and user-friendly, although now slightly dated, guide to the research literature on psychotherapy, with particular emphasis on effective self-help methods.

Singer, M., and J. Lalich. 1996. *Crazy Therapies: What Are They? How Do They Work?* San Francisco: Jossey-Bass. An entertaining and informative look at New Age therapies of various stripes and unethical therapist practices, as well as a helpful guide for mental health practices to avoid.

Sommers, C. H., and S. Satel. 2005. *One Nation under Therapy: How the Helping Culture Is Eroding Self-Reliance.* New York: St. Martin's Press. A thoughtful social commentary on the pernicious consequences of "therapism"—the view, pervasive in American popular psychology, that most people are exquisitely fragile and require psychological help in the wake of stressful events.

# APPENDIX II

## *Recommended Web Sites for Distinguishing Effective from Ineffective Psychological Treatments*

American Psychiatric Association Practice Guidelines for the treatment of mental disorders: http://www.psych.org/psych_pract/treatg/pg/prac_guide.cfm

Bandolier (site for evidence-based thinking regarding medicine and mental healthcare): http://www.jr2.ox.ac.uk/bandolier/

Center for Evidence-Based Mental Health: http://www.cebmh.com/

Empirically supported psychological treatments (from Division 12, the Society for Clinical Psychology, of the American Psychological Association): http://www.apa.org/divisions/div12/rev_est/

Empirically supported psychological treatments for children and adolescents (from Division 53, the Society of Child and Adolescent Psychology, of the American Psychological Association): http://www.wjh.harvard.edu/%7Enock/Div53/EST/index.htm

*Journal of Consulting and Clinical Psychology* (professional journal dedicated to scientific research on psychological treatment and assessment): http://www.apa.org/journals/ccp/

NARSAD (organization dedicated to the scientific study of schizophrenia, mood disorders, and other serious mental illnesses): http://www.narsad.org/

National Institute of Mental Health: http://www.nimh.nih.gov/

Psychologists Educating Students to Think Skeptically (PESTS, an organization dedicated to teaching students and the public to recognize the difference between science and pseudoscience): http://www.scottsdalecc.edu/ricker/pests/

*Psychological Science in the Public Interest* (professional journal dedicated to the scientific evaluation of claims bearing on public policy): http://www.blackwellpublishing.com/journal.asp?ref=1529-1006&site=1

Quackwatch (site devoted to medical and mental health fads): http://www.quackwatch.org/

Science-based medicine (site devoted to scientific controversies in medical and mental health): http://www.sciencebasedmedicine.org

*Scientific American Mind* (popular magazine dedicated to the science of psychology and neuroscience, including facts and fictions in mental health): http://www.sciammind.com/

*Scientific Review of Mental Health Practice* (journal dedicated to distinguishing science from pseudoscience in mental health): http://www.srmhp.org/

*Skeptical Inquirer* (popular magazine dedicated to evaluating controversial and extraordinary claims): http://www.csicop.org/si/

Society for a Science of Clinical Psychology (SSCP): http://www.bsos.umd.edu/sscp/